A Nation at Work

A Nation at Work

The Heldrich Guide to the American Workforce

Written and edited by

HERBERT A. SCHAFFNER

AND

CARL E. VAN HORN

Rutgers University Press
New Brunswick, New Jersey, and London

Library of Congress Cataloging-in-Publication Data

A nation at work: the Heldrich guide to the American workforce/written and edited by Herbert A. Schaffner and Carl E. Van Horn

p. cm.

Includes bibliographical references and index.

ISBN 0-8135-3188-8 (cloth : alk. paper) — ISBN 0-8135-3189-6 (pbk : alk. paper)

1. Labor market—United States. 2. Labor supply—United States. 3. Manpower policy—United States. 4. Employment (Economic theory). 5. Employees—United States.

I. Schaffner, Herbert A., 1959- II. Van Horn, Carl E. III. John J. Heldrich Center for Workforce Development.

HD5724 .N155 2003

331.1′0973—dc21 2002068045

British Cataloging-in-Publication data for this book is available from the British Library

Graphics by Chris Lit Van Cleaf

Manufactured in the United States of America

Contents

Illustrations

Figures

Tables

Preface and Acknowledgments

This book grew out of the work of the John J. Heldrich Center for Workforce Development, an institute for applied research on the workforce, headquartered at Rutgers University in New Brunswick, New Jersey. Founded in 1997, the Heldrich Center provides research, policy design, and strategic advice regarding labor and workforce concerns to corporate, state, and federal government, nonprofit, labor, and foundation clients. The center seeks to be a leading academic-based center of excellence dedicated to ensuring a skilled, high-performance, high-opportunity workforce for the twenty-first century. A cornerstone of the Heldrich Center's work is to educate businesses, policymakers, union leaders, academia, media, and the public about the workforce development system and its role in our changing economy and workplaces.

Our interest in these activities kept us thinking about a book series linked to the Heldrich Center and our research that would be published through Rutgers University Press. We nodded in agreement when a visiting faculty advisor a few years ago mentioned that a thoughtful and accessible guide to the workforce seemed like a good fit for this series and for our goals, but we assumed that a number of such books were already in print. At the time, we were caught up in a number of other pressing short-term projects, but eventually we took up the book discussion again. After digging through the literature, including mainstream publications, we could not find a book similar to the one taking shape in our conversation. The more we talked and traded notes, the more worthwhile it seemed to begin the trek over the high research mountain ranges of an original reference work that would provide a broad audience with an engaging and crisp overview of major workforce trends in the United States.

Well, we are glad and relieved to have arrived at our destination. We are grateful to those who helped us do so. We benefited from the ideas and suggestions of our Heldrich Center colleagues, and in particular from the substantial research and editorial assistance provided by Heldrich colleagues Karen Dixon, Laurie Santos, and Ariana Funaro. They each made important contributions. Madia Logan supervised the permissions and formatting duties involved with this project, and they were considerable. Her hard work, skill, and intelligence are deeply appreciated. Elayne Marinos pitched in to address late-order editing and formatting issues; her insights and contributions were also deeply appreciated. Chris Lit of the Center for Government Services is to be commended for her excellent charts delivered on a tight deadline. Executive director Bill Tracy provided moral support for the project and needed infusions of Irish humor. As always, we cannot forget the tremendous support provided by our founder and National Advisory Board chair, John Heldrich, for all of the center's activities and for this project in particular.

Introduction

What do you do?

In some cultures this might be a rude conversation opener. But in the United States, it is a popular and productive conversation staple of our time.

A few decades ago, jobs were important, but they had a place and a limit—eight hours a day and a short commute—and they left time for other things to do. "It's a job," or "it's a paycheck," or "it's a living"—these were laconic acknowledgments of the rules of adulthood and responsibility. People managed their expectations with a certain realism about what a single individual could do in the economy. Work roles were limited, defined, and narrow for women who had jobs outside the homes. Men had enough time to be visible in their communities, coaching sports, leading Boy Scout troops, seeing their friends on a regular basis. Getting a job was a matter of local contacts and culture. Workers went into their fathers' business, grew up with a particular firm, knew which factory was hiring, or joined a union or went into public service. Networking to explore career opportunities across the nation and the world was virtually unknown; leapfrogging from job to job was a matter of personal shame and dishonor. The editors of this book remember these rules. Carl Van Horn's father worked as a foreman in the same Pittsburgh steel mill for forty years. Herbert Schaffner's father grew to civic prominence as a small-town lawyer committed to the same firm, the same clients, the same causes for three decades—just as *his* father had done.

For postwar generations throughout the 1970s, the business of America was business. But in many towns and suburbs, it wasn't *our* business. It was the concern of one or two powerful people in the big house on the heights and their glamorous bosses far away in large cities. They would take care of us; we wouldn't ask many questions. A better life was entwined in the support and quality of one's community and family networks and the slow accumulation of assets. Jobs were treasured for their security. In his memoir, *Man of the House,* Tip O'Neill remembered his upbringing with images familiar to generations: "You don't get rich working for the city, but we always had enough to eat. Still, we never threw anything away, because there was always somebody in the neighborhood who could use your old shirt, your hat, your coat—even your old shoes. My father used to form organizations to collect food and clothing, and to distribute it secretly so that poor people could be helped without being embarrassed. At Christmas Eve and Easter we would prepare food baskets for the needy, which we'd leave at their doorsteps in the dark of night. There was a lot of goodwill in our neighborhood; in those days people really looked out for one another."

We do not recall these memories to nostalgically hail the past as a golden era gone by. Clearly, many social structures and dynamics of post–World War II

America were repressive, harsh, and fundamentally unfair. But this book was developed and written because of a startling revolution that catapulted the workplace into a position as arguably the most dominant institution in the new global economy and contemporary American life.

The workplace is at the center of far-reaching economic and cross-cultural changes. These include advances in information technology, globalization, the importance of niche markets and products, the spread of large financial institutions and global financial networks, flattened management structures, and the demise of the social contract between workers and employers. These developments make it possible for work to occur in many places, including the home, the hotel room, the office, and places around the world, extending the hours and reach of the workplace.

Today, the nature of work is entangled in new categories of personal difficulty: conflicts between work and family, lack of pension security, and access to lifelong learning and skills. Working adults of many classes and walks of life face a frantic juggling act of meeting the demands of high-productivity workplaces, coping with child-care and elder-care responsibilities, performing volunteer duties, and managing the home.

The workplace is increasingly becoming the foundation for social change and the distributor of health, retirement, and other benefits, which in other industrialized countries are provided by government. Worker training programs are becoming the principal path of advancement for everyone who does not go directly from high school to college—nearly half of our young people. The ramifications of welfare reform have become a dominant field of policy analysis and debate. The competitive strength of the workforce ranks as a top issue for governors and business leaders in countless reports and surveys.

The workplace is now our most diverse national institution, and its diversity will only grow. Our workplaces are absorbing people of many nations, backgrounds, and walks of life—as we see in the movement to provide workplace benefits to gay couples, decisions to increase the numbers of highly skilled foreign nationals allowed to work in high-tech companies, and the continuing struggle of talented women executives to open the doors to CEO suites. From this diversity comes much strength—as seen in how men and women at the grassroots family level are redefining their work roles. The 2000 Census data shows more fathers are primary parents, and a wave of powerful literature by women scholars is examining new directions for women seeking lives that encompass being good parents and successful professionals. "The nuclear family, in which mother is the linchpin of family life and parents alone do child care, rarely works anymore," wrote Joan Peters in *When Mothers Work*.

At the same time, the workplace is a social institution in perpetual flux and tumult, absorbing the blows of economic and world events in real time. Workers form the front lines of issues ranging from race discrimination and health security to global terrorism and environmental safety. As the minority population of the United States continues to grow in size and income, and as businesses seek new global markets, fully incorporating the values of fair treatment and equality of opportunity will be essential goals for leaders seeking to ensure a high productivity workforce. The lack of national health insurance planning in the United States translates into ongoing struggles at the workplace as workers seek good coverage and employers scale back health benefits during slower economic times. Most prominently, the terror threats and security response of post–September 11 America have made workers far more conscious of the safety of their workplaces, urban centers, foreign travel, and business travel in general. In this book, we will note how these emerging challenges may change the lives of American workers.

A Nation at Work addresses fundamental economic, demographic, policy, and business facts about how the workforce and workplace will take shape in this year and the years ahead. These include how workers are adjusting to permanent job insecurity and the lost employer-worker compact, the aging of the baby boomers, and new roles for women. We examine the deep and substantial barriers to opportunity for the working poor, the implications of new and illegal immigrants in the workforce, and the growing importance of lifelong learning and high-tech skills. Reflecting our center's mission, we provide new perspectives and analysis of the roles of education and training institutions in strengthening the workforce, and the impacts of how earned income is distributed.

A Nation at Work has two parts. Part 1 contains three chapters on essential topics about the American workforce and is illustrated with more than thirty-five figures. In part 2, we gathered insightful essays from the nation's very best journalists and analysts who have written about the workforce and the new economy in recent years. We included articles by Jason DeParle and Louis Uchitelle of the *New York Times;* Sue Shellenbarger of the *Wall Street Journal;* Nina Munk of *Fortune;* E. J. Dionne of the *Washington Post;* Ann Crittenden, author of *The Price of Motherhood;* Nina Munk and Thomas Stewart of *Fortune;* Naomi Klein, author of *No Logo;* and Ellen Galinsky of the National Work and Family Institute. We have also included speeches by Alan Greenspan, Leo Reddy, leading economists, and business leaders.

There are plenty of facts and data incorporated throughout the volume, including research tables, Internet sites, periodicals, books, magazines, and nonprofit organizations. This information points readers to the government agencies, researchers, consultants, and academics who can explore key themes and chapters in greater detail.

We hope this book describes and explains the profound changes under way in the American workforce and workplace and helps its readers reach better understandings about their own work and the world of work around them.

Part I

THE WORKFORCE, THE ECONOMY, AND PUBLIC POLICY

Chapter 1

Social, Economic, and Demographic Trends

Who Are America's Workers?

DURING THE POSTWAR PERIOD, two images became icons for the identity of America's workers—the black-shell briefcase and the hard hat. These were our fathers' images. One suggested the authority, secrecy, and closed nature of professional and business life, where men ran the affairs of the world. The second suggested the status of the skilled working man who was well paid and generally respected for the work he did with his back and hands, erecting the great buildings and bridges of a dominant industrial power.

In the twenty-first century, the economic culture suggests new images for who we are as workers. The cell phone is ubiquitous among professional, blue-collar, and technical workers, suggesting the importance of communications and mobility among all levels and niches of the workforce. Who would have known even ten years ago that the symbol one finds using the shift bar for number 2 on a computer or typewriter—the @—would become the unifying sign shared by tens of millions of workers in a national network of email addresses—each the unique property of just one person. Our email correspondence is the national lunchroom of the workplace, forming the vast superhighway of day-to-day communication for all manner of people, whether they are @ work, @ home, or @ rest.

Compared with three or four decades ago, the U.S. workforce is composed of more women, more minorities, more immigrants, more nonunion workers, more service workers, and more educated workers. The proportion of women workers grew from 32 percent of all civilian women in 1948 to 57.7 percent in 1992 and 60.4 percent in 2000 (see fig. 1). During this post–World War II era, workforce participation for men *declined* from 86.7 percent to 75 percent (Bureau of Labor Statistics 2000a).

Money has everything to do with our understanding of work. People get out of their beds every morning and go to work for money. While satisfaction in a job well done and job quality are important to individuals, it is undeniable that people work for money. Any reading of labor force data reveals that historic

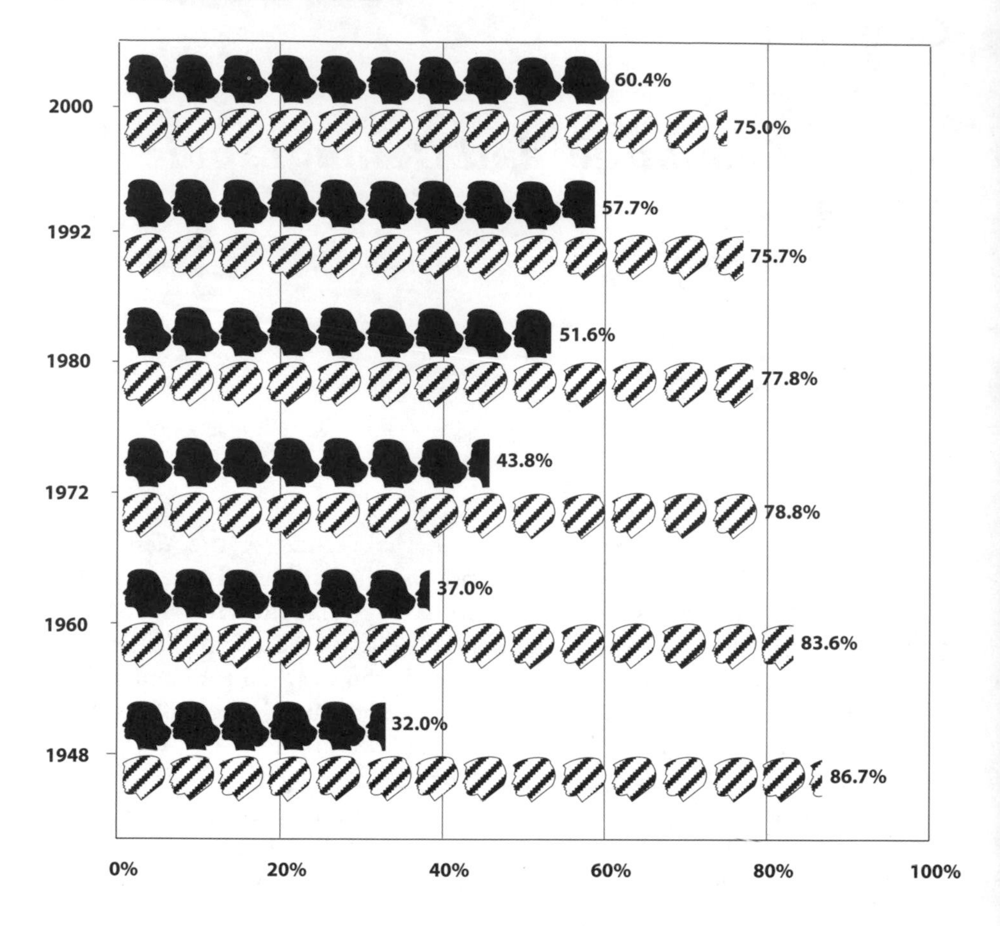

Fig. 1. Workforce participation by gender, 1948–2000. *Source:* U.S. Bureau of Labor Statistics.

divides exist and continue to exist between the earnings of men and women and among the earnings of whites, Asians, blacks, and Hispanics. Incomes of blacks and Hispanics have remained well below the incomes of whites and Asians for decades, although black income has increased since 1967, while Hispanic incomes have remained stagnant (U.S. Census Bureau 2000b). Women's earnings have gradually increased over the past four decades in comparison to men, but, overall, women still make less than seventy-five cents to every dollar made by men. Black men, who made only fifty-seven cents for every dollar made by white men in 1967, now make about seventy cents for every dollar made by white men.

Manufacturing jobs, nearly one in four jobs in 1950, dropped to 13 percent of the workforce by 1998 and are projected to continue shrinking over the next six years. In addition, part-time work is up in today's workforce, unionization is down, and job tenure is short, even for CEOs.

Americans are working harder, too. Workers in the United States average more hours per week on the job than any other Western industrialized nation, according to International Labor Organization and United Nations data. By the late 1990s, nearly half of all workers reported they had to work mandatory overtime (Van Horn and Dautrich, *Work Trends* 1999). Between 1979 and 1998, the number of people holding more than one job increased by 3.4 million. Women accounted for most (72 percent) of that increase. By 1998, nearly half (47.3 percent) of all multiple jobholders—or "moonlighters"—were women, compared with less than 30 percent two decades earlier (Costello and Stone 2001).

During the 1990s, immigrants streamed into America's workforce, particularly from Central America and Asia. Foreign-born individuals made up 5.9 percent of the population in 1960. Today, foreign-born workers make up nearly 13 percent of the U.S. workforce (U.S. Department of Labor, *Report on the American Workforce* 2001). Early in 2001 demographers poring over 2000 census data discovered that Hispanics had become the largest minority ethnic population in the United States, reflecting an extraordinary surge in immigration. Indeed, new census data shows that minorities make up 40 percent of our nation's children and 28 percent of the adult population. By 2020, Department of Labor figures show the Hispanic population is projected to add more people to the United States every year than all other ethnic groups combined. Non-Hispanic whites, who now make up more than 71 percent of the population, are projected to compose about 62 percent of the population in 2020 (see fig. 2).

The composition of the overall U.S. workforce is also older. In 1975, 41 percent of the workforce were between the ages of thirty-five and fifty-four. Today, half of U.S. workers are in this age group, the so-called baby boomers. The workforce is aging with them, and the population of older Americans—people over fifty-five years of age—will nearly double over the next half-century. The Bureau of Labor Statistics (BLS) projects the share of the workforce aged fifty-five and over will grow by 48 percent between 1998 and 2008, by far the largest projected growth of any age group, gender, race, or ethnic identification (U.S. Department of Labor 1999).

But as the workforce ages, experience is losing some of its edge in the workplace. The "creative destruction" of innovation and change characteristic of global competition offers advantages to younger, tech-savvy, mobile workers. Nina Munk of *Fortune* observed in 1999 that "in just four years, for the first time ever, there will be more workers over 40 than there are workers under 40. All those people—the 78 million baby boomers—are competing for a limited number of top jobs. For those who have made it (status, money, fan mail, a title, a corner office), there's no problem; but for the millions who are just decent, everyday performers, it's another story. These people are squeezed: they can't rise to the top (there's no room), and right behind, ready to overtake them is another generation. In years gone by, executives in this position spoke of reaching a plateau—if their path no longer led upward, at least they were in a stable, safe place. Now the plateau is a narrow ledge. Suddenly at an age when they expected to be at the peak of their careers, growing numbers of fortysomethings are slipping backward."

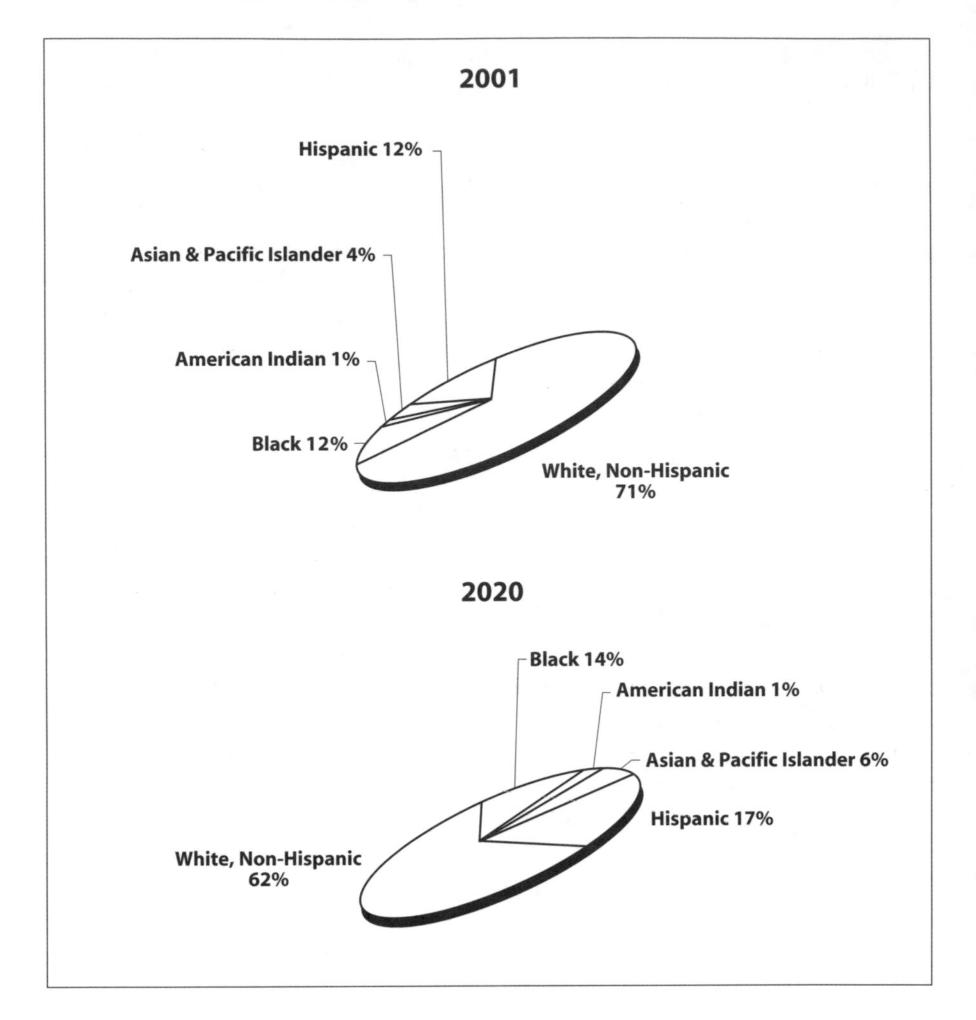

Fig. 2. U.S. population by race, 2001 and 2020. *Source:* U.S. Bureau of the Census.

Working Hard but Losing Ground. Economic researchers have shown that income inequality has soared in America since the early 1970s. While the wealthiest have enjoyed vast increases in income during the past twenty-five years, middle-income families have made relatively little progress. Between 1973 and 1980 the average family's real income did not grow at all. From President Ronald Reagan's first term in 1981 through President Clinton's reelection in 1996, average family real income grew by a total of just 9 percent (Levy 1998).

One reason for this stagnation is that workers who belong to unions are much harder to find today than thirty years ago. During the rise of organized labor in the early twentieth century, union membership grew from 3.4 million in 1930 to 10 million in 1941. Labor's share of the workforce peaked in 1954, when 35 percent of all U.S. workers belonged to unions. In the year 2000, 13.5 percent of the nation's workforce belonged to unions. Since 1983, when detailed records were kept, the share of unionized wage and salary workers in private industry has declined to 9 percent but increased slightly in government, where 37 percent of workers are union members (U.S. Department of Labor 2000c)

In 1999, of the 16.5 million union wage and salary workers, 9.4 million (57 percent) worked in private nonagricultural industries and 7.1 million (43 percent) worked in government at all levels. About one in four wage and salary workers employed in the transportation and communication/public utilities industries were union members (see fig. 3).

Many working Americans remain poor and near poor despite work. In 2000, the unemployment rate was just 4 percent, but 11.3 percent of the population—or 31.1 million people—lived at or below the official poverty level. In the year 2000, 45 percent of people living in families with incomes below the poverty line had at least one full-time worker in each family, a large increase since 1993, when 36 percent of poor people in families had a full-time worker.

The role and opportunities of disabled workers became a major issue in the later years of the twentieth century and remains important today. There are approximately fifty million Americans—or 20 percent of the total population—with a disability, according to the U.S. Census Bureau and the American

	Union Members (in thousands)	Percentage of Union Membership (%)	Members as % of Wage & Salary Workers
Total Union Members	16,477	100	13.9
Agriculture	43	0.3	2.5
Private Nonagriculture	9,376	57	9.5
Mining	57	0.4	10.6
Construction	1,187	7	19.1
Manufacturing	3,024	18	15.6
Transportation	1,136	7	25.5
Communication, Public Utilities	729	4	25.4
Wholesale Trade	248	2	5.4
Retail Trade	1,030	6	5.1
Finance, Insurance, Real Estate	156	1	2.1
Services	1,809	11	5.5
Government	7,058	43	37.3

Fig. 3. Union members by industry, 1999. *Sources:* U.S. Department of Labor; AFL-CIO.

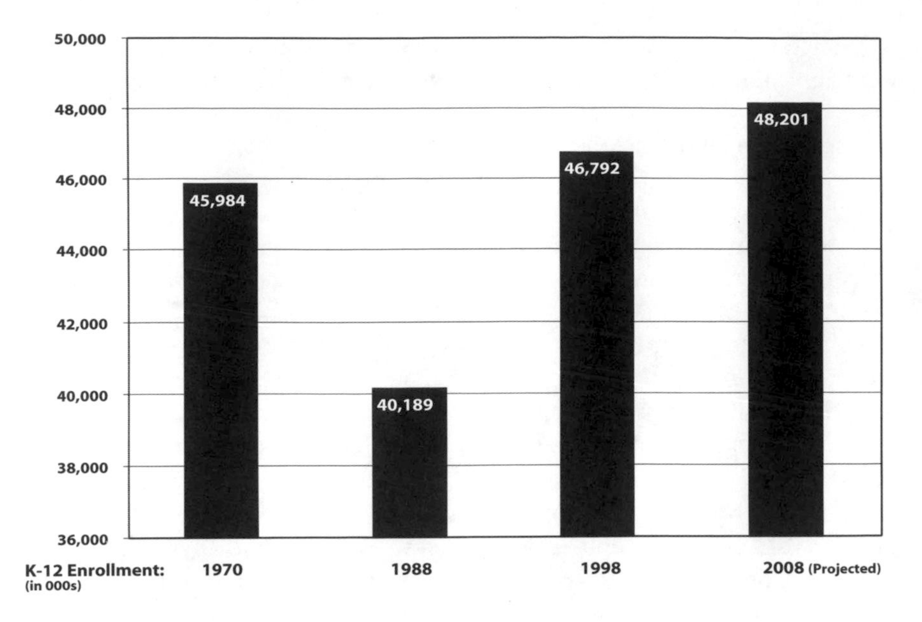

Fig. 4. K–12 enrollment, 1970–2008. *Sources:* U.S. Department of Education, National Center for Education Statistics; Digest of Education Statistics (NCES 1999-036) (based on common core of data); and Projections of Education Statistics, 1998–2008 (NCES 980016).

Association of Disabled Persons. Nearly twenty-five million U.S. citizens are severely disabled. Only about 30 percent of those with significant disabilities are working, compared to 80 percent of the general population—yet studies show the vast majority of people with disabilities want to work. The average monthly earnings of a disabled worker is 18 percent less than workers without disabilities. The severely disabled worker earns even less—only 64 percent of the workers with no disabilities. (Monthly earnings for nondisabled between the ages of thirty-five to fifty-four is $2,446, compared to $2,006 for workers with a nonsevere disability and $1,562 for workers with a severe disability).

As a new "echo boom" of children enter grade school, Americans are seeking higher education in greater numbers than ever before, as show in fig. 4. Between 1988 and 1998, according to the National Center for Education Statistics figures, enrollment in grades pre-K through twelve grew by more than 16 percent, and the NCES projects growth to increase by a little more than 3 percent through 2008. Enrollment in private and public colleges and universities grew by 16 percent between 1978 and 1998 (see fig. 5). Expenditures by public colleges alone climbed from less than $20 billion in 1960 (in constant 1999–2000 figures) to nearly $180 billion in 1999 (U.S. Department of Education 2000).

Trends established by the U.S. Department of Commerce's *Falling through the Net* surveys show steadily rising numbers of Americans with computer and Internet access. The pervasive presence of technology and communications in the lives of most Americans presents employers and policy makers with the abil-

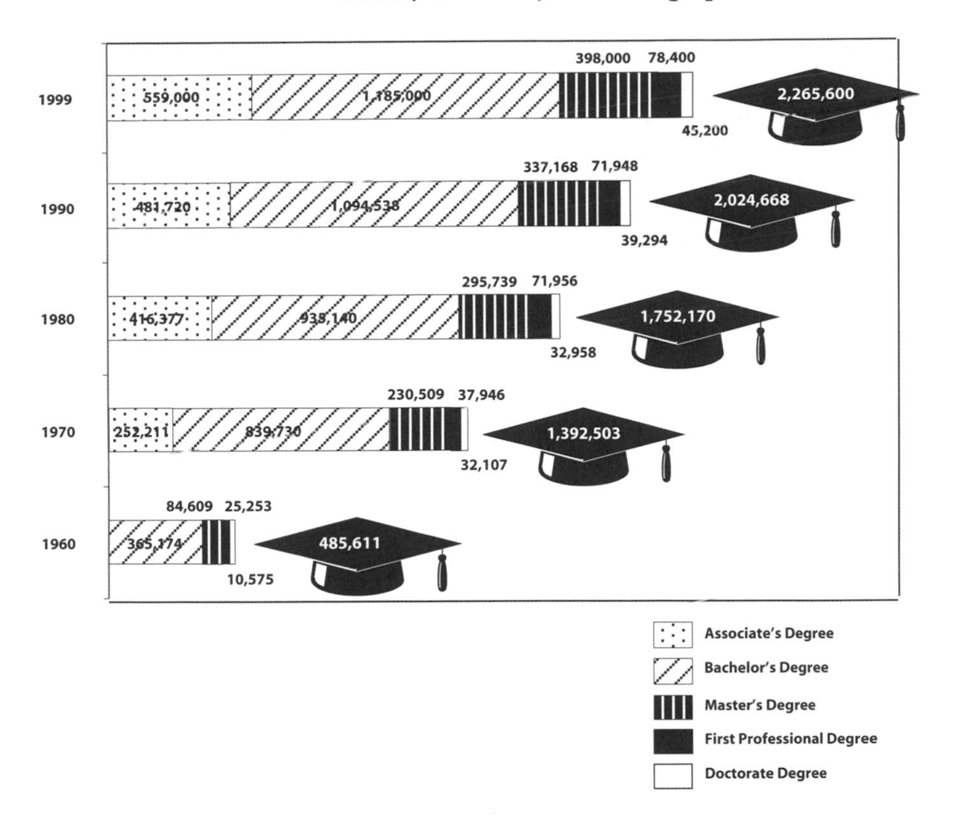

Fig. 5. Enrollment, by degree, in private and public colleges and universities, 1960–1999. *Source:* NCES, Digest of Education Statistics.

ity to link workers and workplaces in hosts of new ways. More than half of all households had computers by the year 2000, up from 42.1 percent in December 1998. The numbers of Americans online jumped by an extraordinary 31.9 million between 1998 and 2000, from 32.7 percent to 44.4 percent. As noted by the Department of Commerce, "the rapid uptake of new technologies is occurring among most groups of Americans, regardless of income, education, race or ethnicity, location, age, or gender." Indeed African Americans and Hispanic Americans from nine to twenty-four years old—the up-and-coming generations—showed some of the fastest rates of increase in Internet use of all groups. Black children between the ages of nine and seventeen years saw a 63 percent increase in online use over the twenty-month span between 1998 and 2000.

The Digital Divide Is Closing. The American workforce is wired and eager to use their knowledge for personal advancement. As the Heldrich Center and the University of Connecticut found in their *Work Trends/Nothing but Net* report (Van Horn and Dautrich 2000), workers who make robust use of personal computer and Internet applications tend to have higher incomes and more education.

Nonetheless, illiteracy remains a profound barrier to economic opportunity for many Americans. According to the 1992 National Adult Literacy Survey, forty-four million American adults—about 20 percent of the total adult population—function at the lowest of the five literacy levels and have difficulty with basic reading, writing, and computational tasks. Nearly two-thirds (62 percent) of those with inadequate literacy skills have not completed high school. The United States has more adults languishing at the lowest level of literacy than Switzerland, Sweden, The Netherlands, Germany, and Canada (International Adult Literacy Survey 1997).

Low literacy levels not only pose barriers to an individual's upward mobility but also harm society. Those with minimal literacy skills are not prepared to learn new skills and more complex applications in any industry. This hampers productivity and slows the introduction of technology.

Trends to Watch

1. The percentage of women working at least part time has increased from 41 percent in 1967 to 60 percent in 1999, and the proportion of these working women with full-time jobs climbed from 52 to 70 percent (U.S. Department of Labor 2000c).
2. New immigrants will account for almost two-thirds of the nation's population growth by the year 2050 (U.S. Census Bureau 2000a).
3. According to the Employment Policy Foundation's projections, from 2000 to 2008 an additional 24 million workers will need to be replaced due to retirement and death if the economy continues to grow at its present rate. The result will be a shortage of 4.6 million workers, of which 3.5 million will need college-level skills.

Related Reading in Part 2

Chapter 8:
"Finished at Forty," Nina Munk
"The H-1B Straitjacket: Why Congress Should Repeal the Cap on Foreign-Born Highly Skilled Workers," Suzette Brooks Masters and Ted Ruthizer
"Labor Movement: Mexicans Transform a Town in Georgia—and an Entire Industry," Joel Millman and Will Pinkston

Where Do We Work?

Over the past two decades, job growth in the southern and western United States has far outpaced job growth in the northeastern and midwestern states. The states with the fastest job growth between 1994 and July 2001 included Nevada at 50.5 percent, Arizona at 38.4 percent, Colorado at 32.2 percent, and Utah at 30.6 percent, followed by Florida at 28.4 percent, and Texas at 26.7 percent (U.S. Department of Labor 2001). (See fig. 6.) In the Northeast, Washington, D.C.,

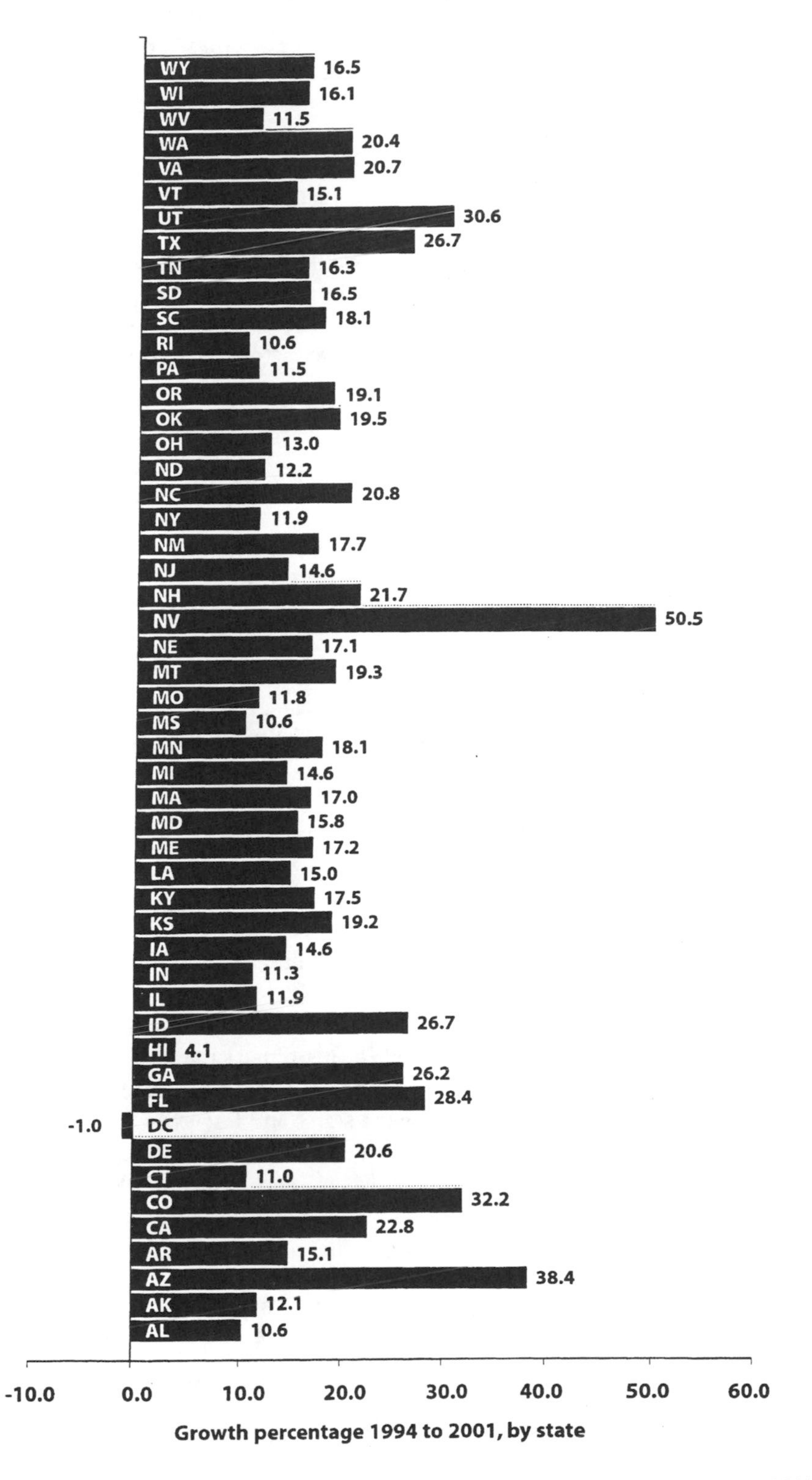

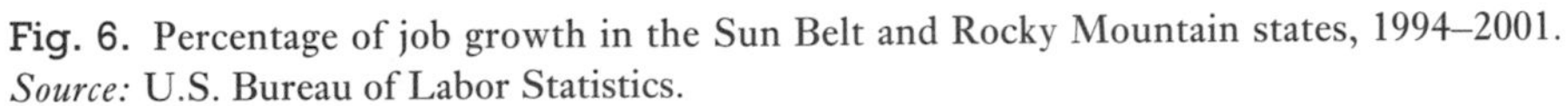

Fig. 6. Percentage of job growth in the Sun Belt and Rocky Mountain states, 1994–2001. *Source:* U.S. Bureau of Labor Statistics.

Rhode Island, Pennsylvania, Connecticut, and New Jersey had less than 15 percent job growth during this time period.

During the rise of the industrial economy in the early twentieth century, the northeastern states—abundant in natural resources and existing population centers—were the economic and job-creating hubs of the nation. As manufacturing declined in the United States, the new economy arose, fueled by information technology and serviced by networked, online back-office centers. Businesses could now locate where taxes were low, land was inexpensive and abundant, and states were eager to attract new business. These factors fed development and job growth in a swath of states from North Carolina and the suburban office park south to the Rockies, with their high quality of life, and extending to Silicon Valley and the Silicon Rainforest of the Pacific Northwest. The most desirable high-tech employers offering high-growth, high-skills jobs found that locating their companies in desirable, ruggedly beautiful west and northwest locations made their firms more appealing to the best college graduates.

The growth in population—and job opportunities—in the American West has been nothing short of remarkable. Between 1990 and 1998, the city of Henderson, Nevada, a suburb of Las Vegas, has nearly doubled in size, growing from 64,948 to 122,339. America's fastest growing cities in the 1990s were not traditional major urban areas. The thirty fastest-growing cities of more than 100,000 people in the United States between 1990 and 1998 sort out this way (Wood 1998):

- 23 of these cities are in the West (of Mississippi)
- 13 are in arid, desert states: five in Arizona, five in Texas, three in Nevada
- 28 of the 30 cities have populations of less than 500,000, most have less than 200,000
- Only one city—Chesapeake, Virginia—is found in the Northeast, Mid-Atlantic, or Southeast

Job creation and opportunity are linked to this remarkable regional growth. A detailed analysis of BLS data published in the January 30, 2001 *New York Times* showed a correlation between fast-growing states and fast-growing occupations. For example, securities and financial services workers are driving job growth in Nevada, which was projected at 54 percent between 1998 and 2008.

Much has been written and said about the potential of telecommuting and telework to allow workers to live and work where they prefer, no matter the distance. The media and numerous leading surveys have documented that the possibilities of telework are of great interest to workers, who in large numbers would prefer the option to do so. But telecommuting is not yet catching on as a widespread practice. Long-form census data released in 2001 found that the fraction of Americans breaking free of offices and cubicles barely nudged, moving from 3 percent in 1990 to 3.2 percent in 2000 (Kulish 2001). In light of the economic and social consequences of the terror attacks on the United States, more employers may offer telecommuting and telework opportunities for workers not only in New York but also other city centers as security measures make automobile commuting more difficult.

It should be emphasized that the mild recession and retrenchment of business investment in early 2001 followed by the economic impact of the terror attacks dampened many state economies for 2002 and 2003 after a decade-long boom. Job losses in September and October 2001 alone accounted for nearly two-thirds of the 1.2 million jobs lost since the U.S. recession officially began in March of that year.

Heavy job losses directly related to the attacks were felt in the travel, tourism, airlines, lodging, and recreation industries, and in the states and cities where these industries are significant. According to a widely noted study released by the Milken Institute in January 2002, the nation's most popular tourist destinations, including cities such as Las Vegas and Honolulu, as well as its largest cities, are projected to suffer the most job losses as a result of the attacks. For example, Las Vegas is projected to see a 5 percent loss in jobs, Reno a 3.1 percent loss, Myrtle Beach a nearly 4 percent loss, New York City a 3.2 percent loss. New York City was projected to lose the most jobs in numerical terms, nearly 150,000, followed by Los Angeles and Chicago at approximately 69,000 and 68,000, respectively. Ranked among the most affected metro areas in percentage of jobs lost due to the attack were Atlantic-Cape May, New Jersey; Orlando, Florida; Wichita, Kansas; Flagstaff, Arizona; Fort Worth, Texas; Seattle, Washington; and a number of small Florida cities (Devol 2001). Should these carefully calibrated projections come to pass, states such as Nevada, New York, and Florida can be expected to lose population as well as jobs through 2004.

How Much Do We Earn?

While it is commonplace to meet a new person and ask "What do you do?" it remains a towering social taboo (and matter of intense curiosity) to ask "what do you earn?" An individual's earnings and income have a strong connection to personal opportunity in the United States, which has wide income disparities. Figure 7 lists the mean hourly and annual wages of a roster of familiar occupations. But our individual earnings must be viewed in the context of the larger, national patterns taking shape in how work is compensated in the United States.

Income Trends. Although Americans of all income levels are working longer hours in the past ten years than they did ten years ago, wealthier Americans are seeing far greater increases in wages and income than citizens further down the income ladder. The most accurate and comprehensive income data published show dramatic increases in the gaps between rich, poor, and middle-income Americans through the 1980s and 1990s. According to a 2001 Congressional

Occupation	Hourly	Annual
Cashier	8.43	13,000
Cook	8.97	16,000
Janitor/Cleaner	9.55	17,000
Secretary	13.49	28,000
Truck Driver	14.04	30,000
Computer Operator	14.14	29,000
Social Worker	16.08	32,000
Legal Assistant	17.29	35,000
Electrician	18.09	39,000
Police/Detective	19.57	40,000
Plumber, Pipefitter, and Steamfitter	20.08	42,000
Accountant/Auditor	20.38	42,000
Registered Nurse	20.71	36,000
Pre-Kindergarten Teacher	21.43	40,000
Aircraft Engine Mechanic	21.80	45,000
Computer Programmer	22.12	45,000
Insurance Sales	22.57	42,000
Editors and Reporters	23.35	47,000
Architects	25.83	54,000
Railroad Conductors	26.78	29,000
Social Work Professors	26.45	45,000
Secondary School Teachers	27.84	53,000
Computer System Analyst	27.90	58,000
Financial Managers	32.85	69,000
Political Science Professors	33.44	65,000
Lawyers	36.52	76,000
Physicians	37.20	77,000
Physicists and Astronomers	37.74	78,000
Engineering Professors	38.55	75,000
Petroleum Engineers	43.02	91,000
Law Professors	60.32	113,000
Airline Pilots and Navigators	79.31	97,000

Year 2000

Fig. 7. Mean hourly and annual earnings for selected occupations in the United States (based on mean weekly hours). *Source:* U.S. Bureau of Labor Statistics.

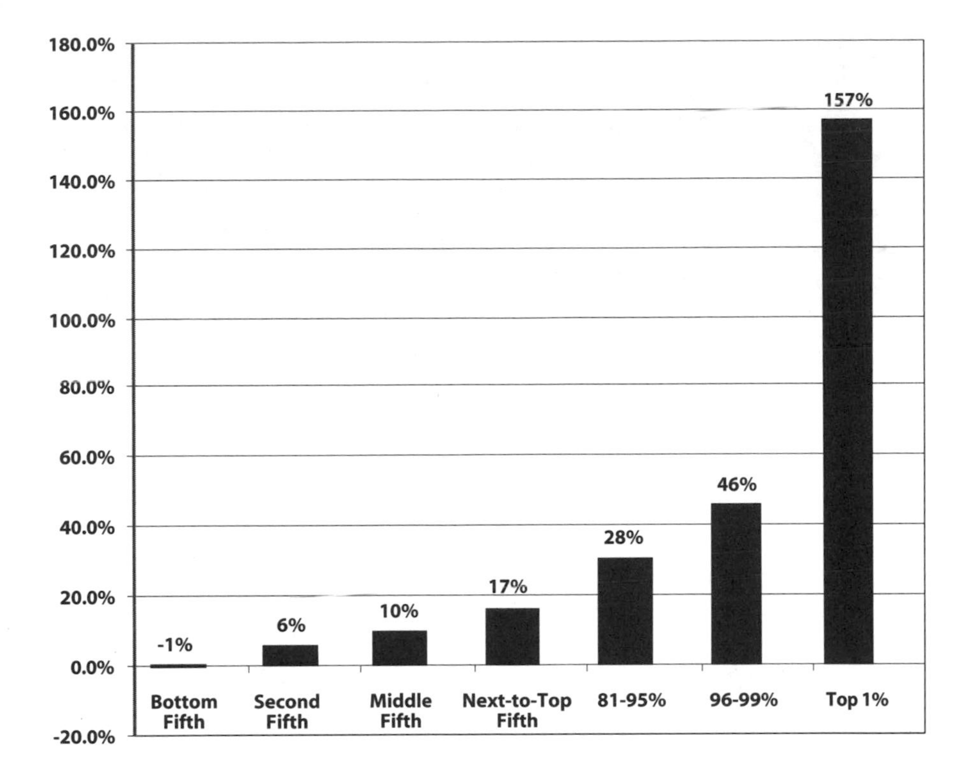

Fig. 8. Change in after-tax income, by U.S. household income categories, 1979–1997. *Source:* Congressional Budget Office, Center on Budget and Policy Priorities.

Budget Office (CBO) study and a related paper by the Center on Budget and Policy Priorities, the average after-tax income of the poorest one-fifth of U.S. households did not grow at all between 1979 and 1997. During this period, however, average after-tax income soared by 157 percent for the richest 1 percent of U.S. households. The gap between the rich and poor, and the rich and the middle class, was wider in 1997 than at any other time since 1979, and according to data it is projected to continue growing (see fig. 8).

Even during the economic boom of the 1990s, income disparities did not stop growing; in fact, they mushroomed. From 1989 to 1997, the average after-tax income of the top 1 percent of households grew 36 percent ($180,000 per household) while the incomes of the middle fifth of households grew just 6 percent. The CBO reports that the rapid rise in the share of income going to the top of the distribution continued at least into 1998 and 1999. Overall, the share of the entire national income held by the top 1 percent of the population grew from 7.5 percent in 1979 to 13.6 percent in 1997 (see fig. 9).

Although the money gap among classes widened throughout the 1990s, the strong job growth of the last few years of the 1990s did produce gains for many U.S. households. Black household income reached an all-time high in 1997 and

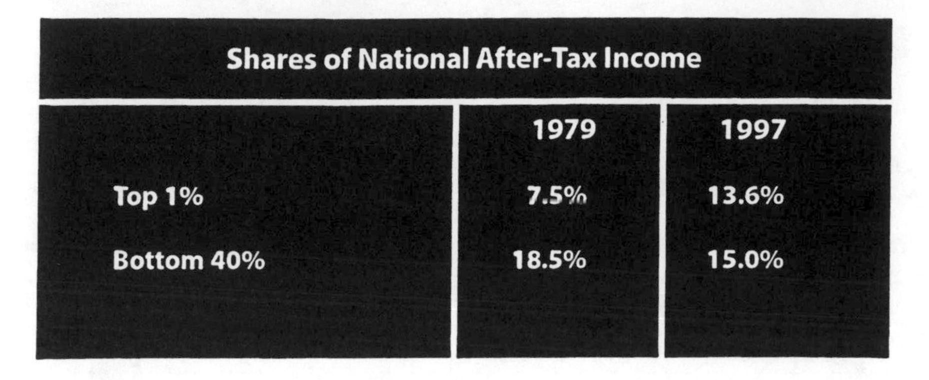

Shares of National After-Tax Income

	1979	1997
Top 1%	7.5%	13.6%
Bottom 40%	18.5%	15.0%

Fig. 9. Share of national after-tax income, 1979–1997. *Source:* Congressional Budget Office, Center on Budget and Policy Priorities.

remained there in 1998, according to census data. In 1999, Hispanic households recorded their highest median incomes since 1972. Due to the economic surge of the late 1990s, income gaps among minority and white households, skilled and unskilled workers, and men and women workers were slightly moderated. During 2000 and 2001, the U.S. economy began to slow down, a decline that was accelerated by the effects of the 2001 terror attacks. Layoffs and cutbacks will likely end this progress for the short-term.

Non-Hispanic white households had a median household income of $44,366 in 1999, compared to $30,735 for Hispanic households; $27,910 for Black households; and $51,205 for Asian/Pacific Islander households (see fig. 10). In 1986, the median income of white households was 83 percent higher than black households and 46 percent higher than Hispanic households. In 1999, that gap had closed to 59 percent between white and black households and 44 percent between white and Hispanic households. In 1999 Asian households had a 15 percent higher household income than non-Hispanic white households, an advantage that has held since 1988, when census takers began collecting Asian/Pacific Islander data.

The historic income gap favoring men over women continues to persist. While men's median income grew to $25,212 in 1997, women's median income was $13,703. However, as noted in figure 11, median income for women has grown steadily in relation to men's income over the past fifty years, slowly closing the gap. Women now realize fifty-four cents on every dollar of income received by men, as their share of the labor force has increased. When examined by earnings only, which excludes asset accumulation through investments, real estate, and other income where men enjoy historical advantages, full-time working women have closed the gap to seventy-four cents on the dollar in 1997 from fifty-eight cents on the dollar in 1967.

The roles of women in parenting and providing childcare also dramatically impact their ability to receive fair and adequate compensation in the American

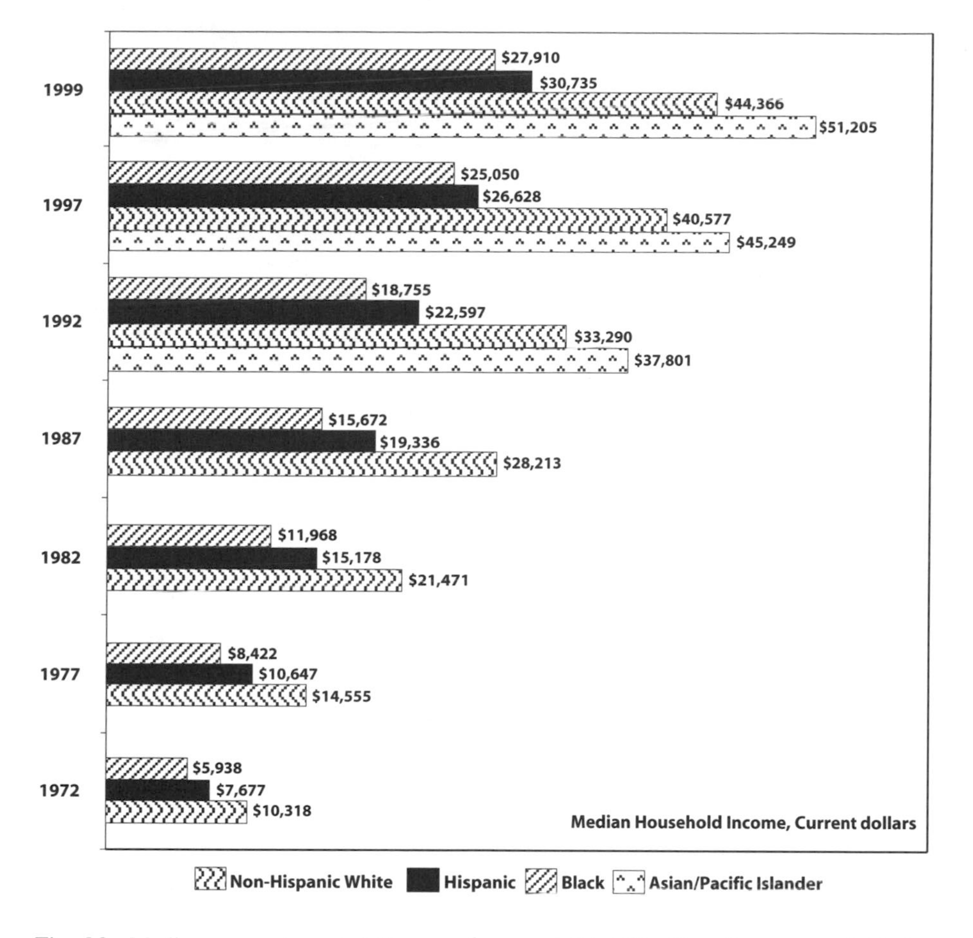

Fig. 10. Median pre-tax household income, by race, 1972–1999. *Note:* Data not available for Asian/Pacific Islanders 1972–1987. *Source:* U.S. Census Bureau.

economy. A growing literature, including the powerful book *The Price of Motherhood* by Ann Crittenden, provides conclusive evidence that the arrangements of America's economic and social structure systemically penalize women for their role in most families as the primary caregiver to children.

When one compares the earnings of all male and female workers, both full *and* part time (which includes many women in parenting and caregiving roles), the average earnings of female workers amount to only 59 percent of men's earnings, Crittenden finds. In addition, the pay gap between women who are mothers and women who are not is growing dramatically. Crittenden cites studies by economists, including Jane Waldfogel of Columbia, that show that during the late 1970s the difference between men's and women's pay was about the same for all women. "Non-mothers earned only slightly higher wages," writes Crittenden. "But over the next decade things changed. By 1991, thirty-year-old American

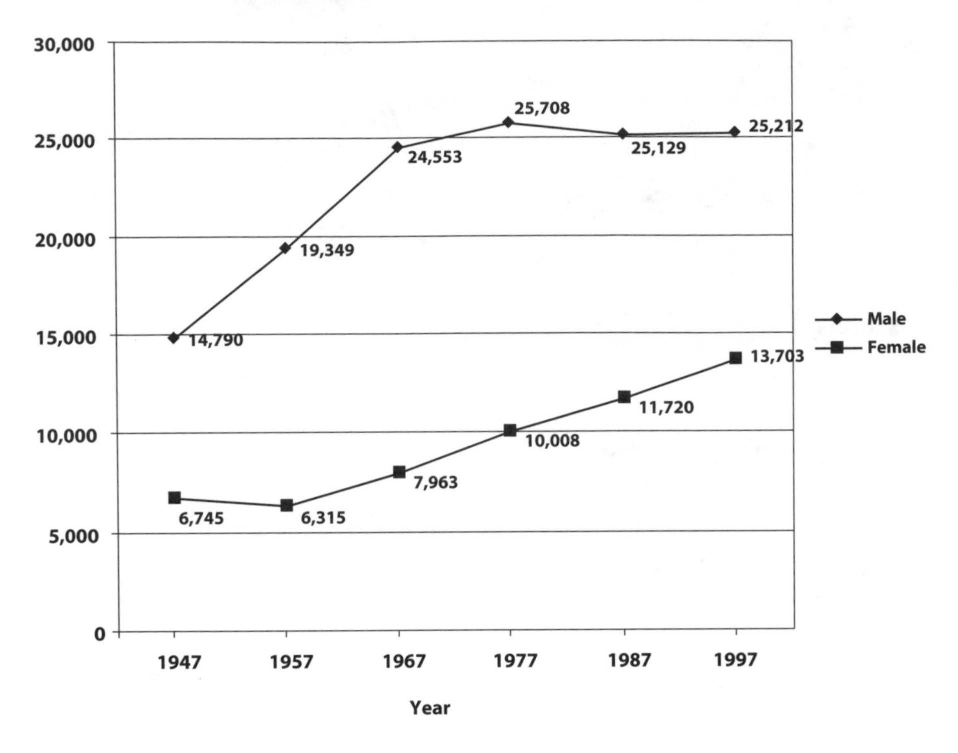

Fig. 11. Median salary of women compared to men, 1947–1997, in 1997 dollars. *Source:* U.S. Census Bureau, *Measuring Fifty Years of Economic Change,* March Population Survey Series (Washington, D.C.: U.S. Census Bureau, 1998).

women without children were making 90 percent of men's wages, while comparable women with children were making only 70 percent. Even when Waldfogel factored out all the women's differences, the disparity in incomes remained—something she dubbed the 'family wage gap'" (Crittenden 2001, 95).

The family wage gap also affects fathers, according to Crittenden and others. One survey found that fathers at the management level in Fortune 500 companies from dual-career families (rather than the "traditional" model of a wife working at home) earned almost 20 percent less than men whose wives were at home and received fewer promotions (Stroh 1994). In general, the United States has refused to follow the lead of European nations in making provision for the imputed value of unpaid work at home when tabulating national economic statistics, Social Security, and other entitlement benefits and setting fair family leave policies and other aspects of economic security.

Younger women (twenty-five to thirty-five) in white-collar occupations with the largest increases in the numbers of full-time working women over the past decade are earning the same as men in these fields, regardless of parental status or hours worked (Employment Policy Foundation, April 2001). Soaring partici-

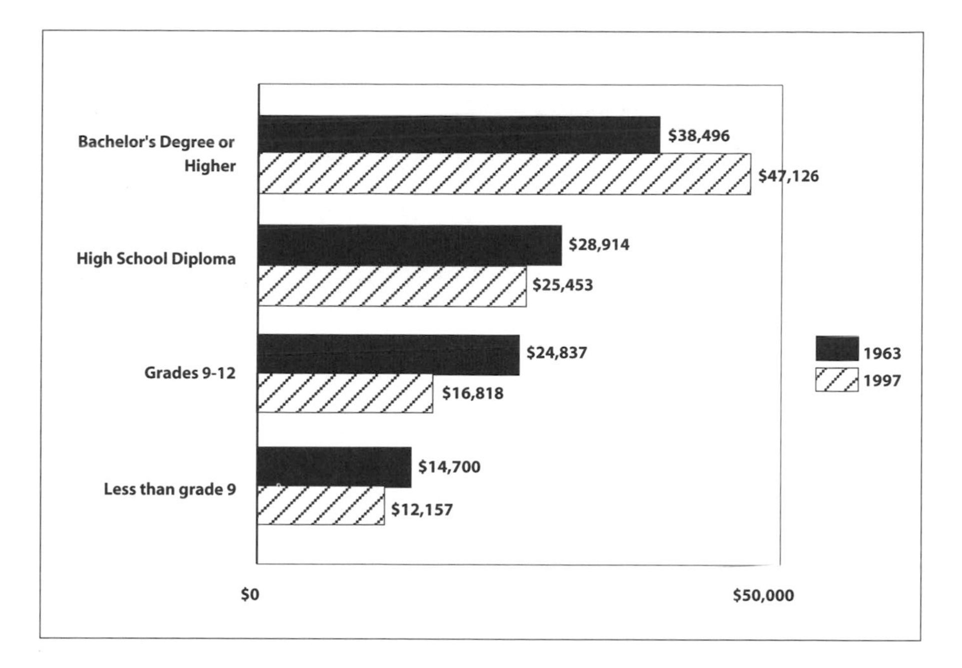

Fig. 12. Median income for men, by educational level, 1963–1997. *Source:* U.S. Census Bureau, *Measuring Fifty Years of Economic Change,* March Population Survey Series (Washington, D.C.: U.S. Census Bureau, 1998).

pation by women in fields that include veterinarians, public administrators, math and science teachers, industrial engineers, dentists, members of the clergy, and physicians' assistants are closing pay disparities between younger men and women. However, gender pay gaps in these fields persist for women over the age of thirty-five, in large part, we may surmise, because many of them leave full-time or fast-track careers to raise their families.

More than any other factor, personal income is determined by one's education and skill attainment. The information economy and globalization of production have eliminated millions of lower-skilled manufacturing jobs in the United States and replaced them with technology-driven jobs requiring higher levels of skills. As seen in Census Bureau figures, the gap in median income between men who have a high school degree and men who have a bachelor's degree or higher grew from about three-quarters in 1963 ($28,914 versus $38,496) to about one-half in 1997 ($25,453 versus $47,126). Looked at another way, the economic premium for achieving a bachelor's degree grew 22 percent since 1963, while men's incomes have actually *declined* in all other educational groups (fig. 12). Women have experienced increases in income at all educational levels, however, since 1963 (fig. 13).

Occupations requiring greater formal education, at least an associate's degree, accounted for 25 percent of all job growth in 1998. By 2008, it is expected

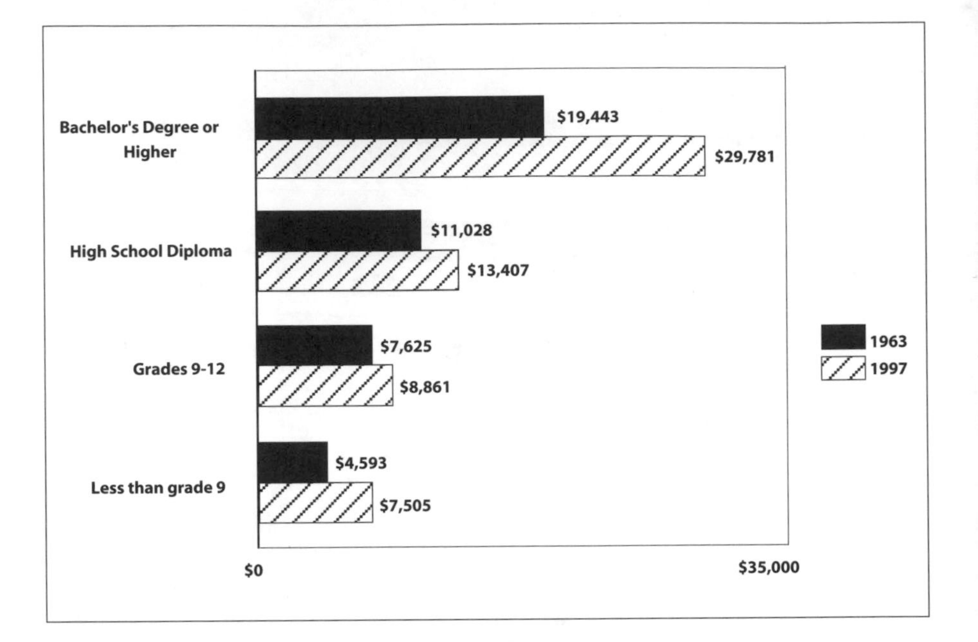

Fig. 13. Median income for women, by educational level, 1963–1997. *Source:* U.S. Census Bureau, *Measuring Fifty Years of Economic Change,* March Population Survey Series (Washington, D.C.: U.S. Census Bureau, 1998).

that 40 percent of job growth will come from jobs requiring at least an associate's degree (Fullerton 1999). Another key income trend is that family incomes for married-couple families with two earners grew in the past two decades as wives entered the labor force.

The surge of married and single women into the labor market reflected not only changing social mores in the United States but also raw economic necessity. Until the late 1970s and then with finality the recession of the early 1980s, the income gap between workers (particularly men) with a high school education only and those with college degrees was actually closing. Unionization, the value of the dollar internationally, and many other factors contributed to a good standard of living for skilled and semiskilled single-earner working families. Then the blue-collar recession of the early 1980s decimated the manufacturing and industrial centers of the northeastern United States. Between 1979 and 1984, about 5 percent of the U.S. labor force were displaced from their jobs, and 70 percent of these workers did not find new jobs within two years or they were reemployed at lower wages (Levy 1998).

White and black male workers with less than a high school education were devastated by these changes. The lower-skilled mining, manufacturing, and agricultural jobs that were at one time respected, though tough-and-dirty pathways to the middle class, vanished by the tens of thousands. Economist Frank Levy notes that between 1970 and 1996 the labor force participation of prime-age white men fell from 97 percent to 93 percent, and among high school dropouts in this group the rate declined from 94 percent to 80 percent. This trend was particularly devastating for black men, who had slowly begun reaping the economic benefits of civil rights, affirmative action, and social change through the 1970s, gaining entry to better-paying jobs and sending their children to college for the first time. As Levy (1998) writes in *The New Dollars and Dreams,* "Since the mid-1970s, slow wage growth, the falling demand for less-skilled men, crime, and the end of affirmative action, have combined to slow substantially the progress of black males."

Millions of veteran blue-collar workers and families spent most of the 1980s seeking skills and hope for their careers. Many became self-employed, entered job-training programs, moved, or worked off the books. During the early 1990s, however, the country experienced a recession that affected many white-collar workers as well. Corporate mergers and downsizing, the massive effects of the savings and loan crisis, and budget cuts in the defense department and related industries all combined to eliminate millions of jobs. Between 1985 and 1989, AT&T alone reduced employment by 76,000 workers. Outplacement firm Challenger, Gray, and Christmas tabulated layoff announcements by major corporations growing from 111,285 in 1989 to 555,292 in 1991 (Levy 1998). Many of these workers eventually found new jobs in technology and service firms, but the U.S. job market had become fundamentally less secure, limiting wage growth as job instability and worker fears gave employers new leverage over salary and wage increases. Thus was heralded a new era of anxiety for all workers. In the recovery years between 1993 and 1995, about 2.7 percent of managers and administrators lost their jobs each year. This rate was lower than the 5 percent rate for blue-collar workers, but both rates were at levels normally found in a deep recession—not an economic recovery (Levy 1998).

Benefit Trends and Costs. Health care and pension benefits are essential to the financial security of working Americans. From the 1950s to the early 1980s, more and more employers added health care and pension benefits for their employees. But in the past two decades this trend has reversed. Increasing health care costs, growing international competition, and changes in the American political and corporate environment have led employers to dramatically reduce employer-provided health care insurance and pension security.

Between 1989 and 1997, the percentage of full-time workers with medical benefits fell from 92 percent to 76 percent. The percentage of employees participating in "defined benefit" plans that guarantee a retirement benefit declined from 59 percent in 1991 to 50 percent in 1997 (see fig. 14). By the year 2000, forty-four million Americans were uninsured, about 17 percent of the nonelderly population. Between 1988 and 2000, the number of uninsured has grown by an average of about one million per year (Kaiser Commission on the Uninsured 2000).

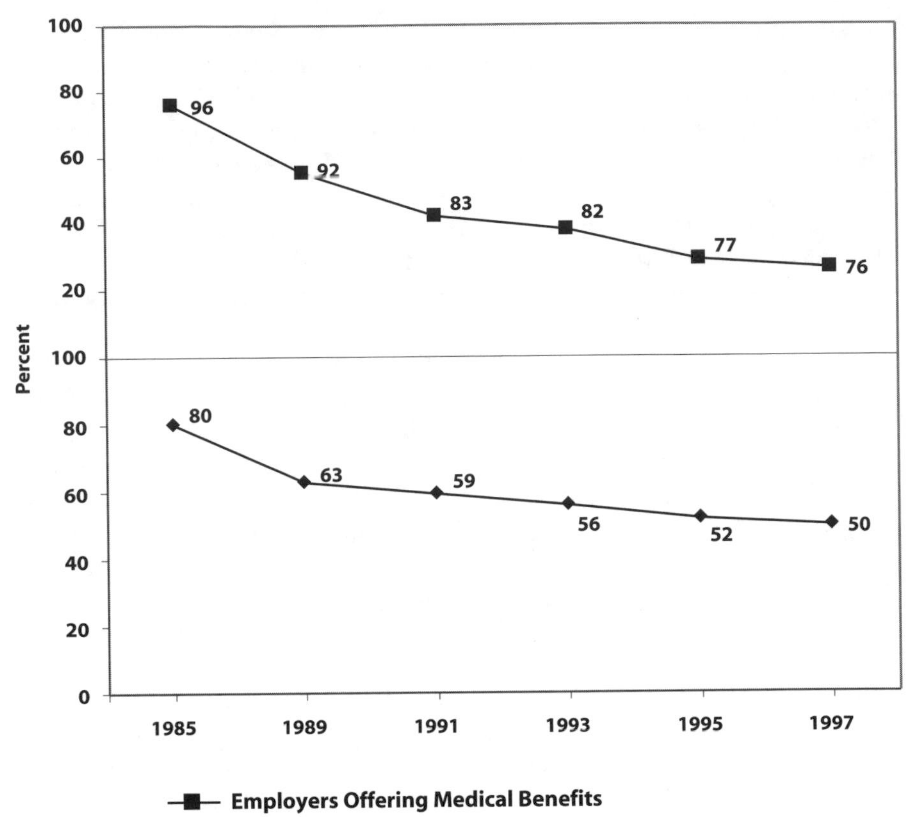

Fig. 14. Percentage of employers offering medical benefits and defined benefit (guaranteed) pension plans, 1985–1997. *Note:* Data not available for 1987. *Source:* U.S. Bureau of Labor Statistics.

Government health care assistance for low-income Americans—whether they work or not—is provided through the Medicaid program. It has expanded gradually since its inception to provide health coverage for increasing numbers of children who are born into and live in or near poverty. In 1996 Congress passed a new federal initiative, known as the Children's Health Insurance Program (CHIP), to provide health care for the children of low-income workers without employer-provided health care coverage. Under this program—which provides health care to as many as 3.3 million children in 2000—states use federal funds to provide basic services to children under the age of eighteen whose families earn up to $34,100.

The nearly two-decade ascent in health insurance costs and premiums so familiar to U.S. workers paused during the mid-1990s, when the rate of growth in medical costs flattened. The growth of managed care had tamped down some of the most inflationary aspects of the health care system—such as multiple tests and emergency room care. However, health care costs began climbing again during 2000 and 2001, when monthly premiums for employer-sponsored health insurance rose 11 percent from the previous year and the share of premium payments paid by workers did not decline as it had during the late 1990s. During 2000 and 2001, workers paid a national average of 15 percent of single coverage premiums and 27 percent of family coverage premiums.

Kaiser Family Foundation/Health Research and Educational Trust data show the portion of employers offering health benefits to their workers increased to 67 percent in 2000 from 54 percent in 1998. However, the difficulties workers face in receiving health insurance through their employer is not limited to being offered some form of care. It also has a great deal to do with the workforce size of their employer, as well as their income. An overview of employer health coverage trends published by the Kaiser Foundation illustrates key trends that unfolded during the 1990s. Forty-seven percent of workers at small firms with fewer than 100 employees received health coverage at work in 1988, and that number declined to 41 percent in 1993 and rose slightly to 43 percent in 1997. This is less than half of the small employer workforce!

However, it is also critical to note the gap between the percent of employees who are actually offered health insurance by these employers and the share of these firms that offer *some* form of insurance to some employees. In smaller firms, workers often fall through numerous gaps in the health insurance coverage net. They must work for certain periods of time, certain numbers of hours per week, or relatively high premiums in order to receive coverage. In 1997, 70 percent of firms offered some form of insurance, but they only offered insurance to 57 percent of their workers. Of this group of workers, about 75 percent enrolled in the offered program.

In a related analysis of smaller firms, in this case those with workforces under 200 workers, Kaiser Foundation analysts found that firms with predominantly low-wage workforces were less likely to offer benefits than larger firms. Among small employers in which less than 35 percent of the workforce earned under $20,000 per year, 85 percent offered health benefits. Among firms in which 35 percent or more of the workforce earned over $20,000 per year, only 35 percent offered health benefits.

In firms with more than 100 employees, the rate of those actually covered declined from 80 percent in 1988 to 73 percent in 1997. Of these larger firms, 91 percent had some form of health insurance, and 85 percent of workers were actually offered coverage. Of this group, 86 percent of workers enrolled in the offered program (Long and Marquis 1999).

During 2000, 41 percent of workers were enrolled in Preferred Provider Organizations (PPOs), 29 percent were enrolled in Health Maintenance Organizations (HMOs), and 22 percent in Point of Service (POS) plans. The expansion of subsidized health care through CHIP funds and the boom years of the late 1990s began to help more low- and moderate-income working families secure affordable health care. However, these developments provided only incremental progress to reverse the long-term trend of the past fifteen years, during which the number of Americans without health insurance has soared. The misfortunes of the American economy in 2001 and 2002 have increased the numbers of uninsured, and a Kaiser Foundation analysis released in 2002 projects substantial cuts in health coverage as the unemployment rate continues to rise.

Who Are the Uninsured? The vast number of the uninsured in America are nonelderly, working adults and their children. The elderly and children in poor families receive health coverage through Medicare and Medicaid. Poor single parents with children are most likely to have Medicaid coverage (54 percent) and are least likely among poor families in general to be uninsured (31 percent). Almost three-quarters (74 percent) of the uninsured are in families where at least one person is working full time.

The uninsured are largely low-income workers and their families. Nearly a third of workers earning under $20,000 a year are uninsured, compared to only 5 percent of workers earning more than $50,000 a year. The vast majority of uninsured workers (70 percent) are not offered these benefits by their employers.

However, during the late 1990s analysts noted increases in the numbers of poor, nonworking parents who lost their Medicaid coverage while they were still eligible. The passage of the new welfare law in 1996 and related restrictions on immigrants triggered declines in the numbers of poor people on assistance, leading to unintended drops in health coverage as many individuals mistakenly believed they were no long qualified for Medicaid or failed to follow new rules and guidelines for applying. The combination of a slowing economy—and its impact on layoffs and the provision of health benefits by employers—with losses of Medicaid coverage for eligible low-income families could dramatically expand the number of uninsured in the years ahead.

Who in America is the most at risk of being uninsured? The Kaiser Commission on Medicaid and the Uninsured reports the following (see figs. 15, 16, and 17):

- Young low-income men between the ages of nineteen and thirty-four are uninsured in far greater numbers (54 percent) than low-income women in the same age bracket (36 percent). Since low-income men are far less likely to be single parents, it is far harder for them to enroll in Medicaid. Rates of coverage rise with age.
- Children are less likely to be uninsured than adults, yet nearly twelve million children were uninsured in 1997. The vast majority (eight million) of these children were from low-income families.
- Low-income minorities are at particular risk of being uninsured. More than half of low-income Hispanic adults are uninsured, while about 29 percent of low-income blacks and 29 percent of low-income whites are uninsured.

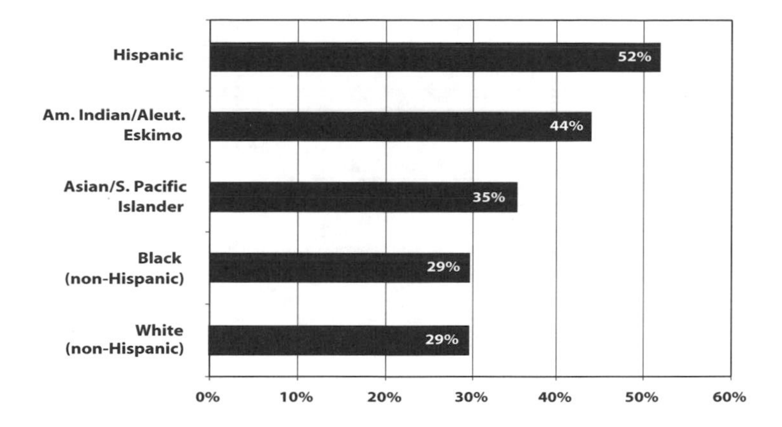

Fig. 15. Percentage of uninsured low-wage workers (less than $20,000 a year), by race, 1997. *Source:* Urban Institute estimates based on March 1998 Current Population Survey.

- Low-wage workers in small businesses are at substantial risk of being uninsured—with 60 percent of low-wage workers employed in businesses with fewer than 100 employees having no insurance.
- Health insurance is more prevalent in some industries than others. Half of all low-wage construction workers are uninsured, and workers in agriculture, business, and repair services are denied wide access to insurance.

Consumer Spending and Saving. Incomes rose only slightly for middle- and low-income Americans during the 1990s, but many extended their purchasing power by saving less and borrowing more. Personal savings rates (savings as a

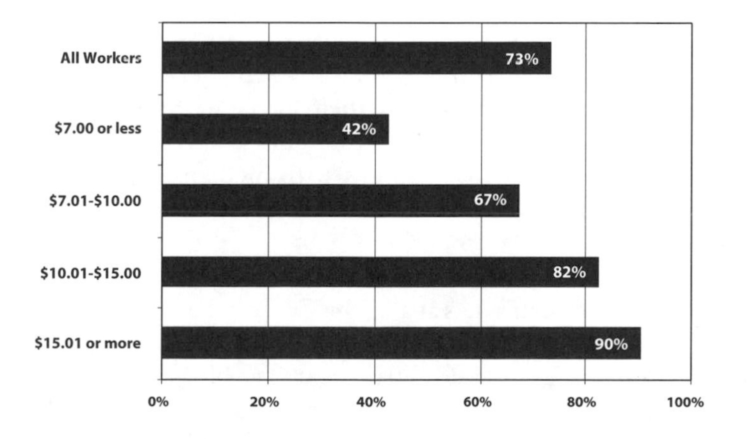

Fig. 16. Percentage of workers with employer coverage, by wage, 1996. *Source:* Calculations based on Cooper and Schone 1997.

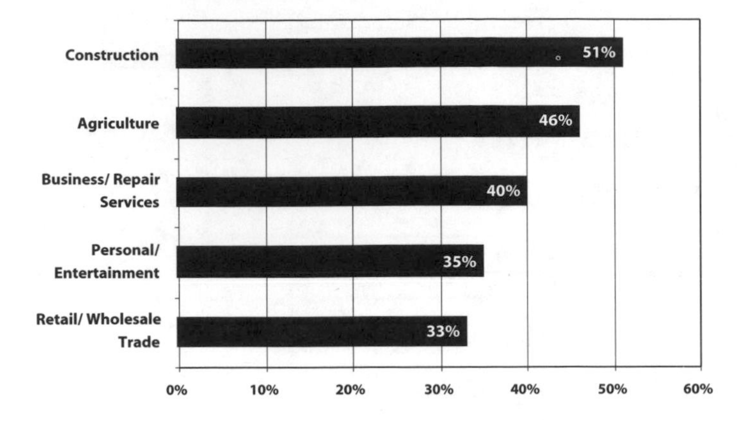

Fig. 17. Percentage of uninsured workers, by industry, 1997. *Source:* Kaiser Commission and Urban Institute estimates based on March 1998 Current Population Survey.

percent of personal income) plunged from 9 percent in 1982 to 2.1 percent in 1997 and just 0.5 percent in 1998, according to the U.S. Department of Commerce/Bureau of Economic Analysis data. Consumer credit grew at a rate of 9.5 percent in 2000, exceeding 10 percent in the first quarter of 2001, as compared to 7.9 percent in 1996 (Federal Reserve Bank of St. Louis 2001). Auto finance companies loaned nearly $21 billion for car purchases in 2000, as compared to about $17 billion in 1996. As noted by Jill Fraser in *White Collar Sweatshop*, "For countless people, the only way to obtain what seemed a fair reward for all their hard work was to push household borrowing to dangerous and unparalleled heights" (Fraser 2001, 39).

The long-term decline of personal savings in the United States may have serious implications for the economic security of American households. Most American families have inadequate savings to see them through financial emergencies, much less to help them prepare them for a long-term secure retirement. Analysis by economist Edward Wolff (2000) of New York University and the Century Foundation show that families with median or lower earnings, on average, have financial reserves sufficient to cover little more than one month's worth of expenses.

Savings and capital gains are faraway hopes for many Americans—many of whom do not have pension assets at all. The Century Foundation analysis found that 43.5 percent of American workers do not have access to an employer-sponsored pension plan, and nearly 80 percent of small-business employees have no pension coverage whatsoever. Despite the Wall Street boom of the 1990s, in the year 2000 only a third of American households owned more than $5,000 worth of stock. The median value of the financial assets of American families is just $13,000, according to the Wolff analysis.

POLICY BRIEF: PENSION PLANS AND SOCIAL SECURITY

Adapted with the permission of the Employee Benefit Research Institute

Employee Benefit Research Institute

Pension Plans

The first pension plan in the United States was established in 1759 to benefit widows and children of Presbyterian ministers. The first corporate plan was adopted more than a century later by the American Express Company. During the next century, some four hundred plans were established, primarily in the railroad, banking, and public utility industries. The most significant growth has occurred since the mid-1940s; now more than forty-five million active participants are covered by more than 708,000 private pension plans.

Pension contributions and participation are encouraged by the federal government and the tax system. An employer's contribution to a qualified plan is immediately deductible in computing the employees' taxes but only becomes taxable to the employee on subsequent distribution from the plan. In the interim, investment earnings on the contributions are not subject to tax. These preferential rules require that the employer comply with rules set out in the Employee Retirement Income Security Act (ERISA) of 1974 and administered by the U.S. Department of the Treasury and the Department of Labor. These rules are designed to protect employee rights and guarantee that pension benefits will be available for employees at retirement. In addition, plans must satisfy a set of nondiscrimination rules. In defined benefit plans, the employer agrees to provide the employee a specific benefit upon retirement based on a specific formula. In defined contribution plans, the employer makes provision for contributions to an account established for each participating employee. The final retirement benefit reflects the total employer contributions, any employee contributions, and investment gains or losses.

ERISA and a series of other federal laws and changes limit the amount of employee and employer contributions that may be made to a plan. They also limit the maximum benefits allowed under a defined benefit plan. Beginning January 1, 2002, there is an overall limit of $200,000 on annual compensation that can be considered for calculating benefit and contribution limits.

Social Security and Medicare

The Social Security Act and related laws establish a number of programs designed to provide for the needs of individuals and families, protect aged and disabled persons against the expenses of illnesses that could otherwise exhaust their savings, keep families together, and give children an opportunity to grow up with good health and security. When Social Security became effective in 1937, it applied only to workers in agricultural industry and commerce—about 60 percent of all workers. Currently, about 95 percent of all jobs in the United States are covered.

Social Security is designed to replace a portion of earnings a worker loses upon retirement or disability. Medicare pays a part of the medical expenses of the aged and disabled. The Social Security program provides a much wider variety of benefits than is generally recognized —in 1999, only 43 percent of benefits under these programs were awarded to retired workers. The following benefits are provided under Old Age, Survivors, and Disability Insurance (OASDI), the group of programs frequently referred to as Social Security:

- Monthly benefits to eligible workers over sixty-two and their eligible spouses and dependents
- Monthly benefits to disabled workers and their eligible spouses and dependents
- Monthly benefits to the eligible survivors of deceased workers

To become fully insured, workers generally need to work about ten years. Benefits are based on the primary insurance amount (PIA), the monthly benefit amount payable to the worker upon retirement at the normal retirement age or, if entitled, earlier due to disability. The PIA is derived from the worker's taxable annual earnings, averaged over the individual's adult years and indexed to changes in average earnings nationally. To assist in achieving social adequacy, benefits replace a larger percentage of indexed preretirement earnings for persons with low average lifetime earnings. The 1983 Social Security Amendments made significant changes in benefit eligibility. While reduced benefits will continue to be paid at sixty-two, the normal retirement age—previously age sixty-five—will be increased in the future.

Social Security benefits are reduced or eliminated altogether if a participant is under the full benefit age or normal retirement age after retiring and his or her earnings exceed an amount specified by law. In 2000, the Social Security Administration set the maximum monthly Social Security benefit at normal retirement age at $1,660 and the amount that can be earned annually before earnings are cut will be $11,280 at sixty-two—normal retirement age. Once monthly benefits begin, they generally are adjusted automatically each December to reflect changes in the cost of living. Cost-of-living adjustments are normally payable beginning in January. Prior to 1986, these adjustments generally occurred only if the consumer price index (CPI) increased by 3 percent or more from the last automatic adjustment. In 1986, Congress passed legislation eliminating the requirement that the CPI had to rise at least 3 percent before a cost-of-living benefit increase would take effect. Under the 1986 law, any rise in the CPI in the preceding twelve-month measurement period calls for an equivalent increase in benefits.

Social Security benefits for some are subject to income taxes based upon a beneficiary's total income range. For example, single taxpayers with incomes of more than $25,000 but not over $34,000 can have up to 50 percent of their benefits subject to federal income taxes. For incomes exceeding $34,000, up to 85 percent of benefits are subject to taxation.

The Medicare program has two parts: Part A, the mandatory program of hospital insurance, and part B, the voluntary program of Supplementary Medical Insurance. Part A benefits are provided automatically on the basis of past work. Part B benefits are available only if individuals choose to pay a monthly premium. These two separate but coordinate health insurance plans are for individuals sixty-five or older. Medicare coverage was extended to certain severely disabled persons under sixty-five and to some individuals suffering from kidney disease in 1972. For both programs, approximately 90 percent of those enrolled are aged; the rest are disabled. Medicare benefits payments for 1999 totaled $205.9 billion, of which hospitalization benefits accounted for more than 50 percent.

Executive Compensation, Stock Options, and Alternate Forms of Compensation. The average CEO of a major corporation received a compensation package totaling $20 million in 2000, including nearly 50 percent more in stock options and 22 percent more in salary and bonus than in 1999 (*New York Times,* April 1, 2001). During this same year, the Standard and Poor Index fell 10 percent in 2000, and the NASDAQ Index fell 39 percent. Typical white-collar and blue-collar workers received raises that averaged about 3.5 percent, according to *Business Week* (April 16, 2000) which also highlighted the inequality between executives and rank-and file-workers. The average CEO made about 42 times the average blue-collar worker's pay in 1980, 85 times in 1990, and a staggering 531 times as much in 2000. Not surprisingly, these gaps contribute in some firms to poor employee morale, lost productivity, and more turnover (AFL-CIO 2001). In contrast, work teams with small pay gaps between leaders and staff perform at higher levels.

Numerous media stories describe CEOs and other executives who continued to receive generous pay increases despite poor corporate performance. For example, William Esrey of Sprint collected pay totaling more than $218 million in a five-year period when the company's stock underperformed the S&P 500 by 34 percent. CEO M. Douglas Ivester of Coca-Cola, who resigned abruptly after a disappointing two-year tenure, "received an $18 million severance package. Then Coke's board ignored a shareholder-approved bonus plan and gave the new chairman, Douglas N. Daft, a $3 million bonus although Coke missed its financial goals. In the process, the company lost its tax deduction on the bonus, since it was unrelated to performance" (Leonhardt 2001).

The exponential growth in executive pay has also drawn enormous criticism for economic hypocrisy as CEOs have reaped huge gains while laying off massive numbers of workers and reducing pay for many more. The high-tech boom of the 1990s drove a war for executive talent among hot dot-coms and other technology companies and the old economy firms where many prospective CEOs and top executives worked. While CEO salaries had been growing at an astonishing pace since the 1980s, the 1990s boom spurred a financial arms race among boards of directors that many believe fundamentally altered the compensation landscape of U.S. firms. Dangling massive compensation packages that included stock options and perks, tech companies lured talent from existing employers, and firms of every nature brought out the "golden handcuffs" to secure executive talent.

The bulk of the compensation boom for executives —75 percent in 2000—has come in the form of long-term compensation, usually stock options (*New York Times,* April 1, 2001). Stock options became popular during the 1990s as short-on-cash technology companies lured and retained talent with stock options that often performed well in the market, for a few years at least, creating thousands of paper millionaires. CEOs and top executives were raking in options while companies were also increasing cash and bonuses. As the stock markets cooled off, many option packages went underwater, their share value declining below the strike price the day the executive was awarded the options. Half of all options granted from 1997 to 1999 at non–S&P 500 companies had gone underwater by April 2000, according to research performed by Brian Hall (2000) at Harvard Business School. While options proved effective in recruiting top executives to new, riskier start-ups, they did not engender loyalty if the initial public offering did not perform as expected. As options became less lucrative, executives and recruiters sought to include more cash, incentive plans, restrictive stock, and other pay in their overall package.

Bonuses became popular for luring younger, entry-level workers, as well. The widely respected journalist Louis Uchitelle of the *New York Times* pointed out that signing bonuses were proliferating and reaching well beyond upper-level managers and skilled technicians (*New York Times,* June 10, 1998). He cited examples, including the Department of Labor's offer of bonuses to attract young economists and PriceWaterhouse's hiring bonuses of $10,000 to newly hired management. Reportedly, the 1998 class of Cornell MBAs received an average bonus of $17,500, nearly double the 1996 average of $9,400.

There are other aspects of compensation driving a wedge between top corporate managers and other workers in their organizations. A landmark article by Ellen Schultz—"As Firms Pare Pensions for Most, They Boost Those for Executives," in the June 20, 2001, edition of the *Wall Street Journal*—describes "a little-known sideshow to the spectacle of surging executive compensation in recent years." While corporations across the country continue to seek and find new ways to freeze or trim pension, medical, and other retirement benefits for rank-and-file workers, companies are drawing up entirely different rules for elite executives guaranteeing extremely generous pension and retirement benefits. As Schultz notes, these inequities escape wide notice because disclosure requirements are weak and details of these transactions can be easily hidden. Because firms are not required to set aside cash for special executive pensions, as they do for rank-and-file plans, many of these golden retirement parachutes constitute unfunded liabilities unknown to many shareholders.

To save money, many firms have adopted sophisticated pension management strategies for virtually all workers that reduce benefits and save money by slowing the rate that pension benefits accumulate, and by eliminating the sharp buildup of benefits in an employee's last few years of service. For top executives, however, many firms are offering pensions that pay as much as 50 percent of their current salary, provide generous annual cost-of-living increases, and guarantee benefits will be paid if the company changes owners.

According to Schultz, for example, Hershey Foods Corporation switched most workers to a cash-balance plan during the late 1980s, but retiring CEO Kenneth Wolfe will receive benefits under the earlier, traditional, and more generous formula, which will pay $1.3 million per year. In another example, Motorola cut its pension liability for rank-and-file workers by switching to a pension-equity plan, while its liability for executive pensions grew from 8.2 percent to 8.7 percent in a plan servicing just seventy-one people.

Contingent Workers. In order to save money and to have greater flexibility in managing their workforces, many firms during the late 1980s and 1990s increased their reliance on subcontractors and temporary workers to deliver services or manufacture products. The American workforce in the economy has become increasingly divided into two strata—a group of core workers, who perform the operations at the heart of a company's business, and a second, rapidly growing and changing layer of contingent workers. The temporary, part-time, and contract workers and consultants that make up the contingent workforce are employed to perform specific tasks for limited time periods.

Contingent workers cut labor costs for employers because they are paid less and often get no pensions, health benefits, paid sick days, or vacations. When their tasks are accomplished, contingent employees go to another job or to the unemployment rolls. This fluid, less-expensive layer of the company's total workforce can be thinned out or fattened as business demands require.

This shift in employment practice undercuts financial security and confidence for workers. The Bureau of Labor Statistics estimates that contingent workers make up between 2 and 5 percent of the workforce, including up to as many as six million workers. BLS data exclude many consultants, contractors, and part-time workers other analysts include as part of the contingent or independent labor force. Nontraditional or contingent workers earn less than their counterparts in traditional jobs, according to BLS data. Contingent workers have median weekly earnings of $285, compared to $416 per week for workers with traditional jobs, about two-thirds of what traditional workers earn. As one expert told the August 7, 2000 *Wall Street Journal* about a case before the National Labor Relations Board that argued that temporary workers should be allowed to organize and be eligible for the rights and privileges of full-time workers: "There's a growing awareness that temporary workers get the worst of both worlds. They're employees in that they don't have much control over their own time like independent contractors do, but they're not employees in terms of benefits and pay."

Part-time and contingent work have generated much of the job growth since the 1970s. Most of the growth in part-time jobs consisted of involuntary part-time workers—people who would prefer to work full time. While voluntary part-time employment rose by 53 percent between 1970 and 1992, involuntary part-time employment increased by 178 percent over that same period, but that trend stabilized during the high-growth 1990s. Only 22 percent of contingent workers received health coverage from their employer (U.S. Department of Labor 1999).

In the early twenty-first-century workforce, temporary workers are also being hired to perform many technical and professional jobs. During the year 2000, Microsoft was sued by a large number of engineers who worked at the company for years at a time. They argued that Microsoft simply renewed one-year contracts that did not allow the workers to obtain health, pension, and other benefits despite their long-term service.

Obviously, contingent workers provide employers with greater flexibility, and many people, especially heads of households with young children, prefer the flexibility that part-time work provides. Frustration arises, however, when people who want to work full time are denied that opportunity. Further, the growth in the contingent workforce reinforces the gap between high- and low-wage earners and the divide in America between those people who work with an economic safety net—and those who do not.

Trends to Watch

1. In 1998, median household income reached a new peak of $39,744, the highest since the previous historic peak of $38,837 in 1989, at the end of the 1980s boom (1999 dollars).
2. The Internal Revenue Service and the Congressional Budget Office show that tax burdens on Americans with the highest incomes declined during the 1990s. Between 1979 and 1997, the top 1 percent of taxpayers experienced the largest percentage-point drop in their effective tax rate than any other income group. The amount the top 1 percent paid as a portion of their income declined from 37.3 percent to 33 percent.
3. Unionized workers earn 30 percent more than nonunion workers; the wage differential is even greater for minorities and women who are members of unions.
4. According to the National Center for Employee Ownership, nearly eight million workers participate in employee stock ownership plans or stock bonus plans, and at least six million are in broad stock option plans.
5. The thirty highest-paid women in the corporate world earned an average total compensation of $8.7 million, as compared with $112.9 million for the thirty highest-paid men, a ratio of 1 to 13 (Institute for Policy Studies 2001).
6. Gross national savings as a percent of gross domestic product is lower in the United States than most industrialized nations. According to the Organization for Economic and Cooperative Development (OECD), in 1996 this figure was 15.6 percent for the United States, as compared to 17.1

percent for Canada and 19.7 percent for France. Only Great Britain had a lower figure of 13.9 percent.

7. The median income for married-couple families, with women in the paid labor force, has continued to grow, whereas the median income for other married-couple families has remained flat since 1973. Since 1951, the labor force participation of women, as a proportion of all married couples, has nearly tripled to 62 percent.

Related Reading in Part 2

Chapter 4:
"Notions of New Economy Hinge on Pace of Productivity Growth," Louis Uchitelle
"A Decade of Difference: The Newly Improved U.S. Economy," Jack Guynn
"Manufacturing Amidst Economic and Market Jitters—Still America's Best Bet for Growth," W. R. Timken Jr.
"What We Work for Now," Jerome M. Segal

Who Are the Working Poor and Unemployed?

The United States entered the twenty-first century in the midst of its longest peacetime economic expansion in history, with the lowest unemployment rates in thirty years. In many economic sectors, particularly the emerging information and service-driven industries, there were more jobs than workers with the requisite skills to fill them. Despite steady job growth throughout the 1990s, concurrent increases in income among the working poor were slow in coming. Changes in public-assistance laws combined with the growing economy meant that millions of low-income adults moved from welfare to work. Specifically, welfare rolls were cut in half from 1996 to 2000, but the percentage of families living below the poverty line declined from 12.2 percent to only 11.1 percent over that same period. This modest progress was reversed in 2001 and 2002 as poverty rates rose and median incomes fell after the 2001 terror attacks and national recession.

Lower-income, lower-skilled workers, who often are the last to be hired in good times, are the first to be laid off in a downturn. In fact, less-skilled, less-advantaged workers face increasingly poor labor market prospects over time, getting worse with each recession. As noted by David Smith and Stephen Woodbury in a 1999 Urban Institute/Department of Health and Human Services analysis, there is a consensus among labor economists that the demand for low-skilled labor is in long-run decline, mainly as a result of technological change. More jobs will be created requiring basic computer literacy as threshold skills. As the demand for low-skilled labor relative to other workers decreases, the number of workers competing for low-wage jobs has been rising and is expected to continue rising as single parents cannot remain on or return to welfare rolls because they have exhausted their time limits or triggered sanctions under the welfare law rules. In a long and/or steep recession, it can be expected that the numbers of low-skilled workers in the labor market will continue to swell while the potential job pool shrinks. This will raise concerns for state and federal policy makers in the 2000-2002 recession, who must address how the increasing pool of low-income parents who have exhausted unemployment insurance and their eligibility for cash assistance can support themselves and their families.

Throughout the 1960s and the early 1970s, the poverty rate in the United States declined dramatically, from more than 20 percent to less than 12 percent (see fig. 18). From that point forward, the poverty rate climbed steadily upward. By the late 1990s, the strong economy finally began to chip away at the poverty level. In 1998, the poverty rate dropped from 13.3 percent to 12.7 percent; and in 1999, the rate dropped to 11.8 percent. The number of people with family incomes below the official poverty level in 1999 was 32.3 million, down from 35.6 million people in 1997.

In 1999, the poverty rate for African Americans fell to a record low of 23.6 percent, down from the previous low of 26.1 percent in 1998 but still considerably higher than the overall level of poverty in the U.S. population. This percentage was still about three times the poverty rate for white non-Hispanics (7.7 percent). The white non-Hispanic rate was the lowest for this group since 1979; the poverty rate for Hispanics in 1999 declined from 25.6 percent in 1998 to 22.8 percent, nearly the lowest ever for this group. For American Indians and Alaska Natives, the 1997–99 poverty rate was 25.9 percent, higher than for white non-Hispanics and Asians but not statistically different from blacks and Hispanics. While the progress is encouraging, these disparities in poverty rates illustrate again the wide economic divides facing workers of color in America.

This American dilemma is also manifested by the linkage of immigration and poverty. In 1999, the poverty rate among noncitizen immigrants was 21.3 percent, down from 22.2 percent in 1998. While many new immigrants are working, they are still poor. Many of those whom the federal government classifies as poor are children and adults not in the labor force. The difficulties facing recent immigrants in the labor force are seen in their low educational attainment compared to the native-born population. About 50 percent of recent immigrants have only a high school education or less, while only 38 percent of the U.S.-born population have not gone on to college.

While work has long been a means of alleviating economic hardship and of providing economic security, having a job does not guarantee an escape from poverty. In 1999, nearly seven million individuals had incomes below the poverty line but worked at least twenty-seven weeks of the year (about 5.1 percent of the workforce). Nearly four million people in families where one member works at least twenty-seven weeks a year are classified as poor.

Working full time does substantially lower a person's probability of being poor. Among persons in the labor force for twenty-seven weeks or more in 1999, 3.9 percent of those usually employed full time were in poverty, compared with

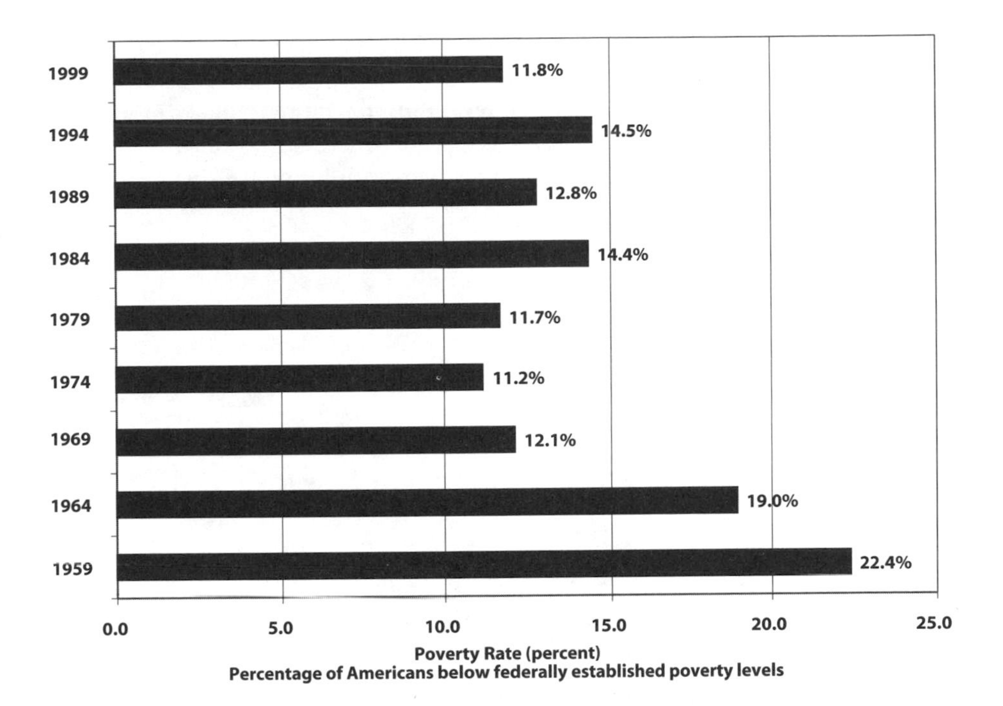

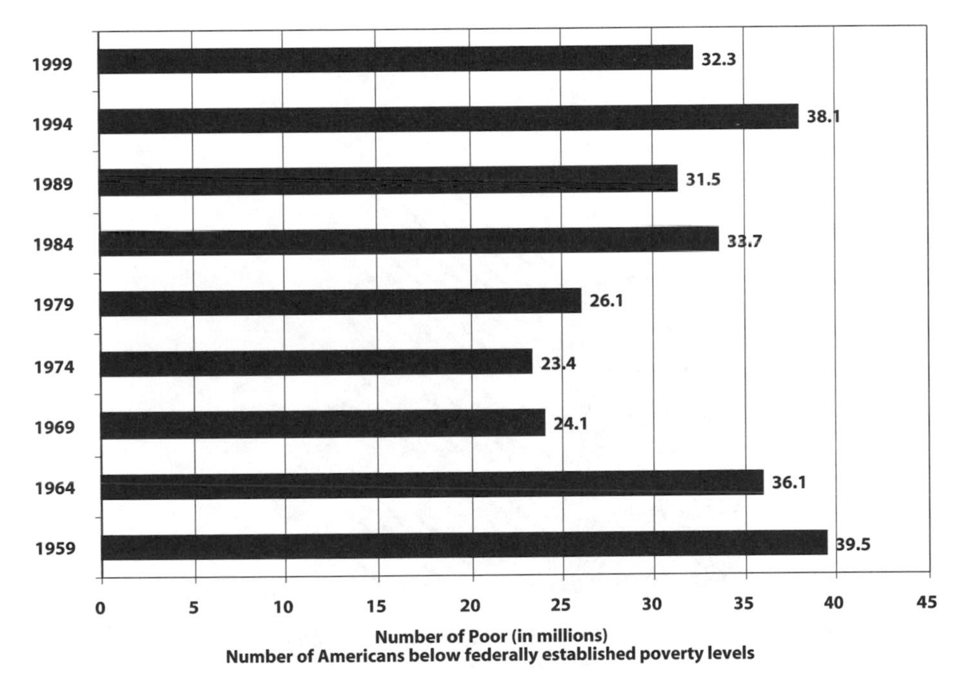

Fig. 18. U.S. poverty rates and number of poor, 1959–1999. *Source:* U.S. Census Bureau, Current Population Survey.

10.5 percent for part-time workers. Nonetheless, the majority of the working poor—64 percent—were full-time workers. Only a very small proportion of the working poor (3.5 percent) actively sought a job for more than six months in 1999. Between 1979 and 1997, there was a steady increase in the percentage of poor families with children where one adult works full time (see fig. 19)

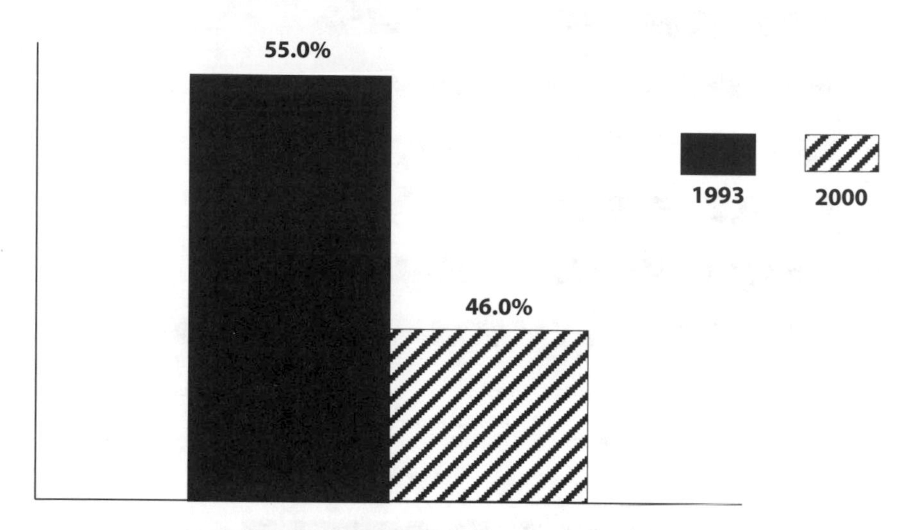

Percentage of poor people in families where there is no full-time worker in family

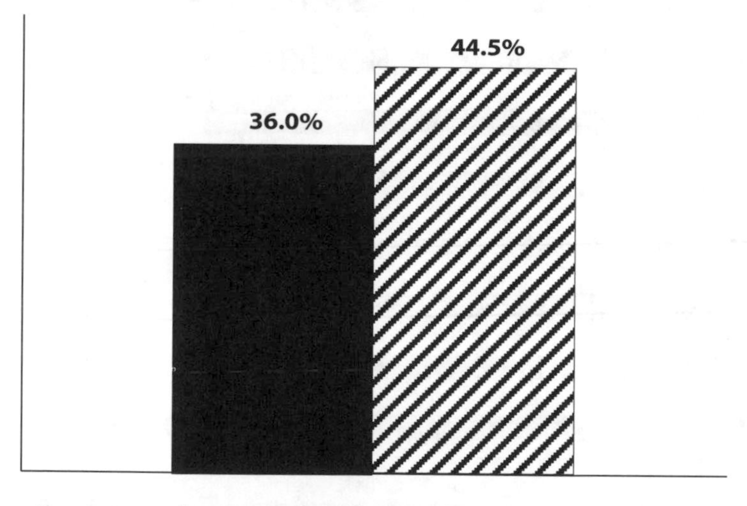

Percentage of poor people in families with at least one full-time worker in family

Fig. 19. Percentage of poor people in families with and without full-time workers, 1993 and 2000. *Source:* U.S. Census Bureau.

Although the strong economy of the 1990s benefited workers across racial groups, the tight labor market conferred the greatest financial benefits on white workers. While the unemployment rate was lower in 1999 for all ethnic groups than in many years, whites experienced a greater cut in unemployment than either blacks or Hispanics, and they enjoy the lowest rate of unemployment today.

People become and remain unemployed for a variety of reasons. Many lose their jobs or have completed temporary jobs and are seeking new work. Much smaller numbers of workers leave their jobs voluntarily. A substantial portion of the unemployed are reentering the workforce after leaving for personal or educational reasons. Even during the peak of the economic boom in the late 1990s, the tight labor market did not eliminate unemployment. Research by former U.S. Department of Labor chief economist William Rodgers of the College of William and Mary shows that 33 percent of the nation's untapped labor pool of thirteen million people in 1999 would like to be working but have dropped out of the active labor force (Rodgers 2000).

POLICY BRIEF: POVERTY AND ITS ROLE IN U.S. POLICY

Understanding trends in poverty begins with understanding what the numbers mean and how families and individuals are counted as poor. According to the U.S. Census Bureau, the federal government uses a set of money income thresholds that vary by family size and composition to determine who is poor. If a family's total income is less than that family's threshold, then that family, and every individual in it, is considered poor. The poverty thresholds do not vary geographically, but they are updated annually for inflation using the Consumer Price Index (CPI-U). The official poverty definition counts money income before taxes and does not include capital gains and noncash benefits, such as public housing, Medicaid, and food stamps. However, family and individual income as it relates to the poverty line determines eligibility for national and state safety-net programs designed to provide basic cash, food, and medical assistance to needy families and individuals. The nature and amount of this assistance has long been a source of intense political and policy controversy.

In 1996 a GOP-led Congress passed and President Clinton signed the Personal Responsibility and Work Opportunity Act, or PRWOA. This law eliminated the open-ended entitlements of AFDC (Aid to Families with Dependent Children) and replaced them with defined time-limited block grants to the states under TANF (Temporary Assistance to Needy Families). The most notable and far-reaching changes the PRWOA makes to social service provision in the United States includes detaching Medicaid eligibility from TANF eligibility, distinct work requirements, time limits, and heightened child support enforcement. The aid is more flexible in its delivery because it is almost wholly left to individual states' discretion. Unless it is clearly stated in the words of the statute, the federal government has no authority to interfere with the business of the states regarding

TANF. On the other hand, the safety the statute provides is much more politically vulnerable to shifting realities in state politics and government. As of 2001, TANF authorizes spending of $16.4 billion per year on assistance distributed in block grants to states.

The TANF block grants to states may be spent on anything "reasonably calculated to accomplish the TANF purposes," such as ending dependency by promoting work, prevention of out-of-wedlock births, promoting two-parent families, and providing assistance to families with children. Under TANF, however, no assistance can be provided to families who have received benefits for more than a cumulative sixty months. The time limit is at the states' discretion, however, and can be shortened. Only families with children and expectant mothers are eligible for benefits under TANF.

Under the PRWOA, recipients must be employed after two years of assistance. The work requirement for two-parent families is thirty-five hours per week; for single parents it is twenty hours per week. Single parent families with children under six years old can be exempted from the work requirement if the state chooses. Adults who are not employed and not exempt from the work requirement must be involved in some form of community service while searching for employment. Work participation rates are strictly defined under TANF for each year. Failure to comply with the work requirements of the state can result in sanctions—a loss or reduction of benefits.

Low-income families qualify for federal food assistance in the form of the food-stamp program administered by the U.S. Department of Agriculture if their gross incomes are no more than 130 percent of the poverty line ($1,848 per month for a family of four) or their net incomes are no more than 100 percent of the poverty line ($1,421 per month for a family of four). In March 2001, 17.3 million people received food stamps in 7.4 million households. The number of people receiving food stamps has dropped 38 percent since it peaked at just under twenty-eight million in March 1994.

A little more than half of all food-stamp recipients are children; another 23 percent are elderly or persons with disabilities. About nine out of ten food-stamp households contain a child, an elderly person, or a person with a disability. About 90 percent of all food-stamp households have gross incomes below the poverty line. Today, most states provide food-stamp benefits in the form of an EBT (electronic benefit transfer) card that allows recipients to use swipe-card technology to purchase their groceries.

The maximum food-stamp benefit a family of four can receive is $434 per month, but the vast majority of food-stamp households receive less than the maximum. In 2001, the average food-stamp benefit amounted to less than seventy-five dollars per month, or eighty-one cents per person per meal (Super 2001). USDA studies show that more than three-quarters of those who apply for food stamps do so for these events: a substantial drop in earnings, exhaustion of unemployment benefits, or the departure of a wage earner who had been supporting the household.

As cash assistance rolls have fallen since the mid-1990s, the number of people receiving food stamps has also fallen swiftly, at a rate of decline that far outstrips the rate of decline in the number of people eligible for food stamps. From 1995 to 1997, the decline in the number of people receiving food stamps—4.4 million—was five times greater than the decline in the number of people living in poverty (Dean and Parrott 1999). Analysts cite the complexities in the food-stamp application process as a critical factor in declining participation. Federal mandates to reduce fraud and error in the food-stamp program motivated many states to impose onerous paperwork requirements on recipients, particularly those who were working. Many eligible recipients would continue to receive benefits under a simplified, commonsense application process. USDA officials, with other experts, are examining ways to continue accountability but reduce complexity to ensure more eligible people receive benefits.

Poverty Despite Work. A family cannot lift itself above the poverty threshold defined by the federal government with one earner working full time at the federal minimum wage of $5.15 per hour, last set by Congress on September 1, 1997. A full-time worker (forty hours per week for fifty-two weeks) could earn only $10,712 a year at this wage. A family of four supported by a full-time, year-round minimum-wage worker will fall short of the poverty line by 25 percent, even after receiving the federal Earned Income Tax Credit (Super 2001). (The EITC is a refundable tax credit that offsets payroll taxes for working poor families and can also provide an additional wage supplement.) The percentage of American families living below the poverty line with one person working full time has actually increased during the 1990s.

Simply rising above the poverty line is not enough for achieving even modest economic security. While the official federal poverty line sets a minimum threshold of poverty, families earning more than the poverty rate can still have trouble making ends meet. For example, the income for a family of three living between 100 percent and 200 percent of the poverty level would range from approximately $12,803 to $25,604. For a near-poor family of four in this group, income would range from approximately $16,401 to $32,800; raising two children on less than $30,000 a year would allow at best modest housing and money to pay food and bills but virtually nothing else. *Work Trends* data gathered in 1999 show that the majority (85 percent) of adults with incomes under 200 percent of poverty are working but describe difficulties in paying for basic shelter and necessities (Van Horn and Dautrich 1999b).

Some economic historians, such as Robert Fogel, point out that today all workers have access to better health care and live longer, healthier lives than past generations of workers. He further argues that technical and economic progress means that Americans work fewer hours today than at any other time, creating more leisure time. According to Fogel, perceived inequality is actually a reflection of how different workers choose to use all this free time and that the real problem the poor face is what to do with this increased leisure. It is debatable whether the working poor and unemployed would agree with this assessment and whether they consider the time they do not spend working as either free or leisurely (Fogel 2001).

A Demographic Portrait of the Working Poor. The working poor and unemployed are not a homogenous group. The 1999 *Work Trends* report, *Working Hard but Staying Poor,* developed a profile of the working poor based on extensive national interview data with poor and near-poor Americans. The typical worker earning less than 200 percent of the federal poverty rate is a single white woman between the ages of thirty and forty-nine who works one full-time job for forty hours a week that she has held for at least a year. This typical working-poor American earns less than $25,000 a year, is paid by the hour, has a child under the age of eighteen, and has little or no paid vacation time. The typical poor worker has not received cash welfare but at some time may have received some form of financial help from the government, most likely an Earned Income Tax Credit. Gender, race, age, and education are important factors that contribute to the likelihood that a person will live in poverty.

In 1999, women were more likely than men to be poor or near poor. Among workers earning less than 200 percent of the federal poverty rate, 59 percent were women, while less than half (41 percent) were men. In addition, younger workers were far more likely than older workers to be living in poverty. Almost one-third (32 percent) of workers age eighteen to twenty-nine, and 53 percent of those age thirty to forty-nine, earn less than 200 percent of the federal poverty rate. In contrast, only 15 percent of workers over the age of fifty earn less than 200 percent of the federal poverty rate.

Across the spectrum of the working poor, however, workers expressed concerns not only with earning enough money to support their families; job security, spending time with family, and planning for retirement also loom large in the minds of working people (see fig. 20).

Almost two-thirds (64 percent) of workers earning less than 200 percent of the federal poverty rate have completed four years of high school or less, the *Work Trends* survey found. The working poor not only have less formal education, they have less access to computers, the Internet, and other forms of information technology necessary for many jobs. Less than half of the working poor use a computer at work or school or have access to a computer at home (48 percent and 42 percent, respectively). More than half (54 percent) have no access to the Internet. The millions of low-income adults and families lacking computers and Internet access will need new bridges to cross the digital divide if they are to be included in a high-performance, high-skills workforce.

What Are the Barriers to Escaping Poverty? Although the strong economy of the 1990s allowed more low-income workers to obtain jobs, the working poor and those who remain unemployed still face significant barriers to economic opportunity and upward mobility. As of this writing, the economic

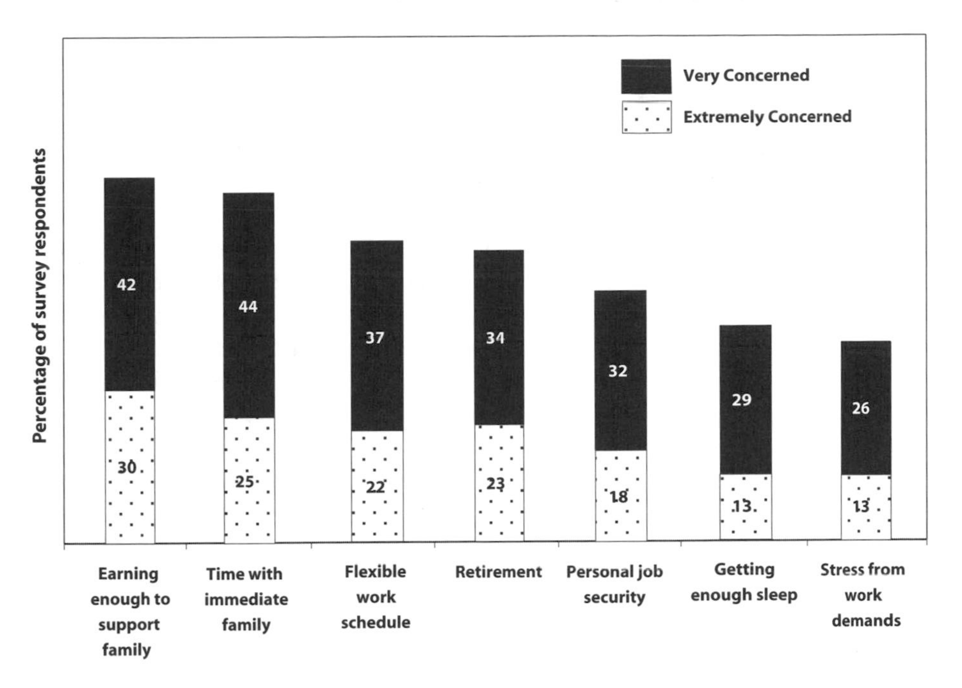

Fig. 20. Percentage of working poor who feel very or extremely concerned about life issues. *Source:* Van Horn and Dautrich 1999b.

slowdown since 2001 has forced more than 2.7 million additional Americans out of work. Obviously, the principal labor market problems associated with people whose incomes fall below the federal poverty level include not having a job or having a job that pays a low wage or is part time. Often the main causes of either not working or holding a low-paying job are lack of education and training. But even those with high school educations or better may face problems with transportation services, or live in neighborhoods with few good jobs, or face racial and ethnic discrimination. At a time of economic transition or emergency—as witnessed in this nation after September 11—large groups of productive, veteran workers can be dislocated from their jobs.

Moreover, the high cost of acceptable day care for young children—if it is available—prevents many poor parents from working even part time. If the costs of childcare could be lowered by fifty cents per hour, the result would be an 18 percent rise in labor force participation by unmarried women with children and a 39 percent rise for unmarried high school dropout mothers, according to estimates prepared by the National Bureau of Economic Research.

Although some child care subsidies are available for low-income working families, funds are severely limited. For example, the Head Start program for young children of low-income parents serves slightly less than half of eligible children. According to the U.S. Department of Health and Human Services (1999), only one out of ten children who would be eligible for child care assistance receive any. Despite expansions of the federal child care tax credit during the 1990s, the amount of aid available for working families making $25,000 or less amounts to no more than $718 per year.

Clearly, economic growth and a strong labor market were not enough to lift many people out of poverty during the expansion of the 1990s. Lack of education, training, childcare, and other issues create roadblocks for workers struggling to better their situation. Despite rising incomes among the working poor, a growing skills gap among workers with less formal education threatens these advances.

Incomes for lower-skilled workers have been hurt by the decline of unions in the private labor force, giving employers additional power and leverage over wages and benefits. A Human Rights Watch study (Compa 2001) notes that more than twenty million U.S. workers, including farmworkers, domestic workers, and independent contractors, are not covered by any U.S. labor-rights legislation whatsoever and can therefore be terminated for whistle-blowing, union organizing activities, or other arbitrary reasons.

During times of rising unemployment, low-wage workers are more likely to be laid off, and, in addition, they are far less likely to receive unemployment insurance benefits than other unemployed workers, according to research by the General Accounting Office, the National Governors' Association, the Urban Institute, and other researchers. In March 1995, only 18 percent of unemployed low-wage workers were collecting unemployment insurance (UI) benefits, compared to about 40 percent of higher-wage unemployed workers. UI regulations tend to bar low-wage workers from benefits because of earnings and eligibility requirements that emphasize relatively long work experience and because workers in the worst-paying jobs tend to quit voluntarily in greater numbers than others. Because welfare benefits are now subject to time limits, low-wage workers who have received welfare in the past and are nearing their time limits but do not qualify for UI may have very limited amounts of assistance they can receive if they lose their jobs. (See "Policy Brief: Unemployment Insurance and Low-Income Workers in the New Economy's First Recession" in this chapter.)

As governors and federal officials grapple with the massive layoffs of late 2001, some experts are optimistic that the number of former welfare recipients able to qualify for unemployment insurance will be greater than in the past, because so many had been working over the course of the late 1990s.

Dislocated Workers in the Slowing Economy. The dramatic changes experienced in the U.S. economy during 2001 have resulted in hundreds of thousands of layoffs, many of these of experienced workers in industries directly affected by the acts of terrorism against the United States. These events and the mixed economic prospects of the coming years raise concerns about the social and economic implications of mass layoffs that have not been widely discussed in recent years when the business and financial pages were dominated by coverage of the tight labor market. As has been shown in the extensive literature examining the effects of mass layoffs on dislocated workers since the late 1970s, layoffs generate not only short-term disruption but also a range of long-term negative consequences.

Among the issues of concern, dislocated workers in huge numbers slip into lower income brackets, experience physical and mental health problems, suffer through family breakdowns, and confront the need to move their families to new communities or commute long distances to find work. If the vast research of these effects is ignored by policy makers and officials, much of the progress made by moderate-income workers in recent years will be lost.

For example, a 1999 study by Cynthia Rocha and Felicia McCant examined the well-being of families displaced by a plant closure (Rocha and McCant 1999). The researchers followed about two thousand union workers laid off when one of the nation's leading garment manufacturers closed a large plant in the southeastern United States. Workers were provided with generous severance packages and access to retraining activities.

During the two-year period in which these workers were studied after the closing, only 22 percent found new jobs, and those workers who did find employment experienced an average pay cut of 27 percent. In the months after the closing, the majority of workers reported feeling more anxious than normal, nearly 85 percent were experiencing some symptoms of depression, and nearly half were clinically depressed. Many workers worried about health insurance and their families. Retraining programs had little positive effect on worker well-being and, as other major studies have shown, have not on the whole proven effective in helping older, more veteran workers recapture lost earnings (see Jacobson et al. 1993; LaLonde 1999).

In 2001, a new generation of dislocated workers are experiencing these harsh realities as tens and hundreds of thousands of hospitality, airline, and service employees find themselves out of work in an uncertain economy. In the years to come, these workers face an additional set of challenges: the demand of employers for workers with highly specific, often technology-related skills that can be demonstrated and immediately put to use. A *Work Trends* survey (Van Horn and Dautrich 2001b) released in the fall of 2001, as the nation experienced its twelfth straight month of declining industrial output, found that 74 percent of American workers believed that it was very or extremely important that employers and government provide career counseling to help laid-off workers understand what jobs they are qualified for and to help them find those jobs. In addition, 62 percent of American workers said that it was very or extremely important that employers and government provide financial assistance for training to upgrade laid-off workers' skills to make them more competitive in the labor market.

Trends to Watch

1. Poverty has risen in both the number and share of those employed full time and year-round since 1973 (Barrington 2000).

2. The average length of unemployment has increased from approximately twelve weeks during the 1960s to more than seventeen weeks during the 1990s (Progressive Policy Institute 1998–2002).
3. Full-day child care costs $4,000–$10,000 a year—at least as much as college tuition at a public university. Yet, one out of three families with young children earns less than $25,000 per year.
4. The U.S. economy lost more than 900,000 jobs between March and October 2001, the largest drop in that amount of time since the 1991 recession.

Related Reading in Part 2

Chapter 4:
"Mass of Newly Laid-Off Workers Will Put Social Safety Net to the Test," Jason DeParle
Chapter 5:
"Scrubbing in Maine," Barbara Ehrenreich
"No Shame in (This) Game," Katherine S. Newman

An Emerging Work-Based Safety Net? Responding to Poverty and Unemployment in the Twenty-first Century

The complexity and long-standing nature of the problems of the unemployed and working poor have vexed policy specialists for decades. But the need for skilled labor throughout the economy underlines the importance of improving education, training, and employment opportunities for the unemployed and working poor.

Even in the best of times, such as the late 1990s, some people remained unemployed or underemployed (involuntarily working part time instead of full time). As noted earlier, gender, race, and educational attainment are factors in the numbers of people who are unemployed or are not in the labor force. According to the Bureau of Labor Statistics, 82.5 percent of men eighteen to thirty-four were employed in 1978–98, compared to 67.7 percent of women of the same age. More than three-fourths (77.6 percent) of white workers were employed during this time, compared to 64.7 percent of black workers and 70.5 percent of Hispanic workers. Likewise, educational attainment among all groups significantly influences a worker's chance of being employed. Among all workers, 9.2 percent without a high school diploma were unemployed, compared to 2.9 percent of those with a college degree.

During the latter half of the 1990s and into the twenty-first century, a number of policy and demographic changes have affected the prospects of unemployed and working-poor people in the United States. These include a succession of laws opening trade barriers, which have the effect of moving low-skilled jobs to less-developed countries, and reform of the welfare system, which requires work instead of cash-transfer payments. By and large, most long-time observers believe that the working poor are facing more adverse circumstances than low-income Americans did before the 1980s. The turbulent, knowledge-driven nature of job creation in the new economy has created few safe harbors for those without substantial skills or work experience. Among the barriers in the twenty-first century facing those who leave welfare, foreign-born workers, low-income workers, and other working poor are shortfalls in work skills and education, difficulty in retaining jobs and moving up the income ladder during employment, and a continuing political culture that discourages reliance on public-assistance programs even for eligible families.

Despite increasing participation in the labor force and surpluses in state welfare and public-assistance budgets, Americans who live below the federal poverty line have not seen their lot improve during the past decade. In a careful analysis of data, the Center on Budget and Policy Priorities (Dean and Parrot 1999) found that despite a strong economy, between 1995 and 1997 the poorest one-fifth of single-mother families experienced a decline in income; a 2001 report using a similar analysis (Porter and Dupree 2001) found that during the 1990s there was no progress in reducing poverty among families headed by single working mothers, despite the growing economy, due to contractions in government safety-net programs. Fewer than one-third of families that left welfare since the passage of TANF subsequently received food stamps even though most families had incomes low enough to qualify, according to studies by the Urban Institute. Similarly, parents received Medicaid in only one-third of the families that left welfare, and children received Medicaid in fewer than one-half of the families (Loprest 1999b).

Adults leaving welfare to find jobs do not always find steady employment, and their average annual incomes remain below or near the poverty line (see U.S. General Accounting Office 1999; Brauner and Loprest 1999; Loprest 1999b; Sweeney and Schott 2000). Researchers have found that eight in ten former welfare recipients studied were employed sometime during the year after leaving welfare. But when a more stringent measure is applied—whether those who left welfare were employed at one point in time—researchers found that employment rates were much lower, running from 51 percent to 75 percent. Brauner and Loprest (1999) have also found that in many states those who leave welfare are not earning enough to raise their incomes far above the poverty level, and nearly a third of those who left welfare for at least a month between 1995 and 1997 had returned to welfare and were receiving benefits in 1997.

Former welfare recipients who find jobs often have higher incomes than other near-poor and low-income mothers (Loprest 1999). But, as Loprest and other researchers have shown, women in each of these groups confront barriers to continuing work as they struggle to make ends meet. Among the most significant obstacles to work for former welfare recipients are low education, no recent work experience, caring for children under the age of one, and being a nonnative English speaker (Zedlewski 1999; see fig. 21). It can be concluded that the new economy has not positively affected the way low-income people cycle in and out of unstable, poor-paying jobs.

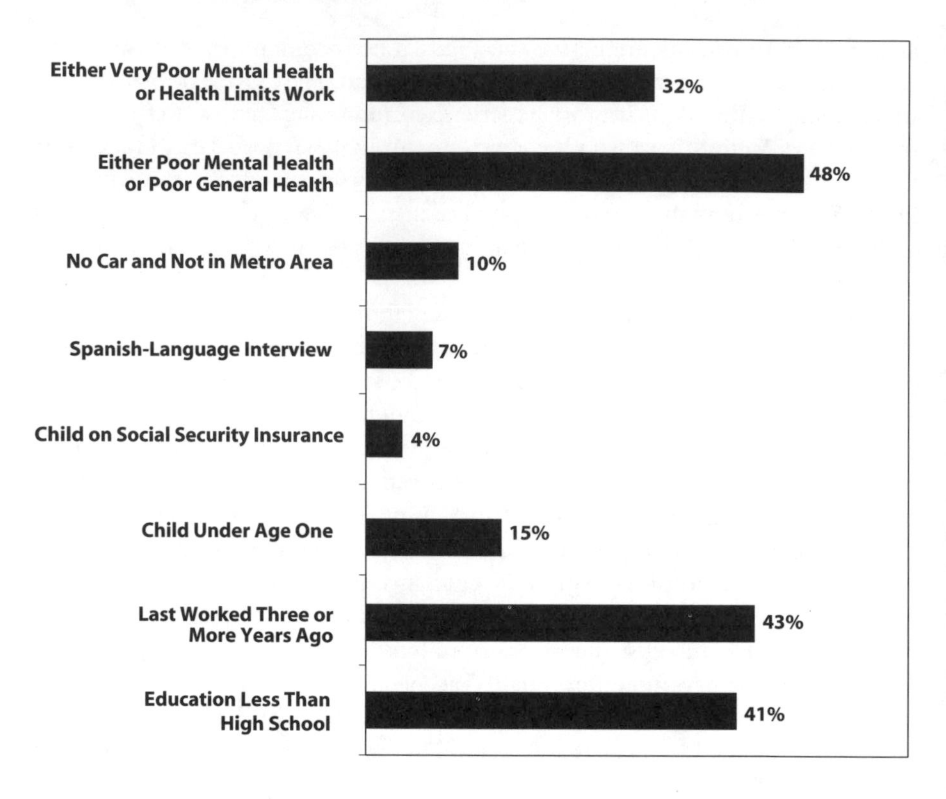

Fig. 21. Percentage of welfare population with various barriers to full-time work. *Note:* National sample of adults who are primary caretakers of children and likely to be subject to work requirements. *Source:* Zedlewski 1999.

A comprehensive survey of 5,200 families who have left the welfare rolls since 1996 provides additional evidence that work does not bring prosperity for all (Children's Defense Fund 2000). Many of the families surveyed by the Children's Defense Fund (CDF) were working, but they were still falling behind. Fifty-eight percent of those who were working had family earnings below the poverty line, and more than half of employed parents were unable to pay the rent or buy food, could not afford needed medical care, or had their telephone or electric service disconnected. Many of the working families who were eligible for food stamps and other assistance were not enrolled in these programs. Child care was cited more frequently than any other reason for not working. What was interesting about the study is that families who worked and received some combination of support, such as health coverage, child care assistance, and food stamps, were more likely to maintain consistent and stable employment and reported improvements in their family well-being.

The difficult experiences of the vanguard of former welfare recipients entering the workforce in the late 1990s—during a time of spectacular economic growth—underlines the need for supporting low-income workers while they make the transition from public assistance. Whether it is health care or food stamps, safety-net assistance should be based and accessed in the workplace and in government offices. Otherwise, poverty will continue to generate human and social costs, as poor adults and children receive less health care, attend underperforming schools, live in dangerous neighborhoods, and have little access to the skills and technological tools needed for success in the labor market.

How might policy makers build upon TANF to strengthen assistance to individuals who have lost their jobs or have poor-paying jobs? A significant problem for the working poor is being able to build seniority on jobs in order to build their earnings. Some experts suggest that states could provide stipends to support parents working in low-wage jobs to encourage long-term employment. In addition, worker stipends could be linked with training and other services to encourage job retention and advancement.

Short-term emergency aid is another tool states have used successfully. Many low-income families experience temporary crises for which they have no resources to address—such as a nonfunctioning car or an ill child. Many states currently operate emergency assistance programs that help low-income families avoid eviction or utility cutoffs. Also, twenty-three states have cash-diversion programs that provide payments to families, often in lieu of welfare benefits.

As we head further into the first decade of the twenty-first century, it is clear that several implacable trends will continue to alter the nature and prospects of unemployment and poverty:

- A growing number of immigrants in the labor force, many undocumented and low-skilled
- Continued barriers to participation in public-assistance programs
- Increasing importance of new skills to acquire and keep jobs
- Cost barriers to big-ticket needs, including affordable health care, retirement security, and quality education
- Expanded accessibility and availability of learning and distance technologies on the job

Minimum and Living Wage Laws. Since 1938, the federal government has established a floor in wages paid to most non-farmworkers. Known as the minimum wage, this floor was most recently set in 1997 at $5.15 per hour and has not changed since. Supporters of minimum-wage laws complain that the wage should be increased substantially because it has not kept pace with inflation; today's minimum wage is only worth $4.66 in 1997 dollars. As noted above, a person working full time at the minimum wage still earns less than poverty level.

Opponents of increasing the minimum wage argue that the market should set the compensation at the appropriate wage level at which employers will attract and retain employees. Moreover, they say that increasing the minimum wage discourages small and medium-sized businesses from creating new jobs and actually leads to higher unemployment.

Researchers differ on how effectively minimum-wage increases assist low-income workers. According to the Economic Policy Institute, of the 8.4 million workers whose wages and incomes would increase with a one-dollar raise in the minimum wage, 2.7 million (32 percent) are the parents of 4.7 million children. Of the 2.7 million parents who earned at or near the minimum wage in 1999, 63 percent had family incomes below $25,000. Mark Turner of the Urban Institute points out that fewer and fewer workers are paid the minimum wage, however, and, in fact, most of the workers earning minimum wage are not technically poor—that is, they do not have incomes below the poverty line.

However, a growing body of research demonstrates that the minimum wage accomplishes its goal of lifting the incomes of low-income working families and establishing a floor on the low end of the labor market—all without leading to significant layoffs among minimum-wage workers. While some economists believe that increasing the minimum wage leads to job losses among that working population, studies by David Card and Alan Krueger (1995) and others during the 1990s disproving this connection are well regarded.

Within the past decade, support has grown for the enactment of so-called living-wage laws in many U.S. cities. These laws require firms with municipal contracts and subsidies to pay their workers wages high enough to keep them out of poverty. (A catalog of the living-wage ordinances passed in more than fifty U.S. municipalities was created by the Political Economy Research Institute of the University of Massachusetts. It is excerpted in fig. 22). The living-wage movement has received higher marks for its antipoverty effects since the landmark Baltimore law passed in 1994, widely considered to be the first of its kind. Much attention has been paid to research by Michigan State University professor David Neumark—a staunch minimum-wage increase opponent—who found in his study of twelve cities with living-wage laws that they did not lead to job losses but reduced urban poverty and helped lift wages for other low-income workers (Adams and Neumark 2000). Other research has concluded that these laws do not significantly increase the cost of city contracts, nor do they result in layoffs. (See studies by the Weisbrot and Storza-Roderick [1998] and the Economic Policy Institute [2001].)

Skills and Job Training Support. Skills and education are at a premium in today's workplace, putting low-skilled workers at a disadvantage in the labor market. Changing occupational demands have rendered certain skills obsolete as the high-tech workplace puts new demands on workers. Lower-skilled, well-paying jobs are increasingly scarce as assembly-line manufacturing declines as a percentage of the American economy. Many of these lower-skilled workers are the first to lose their jobs when the economy slows down, and they are the least likely to be able to respond and adapt to fluctuations in the business cycle and changes in the workplace.

Location	Outcome	Coverage	Main Provisions
Alexandria, VA	Passed 2000	City contracts over $30,000	$8.20 w/benefits, or $9.83 without.
Baltimore, MD	Passed 1994	Service contracsts over $5,000	$6.10 in FY 1996, $6.60 in FY 1997 $7.10 in 1998, $7.70 in 1999, subj. to Board of Estimates approval.
Boston, MA	Passed 1997, amended 1998	Service contracts of at least $100,000 or subcontracts of at least $25,000	$8.23, indexed annually on July 1 to whichever is higher of the adjusted poverty guidelines or 110% of the state minimum wage.
Cleveland, OH	Passed 2000	Service contractors	$8.20 per hr., going to $8.70 on Oct. 1, 2001, to $9.20 on Oct. 1, 2002, and will be adjusted according to inflation after Oct. 1, 2003.
Detroit, MI	Passed 1998	Service contracts, subcontracts, and subsidies over $50,000/yr.	Indexed to poverty rate for a family of 4 w/health benefits, or 125% of poverty level without benefits.
Hudson Cty., NJ	Passed 1999	Service contracts.	150% of the federal minimum wage.
Los Angeles City, CA	Passed 1997	Service contracts and subcontracts over $25,000, concessionaires, and subsidies over $100,000/yr.	$7.25 w/health benefits, or $8.50 without.
Milwaukee City, WI	Passed 1995	Service contracts and subcontracts over $5,000.	Poverty level for family of 3.
Milwaukee Cty., WI	Passed 1997	Select service contracts.	$6.26, indexed to prevailing wage.
Milwaukee Sch.Bd.	Passed 1996	Public School System employees and service contracts.	$7.70
New York, NY	Passed 1996	Security, temporary office, cleaning and food service contracts.	Prevailing wage.
San Antonio, TX	Passed 1998	Tax abatement recipients.	$9.27 to 70% of service employees in new jobs, and $10.13 to 70% of durable goods employees.
San Fernando, CA	Passed 2000	Service contractors (including employees of temp. agencies), city employees	$7.25 w/benefits, or $8.50 without.
San Francisco, CA	Passed 2000	Service contracts of more than $25,000, leases at the San Francisco Int'l. Airport, in home support service public authority (homecare workers).	A min. of $9/hr., rising to $10 by 2001, w/2.5% cost of living increases in each of the following 3 years. Health care benefits provided through a separate ordinance.
St. Paul, MN	Defeated in 1995, passed in 1997	Subsidies over $100,000/yr.	100% of poverty level for family of 4 plus benefits, or 110% benefits.
Toledo, OH	Passed 2000	Service contracts over $10,000 (for firms with >25 employees) and >$100,000 (for firms with >50 employees). Covers tenants in develments receiving subsidies.	$8.58 w/health benefits (indexed at 110% of the federal poverty level for a family of 4), or $10.14 w/o health coverge (130% of the poverty level).
Tucson, AZ	Passed 1999	Service contracts.	$8.00 w/health benefits, or $9.00 w/o.

Fig. 22. Examples of living wage ordinances that cover contractors and recipients of public subsidies. *Source:* Economic Policy Institute/Political Economy Research Institute, University of Massachusetts.

POLICY BRIEF: UNEMPLOYMENT INSURANCE AND LOW-INCOME WORKERS IN THE NEW ECONOMY'S FIRST RECESSION

Adapted from Rethinking Income Support for the Working Poor

Richard Hobbie, David Wittenburg, and Michael Fishman

(As low-wage workers lose jobs in the economic slowdown of 2001 and 2002, policy makers will need to examine the relationship between unemployment insurance and welfare benefits to ensure that layoffs do not leave families and workers with no means of support.)

The purposes of unemployment insurance (UI) are to provide temporary and partial wage replacement to involuntarily unemployed workers who were recently employed and to help stabilize the economy during recessions. UI is a federal-state system in which states have established their own programs within a federal framework authorized by the Social Security Act of 1935 and the Federal Unemployment Tax Act of 1939. Employers generally pay unemployment taxes to cover the costs of unemployment benefits paid to their laid-off workers. The weekly benefit amounts for eligible workers typically are about half of lost wages, up to state-determined maximums, and up to twenty-six weeks of benefits usually are available.

To be eligible for a weekly UI check, workers generally must have worked in UI-covered employment, earned enough in their base years to quality for UI, and lost their jobs through no fault of their own. While receiving UI, they must be able to work, be available for work, and not refuse an offer of suitable work. Individuals who have no reported work experience in the past eighteen months generally are ineligible for unemployment insurance.

Most jobs are covered by UI. . . . The monetary qualification requirements of UI are complex. All states have minimum employment and earnings requirements that individuals who work in UI-covered employment must satisfy to qualify for UI. For those who qualify, the level of UI benefits is determined by the amount of earnings they have in a recent one-year period called a base year. In nearly all states, UI claimants must:

- Have wages in a base year
- Have earned a certain amount of wages in a calendar quarter in which they had the highest wages, often called high-quarter wages (HQWs)
- Meet a distributional requirement for earnings during the base year, which is usually earnings in at least two quarters and some minimum amount in the base year
- Have wages in the base year that exceed an amount that is usually a multiple of their HQW or weekly benefit amount (WBA)

If former welfare recipients obtain stable, full-time, even low-wage employment, they are likely to qualify for UI because state qualifying requirements are relatively low. For example, workers earning a gross wage rate of six dollars per hour for forty hours per week for a full year would be monetarily qualified in all states. However, the UI benefits for those who quality for the minimum base year earnings generally are quite low. Consequently, those who apply and qualify under the minimum requirements may not receive enough to support their families; others may not even apply for UI benefits because the benefits levels are so low.

Many former welfare recipients who leave welfare for work and lose their jobs could be left without a source of income support if they reach their time limit for TANF and fail to qualify for UI. States may want to consider strategies for expanding unemployment assistance and employment opportunities for former TANF recipients to provide a temporary safety net in the event of unemployment. Some strategies focus on the UI system, others take advantage of state flexibility under TANF and other state programs.

Strategies to assist former welfare recipients who lose their jobs include expanding UI coverage to include the self-employed, changing the definition of the base year, increasing benefits for former welfare recipients with children, reducing UI costs for employers paying benefits to former welfare recipients (thereby creating an incentive to hire welfare recipients), or allowing welfare recipients to earn back part of their time limit under TANF if they meet certain requirements.

Empirical studies unanimously agree that higher-skills training boosts wages and reduces unemployment over the long term. Training therefore generates benefits for individuals, companies, and society as a whole. Individuals with more training make more money, enjoy better job security, and therefore pay higher taxes and are less likely to need government safety-net programs. For example, displaced workers with more education return to the workforce faster, and receive higher wages, than those workers with less education (U.S. Department of Labor 1999). Until employer-supported training becomes more uniform and widespread, most economists agree with John H. Bishop, who wrote in *The Impact of Previous Training on Productivity and Wages* that "modest governmental efforts to stimulate general on-the-job and employer-sponsored formal off-the-job training would appear to be in order" (Bishop 1994, 64).

Workers themselves believe that obtaining more skills training reduces their risk of being left behind. The working poor and unemployed report they are lagging behind in obtaining these skills and accessing information technology. Less than half (42 percent) of the working poor and even fewer (33 percent) of those living below the poverty line have access to a computer at home, compared to nearly three-fourths (71 percent) of other Americans (Van Horn and Dautrich 1999b; see fig. 23). The *Working Hard but Staying Poor* survey (Van Horn and Dautrich 1999b) found most of the working poor want more training and education to obtain the jobs they want, but few have the prospects of obtaining this assistance: 81 percent of the working poor would enroll in an education or training program if it were offered by their employer, but only

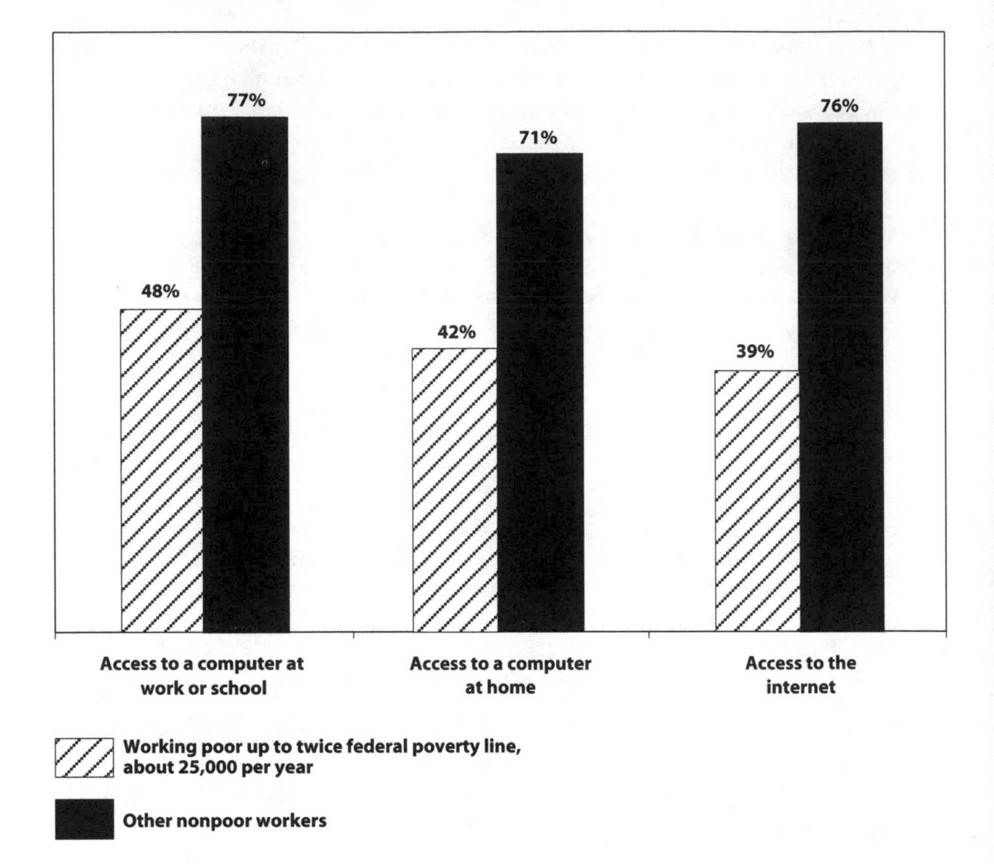

Fig. 23. Percentage of poor and nonpoor workers with access to technology. *Source:* Van Horn and Dautrich 1999b.

18 percent of the working poor have received financial support from their employer to do so.

Careful analysis of actual training programs underscores the merit of these principles. Successful training programs that placed former welfare recipients in higher-paying jobs, including the Center for Employment Training and Project Quest, focused on particular industries and occupations, cultivated close ties with employers to design training, and used aggressive outreach efforts to develop opportunities for graduates in those targeted sectors (Bartik 2000). According to Timothy Bartik, an economist, "training programs may be more politically viable (for welfare leavers) as part of a workforce advancement program available to all low-wage workers" (3). GAPS, a program developed by the Pittsburgh Foundation, is drawing national attention for its success in helping welfare leavers find and keep good-paying jobs. The program is organized at the local level and encourages long-term relationships between clients and their case managers from community organizations in order to promote the kind of flexible, day-to-day help people need to make the transition to work (Clines 2001).

The Earned Income Tax Credit. The federal Earned Income Tax Credit (EITC) program is a strong component of the work-based safety net. It has enjoyed high marks for effectiveness and has received political support at the national and state levels. The EITC was developed to help poor working families cope with high Social Security and Medicare payroll taxes and decrease poverty. The EITC is often referred to as the "making work pay" policy because it is grounded in the theory that every family who has an adult working full time deserves to live above the poverty line. Indeed, 4.8 million people, including 2.6 million children, are lifted out of poverty each year because of the EITC. The income and family criteria have expanded three different times since 1975 (in 1986, 1990, and 1993) to allow more working Americans to participate, including those without children. Since 1997, fifteen states have joined the federal government in providing incentives to work by allowing poor families to be eligible for a state EITC in addition to their federal entitlements.

The EITC is refundable at the federal level and in most states. Based on income from employment and family size, a family is eligible for a certain amount of money in credit. If a family's credit amount exceeds its tax liability, the family receives a refund in the form of a check. Unlike other benefits, the EITC allows families' credit eligibility to increase as income increases, until they reach a specified maximum credit benefit. Once a family's income increases enough to afford the maximum benefit level, the credit value decreases. The family is still eligible for some credit, however, until its earnings reach a particular amount. For example, a family with two or more children in 1999 received forty cents per dollar earned until their income reached $9,540, at which time the family was eligible for $3,816 in credit. As the income of that family continued to increase, the credit decreased until the family's income was $30,580, at which time the credit was entirely phased out (see fig. 24).

Even with minimum-wage increases, the regressive nature of most state taxes is enough to push working families into poverty. While the federal EITC provides help in defraying the cost of federal income taxes, low-income people still pay a disproportionate amount of their income in state and local income taxes. As a response to this problem, fifteen states have supplemented the federal EITC with their own state EITCs. These states are Colorado, the District of Columbia, Illinois, Iowa, Kansas, Maine, Maryland, Massachusetts, Minnesota, New Jersey, New York, Oregon, Rhode Island, Vermont, and Wisconsin. The state EITC can either be refundable or nonrefundable. Nonrefundable EITCs offset a family's tax liability until it reaches zero. If a family's credit exceeds its tax liability, that amount is forfeited, whereas with refundable credits, a family receives that money in the form of a check.

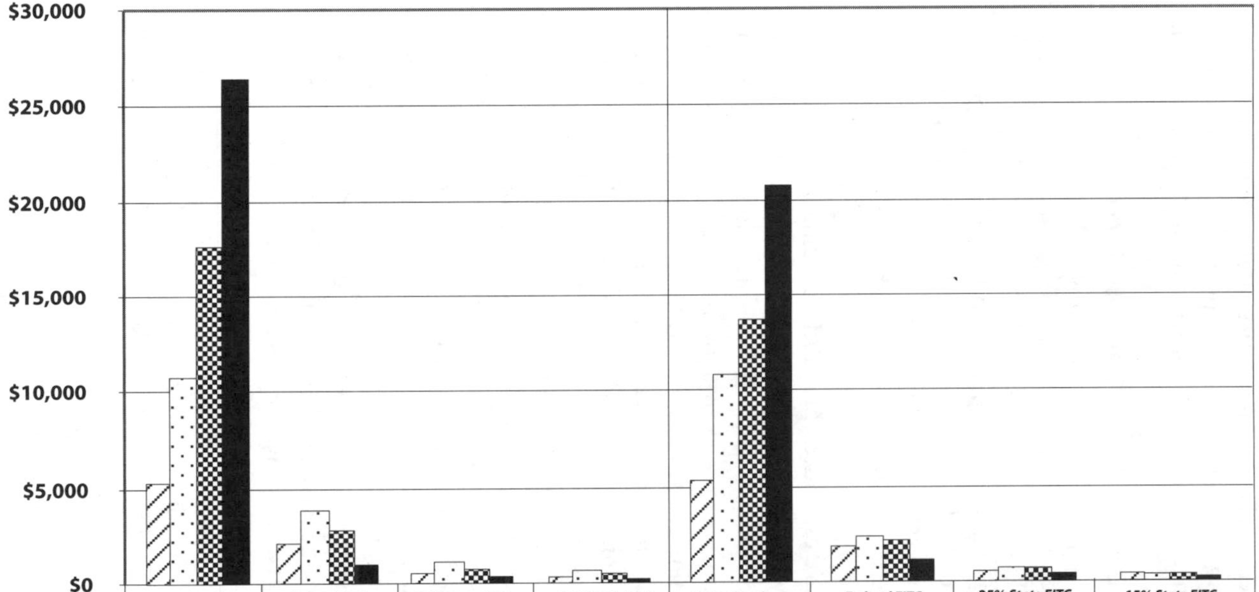

	Family of Four With Two Children				Family of Three With One Child			
	Gross Earnings	Federal EITC	25% State EITC	15% State EITC	Gross Earnings	Federal EITC	25% State EITC	15% State EITC
Half-Time Minimum Wage	$5,350	$2,140	$535	$321	$5,350	$1,819	$455	$273
Full-time Minimum Wage	$10,700	$3,888	$972	$583	$10,700	$2,353	$588	$353
Wages Equal Federal Poverty Line	$17,600	$2,854	$714	$428	$13,700	$2,192	$548	$329
Wages Equal 150% of Poverty Line	$26,300	$1,022	$256	$153	$20,600	$1,089	$272	$163

Fig. 24. Structure of the federal Earned Income Tax Credit (EITC). The federal EITC only applies to households with earnings, with the amount of the credit initially rising as earnings increase. The credit is capped at $3,888 for a family with two children and $2,353 for a family with one child—the credit phases out gradually. Low-income workers without a qualifying child may also receive a federal EITC, but maximum credit for individuals or couples without children is about $353 in 2000, much lower than the credit for families with children. *Source:* Center on Budget and Policy Priorities.

Free Trade and Unemployment. Researchers agree that the rapid globalization of markets for goods and capital affects job opportunities and the mix of businesses in the United States. Where they differ is whether the impact of global trade is positive or negative. It does seem, however, that a strong case can be made that in the short run, low- and moderate-skilled workers in the manufacturing sectors have been hit hardest by the movement of businesses to lower-wage countries. Additionally, few Americans are not offended by the prevalence of child labor, dangerous working conditions, and extremely low wages among developing industrial nations. Disagreements occur, however, over whether and how U.S. policy makers should intervene to influence business practices through trade agreements. Think tanks, elected officials, academics, nonprofit groups, and citizens will continue to debate how to ensure that the benefits of trade are shared more fairly and that the victors of globalization compensate the losers.

While most agree that ultimately countries need to adopt shared labor standards, fierce debate rages about how and when to arrive at core standards for how workers are paid and treated. On one side, labor unions and human rights activists argue that trading nations must meet internationally agreed minimum labor standards to be granted access to Western markets. Competition for the flight of Western jobs and capital to developing countries has sparked a race to the bottom, where human and labor rights are sacrificed in the name of economic progress. Examples cited by critics of globalization include the devastation of small corn farmers in Mexico (where corn is the fundamental food of that culture going back thousands of years). The liberalization of agriculture tariffs allowed cheap corn grown and harvested by agribusiness megagrowers in the United States to flood the Mexican market. As these sales strengthened the already powerful agribusiness concerns in the United States, they further drove out small farms in this country. The elimination of so many small farms has destabilized rural economies in Mexico and spurred more immigration northward.

Developing countries have fought vigorously against core labor standards, however, arguing that these will only drive down worker incomes, create unfair trade barriers, and prevent further progressive economic growth. These nations believe that instead of creating a level playing field, standards will be manipulated by powerful countries to suppress competition. Developing nations cannot compete with more advanced industrialized nations in wages and living standards, they argue. Forcing them to meet unrealistically high standards will only defeat their march toward progress, civil society, and rising prosperity before it can begin. Humanitarian and financial aid will be more effective in raising living standards, these nations tend to argue.

International labor standards generally refer to the following areas:

- Freedom of association
- Minimum living-wage levels
- The right to organize and bargain collectively
- Prohibition of forced or compulsory labor

- Restrictions on the use of child labor
- Guarantee of acceptable working conditions

These standards could be implemented and enforced by expanding the role of international organizations, such as the International Labor Organization, and attaching conditions to trade agreements, as was done in NAFTA, or perhaps by inspiring voluntary private sector initiatives through labeling and codes of conduct. Whether or not individual economies adopt transnational labor standards, a number of leading economists argue that living and working standards cannot improve when nations are isolated behind closed national and economic borders.

As Jeffrey Sachs of the Harvard Institute for International Development has written, "the fundamental gain to be derived from globalization, the fact that poor countries can take advantage of all the world's knowledge both in its disembodied form and as it is embodied in capital technology. It gives them a unique opportunity to catch up with the more advanced countries without having to reinvent the proverbial wheel—or fax machine, cellular telephone, biotechnology, or whatever area of knowledge is embodied in the goods that are engaged in international trade and financial flows . . . globalization gives developing countries an unprecedented opportunity to catch up with the more advanced economies" (Sachs 1996, 4).

Trends to Watch

1. Employers eliminated more positions in 1998 and 1999—677,795 and 675,132, respectively—than in any other year during the 1990s (*U.S. News and World Report*, July 2, 2001).
2. During the 1970s, when the minimum wage was higher in real terms, a full-time working parent of two earned enough to lift their family above the poverty line ($13,423 in 1999 dollars). Today, that same family would be $2,700 below the poverty line (J. Bernstein 2000).
3. Welfare recipients made up 2.1 percent of the population in the United States in June 2001, the lowest since 1964.
4. According to a Public/Private Ventures study, less than 1 percent of companies account for 90 percent of all dollars spent by business on training (Stillman 1999).

Related Reading in Part 2

Chapter 4:

"The New Antiglobalists: Exploring the Psychology of Seattle, Washington, and Beyond," William Finnegan

"The Discarded Factory: Degraded Production in the Age of the Superbrand," Naomi Klein

Chapter 5:

"Shock Absorbers in the New Economy," Chris Benner

What Kind of Work Do We Do?

By the middle of the twentieth century, the U.S. economy was the world leader in manufacturing what people drive, eat, use, or wear. In the early twenty-first century, the United States now leads the world in tapping knowledge and technology to create, market, and sell value-added and expert information and services.

Between 2000 and 2010, the most reliable statistics project that total employment is expected to grow from 145 million workers to 168 million, a rate of 14 percent. Nearly all of our job growth is expected to be in service-producing industries that include finance, insurance, real estate, government, transportation and public utilities, and wholesale and retail trade (U.S. Department of Labor 1999). These industries are expected to account for about 19.1 million of the 19.5 million new wage and salary jobs generated by 2008. Jobs in the manufacturing sector are expected to continue declining, as they have since the late 1970s. Manufacturing employment made up 16.1 percent of the labor force in 1988, declined to 13.4 percent in 1988, and is projected to be only 11.6 percent in 2008. Total manufacturing jobs declined from more than 21 million in the 1970s to approximately 18 million in 2000, despite overall population growth (see fig. 25).

In this knowledge-powered workforce, what kinds of jobs—occupations—can we expect to be in demand through the end of this decade? The BLS data underscores the reality of the modern workforce. Knowledge does indeed rule. Professional specialty occupations such as computer systems analysts, teachers, and scientists are the fastest-growing occupational groups through 2008.

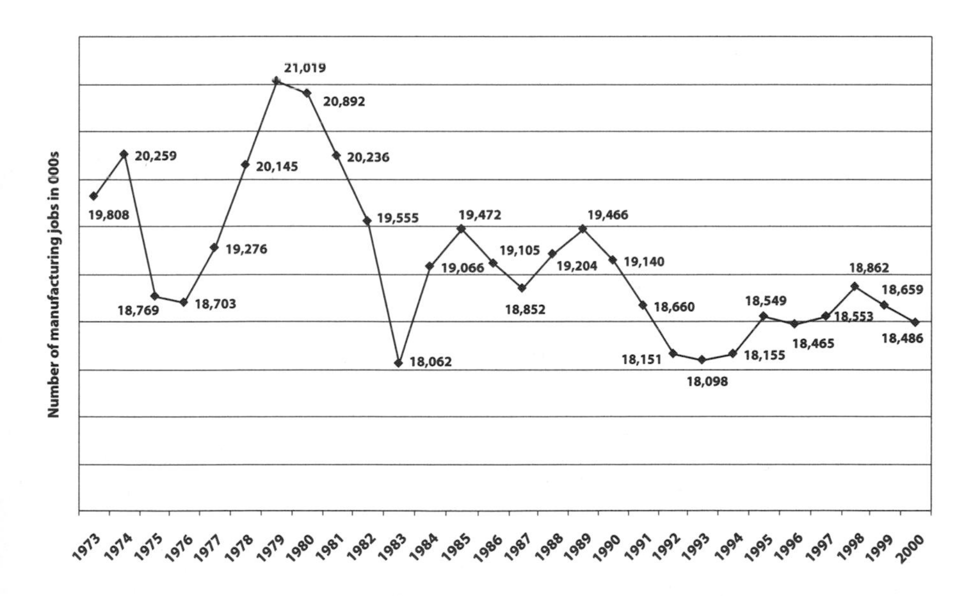

Fig. 25. Number of manufacturing jobs, 1973–2000. *Source:* U.S. Bureau of Labor Statistics.

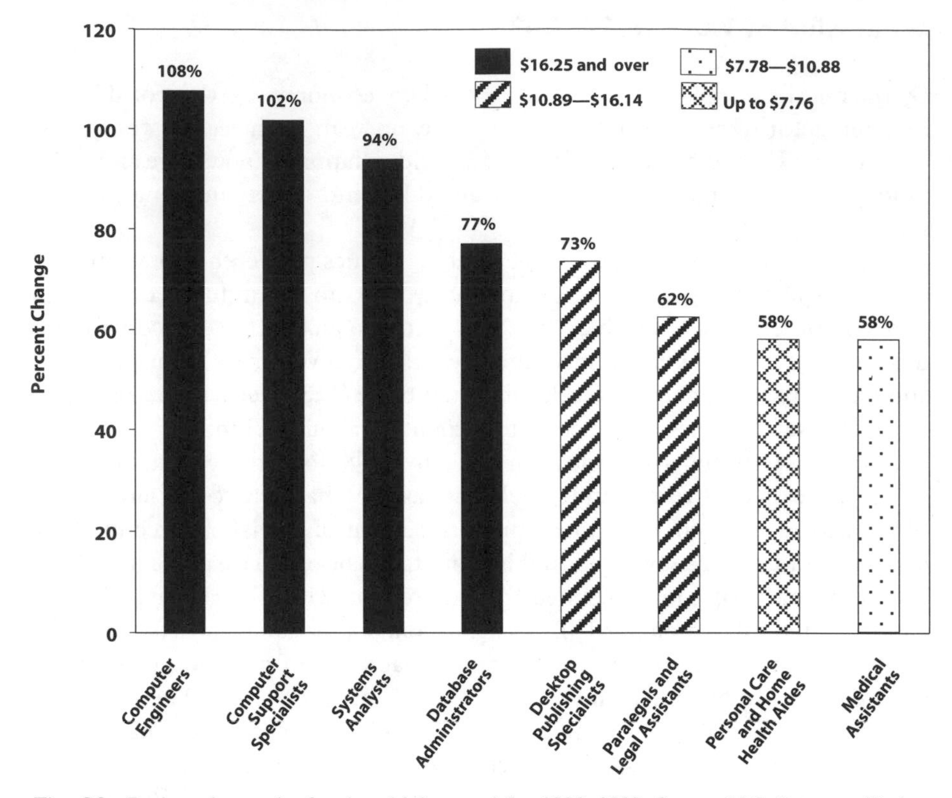

Fig. 26. Projected growth of various high-wage jobs, 1998–2008. *Source:* U.S. Bureau of Labor Statistics.

In an analysis of the twenty jobs projected to grow the fastest, produce large numbers of new jobs, and provide high pay, half of these occupations are involved with computer technology, health care, and education. In fact, computer-related jobs make up the four fastest growing occupations in the economy. By 2008, the number of computer engineers, computer support specialists, systems analysts, and database administrators are expected to increase by 108 percent, 102 percent, 945 percent, and 77 percent, respectively (see fig. 26).

More than 10 percent of the entire U.S. workforce is dedicated to health services or employment in health care settings. Health professionals (physicians and nurses), paraprofessionals (nurse aides, home health aides), and nonpatient care workers employed in health service settings (food service workers, administrators), compose more than 14.6 million people, a substantial chunk of the labor market.

More than ten million of these workers are trained health service workers and professionals. The aging of the population overall—combined with scientific and technological advances in medical treatment, increased expectations for good health by the society as a whole, and the appeal and financial security of many jobs in the health workforce—all contribute to high rates of growth in the health care field. As the massive baby boom cohort ages, expect the health care workforce to continue to be a source of well-paying jobs.

The Automobile and Temporary Help Industries. A well-documented U.S. Department of Labor study of the automotive and temporary help industries examines how the notion of just-in-time production that revolutionized manufacturing in the United States has now become a tool for managing the workforce through temporary help. The study, titled *"Just-in-Time" Inventories and Labor: A Study of Two Industries, 1990–1998*, notes that the automobile and temporary help supply industries reflect the flexible, just-in-time mode of production that many U.S. industries have adopted to reduce costs in a period of heightened worldwide competition.

No study of the American workforce is complete without providing important details about the manufacturing workforce. Nearly a million people, about 5 percent of the manufacturing workforce, work in the motor vehicles and equipment industry. A greater proportion of these manufacturing workers are production workers than in the manufacturing sector as a whole (75 percent to 69 percent). More than 35 percent of employees in the auto industry are unionized, compared to 16 percent of workers who are unionized in the manufacturing sector overall. Auto employees' workweeks are longer and their hourly wage rates are higher than the averages in the manufacturing sector overall. Most of these workers receive health and pension benefits.

From the end of the 1980s through the 1990s, motor vehicle manufacturers faced tough competition while consumer demand for their product leveled off. As prices for cars continued to rise—and quality improved—car buyers held onto their vehicles longer, leading to plant overcapacity. As a result, car manufacturers needed to reduce costs while maintaining or improving quality and keeping prices under control. The industry responded by adopting just-in-time lean production techniques. More competition was introduced to parts producers, who were expected to meet higher quality and delivery standards. Suppliers were also asked to perform more design, development, and management of parts. These changes led to more efficient, unified, and standardized products, further reducing costs. Workers were cross trained to perform quality control, repair, housekeeping, and maintenance, in addition to producing cars, and they were given more authority over work processes and decisions on the factory floor.

These initiatives grew out of the collective bargaining process and had the full support of the United Auto Workers. Union negotiators saw the benefits of accepting work rule and design changes in order to strengthen job stability and lessen outsourcing of jobs for their members. As the automotive industry's productivity began to soar, labor costs stabilized. Workers were getting more done and working longer hours. During the postrecession 1991–98 period, worker productivity grew by an average of at least 3 percent per year for assembly, parts, and stampings workers, while unit labor costs declined for these workers—as much as 5.4 percent per year for stampings workers and 2 percent annually for assemblers. The successful adoption of just-in-time techniques staved off further industry losses, restored jobs, and empowered more workers on the factory floor.

As noted in this guide, the growing numbers of workers in nontraditional temporary, freelance, free agent, consulting, and similar jobs have attracted wide attention in recent years and pose important questions for the ongoing stability and security of families and broader social structures. In the Department of Labor report—and other ongoing research—researchers have studied particularly closely temporary workers who receive job assignments through help supply services companies, so-called temp agencies or manpower firms.

The workforce in the temporary help industry grew from just 0.6 percent of the workforce in 1982 to 2.7 percent in 1998 as a percentage of the private economy (U.S. Department of Labor 1999b). Employers have always used temporary workers during early periods of growth after a recession or for seasonal or unusual projects within the firm. But in the 1990s many employers hired temporary workers as a principal workforce strategy. For employers, the cost advantages can be substantial. Temporary workers seldom receive health or pension benefits and, as is patently obvious, can be hired and fired at a moment's notice. Moreover, the costs of finding—and managing—temporary workers is often delegated to large firms that specialize in providing these services to large companies. As global competitive pressures increase, and the need continues for quarter-to-quarter profitability, the temporary worker is becoming a favorite short-term strategy. According to the Department of Labor study: "The corporate work environment reflects a market that is less regulated, more affected by international trade, and more subject to rapid change than ever before. The resultant volatility has led to the desire for a more flexible labor 'infrastructure.' To meet this need for flexibility, business increasingly is contracting labor for a specific purpose and for a specific duration. Just-in-time in the materials market is being met by just-in-time in the labor market, as expenditures for labor are determined more by the bottom line than by norms and traditions" (U.S. Department of Labor 1999b, 22).

According to the study, those who supply temporary help are also competing and working to improve the quality and reliability of these workers for employers, thereby again shifting costs traditionally borne by employers to the agency instead. Temporary workers often receive certificate skills and other training through their sponsor agencies, who provide all the instruction and training required for word processing and other computer-based jobs. In the past decade, as the information economy began to grow rapidly, employers sought to hire on a temporary basis thousands of highly qualified technology professionals such as computer programmers, paying them well but avoiding long-term commitments and benefits. Corporations could ramp up skilled labor during periods of intense technology development while retaining the freedom to easily reduce workforce size as circumstances warranted. The concept of a just-in-time workforce makes economic sense for many companies, but many questions linger about how these strategies will affect a changing worker-employer compact.

Workers do expect less loyalty from employers and understand they must upgrade skills and jobs to maintain their economic security. The numbers of highly skilled consultants and contractors as well as lower-skilled temps are growing. But there is no evidence to suggest that the vast mainstream of the workforce is prepared to waive their rights to steady jobs and join the free-agent nation. Survey evidence shows that despite the historic growth of the economy during the 1990s, more Americans worried about their financial security in those years than in less glittering periods of prosperity decades earlier. The rising number of workers without health insurance is of such widespread grassroots concern that decent health coverage has been a top priority on the nation's political agenda for nearly a decade. The provision of benefits and security remains important to employee job satisfaction and a signal concern to employers seeking to build a high-quality competitive workforce.

Even in the halls of new economy titans, the vaunted appeal of the high-tech free-agent life hit its limits. At Microsoft, temporary engineers and others working on a succession of temporary contracts at good pay began to organize and lobby for the benefits of permanent staff. At Amazon.com, workers sought union representation to achieve more stable wages and benefits, triggering a tough management backlash. And with the collapse of the dot-com revolution and its frenzied job market, the nation's magazines featured story after story of young professionals experiencing their first layoff—their first taste of genuine economic insecurity. Many returned to old-economy firms, sought more stable careers, and, as of 2002, applied to law and professional schools in skyrocketing numbers. Yet, it is in the information technology sector that we are seeing how a new employer-worker compact may take shape.

The Permanent Information Technology Revolution. Information technology (IT) has become what one observer called the crude oil of the millennium economy, the basic commodity of a global market in finding, transmitting, storing, using, and organizing knowledge. According to Michael R. Pakko (2002) of National Economic Trends, the total nominal expenditures on computers and peripheral equipment in the United States tripled over the decade, rising from $49 billion in 1990 to nearly $150 billion in 2000. Investment in information and communications technology throughout the economy accounted for an astounding 40 percent of total U.S. business investment; it should be noted that corporate spending on the year 2000 bug and systemwide upscaling to e-business capability represented a massive short-term boost in this type of investment.

Employment in the core IT occupations—computer scientists, computer engineers, systems analysts, and computer programmers—has experienced astonishing growth since the 1980s. The number of computer systems analysts, scientists, and computer programmers in the workforce grew from 719,000 in

1983 to 2.1 million in 1998, an increase of 190 percent, more than six times faster than the overall U.S. job growth rate of 30.4 percent. However IT workers are measured, analysts agree that the number of core IT workers will grow dramatically between 1996 and 2006. The more conservative figures provided by the Department of Commerce indicate that the United States will require more than 1.3 million highly skilled IT workers to fill new jobs and replace workers who leave existing jobs (Carol and Sergeant 1999).

In contrast to the rest of the labor force, IT workers are most likely to be men with high levels of formal education. The bulk of the IT workers are also in finance, insurance, real estate, and manufacturing. More than 65 percent of core IT workers possess a bachelor's degree or higher (Carol and Sergeant 1999). Not surprisingly, compensation levels for IT professionals are high and rising. *Information Week*'s 1999 National IT Salary Survey found a median annual salary increase of 8.9 percent for all IT workers, 9.2 percent for managers, and 8 percent for staff.

Women and minorities are underrepresented in the professional IT workforce (Technology Association of America 1999). Women are underrepresented in fast-growing occupations, including programmers (69 percent men), computer systems analysts and scientists (72 percent men), and electrical and electronic engineers (92 percent men). African Americans and Hispanics are also underrepresented in these key positions and in the IT workforce as a whole.

The rapid expansion of the IT workforce raises many issues for public and private employers, unions, policy makers, and others who care about how we manage and regulate the workforce. What kind of jobs does the new infotech economy create? How many of these jobs provide good wages and benefits? Will this industry continue to experience the hiring peaks and plunges of the dot-com revolution? As noted by sociologists Erik Wright and Rachel Dwyer,

> American success is founded on "flexible" labor markets, which allow employers—especially in the context of globalization, NAFTA, and the WTO—to hire and fire employees relatively easily, reorganize employment structures in response to market conditions, and adjust wages as needed, especially in a downward direction. As a result, job growth is accompanied by persistent poverty, continuing high levels of inequality, and the growth of poorly paid, dead-end service sector jobs. While these critics acknowledge the recent American success at creating jobs, they also argue that the jobs are "lousy"—with low pay and little chance for improvement.
>
> Are the critics right? Is the American "jobs miracle" based on the expansion of lousy jobs? More precisely, what is the distribution of job quality—the balance of good and bad—in the current expansion, and how does this distribution compare to earlier job expansions? Before celebrating the American model, and urging its emulation elsewhere, we need answers to these questions.(Wright and Dwyer 2000, 2)

(Wright and Dwyer's answers to these questions are published in MIT's *Boston Review* online.)

While it is true that many jobs created during the 1990s were good jobs, it is also true many of these new jobs did not pay well at all. Their analysis shows that the bulk of the job creation that took place during the 1990s expansion occurred at the top *and* bottom of the earnings ladder. The study finds that while job growth for white Americans was concentrated at the good end of the spectrum during the 1990s, job growth for blacks and Hispanics was concentrated at the low-paying end.

The authors distributed new jobs by occupational category along deciles according to pay. The highest-paying jobs of similar types were grouped together, on down to the lowest-paying jobs of similar types. Then, jobs created in each of the categories were calculated. According to the authors' classification, many new jobs did pay well. According to the analysis, 20 percent of the net expansion of jobs during the 1990s came from those job categories in the highest tenth of pay. But the second largest decile was that containing the number of jobs created in categories with the lowest tenth of pay—17 percent of net job expansion occurred in the lowest decile! The smallest share of new jobs were created in the middle (fourth and fifth) deciles of the spectrum. Using this methodology, the authors found that job growth during the 1960s occurred in greater numbers in the middle deciles, with far less growth at the bottom of the pay decile scale.

According to Wright and Dwyer, 62 percent of the net job expansion during the 1990s for white men and nearly 90 percent of net job growth for white women occurred in the top three deciles of the well-paying job types. For black men and women, and Hispanic men and women, job expansion was concentrated among lower-paying jobs. The bottom two-tenths of job categories accounted for 50 percent of the net job expansion for Hispanic women, 35 percent for Hispanic men, 25 percent for black women, and 28 percent for black men. The Wright-Dwyer analysis provides additional powerful evidence of the stubborn and massive divisions that still characterize the American workforce.

An alternative view is provided by the U.S. Department of Labor and the Council of Economic Advisors. Of the twenty million jobs created between 1993 and 1999, the analysis found, 81 percent paid above-median wages. Among the above-median wage jobs, 65 percent were in the top third highest-paying job categories. The analysis found that roughly 68 percent of all net job growth was among good jobs, and roughly 50 percent of all net job growth was in jobs in the top three deciles of the earnings distribution. In fact, both of these analyses agree that a solid number of high-paying jobs were created during the 1990s expansion, but the Wright-Dwyer analysis shows that many new jobs did not pay well and that fewer new jobs were created in the middle deciles.

Regulating Safety on the Job. Changes in the types of work performed by Americans, combined with the effective work of the U.S. Department of Labor's Occupational Safety and Health Administration (OSHA) and the initiative of thousands of employers and many unions, have contributed to reductions of injuries and deaths on the job. Since 1971, the U.S. occupational injury rate has

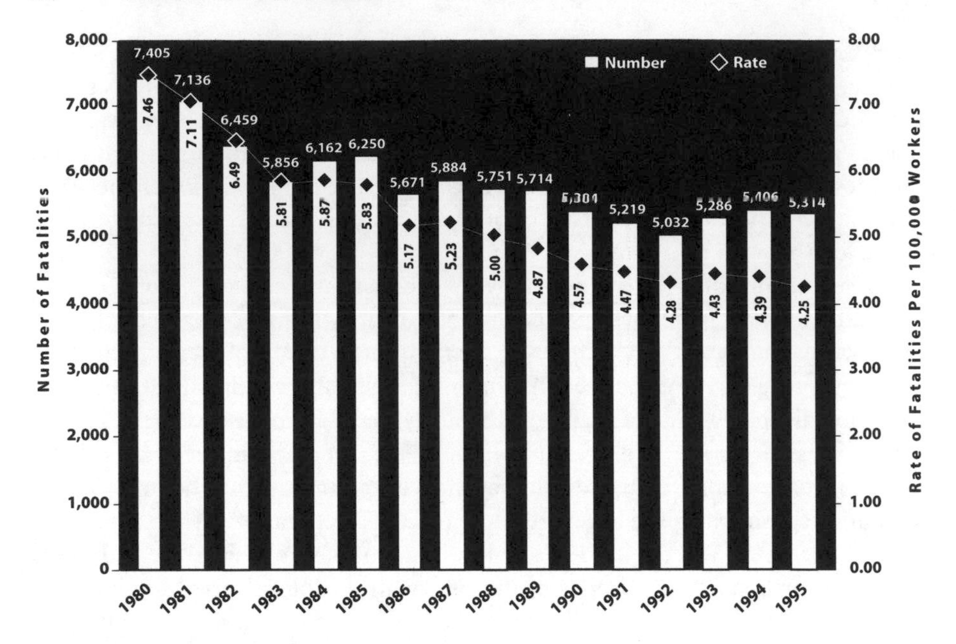

Fig. 27. Number and rate of worker fatalities, 1980–1995. *Source:* National Institute for Occupational Safety and Health.

decreased by 40 percent and the death rate has decreased by 60 percent, as shown in figure 27. However, many workers continue to face profound health concerns, including those related to increases in job-related stress, sleep deprivation, and work hours not measured by OSHA statistics. Workers have spoken through various national surveys about their increasing work demands, the effects of increased work on their wellness and health, and their difficulties in meeting the demands of work while being parents and members of a community.

In the Heldrich Center's 1998 *Work Trends* survey on balancing work and family, nearly half (46 percent) of American workers report spending more than forty hours on the job, with a significant number (18 percent) working more than fifty hours per week (see fig. 28). In light of these long work hours, and the difficulty workers express of spending enough time with family, it appears many are sacrificing the amount of time they sleep. An overwhelming 87 percent of workers told *Work Trends* that they are concerned with getting enough sleep.

The importance of these concerns to the nation are reflected in the rise of the work-family beat in journalism, with regular columns appearing in many newspapers, hundreds of magazine cover stories, and a new wave of research and literature focused on work-related stress. Juliet Schor's *The Overworked American*, Richard Sennett's *The Corrosion of Character*, and Jill Fraser's *White-Collar Sweatshop* are just a few of the nationally recognized books that have explored these trends in depth. The accumulation of data and anecdote compiled

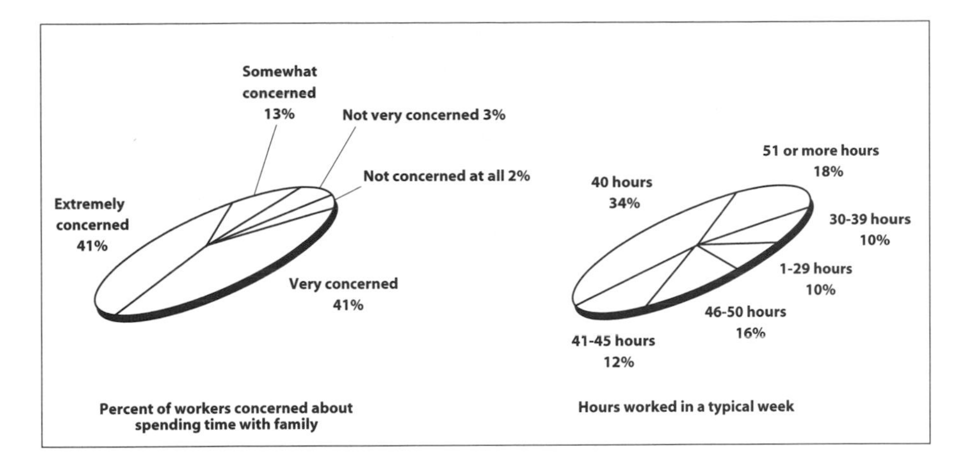

Fig. 28. Percentage of workers concerned about work and family balance. *Source:* Van Horn and Dautrich 1999a.

in these investigations are overwhelmingly—and powerfully—repetitive in their drumbeat description of a modern society out of balance. Passage after passage reads as this one does from Fraser's *White-Collar Sweatshop*:

> Just think about it for a moment. People are working ten or twelve or more hours a day. They're working through their lunch hours, during their commutes to and from the office, in squeezed in spare moments during their evening hours, and whenever else they absolutely need to on weekends and holidays. And many of them still feel that they cannot keep up, that their workloads are excessive.
>
> When the American Management Association conducted an overnight fax survey of its members to explore what it called "the emotionally charged workplace," its results were disturbing. Fifty-one percent of those surveyed cited "frustration" and 49.4 percent "stress" in response to a question about the which emotions best described their feelings throughout the workday. The problem of "having more to do than time to do it" ranked highest on a five-point scale that measured respondents' intensity of feelings.
>
> The National Center for Health Statistics, a division of the U.S. Dept. of Health and Human Services, tracked forty thousand workers to learn that more than half reported feeling either a lot or a moderate amount of stress during the two weeks prior to the survey. In the majority of instances, that stress was work-related. Clearly, the problem abounds. More than 40 percent of professional and clerical workers surveyed by Gallup complained about stress on a daily or almost daily level. (2001, 30)

Trends to Watch

1. According to the *The Digital Work Force* (Carol and Sergeant 1999), the number of computer systems analysts, scientists, and computer programmers in

the workforce grew from 719,000 in 1983 to 2.1 million in 1998, an increase of 190 percent, more than six times faster than the overall U.S. job growth rate of 30.4 percent.

2. Inflation adjusted data from the Department of Commerce indicates that in 1992 the average salary for a worker in an IT-producing industry was $41,300. By the end of the 1990s, the average salary exceeded $58,000.
3. Among the jobs declining the fastest by number, according to the Bureau of Labor Statistics, are private child care workers, sewing machine operators, computer operators, and typists.

Related Reading in Part 2

Chapter 4:
"The Real Foundation of the Software World: Behind-the-Scenes Programmers Are Bricklayers of Internet Economy," Steve Lohr
Chapter 7:
"Rig de Rigueur: Eighteen Wheels and a Laptop," Robert Strauss

Chapter 2

Recruiting, Educating, and Training the Workforce

THE CHANGES WROUGHT BY information technology, deregulation, and a global economy have created a historic transformation in the nature of work. Where a century ago the brute strength of physical labor made the economy move, today fiber optics, satellites, and Pentium chips carry our most precious resources—the data and ideas of the information revolution. Computer literacy has become a basic skills requirement for three out of every four workers.

Today's workforce is not the one our parents knew. In the 1950s, six out of every ten workers were unskilled. Today, six out of ten workers are *skilled.* And the need for skilled workers continues to grow. Huge majorities of American CEOs and senior executives point to the lack of skilled workers and sufficient workforce training as the leading barriers to growth. According to analyst Richard Judy of the Hudson Institute (cited in Porter 2002), 60 percent of future jobs will require training that only 20 percent of present workers possess.

But it should be noted that the identification of the problem by employers is in itself part of the solution. Despite the shortage of workers with the ready package of skills employers sought during the 1990s' economic expansion—a heavily covered topic in virtually every media forum—employers proceeded to hire lower-skilled workers and provide the training needed, either formally or on the job. Federal Reserve chair Alan Greenspan noted:

> As it turned out, however, the capacity for American businesses to absorb the less educated part of our workforce seems to have been far greater than these anecdotes implied. The unemployment rate for adults with a high school education or less fell from 4.75 percent in 1998 to around 4 percent by the middle of last year. And, while the proportion of small-business managers who worried about labor quality has remained elevated in the past few years, it did not increase further in spite of the decline in unemployment.
>
> One explanation for this phenomenon is the often-observed multiplier effects of technological breakthroughs. . . . today's increasingly user-friendly software has enabled workers with far less education and skills to engender value added from new technologies that their older brothers and sisters could not have foreseen a half generation earlier. (Greenspan 2001, 1)

The education and training establishment is a big business. According to *The Book of Knowledge* (Moe 1998), a Merrill Lynch report, education and training activities account for nearly 10 percent of the gross national product in the United States, or nearly $1 trillion. Even though the United States invested heavily in workforce preparation in the early years, it still lags behind most other industrialized nations in workforce skills upgrading and retraining after people complete secondary education. According to Organization of Economic Cooperation and Development (OECD) figures, the share of public investment in total adult training and education investment is less than 50 percent, while most industrialized nations make public investments that are well over 60 percent (see fig. 29).

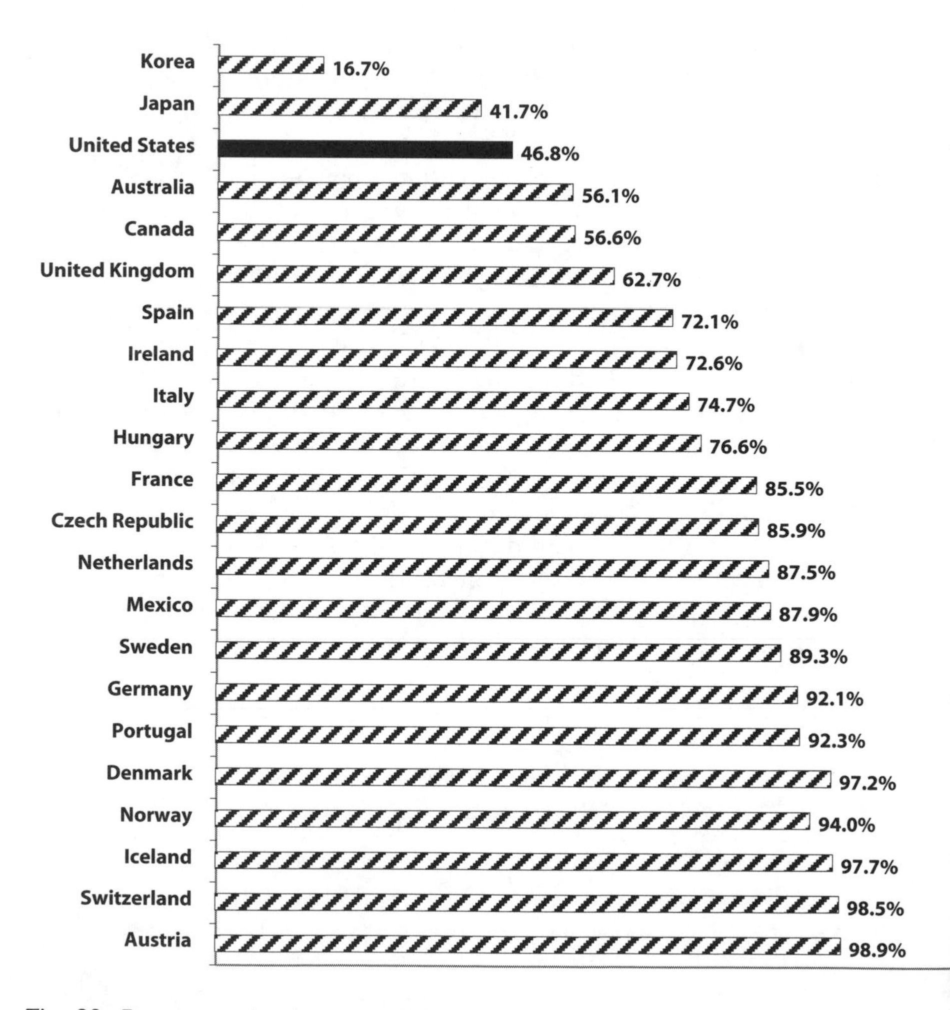

Fig. 29. Percentage of various countries' public investment in adult training and education. *Source:* Organization for Economic and Cooperative Development (OECD).

Analysts argue that U.S.-based education and training policies and programs concentrate too heavily on the early years and should focus more on the lifelong learning needs of workers. Education is not a distinct phase from which we graduate, but a permanent temperament. In the same way that we ideally seek to promote and protect physical health from infancy through old age, so it is we should understand education as the promotion of appropriate knowledge at every step of life, from preschool through elementary grades, high school, college, and graduate education, professional development, or job training. Effective education should no longer be understood as going to a good high school or college, but as a lifelong endeavor that combines the teaching of basic knowledge with training in the concrete skills needed to survive and prosper in a knowledge-based economy. In the United States, federal and state training dollars reach but a scant 5 percent of those eligible.

There is little doubt that additional education and training pays off for individuals and for companies. An analysis of census data (Eck 1993) shows that skills training creates an average increase of 26 percent in wages for high school graduates and 33 percent for those with one to three years of college (see fig. 30). Census data also show that mean monthly incomes for workers with a bachelor's

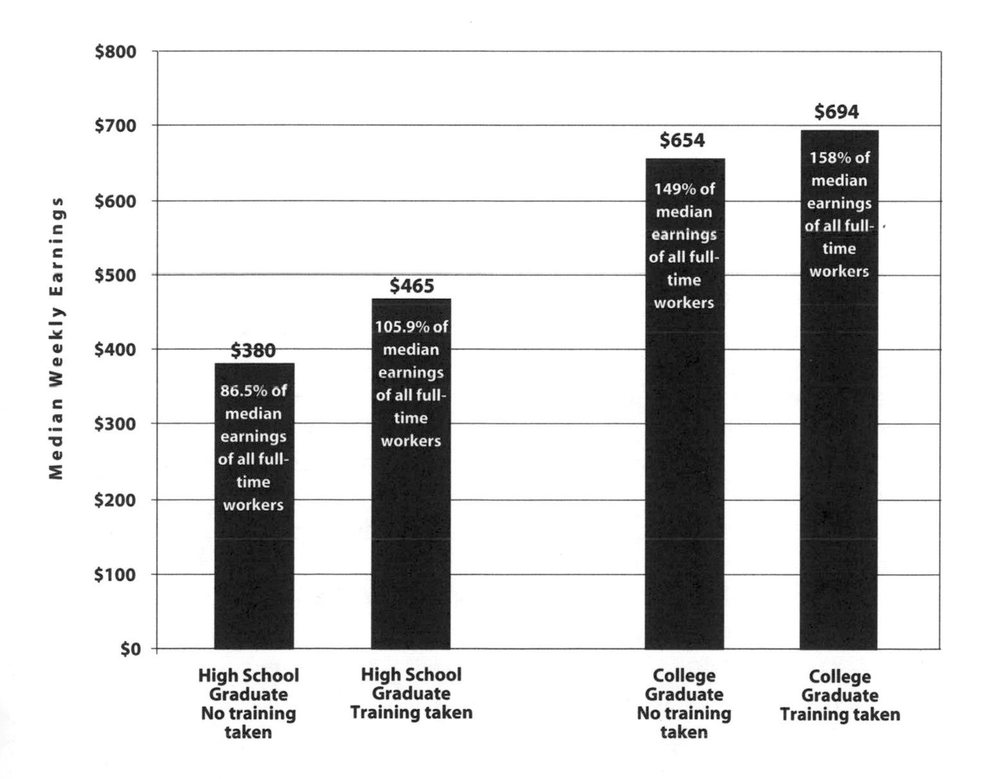

Fig. 30. Median weekly earnings of workers with and without training. *Source: Monthly Labor Review*, October 1993.

degree are nearly twice those of workers with a high school degree only. Researchers Duane Leigh and Andrew Gill (1997) published research showing that even one year of community college increases hourly wages by 8 percent for males and 5 percent for females under twenty-one.

For employers, investments in workplace training generate substantial returns to productivity and growth. Formal training programs have been shown to increase firm productivity by roughly 15 to 20 percent on average, with associated gains in individuals' innovative abilities and wages (Committee for Economic Development 1996). Companies who invested the most in workplace learning saw higher sales and gross profits per employee than companies who invested less in workplace learning (Bassi and Van Buren 1999, 2000).

After nearly two decades of national debate about education reform initiatives at the state and local levels, American public school students still test far below students in other Western nations in math and science and other fields. One out of eight seventeen-year-olds in the United States cannot read, write, or do basic math. One million high school students drop out of school every year. Progress in reading, math, and science scores among high school graduates has been painfully slow.

The fundamental new reality of the marketplace is forcing change in what executive Lea Soupata of the United Parcel Service calls the knowledge supply chain—public schools, colleges, trade schools, churches, community volunteer groups, parents, and government agencies. Because the new economy has created an unprecedented demand for skilled workers far into the future, institutions from across the private sector are plunging ahead to meet it. Technology and the Internet are fueling this competition by wiring networks that allow learning to take place anywhere, at any time, to far more people of various means than ever possible before. This new paradigm presents both a challenge and a historic opportunity for parents and educators to shape how these changes will take place in order to improve an education system that reflects wider economic imperatives and serves students, workers, and families effectively.

Still, there remain profound mismatches between what people learn and the skills they need to work successfully. In a comprehensive survey of New Jersey employers completed in 1995 for the Education Commission of the States and the State Higher Education Executive Officers, employers reported that no more than a third of recent college graduates were "highly prepared for work," and a majority of employers felt that graduates of four-year institutions were "prepared for work but could be better." Employers told researchers that qualities such as integrity and honesty (84 percent) and skills such as listening (73 percent), reading (70 percent), and oral communication (68 percent) were among the most important. But in assessing whether graduates in each skill area were highly prepared, employers answered the following:

Integrity and honesty—only 38 percent highly prepared
Listening—only 19 percent highly prepared

Reading—only 33 percent highly prepared
Oral communication—only 18 percent highly prepared
Knowing how to learn—only 17 percent highly prepared (Van Horn 1995)

Even Ph.D. students are ill prepared for the realities that face them on their ladder of career opportunities, found a major study published in 2000 by researchers at the University of Wisconsin at Madison. Chris Golde directed the survey, which found a "three-way mismatch" among the purpose of doctoral education, the aspirations of students, and the realities of their careers. Two-thirds of the Ph.D. students surveyed said they definitely wanted to become full-time, tenure-track faculty members, while a quarter of them said they may be interested in such posts, even though in most fields no more than half the students would realize that goal. At the same time, more than half of the students surveyed said they were not prepared for the various activities that most faculty members spend their time doing, such as teaching. Finally, students were less able to learn about nonacademic careers and were often not encouraged to explore these options.

Three massive clusters of programs and organizations dominate the supply chain for the education and training of America's workforce:

- Public and private K–12 schools, colleges, and universities
- Private employer training programs
- The publicly funded patchwork of education and training programs and providers commonly known as the workforce development system

Schools, Colleges, and Universities

With as much as 10 percent of the nation's gross domestic product directed toward education and training in the public and private sectors, more attention and debate is needed on how secondary and higher education translates into results for customers—the students—in the workforce. Who graduates from our secondary and higher education schools? What jobs do they obtain? How can schools better prepare students for work and success?

After decades of testing and debate over school reform, education remains an enduring problem among citizens and policy makers because of the stubborn perception that, despite these efforts, many Americans who graduate from secondary and postsecondary schools are ill prepared for the challenges of the workforce. Education and business experts agree that higher literacy and basic skill levels are essential if today's children are to be prepared for even entry-level positions in the modern workforce.

The money and numbers of people enrolled in education programs are staggering. In 1999–2000, K–12 expenditures reached $308 billion, an increase of 65 percent from the $202 billion figure in 1990 (see fig. 31). The number of children

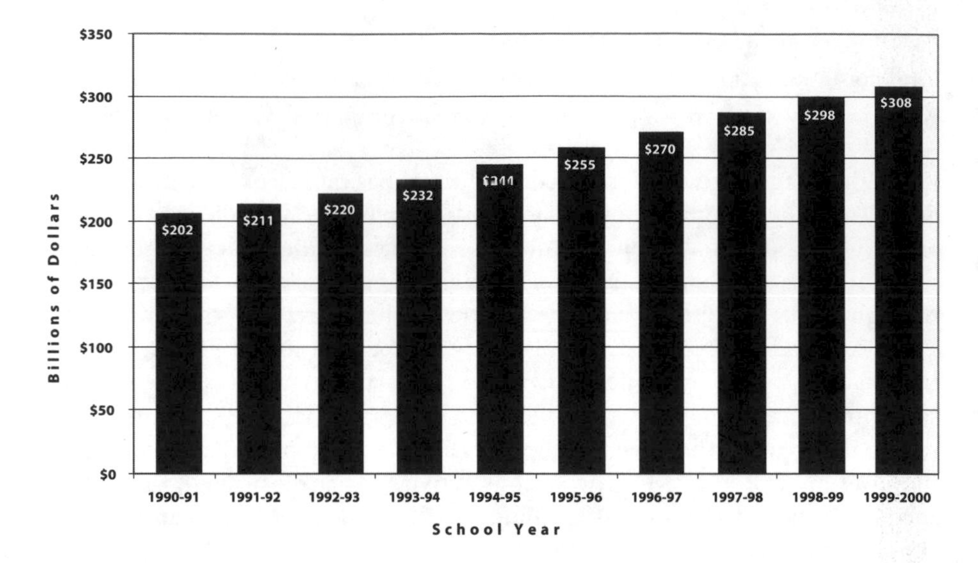

Fig. 31. Public elementary and secondary school expenditures, 1990–2000. *Source:* U.S. Department of Education, National Center for Education Statistics, *Common Core of Data, National Public Education Financial Survey and Digest of Education Statistics* (Washington, D.C.: U.S. Department of Education).

enrolled in grades K–12 remained relatively flat during the early 1980s but is steadily growing from more than forty-six million in 1990 to projected levels of nearly fifty-five million in 2007. The baby boomers' children, who entered elementary grades in the late 1980s and 1990s will create a demographic bulge that will require increases in teachers, classroom space, and other resources well into the next decade. The U.S. Department of Education projects student populations to grow by 18 percent in grades nine through twelve between 1996 and 2006 (see fig. 32).

The importance of education to the first generation born in the new economy will increase the pressure on educators and policy makers to bridge the broken connection between traditional classroom education and the skills needed to thrive in the fluid, highly mobile workforce of the future. Additionally, educators, administrators, and policy makers must also learn to better serve the growing wave of working adults who are returning to the classroom in numbers at all-time highs.

Despite decades of talk about improving education, American workers are not confident that the schools are doing all they can to properly prepare young people for the workplace. In a survey conducted in 2000 (Van Horn and Dautrich 2000b), working Americans expressed serious reservations about the preparation of students graduating from the nation's high schools, colleges, and universities. More than half of the workers surveyed in the report gave high schools nothing better than a grade of C on how well they prepare students to succeed in today's

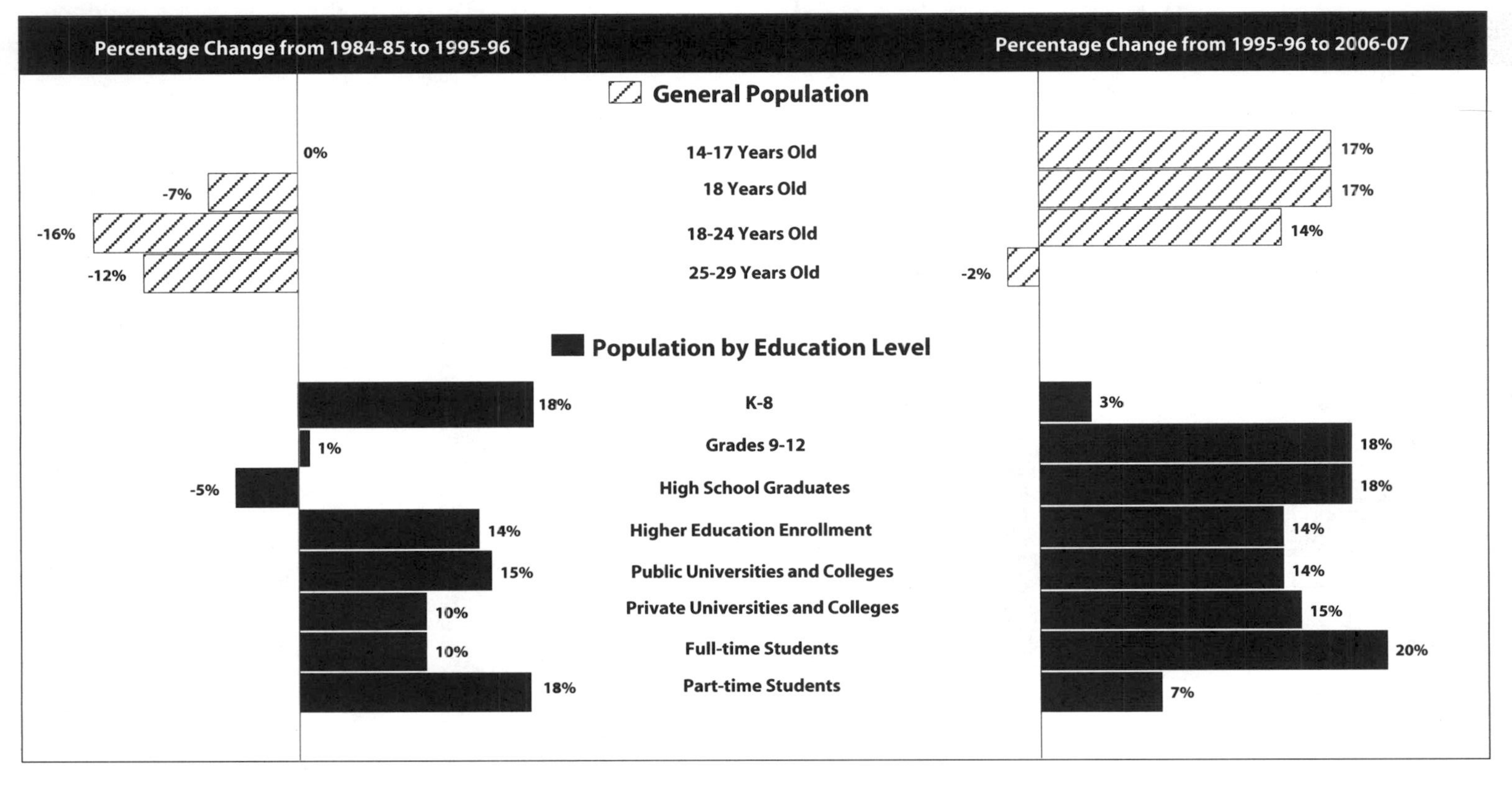

Fig. 32. Percentage change in high school and college enrollment, 1984–2007. *Source:* Van Horn and Dautrich 2000b.

workforce, as shown in figure 33. One-third (32 percent) of workers gave high schools a B. The majority of workers indicated the primary purpose of high school is to provide students with basic skills and prepare them for college.

The majority (70 percent) of workers gave colleges and universities a B or better on how they prepare students to succeed in their careers. Almost two-thirds (64 percent) of Americans said the primary purpose of a college educa-

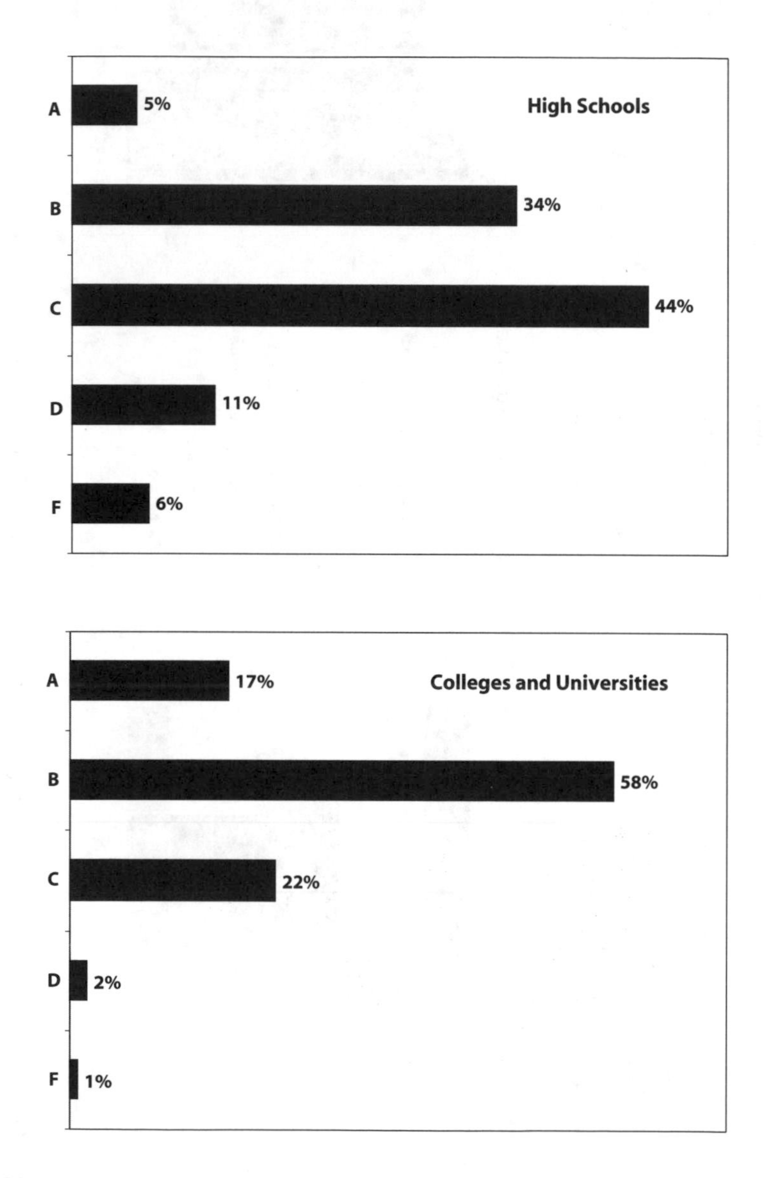

Fig. 33. U.S. workers' grades of schools and universities on effective workforce preparation. *Source:* Van Horn and Dautrich 2000b.

tion is to prepare students for specific careers. While a majority of the Americans surveyed said they believe education has improved since they went to school, fewer than 40 percent were very satisfied with how effectively their own education prepared them for their jobs and careers.

Workers made clear a number of the reasons for their dissatisfaction. They rated general, all-around skills and personal attitudes as being far more important for schools to provide than specific skills. The vast majority of workers report that communications skills, basic literacy, and critical thinking skills (87 percent, 81 percent, and 81 percent, respectively) are very important, while only 50 percent said computer skills are very important.

In addition, almost all workers (92 percent) reported that maintaining honesty and integrity at work is very important, and just as many said that taking individual responsibility and having a good work ethic is very important. Workers said in huge majorities that schools should help students learn these skills, attitudes, and behaviors. However, they did not believe schools were accomplishing these goals and said on-the-job training provided the best preparation for the workforce. Workers in vast majorities believed that on-the-job training methods were far more effective work preparation methods than formal education in school or formal training after school (see fig. 34).

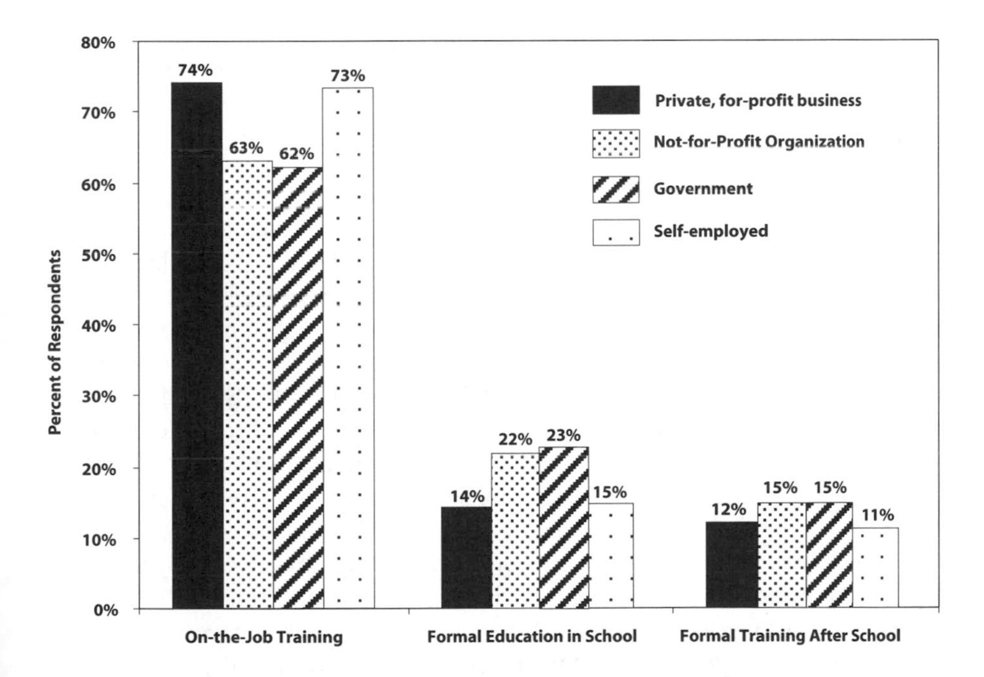

Fig. 34. U.S. workers' opinions of the effectiveness of work preparation methods, by sector, 2000. *Source:* Van Horn and Dautrich 2000b.

Driven by concerns about how well young people are prepared for the challenges of the information-technology economy, private and public sector leaders have largely endorsed and funded three disparate strategies for transforming our nation's schools and postsecondary institutions. These strategies involve creating school-to-work partnership programs; employing the Internet and information technology to improve learning; and forging business–public school alliances to improve literacy in reading, math, and science. Although not every business, education, or government leader supports all of these approaches, they do enjoy significant funding and widespread support and can be implemented through community-based partnerships. Policy analysts are studying the effectiveness of these approaches. At this juncture, we know enough to say that each of these approaches is working well in at least some communities, but debate rages around future policy directions. What follows is a current assessment of these three major policy shifts in how educators are preparing students for the workforce.

School-to-Work Partnership Programs. During the 1980s and 1990s, educators, parents, business and community leaders, government agencies, and many others debated how to better help students make the transition from secondary schools to colleges and careers. As many as three-fourths of the high school students in the United States entered the workforce in that period without college degrees, and many lacked the academic and entry-level occupational skills necessary to succeed in the changing workplace. This situation was compounded by the decline in earnings of high school graduates relative to the earnings of individuals with more education and by the high dropout levels of economically disadvantaged and minority students and those with disabilities. Concurrently (and to the present day), trade liberalization in a global economy, increasing public and private technology investments, and innovations in personal computers and devices combined to increase the importance for young workers in the United States to possess solid literacy as well as high-tech skills. Business, civic groups, parents, and policy makers began to pay very close attention to the issue of improving public schools to make sure more students graduated with more of the tools employers required—and a willingness to learn more tools.

In 1994, Congress and President Clinton created the School-to-Work Opportunities Act (STWOA), a five-year initiative designed to better prepare students for the workforce of the future and encourage a wide understanding that learning takes place not only in school but also on the job and over a lifetime. The STWOA established five-year federal grants to be used by states as seed money to implement a system of school-to-work partnerships among employers, organized labor, educators, and public agencies and other groups responsible for economic and workforce development, education, and human services.

The legislation was designed to encourage a number of goals, including increasing the number of students achieving high-level academic and occupational skills, and expanding opportunities for all students to participate in postsecondary education and to move into better-paying jobs. The law aimed to improve learning experiences for low-achieving youth, school dropouts, and youth with disabilities and assist them in obtaining good jobs and pursuing postsecondary education. The law established a framework in which all states can create school-to-work systems that are part of comprehensive education reform and career preparation, leading to increased opportunities for minorities, women, and people with disabilities by enabling them to prepare for careers from which they traditionally have been excluded.

Between 1994 and 1999, the legislation awarded $1.5 billion to create school-to-work systems in thirty-four states. While the bulk of funding was provided to localities by states using their federal grants, some local partnerships were funded directly by the federal government. By the fall of 1997, states had funded 1,106 local partnerships through STWOA dollars.

The STWOA anticipated that the network of school-to-work systems would be implemented as state and local partnerships saw fit while meeting three broad criteria: incorporating career development programming in schools, changing curricula to integrate academic and vocational instruction, and linking work-based learning to the school curriculum. Still, analysts including those at the Heldrich Center at Rutgers University have found that the states would have benefited from more clarity of direction from the federal rule writers. According to Van Horn and Erlichson (1999, 7), *School to Work Governance: A National Review*, "Most important is that there is not a standard definition of what School-to-Work is or what the goals of the initiative should be. There are multiple names for the initiative both among the states and sometimes within a single state".

Estimating the progress and effects of this legislation is difficult. As noted in the Mathematica Policy Research evaluation published in 1999: "School-to-work implementation generally involves broad and diverse initiatives that in varied ways touch most or all students, so it is impossible to distinguish between participants and an unaffected comparison group." In fact, the legislation was designed to expire in five years: "Because STWOA funding was meant to be short term, the legislation envisioned an infrastructure of leadership entities and policies. Partnerships at the state and local levels would lead to the development of STW systems. These collaborations would coordinate the efforts of educators, private-sector firms, labor unions, parents, students, and community groups" (Hershey et al. 1999, 4).

Among the most encouraging signs of success of the school-to-work movement is the rapid spread of partnerships across the country and the involvement of critical stakeholders in those partnerships. In twenty states, more than 90 percent of secondary school districts include school-to-work partnerships, and another six states have partnerships in at least 75 percent of their districts. From 1995 to 1997, business and industry involvement in these partnerships have increased substantially to about or above 50 percent in most school-to-work activities.

Education and training organizations are included in virtually all school-to-work partnerships, but researchers have found substantial participation by significant independent sector groups. Nearly two-thirds of all partnerships cite a community-based or nonprofit organization as a member, often a long-standing education-business alliance or youth organization. Almost 70 percent of partnerships include at least one alternative education provider.

Generally, school-to-work partnerships have successfully established roles providing school districts with training and technical assistance, informal guidance, inspiration, and collaboration, often without high-level support from state agencies, which are paying less attention as federal funding has ended. Unfortunately, partnerships will no longer receive federal dollars and to survive they have begun and must continue acquiring new resources and partners, according to the federal evaluation of the school-to-work law (Hershey et al. 1999).

The only substantial impact school-to-work efforts have had on school curricula is an increase in structured career programs that have begun at about a quarter of partnership schools. Highly structured, European-style career programs discussed by the federal law—programs that combine academic and vocational learning around a career or industry focus, with links to work-related opportunities—are relatively unpopular. Parents and students remain wary of what seems like early career decisions and activities that might lead students away from four-year colleges. Participating schools and organizations place more emphasis on recommending how to link existing courses and opportunities to prepare for broadly defined career areas.

Mathematica and other evaluations have found that since school-to-work programs began, work-site visits and job-shadowing opportunities are fairly widespread and school-listed job and internship placements are increasing. A report issued in 2000 by the Public Forum Institute—based on a series of dialogues with educators, parents, students, employees, labor representatives, and other partners—found that key participants in school-to-work programs emphasized the success of its mission. According to the report, 84 percent of student participants and 81 percent of businesses noted that school-to-work students met or exceeded their expectations. Similarly, 81 percent noted that the program helps students meet challenging academic standards, and 96 percent emphasized that it helps students better prepare for college.

The school-to-work movement has followed a familiar pattern: high hopes and inspiration as the final, compromise legislation is enacted; frustration as the law is put into effect and competes with many other priorities; evaluation and assessment that determines ongoing funding support; and, finally, the push among core believers and supporters to keep school-to-work programs part of an ongoing program. These experiences of the 1990s underscore the key idea at the core of all this debate. The country is still searching for ways to provide young people not attending four-year colleges with a quality education without categorizing them negatively. This sector of the population needs higher-skills training, better work preparation, and opportunities for certificates and college degrees.

Information Technology, the Internet, and Education. The Internet and technology have the potential to profoundly change how schools operate and teach children. The wiring of America's schools in the late 1990s was largely funded by a new federal telecommunications law that levied a telephone bill surcharge to finance a national telecommunications infrastructure. The so-called e-rate program allocated funding to ensure schools received discounts for Internet access, internal connections, and other technology needs; funding distribution was based on the income levels of students within a school and whether a school's location was urban or rural. By 2000, almost all public school buildings in the United States were connected to the Internet, compared with only 35 percent in 1994 (U.S. Department of Education 2000; see fig. 35).

In 1994, only 3 percent of classrooms had computers with Internet access; by the fall of 2000, the number of wired classrooms jumped to 77 percent, according to the National Association of Colleges and Employers (NACE) (Cattagni and Farris 2001). Six in ten schools with large numbers of low-income students had their classrooms wired for the Internet, whereas eight in ten classrooms in schools with a small number of low-income students had Internet access.

Home access is an important companion to the efforts of schools to provide broad-scale instruction and availability for computers and the Internet. When the Internet and computers are available at home, students can do research, take online courses, and communicate with teachers and other learners; parents can communicate with schools and teachers; and families can connect with ommunity and government services. According to the U.S. Department of Commerce (2000) and its surveys of digital access, the share of households with Internet access has grown dramatically. Between December 1998 and August 2000, the share of households with Internet access nearly doubled, from 26.2 percent to 41.5 percent. Still, the digital divide widened slightly. The gap in Internet access between African American households and the national average grew from 15 percent in 1994 to 18 percent in 2000. At the same time, the gap between Hispanic households and the national average grew from 14 percent to 18 percent. Those learners without Internet access at home must rely on schools, libraries, and community centers to get online.

	1994	1995	1996	1997	1998	1999	2000
% of Public Schools with Internet Access	35	50	65	78	89	95	98
% of Instructional Rooms with Internet Access	3	8	14	27	51	64	77

Fig. 35. Percentage of public schools and instructional rooms with Internet access, 1994–2000. *Source:* U.S. Department of Education, National Center for Education Statistics, "Survey on Advanced Telecommunications in U.S. Public Schools," 1994–2000.

As people gain access to computers and the Internet, leading entrepreneurs, analysts, educators, and policy makers are asking in what ways computers and the Internet can improve how kids learn. Some studies from the private sector and government indicate that the Internet's potential benefits for education, if well executed, are breathtaking. They include increasing student motivation, encouraging higher-order thinking, expanding parent involvement, decreasing administration and paperwork, and providing tools for teachers to communicate individually with students anytime, anywhere. Following are some widely cited findings.

1. A New York City computer pilot program, which focused on remedial and low-achieving students, showed gains of 80 percent for reading and 90 percent for math when computers were used to assist in the learning process (see Guerrero et al. 1990).
2. When learning methods such as peer tutoring, adult tutoring, small class sizes, longer schooldays, and computer-based instruction are compared, computer-based instruction is the least expensive instructional approach for raising mathematics scores by a given amount (see Fletcher, Hawley, and Piele 1990).
3. Studies of school-age children with disabilities who used computer-assisted learning techniques showed that almost three-quarters were able to remain in a classroom and nearly half were able to reduce school-related services (National Council on Disabilities 1995).

Before these benefits can be fully realized, however, educators, parents, and policy makers face significant challenges. Robert McClintock, codirector of the Institute for Learning Technologies at Columbia University Teachers' College, points out that the Internet does not just act within the education system, its acts upon it—fundamentally changing the educational process as it becomes part of it. The Internet transfers initiative and control to students, who can tap into a mind-boggling range of educational resources outside the classroom and their teachers. Will this freedom of choice ultimately undermine the hierarchical teacher-student relationship and other longstanding traditional structures, and is this good or bad? The Internet challenges teachers to integrate new, advanced technologies into daily teaching and to adapt to ways the Internet changes students. Teacher development and training is also absolutely crucial for the potential of these technologies to be realized.

Research by the Benton Foundation and the President's Committee of Advisers on Science and Technology have analyzed the fundamental issues in training teachers to adapt to and use the Internet. These include evaluating content; redesigning curriculum; structuring student use of the Internet; assessing student learning, issues of access, and community involvement; and, perhaps most important, addressing the student-centered nature of Internet-aided learning. The bipartisan congressional Web-based Education Commission, created by

Congress and the White House in 1999, released a significant report in 2000 that reviewed best practices in using technology to improve learning and to prepare students for the future in a new economy. The report summarized its findings this way:

> The Internet is not a fad. It is not just another in a long line of technologies that have promised a quick fix for education. Its reach and impact on all aspects of society are unprecedented. The interactivity of this new technology makes it different from anything that came before. It elicits participation, not passive interest. It gives learners a place for communication, not isolation. It is not a new form of television. It is a new way of learning. (Kerrey et al. 2000)

Internet and computer access barriers are being surmounted in many communities, but in K–12 education, adequately preparing teachers to use technology is still a substantial challenge. Consider these findings:

- An evaluation of school technology budgets by the CEO Forum on Education and Technology found that just 6 percent of K–12 technology budgets are dedicated to training (see fig. 36; Moe 2000).
- A survey by *Government Technology* magazine published in October 2000 found that 53 percent of states have allocated just one to five hundred dollars per teacher for in-service professional development programs designed to train teachers how to use technology in classrooms.
- A 1998 Department of Education survey found that only 20 percent of teachers say they feel prepared to integrate technology into the classroom.

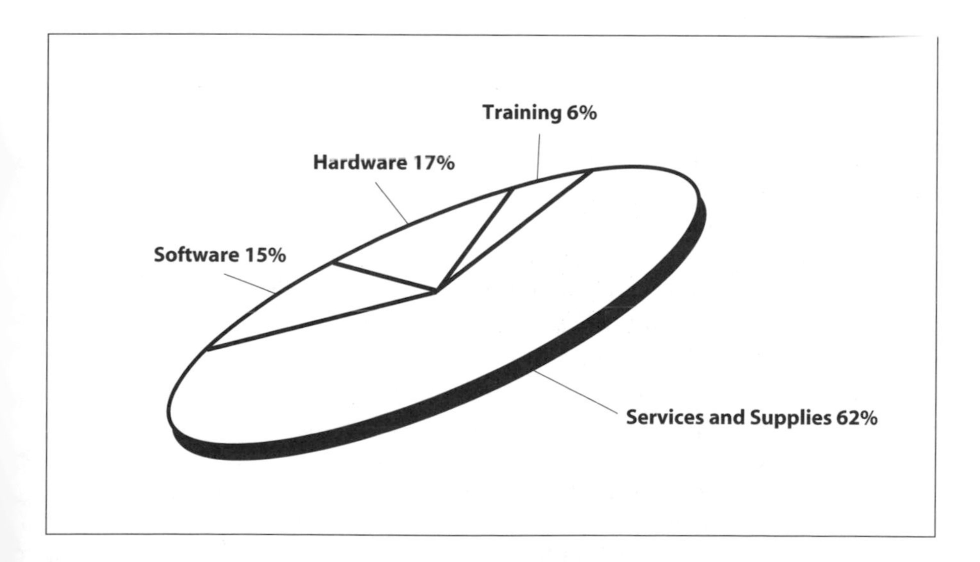

Fig. 36. K–12 technology budgets for 1995–1996 school year. *Source:* Moe 2000.

Several state governments are undertaking dramatic efforts to surmount technological barriers to effective education. Many states are making swift progress toward integrating technology into the classroom and increasing the number of students with access to high-speed online learning resources. One survey found that 72 percent of the states are supporting at least ten new projects and investing up to $1 million in exploring new ways of using technology in the classroom. Fifty-four percent of the states have provided at least half of the students in the state with high-speed Internet access. Meanwhile, more than half of the states reported that technology training or proficiency is a requirement at state higher-education institutions for teacher certification.

Lifelong Learning: The Business–Public School Alliance. Effective education should no longer be understood as going to a good high school or college but as a lifelong endeavor that combines the teaching of basic knowledge with training in the concrete skills needed to survive and prosper in a knowledge-based economy. Community and state colleges and higher education institutions have become vital stepping stones of upward mobility for those with middle- and moderate-incomes. Adults are interested in both general education and training and job and industry-specific training. Community colleges often work closely with job agencies, employers, and unions in developing customized courses designed to meet the career needs of local workers and professionals.

The number of community colleges has grown from 1,091 in 1970 to 1,600 in 1998, and 44 percent of all undergraduates in higher education overall were attending community colleges in 2001. Nearly 33 percent of community college students receive financial aid.

About ninety-nine million adults—or 46 percent of the national population—participated in one or more adult education programs over the course of a year, according to 1999 NCES data. This is a staggering increase since the early 1990s when the NCES found that about fifty-eight million adults participated in adult education in 1991. The increase in the number of adult education participants in the United States between 1991 and 1999 is about double the number of all persons enrolled in higher education for the same time period (Kim and Creighton 2000).

Still, working adults face considerable barriers in acquiring the education they seek. Among adults interested in continuing education, a recent survey found that 54 percent reported lack of time as a barrier; 40 percent reported that courses were not available at convenient times; 25 percent considered the distance to classes to be too far; and 56 percent reported lack of financial resources. In addition, many undergraduate students leave college with outstanding loans that must be repaid during the first years of their careers.

In 1997, Congress and President Clinton enacted two new tax credits to ease the burden of costs of undergraduate education and adult degree-earning or skill-based courses. The new HOPE college tax credit provides a maximum of $1,500 a year of income-tax relief for taxpayers or their dependents during the first two years of college. Each taxpayer's household may receive an additional lifelong-learning tax credit that equals 20 percent of the first $5,000 ($10,000 after 2002) spent on tuition and fees for postsecondary education. The maximum lifelong-learning credit is $1,000 per tax return per year ($2,000 after 2002).

Trends to Watch

1. The Department of Education projects by 2010 an increase of 24 percent in higher education enrollments for people under twenty-five and an increase of 9 percent for people over twenty-five (Cattagni and Farris 2001).
2. According to NCES projections, states expecting the largest growth in the annual numbers of high school graduates by 2007 include Nevada (102 percent), Arizona (65 percent), Hawaii (45 percent), Connecticut (34 percent), Washington (34 percent), Maryland (36 percent), and Colorado (32 percent). Growth rates are relatively flat in many midwestern states. Many states saw huge dips in the numbers of high school graduates during the late 1980s.
3. Sixty-seven percent of teachers are over forty, and another 22 percent are between thirty and thirty-nine, as of 2000. More than 2.5 million teachers will need to be hired in the next ten years as this generation retires.
4. The telephone took seventy years to reach fifty million users; the computer took twenty years to reach that number; the World Wide Web took just four years.

Related Reading in Part 2

Chapter 7:
"The Knowledge Web," Michael Moe
"A Vision of E-Learning for America's Workforce," The Commission on Technology and Adult Learning, American Society of Training and Development / National Governors Association Center for Best Practices
Chapter 8:
"Gray Flannel Suit? Moi?" Thomas Stewart

Employer-Based Training and Education

Employer-based training is widespread in the U.S. economy. Between 70 and 80 percent of U.S. companies with more than fifty employees report that they offer their employees some kind of formal training, according to reports by the U.S. Bureau of Labor Statistics (BLS), the National Center on the Educational Quality of the Workforce (NCEQW), the American Society for Training and Development (ASTD), and many other sources.

Informal training comprises on-the-job instructions, mentoring, and discussions that are in large part intrinsic to any work and inseparable from other forms of work activity. Formal training is planned in advance and has a structured format and a defined curriculum. Six of every ten companies provide tuition reimbursement to their employees, according to the International Foundation of Employee Benefits Plans. These benefits reimburse employees for courses taken in various settings, including undergraduate, graduate, and vocational and technical institutions. Today, employers are spending more on training than ever before.

- Employers with fifty or more workers found that 69.2 percent of employers increased their spending on formal training during the early 1990s, while just 5.2 percent lowered them, according to a Bureau of Labor Statistics survey (U.S. Department of Labor 1995).
- The ASTD's 2000 report on firms participating in its long-term benchmarking study found that companies spent 11 percent more on training in 1998 than in 1997. This increase slowed from the pace of previous years, when firms spent 20 percent more on total training expenditures in 1997 compared to 1996.

Where costs can be spread over larger numbers of employees, where training is required for workers to retain productivity and wage growth, where the demands of technology and global competition force rapid workplace changes—all these factors encourage employer training investments. Employers who have made large investments in physical capital relative to the number of workers, or who have hired workers with higher average education, are more likely to train workers within their establishments.

Companies that underinvest in training do so because they have high employee turnover, because they are reducing their workforce, they face short-time horizons for training investments, or they lack information about defining and measuring knowledge and competencies. In data from an earlier BLS survey (U.S. Department of Labor 1995), the most frequently cited reason establishments of all sizes gave for offering formal job skills training was that training was necessary to provide skills specific to their organization. Other important reasons for offering formal job skills training were to keep up with changes in technology or production methods and to retain valuable employees—each of these reasons was cited by at least half of those providing formal job skills training.

The same data found that establishments that provide formal basic reading, writing, arithmetic, or English skills said they did so to reduce error and waste (56 percent) and because basic skills were thought to be critical to technology or production methods (52 percent). About one-quarter of all establishments reported that they offered basic skills training to meet safety and health requirements.

Firms employing high-performance work practices such as creating work teams, reorganizing work sites, and tracking performance are more likely to invest in formal off-the-job training. According to economists Lynch and Black

(1995), employers who use benchmarking or have introduced Total Quality Management (TQM) into their establishments are also more likely to provide formal training. Both TQM and benchmarking require workers to take on more responsibilities for quality control and problem solving. Similar findings are reported from the BLS Survey of Employer-Provided Training. Researchers Duane Leigh and Kirk Gifford (1999) reached the same conclusion in a separate study that showed firms practicing organizational transformation and other high-performance workplace practices are more likely to pay for formal training to train a greater share of their workforces. According to their analysis, formal training for workers affected by organizational transformation is about three times as likely (27 percent) as for workers unaffected by any source of workplace change (8.2 percent).

The types of training offered by companies differ by their industry. Basic skills training is more likely to occur in manufacturing industries, whereas training in specific and workplace-related skills are more likely to occur in nonmanufacturing industries. While manufacturing firms as a sector offer less training than the financial, service, and professional industries, a greater percentage of manufacturing employees tend to take advantage of training opportunities as a share of their workforce.

Private sector investments in training and education vary widely by sectors of the economy. Training expenditures tend to be highest in the information technology and the transportation and public utilities sector (Bassi and Van Buren 1999). The IT and services sectors spent the most on training as percentage of payroll (2.1 percent), and the health sector spent the least (1.2 percent). But some of the nation's leading firms with strong training commitments, such as Motorola and Verizon, typically spend up to 4 percent of their payroll on education and training (Van Horn 1996). The majority of these funds go to wages and salary of training staff, approximately 41 percent, with the next largest chunk going to outside companies for training products and services, about 27 percent for the average firm.

Firms tracked by ASTD in their benchmarking studies spend the most on training in technical processes, procedures, and information technology skills. Managing and supervisory skills, professional skills, and occupational safety were the second most common types of training on which firms spent money. Benchmarking firms spent the least on basic skills, executive development, and business practices training (ASTD 2000).

It has been widely established that workers who already have the highest education and most skills are more likely to receive training than those with lower education and skills. However, national survey data show that nondurable manufacturing, mining , and construction employers provide the largest number of training activities per employee. The most frequently offered types of formal skills training are computer training, professional/technical training, and production/construction–related training (U.S. Department of Labor 1995). White males are more likely to receive training that nonwhite males, particularly among older workers. Race does not seem to affect training receipt among women or low-income workers, but it is generally believed that economically disadvantaged and lower-skilled workers are less likely to get postschool training. It has also been widely shown that the longer workers remain with a firm the more likely they are to receive formal company-sponsored training.

A wide array of organizations and institutions provide employee training. Three of four employees are training by other company personnel; nearly half receive training from outside providers; 36 percent are training through lectures, conferences, and seminars during work hours. Only 17 percent have received employer-provided training from educational institutions (BLS 1995).

The influence of unions and collective bargaining agreements can also be felt in the area of progressive, far-reaching lifelong and work-based learning models. The 1999 negotiations between the United Auto Workers and Ford Motor Company led to the creation of the Family Service and Learning Centers. Other collective bargaining agreements have prevented the loss of jobs through a commitment to retraining on the part of employees and management. For example, NYNEX and the Communications Workers of America (CWA) reached an agreement in 1994 that prevented the downsizing of more than sixteen thousand workers through retirement incentives and the creation of educational programs to establish a smaller and better-skilled workforce (Committee for Economic Development 1996). Established in 1986 through the collective bargaining process between AT&T and CWA, the Alliance for Employee Growth and Development is one of the most successful labor/management ventures in the United States to provide continuous learning to employees.

These partnerships and programs emphasize continuous education and individual enrichment, as well as the more typical training for job-specific technical skills and career advancement, a vital trend. A few corporations are supporting community organizations that provide lifelong learning opportunities. The Ford Motor Company and the United Auto Workers Union joined to create the Family Service and Learning Center (FSLC), aimed to "meet the diverse needs of working families, individuals, retirees, and their communities . . . [T]he FSLC effort acknowledges that our workplaces are part of our communities, and our needs and concerns as employees are intertwined with those of our communities" (Ganzglass et al. 2001). The FSLC offers family education and services (including adult education programs), early childhood education services, and community service education and outreach in more than thirty locations nationwide.

While the bulk of training in private firms still takes place in the traditional classroom format, e-learning technologies are growing in popularity. According to *Training*'s 1996 report, 83 percent of training is delivered through instructor-led courses, compared to only 17 percent delivered through other methods, such as the Internet.

There is no doubt, however, that e-learning is on the rise. From 1994 to 1995, the number of companies using interactive/multimedia computer-based training increased by 25 percent, and the number of companies using the Internet or network-based learning increased by 300 percent. In 1996, nearly 40 percent of companies were using electronic performance support systems, according to ASTD (1997).

Internet-based education and training are provided by numerous and varied organizations. The U.S. Department of Education reported that 60 percent of all 1997–98 distance-learning programs were offered via the Internet (Olsen 2002). Many corporations have and are creating partnerships with large online universities such as the University of Phoenix to outsource their entire training infrastructure, most of it presented online; a number of national private and public universities, including Massachusetts of Technology and Rutgers University, make hundreds of courses and entire degree programs available online.

Trends to Watch

1. In 1994, 57 percent of employers reported that the level of formal training they provided had increased since 1990; only 2 percent reported a decrease (U.S. Department of Labor 1995).
2. Among U.S.-based publicly traded firms during 1996, 1997, and 1998, companies that invested more in training per employee than the average company had a total stockholder return (TSR) that was 86 percent higher than firms that spent less and 45 percent higher TSR than the market average (Bassi and Van Buren 2000).
3. According to BLS employer data, 69.2 percent of private firms raised their expenditures on formal training during the early 1990s, while just 5.2 percent lowered them.

Public Training and Skills Programs

In the first three decades of the twentieth century, the United States faced the technological challenge of adapting our economy and society to benefit from the invention of electricity and the spread of mass production. The high school movement in the United States, whereby nearly all students were expected to remain in school at least until the age of sixteen, helped produce an educated and skilled workforce to meet this challenge. Following World War II, the GI bill that supported continuing education and training for returning servicemen and women also helped the growing economy meet the need for talented workers. Today, as the nation faces a similar epochal transformation, the question facing elected policy makers and other leaders is how to help spur a wave of technology-literate workers who can meet the demands of the information economy with broadly shared gains in income.

Despite its imperfections, the public workforce development system provides a cornerstone of the nation's ability to meet this challenge. Local, state, and federal governments have made substantial investments in workforce development programs. In fiscal year 2000, the U.S. government budgeted and spent about $53 billion combined on the conduct of education and training in America, including primary, elementary, postsecondary, vocational, and special education, adult job training and education, related research, and veteran's education and training programs. The states, of course, spent billions more.

If we follow the nation's money, how is the U.S. budget for education and training—for developing the knowledge and skills of its people, our most precious resource—divided? Where are increases in federal spending being made over the years? Federal spending in education and training as a percentage of the total U.S. budget reached as high as 5 percent in 1975 and 1976 ($43 billion in constant 1992 dollars) and was cut in half during the 1980s to as low as 2.5 percent in 1987 and 1990 ($33.7 in constant 1992 dollars). Education and training outlays grew slightly during the 1990s to reach 3 percent in 1995 ($42.2 billion in constant 1992 dollars) and 2000 ($43 billion in constant 1992 dollars). Here's how these federal dollars were divided in the U.S. budget for 2000:

Dollars given directly to organizations and individuals:
$1.3 billion—Elementary, secondary, and vocational education
$11.5 billion—Higher education (tuition grants and assistance)
$1.3 billion—Training and employment
$957 million—Health
$1.7 billion—Veterans' education, training, and rehabilitation
$3.2 billion—Other
$20 billion—Total, direct

Dollars given as grants to state and local governments:
$18.7 billion—Elementary, secondary, and vocational education
$122 million—Higher education
$479 million—Research and general education aids
$5.3 billion—Training and employment
$7.2 billion—Social services
$512 million—Other
$32.4 billion—Total, grants

Or, looked at another way, by major categories of discretionary spending (not mandated on an ongoing basis but requiring approval each year) and tax subsidies and exemptions provided for individuals, federal spending breaks down this way:

Preschool—$5.26 billion
Elementary and secondary education—$18.5 billion
Postsecondary and college education—$13.3 billion
Higher education tax subsidy (Hope Scholarships)—$4.9 billion
Workforce development—$6 billion
Lifelong learning tax credit—$2.3 billion

Post-secondary Education and Other Training

Hope Scholarships: With Hope Scholarships, students in the first two years of college or other eligible postsecondary training programs can get tax credit of up to $1,500 for tuition and fees.

Lifetime Learning Credit: Students beyond the first two years of college, or those taking classes parttime to upgrade their job skills can receive a 20 percent credit for the first $5,000 of tuition and fees for each year through 2002. After the year 2002, the credit is available on the first $10,000 in tuition and fees.

Pell Grants: This program provides grants to low- and middle-income undergraduate students.

Student Loans: Federal Family Education Loan program guarantees commercial loans, and the Direct Loan Program provides loans directly to schools and students.

Learning Anytime, Anywhere Partnerships: Provides grants to partnerships of two or more independent organizations to ensure that high-quality learning opportunities are available to distance education students.

Montgomery G.I. Bill–Active Duty and Selected Reserve: Veterans and reservists receive education benefits for degree and certificate programs, flight training, apprenticeship/on-the-job training, correspondence courses, and other training.

Veterans Educational Assistance Program: Benefits may be used for degree and certificate programs and other training.

Workforce Development

Exclusion for Employer-Provided Educational Assistance: A tax-exemption for employer-provided educational assistance for undergraduate courses that begin before June 1, 2000. Employers may continue to provide up to $5,250 per year in educational assistance to each employee on a tax-exempt basis for courses beginning before that date, regardless of whether the education is job-related.

Workforce Investment Act of 1998: Provides job search, employment counseling, and training services to adults, dislocated workers, and youth.

One-Stop Delivery Systems: In a single neighborhood resource center, one-stops provide information about and access to a wide array of job training, education, and employment services.

Adult Education and Literacy: Funds state and local programs to help educationally disadvantaged adults—including welfare recipients and immigrants—develop basic skills (including literacy), complete secondary education, and learn English.

America's Learning Exchange (ALX): Part of America's Career Center Kit, ALX is an Internet program, which makes it easier for employers and individuals to find the training they need.

Manufacturing Extension Partnership: Helps smaller manufacturers work with education and training providers to match their capabilities with manufacturers' requirements. Companies are assisted by more than 400 nonprofit linked centers and offices around the country.

Fig. 37. Federal initiatives supporting workforce education and training. *Source:* U.S. Department of Labor et al. 1999.

These categories are quite broad, but they do demonstrate that as a policy, federal lawmakers invest far more in education received before adulthood than after it. The overlap and duplication of all federal spending on workplace issues was made clear in a 1995 General Accounting Office report (U.S. Department of Labor 1999). The analysis examined the entire federal budget, estimating that the federal government spends more than $35 billion on 163 workplace-related programs administered by fourteen separate agencies (see fig. 37); while this figure would be slightly higher today, the way the funds are divided among these various agencies has not changed markedly.

POLICY BRIEF: THE WORKFORCE INVESTMENT ACT

An important law governing how states and local governments allocate training funds and ensure program performance is the Workforce Investment Act (WIA) of 1998. In partnership with elected officials and state agencies, the WIA provides state and local Workforce Investment Boards (WIBs) the authority to carry out changes in the workforce development system to meet the nation's needs for a high-performance, high-skills workforce. According to the law, 85 percent of WIA funds ($630 million in federal funds in 2001–2) are allocated to WIBs; the remaining 15 percent of WIA funds ($94.5 million) may be used by states for discretionary purposes, such as administration, statewide initiatives, or competitive grants. More important, the policy and strategic role of WIBs provide a platform to influence and shape the spending of billions more in federal dollars.

By strengthening WIBs, the authors of the WIA addressed the long-stated need to unify, streamline, and make more effective the patchwork of private and public spending on skills training and employment education. The chief elected official of a county or counties appoints WIB members. WIB membership must include private sector businesses—as a majority—along with organized labor, community-based organizations, educational institutions, the state employment services, human service advisory councils, and economic development agencies.

WIBs charter or designate so-called one-stop career centers, which are intended to connect employment education and training services into a coherent network of resources at the local, state, and national level. One-stop centers link employers to applicants and provide adults and young people with access to employment and training opportunities and information. Services provided by these centers include the following:

- Information about local, state, and national labor markets
- Job and career resources
- Job listings
- Hiring requirements
- Job referral and placement and quality of education and training programs

Services provided by one-stops to employers include the following:

- Recruitment and prescreening of qualified applicants
- Easy access to post job listings on America's Job Bank
- Job and industry growth trends and forecasts
- Wage data and other valuable labor market information
- Compliance information on federal legislation

WIA enhances the private sector's authority over workforce programs and the allocation of funds. Job seekers are given greater choices in how to use workforce services and funding to manage their careers. Adults who are eligible to get government funds for training under WIA include disadvantaged job seekers who have not found a job after making a required job search.

By controlling education and training funds in their communities, WIBs are in a position to stimulate broad-based changes in their community's education system. Through their strong private sector membership and charter to assess employer needs, WIBs can provide a concrete picture of the skills and proficiencies demanded by employers in their area. These employment requirements can influence education and training programs at all levels.

The WIA establishes the principle of systemwide performance measures, requiring that workforce development programs provide more information to customers about the labor market and the quality of education and training programs nationwide, including information on customer satisfaction and program quality. The WIA also establishes youth councils so that for the first time a local governing body will oversee and distribute federal grants and support for programs that develop the skills, capabilities, and success of at-risk and low-income young people. Programs will be accountable, performance-based, and evaluated by results against benchmarks.

These changes have implications for policy makers, who have historically approached workforce development issues from a narrow perspective. Education interests promoted education reform strategies; labor advocates focused on determining the needs of low-income job seekers, while others concentrated on determining the needs of businesses. These three areas should be seen as elements of a dynamic relationship. Leaders in these three disciplines—education, public service, and business—can collaborate through the role of WIBs to create new approaches that recognize the cross-cutting reality of education and training in the new world workforce.

The WIA is the fourth piece of enabling legislation passed by the U.S. government since World War II to provide state and local workforce systems with rules and structures intended to make job training and education services cohesive and effective as well as accessible to those who need help. Few observers have questioned the high intentions and goals of the crafters of these laws; but as these services were carried out in communities, they encountered persistent problems. While some local and state organizations developed and managed excellent organizations, the national system as a whole continued to be plagued and criticized for multiple funding streams, lack of accountability and reporting requirements, fragmented services, and a lack of coordination with employers. To critics of publicly funded programs, the longstanding flaws in the system resisted one national reform effort after another.

WIA enjoyed bipartisan support in Congress and a good deal of interest in the states and at the community level for its ambitions to provide far more cooperation and alignment of services and funding and to encourage, reward, and, in some cases, require more accountability, wider access to services, more emphasis on work first, more emphasis on incumbent workers and youth programs, and better information for consumers and employers.

Since its passage in 1998 it is clear that many states and communities have taken advantage of the opportunities the law provides. The system is responding, and the law's emphasis on giving employers a decisive role has been strikingly effective. (For descriptions and examples of workforce development strategies and system management at the state level and best practices at the local workforce agency levels, see Ganzglass et al. 2001; U.S. Department of Labor and Heldrich Center 2001).

However, it is also clear that the workforce system faces substantial obstacles to change. While WIA encourages and calls for a more unified system, it has not consolidated areas of federal funding for job training and placement activities or provided sufficient resources for states to take such far-reaching unification measures on their own. Therefore, the system remains fragmented. WIBs and staff must coordinate among different, inconsistent policies and rules for various federal programs. Accountability measures vary from program to program, with complex definitions and methodology. And, WIBs must negotiate—but cannot dictate—to other federally funded programs. WIA authorizes integrated one-stop career centers but does not provide WIBs with the leverage to accomplish this goal.

Customized Training. Many states embarked on large government-funded customized training programs during the 1990s. These programs assist employers with targeted grants for providing training programs for an employer's workforce, in hopes of improving a firm's ability to compete and encourage the company to keep jobs and firms within state borders. Nearly every state has some version of this program. The budgets include more than $110 million in California to assist 2,300 employers; $31 million in Michigan to assist more than 360 employers; more than $3 million in Connecticut to assist 500 employers; and about $30 million in Pennsylvania to assist around 200 employers (National Governors' Association Center for Best Practices/Regional Technology Strategies 1999, table 9).

These programs have had varying levels of impact for employers and workers. A Michigan customized training grant program was found to have a positive and sustained effect on the quality of goods produced at the firm but did not lead to improvement of workers' wages. One study of training grants in California and Illinois found that the grants funded training activities that would have taken place anyway (Osterman 1992), but more recent studies of the California program found that customized training led to improved job stability and higher earnings for trainees.

The John J. Heldrich Center for Workforce Development performed an evaluation of New Jersey's Workforce Development Partnership Program. The Heldrich Center found that the state's individual training grant program assisted dislocated workers to recover lost wages and to become and remain employed. A large majority of the workers who received vouchers through the program said they were satisfied with the program and believed they received valuable training. The evaluation also found that the state's customized training grant program helped firms provide more training to employees, who often had few previous opportunities to improve their skills. Firms that received the customized training grants said they were very satisfied with the program and believed that the additional training made possible by the grant played a significant role in allowing them to increase employee productivity and firm profitability.

The Effectiveness of Public Training Programs. Over the years, government and independent analysts have grappled with the challenge of evaluating the effectiveness of publicly funded training and skills programs and services, both for job seekers and for the government dollar. The federal government, and to a large extent most states, focus basic skills training and work support programs on disadvantaged youth and adults, as well as dislocated workers, whose skills are outmoded or nonvalued because of economic and technological changes. These federally funded services are offered on a voluntary basis with the exception of mandatory work and training activities required of adults receiving cash assistance.

The primary federal law governing job training programs for economically disadvantaged and other individuals (excluding welfare recipients) is the Workforce Investment Act. From 1991 through 1996, the Job Opportunities and Basic Skills (JOBS) program was the principal law controlling mandatory training programs for welfare recipients. That program was repealed in 1996 and replaced by the new national law governing the welfare system, TANF, which incorporated a work-first philosophy that required adults on assistance to participate in job-search and on-the-job training activities before receiving classroom education (or excluding it altogether).

For many years, the federal government has also invested in programs aimed at helping young people move into their first jobs and in targeted efforts to bridge disadvantaged out-of-school youth to employment. Federal youth programs for in-school youth have included the Summer Training and Employment Program (STEP), the Summer Youth Employment and Training Program (SYETP), and other summer-job programs. Lawmakers have discontinued many of these programs over the years, with some states and/or federal Department of Labor initiatives continuing limited operation. The United States has also funded substantial efforts directed at low-income, out-of-school youth, including short-term Job Training Partnership Act (JTPA) programs; the residential, high-intensity Job Corps program; and initiatives targeted at young, poor, single mothers.

The multifaceted patchwork of federal and state training programs evaluated over the last two decades fall into four basic types of service: job search assistance, short-term classroom training, long-term classroom training, and subsidized employment. Dozens of reliable evaluations have been performed on these programs. A number of major reports—including *What's Working and What's Not* (U.S. Department of Labor 1995); *Evaluating Government Training Programs for the Economically Disadvantaged* (Friedlander, Greenberg, and Robins 1997); and *Strategic Plan: Fiscal Years 1999–2004* (U.S. Department of Labor 2000d)—have studied the entire bookshelf of evaluation literature and the implications of these studies for the effectiveness of skills training and bridge-to-work efforts. The evaluations yield common themes that show that longer-term training programs that include both classroom and on-the-job training are more effective, particularly for adults.

Results from successful programs overall are significant but moderate. When they work, training services provide benefits in money earned and reduced time of unemployment, but, on average, they rarely lift disadvantaged people out of poverty. Many training services have proved to be cost effective. Evaluations of JTPA, Job Corps, and welfare-to-work programs, among others, show returns of $1.40 or more per dollar invested by the government (U.S. Department of Labor 1995). Less-expensive services such as job-search assistance tend to be cost effective and helpful in the short term for more experienced, adult workers.

Training programs generally yield mixed results for youth training and work programs; in particular, short-term training and jobs programs for youth have not shown positive results. Programs that link classroom training of this nature to job opportunities and work experience show better results, as demonstrated in evaluations of the San Jose Center for Employment and Training (CET).

The literature examining the effects of long-term classroom-based academic and occupational training is somewhat contradictory. The intensive, costly, residential Job Corps program has shown that long-term initiatives can be very effective in helping disadvantaged youth. It is unlikely in the extreme, however, that lawmakers would provide the substantial new funds required to provide Job Corps–quality experiences to the numbers of young people who would benefit. One evaluation of long-term community college training for dislocated workers found earnings increases of 6 to 7 percent per year of education completed (U.S. Department of Labor 1995); however, a 1997 analysis of similar programs found poor rates of return (Alsalam 1998; Kodrzycki 1997). Other evaluations of long-term programs for dislocated workers show that the programs have led to higher earnings but have not reached the majority of workers in communities. Early intervention and job-search programs targeting dislocated workers have reduced time of unemployment, according to studies performed in a number of states.

On-the-job training (subsidized by government dollars) has proved to be effective, particularly over long periods of time. One major evaluation of the JTPA program found that adults receiving on-the-job training or job-search assistance showed annual income gains of more than one thousand dollars by the study's final year. Gains were particularly significant for welfare recipients who participated in on-the-job training (Orr et al. 1994; U.S. Department of Labor 1995).

Providing basic education to improve literacy has proven to be extremely effective. High literacy levels and literacy training are indicators of success in the workplace, which is measured by workers' gainful employment, higher earnings, improvement in self-image, and the perception that personal goals are being achieved (Beder 1999). A U.S. Department of Education program providing family-centered literacy education increased children's school-readiness test scores and adult basic education test scores (St. Pierre and Noonan 1998).

The majority of participants in adult literacy programs are Hispanic (38 percent) and white (32 percent), according to 1996 figures released by the National Literacy Summit. Nearly half (47 percent) of participants in these programs are between twenty-five and forty-four. According to the Literacy Summit figures, participants realized a variety of benefits and outcomes from their enrollment in adult education programs, including the following:

- Entering a more advanced training program (28 percent)
- Finding a job (25 percent)
- Gaining needed skills to either keep an existing job or advance to a better one (23 percent)
- Achieving citizenship (9 percent)
- Registering to vote (9 percent)
- Leaving public assistance (6 percent)

The average basic skills and education levels of welfare recipients are far below that of America's workers. Various studies estimate that between one-third and one-half of low-income workers overall are functionally illiterate—which means, among other things, that they would have difficulty filling out a job application. For example, the National Adult Literacy Survey conducted by the National Center for Education Statistics and the Educational Testing Service in 1992 found that approximately 50 percent of welfare recipients fall into the lowest skill level, as measured by this survey, and an additional 25 percent scored at the second lowest level. The implications of these findings are drastic: "The new welfare legislation emphasizes work placement first, but the NALS study clearly showed that up to seventy-five percent of the welfare recipients perform at Levels 1 and 2, which is below the level required of unskilled laborers and assemblers" (Knell 1992, 10). This finding does not mean that these individuals cannot work at all, but the jobs for which they are qualified are often low paying and unstable.

In response to these findings, some argue that improving adult literacy and basic skills education must be the central component of adult, postsecondary education. Speaking of this problem, the National Adult Literacy report concluded, "Welfare dependency can be reduced in two ways: 1. by increasing literacy levels in the general population to reduce the risk of falling into dependency; and 2. by raising the literacy levels of those already on welfare to help them become more financially self-sufficient" (11).

Even though the TANF program emphasizes work first, several welfare-to-work and workforce development programs enable welfare recipients to pursue education and training. Moreover, several states, such as Maine, Illinois, Kentucky, Michigan, and Iowa set aside portions of their TANF funds to pay for postsecondary education and to provide cash assistance, child care, or transportation services to needy parents enrolled in postsecondary education (Friedman 2000; Golonka and Matus-Grossman 2001).

Recruiting the Workforce

In the robust economy of the past decade, many employers have struggled to find and retain qualified workers, leading them to look for ways to accelerate their hiring cycles and widen the scope of their recruiting efforts. Concurrently, the information age has arrived, and new technologies are having profound implications for life in the workplace. In certain sectors of the economy, particularly technology-related fields, unemployment has hovered near zero as the number of information technology jobs outpaced the number of available workers. Other sectors of the economy have experienced similar shortages of qualified workers.

The strong labor market of the 1990s has receded, but the record-breaking expansion of that time has left us nonetheless with several large-scale changes in how employers secure the employees they need and what workers expect from employers. For most of the 1970s and 1980s, unemployment remained well above 5 or 6 percent. It was a buyers' market—with employers holding the advantage as they doled out the best salary offers to a lucky few. Many college graduates were grateful to get a foot in the door of what they considered to be good companies. Mergers, downsizing, and global competition had eliminated layers of jobs; companies were hiring cautiously through the early 1990s. It was commonplace for students to lament the shortage of jobs and for universities to begin talking about placement rates as a selling point. Although it was certainly an exaggeration, journalists wrote sorry tales about bright college graduates working in coffee bars or drifting through an assortment of menial jobs.

As the economy heated up to annual growth rates of 4 and up to 5 percent and entire new industries were born, the labor market advantage shifted dramatically to the seller—the job seeker. Employers jacked up entry-level salaries for college and professional school graduates and started offering hiring bonuses and other perks to college graduates with little or no work experience. Human resource specialists shifted from talking about force reductions and downsizing to their need to win the war for talent.

Entry-level salaries for some college graduates increased by 10 percent per year in 2000 and 2001, compared with 2- and 3-percent increases in the early 1990s, according to the National Association of Colleges and Universities. The average salary for computer science graduates landing jobs in 2000 was $48,500, while graduates in accounting averaged $37,200 and liberal arts graduates averaged $29,100 (NACE 2000). Starting salary offers continued to increase for many new college graduates through 2001. For example, the average salary offer in 2001 to economics/finance graduates was $40,577, up 8.2 percent since July 2000. Business administration majors also attracted attention from a variety of employers; their average offer rose 6.8 percent to $38,449 in 2001.

The competition and compensation for top-level executives also shot skyward during the 1990s boom. Demand for executives reached a crescendo in 1999, growing 14 percent over the previous year, according to a 2000 survey by the Association of Executive Search Consultants. In fact, national demand for senior executives making between $500,000 and $1 million soared 32.2 percent between 1999 and 2000. The U.S. Bureau of Labor Statistics projects that the number of jobs for top executives and general managers will increase by 2.4 million, or 16 percent, from 1998 to 2008.

Since the peak of the 1990s, the economy has slowed down substantially. Financial visionaries discovered that, yes, there is a business cycle. Working parents discovered that there is a limit to the amount of consumer debt they will carry. Corporate CEOs discovered the pain of quarterly earnings statements and recalled their old standby, the layoff.

The U.S. economy and workers will continue to reap the benefits of America's leadership in technological innovation, research and education, powerful financial markets, and entrepreneurial culture. But the frenzied market for talent that workers enjoyed during the late 1990s is unlikely to be repeated: young college graduates offered thousands of stock options with their first or second jobs; workplace perks that included massages, catered gourmet lunches and breakfasts, pets, and free dry-cleaning pickup; compensation packages that included free cars, personal technology gadgets, and liberal work-at-home provisions (for more on this period, see Girion 2000).

Observers widely noted that many lucrative job offers made in 2000 were rescinded the next year. The repossession of luxury cars is soaring in the Silicon Valley area; even the absurdly inflated housing market in northern California is beginning to cool. Applications to law and business schools are increasing as college graduates return to the traditional stepping stones to career success. Those firms in a tight job market are switching their emphasis to retention, paying bonuses, and increasing salaries to keep more of their best workers on the payroll and to avoid the costs and uncertainties of endless recruiting.

It should also be noted that the war for talent in the late 1990s was driven by small but influential high-growth sectors of the economy that were chasing a small pool of highly educated workers. Only rarely does a high school graduate enjoy this kind of attention from an employer, and the same is true of many college graduates who do not graduate from Ivy League and elite institutions.

Telecommuting and Other Flex Options. For years, telecommuting and other family friendly benefits were offered only at larger, more progressive companies, often those known as the best companies to work for. Telecommuting is not a practical option for many workers. *Work Trends* research by the Heldrich Center found that 41 percent of workers would take advantage of telecommuting if it were offered—though only 17 percent of these workers said that their employers offered the option.

At the height of the robust labor market of the 1990s, more employers were embracing telecommuting as an appealing perk to help attract talent. In a survey conducted by outplacement firm Challenger-Gray-Christmas in 2000, 62 percent of human resources executives said telecommuting opportunities were being offered to attract new employees and retain existing staff. Another earlier survey by the firm found that nearly half of human resources executives said telecommuting would be the biggest workplace trend in the twenty-first century.

Telework could become more popular as employers respond to the powerful demographic pressures shaping the labor force. As baby boomer workers feel the pull to spend more time with growing families and/or care for aging parents, they are placing more and more importance on having flexible schedules at work. Generation Y workers—eighteen to twenty-five—tell researchers that they want flexibility and balance from their employers, as well as money and opportunity. A PricewaterhouseCoopers 2000 survey of more than twenty-five hundred graduating college students from around the world found these students' most important goal was to balance work and personal life through employer-provided telework and flexible scheduling programs. Other benefits workers see as supportive of family issues have risen in favor, including onsite child care, full healthcare coverage and other benefits for nonmarried partners, the use of tax-exempt accounts for child care and elder care, and onsite concierge services to perform employees' personal errands.

Telework is also the focus of new debate among sociologists, urban planners, and policy analysts about its potential for addressing spatial mismatch in the job market. That is, lower-income, lower-skilled adults of color living in inner-city neighborhoods face additional barriers to meaningful work because of the resistance of employers to locate their offices and businesses within the borders of large cities. Research shows that distance *does* matter for people of color seeking job opportunities (Moss and Tilly 2001). Analysis of major studies shows (1) employers hold a largely negative view of inner-city areas, (2) these views affect their assessments of the skills and abilities of inner-city residents, and (3) at least some employers adopt recruitment strategies explicitly based on excluding applications and employees from inner cities.

Supporting Education and Training Opportunities. Education and training has also become a highly important benefit employers offer employees. In June 2000, the American Society of Training and Development and the Society for Human Resource Management (SHRM) released a detailed and well-documented study that provided convincing evidence of this trend. The study examined how seven major companies, which they called exemplary practice partners, used employee growth and career initiatives to find and keep employees. These companies included Dow Chemical Company; Edward Jones; Great Plains; LensCrafters; Sears, Roebuck and Company; Southwest Airlines; and South African Breweries.

Each of these companies experienced lower turnover rates and higher employee satisfaction ratings than the average company in its sector of the industry. The companies told the researchers that their success is due in large part to the investments they make in their people through human resources policies, including their employee growth and career development initiatives. The following similarities were found among the firms:

- Employees were responsible for their own development, but they were generously supported (and held accountable) by managers, leaders, coaches, mentors, and teams.
- Each organization supported training from the very highest levels, realizing that building the knowledge capacity of their workers was a necessary strategy for business success.
- Each company had a strong identity and culture in which employees were understood to be one of the main reasons for the business's success.
- Funding and staff had been put in place to support human resources' efforts to attract and retain employees.

Online Recruitment: The Internet Moves to the Center Stage. Although traditional recruitment methods such as print ads and in-house referrals continue to dominate the recruitment process of most firms, employers are increasingly turning to the Internet to locate and hire new workers. Most large employers now post some or all of their job openings on company Web sites. Most also post jobs on specialized or general Internet job boards, which number in the thousands. In 1995, there was an estimated five hundred online labor exchange sites. Depending on how they are classified, as of 2000 there were somewhere between 5,000 and 100,000 online job sites—not including company Web sites.

The spectrum of employment-related Web sites includes major career hubs, smaller boutique sites that focus on particular audiences, and online newspapers and trade magazines. Publicly funded workforce development sites have also been developed by federal, state, and local governments. The most prominent public sector site is America's Job Bank—a partnership between the U.S. Department of Labor and state workforce development systems.

In 1999, the Internet recruiting business was valued at approximately $250 million, and it is expected to grow to $5.1 billion by 2003, according to figures compiled by *BusinessWeek* and others. A 1999 study by the Conference Board found that the volume of help-wanted ads placed in newspapers has abruptly stopped growing in all areas of the country—suggesting that more and more employers are posting jobs on the Internet. Moreover, Yankelovich Partners' recent study of three hundred large U.S. employers found that two of five firms plan to invest more resources into Internet recruiting during the coming year.

A 1999 Heldrich Center survey of New Jersey employers with fifty or more employees found that nearly three-fourths (71 percent) of New Jersey firms have a Web site that can be viewed by the general public. Forty-one percent of New Jersey firms post jobs on their company Web site, and almost half (48 percent) post jobs on a third-party Internet recruiting Web site.

Use of online recruiting is expected to grow. Among those New Jersey firms that currently do not post jobs on their company's Web site, 43 percent plan on doing so in the future, the Heldrich survey found. Among those that currently do not use Internet recruiting sites, 40 percent plan on doing so in the future. Among all New Jersey firms, nearly two-thirds (63 percent) say they expect their firm's use of Internet recruiting sites to increase in the future (see fig. 38).

Where are jobs being posted? The Internet Business Network 1999 Electronic Recruiting Index estimates that there were more than twenty-eight million Internet job postings in 1998. Approximately 61 percent of these postings were to corporate Web sites, a third (32 percent) were posted on Internet recruiting sites/job boards, and 7 percent were posted to Usenet. More than eight in ten employers who do not currently post job openings on their own Web site or a third-party Web site plan to do so in the future.

Proponents of Internet recruiting cite several advantages over other methods, including greater information availability and exchange, speed, and wider distribution. Internet job posting also costs less than traditional recruiting methods. Merrill Lynch estimates that recruiting online saves $1,000–$11,000 per hire for the typical employer.

Research by the Heldrich Center and other labor market specialists, however, provide some countervailing evidence on the efficacy of Internet recruiting. In addition to using the Internet, New Jersey employers employ a number of well-established strategies to find workers, including newspaper help-wanted ads,

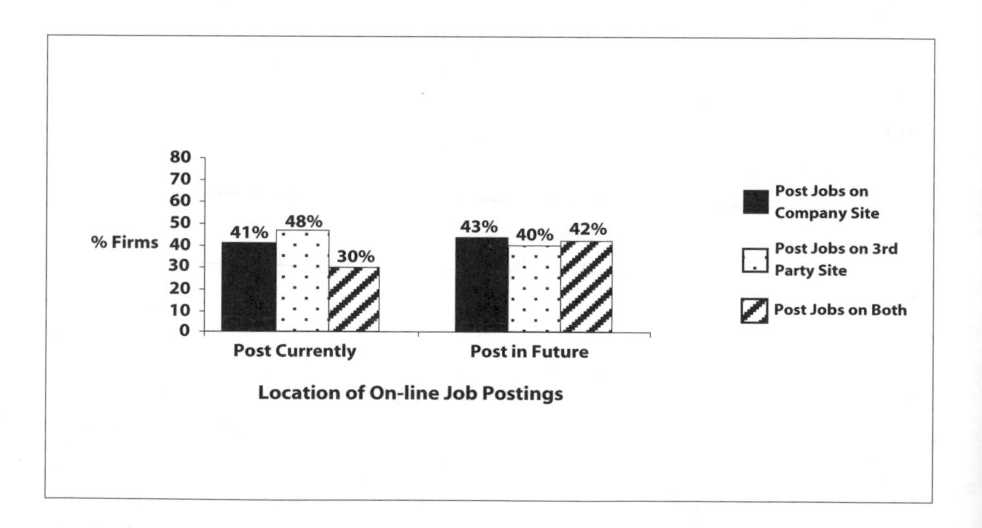

Fig. 38. Percentage of online job postings among employers in New Jersey, 1999. *Source:* Heldrich Center for Workforce Development.

campus job fairs, headhunters or private placement agencies, and in-house referrals. Heldrich Center surveys show a majority of New Jersey firms still rely heavily on referrals from existing employees and newspaper want ads (96 percent and 91 percent, respectively). In addition, almost three-fourths (71 percent) of New Jersey employers accept referrals from schools, colleges, or training agencies to meet their staffing needs.

Placement professionals are also turning to the Internet to find qualified job candidates. Among employers who utilize private placement firms or headhunters, 30 percent report that those firms use Internet recruiting sites to post job openings. Interestingly, more than a third (37 percent) of firms using private placement firms did not know if those firms used Internet recruiting sites to post their job openings.

The process by which workers find jobs and employees find workers is changing rapidly, and Internet-based recruiting is playing an important role in the labor exchange process. According to economists Peter Kuhn and Mikal Skuterud (2000), 15 percent of unemployed job seekers used the Internet to find a new job, more than had used such traditional methods, such as contacting private employment agencies, friends and relatives, schools, universities, or union and professional listings.

Currently, the Internet is just one method among many that employers can use to find qualified workers. Employers often use their own Web sites and third-party Internet job sites for recruitment. Users of third-party Internet job sites also appear more satisfied with online recruiting than employers who post only to their company's Web site. Despite the allure of saving money by using the Internet for recruiting, neither type of user believed that online recruiting has actually reduced the cost of finding new employees.

Although online job postings are likely to be managerial or ones that require at least some college education, a significant number of jobs posted online are entry level and require less than a college education. In addition, some employers report that they do not post lower-skilled jobs online because they do not believe that job seekers interested in these jobs have access to computers or the skills to conduct online job searches. The fact that many entry-level jobs and jobs that require less than a college education are currently posted online is good news for workers with less formal education or job experience. However, unless these individuals have the access to the Internet and skills they need to participate in the online labor market exchange, and unless more employers are willing to post entry-level jobs online, workers with less formal education will benefit less from Internet recruiting.

Related Reading in Part 2

Chapter 6:
"Work at Home? First, Get Real!" Susan Garland
"Child Care, the Perk of Tomorrow?" Steven Greenhouse
Sidebar: "General Description of Hewlett Packard's Domestic Partner Benefits"

Chapter 3

Regulating the Workforce

THE RULES AND LAWS that govern how workplaces are designed, how workers are treated, and what worker rights are and how they can be defended compose an important substrata in the foundation of the workforce. Fights over many of these laws have involved millions of workers and employers, but in many areas they have been settled. The bodies of employment law in areas such as child labor, work hours, and compensation are well established and relatively stable, and they are well covered in many sources.

In this chapter, we focus on those arenas of regulation where change and conflict are shaping the final regulatory landscape: how people with disabilities will access the workforce and workplace; how workers and government will address unfair treatment in the workplace due to race and gender; and how workplaces will be kept safe. While other areas of employment law and regulation are of course essential, we have restricted our focus to landmark fields of policy that are still in flux and under debate.

Opening the Workforce to People with Disabilities

People with disabilities have often been excluded from the workplace. Employers' discrimination and discomfort regarding hiring people with disabilities, as well as lack of physical access to the workplace, have kept many otherwise qualified workers from obtaining regular employment. In addition, federal laws regarding Social Security income and Medicare have prevented many people with disabilities from entering the workplace for fear of losing their health benefits. Today, despite an increased awareness among employers and laws to encourage access, people with disabilities still experience higher levels of unemployment than people without disabilities. The explosion of technology in the workplace is opening doors for the disabled. Employers now have increasingly affordable technology to allow workers to do their jobs from home or other locations.

Since the 1960s, a number of regulations have been enacted to prevent discrimination and make the workplace and public facilities accessible to people with disabilities, including the Rehabilitation Act of 1973, one of the first attempts by Congress to enforce nondiscrimination of people with disabilities in the federal workplace. The most significant parts of the Rehabilitation Act include section 501, which requires nondiscrimination and affirmative action in federal employment; section 502, which requires accessibility in federal buildings; section 503, which requires affirmative action in employment by federal contractors; and section 504, which requires affirmative action of recipients of federal funds.

In 1990, Congress passed the Americans with Disabilities Act (ADA). The goal of the act is to make workplaces, transportation, telecommunications, and the public arena fully accessible to people with disabilities and to ensure that workers with disabilities have the same job and career opportunities as other workers. The ADA prohibits discrimination against individuals with physical and mental disabilities in employment, housing, education, and access to public services. The employment provisions of the law prohibit discrimination in hiring or firing people with disabilities qualified for a job, inquiring about a disability, limiting advancement opportunities or job classifications, using tests that tend to screen out people with disabilities, or denying opportunities to anyone in a relationship with a person with disabilities. Both the Equal Employment Opportunity Commission (EEOC) and the Department of Justice are responsible for enforcing the ADA. Private employers of fifteen people or more; federal, state, and local governments; employment agencies; and labor unions are covered under the ADA.

Despite its laudable goal, the ADA has not been without controversy, beginning with how the act defines disability, a definition that is open to a certain degree of interpretation. The ADA defines a disability as a physical or mental impairment that substantially limits one or more of the major life activities of the individual, a record of such impairment (cancer, for instance), or being regarded as having such an impairment (such as a disfigurement that does not limit major life activities but may be viewed by others as doing so). In addition, the ADA requires that "reasonable accommodation" be made in the workplace for qualified individuals with disabilities. Reasonable accommodation is considered to be any modification or adjustment to a job or work environment that will enable a qualified applicant or employee with a disability to participate in the application process or to perform essential job functions. It can include providing special equipment or making a workplace more accessible. It can also mean allowing an employee to work at home or on a nontraditional schedule. Under the act, employers are not required to provide accommodations that impose an undue hardship ("action requiring significant difficulty or expense") on their business operations, nor are they required to hire people who are not qualified candidates simply because they have a disability. However, this provision has not been enough to allay the fears of many employers.

With the passage of the ADA, many employers feared that they would be forced to make costly accommodations for people with disabilities, hire people with disabilities who are not qualified for the job, or be sued by disgruntled workers claiming discrimination under the ADA. Many employers have overcome their fear of hiring people with disabilities, made reasonable accommodations, and found the requirements of ADA to not be unduly burdensome. Others have resisted making the accommodations and changes necessary for an accessible workplace.

From 1993 to 1999, the EEOC, along with the U.S. Department of Justice, resolved nearly 130,000 ADA charges. According to a report in the May–June 2000 issue of the American Bar Association's *Mental and Physical Disability Law Reporter,* employers win more than 95 percent of the time in ADA suits and prevail in 85 percent of the administrative complaints handled by the EEOC.

In addition, a 1999 U.S. Supreme Court decision narrowed the definition of disability to exclude certain people from protection under ADA. The Court held that a person is not disabled, and therefore not protected from discrimination under the Americans with Disabilities Act, if medication or other corrective devices diminish his or her impairment (taking medication for depression, for instance, or wearing corrective lenses). In February 2001, the Court dealt what could be another blow to ADA protection when it ruled in favor of states' rights by deciding in *University of Alabama* v. *Garrett* that state employees cannot sue for money damages under ADA when they are discriminated against on the basis of disability. The decision narrows the law as written by Congress by excluding state governments as parties that can be sued for financial damages under ADA. However, state governments can still be sued or ordered to provide other forms of injunctive relief that require states to take actions such as building wheelchair ramps or reinstating fired employees. In the wake of these rulings by the U.S. Supreme Court, California has passed a law that restores the scope and purview of ADA within its borders, and other states may follow.

It is likely that ADA will continue to be litigated in the courts as advocates for the disabled, state governments, courts, and employers continue to struggle to define the reach, scope, and regulatory requirements of the act. It is clear that the Americans with Disabilities Act was a critical step in the fight to provide unfettered access to the workplace for people with disabilities, but barriers to participation remain.

If the general public was at all unsure about the very real obstacles people with disabilities confront in the workplace, the tragic consequences of the World Trade Center attacks wiped them away. Many disabled workers in wheelchairs or with other walking problems were unable to escape the buildings when their coworkers did, because only the long stairways were available as a way out.

Ticket to Work and Work Incentives Improvement Act of 1999. During the late 1990s, the government, national foundations, and nonprofit research groups increased the amount of resources devoted to the problem of unemployment among people with disabilities. Today, many people with disabilities who want to work fear losing their health care coverage because getting a job may make them ineligible for benefits such as Medicare and Medicaid. Many people with disabilities cannot obtain private health care and cannot afford to pay their medical expenses, even if they work. Not working, or working very little, is frequently in their best interests if it means holding onto their health care. In this situation, many people who want to work and can work choose to remain unemployed.

To remedy this situation, the federal government in 1999 passed the Ticket to Work and Work Incentives Improvement Act (TWWIA). The purposes of the act are to provide the following to individuals with disabilities: (1) health care and employment preparation and placement services to reduce dependency on cash benefits; (2) Medicaid coverage (through incentives to states to allow them to purchase it) needed to maintain employment; (3) the option of maintaining Medicare coverage while working; and (4) return-to-work tickets allowing them access to services needed to obtain and retain employment and reduce dependence on cash benefits.

Between 2000 and 2002, the U.S. government took additional steps, reflecting bipartisan consensus that chronic unemployment for people with disabilities had become a major national priority. The Social Security Administration enacted a number of regulatory changes that made it easier for people with disabilities who received disability benefits to return to work. The U.S. government committed to hiring 100,000 new federal employees with disabilities by 2005. The U.S. Department of Labor now has an Assistant Secretary of Disability Employment Policy to coordinate efforts and maintain a focus on employment of people with disabilities.

The Workforce Investment Act and Access to Government Services. This renewed attention on reducing unemployment among people with disabilities has focused advocates and experts on how people with disabilities can better access federal workforce programs and services designed to help all job seekers improve their skills and find work. In this instance, accessibility is about far more than physical accessibility to government buildings and facilities (almost all of them are now designed and/or retrofitted so they are physically accessible to people with disabilities). Rather, the issue is how to improve accessibility to federal and state programs and services.

These concerns are being addressed at the nation's one-stop career centers as they are governed by the Workforce Investment Act. One-stops are addressing what it means to be accessible to people with disabilities, whether barriers are physical, virtual, psychological, or informational, and how to make the necessary accommodations (Hoff 2001).

Workplace Discrimination and People with Disabilities. The EEOC reports that since the ADA law took effect, it has collected more than $300 million on behalf of twenty thousand people through lawsuits, settlements, mediation, and other enforcement actions. In addition, the agency has helped more than ten thousand individuals settle disputes over training, education, job referrals, union membership, and other issues. A national mediation program begun in 1997 and expanded in 1999 has resolved more than 60 percent of two thousand ADA charges brought before the commission in about half the time for that of administrative review. The commission has successfully resolved about 90 percent of ADA suits filed in district court either by settlement or favorable court or jury decision. In the appellate courts, the EEOC has filed nearly one hundred amicus curiae briefs in cases confronting fundamental issues on how the ADA should be applied. Significant cases argued and won by the EEOC include the following:

- In the first lawsuit filed by EEOC under the ADA, EEOC won a jury verdict finding the defendant had unlawfully fired its executive director due to the assumption that he could no longer perform his job because he had been diagnosed with terminal brain cancer. The former director was awarded $222,000.
- In a suit against Chuck E. Cheese's, EEOC claimed that a district manager fired a custodian with a developmental disability because the company did not employ "those type of people." A jury awarded the custodian back pay, $70,000 in compensatory damages for emotional distress, and $13 million in punitive damages (the punitive damages award was later reduced to $230,000 because of the statutory cap on damages). The judge also ordered the company to give the custodian his job back.
- In *EEOC* v. *Chomerics, Inc. et al.*, the commission claimed that a chemical worker's coworkers and supervisor harassed and mocked him because of his disability (cerebral palsy). The company agreed to provide the worker with $98,000 in back pay and compensatory damages.
- In the EEOC's case involving Wal-Mart Stores, a jury found the store's hiring official had illegally asked a job applicant about his disability (amputated arm) in a job interview and then refused to hire him. The applicant was awarded $7,500 in compensatory damages and $150,000 in punitive damages.

The Justice Department cites a decade of numerous accomplishments in enforcing ADA that include victories for people seeking access to services, facilities, jobs, and economic opportunity. Towns in North Dakota, Wisconsin, Montana, Ohio, and other states agreed to improve and expand access to public buildings and services for people with disabilities. Courts in Utah and Washington, D.C., were ordered to improve access for the deaf and blind. The Houston, Texas, and Oakland, California, police departments agreed to take the necessary steps to ensure that people who are deaf or hard of hearing can communicate effectively with police officers. Through cases involving an injured Denver police officer, a dyslexic New York plumber, and disabled police and fire officers in Illinois, the

Department of Justice enforced the employment provisions of ADA. The department worked with professional licensing and college testing services to provide the necessary materials and devices for deaf students and other students with disabilities to prepare for and take professional and precollege exams.

Affirmative Action

The long history of federal law and policy regarding discrimination in hiring and promotion within the workforce began in 1941, when President Franklin D. Roosevelt issued an executive order affirming employers and labor unions to take steps to encourage full participation in the national defense program by all citizens of the United States, regardless of race, creed, color or national origin. This order was the first to establish a mechanism for the U.S. government to process discrimination complaints.

President Harry S. Truman's 1948 order to fully desegregate the armed forces was woefully overdue after the sacrifices of black soldiers and airmen in World War II, but it did set a precedent for additional actions by the federal government. In 1961, President John F. Kennedy called for a more proactive and broad-scale approach to ending discrimination at work in Executive Order 10925, which established the President's Committee on Equal Employment Opportunity, whose purpose was to end discrimination in employment by the government and its contractors. The order required every federal contract to include the pledge that "the Contractor will not discriminate against any employee or applicant for employment because of race, creed, color, or national origin. The Contractor will take affirmative action, to ensure that applicants are employed and that employees are treated during employment, without regard to their race, creed, color, or national origin."

The practice of affirmative action became more controversial as the federal executive branch under presidents of both parties in the late 1960s and 1970s introduced the concept of corrective measures such as numerical goals and timetables to correct or compensate for past or present discrimination or to prevent discrimination for recurring in the future. Affirmative action laws now operate in areas including employment, public contracting, education, and housing. Controversies in recent years over the appropriate extent and scope of affirmative action have focused largely on employment and contracting programs. Supporters of affirmative action have long argued that concrete hiring measures are necessary to actually meet the goals of civil rights and affirmative action laws, while critics have maintained that targets are in fact rigid quotas that lead to new discriminatory practices.

How did affirmative action evolve beyond the government's own hiring practices? Laws regarding employment discrimination were extended to private employers in the Civil Rights Act of 1964, the nation's most influential civil rights law ever enacted. It declared "no person in the United States shall, on the ground of race, color, or national origin, be excluded from participation in, be denied the benefits of, or be subjected to discrimination under any program or activity receiving federal financial assistance."

The act empowered the courts to order affirmative action steps such as reinstatement and hiring of employees to redress discriminatory actions by employers. In 1965, President Lyndon B. Johnson argued that affirmative action required more than a commitment to race and ethnic-blind treatment. As he said in his 1965 commencement address at Howard University, equality must be vigorously promoted: "You do not take a person who for years has been hobbled by chains and liberate him, bring him up to the starting line of a race and then say, 'you're free to compete with all the others,' and still justly believe that you have been completely fair. Thus it is not enough just to open the gates of opportunity. All our citizens must have the ability to walk through these gates."

On September 28, Johnson issued Executive Order 11246, which expanded the obligations of government contractors to apply affirmative action principles to all of their operations, stating that "it is the policy of the Government of the United States to provide equal opportunity in federal employment for all qualified persons, to prohibit discrimination in employment because of race, creed, color, or national origin, and to promote the full realization of equal employment opportunity through a positive, continuing program in each department and agency." In two years, the order was amended to prohibit discrimination on the basis of sex. Authority to enforce and administrate these orders was transferred to the U.S. Department of Labor.

Acting on the basis of the expanded mandate for affirmative action, the Labor Department during the administration of President Nixon issued new regulations that required written action plans, goals, and timetables for federal contractors. The Department of Labor issued the so-called Philadelphia Plan in 1969, requiring that contractors bidding for federal work in that city submit affirmative action plans containing goals and timetables for minority employment.

In 1971, the Nixon administration expanded the use of employment goals and timetables in Revised Executive Order No. 4. The order required that affirmative action plans for federal contractors include "an analysis of areas within which the contractor is deficient in the utilization of minority groups and women, and further, goals and timetables to which the contractor's good faith efforts must be directed to correct the deficiencies." The goals as stated in the order were not to be "rigid and inflexible" but targets that could be "reasonably attainable by means of applying every good faith effort to make all aspects of the entire affirmative action work."

In 1979, President Carter transferred responsibility for the federal equal employment opportunity program from the Civil Service Commission to the Equal Employment Opportunity Commission, which directed agencies to develop, submit, and implement five-year employment and affirmative action plans. A 1987 directive from the EEOC gave federal agencies more flexibility in achieving goals.

The Civil Rights Act of 1991. The Civil Rights Act of 1991, which amended Title VII of the 1964 Civil Rights Act and other civil rights statutes, aimed to counter the effects of nine U.S. Supreme Court decisions that had restricted the scope of federal protections against employment discrimination. Reversing the 1989 U.S. Supreme Court ruling in *Pattern* v. *McLean Credit Union,* the act prohibits racial discrimination in all phases of the making and enforcement of contracts. In response to a second 1989 Court decision, *Wards Cover Packing Co.* v. *Atonio,* the act states that in order for employers to prevail in disparate impact cases, they must demonstrate that seemingly neutral employment practices that have a disparate impact on women and minorities are job-related and consistent with business necessity.

As noted in Andorra Bruno's Congressional Research Service report, *Affirmation Action in Employment: Background and Current Debate*, the Civil Rights Act of 1991"ignited a national debate about quotas."

> The Bush Administration maintained that the bill, as introduced, would force employers to adopt numerical hiring and promotion quotas for women and minorities to avoid lawsuits. President Bush had vetoed a similar 1990 civil rights bill. Citing explicit anti-quota language in the 1990 and 1991 bills, proponents rejected the contention that the legislation would encourage the institution of quotas. President Bush signed the compromise version of the Civil Rights Act in November 1991. . . . Many supporters and opponents of the legislation, however, argued that the bill President Bush ultimately signed was little different from the prior versions he had criticized as quota bills. (Bruno 1999, 13)

During this time, public opinion was divided on affirmative action. In most surveys, blacks consistently expressed a greater need for affirmative action than whites. A series of polls found that among affirmative action practices, providing job training and educational classes for minorities and women were far more popular than setting targets or ceilings on hiring. A December 1997 CBS News/*New York Times* poll found that 69 percent of those polled favored government funding for job training programs for minorities to help them get ahead in industries where there are few minorities. Sixty percent of respondents favored outreach programs to hire more minority workers.

The Growing Affirmative Action Backlash and Debate. Policy makers, employers, the public, and the media have debated an array of views about affirmative action. During the late 1980s and early 1990s, the topic became a hotly argued national issue and a number of high-profile affirmative action cases were argued before the U.S. Supreme Court. These cases included the following:

- *Local 28, Sheet Metal Workers* v. *EEOC,* 1986: the Court upheld a federal district order reinstating a nonwhite membership goal of 29 percent for a union that persistently refused to admit blacks.

- *United States* v. *Paradise,* 1987: the Court ruled that temporary one-black-for-one-white promotion quotas imposed by a district court on Alabama state troopers did not violate the equal protection clause of the Fourteenth Amendment.
- *Wygant* v. *Jackson Board of Education,* 1986: the Court considered a collective bargaining agreement between a school board and a teachers' union that gave hiring preference and layoff protection to minority teachers. The agreement had resulted in a group of white teachers being laid off while minority teachers with less seniority kept their jobs. The Court ruled this provision to be unconstitutional.
- *Johnson* v. *Transportation Agency,* 1987: the Court reviewed a voluntary affirmative action plan adopted by Santa Clara County that resulted in the promotion of a well-qualified woman over a well-qualified male, who had scored higher in the initial interview. The job fell outside of the listed occupational categories that were considered traditionally segregated. The justices ruled that the affirmative action plan did not violate Title VII of the Civil Rights law in seeking a moderate, gradual approach that was minimally intrusive on other workers.

After the 1994 elections that led to Republican majorities in the U.S. Senate and House of Representatives, critics of affirmative action lobbied and worked with the legislative majorities in these bodies to pass legislation banning what critics called "racial and gender preferences." At the same time, anti–affirmative action forces organized major statewide efforts to terminate state affirmative action laws, most notably in California.

In 1996, voters in California approved Proposition 209, a controversial ballot initiative that banned state laws and policies that offered support or preferential treatment by race or gender. The American Civil Liberties Union (ACLU) and a coalition of civil rights and other groups filed suit to block enforcement of Proposition 209. U.S. District Court Judge Thelton Henderson issued a preliminary injunction, ruling the ACLU was likely to prevail on the merits of its case. A panel of judges from the Ninth Circuit of Appeals overruled the district court, but the Clinton administration and the ACLU coalition challenged the ruling and sought a new hearing before the ninth circuit. As of today, no hearing has been granted, but an injunction remains in effect on Proposition 209. Many experts believe the case will ultimately end up in the U.S. Supreme Court.

As the 104th Congress took office in 1995, another event appeared to strengthen the hand of affirmative action foes. The U.S. Supreme Court ruled in the case of *Adarand Constructors, Inc.* v. *Pena* that federal affirmative action programs to benefit minorities must meet stringent strict-scrutiny standards, meaning that such programs must be narrowly tailored to serve a compelling governmental interest. The Clinton administration had already undertaken a review of all federal affirmative action programs. Meanwhile, leadership in the

104th Congress wrote sweeping bills aimed at virtually eliminating federal affirmative action. Although the legislative effort generated national publicity and controversy, the two leading bills, H.R. 2128 and S. 1085, never made it out of committee. By the conclusion of the Congress, only two specific provisions benefiting minority businesses were repealed: a Federal Communications Commission program that gave tax breaks to companies selling broadcast companies to minority-owned businesses, and a provision setting a 10 percent goal for the Agency for International Development to contract with minorities and women.

The 105th Congress followed a similar course. Republicans introduced broad, high-profile bills that became lightning rods for debate and fodder for their supporters. Sponsors and rank-and-file legislators would not, however, risk the political fallout of holding actual votes on the measures. These bills included H.R. 1909, the so-called Civil Rights Act of 1997; H.R. 3330, which would have prohibited universities and colleges from participating in virtually any affirmative action programs; and S. 46 and S. 188, which would have eliminated these programs in employment law. One provision placing limits on the Defense Department's disadvantaged business program was enacted.

In the executive branch, President Clinton addressed the results of the White House study on affirmative action and the *Adarand* decision. According to Clinton (1995), "this review concluded, that affirmative action remains a useful tool for widening economic and educational opportunity. . . . When affirmative action is done right, it is flexible, it is fair, and it works." On the *Adarand* ruling, the President emphasized that it did not dismantle affirmative action, but rather set stricter standards to mandate reform. Clinton directed federal agencies to comply with *Adarand* and apply four standards to affirmative action programs: no quotas in theory or practice; no illegal discrimination of any kind; no preference for people who are not qualified for any job or other opportunity; and, as soon as a program has succeeded, it must be retired. The Justice Department began working with federal agencies shortly thereafter to ensure their compliance with *Adarand* and these principles.

POLICY BRIEF: AFFIRMATIVE ACTION—PROS AND CONS

Andorra Bruno's 1998 Congressional Research Series report provides an excellent in-depth analysis of judicial action concerning affirmative action and the recent debate among leading intellectuals, policy makers, and journalists about the social and economic benefits of affirmative action—or its elimination. Among the influential arguments on both sides are the following:

- Supporters characterize affirmative action as appropriate compensation for generations of past injustice. Affirmative action remains necessary to address past economic and social discrimination and injustices suffered by minorities. Sociologist Orlando Patterson argued that racism has harmed middle-class

African Americans, who are in direct competition with whites for jobs, status, and power; who are isolated from networks of influence; and who need affirmative action to level the playing field that has favored whites for three hundred years.

- Supporters believe affirmative action is needed to address ongoing discrimination in the labor market. In *Defense of Affirmative Action,* Barbara Bergman argues that "we cannot expect a great deal of progress in integrating the workplace by race and by sex without a systematic program that pushes people to act differently" (1996, 133).
- Opponents claim affirmative action can never compensate for past injustices. In Shelby Steele's *The Content of Our Character,* the English professor argues that affirmative action "indirectly encourages blacks to exploit their own past victimization as a source of power and privilege," rather than look to "present achievements" (1990, 118). Other observers claim that the lower economic status of various minority groups is due to other factors beyond discrimination.
- Economist Glenn Loury is among the leading critics of affirmative action who argue that discrimination is much less of a problem today than it was in the past. Today's black middle-class live in an era of equal opportunity, Loury holds, and minorities on the whole continue to receive fair, nondiscriminatory treatment in the absence of affirmative action.
- Critics also charge that affirmative action violates the constitutional guarantee of equal protection of the laws by permitting discrimination based on race and ethnic origin. They argue that in making race and ethnic affiliation increasingly important, affirmative action programs betray the constitutional ideal of color blindness. But leading legal scholar Randall Kennedy has argued in response that the colorblind theory of the Constitution is not the only way to interpret the Fourteenth Amendment's equal protection clause. Rather, Kennedy believes, the great cases of the Supreme Court "stand for the proposition that the Constitution prohibits any arrangements imposing racial subjugation—whether such arrangements are ostensibly race-neutral or even ostensibly race-blind" (1991, 54).
- Steele and Glazer have also argued that affirmative action results in reverse racism by fostering preferential policies that unfairly deny opportunities to white males not guilty of discrimination. Supporters respond that reverse discrimination is not a widespread problem and that relatively few reverse discrimination complaints are filed and even fewer are found to be credible. Many proponents of affirmative action also reject the idea that the injuries done to whites by preferential policies can be equated with the harm inflicted on blacks. As English professor Stanley Fish wrote: "Blacks have not simply been treated unfairly; they have been subjected first to decades of slavery, and then to decades of second-class citizenship, widespread legalized discrimination, economic persecution, educational deprivation, and cultural stigmatization" (1993, 130).
- Critics maintain that affirmative action undermines the importance of colorblind merit selection in the competition for job and economic opportunity and

the importance of human merit as an ideal. In response, supporters emphasize that traditional measures of merit are unfair to African Americans who have enjoyed only a few decades of civil and human rights, and that in the multitude of hiring decisions across the nation many factors as well as merit have played and do play a role in the allocation of opportunities—such as personal connections, social background, and ethnicity.

Evaluating Affirmative Action. The body of research regarding the benefits of affirmative action to its recipients is ambiguous. A number of respected researchers have examined the wage and employment effects of affirmative action with a variety of findings. Most analysts do agree that the early years of affirmative action correlate with improved employment outcomes and increased wages for black Americans. Key conclusions of the major evaluations include the following:

- Affirmative action during the 1970s benefited black males at all skill levels, although skilled workers benefited the most. Jonathan Leonard's studies of employment rates among contractors who did and did not operate within affirmative action rules found that protected groups' employment was higher at contractors operating within compliance across all skill levels. Only white women did not share in occupational gains.
- In examining hiring rates between 1966 and 1980 at firms that reported to the EEOC and firms that did not, researchers James Smith and Finis Welch found that the percentage of black workers employed at EEOC-covered firms, particularly black officials and managers, increased greatly in that time (1984, 276). The greatest growth in hiring among blacks occurred in the early years of affirmative action, between 1966 and 1970. The percentage of white men and women working at the EEOC-covered firms decreased.
- Federal contractors had higher shares of workforce that were African American, William Rodgers and William Spriggs found in their analysis of hiring data between 1979 and 1992, though the direct impact of antidiscrimination efforts on the part of the government is fairly small (1996, 290–93).
- Richard Freeman argued that nonwhite workers experienced significantly greater gains in earnings and promotions because of the role of affirmative action in increasing demand for black labor. His analysis of wage, income, and occupational data from the late 1940s through the 1970s found overwhelming evidence that personnel policies were themselves changed by federal equal employment opportunity and affirmative action pressures (1981, 247–70).
- Dave and June O'Neill examined the changes in black wages and found that it was not later affirmative action regulations but the 1964 Civil Rights Act that produced the largest increase in earnings (1992, 96).

- James Smith and Finish Welch observed a substantial increase in black workers' wages between 1967 and 1972, triggered in large part by affirmative action. By 1975–76, however, they found that these policies no longer had an effect on the racial wage gap (1986, 93).
- Harry Holzer and David Neumark in an analysis of employer survey data found that firms practicing affirmative action had a track record of raising the relative wages of women and minorities (1996, 23).

Discrimination: Perception Is Reality. The perception of race also looms as a continuing barrier to the productivity and potential of the workforce. *A Workplace Divided,* a major survey conducted in late 2001 by the John J. Heldrich Center and the Center for Survey Research and Analysis at the University of Connecticut found black and white Americans have sharply different perceptions of how minorities are treated in the workplaces (Van Horn and Dautrich 2002). According to the data found, White workers are far more likely than workers of other races to believe that everyone is treated fairly. In contrast, half of the African American workers said that their ethnic group was the most likely to be treated unfairly, compared to just 10 percent of whites and 13 percent of other minority workers. In addition, the survey found that far more African Americans and Hispanic Americans than white workers reported having personally experienced unfair treatment at work.

This perceptual divide is also reflected in how Americans view the importance of affirmative action and other policies for increasing diversity in the workforce, while African American support for these policies dwarfs the support of white workers.

Workers across the ethnic and income spectrum were agreed that employers (50 percent) and workers (16 percent) are primarily responsible for addressing employment discrimination, not government. However, minority workers expressed dissatisfaction with how employers had addressed these concerns and incidents of discrimination. While 86 percent of white workers and nearly three-fourths of workers of other races agree that their employers take discrimination seriously, far fewer (61 percent) African Americans do.

Almost two-thirds (63 percent) of the nearly all minority workers who believed they were treated unfairly said in the survey that their employers ignored their complaints and took no action in response to reported incidents. Fifty-seven percent said their employers did not respond in a prompt or satisfactory manner. Workers said discrimination primarily took the form of being passed over for promotion (28 percent), being assigned undesirable tasks (21 percent), and being subjected to racist comments (16 percent).

While virtually all white workers (94 percent) believe employment practices in hiring, promotion, assignment of responsibilities, salaries, and a safe working environment are fair to all, nearly half (46 percent) of African American workers and 12 percent of workers of other races said they are not likely to be treated fairly.

African American workers were far more likely than white workers or workers of other races to support the idea of affirmative action to address past discrimination. Half (50 percent) of African Americans agreed with this kind of affirmative action, and 33 percent strongly agreed. In stark contrast, only 15 percent of white workers similarly agreed, with only 4 percent voicing strong agreement for affirmative action.

The survey showed in stark and powerful terms that despite the economic expansion of the 1990s and the modest income growth seen for African American and Hispanic families in that period, black and white America still perceive opportunity in the workplace from different aspects of the economic prism. Many workers believed they could go as far as hard work and skill would take them; but for others, this same level of effort and talent may not be rewarded. As is well known, these differences can bring opportunity costs to the economy as a whole.

Related Reading in Part 2

Chapter 5:
"No Shame in (This) Game," Katherine S. Newman

Health and Safety in the Workplace

The Occupational Health and Safety Act was enacted in 1970, at a time when the media, lawmakers, the general public, activists, and many employers were paying attention to the escalating dangers of the workplace in the growing industrial economy of the United States. During the 1960s, disabling injuries increased 20 percent during the decade, and fourteen thousand workers were dying on the job each year (Fleming, 2001). Today, this legislation and the Occupational Safety and Health Administration provide the main pillars of regulatory health and safety protections for American workers. The act established three permanent agencies:

- The Occupational Safety and Health Administration (OSHA) within the Labor Department to set and enforce workplace safety and health standards
- The National Institute for Occupational Safety and Health (NIOSH) in what was then the Department of Health, Education and Welfare to conduct research on occupational safety and health
- The Occupational Safety and Health Review Commission (OSHRC), an independent agency to adjudicate enforcement actions challenged by employers.

Known initially as the safety bill of rights, the law charged OSHA with assuring safe and healthful conditions for working men and women. When the agency opened in April 1971, OSHA covered 56 million workers at 3.5 million workplaces. Today, 105 million private-sector workers and employers at 6.9 million sites are covered by OSHA regulations on workplace safety and health issues. The U.S. occupational injury rate is 40 percent lower in 2000 than when OSHA was chartered in 1971. Deaths from occupational injuries are at an all-time low—60 percent lower than thirty years ago (Fleming 2001).

The act covers all employers and their employees in the fifty states, the District of Columbia, Puerto Rico, and all other territories under federal government jurisdiction. Coverage is provided either directly by OSHA or through an OSHA-approved state occupational safety and health program. The act applies to employers and employees in such varied fields as manufacturing, construction, longshoring, agriculture, law and medicine, charity and disaster relief, organized labor, and private education. Such coverage includes religious groups to the extent that they employ workers for secular purposes. Not covered by the act are self-employed persons or farms at which only immediate members of the farmer's family are employed. Employees of state and local governments (unless they are in one of the states with OSHA-approved safety and health programs) are also not covered by OSHA.

The act assigns to OSHA two principal functions: setting standards and conducting workplace inspections to ensure that employers are complying with the standards and providing a safe and healthful workplace. OSHA standards may require that employers adopt certain practices, means, methods, or processes reasonably necessary to protect workers on the job. It is the responsibility of employers to become familiar with standards applicable to their establishments, to eliminate hazardous conditions to the extent possible, and to comply with the standards. Compliance may include ensuring that employees have and use personal protective equipment when required for safety or health. Employees must comply with all rules and regulations that are applicable to their own actions and conduct.

Even in areas where OSHA has not issued a standard addressing a specific safety hazard, employers are responsible for complying with OSHA's "general duty" clause, which states that each employer "shall furnish . . . a place of employment which is free from recognized hazards that are causing or are likely to cause death or serious physical harm to his employees."

States with OSHA-approved job safety and health programs must set standards that are at least as effective as the equivalent federal standard. Most of the state-plan states adopt standards identical to the federal ones (two states, New York and Connecticut, have plans that cover only public-sector employees).

Federal OSHA standards fall into four major categories: general industry (29 CFR 1910); construction (29 CFR 1926); maritime—shipyards, marine terminals, longshoring (29 CFR 1915-19); and agriculture (29 CFR 1928). Each of these four categories of standards imposes requirements targeted to that industry, although in some cases they are identical across industries. Among these uniform standards are access to medical and exposure records, personal protective equipment, and hazard communication. Other types of requirements are imposed by regulation rather than by a standard, covering such items as record keeping, reporting, and posting.

Employees are granted several important rights by the act. Among them are the right to complain to OSHA about safety and health conditions in their workplace and have their identity kept confidential from the employer, to contest the time period OSHA allows for correcting standards violations, and to participate in OSHA workplace inspections. Private-sector employees who exercise their rights under OSHA can be protected against employer reprisal, as described in section 11(c) of the OSHA act. Employees must notify OSHA within thirty days of the time they learned of the alleged discriminatory action. This notification is followed by an OSHA investigation. If OSHA agrees that discrimination has occurred, the employer will be asked to restore any lost benefits to the affected employee. If necessary, OSHA can take the employer to court. In such cases, the worker pays no legal fees.

Over the past three decades, the agency has responded to tragic workplace events with new strategies and regulations. Examples include OSHA's standard for preventing grain elevator explosions, its process safety management standard for forestalling chemical catastrophes, and its focus on health issues such as blood-borne pathogens and musculoskeletal disorders. "OSHA was created because of public outcry against rising injury and death rates on the job. Through the years, the agency has focused its resources where it can have the greatest impact in reducing injuries, illnesses, and deaths in the workplace" (Fleming 2001, 24).

Fleming also notes that "OSHA's enforcement strategy has evolved from initially targeting a few problem industries to zeroing in on high-hazard industries and, more recently, pinpointing specific sites with high injury rates. Education and outreach have played important roles in dealing with virtually every safety or health issue" (2001, 24).

OSHA published its first standards in May 1971, including permissible exposure limits for more than four hundred toxic substances. Some of these rules remain in effect today. OSHA's first original standard limited worker exposure to asbestos, a proven carcinogen. Standards for a group of carcinogens, vinyl chloride, coke oven emissions, cotton dust, lead, benzene, dibromochloropropane, arsenic, acrylonitrile, and hearing conservation followed. Early standards responded to health issues well known to the occupational safety and health community.

According to Fleming, "Initially, the agency emphasized voluntary compliance with inspections dedicated to catastrophic accidents and the most dangerous and unhealthful workplaces. Later, the agency adopted a tough stance that evolved to a more targeted approach based on significant hazards. OSHA further refined its inspection targeting system in the late 1970s to focus 95 percent of health inspections on industries with the most serious problems" (2001, 28).

In the 1980s, OSHA focused on reducing regulatory burdens where possible and emphasizing and encouraging employee self-reporting and compliance. Its goal was to provide a balanced mix of enforcement, education and training, standard-setting, and consultation activities. The agency introduced major new health standards during this decade that included employee access to medical and exposure records maintained by employers; hazard communication; and more stringent requirements for asbestos, ethylene oxide, formaldehyde, and benzene. Safety standards covered a wide range of issues, such as updated fire protection and electrical safety, field sanitation in agriculture, grain handling, hazardous waste operations and emergency response, and lockout/tagout of hazardous energy sources.

During the 1990s, OSHA reexamined its goals as part of the Clinton administration's "Reinventing Government" initiative, looking for ways to leverage its resources and increase its impact in reducing workplace injuries, illnesses, and deaths. The agency reorganized its area offices to provide rapid response to worker complaints and workplace tragedies as well as to focus on long-term strategies to lower job-related fatalities, injuries, and illnesses. OSHA instituted a phone-fax policy to speed the resolution of complaints and focus investigation resources on the most serious problems (Fleming 2001).

Many standards published during the 1990s relied on a performance-oriented approach—setting specific goals for workers' safety and health—but providing flexibility in how those goals were to be met. Major safety standards included process safety management, permit-required confined spaces, fall protection in construction, electrical safety-related work practices, and scaffolds.

In 1991, OSHA introduced a blood-borne pathogens standard to address biological hazards. During the 1990s, the agency also updated its asbestos, formaldehyde, methylene chloride, personal protective equipment, and respiratory protection standards; developed a standard covering lead exposure in construction; and issued rules to protect laboratory workers exposed to toxic chemicals. OSHA also issued guidelines for preventing workplace violence in health care and social services work and in late-night retail establishments.

The agency shifted its resources for workplace inspections to focus on serious violators, proposing sizable penalties for egregious safety and health problems. In 1990, Congress increased maximum penalties for OSHA violations from $1,000 to $7,000 for serious violations and from $10,000 to $70,000 for willful and repeat violations (Fleming 2001).

During the Clinton administration, OSHA, unions, advocates, and employers wrangled with the importance of improving how workplaces are designed in order to prevent repetitive motion injuries. So-called ergonomics injuries are caused by heavy lifting, repetitive work, and poorly designed jobs. OSHA generally argued for the importance of a new ergonomics standards. On November 23, 1999, OSHA issued its proposed ergonomics standard that would require employers to set up control programs for any jobs where these disorders are reported. A second kind of action for problem jobs would include more detailed analysis, control, training, and action.

OSHA mounted a new emphasis on partnerships during the 1990s. Participation in the agency's Voluntary Protection Programs increased eightfold, and OSHA formed partnerships with a number of companies and associations, including ConAgra Refrigerated Foods, the Associated General Contractors, and the Associated Building Contractors.

As the new century began, OSHA expanded its outreach program with new compliance assistance specialists slated to join every area office to provide safety seminars, training, and guidance to employers and employees upon request. More and more the agency used its Web site to provide information to its customers. As of 2002, nearly 1.4 million people visited the Web site each month—a total of 23 million hits—and as many as 300,000 people download OSHA's Expert Advisor software every month. The agency recently added a small business page, a partnership page, and a workers' page to its Web site to make its information more readily available and easily accessible. The workers' page enables concerned employees to file complaints online. Along with its counterparts in the European Union, OSHA set up a Web site on job safety and health issues of concern to many countries (Fleming 2001).

How OSHA Inspections Work. To enforce its standards, OSHA is authorized under the act to conduct workplace inspections. Every establishment covered by the act is subject to inspection by OSHA compliance safety and health officers who are thoroughly trained in OSHA standards and in the recognition of safety and health hazards. Similarly, states with their own occupational safety and health programs conduct inspections using qualified state CSHOs.

OSHA conducts two general types of inspections: programmed and unprogrammed. Unprogrammed inspections respond to fatalities, catastrophes, and complaints, the last of which is further detailed in OSHA's complaint policies and procedures. Following are some of the types of violations that may be cited and the penalties that may be proposed:

- Other-than-serious violation: A violation that has a direct relationship to job safety and health but that probably would not cause death or serious physical harm. A proposed penalty of up to $7,000 for each violation is discretionary. A penalty for an other-than-serious violation may be adjusted downward by as much as 95 percent, depending on the employer's good faith (demonstrated efforts to comply with the act), history of previous violations, and size of business.
- Serious violation: A violation where there is substantial probability that death or serious physical harm could result and that the employer knew, or should have known, of the hazard. A mandatory penalty of up to $7,000 for each violation is proposed. A penalty for a serious violation may be adjusted downward, based on the employer's good faith, history of previous violations, the gravity of the alleged violation, and size of business.

- Willful violation: A violation that the employer has intentionally and knowingly committed. The employer either knows that what he or she is doing constitutes a violation or is aware that a hazardous condition exists and has made no reasonable effort to eliminate it. An employer who willfully violates the act may be assessed a civil penalty of not more than $70,000 but not less than $5,000 for each violation.
- If an employer is convicted of a willful violation of a standard that has resulted in the death of an employee, the offense is punishable by a court-imposed fine or by imprisonment for up to six months, or both. A fine of up to $250,000 for an individual or $500,000 for a corporation (authorized under the Comprehensive Crime Control Act of 1984 [1984 CCA], not the OSH Act)s may be imposed for a criminal conviction.
- Repeated violation: A violation of any standard, regulation, rule, or order where, upon reinspection, a substantially similar violation is found. Repeated violations can bring a fine of up to $70,000 for each such violation. To be the basis of a repeat citation, the original citation must be final; a citation under contest may not serve as the basis for a subsequent repeat citation.
- Failure to correct prior violation: Failure to correct a prior violation may bring a civil penalty of up to $7,000 for each day the violation continues beyond the prescribed abatement date.

If an inspection was initiated as a result of an employee complaint, the employee or authorized employee representative may request an informal review of any decision not to issue a citation. Employees may not contest citations, amendments to citations, penalties, or lack of penalties. They may contest the time in the citation for abatement of a hazardous condition. They also may contest an employer's Petition for Modification of Abatement (PMA) that requests an extension of the abatement period. Employees must contest the PMA within ten working days of its posting or within ten working days after an authorized employee representative has received a copy.

When issued a citation or notice of a proposed penalty, an employer may request an informal meeting with OSHA's area director to discuss the case and seek a settlement. The employer may contest the citation and the penalty for a period of fifteen working days from the time the citation and proposed penalty are received, where the appeal is heard by the Occupational Safety and Health Review Commission (OSHRC). The commission is an independent agency not associated with OSHA or the Department of Labor. The commission assigns the case to an administrative law judge. Once the administrative law judge has ruled, any party to the case may request a further review by OSHRC.

OSHA, Politics, and Controversy. Many of OSHA's standards and protections were developed in response to formidable threats to human life and human safety and enjoyed broad support, particularly for workers in chemical, manufacturing, mining, and heavy industries where exposure to machinery and toxic compounds were proven to be deadly. However, political pressure and controversy have flared frequently around OSHA and state safety actions and how workplace safety concerns should be addressed.

OSHA has been criticized on one side by unions, progressives, and advocates for working too closely with business and failing to pass tougher standards; this side argues that without the threat of inspections and enforcement, too many employers will skirt the law. Small businesses and their advocates, as well as larger employers, have criticized OSHA for excessive regulations and excessive enforcement. "Surveys of small business owners have repeatedly shown that they consider OSHA to be the most difficult of federal regularly agencies to deal with," notes a 2000 Congressional Research Service report. "[Big business's] concern is more that 'reasonable' standards be written so that they know exactly what is expected of them" (Rappaport 2000, 4–5). Small business owners also complain that OSHA citations and requirements are too complex and too technical for them to realistically implement and that OSHA should invest more resources in providing technical assistance to employers.

Workplace safety advocates could point accurately to a number of disturbing trends in major industries that have demonstrated the need for a vigilant OSHA. Workers in fishing and logging industries still sustain shockingly high rates of workplace injury. Declines of union representation in certain heavy manufacturing and extraction industries may provide more leeway for employers to cut corners. Major declines in safety performance and systems in some poultry and meat processing plants caused alarm. Most importantly, through the 1980s and 1990s, workplace safety specialists and scientists identified a national concern in the number of workplace injuries associated with poor ergonomics design and believed that employers needed to install systematic programs to reduce injuries caused by repetitive motion, excessive force, awkward postures, and heavy lifting.

Numerous medical associations and groups—including the American College of Occupational and Environmental Medicine, the American Occupational Therapy Association, the American Public Health Association, the American Industrial Hygiene Association, the American Association of Occupational Health Nurses, and the American Nurses Associations—urged OSHA to move forward in developing an ergonomics standard. The AFL-CIO and many labor groups were also strong advocates.

Throughout the 1990s, a multifaceted, controversial legislative debate over the ergonomics legislation was waged by organized labor, safety advocates, medical experts, business groups, and members of Congress. Both sides believed passionately in their view of the issue. The business and safety coalitions worked intensely to lobby public opinion and members of Congress. Bills proposing and opposing the standard were passed, scratched, vetoed, and sunk. The role of federal regulation in keeping workplaces safe was a focus of debate. Businesses argued they would do a better job of maintaining workplace safety without regulation; worker advocates insisted that history taught that enforcement was needed to prevent some employers from taking worker safety lightly and that the regulations would in fact save employers money in the long run.

Republican congressional leaders, spearheaded by Tom DeLay, aggressively went after OSHA and the ergonomics standard in the mid-1990s. As noted by City University of New York (CUNY) political scientist Vernon Mogensen, whose book *Office Politics* covered many of the issues in the ergonomics battle, "punishment came in the form of Congress prohibiting OSHA from conducting research on the RSI standard, and cutting its already meager budget by close to $20 million to preclude any possibility of the safety agency's interfering with the movement of the invisible hand. However, supporters of the ergonomic standard won a surprising victory in 1996 with help from an unexpected source. Thirty-four moderate House Republicans committed the heresy of voting with the Democratic minority to permit OSHA to resume work on its proposed ergonomic standard." (1999)

OSHA proposed an ergonomics program in November 1999 to prevent 300,000 work-related injuries and save $10 billion annually in medical and workers' comp costs. As noted by former assistant U.S. Department of Labor secretary Charles Jeffress, "the ergonomics proposal is the most flexible standard OSHA has ever written. It focuses specifically on high-risk jobs—manual handling and production jobs—in which sixty percent of all MSDs occur. That means that seventy-five percent of general industry employers would not need to take any action unless one of their employees actually suffered an injury that the employer determined to be related to routine tasks on the job" (Jeffress 2000, 40). The standard also gave employers many ways to achieve compliance, including quick-fix options for jobs that could be fixed right away, a grandfather clause to recognize programs already in place, and the option to discontinue programs when no longer needed.

Still, employers were fiercely opposed. When George Bush became president, reversing the ergonomics standard was one of his first executive orders. The fight over the ergonomics standard in Washington illustrates quite powerfully the political stakes involved. For years, business lobbies worked with Republican members of Congress to stall OSHA's release of the ergonomics standard. While health and safety advocates, scientists, doctors, and state leaders testified to the importance of a standard and appeared frequently before Congress and the public to plead for swift action, a coalition of Republican members passed bills requiring that additional studies needed to be completed before the standard could be issued.

Even when negotiators of both parties agreed to a compromise that would have permitted OSHA to issue the final rule—with a delay of the enforcement and compliance requirements until June 1, 2001—Republican congressional leaders, acting at the behest of the business community, overrode their negotiators and refused to stand by the agreement. The debate over the role of regulation in keeping the workplace safe has become more intense with the election of a conservative presidential administration; whether unions and advocates will successfully appeal to workers on the basis of their own self-interest and safety remains to be seen.

Related Reading in Part 2

Chapter 6:
"Should Washington Implement National Ergonomic Standards?" Edward Potter
"Home-Office Debate Isn't New," Eileen Boris and Nelson Lichtenstein
"Right to Refuse Unsafe Work," Communications Workers of America
"Fishing for a Living Is Dangerous Work," Dino Drudi
"Logging Is Perilous Work," Eric F. Sygnatur

Part II
THE ECONOMY AND THE WORKFORCE
A Critical Reader

Chapter 4

Globalization, Technology, and Trade

THIS FIRST SELECTION of readings provides varying perspectives on the dominant story of the 1990s U.S. economy and workforce—the decade's soaring growth, innovation, and productivity. The U.S. Department of Commerce's *Digital Economy* report lays out the core argument that information technology innovations were directly related to the growth of the new economy and increased worker productivity that drove the 1990s boom. Louis Uchitelle describes a different mood early in 2001, as an economic slowdown punctured beliefs about the productivity miracle of the U.S. economy and the widespread optimism of the late 1990s among economists led by Federal Reserve Chair Alan Greenspan. Jack Guynn praises the fundamentals of the U.S. economy and the potential of the Internet and other innovations to provide powerful synergies for continued growth. And Leo Reddy, president of National Coalition for Advanced Manufacturing, emphasizes that manufacturing has adopted and thrived under the economic realities of the 1990s and should continue to grow as technology enhances manufacturing productivity. His vision of the economy is one in which the decline in manufacturing is reversed. W. R. Timken Jr., of the National Association of Manufacturers, however, argues in more partisan, ideological, and hard-nosed terms that manufacturing is vital to our economic future, and owners and stockholders need and should receive more support and assistance from the government.

In contrast, Nancy Mills of the AFL-CIO's Center for Workplace Democracy argues that much of the arguments surrounding a progressive manufacturing workplace are based on an illusion—an Oz-like fantasy of the new workplace. Her observations resonate with E. J. Dionne Jr., who raised concerns about the direction of the economy before it was common to do so, arguing that to revive the economy we must continue to build on economic policies of the 1990s that made work pay for low- and moderate-income workers.

In a less than obvious, but interesting, perspective of what does and should motivate workers to make a living in the current economy, Federal Reserve Chair Alan Greenspan describes his analysis of math and science education in the United States and its importance for the future workforce. Economist Jerome Segal contends that workers today spend most of their earnings on basic necessities, and Steve Lohr portrays the world of highly sought-after software specialists who, after being viewed as nerds for many years, are enjoying the high-rolling attention and perks lavished on them by the private sector.

William Finnegan introduces us to talented young progressives leading the antiglobalism coalition that stamped its influence on world politics and public opinion in Seattle in 1999. Naomi Klein tells us how today's workers receive few protections in the overseas factories where American consumer goods manufacturing is outsourced. The next piece argues for the benefits of free trade to all workers and U.S. society generally. Ernest H. Preeg, of the Hudson Institute, takes the stance that most workers and consumers benefit from free trade in the form of higher-skilled, better-paying jobs and more affordable consumer purchases. To balance these perspectives, *New York Times* columnist Thomas L. Friedman uses his empathy, clarity, and common sense to demonstrate inconsistencies in the views of organized labor on free trade while showing that he understands the enormous difficulties unions face in the new economy.

Three of the selections in this section inform our understanding of the effects of the 9-11 terror attacks. Jack El-Hai, from the *Atlantic Monthly,* describes the business of workplace recovery centers, noting that "power outages, dead phone lines, and crashed Internet servers" are possibilities more chilling to companies than terror attacks. Excerpts from an *Atlantic Monthly* dialogue between noted journalists Michael Lewis and James Fallows, passing from pre– to post–September 11 America, captures the unmistakable transition from one era to another in this country. Finally, Jason DeParle, of the *New York Times,* analyzes how the mass layoffs after the attacks have posed a significant new test for the revamped U.S. social safety net, as systems that were overhauled in 1996 face their first test of a national recession.

Information Technology and the New Economy

U.S. DEPARTMENT OF COMMERCE

Two remarkable developments occurred in the second half of the 1990s. After quietly improving in speed, power, and convenience since 1969, the Internet burst onto the economic scene and began to change business strategy and investment. At the same time, the U.S. economy has enjoyed a remarkable resurgence. Productivity growth, one of the most important indicators of economic health, doubled its pace from a sluggish 1.4-percent average rate between 1973 and 1995 to a 2.8-percent rate from 1995 to 1999.[1]

Evidence is increasing that these two phenomena are not coincidental but derive substantially from the same phenomenon: the synergistic convergence of dramatic increases in computer power, an explosion in connectivity, and increasingly powerful new software. These advances in technology have produced sharp declines in the prices of computer processing, data storage and retrieval, and communications that are in turn driving both the surge in Internet activity and the increases in business investment in IT hardware and software. Such investment has been a major source of recent U.S. economic strength.

The advances in computer power overwhelm imagination. Since the 1960s, the number of transistors per microprocessor chip has been doubling roughly every eighteen to twenty-four months, resulting in a massive increase in processing capability and sharply declining costs.[2]

Technologies associated with computer use, such as data storage technologies, have also shown dramatic improvements in performance and even more dramatic cost reductions. The capacity of today's hard-disk drives is doubling every nine months and the average price per megabyte for hard-disk drives has declined from $11.54 in 1988 to an estimated $.02 in 1999.[3] As a consequence of technological advances in microprocessors, storage, and other components, already steep annual declines in computer costs from 1987 to 1994 accelerated sharply beginning in 1995.

Similar improvements have occurred in communications technologies. In recent years, for example, wavelength division multiplexing, digital subscriber lines, and cable modems have produced exponential increases in the speed of data communication and the carrying capacity of the communications infrastructure. The carrying capacity of fiber is currently doubling every twelve months.[4]

"Digital Economy 2000." Report prepared by the Office of Policy Development, Economics and Statistics Administration, U.S. Department of Commerce. Authors include Patricia Buckley, Sabrina Montes, David Henry, Donald Dalton, Gurmukh Gill, Jesus Dumagan, Susan La Porte, Sandra Cooke, Dennis Pastore, and Lee Price.

Between 1994 and 1998 (the last four years for which data are available), the price of telecommunications equipment declined by 2 percent per year.

Price declines for computers and peripheral equipment and for communications equipment have spurred major increases in business IT investment and extraordinary growth in U.S. production of computers, communications equipment, and semiconductors. Output growth in these industries has jumped from about 12 percent a year in the early 1990s to roughly 40 percent in the past six years.

In addition, the declining costs of computing and communications are helping to drive complementary investment in new software that harnesses and further enhances the productive capacity of IT hardware and infrastructure. Overall, U.S. businesses have increased their investments in new software from about $28 billion in 1987 to $149 billion in 1999.[5]

The new economy is being shaped by developments not only in computer hardware and software but also in electronic connectivity. Larger businesses have been increasing efficiencies through standardizing and automating routine transactions electronically for some time. Until recently, however, most small and medium sized businesses found that the costs of necessary hardware, software, and communications service for these systems exceeded the benefits.

The advent of the Internet as an instrument of commerce fundamentally altered this equation by cutting the costs of software and communications services needed to conduct electronic transactions. Beginning in the mid-1990s, as a result of the convergence toward digital formats and the development of de facto standards for digital networks, such as the Internet's technical specifications, the expansion and commercialization of the Internet made connecting computers and communications devices easier and cheaper. Commercial opportunities on the Internet and the falling costs of computer and communications hardware created an extraordinarily fertile environment for innovations that are creating new value and new efficiencies for businesses of all sizes.

The Internet is both an effect and a cause of the new economy. It is, in part, a product of the powerful technological and economic changes that are shaping a new epoch of economic experience. However, as this report shows, the Internet and related networking technologies are also increasingly the new economy's medium.

Networks, like telephone networks or the Internet, are subject to a phenomenon called "network effects" or "network externalities." Establishing a network involves large, up-front fixed costs (for example, purchasing equipment, laying new cable, or developing new software), but adding an additional user to an existing network costs very little. Conversely, the value of a network to participants is low when the number of participants on the network is low, but rises rapidly as network participation expands. For example, a network of a single telephone is of no use. Adding another telephone increases the value of the network because now calls can be made between the two phones. As phones are added, the number of possible connections rises almost as fast as the number of phones squared.[6]

Any person with a phone can reach more people, so the network's value to them increases.

Similarly, as the number of people online has grown, so has the value of being online to each Internet user. Moreover, as the Internet gains popularity, its technological specifications have become a default standard, encouraging new hardware and software innovations that use Internet technology as a platform.

Fundamental engineering breakthroughs alone do not have important economic effects until their costs and applications become favorable. For example, by the mid-1970s, Xerox PARC had already made several breakthroughs underpinning today's IT revolution: a microcomputer with a mouse, graphical user interface, and Ethernet communications capabilities. But there was no mass market for their machine, which at the time cost about $25,000 each to produce, especially given its slower processing speed and the absence of applications software that drives computer use today. In contrast, technological advances in recent years have brought IT costs down to a far more commercially attractive range, and new software applications for networked systems have been developed.

Nothing approaching the activities now conducted over the Internet was possible a few years ago. Push back the technology or cost declines in any one of the four elements—computer processing, data storage, software, or communications—just a few years and the Internet activities we now view as commonplace would be too frustrating or too costly for a mass market. Likewise, roll back any one of those elements and business would have found IT investment to be far less productive. As applications software is developed to exploit the continuing plunge in hardware prices in coming years, businesses and consumers will find new ways to create value and increase efficiency.

Notes

1. If productivity growth had remained at 1.4 percent for the past four years, nonfarm output would have been $300 billion lower in 1999, the equivalent of about $1,100 in lost output for every person in the country.

2. Doubling every eighteen months is closely equivalent to increasing by a factor of ten every five years and by a factor of one hundred every ten years. This phenomenon is know as "Moore's Law" and was first noted by Gordon Moore, cofounder of Intel, in 1965. Intel, "What Is Moore's Law?" at the Intel Museum's home page: http://www.intel.com/intel/intelis/museum/.

3. David Clark, senior research scientist at MIT's Laboratory for Computer Science, cited in Jeff Hecht, "Wavelength Division Multiplexing," *MIT's Technology Review* (March–April 1999).

4. Skeptics argue that software upgrades do not represent increases in performance but only the addition of bells and whistles that offset improvements in processing speed. However, that view ignores the directions taken in the business uses of their software investments. Businesses are deploying software to combine cheaper computer power with more reliable communications to create extraordinary efficiencies and improve decision making within their own operations and supply networks. For example, over a three-year period, Wal-Mart achieved a 47 percent increase in sales on only a 7 percent increase in inventories by using a relational data-

base system running on massively parallel computers. The system allows vendors to access almost real-time information on sales and customer transactions and handles 120,000 queries each week from seven thousand suppliers. Businesses are also investing in software to integrate information and reduce staffing in other activities, such as production operations, human resources management, payroll, and sales force activities. "High-Tech Complements Human Touch," *Discount Store News* (October 1999).

5. The number of possible connections is technically $n(n-1)$. This contrast between the change in cost and value of a network as it grows is sometimes labeled "Metcalfe's Law." Carl Shapiro and Hal Varian, *Information Rules: A Strategic Guide to the Network Economy* (Boston: Harvard Business School Press, 1998), 184.

6. Robert X. Cringely, *Accidental Empires* (New York: Harper Business, 1992), 83.

Notions of New Economy Hinge on Pace of Productivity Growth

LOUIS UCHITELLE

Rising prosperity still bathed the nation a year ago when Alan Greenspan opened the annual symposium of Federal Reserve policy makers in this mountain resort with a confident boast that the strong gains in worker productivity that seemed to underlie the robust expansion of the 1990s would continue.

That contention appears to haunt him today. The nation's boom has collapsed despite the faith of Mr. Greenspan, the Fed chairman, that the ever-greater efficiencies of the information age would keep on raising profits, incomes, and employment at a healthy pace. Instead, the nation is barely skirting a recession, stock prices have fallen, the budget surplus is shrinking, and the new economy is losing its charm. Adding injury to insult, the government just last month took the accelerating productivity figures that Mr. Greenspan cited so proudly a year ago and revised them downward. Instead of growing at an annual rate of 3.4 percent in 1999 and 2000, productivity—the amount that a worker produces in a hour—grew at a significantly slower rate of 2.6 percent a year during the best years of the economic boom.

"He must have an awful lot of egg on his face," Dean Baker, codirector of the Center for Economic and Policy Research, said in a telephone interview from Washington.

But don't tell that to Mr. Greenspan. With the Fed's leadership once again gathered here for this year's symposium, the message remained upbeat for the 100 or so experts from government, academia, and Wall Street who were invited here. Most expressed their confidence that the vast changes wrought by computer technology are providing a solid foundation for long-run prosperity.

And despite the new figures casting doubt on some of those views, the general mood was that the new economy—promising strong growth with little inflation—would endure once the current slowdown ends.

"The preponderance of evidence suggests a continual increase in productivity growth," Lawrence H. Summers, president of Harvard University and Treasury secretary in the administration of President Bill Clinton, declared in an interview here, reaffirming Mr. Greenspan's optimism a year ago.

Mr. Greenspan himself sat through the conference sessions in silence, but he has made clear to other Fed policy makers that he still believes that the productivity miracle is alive and well.

New York Times, September 3, 2001. Reprinted with permission of *New York Times*. Louis Uchitelle reports on economics and business for the *New York Times*.

Still, the latest government figures gave ammunition to critics who have long argued that the rapid productivity gains reported in the late 1990s were more of a mirage caused in part by unsustainable business investment. That also led to a spurt in growth that temporarily forced companies to use labor more efficiently.

Much is at stake in this debate. The optimists think that the productivity growth rate will stay above 2.5 percent annually over the long run. The pessimists, by contrast, think that the improvement has been more mundane, more like the 2 percent that the government now says is the average annual rate since 1990.

The impact of that seemingly small gap is enormous. Productivity is the principal contributor to economic growth. It determines whether corporate revenue is rising fast enough to increase wages and profits. When there is enough revenue and profit from productivity, companies are under less pressure to raise prices, so there is less inflation.

Similarly important, the government's projection that it will accumulate a $3.4 trillion budget surplus between now and 2011 relies on a rate of productivity growth of at least 2.5 percent. A more modest gain of 2 percent would mean that the surplus would be roughly $800 billion lower, according to Dan Crippen, director of the Congressional Budget Office.

Mr. Crippen, in a telephone interview from Washington, noted that $800 billion is enough to pay for all of the nation's military expenses for two years and to cover prescription drugs for the elderly for more than a decade. "Probably the biggest uncertainty in our projections is whether the increase in productivity is sustainable," he said.

Mr. Greenspan has argued that an accelerating rate of productivity growth is the chief explanation for the boom that started in the mid-1990s as American companies increased their investments in computer-based information technologies, including the Internet. The productivity growth rate measures the increase in output from each hour of work. From that increase, companies are able to generate higher revenue, adding to profits and to wages for workers without having to raise prices. Profits and wages did in fact rise for nearly five years. The prosperity was real.

But now that the boom has collapsed into sluggish growth, productivity's contribution to that prosperity is uncertain. The revised productivity figures suggest that temporary factors—an exuberant stock market, excessive business investment, a surge in debt-financed consumer spending, for example—all played important roles. The Fed's conference here was the first high-powered challenge to a growing view that the new economy lacks staying power.

"There is a lot at stake," said Martin N. Baily, a senior fellow at the Institute for International Economics and a former chairman of President Clinton's Council of Economic Advisers, who presented a paper at the conference. "Profits will not be as strong, and with less profits business investment in the new technologies will not be as strong and the stock market won't be strong."

There were some skeptics here. One of them, Henry Kaufman, a Wall Street economist and consultant, says that Mr. Greenspan, having committed himself to the idea of accelerating productivity, cannot easily get off that horse without frightening the markets.

But Mr. Kaufman's dissent was distinctly in the minority. Mr. Summers, coauthor of a paper presented here, spoke for the majority, and so did Martin Feldstein, a Harvard economist who served for a while as President Ronald Reagan's chief economic adviser.

"The key question is whether productivity at 2.5 percent is going to continue," Mr. Feldstein said at the final session, summarizing the conference's findings. "My answer is yes. You cannot know this just by looking at the data; you have to look at the economy itself. The information revolution is going to keep us going."

The main argument for those who are optimistic about productivity centers on the belief that hundreds of thousands of companies outside the high-technology sector are still in the process of incorporating the new technologies and changing their practices. They think that these companies have considerable room to improve their efficiency.

But a few experts worry that the efficiencies might be slow in coming. "I cannot say that the optimists are wrong," Mr. Baily said. "I can only say that if I were planning the future, I would count on only 2 percent."

The overall economy can grow and generate prosperity only as fast as the workforce itself grows and each worker increases his or her output. The working-age population is expanding at barely 1 percent a year, so most of the nation's gain in prosperity must come from productivity.

Mr. Greenspan has spoken of a potential growth rate of 3.5 percent to 4 percent a year. His critics—those who doubt that the computer-based technologies are all that special—see 3 percent, or slightly less, as the limit for economic growth.

Whatever the truth, embracing the higher figure gave Mr. Greenspan justification to hold down interest rates even as the economy surged—and to cut rates quickly as the slowdown developed. After all, why turn off the boom to fight an inflationary threat that may never materialize?

"There is no question," Mr. Baily said, "that if you believe in the new economy, it lowers your estimate of what inflation will be. That has given the Fed the freedom to act aggressively in cutting interest rates, and the freedom to keep rates down when the upturn finally comes."

But what if those assumptions prove too optimistic? The Congressional Budget Office produced the budget-surplus projections that the Bush administration has cited to justify its $1.3 trillion tax cut. Those who want to privatize a part of Social Security would tap the surplus to help pay the costs.

So far, in making its projections, the budget office has tilted toward the Greenspan camp. It assumed, in its latest revisions announced last week, that productivity would grow at a 2.5 percent annual rate for the next ten years, down only slightly from its earlier projection of 2.7 percent, but well above the 1.4 percent average rate of productivity growth from 1973 to 1995.

"Last January, we bought into some aspects of the new economy," Mr. Crippen said. "We did not buy into all of it. Historically speaking, our assumptions are not abnormally high."

Note

The following correction to this article was published September 7, 2001: "A front-page article on Monday about the debate over productivity of the economy attributed a phrase erroneously to Alan Greenspan, chairman of the Federal Reserve. While Mr. Greenspan's statements have implied that he believes the economy can achieve a maximum growth rate near 3.5 to 4 percent a year without rising inflation, he has not publicly specified rates."

A Decade of Difference

The Newly Improved U.S. Economy

JACK GUYNN

As our record-breaking expansion heads toward the halfway mark of its tenth year, you'd be hard-pressed to think of a better place to consider what's gone right with the economy than right here in Gwinnett County. Everything that distinguishes the U.S. economy from the rest of the world—high technology, labor mobility, entrepreneurship—is on display here in abundance.

I'm going to resist the urge to recite Gwinnett's awesome growth figures this afternoon, but because I'm a policymaker, I would like to begin with a show-of-hands survey.

- How many of you lived outside the Southeast in 1990?
- How many of you lived outside the state of Georgia, but still in the Southeast, in 1990?
- How many of you lived in Georgia in 1990 but not in Gwinnett County?
- And how many of you lived in Gwinnett County in 1990?

Now, let me ask you this: Do you live in a "new" Gwinnett County? The answer, I suppose, is "new compared to what?" or "it depends"—and I leave it to you to decide. But reasonable people can disagree about the answer without disputing one central fact: there are a lot more of you in Gwinnett County today than there were ten years ago: 524,000 today versus around 353,000 in 1990. Or, to put it another way, more people have moved to Gwinnett since 1990—171,000—than *lived* here just two decades ago (167,000 in 1980).

The debate I've just suggested—is Gwinnett new or not?—resembles one that's been raging among economic policy makers lately. No one disputes that we've witnessed some profound changes in the U.S. economy since 1990 (although, since this is economics we're talking about, few agree about what those changes are). The question is whether they add up to a fundamentally "new" economy.

I've got some thoughts of my own to share with you on that question. But I'd like to begin this afternoon by looking at how things have improved for the U.S. economy, circa 2000, through the lens of what has changed since 1990.

Address given to the Gwinnett County Chamber of Commerce, Duluth, Georgia, on September 18, 2000. Reprinted with permission of Vital Speeches of the Day. Jack Guynn is president and CEO of the Federal Reserve Bank of Atlanta.

Faster, Smarter, and More Productive

Let me start with productivity. Ten years ago last month, on August 2, Iraq invaded Kuwait after Kuwait spurned an old-fashioned shakedown by Saddam Hussein. Now, if tomorrow you heard that Iraq was once again preparing to invade Kuwait, how would you get more information on developments there? You could turn on your radio and wait for a wire report, of course. Or you could tune into CNN or wait for your morning paper. You might have done any of those things ten years ago, too.

Today, though, you could gather as much information as any newsroom by simply firing up your computer and checking out dispatches from the *Kuwait Times*, or the *Jerusalem Post*, or Egypt's *Middle East Times*. This is the very definition of productivity improvement, and you can do it because you've got access to the Internet. And you can use the Internet because in 1990, British engineer Tim Berners-Lee invented the World Wide Web at CERN, the European Particle Physics Laboratory in Geneva, Switzerland.

It's easy to forget sometimes, but the Internet isn't new. It actually dates to 1969, when the U.S. Department of Defense created a decentralized computer network called ARPAnet to facilitate communications during a nuclear attack. ARPAnet, of course, evolved into the Internet as other networks connected to it. But until Tim Berners-Lee set out those first World Wide Web specifications to help CERN's physicists work together, the Internet's productivity-enhancing potential remained mostly unfulfilled.

I don't mean to suggest that the Internet is responsible for all or most of the productivity gains we've seen in the current expansion. (And I'll have more to say on this later.) But as an analogue for the sheer neck-snapping speed with which telecommunications, data processing, and personal computers improved productivity in the current expansion—from Tim Berners-Lee's PC to every single one of ours in less than ten years!—I like the Web just fine.

The Napsterization of Finance

The second distinguishing factor of the current expansion is a transformation of the financial system. Think back again to 1990: It was the first full year of operations for the Resolution Trust Corporation, which was established in 1989 to liquidate the assets of thousands of failed savings and loans. There are, of course, lots of reasons why the S&L industry failed. But they all have their roots in post–depression era legislation that divided the financial services industry into rigid sectors while prohibiting competition between and among them.

Last year, Congress passed the so-called Gramm-Leach-Bliley Act. Among Gramm-Leach-Bliley's most important provisions was a repeal of the centerpiece of those 1930s-era statutes, the Glass-Steagall Act. With the passage of

Gramm-Leach-Bliley, banks are now (officially) permitted to own insurance companies, and brokerage houses are able to operate banks. And while the financial services industry has evolved much more quickly than the law, Gramm-Leach-Bliley nevertheless signaled that old era—the one that was still very much with us ten years ago—had officially ended.

What we're witnessing in the new era, I think, is what my Atlanta Fed colleague Bob Eisenbeis calls the Napsterization of finance. If you've got a teenager at home, you know what I'm talking about. Napster is a so-called peer-to-peer distribution service, meaning that it allows me to download onto my computer a digital recording from someone else who already has it. The recording industry, of course, calls this "stealing" (and they may or may not be right), but I think Napster is a fascinating example of what economists call disintermediation: the elimination of the middle man.

And it's increasingly happening in finance. Consider this: Two years ago, more than a third of all small business loans in Georgia were originated by banks with no presence here at all. In Florida last year, not a single Florida-based bank ranked in the top ten in terms of market share. And throughout the 1990s one of the nation's leading industrial and consumer lenders has been General Electric, maker of jet engines, dishwashers, and situation comedies.

Obviously, disintermediation has not been an entirely positive development for the old intermediaries—although I think there will always be a place for traditional community bankers to help customers find their way in an increasingly complicated financial world. But for the economy, disintermediation has been absolutely essential: Today, investors and entrepreneurs can find each other with greater ease and at lower cost than at any time in history. Without question, this has been one of the most important reasons for the economy's record-breaking performance these last nine years.

Embracing the One Sure Thing

The expansion's third distinguishing factor is a willingness by the American people to embrace uncertainty. Ten years ago, you may recall, Americans were in awe of the so-called Asian miracle. The success of Japan in particular had launched an epidemic of envy, worry, and even fear across the United States. In less than half a century, Japan had transformed itself from one of the world's most wretched countries into one of its richest; it seemed to be doing something right. That something was industrial policy, and many Americans thought we should pursue one, too.

With hindsight, of course, it's obvious that the Japanese approach had some problems. Above all, Japan's experience over the past ten years demonstrates that markets make much better decisions about the allocation of resources than policy makers. And while it's true that American-style layoffs remain mostly unheard of in Japan, it's also the case that Japan's reliance on industrial policy led it into a recession that has lasted most of the last decade.

The willingness of Americans to accept the dictates of global markets, good and bad, distinguishes the United States not just from Japan but from much of the rest of the world as well. In Europe, for example, the objective of labor practices remains (as it has for decades) to provide workers with *certainty:* with the assurance that their jobs and their paychecks will be there tomorrow, no matter what. The problem is that global markets make no such assurances. As a result, some of Europe's leading companies—despite chronic double-digit unemployment in their own home countries—are sending some of the best jobs overseas.

Here in the United States, transfers, layoffs, plant closings, and worse have been with us a long time. As recently as ten years ago, though, we took them as a sign that we had been outsmarted and outhustled by our international competitors. Now we know otherwise. Now we understand that as capital has become quicksilver, mobile and international markets merge into one, the American tolerance for uncertainty is a crucial competitive advantage.

Who Wants to Be an Entrepreneur?

A fourth, related change from a decade ago is an increased capacity for entrepreneurial risk. Think back again to 1990. Quite apart from concerns about hostilities in the Gulf, there was, I recall, a fairly severe case of economy-induced anxiety gripping the country. The title of a 1992 bestseller perhaps best captured the mood—*America: What Went Wrong*. There was, of course, absolutely nothing wrong, but in the early 1990s, a great many people thought there was.

Today, I'd say the mood is captured not by any particular book but by a television show: "Who Wants to Be a Millionaire?" If ten years ago everyone you encountered knew at least somebody who'd been laid off, today everyone knows somebody who's gone to work for a startup. Yes, it's true that the current mood is as overdone as it was ten years ago. And it's also true that many—maybe even most—high-tech startups won't amount to much in the long run. But the point is not that 999 startups fail for every one that succeeds. The point is that one thousand try something completely new, completely different—and that in terms of innovation and value creation, the successes redeem the failures thousands of times over. These folks are making venture capitalists of us all—and the United States the envy of the world.

Productivity improvements, financial innovation, a willingness to embrace global uncertainty, and a newfound spirit of entrepreneurialism: All four developments distinguish the current expansion from previous periods of growth, and all four are very much on display here in Gwinnett County. But public policy has been an important factor also, and here, too, there's been one more change for the better over the past decade.

Fiscal and Monetary Policy: Pulling in the Same Direction

In 1990, the U.S. government ran a deficit of $221 billion. That fall, some of you may remember, President George Bush and congressional leaders cloistered themselves at Andrews Air Force Base, where they hammered out legislation that began to bring spending in line with revenue through a combination of spending cuts and tax increases. In 1993 and 1997, President Clinton signed legislation that continued the job.

As we approach the end of fiscal year 2000, the federal government is going on three consecutive years of budget surpluses. And while the good old U.S. economy deserves most of the credit for the budgetary heavy lifting, fiscal restraint (such as it is) has also played an important role in the economy's performance. Businesses no longer have to compete against the federal government for financial resources. And the so-called inflation premium has largely disappeared from interest rates now that fiscal and monetary policies are pulling in the same direction. As election season approaches and you begin to hear lots of rhetoric about fiscal policy, I hope you'll keep in mind that the budget surplus is already providing dividends.

Now let me mention one thing that hasn't changed since 1990. I'm talking, of course, about monetary policy. I know, on the face of it, any claim that monetary policy hasn't changed seems a little incongruous. The FOMC has, after all, increased the fed funds target rate 175 basis points since June of 1999; "unchanging" hardly seems to describe our disposition. But the FOMC's actions over the past fifteen months—indeed, over the past two decades—have been in service to a principle that truly has become immutable: the principle that low inflation, if sustained over time, will be followed by strong economic growth and low unemployment. For too long, though, this ideal was an exercise in academic conjecture, usually because monetary policy makers made a mistake and allowed inflation into the economy.

The extraordinary expansion is evidence that low inflation *works.* Since 1990, it has encouraged businesses to invest in productivity-enhancing innovations and allowed financial resources to flow to their most efficient uses. It has ensured that Americans' willingness to live with uncertainty accrued to our benefit and guaranteed that the budding entrepreneur has something to fall back on if things don't work out. Low inflation has, in short, been the difference in the economy's four distinguishing factors.

Productivity Gains: How Much Longer? (And How Significant?)

All of this takes me back to the question I led off with: Do we have a new economy? I suggested earlier that the answer is "it depends" or "new compared to what?" Let me explain what I mean.

The new economy debate is fundamentally about productivity, which is generally defined as output per worker per unit hour. Productivity matters because, along with the size of the labor pool, it determines how much an economy can produce. The issue is particularly important now, with labor markets as tight as they are: If the economy is going to continue to meet surging demand, then productivity is going to have to grow, too.

And in the current expansion, as I suggested earlier, it has. From 1972 to 1995, annual productivity growth averaged an anemic 1.4 percent. From 1996 to 1999, though, it doubled, to 2.8 percent, and from the second quarter of 1999 to the second quarter of 2000 it grew a staggering 5.3 percent. So what, exactly, do I mean by "it depends"? Well, to be precise, it depends on whether the recent upshift in productivity growth is truly *permanent.*

Productivity growth generally results from two developments. The first is capital deepening, which is just what it sounds like: giving workers more resources—deeper capital—to do their jobs with. The second development is the arrival of some new technology that truly, permanently changes the way things are done.

A few minutes ago I said that the Internet, telecommunications, data processing and other information technologies are driving the productivity surge we've witnessed in the second half of the current expansion. True enough. But it's also quite likely that a good portion of the increase resulted from old-fashioned capital deepening. Because, in fact, several years before productivity broke out of its slump, investment (or what economists call fixed private nonresidential investment) exploded, too: from 2.5 percent between 1980 and 1991 to 10.3 percent from 1992 to 1999. You would expect to see some productivity improvement after an investment surge like that.

But the critical issue is not whether technology has fundamentally improved the way things are done (as I believe it has), but *whether it will continue to improve at the same rate in the future.* In some ways it reminds me of the debate over the so-called Asian miracle a few years ago, when GDP across much of Asia was growing at annual double-digit rates: On the surface, it looked like Asia had come up with a new and fundamentally better way to do things. What really happened, though, was that hundreds of millions of workers transitioned from subsistence agricultural production to basic manufacturing. No wonder those economies grew so quickly!

I'm not suggesting that the pre-Internet age in the United States was comparable to subsistence agriculture. Of course not. But the bounce we've received from information technologies may in some ways be comparable to the basic and fundamental shift in productivity we witnessed in Asia. Again, though, the essential question is not whether this shift has taken place but whether it can continue. It didn't in Asia, where the transition was a lot more fundamental, and I'm not sure it will here, either. The World Wide Web, remember, went from one scientist's personal computer to ubiquity in a decade. But if the productivity shift is permanent, then the information technology revolution cannot be a once-ina-lifetime development. It will have to happen again, and be even more profound, in the next ten years. As much as I believe in American ingenuity, that seems a bit much to ask.

On the other hand, though, maybe the productivity shift hasn't been so profound here, after all. That's what I mean by "new compared to what?" For hundreds of millions of Asians, the economy really was new (and truly miraculous) in the sense that basic manufacturing—the move from the fields to the assembly line—permanently improved the human condition. Has the Internet really been *that* profound?

Profound as it has been, the IT revolution probably doesn't compare to productivity developments in our own history, either. It's easy enough to think of some obvious candidates—electrification, the invention of the automobile, the telephone or television—but I'd like to think one more time about Gwinnett County. If, fifty years ago, you could have asked the ancestors of many recent arrivals whether they would consider moving to Gwinnett County (or anywhere else in the South, for that matter), the answer would surely have been "never." There are lots of reasons why the South trailed the rest of the country in economic development, but two of the most important were that it was too hot and too remote.

Let me ask you this: Which is more essential on a smoldering August day—your PC or your AC? Which is more vital to your business—the Interstate or the electronic highway? Maybe it's a close call. Nevertheless, there's no arguing with the fact that Gwinnett County and the rest of the South would not be what they are today without air conditioning and the Interstate highway system. They transformed the region in ways that information technology simply cannot.

So I conclude that we do *not* have a fundamentally new economy. Yes, much of it is new and improved and more productive, too. And that means we can probably grow faster than previously thought. Even so, there are still limits. Economic shocks can still happen. And policy makers can still make mistakes. As long as those three remain, the possibility of inflation remains, too.

Throughout the almost ten-year-long economic expansion, the Fed has avoided rigidly applying all the old economic rules and has allowed the economy room to take account of recent developments. The Fed has also been vigilant in defending the principle that low inflation is an indispensable element in the pursuit of our other objectives of strong growth and low unemployment. And while it's true that inflation remains relatively low, I believe that overall demand growth remains sufficiently close to productive capacity to warrant a cautious monetary policy stance. Consumers and businesses have had no problem generating momentum, but inflation is the one thing that could stop them. With our actions over the past fifteen months, the Fed is determined to help keep that from happening, and to keep the current expansion on track well into the new century.

Manufacturing's Place in the Twenty-first-Century Economy

LEO REDDY

Manufacturing will remain one of the principal means by which wealth is created.
—National Research Council, *Visionary Manufacturing Challenges for 2020*

Wealth generation is the twenty-first century's public policy imperative. The "smart" way to increase the standard of living for all Americans is through wealth creation. Potential pressures on the economy demand greater attention by all to ensure that the factors driving prosperity remain strong and viable. Potential pressure on the economy is reduced if robust growth generates additional revenues to deal with societal needs such as Social Security, education, and health care.[1] Manufacturing is the most effective way for the United States to generate wealth in the twenty-first century economy because it adds value in a way no other economic activity can by manipulating resources into new products.

With greater attention being paid to Internet industries, e-commerce, and the service sector, a belief has emerged that "old" activities, such as manufacturing, no longer matter. In fact, the "old" and "new" economies are not separating, as some suggest,[2] they are converging. The stereotypical "bricks-and-mortar" manufacturer is increasingly turning to information technologies to connect with customers and suppliers.[3] Advanced technologies are embedded at all levels in manufactured products. Only the limits of creativity, technology, and engineering preclude the introduction of a host of new products exploiting advanced materials, biomechanical systems, or human-machine interfaces, just to name a few possibilities.

What is often lost in discussion about the new economy is how much of it depends on the health and vitality of the old economy. Estimates of retail e-commerce are substantial, but are dwarfed in comparison to business-to-business transactions.[4] These business-to-business transactions fundamentally are about the more efficient distribution of physical assets; assets that are eventually transformed into physical products.

At the most basic level, the components of the new economy are themselves manufactured products. Computers and computing equipment are advanced manufactured products requiring specialized facilities, skilled workers, access to a sophisticated technical infrastructure, and responsive supply chains and logistic systems. Computer and electronics manufacturers face significant hurdles, such

Excerpts from speech given at the National Institute of Standards and Technology (NIST). Reprinted with permission of the National Coalition for Advanced Manufacturing. Leo Reddy is president of the National Coalition for Advanced Manufacturing.

as the lack of skilled labor, technical challenges to continue the reduction in physical size while increasing performance and decreasing costs, and the manipulation of new materials. Even if the technological barriers are overcome, the cost-effective mass production of quality products remains a critical problem. The same basic characteristics apply to pharmaceuticals and biotechnology. Problems faced by these industries will become the problems of the entire economy as electronics and biosystems become embedded in everyday products.

Other factors are changing the very nature of what it means to be a manufacturer in the traditional sectors. New technologies, particularly information technology, and the dynamic competitive environment are transforming the manufacturing enterprise and altering relationships between manufacturers and suppliers. Contract manufacturing is on the rise as many of the nation's prominent firms shift focus to design and marketing concerns.[5] Research and technology acquisition are being outsourced at higher rates in search of new sources of talent and innovative ideas while reducing internal expenditures and capacities.[6] Small- and medium-sized businesses that comprise the supply chains for larger manufacturers are being asked to assume new roles and take on new tasks for which they may not be prepared. As technology changes and new processes are introduced, the skills of the incumbent workforce are put to the test and the ability to find entry-level workers with the appropriate skills is taxed.

The significance of these challenges to today's manufacturing base must be viewed in the context of what the twenty-first-century economy needs from its manufacturers.[7] Tomorrow's manufacturer must be flexible with the capability of using communications technology and knowledge sharing systems to respond to changing market demands. Customization will be the norm rather than the exception. A manufacturing system must be adaptable to the changing needs of the consumer but be intelligent enough to provide the right context so the consumer makes smart choices. Physical size will become less and less important as innovative processes allow micro- or nanoscale manufacturing. Finally, a successful twenty-first-century manufacturing operation will reduce production waste, effectively use new materials, and strive toward a minimal environmental impact.

Notes

1. National Academy on an Aging Society, *Demography Is Not Destiny* (Washington, D.C.: Gerontological Society of America, 1999).

2. An example of this false perception is Eamonn Fingleton's book, *In Praise of Hard Industries* (Boston: Houghton Mifflin, 1999). Fingleton is right to praise hard industries but goes too far in the opposite direction in his criticisms of information industries. There is no zero-sum relationship. The sectors are mutually dependent and exert positive influence on each other.

3. The decision announced by Ford, General Motors, and Daimler Chrysler in March 2000 to create "a business-to-business integrated supplier exchange through a single global portal" is the most recent example of how information technologies are transforming traditional

manufacturers. For additional detail on the use of e-commerce techniques by manufacturers, see *Industry Week, Census of Manufacturers: Third Annual Research Report* (Cleveland: Industry-Week, 1999): 7–12; and National Association of Manufacturers, Press Release no. 00-60, February 22, 2000.

4. The Commerce Department's first estimates of retail e-commerce sales reported a fourth-quarter fiscal year 1999 figure of $5.3 billion, which was 0.64 percent of total retail sales for the same period (press release CB00-40, March 2, 2000). The Gartner Group estimates business-to-business (B2B) e-commerce will grow at aggressive rates through 2004, causing fundamental changes to the way businesses do business with each other. Worldwide B2B market is forecast to grow from $145 billion in 1999 to $7.29 trillion in 2004. By 2004, it is estimated B2B e-commerce will represent 7 percent of the forecasted $105 trillion total global sales transactions (press release, January 26, 2000).

5. NACFAM/AMLF Proceedings of the Chicago Meeting, October 20, 1999.

6. NACFAM/AMLF Proceedings of the Detroit Meeting, December 7, 1999.

7. A number of studies in the past three years have looked at this question. For details, see the National Research Council, *Visionary Manufacturing Challenges for 2020* (Washington, D.C.: National Academy Press, 1998); Integrated Manufacturing Technology Roadmapping Initiative, *Manufacturing Success in the Twenty-first Century* (Oak Ridge, Tenn.: IMTI, Inc., 1999); and Agility Forum, *Next-Generation Manufacturing* (Bethlehem, Pa.: NGM Project Office, 1997).

Manufacturing amidst Economic and Market Jitters—Still America's Best Bet for Growth

W. R. TIMKEN JR.

Manufacturing and vehicles are in my blood. Before the Civil War, my great-grandfather was one of the premier carriage manufacturers in the United States. In fact, in 1985 he was chairman of the Carriage Builders National Association. As such, he was chosen to judge the first horseless carriage race—automobile—in the United States, sponsored by the *Chicago Times.* (A race Henry Ford twenty years later said he had wanted to attend more than anything in his life but could not find anyone to loan him carfare to Chicago.)

When he returned from the race, he told my twenty-five-year-old grandfather the automobile was the future, and they set out to be a part of it. They patented the tapered roller bearing in 1898, formed the present Timken Company in 1899, and sold the first tapered-bearing-equipped axles to an automobile producer in St. Louis in 1900. They opened their first plant in Detroit in 1909, and Grandfather was inducted into the Automotive Hall of Fame in 1977.

For my part, I started in the factory in 1958 and began peddling bearings and steel in Detroit in 1962. As I said in the beginning, manufacturing and vehicles are in my blood. For that reason, I was excited to accept the chair of the National Association of Manufacturers, the oldest and largest multi-industry trade association in the United States. This is a critical period for domestic manufacturing and the eighteen million people who make things.

For those of us who watch the economy, this is certainly an interesting, if somewhat nerve-racking, time. Consumer confidence has plummeted. Stock markets are cratering. Manufacturing activity is at recent lows. GDP is zero. It all reminds me of the situation faced by Marine Col. Chesty Puller during the Korean War. His marines were completely surrounded by enemy troops. He called his men together and said: "The enemy is in front of us and behind us. They are to the right and to the left of us. They won't get away this time." In a time of difficulty, Chesty Puller saw and seized an opportunity to think positive and succeed. He got his message across. That's what we at the NAM are determined to do.

Address to the Economic Club of Detroit, Michigan, April 9, 2001. Reprinted with permission of Vital Speeches of the Day and the author. W. R. Timken Jr. is the chairman and CEO of the Timken Company, a trustee of the Manufacturing Institute, and past chairman and CEO of the National Association of Manufacturers.

Now it may seem incongruous for me to stand before you today making positive comments about manufacturing with the economic problems going on, but in fact these difficulties highlight the new economic reality characterized by innovative technology, high productivity, and intense global competition.

Some, though, seem to have questions about the driving forces behind this new economic reality. You know, it reminds me of an old saying: Sometimes, it isn't what people don't know that's the problem; it's the things they think they do know that aren't correct!

Lately, in financial markets, public policy circles, and the country at large, there's been such a certainty about the kinds of companies that are the driving force behind the economy. Some people just know that services and technology companies are the most important parts of the economy. And just as certainly, some people just know that manufacturing is part of the past.

These are serious misconceptions about manufacturing and what makes the American economy tick. So today I want to set out a more realistic view. You've heard about the famous Four Horsemen of the Apocalypse—Death, Disease, War, and Famine. I want to tell you about the Four Horsemen of Prosperity that are shaping the present economy and surely our future.

Laying all the stock market and economic jitters aside, these four Horsemen of Prosperity are the new reality of the marketplace. I am convinced that Wall Street analysts are coming to see the value of these underlying truths and that they will again place a premium on manufacturing when this current slump begins to ease.

The four horsemen are equity values, interest rates, productivity growth, and Internet innovation. Like any team of horses, they are powerful when they pull together. When that happens, they reinforce each other. Here's what I mean:

- Equities of manufacturing companies represent one of the best long-term values in the stock market.
- Low real interest rates spur economic growth here and abroad.
- Productivity growth, advanced through use of technology and a trained workforce, are the keystones of successful wealth creation.
- The technologists have motivated us all to be more innovative in our use of the Internet and Web-based technology.

Let's look at the first of these twenty-first-century realities: how the stock market values in manufacturing. It's useful to recall why stock markets continue to be so important to our business. The central purpose of equity markets and debt is to serve as a vehicle for promising companies to raise the funds they need for expansion and growth. All of them require capital and investment. All require an equities market that soundly values these types of investments. When the capital is available for productivity growth and technological innovation, the revenues and earnings prized by Wall Street follow.

In recent years, Wall Street has strayed from these values. They have placed a higher premium on Internet-based companies that had neither revenues, profits, nor—as was often the case—a workforce. You'll remember the fervor a year ago when the rest of the economy was seen as an aging relic. Everything was going to migrate to the Internet, and all other time-tested measurements of business success were thrown to the wind. Having a new idea and a Web site seemingly replaced them all.

Now that bubble has burst. Financial analysts are coming down to earth again. It is time for them to come back to the original standards that guided markets: revenues, earnings, return on investments, and realistic growth projections. The dot-coms of 2000 have become the dot-bombs of 2001.

How Wall Street values our companies is important for another major reason: our employees have become major holders of our stock. Stock ownership has taken on an entirely new meaning. Today, 77 percent of households' liquid assets are in stocks, compared with only 49 percent in 1985. Stocks have replaced bank products as the investment of choice. People are not just buying equities for their personal accounts. Stock ownership is an important part of many corporate retirement accounts, especially through 401(k)s and stock options. Since 1989, the number of Americans owing stock through these accounts and mutual funds has increased sharply from fifty-two million to sixty-nine million. More than 70 percent of my global workforce of twenty thousand own Timken Company stock. They own 16 percent of the stock! Demonstrating again to Wall Street why fundamental value propositions of revenue and profits are the right kind of investment benchmarks is an important mission. How the Street values manufacturers will determine in many ways what kind of an economy and what kind of a country we have in the future. The markets should take a page from Warren Buffet, whose portfolio is up 27 percent in the past year. He invests in companies that make bricks, ceramics, carpeting, and furniture because he sees that these companies will grow and provide value to their shareholders. Another company that comes to mind is Textron, a diversified manufacturer that produces Bell helicopters, Cessna jets, automobile fuel tanks, equipment to test fiber optic networks and fasteners for computer hardware. Textron has delivered eleven consecutive years of consistent earnings growth and an average return on invested capital in excess of 15 percent. Textron's commitment to continuous improvement has resulted in a range of new products and increased productivity. It is just the kind of company that Wall Street should see as the model for the twenty-first century. Getting analysts and mutual funds to see our perspective again is more important than ever before. We saw a year ago what happens when they don't. It's a two-way street: Publicly traded companies have to redouble their efforts to maximize shareholder value; and Wall Street analysts have an even greater responsibility on their shoulders to make wise valuations. As manufacturers, it is our job to make sure Wall Street is well educated on our businesses. That is one of our highest priorities at the NAM, and it is why we have made speaking with Wall Street a new focus.

The second horseman is low real interest rates. This winter, the Federal Reserve has been wrestling with the aftereffects of its increase in interest rates. They wanted to slow the economy. Boy, were they successful! Growth only started to slow when the Fed began raising interest rates. Manufacturing has gone into a recession. In response, the Fed has lowered interest rates by 150 basis points since January, and real rates are still way too high. Also, unfortunately, reductions often take up to a year to have a positive impact. We can clearly see the negative effect of high rates on economic growth, so getting rates right is key to refueling economic growth. I want to see the Fed reduce rates by 100 basis points.

The third horseman is productivity. And what a horseman he is! In the past four years, manufacturing productivity growth averaged nearly 5 percent annually—double the overall business sector. The productivity increases in manufacturing specifically are among the key factors driving productivity throughout the economy. Without us, productivity growth would be zero. The overall productivity surge is, in turn, the principal reason we enjoyed a high growth, low-inflation expansion in the '90s. The jump in productivity is even more striking in durable goods manufacturing—from 3.4 percent to an astonishing 6.2 percent. Economists have pointed out that productivity has even accelerated as the economic expansion of the 1990s has aged, which is the opposite of the norm.

This unprecedented late-expansion acceleration in productivity growth, along with the rapid investment in new technologies, is not accidental. It reflects the long-lasting positive effects that manufacturing technologies and the business models they support have had on the production process and management of manufacturing firms. New manufacturing processes like Six Sigma and investments in the deployment of computers, robots, and new machine tools are responsible for this steady rise in productivity.

As this audience here in Motown knows full well, these productivity investments also have resulted in a significant increase in vehicle quality. According to the U.S. Labor Department, the quality of vehicles produced between 1967 and 1998 increased at an average annual rate of 2.2 percent. This means that a car built today has more than twice the quality as one built in 1967 in terms of performance, reliability, durability, and type of warranty. Today, owners of new U.S.-made cars experience fewer than 30 problems per 100 cars in the first year of ownership, compared with 104 defects per 100 cars twenty years ago. In turn, this means fewer repairs and a longer useful life.

Going hand in hand with plant investments in technology are capital expenditures for research and development. Almost 60 percent of all the R&D in America is manufacturing R&D. Government supported research programs have been declining while manufacturing has invested more. Three manufacturing industries alone—transportation, equipment, electronics, and chemicals—account for 38 percent of it.

The fourth horseman is the Internet. In one way, some of our Wall Street friends were right to be captivated by the promise of Web-based technology. It is a powerful new force that will, in time, change the way business communicates with its partners, employees, suppliers, and customers. Already at some companies like General Electric, Dell Computer, and Cisco Systems, Internet communicating has been put in place with dramatic and positive impacts.

Where last year Wall Street saw promise in the clicks and not the bricks, this year a new reality is dawning. It shows that the most effective Internet companies will actually be traditional companies that use the Internet more and more for standard business communication and, ultimately, for transactions.

The NAM has followed the emergence of digital manufacturing companies. Recently we released a survey conducted with Ernst and Young, one of the major accounting firms. We found out that, on one hand, only a small number of sales are made over the Internet right now—about 2 percent of all sales of manufacturers; but, on the other hand, nearly 75 percent of companies reported that they have e-commerce initiatives under way to better communicate with suppliers, customers, and employees. Most important, those companies that can use the Internet to view their suppliers' inventory levels reported that their inventory turn rates are 44 percent higher, showing one a powerful insight into the potential use of e-business. In addition to these findings, a similar study by *Industry Week* found that manufacturing was ahead of other sectors in putting e-commerce strategies in place.

What do companies gain from these investments in e-commerce? Let me highlight just a few examples to show you why this is the next big wave in productivity and growth: DaimlerChrysler has developed a new system that uses the Internet to connect all aspects of a vehicle program life cycle called FastCar. The program makes any change to a vehicle program immediately visible, a vast improvement over the old system, which could take up to ninety days to communicate change through the company and the supply chain. It allows suppliers involved in the design process to monitor changes so that, if necessary, their products can be redesigned to fit into the final product. FastCar could end up saving hundreds of millions of dollars during the life cycle of a vehicle program.

Dell Computer changed the way products can be ordered when it started selling PCs over the Internet way back in 1996. Dell lets consumers design their own PCs on the Internet, choosing only the features they want. Only after the order is placed will Dell manufacture the PC or laptop, thereby dramatically reducing its parts inventory. It communicates the order down the line electronically, precluding errors in the customer's product. As a result, the total production time for a Dell PC, from the time the customer places the order until it is shipped, is only six hours.

Just as manufacturing led the way in a massive investment in information technology that has produced the unparalleled burst of productivity we enjoy today, similar investments in Internet technology will produce further record productivity growth.

Manufacturing has huge fixed assets. We don't use them optimally because we don't have the necessary real-time information to make the right decisions. This is what the Internet will provide.

We manufacturers respect both Washington and Wall Street. Public policy decisions are made in one place, investment decisions in the other. We intend to be a greater presence in each—to lobby and to tell our story. But when it comes to manufacturing, all of us need to do more than talk. We need to show off a little—show off our products, our processes, our people, our plants. We need to get policymakers from Washington, financial analysts from New York, even editors and reporters from everywhere into our plants and mills and factories so they can see what we see—and see why we're so proud of it.

I'm not looking at our world with rose-colored glasses. Clearly, we face significant challenges today. The economy is struggling and manufacturing is in recession. But the underlying fundamentals, the bedrock of economic vitality, can still be found in manufacturing. And I believe the solution to our economic problems can be addressed by a focus on one key area. That area is economic growth. For almost two decades, American GDP growth has averaged more than 3 percent a year, and inflation has remained moderate and under control during the whole period. Over these past eighteen years, manufacturing has led that consistent American economic growth and the wealth it has produced. In 1970, the civilian workforce was 80 million people; in 2000, 140 million people—an increase of 75 percent. So much for those who used to run for public office on the "we can't grow the pie" platform people who believed productivity increases created unemployment.

Public policy is a key to continued growth. If we don't get it right and keep it right—on tax policy, entitlement, policy, fiscal policy, regulatory policy, training and education policy—we can strangle this economy along with its promise of durable growth and rising living standards for America, American workers, and their families.

Here's an example of the effect of policy on growth. Back in late 1998, when economic times were better, the NAM began calling for pro-growth tax relief. Back then, when the economy was strong, we called it an insurance policy for growth. But the tax-cut bill that was passed the following year by both the House and Senate was vetoed by President Clinton. I firmly believe that if that tax cut had been signed into law, we wouldn't be experiencing the current sharp downturn in economic growth.

Growth is the reason why the NAM board of directors recently passed a resolution expressing unanimous and unequivocal support for President Bush's $1.6 trillion tax-cut plan. We believe this tax cut would be a shot in the arm for the U.S. economy and a necessary stimulus for long- and short-term economic growth.

Growth is the reason why we supported overturning OSHA's ergonomics regulation. This extraordinarily overreaching and costly regulation based on conflicting scientific data could have crippled manufacturing's ability to be a driver of growth.

Growth is the reason why we are urging the administration, Congress, and industry to work together to develop a strategic national energy plan to increase energy supply, improve energy efficiency, and optimize all energy resources, including natural gas, oil, and coal. With the NAM's calculations indicating that the rising price of oil and gas cost our economy more than $115 billion between 1999 and 2000, it is clear that energy problems already are affecting economic growth.

In short, growth is why NAM does what it does. And growth is the reason why manufacturers need to get involved. You'll remember they used to say that war was too important to leave to the generals. Well, it's time for us in the business community to act on a similar proposition, that politics is too important to leave to the politicians. It's time for us to take our place in America's public life and to fill in the blanks we often just complain about in America's political and public policy debates.

At the NAM, we know that nobody understands better what policies are good for the American economy and people than manufacturers. We make things. We make products. We make prosperity. It's time to make a political difference. If we enter more vigorously than ever into the political arena, then the eighteen million people who make things in America can help to ground that debate in the serious stuff of real life. We can begin to build deeper relationships between manufacturers and the people who represent them in Congress. We can start a dialogue between them and us—a dialogue about who we are and what we make and how we make it—and why manufacturing is not a dismissible part of the past, part of an "old economy," but an essential part of the new—and why we manufacturers feel so strongly about so many issues of public policy.

But it's not just about manufacturers making their voices heard. It's about a united business community speaking with one voice about policies that are good for growth and good for the country—good for business. At its best, politics is a contest of ideas; perhaps more often, it is a clash of interests. Either way, more of us should engage. We need to recognize that people with decidedly different interests and ideas from our own—our adversaries in the public policy debate, such as labor leaders and trial lawyers and environmental interest groups—seem never to disengage. In this, they seem to have us at a disadvantage. We who care about more growth work in the private sector. We have businesses to run, competitors to reckon with, payrolls to meet. Our adversaries, who care about more government, work in the public sector. It seems they live there. Politics is their business. They're at it all the time. That's why we need to work harder, and we are. In fact, our hard work at generating business involvement in the political process is paying off. Three times in less than a year a united business community has gone toe to toe with labor and won.

Permanent trade relations with China was the first recent battle. After Seattle, the conventional wisdom was that we'd seen the chances for any bipartisan free-trade majorities die amid the chaos in Seattle's streets. But the business community unified after Seattle and pulled together. And even though labor mobilized and spent money and ran ads and joined forces with the antiglobalist left nationwide, PNTR for China passed.

The second of these three business victories over labor was the reelection of Congressman Ernie Fletcher in the Sixth District of Kentucky. After he had the courage to vote against the so-called Patients' Bill of Rights in late 1999, he moved to the top of labor's list in the 2000 elections. He was one of their main targets and, again, the common wisdom had it that labor couldn't miss. Labor ran ads, spent $2.5 million against him, tried to mobilize their grassroots, and worked hand in glove with the trial bar and the doctors' lobby to defeat Fletcher. But then manufacturers in and around Lexington, Kentucky, came together to thank Congressman Fletcher for his no vote on the misguided Patients' Bill of Rights. And what began as a unified manufacturing sector grew into a broadly unified business community that hosted plant tours and visits with employees even before the campaign season had begun. Of the NAM'S eighteen million people who make things in America, fifty thousand make things in the Sixth District of Kentucky, and Congressman Fletcher won reelection by fifty thousand votes.

Labor's third defeat, the vote to nullify the ergonomics rule, also confounded the conventional wisdom that warned members of Congress to be cautious since labor's retribution was certain and to be feared and there were easier, less politically risky ways to undo the rule. But, here again, as impressively as ever, the business community unified and energized business around the country. One member of Congress reported that for every call he got from Labor, he got ten from business. And so, with bipartisan majorities in both the House and Senate, Congress voted to send the rule back to OSHA's drawing board.

In closing, I'll remind you that it was de Tocqueville 170 years ago who wrote that an American manufacturing association "is a powerful and influential member of the community . . . which, by defending its own rights . . . saves the common liberties of the country." One hundred and fifty years later, it seems we're proving him right all over again.

Shining Factory on a Mountaintop

NANCY MILLS

I was struck in listening to Leo's remarks, about how much this world that he describes is a world that we in the labor movement would indeed like to have. It almost struck me as this shining factory on a hilltop, on a mountaintop, one in which workers feel free and justified in contributing all their skills, knowledge, and abilities to the success of that firm; where technology relieves the drudgery, tedium, and danger of work; where productivity increases are such that we can share in those gains to improve the quality of our lives. That is the world of work that our members dream about. That's what unions have committed themselves to fighting for.

Unfortunately, we don't see that world of work very much. I decided to use our new technology recently to send out an e-mail to a variety of folks who are much closer to the world of work than I am. These folks were from the industrial unions in the AFL-CIO, and I asked a variety of levels—business agents, research people, and so forth—to give me some reaction to the picture that Leo paints.

I will tell you that the roar of their responses was deafening. Although they see a few exceptions, exceptions that we could all probably point to or names that we would be familiar with—the Champion Papers, Harley-Davidsons, Intec Steels, Detroit Diesels—and, although I will also say that in many of the regular workplaces we see elements, pieces, small pieces of this high-performance workplace that Leo's describing, the fact of the matter is that most of our workplaces are still pretty much command-and-control operations, with very little independent authority for workers to make decisions about how they conduct their work.

I would urge people to read *Prosperity,* if you haven't done so, the book by David Wessell, the Wall Street Journal reporter. The book basically argues that the real productivity increases that we are hoping for, increases caused by computers, for example, we've really yet to see. As David Wessell notes, in many of our workplaces the computers are used more as fancy word processors than as something that really actively changes the way work is performed.

Another recent study describes an analysis of a number of different insurance companies, showing how the computers are being used in very different

Address given to the National Institute of Standards and Technology. Reprinted with permission of the author. Nancy Mills is executive director of the Working for America Institute, AFL-CIO, and former director of the Center for Workplace Democracy, AFL-CIO.

ways. In one case, the computer is actually being used to de-skill workers, and workers are working in huge pools doing nothing but data entry all day long. And that's the case in a number of the large insurance companies. And then, in some of the smaller ones, it's exactly the opposite. Computers are being used to allow up-skilling and to have folks doing much more of their own work to price out policies and so forth.

So there are very broad differences out there in the world of work—both in how technology is being utilized and what its benefits are for American workers.

But I want to be clear. We want the high-performance workplace. We want the high-road workplace. And, we know that what that workplace needs from workers is the following. Workers are going to have to commit to learn what they can do to improve their contribution to the workplace. That's a commitment that workers, in fact, will need to make for that high-performance workplace. They will have to commit to proactively using that knowledge for the good of the firm. And they will have to commit to loyalty to that firm.

Now, this may sound like heresy coming from a labor leader. But let me tell you why. What I'm really saying is that without those commitments, you're not going to get the kind of results that you need. Just training workers or educating them without them having that desire to proactively contribute to the success of the firm isn't going to result in the kinds of productivity increases that we all need or the success that we all want.

So the question is, why don't we get that commitment in many cases? What are the commitments that employers need to make to get that kind of commitment in return? I'm going to just focus very quickly on five. And they're the C words, I'm calling them.

The first is really a question of fundamental choice. Employers have to make a fundamental choice to compete on the high road. There are three more factors, which are factors of commitment to workers. And the fifth and final one is what I'm going to call courage. These are the five C challenges that I think employers have to meet in order to get the kinds of commitments that I was talking about and that workers will need to make to create these high-road, high-performing companies.

This question of choice. Despite all of our rhetoric and proselytizing about the need of companies to invest in their workforce, the fact of the matter is that the market is telling employers something very different. It tells them that there is a choice about how they can compete. Companies can choose to compete by investing in their workforce and making a commitment to that workforce and empowering that workforce. Or, they can commit to a low-road choice, which is to decrease labor costs, and working not through smart automatization or technology, but by simply reducing workers' living standards. That's a choice we believe that many American employers are, in fact, making.

I was reminded the other day that the number of American workers without health insurance has increased from thirty-five million to forty million in just the past five years, and that number is continuing to increase. These are working Americans, people who actively hold a job, who don't have health insurance.

People who go to work, or young workers who go to work today, no longer expect pension plans. An employer contribution pension plan is no longer an established and expected benefit to work. That was unheard of when most of us—I'm looking around the room and we're all pretty gray here—when most of us entered the work world. Most of us would have never imagined that the burden of preparing for one's retirement would have fallen almost entirely on the individual. I don't need to tell this audience about how, as productivity has increased over the past twenty-five years, workers' wages have not kept up with those productivity increases.

On the question of education and training, in particular, our statistics are indicating that the total dollars spent on education and training are, in fact, going down in America as a percentage of payroll. The dollars are being spent more and more on supervisors, managers, and engineers. The recent study by Lisa Lynch and Peter Black indicates that you're much more likely to get education and training in American if you already have high levels of education and training. If you are, however, a lesser-educated and lower-skilled worker, you're much less likely to get any increased education and training.

The first thing that we need to do is make the high-road choice. We would argue that you can make money on either the high-road or the low-road path. The high-road option may cost a little bit more in the short run, but the statistics about increased productivity and increased financial performance, in the long run, are real ones. But we shouldn't forget that employers can and do make the choices themselves. We need to figure out ways to close off the low road as an option.

Let's assume for a second that an employer says he/she does want to go on the high-road path. There are still the three Cs of commitments that we think employers need to make if they're going to get the kinds of commitments that I talked about earlier from their workers. One is that employers have to commit to share the burdens and the cost of preparing workers for the skills they need for the world of work. There's a popular notion now that says basically that workers should go out and prepare themselves. Then, employers are surprised when workers take that investment that they've made, getting more skills and more education, and take it to the next highest bidder.

At the recent Vice Presidential Summit on Twenty-first-Century Skills for Twenty-first-Century Jobs, employers reported that the main reason they were not investing in education and training for their workforce was because they saw their workers being scooped up, stolen, by the employer down the street.

So if employers want commitment and loyalty from their workers, then they're going to have to contribute to paying for it. We're very encouraged by some new high-road regional partnerships that are springing up around the country. Groups of employers and unions, in some cases just groups of employers, are coming together to share the costs and the practices of equipping their workforce with the kind of generic and generalized skills—problem solving, computer usage, teamwork, and so forth—that every employer needs, because they are not company-specific skills.

We encourage you to think about how government can support these high-road regional partnerships, because we think they are an example of real solutions to real problems that employers face.

The second commitment employers need to make is a commitment to employment security. I know this sounds like an old paradigm, but the fact is, without it, we have the Ralph Kramden problem. How many of us are old enough to remember the suggestion box routine? What Ralph Kramden said basically was that you put a suggestion in the suggestion box and then you get a pink slip. Well, unfortunately, this is still a real problem. If we want loyalty and commitment and we want American workers to contribute to the success of the firm, there needs to be an accompanying commitment to their employment security. Nobody is going to make a suggestion that's going to result in the abolition of their work. I think we need to be creative about the employment security question. It's one thing for a major auto company to provide that kind of security. It's something very different for a small machine shop to provide that kind of security. There are ways of linking employers together with other employers, and there are other social safety nets that we ought to be exploring.

The last commitment we think employers need to make to get the accompanying commitment from their workforce is a commitment to share the rewards of success. Sharing takes many forms. We all know that there have been profit-sharing plans and gain-sharing plans, but just good old-fashioned collective bargaining is a way to commit to share the rewards. Workers need to have a say in how the rewards are shared.

The last of the five C challenges is courage. What I mean by this is that employers need to have the courage to give workers the authority to make the decisions—to allow workers to use their knowledge, skills, and abilities to contribute to the success of the firm.

I was struck by your comments, Pamela, about how engineers and managers aren't being prepared to work with production workers. Part of the problem, I think, is that there really is the very deeply held view that managers know all the answers about how things should get done. It takes a tremendous amount of courage for an employer to empower its workers to make decisions.

It's our sense that if employers make the fundamental choice to compete on the high road, if they give the three commitments—sharing the burdens of preparing workers, providing employment security, and sharing the rewards—and if they have the courage to give workers the authority, you'll get the commitment.

I want to just make one last closing advertisement, which is that we don't think it's an accident that unionized workplaces outperform nonunionized workplaces in high-performance settings. This recent study that Lisa Lynch and Peter Black did shows pretty conclusively that unionized—and I'm going to tell the whole truth here—that unionized traditional workplaces, traditional in the sense that they don't have the elements of a high-performance workplace, were the least productive candidates. Nonunion, so-called high-performance, ones were a little bit more productive. But, what beat the pants off everybody was the unionized high-performance firm.

We believe it's because unions provide a way to both structure those commitments that we talked about—the choice, the commitments, and the courage—and also provide a social sanctioning of workers performing their role and their commitments to the employer. Unionized workplaces make it OK to have that balance between the commitments of the employer and the commitments of the worker. Therefore, if unionized workplaces are, in fact, the leaders here—leaders not just in the outputs, the outputs of higher productivity, but they're also the leaders in the inputs—unionized workplaces spend more money on technology. They spend more money on training. Unionized workers avail themselves of training more than nonunion workers do.

If this is the case, then I guess I want to make a pitch here. The country has a tremendous amount to learn about how unionized workplaces, and the exercise of commitments, make the transition to a high-performance workplace easier and more successful. I urge NIST and those of you who are concerned, as we are, about creating workplaces that will provide high-quality jobs for our children and their children and their children's children to learn what works in a unionized workplace. Learn what makes technology, teamwork, education, skills, training, and all the commitments that we've talked about come together and figure out how we can spread that to more American workplaces for the sake of our nation's economy for the future.

Stocks Matter, but Jobs Matter More

E. J. DIONNE JR.

For anyone with an interest in the Great Depression, certain phrases set off chills. So when Anthony M. Santomero, president of the Philadelphia Federal Reserve Bank, declared this week that economic recovery was "just around the corner," he must have been unaware that he was paraphrasing Herbert Hoover.

The Federal Reserve's interest rate cut on Wednesday may, temporarily anyway, restore some of Fed Chairman Alan Greenspan's popularity. Accused of foot-dragging on the matter of priming a sluggish economy, Greenspan now seems in a full-speed-ahead mood to get things moving again.

But the Fed's action also is a sign of how worried the economic masters of the universe are about our nation's slowdown. In the dry language of Fedspeak, "the risks are weighted mainly toward conditions that may generate economic weakness in the foreseeable future." If a good inflation-phobe like Greenspan believes this, it's hard for anyone to disagree.

The question is whether our sustained national experiment with very low unemployment is about to end. The unemployment rate has spiked up, and the news of layoffs suggests the numbers are likely to get worse this year. For all the media focus on stock prices, it's unemployment that has real human and social impact.

With all those cable stations running the market ticker at the bottom of their screens all day long, it's hard to remember that in the economic lives of most people, stocks play a limited role. As David Leonhardt of the *New York Times* put it this week, "Relatively few Americans rely on them for a significant portion of their income." It's an antique notion, I know, but jobs really matter.

During the 1990s, we discovered the virtuous cycle created when unemployment drops sharply. It's not just that people have work to do. Low unemployment also increases the bargaining power of employees. They can command higher wages and better benefits. As a result, the 1990s saw a halt in the growth of income inequality that had been a rule in our country for two decades.

It turns out that rising incomes for people in the middle and at the bottom of the economy have all sorts of positive social spinoffs. During the 1990s, crime dropped sharply and so did welfare dependency. The latest figures released this week show a continued drop in teen pregnancy rates. By most mea-

 E. J. Dionne Jr. is a columnist with the *Washington Post* and senior fellow at the Brookings Institution.

sures, we Americans behave better when we can share widely in economic opportunities.

By contrast, unemployment was higher during the boom of the 1980s, and economic growth was distributed more unequally, tilting toward the top. It also turns out that, according to the careful measures compiled annually by conservative social critic William Bennett, many of the social indicators (including crime and teen pregnancy) were going the wrong way in the 1980s.

Only an extreme economic determinist would assert that low unemployment drives all social improvement. Many good things happened in the 1990s for reasons other than the economy—and probably also for reasons we don't fully understand yet.

But only someone determined to ignore evidence would overlook the link between low unemployment, more progressive tax policies, and general social improvement. During the 1990s, as Robert McIntyre of Citizens for Tax Justice showed in a recent article in the *American Prospect,* income taxes went up only on the top income groups. Because of such innovations as the child tax credit, they stayed the same or went down for most other groups. And for poor working Americans, programs such as the earned income tax credit delivered substantial amounts of new cash.

These lessons are being ignored in the current tax and budget debate. Clearly, all sides want to restore economic growth. But the president's tax program openly and consciously imitates Ronald Reagan's policies. What ought to be at the heart of the current argument is which growth model—the one from the 1980s or the one from the 1990s—is better.

The evidence, on both the social and employment fronts, favors the 1990s. That can be said with full acknowledgment that many of the favorable trends of the decade were driven by technological changes in the marketplace and not just government actions. The question is: Do we want to revert to policies consciously tilted toward the best-off and investors, or do we want to stick with an approach that leans mildly toward greater equality—toward those whose livelihoods depend far more on their work than their portfolios? The second approach made everyone richer, including the very wealthy.

There are many ways to get the economy moving again. The best way would keep everyone moving forward together.

The Economic Importance of Improving Math-Science Education

ALAN GREENSPAN

We are in a period—especially in this country—of rapid innovation that is yielding dramatic changes in the way goods and services are produced and in the ways that they are delivered to final users. These innovations are markedly elevating the skill levels that will be needed if our increasingly sophisticated capital stock is to function effectively in the years ahead. Such considerations are an important element in the ongoing dialogue that our nation's leaders in business, labor, education, and public policy must have if we, together, are to be successful in meeting the rising demand for skilled workers. Success in this area will, in turn, allow us to realize the potential that advances in science and technology have to enhance living standards for a large majority of Americans.

The pressures we face today are not unlike those of a century ago, when our education system successfully responded to the multiplying needs brought about by a marked acceleration in technological innovation. As those advances put new demands on workers interacting with an increasingly more complex stock of productive capital, high school education proliferated—enabling students to read manuals, manipulate numbers, and understand formulae. Students were thus accorded the skills necessary to staff the newly developing assembly lines in factories and the rapidly expanding transportation systems whose mechanical and automotive jobs required a widening array of cognitive skills. For those who sought education beyond high school, land grant colleges sprang up, as states reacted to the increased skills required by industry and especially agriculture, the dominant occupation a century ago.

By today's standard, the required share of "intellectual workers" in our labor force was then still small. But the technological innovations of the latter part of the nineteenth century began to bring an increasing conceptualization of our gross domestic product—that is, a greater emphasis on value added stemming from new ideas and concepts as distinct from material inputs and demanding physical labor. The proportion of our workforce that created value through intellectual endeavors, rather than predominantly through manual labor, began a century-long climb. In 1900, only one out of every ten workers was in a professional, technical, or managerial occupation. By 1970, that proportion had doubled, and today those types of jobs account for nearly one-third of our workforce.

Testimony before the Committee on Education and the Workforce, U.S. House of Representatives, September 21, 2000. Alan Greenspan is chairman of the U.S. Federal Reserve.

Moreover, this simple statistic undoubtedly understates the ongoing increase in the analytic content of work, because there also seems to have been a marked increase in the need for conceptual skills in jobs that a decade or so ago would have been easily characterized as fully manual labor. Indeed, the proliferation of information technologies throughout the economy in recent years has likely accelerated this shift in the skill requirements of many occupations away from routine work and toward nonroutine interactive and analytical tasks.

Another signal of the ongoing rise in demand for conceptual skills in recent years has been the increase in relative wages for college-educated workers. During the 1980s and much of the 1990s, as demand for skilled workers outpaced the supply, the gap between the wages of the college educated and those with a high school diploma or less widened considerably. More recently, as labor markets have tightened, that gap has leveled off. Real wage gains have picked up for workers with less than a college education. But evidence of a high skills premium for workers with college degrees remains—not just for high-tech workers but across a broad range of occupations.

Innovation boosts output per hour and the freed pool of workers seek to exploit other opportunities. Their success is evidenced by the dramatic decline in the unemployment rate since 1992. The capital invested in any endeavor needs human interaction in order to function. But the new jobs that have been created by the surge in innovation require that the workers who fill them use more of their intellectual potential. This process of stretching toward our human intellectual capacity is not likely to end any time soon. Indeed, the dramatic increase in the demand for on-the-job technical training and the major expansion of the role of our community colleges in teaching the skills required to address our newer technologies are persuasive evidence that the pressures for increased learning are ongoing.

At the same time that we have been witnessing these substantial increases in the demand for human input, we see little evidence that the general level of human intelligence has changed much—indeed, has changed at all—over the centuries. Fortunately, human beings exhibit a pronounced ability to stretch their intellectual capabilities when called upon. Hence, while the intellectual output of humans may appear to have an upper limit, that limit seems to be sufficiently flexible to assuage most concerns. Nonetheless, in today's economy, it is becoming evident that a significant upgrading or activation of underutilized intellectual skills will be necessary to effectively engage the newer technologies.

Expanding the number of individuals prepared to use a greater proportion of their intellectual capacity means, among other things, that our elementary and secondary students must broaden their skills in mathematics and related sciences. In my experience, competency in mathematics—both in numerical manipulation and in understanding its conceptual foundations—enhances a person's ability to handle the more ambiguous and qualitative relationships that dominate our day-to-day decision making. The study of science, of course, also advances problem-solving skills.

Early success in problem solving clearly enhances the self-esteem of young people and encourages them to engage in ever more complex reasoning. We all tend to gravitate toward those activities that we do best. This is a self-reinforcing process in which early success promotes further effort in a self-perpetuating direction. This is true of playing Little League baseball or the piano, as well as doing math.

If we are to improve the scientific reasoning skills of our young people, we need to encourage a deeper interaction with numbers and their manipulation to a point at which students are confident and proud of their level of skills—in many instances an outcome they may not have anticipated. One is led to wonder whether the early sharpening of intellectual rigor that occurs when young students struggle to negotiate the complexities of doing multiplication and division the old-fashioned way is not without enduring value. A superficial understanding that does not stretch a child's intellectual capacity, in my experience, cannot galvanize an enhanced reality-based sense of self-esteem.

In this regard, it is discouraging that so many students who clearly demonstrate impressive verbal or other conceptual skills find mathematical procedures intimidating. According to a recent survey of student attitudes toward math conducted by the Department of Education, fewer than half of the high school seniors surveyed said that they like mathematics, a proportion similar to the proportion who felt that they were good at it. Even more disturbing, these proportions were lower than those in the surveys conducted in 1990. Some research indicates that such "math anxiety" has a negative effect on mathematics performance and that strategies for increasing students' confidence in their mathematical abilities are likely to have additional benefits in terms of achievement.[1] If we can enhance their self-esteem and provide them with a strong curriculum and effective teaching, students may well find themselves rising to a level of analytic capability beyond their previous vision.

There is clearly work to be done, for, as you know, the international comparisons of student achievement in mathematics and science that were conducted in 1995 suggested that our fourth graders were among the highest rated around the world but that our eighth and twelfth graders fell short of their peers in other countries. These comparisons heightened the debate about the quality of education that students are exposed to between the fourth and twelfth grades and raised concerns about prospects for a continuing shortfall of American-educated skilled technicians.

To be sure, substantial reforms in math and science education had been under way for some time prior to the 1995 study and have continued since. It is encouraging that the latest results on trends in academic progress from the National Assessment of Educational Progress show some improvement in both subjects. Perhaps that improvement will show up in a narrowing of the gap between our students and those abroad when the results of a follow-up survey of international comparisons are released later this year. Nonetheless, with the conceptual demands on our workers continuing to rise, substantial further progress needs to be made in raising the analytic competency of our graduating high school seniors.

Addressing this issue is crucial for the future of our nation. It is obviously just a matter of time before the bulk of our workforce will require a much higher level of problem-solving skills than is currently evident. And while we have been fortunate to attract so many skilled young people to our shores, we must nonetheless strive to increase math and science achievement so that our students can take advantage of the considerable opportunities that will exist in tomorrow's labor market. In that way, we can realize the potential of technological change for bringing substantial and lasting benefits to our economy.

As a final point, I would stress that, even with the increasing intellectual specialization so necessary if we are to move to an ever higher degree of specialization in our overall economy, we also need to ensure that all students have a broad knowledge of the world at large. Major technological advances are becoming increasingly interdisciplinary. Many academics argue, I believe rightly, that significant exposure to a liberal education—music, literature, and the arts—broadens intellectual awareness, enhancing the ability to reach across disciplines to forge new ideas. Thus, while we must strengthen math and science education to address the requirements of the newer technologies we see on the horizon, we should not lose sight of the advantages of a liberal education.

I do not doubt that many of our most innovative and successful dot-com entrepreneurs are exceptionally, but narrowly, technically focused and educated. But if technology is to fit into a broader society of complex democratic institutions such as ours, it is important that all participants have an adequate awareness of its structure and values. For it is the latter that we as a people endeavor to achieve. Our technologies are only a means to that end.

Note

1. Hsui-Zu Ho et al., "The Affective and Cognitive Dimensions of Math Anxiety: A Cross-National Study," *Journal for Research in Mathematics Education* (May 2000). This article cites a long literature on "math anxiety" among U.S. students and reports that it also has an adverse effect on students in China and Taiwan.

What We Work for Now

JEROME M. SEGAL

Despite all our concerns with self-fulfillment, most Americans work to earn money, just as their forebears did one hundred years ago. The relative costs of necessities have changed, and so has a fair definition of what is necessary. But even with all our economic growth, and even with some items much cheaper than they once were, families still spend about four-fifths of their budgets for core needs, just as their counterparts did a century ago. Perhaps there should be some national introspection about how much we have really gained.

Certainly, we have escaped the overwhelming tyranny of food. In 1901, the Bureau of Labor Statistics reported that in major industrial cities, the biggest expenditure item for families was food—half of spending in low-income families and a third in more affluent ones. In 1999, food took only 15 percent of household spending, and more than a third of that spending was for food prepared away from home. For food from their own kitchens, Americans now use up only 9 percent of their budgets. They can cover that with a little more than a month of work—probably the lowest level of work effort for food in human history. Even households in the lowest fifth of income use only 18 percent of total spending for food. Something similar has happened with clothing. In 1901 it took 10 to 15 percent of the family budget, and now it takes only 5 percent.

What, then, are Americans spending their money on? A common stereotype of the pampered consumer might suggest that large amounts are going for toys and luxuries, but I found while conducting studies for Redefining Progress, a public policy organization in Oakland, California, that this is a misconception. Electronic gadgets, for instance, have a small place in consumer spending—2 percent in 2000. Entertainment takes less than 6 percent.

The largest expenditure item now is housing. Bringing together renters and owners, shelter, including utilities, takes 27 percent of our spending, compared to a very similar 25 percent in 1901. Although our homes today are much more luxurious, safe neighborhoods with good public schools remain out of reach for many.

The big growth category is transportation. In the earliest studies of consumption, transportation wasn't even a separate category; it took only 1 or 2 percent of spending. But then came the automobile, and now we devote more than 20 percent of our spending to transportation. Just to cover that, the aver-

New York Times, September 3, 2001. Reprinted with permission of the *New York Times*. Jerome M. Segal is a senior research scholar in public affairs at the University of Maryland.

age American family works from New Year's Day to March 14. No society in history has worked so much just to be able to get around.

A car may once have been a luxury, but as cities and suburbs have spread out, stores have disappeared from neighborhoods, and work and school have ceased to be within walking distance, nearly all Americans have become car-dependent. And with most women in the formal workforce, many families have two automobiles—not really as a matter of choice, but as a basic need.

Another work-related item virtually unknown a century ago is day care. Self-sufficiency budgets, calculated by many states to determine families' costs for basic needs, allocate 25 to 30 percent of a low-income household's spending for day care.

Though education remains only a minor category of spending—2 percent—this is just on average. For families with children in college—and college is now required for far more jobs than in the past—this expense can be staggering.

So in a century of growing incomes and changing lives, what has been gained? While the energies of Americans are expended to obtain different items than they were years ago, what remains constant is the emphasis on the basics.

In 1901, 80 percent of spending went for food, housing, and clothing. In 1999, 81 percent of spending went for food, housing, clothing, transportation, and health care. A century of economic growth has certainly brought some genuine progress, but it is less clear-cut than we sometimes think.

The Real Foundation of the Software World

Behind-the-Scenes Programmers Are Bricklayers of Internet Economy

STEVE LOHR

Gazing out at the nearly seven thousand software developers assembled in Orlando two weeks ago, William H. Gates recalled how much things had changed since his company, Microsoft, was founded in 1975. Back then, he said, there were fewer people in the software industry than had gathered that morning in the cavernous convention center. "It was a tiny, tiny business," recalled Mr. Gates, Microsoft's chairman.

Software, to be sure, is a big business today. But in many ways, it once again has the up-for-grabs feel of the early days of the personal computer industry, before Microsoft became the dominant force. And that is why big companies like Microsoft, IBM, Oracle, and Sun Microsystems are spending so much time, energy, and money these days trying to woo outside programmers. "It's nice to be in demand, and in a satisfying profession that has turned out to be fairly lucrative," observed Basim Kadhim, a twenty-nine-year-old programmer who telecommutes from Bend, Oregon, to Silicon Valley.

The corporate campaigns are a sign that the industry is entering "a disruptive new era of opportunity in software," according to Richard Doherty, president of Envisioneering, a technology research firm.

The opportunity lies in building all the software needed to make the promise of Internet commerce a reality. So far, e-commerce is in its infancy, rarely going beyond browsing the Web and executing some rudimentary transaction, like buying books online or ordering office supplies on an in-house corporate Web site. And the information is still typed by hand on a computer keyboard.

But for software developers like Mr. Kadhim, the goal is to help build a far smarter Internet, where most exchanges of information would be automated. Before long, for example, information from the purchasing department of a carmaker might be shuttled automatically to and from the accounting department of a parts supplier. Most steps in a transaction would be computer-to-computer communication, eliminating mounds of paperwork and hours of human toil.

New York Times, July 24, 2000. Reprinted with permission of the *New York Times*. Steve Lohr reports on business for the *New York Times* and is the coauthor of *U.S. vs. Microsoft*.

Or a person's cell phone or Palm-like device might be able to automatically match his calendar with the doctor's schedule, suggesting times for a checkup. Thousands of similar labor-saving uses will add up to the next generation of e-commerce, representing the real payoff from the Internet—both in terms of personal convenience and economic productivity.

Software will make it happen. And most of the work will be done not by engineers at the big software houses like Microsoft, IBM, and Oracle, but by the 80 percent of programmers who labor, often in relative obscurity, at old-line companies, Web site contractors, computer consultants, and elsewhere.

Such programmers are in demand because they are the ones who write all the handcrafted software programs that keep the nation's computer-dependent economy running. And many thousands of them now face the task of bringing brick-and-mortar businesses into the future. They are the bricklayers of the Internet economy.

This army of behind-the-scenes programmers will largely determine who the big software winners will be in this, the Internet era of computing.

Today, companies that include Microsoft, IBM, Sun, Oracle, BEA, Hewlett-Packard and others are scrambling to establish their software tools and technology as "platforms," or environments, in which large numbers of programmers will want to develop software applications for the Web. The stakes are high. The market for such e-commerce platform software, according to some analysts' projections, could grow to as much as $100 billion over the next decade.

No one expects any single supplier to become as powerful as Microsoft has been in personal computing, because Internet computing is such a diverse milieu, with many of the key technology standards in the public domain. But the PC era proved the importance of attracting developers. Today, many technologists still believe Apple's Macintosh and IBM's OS/2 were better operating systems than Microsoft's Windows. But Microsoft lured far more developers to write applications for Windows.

"A platform is an ecosystem," noted Charles Fitzgerald, director of business development in the developer division at Microsoft. "And there are a few thousand people at Microsoft whose job it is to help developers."

Microsoft plans to spend $2 billion over the next three years on the tools and training to help software developers build Web applications using Microsoft technology. IBM also puts a $2 billion price tag on its three-year Internet software initiative intended to lure developers to its camp. Other companies are also spending heavily to win over developers.

"Software developers are a hot commodity today, and they increasingly drive platform decisions within companies," explained Valerie Olague, who is leading the IBM program. "We can only be successful if we attract developers."

As a group, the developers seem beyond the reach of conventional salesmanship. They are the kind of people who cultivate deep intellectual interests in particular fields like Japanese animation and science fiction, according to research done for IBM by Renegade, a marketing firm. They share the mind-set that drives a person to stay up all night to solve the puzzle of a few buggy lines of programming code.

Certainly, at industry events, developers want to do more than drink and dance. So IBM is sponsoring gatherings in cities including New York, Seattle, and San Francisco, which feature talks by renowned Internet programmers and team coding contests with handheld computers as prizes.

There is no hard sell. The goal is primarily to prompt the developers to go to IBM's Web site, because increasingly, company Web sites and specialist sites like Slashdot ("News for Nerds") are where developers hang out, exchange tips, and download software to try out.

Developers seem most impressed by the simple beauty of code that works. At the Microsoft Developers Conference in Orlando recently, the crowd yawned when Microsoft executives talked of the company's Internet vision. They clapped politely for the slick videos and chuckled at the early-morning warm-up routine of the comedian Richard Jeni, who began, "I couldn't be more excited to be here if I knew what you guys did for a living."

But the rousing applause came for a string of programming code, written partly in the hot new Internet standard, XML—for Extensible Markup Language—that was projected onto giant blue screens and performed precisely as it was supposed to.

Software programming is problem solving, and developers tend to gravitate to the technology that is the most useful for the task at hand. The young developer from Oregon, Mr. Kadhim, speaks of the appeal of software as a kind of infinitely malleable medium for technical artistry. "You get a rush when you build something and make it work," he said. "It's like cracking a puzzle."

Mr. Kadhim has a Ph.D. in computer science, and he is fluent in programming languages including BASIC, COBOL, C, C ++, Java, and Linux. He calls himself a "Linux lover," referring to a version of the Unix operating system that is distributed free over the Internet and is regarded as a threat to Microsoft's Windows.

Yet in January, Mr. Kadhim joined Fujitsu Software, which makes specialized software tools for COBOL programmers. And he was in Orlando at the Microsoft conference, demonstrating how some of Microsoft's new technology can bring applications written in COBOL, a forty-year-old programming language still widely used in business, onto the Web.

"I'm doing this because it's a challenging software engineering problem—how do you bring so much of the old world into the future?" he said. "So far, most of the Web development amounts to toy applications, interesting but not yet hooked to the core of our economy. And COBOL, whether you like it or not, is at the heart of our economy."

In New York, Elaine Power manages a group of two dozen programmers at Organic, a Web site builder and consultant. Ms. Power, thirty-six, got a taste for computers as a teenager in Britain when she wrote a program in BASIC, a simple programming language, that sent a digital ball bouncing around the screen of her brother's personal computer. The fascination was enough to prompt her to major in computer science in college and eventually learn computer languages ranging from FORTRAN to Java.

Most of the young engineers she works with today program in Java, an Internet programming language developed by Sun Microsystems. They see it as the programming language of the moment and a skill of the future. "Programmers can be very religious about their platform and their tools," Ms. Power said.

But experienced programmers tend to value flexibility rather than religion because the field moves so quickly. In the 1960s, after all, COBOL was the hot programming language, the skill of the future.

"Being a good programmer is a lot like being a good carpenter," said Tim Howes, chief technology officer of Loudcloud, a startup founded by Mr. Howes and three other former executives of Netscape, the Internet pioneer. "You should have a breadth of knowledge and know when to use the appropriate tool—when to use your hammer, your saw, and your screwdriver."

Today, many companies are using a variety of tools when building Web applications rather than becoming overly dependent on any single technology supplier.

Last year, a group of longtime Silicon Valley software developers founded Liquidprice, a reverse-auction Web service, which allows electronics retailers and auto dealers to bid for the business of individual consumers on the basis of where they live and what products they want. To run the service, Liquidprice, based in Cupertino, California, deploys a smorgasbord of software—Oracle for the database, Microsoft for its Web servers, Java as its main programming language, and IBM's Websphere as the development environment for its specialized Web applications.

At each tier, says Piyush Gupta, the president and cofounder, the company has ensured that it can quickly switch to other suppliers. The trickiest one to abandon would presumably be its Web development software, Websphere. Still, it is a tentative win indeed for IBM in the emerging market for Web development software. Liquidprice engineers have written a thin layer of code intended to isolate the company's in-house applications from the IBM software.

"The day Websphere doesn't satisfy me, we'll switch," Mr. Gupta said. "For the smart developers, the world of being locked in to any one software vendor is over."

The New Antiglobalists

Exploring the Psychology of Seattle, Washington, and Beyond

WILLIAM FINNEGAN

For Juliette Beck, it began with the story of the Ittu Oromo, Ethiopian nomads whose lives were destroyed, in vast numbers, by a dam—a hydroelectric project sponsored by the World Bank. Beck was a sophomore at Berkeley, taking a class in international rural development. The daughter of an orthopedic surgeon, she had gone to college planning to do premed, but environmental science caught her interest, and the story of the Ittu Oromo precipitated a change of major. Beck was a brilliant student—"One of these new Renaissance people, so smart they could be almost anything," a former professor of hers recalls. She was intellectually insatiable, and her eagerness to understand the dynamics of economic development propelled her into several academic fields, notably the dry, dizzying politics of international finance and trade. By her junior year, she was teaching a class on the North American Free Trade Agreement. "It was one of the most popular student-led classes we've had," her professor says. "I understand it's been cloned on other campuses."

Beck had found her strange grand passion—international trade rules—at an auspicious time. Besides the popularity of her class, there were the events last November in Seattle, where fifty thousand demonstrators shut down a major meeting of the World Trade Organization. Beck, who is twenty-seven, was a key organizer of the Seattle protests.

"The Spirit of Seattle," she says, crinkling her eyes and grinning blissfully. "Your body just tingled with hope, to be around so many people so committed to making a better world." Beck says things like "tingled with hope" and "making a better world" with no hint of self-consciousness, and in the next breath will launch into a critique of the Multilateral Agreement on Investment, a set of international trade rules that she and other activists have fought against for the last several years. (The MAI would limit the rights of national governments to regulate currency speculation or set policies regarding investment.) This odd fusion of hardheaded policy analysis and utopian idealism has an exhilarating edge, which may account for some of Beck's habitual high spirits.

 William Finnegan writes for the *New Yorker* and is the author of a number of books, including *Cold New World.*

Almost six feet tall, she retains, to a striking degree, both the coltishness of adolescence and the open-faced, all-American social style of the Girl Scout and high school athlete (volleyball, tennis, basketball) she was. Zooming around the scruffy, loft-style offices of Global Exchange, the human-rights organization in San Francisco where she works, she seems conspicuously lacking the self-decor of the other young activists around the place—piercings, tattoos, dreadlocks. It may be that she's simply been too busy to get herself properly tatted up. While we were talking in her office on a recent evening, she tried to deal simultaneously with me and with a significant fraction of the seven hundred e-mail messages that had piled up in her inbox—reading, forwarding, filing, trashing, replying, sighing, grumbling, erupting in laughter. She was determined, she said, to have an empty inbox before she left, in a few days' time, for Washington, D.C., even if it meant pulling consecutive all-nighters.

"Where I grew up, in suburban San Diego, it was so strange," she said. "Politics didn't exist. The only political gesture I ever saw there was during the Gulf War. People drove around waving American flags from the backs of pickups. That was it. When we were teenagers, the consumerism was overwhelming. If you didn't wear Guess jeans, you didn't exist. When I got to Berkeley, I was just like a *sponge*. At one point, I realized that, in my entire education, having gone through good public schools, advanced-placement programs, and all that, I had never learned anything about the American labor movement. Nothing. I don't think I ever heard the term 'collective bargaining' inside a classroom. No wonder we were all so apolitical!"

After college, Beck went to work as an environmental engineer for a small Bay Area firm. The pay was good, and the work was interesting, but she found herself spending most of her time competing with other firms for contracts. "It made me realize I didn't want to be doing work that was all about money." So she made the downward financial leap into the nonprofit sector (and was recently forced to move from chic, expensive San Francisco to cheaper, inconvenient Oakland, where she lives in a group house with no living room). It's a step she says she's never regretted. "I think a lot of people in my generation—not a majority, maybe, but a lot—feel this void," she told me. "We feel like capitalism and buying things are just not fulfilling. Period." She became an organizer for Public Citizen, Ralph Nader's consumer group, which was campaigning, along with labor unions and other allies, to stop the Clinton administration's effort to get renewed "fast track" authority to negotiate trade agreements with limited congressional oversight. (The problem with such authority, according to its opponents, is its bias, in practice, in favor of industry.) The campaign was successful—the first major defeat in Congress for trade advocates in sixty years. "That was a great victory," Beck said happily. "We defeated some of the most powerful forces on the planet."

Those powerful forces, once they had recovered from the shock, responded with a public-relations offensive. William Daley, the secretary of commerce, embarked on a national trade education tour meant to persuade the American people of the wisdom of free trade. Daley was met by protesters at every stop. In Los Angeles, Beck helped coordinate his unofficial reception. "We just *dogged* him." Longshoremen refused to cooperate with the secretary, she said, for what she called "a photo op at the docks." She went on: "They said, 'No way, come down to our headquarters and we'll have an honest discussion on trade.' He said no. These fat cats only want to talk on their terms. Even the kids at a high school in Long Beach where Daley spoke asked him tough questions. We really caused that tour to flop. Daley had a bus full of CEOs and flacks from the Business Roundtable, but a lot of bigwigs flaked when they saw how hokey the whole thing was." Six corporate leaders, including the chairs of Boeing and AT&T, had in fact appeared with Daley at the tour's kickoff, then made themselves scarce when it began to smell of disaster.

Beck's delight in such disasters is wicked and shameless. I recalled a news story she had circulated by e-mail a few weeks before. The story was about Michel Camdessus, the managing director of the International Monetary Fund, getting hit in the face by a fruit-and-cream pie just before he gave a farewell speech to mark his retirement. Beck's cover note exulted, "The head of IMF got his just desserts this weekend—a parting pie shot!"

Beck likes to call the IMF, the WTO, and the World Bank "the iron triangle of corporate rule." In her view, these institutions—their leaders, clients, political allies, and, above all, true bosses, multinational corporations—are frog-marching humanity, along with the rest of the planet, into a toxic, money-maddened, repressive future. And she intends to persuade the rest of us not to go quietly.

In her office at Global Exchange, still crashing through the underbrush of her inbox, she suddenly pulled up short. "Oh, check this out," she said, and pointed to her computer screen. "Have you seen this?"

I had. It was a report prepared by Burson-Marsteller, the Washington publicity firm, which had been leaked and was making the electronic rounds. It was titled "Guide to the Seattle Meltdown: A Compendium of Activists at the WTO Ministerial." Burson-Marsteller's cover letter began, "Dear [Corporate Client]," and characterized the report "not so much as a retrospective on the past, but as an alarming window on the future." The report offered profiles of dozens of groups that had participated in the Seattle protests—from the Anarchist Action Collective to Consumers International to the AFL-CIO—naming leaders, giving Web-site addresses, and including brief descriptions, usually lifted from the literature of the groups themselves. The cover letter mentioned possible "significant short-term ramifications for the business community" because of the "perceived success of these groups in disrupting Seattle" and, more portentously, warned of "the potential ability of the emerging coalition of these groups to seriously impact broader, longer-term corporate interests."

Burson-Marsteller was at least trying to reckon with what had been revealed in Seattle. The press, the Seattle authorities, the Clinton administration, the WTO, and many other interested parties had largely been ignorant of the popular movement being built around them. Suddenly challenged, everyone had scrambled to respond, some (the police) attacking the protesters, others (Bill Clinton) rhetorically embracing them (while his negotiators continued to pursue in private the controversial policies he was renouncing in public), but all basically hoping that the problem—this nightmare of an aroused, mysteriously well-organized citizenry—would just go away. Burson-Marsteller knew better. Its "compendium" had even picked up on demonstrations being planned for April against the World Bank and the IMF during meetings in Washington, D.C. This was before anything about those demonstrations had appeared in what movement activists insist on calling the corporate press.

I say "movement activists" because nobody has yet figured out what to call them. Sympathetic observers refer to them as "the Seattle coalition," but this title reflects little of the movement's international scope. In the United States, the movement is dramatically—even, one could say, deliberately—lacking in national leaders. It is largely coordinated online. I picked Juliette Beck almost at random as a bright thread to follow through this roiling fabric of rising, mostly youthful American resistance to corporate-led globalization.

Global free trade promotes global economic growth. It creates jobs, makes companies more competitive, and lowers prices for consumers. It also provides poor countries, through infusions of foreign capital and technology, with the chance to develop economically and, by spreading prosperity, creates the conditions in which democracy and respect for human rights may flourish.

This is the animating vision of the Clinton administration, and it is a view widely shared by political leaders, economic decision makers, and opinion makers throughout the West. It is also accepted, at least in its outlines, by many important figures in business and government in Third World countries, where it is known as "the Washington consensus."

Critics of this consensus dispute most, if not all, of its claims. Growth, they argue, can be wasteful, destructive, unjust. The jobs created by globalization are often less sustaining and secure than the livelihoods abolished by it. Weak economies abruptly integrated into the global system do not become stronger or develop a sustainable base; they just become more dependent, more vulnerable to the ructions of ultravolatile, deregulated international capital. In many countries, the benefits of economic growth are so unequally distributed that they intensify social and political tensions, leading to increased repression rather than to greater democracy. To the hoary trope that a rising tide lifts all boats, critics of corporate-led globalization retort that in this case it lifts only yachts.

Nearly everyone, though, on both sides of the globalization debate, accepts that the process creates winners and losers. And it is globalization's losers and potential losers—and all those with doubts about the wisdom of unchecked, unequal growth—who propel the backlash that found such vivid expression in Seattle. One odd aspect of that backlash is the ideological opposites it contains. American right-wing isolationists of the Patrick Buchanan variety are as hostile to the international bodies that promote economic globalization as they are to the United Nations. In Britain, unreconstructed Tories continue to loathe and oppose the European Union, a prime mover of globalization. Meanwhile, young British anarchists also hate the EU, and the bulk of the Seattle coalition is being drawn from the American liberal and radical left.

The booming popularity of the movement on college campuses is another odd aspect of its makeup, since American college graduates are unlikely to find themselves, even in the short term, on the losing side of the great globalization ledger. And yet students, whether fired up by their coursework, like Beck, or simply sensing that this is where the subcultural action is now, have been turning out in surprising numbers for mass "teach-ins" on the WTO, the IMF, and the World Bank—even eagerly swallowing solid doses of the economic history and international financial arcana that come unavoidably with these topics.

Kevin Danaher, a cofounder of Global Exchange, sees nothing incongruous about young people getting excited about the dismal science. "Economics and politics have been kept falsely separate, traditionally," he says. "We're just trying to drag capital-investment decision-making out into the public realm. That's the terrain of struggle now. The antiapartheid divestment campaign set the precedent."

Danaher, who in a doctoral dissertation examined the political economy of U.S. policy toward South Africa, was one of the leaders of the American divestment campaign. Since that campaign's contribution to ending apartheid and bringing democracy to South Africa can scarcely be overstated, his bullishness about the prospects for democratizing the rules of the new global economy may be understandable. He talks, somewhat messianically, about replacing the "money cycle" with the "life cycle," but then puts his ideas to the test by running a bustling nonprofit business. Global Exchange, besides its human-rights research and activism—it has mounted corporate-accountability campaigns targeting Nike, the Gap, and, starting this month, Starbucks for their international labor practices—operates two stores in the Bay Area, plus an online store, selling crafts and coffee and other goods bought directly, on demonstrably fair terms, from small producers in poor countries; it also offers "reality tours" of such countries as Cuba, Haiti, and Iran to high-disposable-income travelers not yet ready for cruise ships.

Addressing young audiences, Danaher—who is forty-nine, has a shaved head and a white goatee, and retains enough of the speech patterns of a working-class New Jersey youth to carry off the most populist harangue—makes a cross-generational pitch. He acknowledges the difficulty of understanding what it is that an institution like the World Bank even does, but then urges people to educate themselves and, in recent speeches, to come to Washington in April. "It's going to be Woodstock times ten," he told one college class, pulling out the stops. "I was at Woodstock, I was at Seattle, and Seattle changed *my* butt."

The World Bank lends money to the governments of poor countries. It was founded, along with the International Monetary Fund, after the Second World War to help finance the reconstruction of Europe. When the Marshall Plan usurped its original purpose, the bank had to reinvent itself, shifting its focus to

Asia, Africa, and Latin America, where the elimination of poverty became its declared mission. This was the first in a long series of institutional costume changes. Today, the bank, which is headquartered in Washington, D.C., has more than ten thousand employees, 180 member states, and offices in sixty-seven of those countries, and lends nearly $30 billion a year. It ventures into fields far beyond its original mandate, including conflict resolution—demobilizing troops in Uganda, clearing land mines in Bosnia. The IMF, whose founding purpose was to make short-term loans to stabilize currencies, has similarly had to shape-shift with the times. Also headquartered in Washington, it now makes long-term loans as well and tries to manage the economies of many of its poorer member states.

Both institutions have always been dominated by the world's rich countries, particularly the United States. During the Cold War, this meant that loans were often granted on a crudely political basis. Indeed, the World Bank's first loan—$250 million to France in 1947—was withheld until the French government purged its Cabinet of Communists. In the Third World, friendly dictators were propped up by loans. Robert McNamara, after presiding over the Vietnam War, became president of the World Bank in 1968, and he expanded its operations aggressively, pushing poor countries to transform their economies by promoting industrialized agriculture and export production. There were fundamental problems with this development model. By the time McNamara retired, in 1981, his legacy consisted largely of failed megaprojects, populations no longer able to feed themselves, devastated forests and watersheds, and a sea of hopeless debt.

Bank officials have consistently vowed to improve this record, to start funding projects that benefit not only big business and Third World elites but also the world's poor. Accordingly, projects with nongovernmental organizations and other "civil society" groups, along with efforts to promote access to health care and education, have increased. But World Bank contracts are worth millions, and multinational corporations have remained major beneficiaries. In 1995, Lawrence Summers, then an undersecretary at the Treasury Department—he is now its secretary—told Congress that for each dollar the American government contributed to the World Bank, American corporations received $1.35 in procurement contracts. One of the bank's major proposals at the moment is for the development of oilfields in Chad, in central Africa, and the construction of an oil pipeline running more than six hundred miles to the coast at Cameroon. The environmental impact of this pipeline is predicted by many to be dire, the benefits to the people in the area minimal. The big winners will, in all likelihood, be the bank's major partners in the project—Exxon Mobil and Chevron.

More onerous than ill-advised projects, however, for the people of the global south has been the crushing accumulation of debt by their governments. This debt now totals more than $2 trillion, and servicing it—simply paying the interest—has become the single largest budget item for scores of poor countries. About twenty years ago, the World Bank and the IMF began attaching stricter conditions to the loans they made to debtor countries to help them avoid outright default. More than ninety countries have now been subjected to IMF-imposed austerity schemes, also known as structural-adjustment programs. Typically, these force a nation to cut spending in health, education, and welfare programs; reduce or eliminate food, energy, and transport subsidies; devalue its local currency; raise interest rates to attract foreign capital; privatize state property; and lower barriers to foreign ownership of local industries, land, and assets.

This is where the World Trade Organization comes in—or, rather, where its agenda dovetails with the work of the bank and the IMF. All three institutions have always sought to increase world trade. (The WTO is the successor to the General Agreement on Tariffs and Trade, which began in 1947 and was folded into the WTO in 1995.) But the WTO is the spearhead of the present surge toward economic globalization. It is a huge bureaucracy that makes binding rules intended to remove obstacles to the expansion of commercial activity among the 135 countries that constitute its membership. This means, in practice, an incremental transfer of power from local and national governments (the bodies likely to erect such obstacles) to the WTO, which acts as a trade court, hearing, behind closed doors, disputes among members accusing one another of creating barriers to trade. These "barriers" may be health, safety, or environmental laws, and a WTO ruling takes precedence over all other international agreements. A country found to be impeding trade must change the offending law or suffer harsh sanctions. The effect is to deregulate international commerce, freeing the largest corporations—which, measured as economic entities, already dwarf most of the world's countries—to enter any market, extract any resource, without constraint by citizenries. Speaking anonymously, a former WTO official recently told the *Financial Times,* "This is the place where governments collude in private against their domestic pressure groups."

There is, in other words, little mystery about why the WTO and its partners in free-trade promotion, the World Bank and the IMF, have become the protest targets of choice for environmentalists, labor unions, economic nationalists, small farmers and small-business people, and their allies. Trade rules among countries are obviously needed. The question is whom those rules will benefit, whose rights they will protect.

The fifty thousand people who took to the streets of Seattle chanting "No new round—turn around!" had clearly decided that the WTO was not on their side when it came to steering the direction of global trade. But even that might be too broad a statement—for the coalition that gathered there was wildly diverse, its collective critique nothing if not eclectic. Many of its members would probably not agree, for instance, that trade rules are "obviously" needed. That's my view, but the movement against corporate-led globalization contains many people who accept fewer rules of the capitalist game than I do.

The Direct Action Network (DAN) probably belongs in the deeply anticapitalist category. But the group is less than a year old and extremely loosely structured, so its ideology isn't easy to get a fix on. What does seem certain is that the shutdown (or "meltdown," as Burson-Marsteller has it) of the Seattle ministerial would never have happened without the emergence and furious efforts of DAN.

Juliette Beck was present at DAN's creation. Late last spring, a young organizer named David Solnit, who was well known in the movement for his dedication and ingenuity, and for his giant homemade puppets—Solnit's allegorical figures have appeared in demonstrations from coast to coast—approached Beck with a plan to shut down the Seattle meeting. Dozens of groups, including the AFL-CIO and Global Trade Watch, a leading branch of Nader's Public Citizen, were already planning for Seattle. But no one was talking shutdown. Solnit thought it could be done, and he figured that Global Exchange could help. Beck and Kevin Danaher called in the Rainforest Action Network and a Berkeley-based group called the Ruckus Society, which specializes in nonviolent guerrilla action, and DAN was hatched.

Solnit was the dynamo but not the leader. "DAN is lots of lieutenants, no generals," Danaher says. The word went out, largely over the Internet, about DAN's plans, and dozens of groups and countless individuals expressed interest. The DAN coalition developed along what is known as the "affinity-group model." Affinity groups are small, semi-independent units, pledged to coalition goals, tactics, and principles—including, in DAN's case, nonviolent action—but free to make their own plans. Members look out for one another during protests, and some have designated roles: medic, legal support (avoids arrest), "spoke" (confers with other affinity groups through affinity "clusters"), "action elf" (looks after food, water, and people's spirits). Thousands signed up for training and for "camps" organized by the Ruckus Society, where they could learn not only the techniques of classic civil disobedience but specialized skills like urban rappelling (for hanging banners on buildings), forming human blockades, and how to "lock down" in groups (arms linked through specially constructed plastic tubes). Solnit coordinated a road show that toured the West in the months before the WTO ministerial, presenting music and speakers and street theater, urging people to get involved and come to Seattle.

They came, of course, and the combination of strict civil-disobedience discipline (the only way that the lines around the hotels and meeting places and across key intersections could have held, preventing WTO delegates from gathering) and polymorphous protest (dancers on vans, hundreds of children dressed as sea turtles and monarch butterflies, Korean priests in white robes playing flutes and drums to protest genetically modified food) could never have been centrally planned.

The affinity-group model proved extremely effective in dealing with police actions. Downtown Seattle had been divided by a DAN "spokescouncil" into thirteen sectors, with an affinity cluster responsible for each sector. There were also flying squads—mobile affinity groups that could quickly take the place of groups that had been arrested or beaten or gassed from the positions they were trying to hold. The structure was flexible, and tactically powerful, and the police, trying to clear the streets, resorted to increasingly brutal methods, firing concussion grenades, mashing pepper spray into the eyes of protesters, shooting rubber bullets into bodies at short range. By the afternoon of November 30 (the first day of the meeting), the police had run low on ammunition, and that evening the mayor of Seattle called out the National Guard.

There were hundreds of arrests. Beck, who was teargassed on a line blocking the entrance to the convention center, had credentials, through Global Exchange, to enter the theater where the WTO was supposed to be having its opening session. She went inside, where she found a few delegates milling and an open microphone. She and Danaher and Medea Benjamin—another cofounder of Global Exchange—took the stage, uninvited, and suggested that delegates join them in a discussion. The interlopers were hustled off the stage. Beck elected not to go quietly. Marshals put her in a pain hold—her arm twisted behind her back—and dragged her through the theater. A news camera recorded the event. "Then CNN kept showing it, over and over, them carrying me off, whenever they talked about the arrests," she says. "My claim to fame. Except I wasn't arrested! They just threw me out."

Ironically, the only protesters not following the nonviolence guidelines—a hundred or so "black bloc" anarchists, who started smashing shop windows—were hardly bothered by the police. The black-bloc crews, whose graffiti and occasional "communiqués" run to nihilist slogans ("Civilization Is Collapsing—Let's Give It a Push!"), were masked, well organized, young and fleet of foot, and armed with crowbars and acid-filled eggs. The police in their heavy riot gear could not have caught them if they'd tried. The targeted shops belonged to big corporations: Nike, the Gap, Fidelity Investments, Starbucks, Levi's, Planet Hollywood. Still, other protesters chanted "Shame! Shame!" Some even tried to stop the attacks. There were scuffles, and suggestions that the black blocs contained police agents provocateurs—hence the masks. Medea Benjamin, who had helped produce the original exposé of Nike's sweatshops in Asia, found herself in the absurd position of siding with protesters who were defending a Niketown. And her fear (shared by many) that a few broken windows might snatch away the headlines in the national press proved justified.

The political spectrum represented in the protests was improbably wide, ranging from, on the right, James Hoffa's Teamsters and the AFL-CIO (who fielded tens of thousands of members for a march) to, on the left, a dozen or more anarchist factions (the black blocs were a rowdy minority within a generally less aggressive minority), including the ancient Industrial Workers of the World. All these groups had found, if not a common cause, at least a common foe. Some unlikely alliances were cemented. The United Steelworkers union and Earth First!, for example, had a common enemy in the Maxxam Corporation, which logs old-growth forests *and* owns steel mills, and the two groups are currently working together to end a bitter lockout at a Kaiser Aluminum plant in Tacoma.

Inside the besieged WTO ministerial, there was a rebellion among countries from the global south, which raised the possibility of another, truly formidable alliance with some of the forces out in the streets. The leaders of the poorer countries, though often depicted as pawns of the major powers, content to offer their countries' workers to the world market at the lowest possible wages—and to pollute their air and water and strip-mine their natural resources, in exchange for their own commissions on the innumerable deals that come with corporate globalization—in reality have to answer, in many cases, to complex constituencies at home, many of whom are alarmed about their own economic recolonization. In Seattle, delegations from Africa, Asia, the Caribbean, and Latin America—rattled by the total disruption of the ministerial's schedule and furious about being excluded from key meetings held privately by the rich countries—issued statements announcing their refusal to sign "agreements" produced at such meetings. In the end, no agreements were signed, no new round launched, and the ministerial finished in disarray. This insurgency was often depicted in the American press as a refusal by the representatives of the poor countries to accept higher labor and environmental standards being imposed on them by the West, but that was not the gist of the revolt, which ran deeper and echoed the fundamental questions being asked outside in the streets about the mandate of the WTO.

"Coalition-building is hard," Juliette Beck said. "There's no doubt about it. But it's what we do." We were sitting in a deserted café in some sort of Latino community center one Sunday night in Berkeley, sipping beers. "At Global Exchange, we try to think of campaigns that will appeal to the average Joe on the street. We're really not interested in just organizing other leftists. Big corporations are a great target, because they do things that hurt virtually everybody. My dad, who's very right-wing, but libertarian, hates corporations. The HMOs have practically ruined his medical practice, mainly because he insists on spending as much time with his patients as he thinks they need. After Seattle, he read a column by the economist Robert Kuttner, and suddenly, he said, he got what we're trying to do. Kuttner apparently explained that corporations just naturally grab all the power they can, and when they've grabbed too much there has to be a backlash. That's what led, a hundred years ago, to trust-busting and federal regulation after the robber barons did their thing, and that's what's causing this movement now. It was nice to hear my dad say that."

Across the street was a café/bookshop/community center, this one run by an anarchist collective (we were, remember, in Berkeley) called Long Haul Infoshop, which distributes a radical journal called *Slingshot.* In a special WTO edition, *Slingshot* had derided Global Exchange and "other despicable examples of the corporate left"; another column slammed Medea Benjamin for her defense of Nike. I asked Beck about the attacks from the left. She sighed. "Yeah, there's been a lot of fallout. A lot of people believe property destruction isn't violence. But that wasn't really the issue in Seattle. The issue was what message, what images, we were sending out to the world. There's always going to be disagreement. When it comes to these institutions—the WTO, the IMF, the World Bank—we have reformists and abolitionists. If we're talking about the World Bank, I, for instance, am an abolitionist."

I asked Beck if she considered herself an anarchist.

She shrugged, as if the question were obtuse.

DAN seemed, at a glance, to be an anarchist organization, or at least organized on anarchist principles, I said.

"Sure," Beck said, still looking nonplussed. Finally, she said, "Well, I definitely respect anarchist ways of organizing. I guess I'm still learning what it means to be an anarchist. But the real question is: Can this anarchist model that's working so well now for organizing protests be applied on an international scale to create the democratic decision-making structures that we need to eliminate poverty?"

I took this opportunity to float a theory, somewhat grander and iffier than Kuttner's, about the historical forces that cause anarchism to flourish. Anarchism, I said, first arose in Europe as a response to the disruptions of peasant and artisanal life caused by industrialization and the rapid concentration of power among new business élites. After a good long fight, anarchism basically lost out to socialism as an organizing vision among workers—and lost again, after a heady late run, in Republican Spain, to Communism (which then lost to fascism). But anarchism was obviously enjoying some kind of small-time comeback, and, if today's Information Revolution was even half as significant as both its critics and its cheerleaders like to claim—the most important economic development since the Industrial Revolution, and so on—then perhaps the time was ripening, socialism having been disgraced as an alternative to capitalism, for another great wave of anarchist protest against this latest, alarmingly swift amassing of power in the hands of a few hundred billionaires. Did Beck know that the term *direct action* was used by anarcho-syndicalists in France at the turn of the last century?

She did. She also knew, it seemed, that anarchism has become wildly popular among Latin American students who are fed up with what they call *neoliberalismo* (their term for corporate-led globalization) but disenchanted, also, with the traditional left. And she knew that the students who went on strike and took over the National University in Mexico City for nine months recently were mostly anarchists. But did I know (I didn't) that it had been a structural-adjustment edict from the World Bank that led the Mexican government to raise student fees, which sparked the strike and the takeover?

Beck drained her beer. DAN, whatever its historical analogues, had been thriving since its triumph in Seattle, she said. The network was now directing most of its considerable energies toward the April action in Washington, D.C., which people were calling "A16," for April 16, the day the IMF planned to meet. She was going to Washington herself in a couple of days and then joining a road show, which would start making its way up the East Coast, beating the drums for the big event.

"I Am Funkier Than You," the bumper sticker said, and it was almost certainly true. But the Mango Affinity Group, as the road-show crew had taken to calling themselves, had scored this big, extremely grubby van free from a woman in Virginia simply by asking for a vehicle on the A16 e-mail list serve, so they were not complaining. Liz Guy, an efficient DAN stalwart usually known as Sprout, had pulled together both the crew—eight or nine activists, aged nineteen to thirty-two, including Juliette Beck—and a tight, three-week, show-a-day itinerary that ran from Florida to Montreal before looping back to Washington. I found them in St. Petersburg, bivouacked under a shade tree on the campus of Eckerd College, working on a song.

Beck introduced me. They were a sweet-voiced, ragamuffin group, drawn from Connecticut, Atlanta, Seattle (Sprout), and the mountains of British Columbia. This afternoon was going to be their first performance together, and, judging from the situation as showtime approached and they began lugging their gear into a low-roofed, brutally air-conditioned hall, somebody had blown the publicity. There was virtually no one around except their hosts—two young DAN guys, Peter and Josh, who were hopefully laying out anarchist and vegan pamphlets and books on a table. Peter and Josh, embarrassed, said they had just returned from a Ruckus Society camp. Evidently, they had left arrangements in the wrong hands. "Let's do a skate-by, see where people are," one of them said, and both jumped on skateboards and shot off.

"Woodstock times ten," Kevin Danaher had said. Pure hooey, I now thought. In truth, A16 did not have going for it many of the things that had converged so resoundingly in Seattle. The planning for the protest was far more rushed. The WTO's Seattle ministerial had been, moreover, a momentous gathering, meant to kick off a so-called Millennial Round, whereas the World Bank/IMF spring meetings were strictly routine and scheduled to be brief. Big labor, finally, had no special interest in the World Bank and the IMF, and the AFL-CIO, while endorsing the A16 protest, had decided to concentrate its energies this political season on preventing the permanent normalization of U.S. trade relations with China. A demonstration by union members to press these issues was scheduled to take place in Washington on April 12. And it wasn't the only event threatening to disperse attention from A16. There was a big protest planned for April 9, also in Washington, organized by a movement called Jubilee 2000, to demand debt cancellation for the poorest countries.

The hope, of course, was that all these protests would produce some sort of antiglobalization synergy that might just culminate, on A16, in the type of massive turnout that would certainly be needed to have any chance of shutting down the World Bank and the IMF meetings. On the Internet, as always, anything looked possible. Caravans were being organized all over the country, reconnaissance was being conducted on "targets" in Washington, anticapitalist revolutionary blocs were breaking away from the DAN-centered action with furious objections to mealymouthed talk of "fair trade" and alleged "collaboration with the enemy at large"—to, that is, meetings being held by organizers with the D.C. police to try to prevent bloodshed. (In fact, the D.C. police had gone to Seattle to observe the demonstrations and had spent a million dollars on new riot gear for A16.) Beck had told me, back in San Francisco, "I get so tired of the Internet and e-mail. We couldn't do this work without it, but, really, it's not organizing. There's nothing like face to face."

Now in Florida, Beck, perhaps getting desperate for some F2F, approached two young women who had wandered into the frigid hall, possibly just to get out of the afternoon heat, and started regaling them with a spiel about how the World Bank and the IMF are "partners in crime." The young women, who wore tank tops and looked as if they belonged on a beach somewhere, nodded politely but said nothing. In the background, Damon, a tall, dark-skinned, curly haired musician from British Columbia, strummed a guitar, and the rest of the Mango Affinity Group busied themselves making posters denouncing exploitation.

Blessedly, between the skate-by and Damon's guitar, people began to trickle into the hall. Soon there was an audience of thirty or so, and the show began. Damon disappeared inside a towering, black-suited puppet with a huge papier-mâché head, sloping skull, and cigar stuck between his lips, Beck slapped a "World Bank/IMF" sign on his chest, and he began to roar, "You are all under my power!" The crowd laughed, and he roared, "It's not funny, it's true!" They laughed harder. A political skit followed, with a series of fresh-faced young women getting thrashed by an IMF henchman for demanding health and safety standards, then put to work in a Gap sweatshop. "Right to Organize" also got pounded. Afterward, Beck led a teach-in called Globalization 101, with pop quizzes on the meaning of various trade and finance acronyms and Hershey's Kisses tossed to those who got the answers right. One middle-aged trio—Eckerd faculty, from the look of them—seemed well versed on the topic. Then the Mango members introduced themselves individually—Leigh, from an "intentional community" in Atlanta, and Ricardo, from a Canadian "solar-powered cooperative" where people grew much of their own food. Sprout took the opportunity to encourage people to form affinity groups, explaining what they were and how they worked.

I was struck by Sprout's poise. Talking to dozens of strangers, she somehow made her presentation seem like an intimate conversation, with pauses, eye contact, murmurs back and forth, little encouraging interjections ("Awesome!" "Cool!") when she felt she'd been understood. Twenty-five, physically small, and dressed with utter simplicity—loose shirt, cargo pants, no shoes—she achieved, with no theatricality, an effect of tremendous presence. It occurred to me that Sprout, with her neighborly voice and unerring choice of words, could easily be very successful in a completely different arena. On another sort of road show, for instance—the sort that dot-com start-ups mount, touring and performing for investors and analysts, before taking their companies public. The same was true for Beck. And both women came from cities (Seattle, San Francisco) that were crawling with rich dot-commers more or less their age. What was it that made them choose this raggedy, low-status activist's path instead? While the rest of the country obsessed over its stock portfolio, these brainy young people were working killer hours for little, if any, pay—quixotically trying, as they sometimes put it, to globalize the world from below.

Next on the program was a rousing folk song, with Damon on guitar and Sage, his regular bandmate from B.C., on drums. Their vocal harmonies sounded fairly polished. Then Sprout produced a viola, slipping without fanfare into the tune, and began improvising fiddle breaks of steadily increasing warmth and precision. I caught Beck's eye. Who *was* this woman? Beck could not stop grinning. The Mango group then ruined the soaring mood, as far as I was concerned, by leading the crowd in some mortifyingly corny chants—"Ain't no power like the power of the people, cuz the power of the people don't stop!"

Beck asked for a show of hands. How many people thought they might go to Washington for A16? Fifteen or twenty hands shot up, including those of the two women in tank tops. I was amazed that they had even stayed for the show. A signup sheet was circulated.

Next came nonviolence training, for which ten or twelve people stuck around. Leigh and Sprout led the training, which lasted into the evening and included a lot of "role-playing"—people pretending to be protesters, police, IMF. officials, workers trying to get to work. There were drills in quick decision making among affinity groups: shall we stay locked down or move when threatened with arrest and felony charges? Group dynamics were dissected after each scene. Sprout demonstrated unthreatening body language. Hand signals for swift, clear communication were suggested. Peter and Josh, the two local DAN guys, joined in the training, and it was soon obvious that they had a lot of experience. Peter, who was wiry, bushy-bearded, and soft spoken, firmly refused to be bullied by some of the bigger, more aggressive men in the group. It became clear that effective nonviolent protest needed a cool head, and that bluster wasn't helpful. Toward the end of the evening, Leigh presented a list of things to bring to an action. Most were commonsense items like food, water, and herbal remedies for tear gas. The rationale for others was less self-evident. Maxi pads?

Leigh and Sprout glanced at one another. "If the cops start using chemical warfare, some women start bleeding very heavily," Leigh said. There was a brief, shocked silence. "They're good as bandages, too," she added.

What about gas masks?

"They can become targets," Josh said. "In Seattle, the cops tried to tear them off, and if they couldn't reach them they fired rubber bullets, or wooden bullets, or these wooden dowel rods they had, at the masks. Some people got a lot of glass in their faces. Masks can be dangerous."

The trainees stared.

"One thing that's good to have is big toenail clippers," Peter said cheerfully. "Put 'em in your pocket, and if you're arrested, and just left in a cell or a paddy wagon, somebody can fish them out of your pocket and cut off your cuffs with 'em. They use cheap plastic cuffs when they arrest a lot of people, and if they leave you sitting for ten or fifteen hours it's a lot more comfortable if your hands aren't tied behind you."

Ten or fifteen hours?

"It happens. It happened to me in Seattle."

It had happened to Sprout, too—seventeen hours in an unheated cell alone, doing jumping jacks to try to stay warm.

The tone of the gathering was entirely sober now. Somebody asked about carrying ID during an action.

"It depends whether you want to practice jail solidarity," Beck said. "That's something you need to decide with your affinity group."

None of the trainees knew what jail solidarity was.

"Noncooperation with the system," they were told. It might be widely used in Washington—to clog the jails and courts and try to force mass dismissals of charges.

But the details of jail solidarity could wait for another session, Beck said. It was late. People were tired. DAN would be offering more nonviolence training locally in the weeks ahead, and everybody going to Washington for A16 should get as much training as possible.

We stayed that night with Peter and Josh. They lived in a mobile home near a strip mall in Clearwater. People slept on couches and chairs and on the floor, in the van, on a back porch, and on a tiny plywood dock on a fetid canal behind the trailer. I tried to sleep on the dock, but mosquitoes kept me awake. There was a full moon and low, cotton-puff clouds streaming across it at an unusual speed. The clouds were glowing a sort of radioactive mauve from all the strip-mall lights.

At some point, the mosquitoes woke Beck, who was also on the dock. Out of the darkness, a restless voice: "We need a name. For the movement as a whole. Anti-Corporate Globalization isn't good enough. What do you think of Global Citizen Movement?"

I thought it needed work.

Beck started talking about plans she had for disrupting the Democratic Party's national convention this summer in Los Angeles. She mentioned a Millennium Youth March.

"You're thinking big."

"That's my job."

I wanted to know what would happen in Washington on A16.

"Me, too," she said, and I thought I heard her sigh. "For now, crowd-building is the main thing. That's why I'm really glad I'm on this road show. I kind of feel like I should be in D.C., walking the site, doing messaging, doing logistics, but I'm going to stay with this as long as I can."

"Messaging" meant press releases, banners, slogans—even sound bites for protesters to give to reporters, should the opportunity arise. I had begun to think that, for the American public, effective messaging about the IMF and the World Bank was a hopeless task. In Nigeria and Venezuela, yes, everybody knew and had strong opinions about structural adjustment and IMF debt. That was never going to be true in this country. People might turn out in large numbers, for many different reasons, on A16, but it would basically be Americans expressing solidarity with people in poor countries who are on the receiving end of bad policies. That wasn't a formula for real political leverage. The plight of, say, the Ittu

Oromo would never move more than a few faraway hearts. In the great shakeout of economic globalization, most Americans probably believe, not unreasonably, that they will be among the revolution's winners. As for the big goal—democratizing international decision making in order to eliminate poverty—it seemed to me impossibly abstract.

I was loath to tell Beck that. While she seemed quite dauntless, her identification with her work seemed, at the same time, perilously deep. She once told me that she thought it was significant that she had been born in 1973, the same year that Richard Nixon allowed the dollar to float—"and the IMF should have been allowed to die!" On another occasion, she'd said, "I really feel lucky to be doing this work. When I started studying the World Bank in college, I couldn't believe how evil it was, even while it's supposedly all about fighting poverty. I thought, you know, it would really be an honor to dedicate my life to fighting this evil institution. And that's all we're asking people to do: help us drag these institutions out into the sunlight of public scrutiny, where they belong. They'll shrivel up like Dracula!"

While I tried to doze, Beck reminded me that the World Bank and IMF had pressured Haiti to freeze its minimum wage, that NAFTA was a failure from beginning to end—details available if I needed them—and that the U.S. Supreme Court was hearing a crucial case, which I should watch closely when I got back to New York. It seemed that the federal government was trying to stop the Commonwealth of Massachusetts from boycotting companies that did business in Burma, which uses forced labor.

At dawn, finally agreeing that sleep was hopeless, Beck and I took a canoe that was tied to the dock and paddled off down the stinking canal, gliding past the battered, moldy backdoors of mobile homes. It was a Sunday morning. Everybody in the trailers seemed to be asleep—probably dreaming about their stock portfolios. The mangroves on the banks slowly closed over our heads. We tried to push through. There seemed to be wider, brighter water ahead. Beck was happy to keep going, but I was in the bow, catching spider webs with my face. In the end, we turned back.

The Mango Affinity Group held a morning meeting on the little dock. While trying to decide who would be responsible for grocery shopping, they started goofing on the hand signals developed by DAN for anarchist consensus decision making, cracking each other up. Beck was supposed to be guiding the discussion—facilitating, they called it—but she had the giggles, too. Group morale seemed high.

Bushy-bearded Peter came out of the trailer, yawning and stretching. He started filling a plastic bag with grapefruit from a low, gnarled dwarf of a tree. The fruit looked awful, with upper halves all blackened as if by grime falling from the sky, but Peter assured me they were fine. I cut one open. It was the best grapefruit I had ever tasted.

Inside the trailer, there was a small room devoted to Josh and Peter's book and periodical distribution business. They had a dense, nondoctrinaire selection, with sections on Organizing, Anarchism/Social Theory, Animal Liberation, Punk, Direct Action, Media, Globalization, Feminism/Sexuality, and Youth Oppression/Radical Education. They had ten Noam Chomsky titles, lots of Emma Goldman, a guide to "understanding and attacking mainstream media," arguments against compulsory schooling, even a collection of Digger tracts (seventeenth-century free-love proto-anarchists). Josh and Peter's catalog included an introduction that traced their own political development from 1996, when "we were straightedge as fuck," to more recent days, when "our distro grew greener and more anarchistic."

Elsewhere in the trailer, somebody had put on a Delta blues tape. Out in the living room, I found Josh sprawled on a couch. He was a quiet guy, in his early twenties, with sparse blond muttonchops and small blue eyes. He was wearing a baseball cap and talking to a glum-looking young woman with an elaborately pierced nose. I started asking Josh about himself. He wasn't a student, he said pleasantly. He had realized he could learn more outside school. He didn't have a job. "But I need to get one, just to make money. The problem is, I'm really too busy to work."

Through a window, I could see the Mango Affinity Group loading up the van. Beck and Sprout, the lanky, tireless trade wonk and the barefoot fiddler, had their heads bent together over a map. Today, the road show went to Gainesville. Tomorrow, Valdosta, Georgia.

The Discarded Factory

Degraded Production in the Age of the Superbrand

NAOMI KLEIN

Our strategic plan in North America is to focus intensely on brand management, marketing, and product design as a means to meet the casual clothing wants and needs of consumers. Shifting a significant portion of our manufacturing from the U.S. and Canadian markets to contractors throughout the world will give the company greater flexibility to allocate resources and capital to its brands. These steps are crucial if we are to remain competitive.
—John Ermatinger, president of Levi Strauss Americas division, explains the company's decision to shut down twenty-two plants and lay off thirteen thousand North American workers between November 1997 and February 1999.

Many brand-name multinationals, as we have seen, are in the process of transcending the need to identify with their earthbound products. They dream instead about their brands' deep inner meanings—the way they capture the spirit of individuality, athleticism, wilderness, or community. In this context of strut over stuff, marketing departments charged with the managing of brand identities have begun to see their work as something that occurs not in conjunction with factory production but in direct competition with it. "Products are made in the factory," says Walter Landor, president of the Landor branding agency, "but brands are made in the mind."[1] Peter Schweitzer, president of the advertising giant J. Walter Thompson, reiterates the same thought: "The difference between products and brands is fundamental. A product is something that is made in a factory; a brand is something that is bought by a customer."[2] Savvy ad agencies have all moved away from the idea that they are flogging a product made by someone else, and have come to think of themselves instead as brand factories, hammering out what is of true value: the idea, the lifestyle, the attitude. Brand builders are the new primary producers in our so-called knowledge economy.

This novel idea has done more than bring us cutting-edge ad campaigns, ecclesiastic superstores, and utopian corporate campuses. It is changing the very face of global employment. After establishing the "soul" of their corporations, the superbrand companies have gone on to rid themselves of their cumbersome bodies, and there is nothing that seems more cumbersome, more loathsomely corporeal, than the factories that produce their products. The reason for this shift is simple: building a superbrand is an extraordinarily costly project, needing

 Naomi Klein is a journalist whose work has appeared in the *Toronto Globe and Mail* and the *Village Voice*.

constant managing, tending, and replenishing. Most of all, superbrands need lots of space on which to stamp their logos. For a business to be cost effective, however, there is a finite amount of money it can spend on all of its expenses—materials, manufacturing, overhead, and branding—before retail prices on its products shoot up too high. After the multimillion-dollar sponsorships have been signed and the cool hunters and marketing mavens have received their checks, there may not be all that much money left over. So it becomes, as always, a matter of priorities; but those priorities are changing. As Hector Liang, former chairman of United Biscuits, has explained: "Machines wear out. Cars rust. People die. But what lives on are the brands."[3]

According to this logic, corporations should not expend their finite resources on factories that will demand physical upkeep, on machines that will corrode, or on employees who will certainly age and die. Instead, they should concentrate those resources in the virtual brick and mortar used to build their brands; that is, on sponsorships, packaging, expansion, and advertising. They should also spend them on synergies, on buying up distribution and retail channels to get their brands to the people.

This slow but decisive shift in corporate priorities has left yesterday's non-virtual producers—the factory workers and craftspeople—in a precarious position. The lavish spending in the 1990s on marketing, mergers, and brand extensions has been matched by a never before seen resistance to investing in production facilities and labor. Companies that were traditionally satisfied with a 100 percent markup between the cost of factory production and the retail price have been scouring the globe for factories that can make their products so inexpensively that the markup is closer to 400 percent.[4] And as a 1997 UN report notes, even in countries where wages were already low, labor costs are getting a shrinking slice of corporate budgets. "In four developing countries out of five, the share of wages in manufacturing value-added today is considerably below what it was in the 1970s and early 1980s."[5] The timing of these trends reflects not only branding's status as the perceived economic cure-all but also a corresponding devaluation of the production process and of producers in general. Branding, in other words has been hogging all the "value-added."

When the actual manufacturing process is so devalued, it stands to reason that the people doing the work of production are likely to be treated like detritus—the stuff left behind. The idea has a certain symmetry: ever since mass production created the need for branding in the first place, its role has slowly been expanding in importance until, more than a century and a half after the Industrial Revolution, it occurred to these companies that maybe branding could replace production entirely. As tennis pro Andre Agassi said in a 1992 Canon camera commercial, "Image is everything."

Agassi may have been pitching for Canon at the time, but he is first and foremost a member of Team Nike, the company that pioneered the business philosophy of no-limits spending on branding, coupled with a near-total divestment of the contract workers that make its shoes in tucked-away factories. As Phil Knight has said, "There is no value in making things any more. The value is added by careful research, by innovation and by marketing."[6] For Phil Knight, production is not the building block of his branded empirc, but is instead a tedious, marginal chore.

Which is why many companies now bypass production completely. Instead of making the products themselves, in their own factories, they "source" them, much as corporations in the natural resource industries source uranium, copper, or logs. They close existing factories, shifting to contracted-out, mostly offshore manufacturing. And as the old jobs fly offshore, something else is flying away with them: the old-fashioned idea that a manufacturer is responsible for its own workforce. Disney spokesman Ken Green gave an indication of the depth of this shift when he became publicly frustrated that his company was being taken to task for the desperate conditions in a Haitian factory that produces Disney clothes. "We don't employ anyone in Haiti," he said, referring to the fact that the factory is owned by a contractor. "With the newsprint you use, do you have any idea of the labor conditions involved to produce it?" Green demanded of Cathy Majtenyi of the *Catholic Register.*[7]

From El Paso to Beijing, San Francisco to Jakarta, Munich to Tijuana, the global brands are sloughing the responsibility of production on to their contractor: they just tell them to make the damn thing, and make it cheap, so there's lots of money left over for branding. Make it really cheap.

Exporting the Nike Model

Nike, which began as an import/export scheme of made-in-Japan running shoes and does not own any of its factories, has become a prototype for the product-free brand. Inspired by the swoosh's staggering success, many more traditionally run companies ("vertically integrated," as the phrase goes) are busy imitating Nikc's model, not only copying the company's marketing production structure. In the mid-nineties, for instance, the Vans running shoe company pulled up stakes in the old-fashioned realm of manufacturing and converted to the Nike way. In a prospectus for initial public stock offering, the company lays out how it "recently repositioned itself from a domestic manufacturer to a market-driven company" by sponsoring hundreds of athletes as well as high-profile extreme sporting events such as the Vans Warped Tour. The company's "expenditure of significant funds to create consumer demands" was financed by closing an existing factory in California and contracting production in South Korea to "third party manufacturers."[8]

Adidas followed a similar trajectory, turning over its operation in 1993 to Robert Louis-Dreyfus, formerly a chief executive at advertising giant Saatchi and Saatchi. Announcing that he wanted to capture the heart of the "global teenager," Louis-Dreyfus promptly shut down the company-owned factories in Germany and moved to contracting-out in Asia.[9] Freed from the chains of production, the company had newfound time and money to create a Nike-style brand image. "We closed down everything." Adidas spokesman Peter Csanadi says proudly. "We only kept one small factory which is our global technology center and makes about 1 percent of total output."[10]

Though they don't draw the headline they once did, more factory closures are announced in North America and Europe each week—forty-five thousand U.S. apparel workers lost their jobs in 1997 alone.[11] That sector's job flight patterns have been equally dramatic around the globe. Though plant closures themselves have barely slowed down since the darkest days of the late-eighties/early-nineties recession, there has been a marked shift in the reason given for these "reorganizations." Mass layoffs were previously presented as an unfortunate necessity, tied to disappointing company performance. Today they are simply savvy shifts in corporate strategy, a "strategic redirection," to use the Vans terms. More and more, these layoffs are announced in conjunction with pledges to increase revenue needs of their brands, as opposed to the needs of their workers.

Consider the case of Sara Lee Corporation, an old-style conglomerate that encompasses not only its frozen-food namesake but also such "unintegrated" brands as Hanes underwear, Wonderbra, Coach leather goods, Champion sports apparel, Kiwi shoe polish, and Ball Park Franks. Despite the fact that Sara Lee enjoyed solid growth, healthy profits, good stock return, and no debt, by the mid-nineties Wall Street had become disenchanted with the company and was undervaluing its stock. Its profits had risen 10 percent in the 1996–97 fiscal year, hitting $1 billion, but Wall Street, as we have seen, is guided by spiritual goals as well as economic ones.[12] And Sara Lee, driven by the corporeal stuff of real world products, as opposed to the sleek ideas of brand identity, was simply out of economic fashion. "Lumpy object purveyors," as Tom Peters might say.[13]

To correct the situation, in September 1997, the company announced a $1.6 billion restructuring plan to get out of the "stuff" business by purging its manufacturing base. Thirteen of its factories, beginning with yarn and textile plants, would be sold to contractors who would become Sara Lee's suppliers. The company would be able to dip into the money saved to double its ad spending. "Its passé for us to be as vertically integrated as we were," explains Sara Lee CEO John H. Bryan.[14] Wall Street and the business press loved the new marketing-driven Sara Lee, rewarding the company with a 15 percent jump in stock price and flattering profiles of its bold and imaginative CEO. "Bryan's shift away from manufacturing to focus on brand marketing recognizes that the future belong to companies—like Coca Cola Co.—that own little but sell much," enthused one article in Business Week.[15] Even more telling was the analogy chosen by *Crain's Chicago Business:* "Sara Lee's goal is to become more like Oregon-based Nike Inc., which outsources its manufacturing and focuses primarily on the product development and brand management."[16]

In November 1997, Levi Strauss announced a similar motivated shakeup. Company revenue had dropped between 1996 and 1997, from $7.1 billion to $6.8

billion. But a 4 percent dip hardly seems to explain the company's decision to shut eleven plants. The closures resulted in 6,395 workers being laid off, one-third of its already downsized North America workforce. In this process, the company shut down three of its four factories in El Paso, Texas, a city where Levi's was the single largest private employer. Still unsatisfied with the results, the following year Levi's announced another round of closures in Europe and North America. Eleven more of its North American factories would be shut down and the total toll of laid-off workers rose to 16,310 in only two years.[17]

John Ermatinger, president of Levi's Americas division, had a familiar explanation. "Our strategic plan in North America is to focus intensely on brand management, marketing and product design as a means to meet the casual clothing wants and needs of consumers," he said.[18] Levi's chairman, Robert Haas, who on the same day received an award from the United Nations for making life better for his employees, told the *Wall Street Journal* that the closures reflected not just "overcapacity" but also "our own desire to refocus marketing, to inject more quality and distinctiveness into the brand."[19] In 1997, this quality and distinctiveness came in the form of a particularly funky international ad campaign rumored to have cost $90 million, Levi's most expensive campaign ever, and more than the company spent advertising the brand in all of 1996.

"This Is Not a Job-Flight Story"

In explaining the plant closures as a decision to turn Levi's into "a marketing company," Robert Haas was careful to tell the press that the jobs that were eliminated were not "leaving," they were just sort of evaporating. "This is not a job-flight story," he said after the first round of layoffs. The statement is technically true. Seeing Levi's as a job-flight story would miss the more fundamental—and more damaging—shift that the closures represent. As far as the company is concerned, those 16,310 jobs are off the payrolls for good, replaced, according to Ermatinger, by "contractors throughout the world." Those contractors will perform the same tasks as the old Levi's-owned factories—but the workers inside will never be employed by Levi Strauss.

For some companies a plant closure is still a straightforward decision to move the same facility to a cheaper locale. But for others—particularly those with strong brand identities like Levi Strauss and Hanes—layoffs are only the most visible manifestation of a much more fundamental shift: one that is less about where to produce than how. Unlike factories that hop from one place to another, these factories will never rematerialize. Mid-flight, they morph into something else entirely: "orders" to be placed with a contractor, who may well turn over those orders to as many as ten subcontractors, who—particularly in the garment sector—may in turn pass a portion of the subcontracts on to a network of home workers who will complete the jobs in basements and living rooms. Sure enough, only five months after the first round of plant closures was announced, Levi's made another public statement: it would resume manufacturing in China. The company had pulled out of China in 1993, citing concerns about human rights violations. Now it has returned, not to build its own factories but to place orders with three contractors that the company vows to closely monitor for violations of labor laws.[20]

The shift in attitude toward production is so profound that where a previous era of consumer goods corporations displayed their logos on the facades of their factories, many of today's brand-based multinationals now maintain that the location of their production operations is a "trade secret," to be guarded at all costs. When asked by human-rights groups in April 1999 to disclose the names and addresses of its contract factories, Peggy Carter, a vice president at Champion clothing, replied: "We have no interest in our competition learning where we are located and taking advantage of what has taken us years to build."[21]

Increasingly, brand-name multinationals—Levi's, Nike, Champion, Wal-Mart, Reebok, Gap, IBM, and General Motors—insist that they are just like any one of us: bargain hunters in search of the best deal in the global mall. They are very picky customers, with specific instructions about made-to-order design, materials, delivery dates, and, most important, the need for rock-bottom prices. But what they are not interested in is the burdensome logistics of how those prices fall so low; building factories, buying machinery, and budgeting for labor have all been lobbed squarely into somebody else's court.

And the real job-flight story is that a growing number of the most high-profile and profitable corporations in the world are fleeing the jobs business altogether.

The Unbearable Lightness of Cavite: Inside the Free-Trade Zones

Despite the conceptual brilliance of the "brands, not products" strategy, production has a pesky way of never quite being transcended entirely: somebody has to get down and dirty and make the products the global brands will hang their meaning on. And that's where the free-trade zones come in. In Indonesia, China, Mexico, Vietnam, the Philippines, and elsewhere, Export Processing Zones (as these are also called) are emerging as leading producers of garments, toys, shoes, electronics, machinery, even cars.

If Nike Town and the other superstores are the glittering new gateways to the branded dreamworlds, then the Cavite export processing zone, located ninety miles south of Manila in the town of Rosario, is the branding broom closet. After a month visiting similar industrial areas in Indonesia, I arrived in Rosario in early September 1997, at the tail end of monsoon season and the beginning of the Asian economic storm. I'd come to spend a week in Cavite because it is the largest free-trade zone in the Philippines, a 682-acre walled-in industrial area housing 207 factories that produce goods strictly for the export market. Rosario's population of sixty thousand all seemed to be on the move: the town's busy, sweltering streets were packed with army jeeps converted into minibuses and with motorcycle taxis with precarious sidecars, its side walls lined with stalls selling fried rice, Coke, and soap. Most of this commercial activity serves the fifty thousand workers who rush through Rosario on their way to and from work in the zone, whose gated entrance is located smack in the middle of town.

Inside the gates, factory workers assemble the finished products of our branded world: Nike running shoes, Gap pajamas, IBM computer screens, Old Navy jeans. But despite the presence of such illustrious multinationals, Cavite—and the exploding number of export processing zones like it throughout the developing world—could well be the only places left on earth where the superbrands actually keep a low profile. Indeed, they are positively self-effacing. Their names and logos aren't splashed on the facades of the factories in its own superstores: they are often produced side by side in the same factories, glued by the very same workers, stitched and soldered on the very same machines. It was in the Cavite that I finally found a piece of unswooshed space, and I found it, oddly enough, in a Nike shoe factory.

I was only permitted one visit inside the zone's gates to interview officials—individual factories, I was told, are off-limits to anyone but potential importers or exporters. But a few days later, with the help of an eighteen-year-old worker who had been laid off from his job in an electronics factor, I managed to sneak back to get the unofficial tour. In the rows of virtually identical giant shedlike structures, one factory stood out: the name on the white rectangular building said "Phillips," but through its surrounding fence I could see mountains of Nike Shoes piled high. Its seems that in Cavite, production has been banished to our age's most worthless status: its factories are unbrandable, unswooshworthy: producers are the industrial untouchables. Is this what Phil Knight meant, I wondered, when he said his company wasn't about the sneakers?

Manufacturing is concentrated and isolated inside the zone as if it were toxic waste: pure, 100 percent production at low, low prices. Cavite, like the rest of the zones that compete with it, presents itself as the buy-in-bulk Price Club for multinationals on the lookout for bargains—grab a really big shopping cart. Inside it's obvious that the row of factories, each with its own gate and guard, has been carefully planned to squeeze the maximum amount of production out of this swath of land. Windowless workshops made of cheap plastic and aluminum siding are crammed in next to each other, only feet apart. Racks of time cards bake in the sun, making sure the maximum amount of work is extracted from each worker, the maximum number of working hours extracted from each day. The streets in the zone are eerily empty, and open doors—the ventilation system for most factories—reveal lines of young women hunched in silence over clamoring machines.

In other parts of the world, workers live inside the economic zones, but not in Cavite: this is a place of pure work. All the bustle and color of Rosario abruptly stops at the gates, where workers must show their ID cards to armed guards in order to get inside. Visitors are rarely permitted in the zone, and little or no internal commerce takes place on its orderly streets, not even candy and drink vending. Buses and taxicabs must drop speed and silence their horns when they get in the zone—a marked change from the boisterous streets of Rosario. If all of this makes Cavite feel as if it's in a different country, that's because, in a way, it is. The zone is a tax-free economy, sealed off from the local government of both town and province—a miniature military state inside a democracy.

As a concept, free-trade zones are as old as commerce itself, and they were all the more relevant in ancient times when the transportation of goods required multiple holdovers and rest stops. Pre–Roman Empire city-states, including Tyre, Carthage, and Utica, encouraged trade by declaring themselves "Free cities," where goods in transit could be stored without tax, and merchants would be protected from harm. These tax-free areas developed further economic significance during colonial times, when entire cities—including Hong Kong, Singapore, and Gibraltar—were designated as "free ports," from which the loot of colonialism could be safely shipped back to England, Europe, or America with low import tariffs.[22] Today, the globe is dotted with variations on these tax-free pockets, from duty-free shops in airports and the free banking zones of the Cayman Islands to bonded warehouse and ports where goods in transit are held, sorted, and packaged.

Though it has plenty in common with these other tax havens, the export processing zone is really in a class of its own. Less holding tank than sovereign territory, the EPZ is an area where goods don't just pass through but are actually manufactured, an area, furthermore, where there are no import and export duties and often no income or property taxes either. The idea that EPZs could help Third World economies first gained currency in 1964 when the United Nations Economic and Social Council adopted a resolution endorsing the zones as a means of promoting trade with developing nations. The idea didn't really get off the ground, however, until the early eighties, when India introduced a five-year tax break for companies manufacturing in its low-wage zones.

Since then, the free-trade zone industry has exploded. There are fifty-two economic zones in the Philippines alone, employing 459,000 people—that's up from only 23,000 zone workers in 1986 and 229,000 as recently as 1994. The largest zone economy is China, where by conservative estimates there are 18 million people in 124 export processing zones.[23] In total, the international Labor Organization says that there are at least 850 EPZs in the world, but that number is likely much closer to 1,000, spread through seventy countries and employing about 27 million workers.[24] The World Trade Organization estimates that between $200 and $250 billion worth of trade flows through the zones.[25] The number of individual factories housed inside these industrial parks is also expanding. In fact, the free-trade factories along the U.S.-Mexico border—in Spanish, *maquiladoras* (from *maquillar,* "to make up" or "assemble")—are probably the only structures that proliferate as quickly as Wal-Mart outlets: there were 789 maquiladoras in 1985. In 1995, there were 2,747. By 1997, there were 3,508 employing about 900,000 workers.[26]

Regardless of where the EPZs are located, the workers' stories have a certain mesmerizing sameness: the workday is long—fourteen hours in Sri Lanka, twelve hours in Indonesia, sixteen in southern China, twelve in the Philippines. The vast majority of the workers are women, always young, always working for contractors or subcontractors from Korea, Taiwan, or Hong Kong. The contractors are usually filling orders for companies based in the United States, Britain, Japan, Germany, or Canada. The management is military style, the supervisors often abusive, the wages below subsistence, and the work low-skilled and tedious. As an economic model, today's export processing zones have more in common with fast-food franchises than sustainable developments, so removed are they from the countries that host them. These pockets of pure industry hide behind a cloak of transience: the contracts come and go with little notice: the workers are predominantly migrants, far from home and with little connection to the city or province where zones are located; the work itself is short term, often not renewed.

As I walk along the blank streets of Cavite, I can feel the threatening impermanence, the underlying instability of the zone. The shedlike factories are connected so tenuously to the surrounding country, to the adjacent town, to the very earth they are perched upon, that it feels as if the jobs that flew here from the north could fly away again just as quickly. The factories are cheaply constructed and tossed together on land that is rented, not owned. When I climb up the water tower on the edge of the zone and look down at the hundreds of factories, its seems as if the whole cardboard complex could lift up and blow away, like Dorothy's house in *The Wizard of Oz*. No wonder the EPZ factories in Guatemala are called "swallows."

Fear pervades the zones. The governments are afraid of losing their foreign factories: the factories are afraid of losing unstable jobs. These are factories built not on land but on air.

Notes

1. Landor Web site at www.landor.com.

2. Peter Schweitzer, "People Buy Products Not Brands," J. Walter Thompson White Papers series, undated.

3. "Big Brand Firms Know the Name Is Everything," *Irish Times*, February 27, 1998.

4. Ortega, *In Sam We Trust*, 342.

5. "Trade and Development Report, 1997," United Nations Conference on Trade and Economic Development.

6. Katz, *Just Do It*, 204.

7. Cathy Majtenyi, "Were Disney Dogs Treated Better Than Workers?" *Catholic Register*, December, 23–30, 1996.

8. "Extreme Spreadsheet Dude," *Baffler* 9:79, and *Wall Street Journal,* April 16, 1998.

9. John Gilardi, "Adidas Share Offer Set to Win Gold Medal," *Reuters,* October 26, 1995.

10. *Globe and Mail,* September 26, 1997.

11. Charles Kernaghan, "Behind the Label: 'Made in China,'" prepared for the National Labor Committee, March 1998.

12. *Los Angeles Times,* September 16, 1997. Furthermore, Sara Lee's investors had been getting a solid return on their investment, but the stock "had gained 25 percent over the prior 12 months, lagging the 35 percent increase of the benchmark Standard & Poor's 500 stock index."

13. Peters, *The Circle of Innovation,* 16.

14. David Leonhardt, "Sara Lee: Playing with the Recipe," *Business Week,* April 27, 1998, 114.

15. Ibid.

16. Jennifer Waters, "After Euphoria, Can Sara Lee Be Like Nike?" *Crain's Chicago Business,* September 22, 1997, 3.

17. Nina Munk, "How Levi's Trashed a Great American Brand," *Fortune,* April 12, 1999, 83.

18. "Levi Strauss & Co. to Close 11 of Its North American Plants," *Business Wire,* February 22, 1999.

19. Wall Street Journal, 4 November 1997, B1.

20. Joanna Ramey, "Levi's Will Resume Production in China After 5-Year Absence," *Women's Wear Daily,* April 9, 1998, 1.

21. "Anti-Sweatshop Activists Score in Campaign Targeting Athletic Retailers," *Boston Globe,* April 18, 1999.

22. Richard S. Thoman, *Free Ports and Foreign Trade Zones* (Cambridge: Cornell Maritime Press, 1956).

23. These are International Labor Organization figures as of May 1998, but in Kernaghan's "Behind the Label," the figures on China's zone are much higher. Kernaghan estimates that there are thirty million inside the zones and that there are 400—as opposed to 124—special economic zones inside China.

24. The International Labor Organization's Special Action Program on Export Processing Zones. Source: Auret Van Heerden.

25. This estimate was provided by Michael Finger at the World Trade Organization in a personal correspondence. No official figures are available.

26. Figures for 1985 and 1995 provided by the WTO. Figures for 1997 supplied by the Maquila Solidarity Network/Labor Behind the Label Coalition, Toronto.

The Positive Effect of Trade on U.S. Jobs

ERNEST H. PREEG

The protectionist assault on the longstanding U.S. liberal trade policy has had notable success in recent years. Vilification of the North American Free Trade Agreement (NAFTA), defeat of fast-track legislation, and the failure of the World Trade Organization (WTO) ministerial meeting in Seattle in 1999 testify to the power of the protectionist assault. Even the May 2000 congressional approval of permanent normal trade relations with China was accompanied by a Wall Street Journal/NBC public opinion poll indicating that 48 percent of Americans believed foreign trade is bad for the U.S. economy and only 34 percent believed it is good.

The assault comprises several lines of attack. A vague anticapitalism and antiglobalization ideology is proffered, with particular venom directed at large multinational corporations. Violations of core labor standards and environmental degradation in developing countries are more specific targets. But the most compelling political argument is that trade-liberalizing agreements like the NAFTA and a new WTO round of multilateral negotiations will have widespread adverse impact on U.S. jobs. This charge, however, is not substantiated by recent experience. To the contrary, expanding international trade and investment are providing substantial net benefits to American workers.

There is no question that as trade expands, some American jobs are lost to import competition, just as some new jobs are created in export industries. The same is true throughout the market-oriented U.S. economy, as more competitive firms gain market share from less competitive firms and as new technology applications and changing consumer tastes favor some companies and products over others. In this context the issue of impact on U.S. jobs from trade concerns the relative numbers of jobs gained and lost from trade, the quality of such job gains and losses, and the trade-induced changes in levels of worker income. And in all of these areas the international trade creates substantial net benefits.

Few Existing Jobs Lost

Almost all American jobs threatened by or lost from imports are in the manufacturing sector, but today only 14 percent of the U.S. labor force is in

American Outlook Magazine, May/June 2001. Reprinted with permission of *American Outlook Magazine*.
Ernest H. Preeg is a senior fellow in trade and productivity at the Manufacturers Alliance and an adjunct fellow at the Hudson Institute.

manufactures, thanks largely to consistently high gains in labor productivity over the past two decades. Of this 14 percent, only 3 percent is in industries facing substantial import competition. Textiles and apparel account for almost 1 percent, and the other 2 percent is spread among various industries. The remaining 97 percent of U.S. workers, mostly in the service sector, are therefore, with rare exception, net beneficiaries of trade from export-oriented jobs or as consumers.

Consequently, the number of existing jobs actually lost to trade is also very small. Each year approximately 2.5 million American workers, or 2 percent of the labor force, are "displaced" because of plant shutdowns or abolition of particular jobs. Only some 120,000, or 5 percent, of these lost jobs, however, are caused by imports and foreign direct investment, based on the number of workers certified for Trade Adjustment Assistance (TAA) or NAFTA transitional assistance. This amounts to just one-tenth of 1 percent of the labor force actually losing jobs because of trade. Moreover, three-quarters of these certified workers quickly find jobs elsewhere and do not need to avail themselves of the TAA/NAFTA services and allowances. Public- and private-sector programs to assist displaced workers in upgrading their skills and finding new jobs play an important role in a dynamic, growth-oriented economy, but the very large majority of this assistance is unrelated to trade, and the trade-related 5 percent of displaced workers, if anything receive more generous benefits than the other 95 percent.

Export-Oriented and Transportation Jobs Grow

Export-oriented jobs pay 12 to 15 percent more than the average for all U.S. jobs, largely as a result of higher skill and education requirements. It is difficult to calculate how many new export jobs are created as trade expands, but for a given increase of both exports and imports, more new export jobs tend to be created than existing import-competing jobs are lost. When the overall economy is growing, which is almost all the time, an increase in exports generally produces a direct increase in jobs, whereas a comparable increase in imports often results in a slower growth of industry-wide jobs rather than a loss of existing jobs.

The moderating effect economic growth has on import-related job losses is evident in the thirteen industries that account for more than 80 percent of TAA/NAFTA job loss certification. During 1994–1999, a time of steady growth in the U.S. economy, there was actually a net annual gain of twenty-one thousand jobs for all thirteen industries. Six individual industries also showed positive job growth, while textiles and apparel accounted for three-quarters of industry job losses. With respect to relative pay levels, the six industries with positive job growth provided average annual compensation to workers of $51,000, compared with $30,000 in the textiles and apparel sectors.

A liberal trade policy is especially beneficial to labor in segments of the transportation sector because increases of both imports and exports tend to create jobs there. For example, the number of containers passing through U.S. ports in both directions increased by 42 percent between 1993 and 1998, clearly benefiting jobs in the port cargo handling sector. Long-distance truck drivers likewise benefit greatly from NAFTA because trucks account for 83 percent of surface trade between the United States and Mexico. This trade increased by more than 70 percent between 1994 and 1999 and, partly as a result, there is now a growing shortage of experienced truck drivers, which is exerting upward pressure on wages. Despite this win-win job-creating ability of international trade in these two segments of the transportation sector, the longshoremen and teamsters' unions are outspoken protectionists in the trade policy debate.

All Workers Gain as Consumers

Although the consumer benefits from lower-priced imports can be especially large for lower-income workers because a larger share of their income goes for apparel, footwear, consumer electronics, basic foodstuffs, and other heavily imported products, this basic justification for free trade is often ignored. Prices of many of these products could easily increase by 25 to 50 percent if imports were cut back as protectionists advocate. Similarly, remaining "protections" now double the price of sugar and increase substantially the cost of many other goods to all workers.

The most frequent job-related protectionist argument is that America's current record trade deficit is caused by liberal trade agreements such as the Uruguay Round and NAFTA, and therefore such agreements should be terminated. This is essentially a bogus argument. The rapid expansion of the trade deficit over the past several years has been caused primarily by a low savings rate in the U.S. economy and by manipulation of exchange rates by some foreign governments to commercial advantage—not by trade-liberalizing agreements. To the contrary, agreements that have progressively reduced trade barriers have tended to expand U.S. exports more than imports because other countries' trade barriers are higher than U.S. barriers to begin with. This was starkly evident for NAFTA, where Mexican tariffs, on average, were reduced from about 20 percent to zero for U.S. exporters, while average U.S. tariffs were reduced from only 3 percent to zero. Moreover, U.S. competitors in Europe, Japan, and elsewhere continued to pay 20 percent Mexican tariffs, giving U.S. exporters a large preferential advantage in the Mexican market. In any event, as explained earlier, the number of existing jobs lost to imports, even with a growing trade deficit but within the context of high overall growth in the U.S. economy has been very small.

Judging by these basic points of reference that define how open trade affects U.S. jobs and labor interests, the net assessment is clearly positive and substantially so. The protectionist alliance highlights the personal hardships of individual families where jobs are lost to imports, but this anecdotal approach evades the central issue: the overall impact of trade on U.S. labor. Of course, every family confronted with a job loss, from whatever cause, can encounter hardship, in some cases severe hardship, and support facilities should be and are provided by both the government and the private sector to help them. The case for or against open trade, however, must be based on a full national assessment. Such an assessment, as presented here, demonstrates that (1) only a very small number of American workers are adversely affected by increased imports; (2) many workers benefit from export-oriented jobs or from trade directly, as in the transportation sector; (3) new jobs created from trade are higher-skilled and better-paid jobs than those lost to imports; and (4) as consumers, all workers reap substantial benefits from trade. This is the case for free trade that the protectionists need to address, point by point, but so far they have not done so.

America's Labor Pains

THOMAS L. FRIEDMAN

What's going on with the American labor movement?

In March the Teamsters started lobbying the Clinton White House to award one of the Teamsters' largest employers, UPS, a much sought-after new air route for landing cargo planes in China. At the same time, the Teamsters have been lobbying against the administration's effort to grant China permanent normal trade relations or entry into the World Trade Organization, which would actually spur U.S.-China cargo trade. "It seems that the Teamsters want us to have more cargo flights to China, but no cargo," said one U.S. official. They want more trade in empty boxes. This is almost as interesting as the dockworkers' union marching in Seattle against more globalization and free trade, which is like the milkmen's union coming out against cows. No trade, no dockworkers. No milk, no milkmen. But then you also have the United Auto Workers opposing the trade deal with China, which is strange since today virtually no U.S.-made car can be sold in China, but under the Clinton-negotiated WTO deal all U.S.-made cars can be sold, financed, and distributed in China.

And then, of course, there was the lovely scene during the recent anti-IMF protests in Washington when that hate-mongering isolationist Pat Buchanan joined forces with the Teamsters and their boss, James Hoffa. Mr. Buchanan told cheering Teamsters that as president he would tell the Chinese to either shape up or "you guys have sold your last pair of chopsticks in any mall in the United States," and that he would appoint Mr. Hoffa as America's top trade negotiator.

How did the U.S. labor movement go from being a progressive force to being the leading opponent of free trade and pal of Pat Buchanan? I posed that question to former Labor Secretary Robert Reich, now a Brandeis University professor. His short answer is that U.S. labor unions have come to totally distrust U.S. business and are convinced that free trade is simply a vehicle for moving manufacturing jobs abroad.

"I believe the labor leaders today are being pushed by their rank and file, who never liked NAFTA and who do not trust American business to keep jobs in this country," said Mr. Reich. "Even though the business cycle in recent years has improved things for the country as a whole, labor does not feel that it has really shared fully in the expansion. It feels that manufacturing jobs are still vanishing—whether because of technology or globalization and free trade."

New York Times, May 9, 2000. Reprinted with permission of the *New York Times.* Thomas L. Friedman is an op-ed columnist for the *New York Times* and author of numerous books.

Labor's response, therefore, has been to try to slam America's doors shut, even though it is obvious that globalization and free trade have contributed mightily to America's economic expansion. What to do? Congressman Sander Levin's thoughtful proposal for better monitoring of China's worker and human rights behavior is laudable, but I don't think labor really cares about either.

What we need is a business-government-labor summit that tries to defuse at least some of labor's real concerns in return for a tempering of its opposition to trade.

"If the business community is really serious," says Mr. Reich, "it should combine the China trade deal with legislation that would give labor a ban on the permanent replacement of striking workers, something labor has sought for years, and it would also treble the fines against any company that illegally fires workers for trying to form unions. In recent years more companies have been using the threat of permanently replacing striking workers, and the practice of illegally firing workers for trying to form unions has been on the rise, because the penalty structure is just a slap on the wrist."

This is worth considering. Free trade and the new economy have been very good for the United States, but the gains have been unequally distributed, particularly when it comes to blue-collar workers. My attitude toward labor is: Tell us what we can do to ameliorate that—short of putting up walls and closing doors that will only hurt us all in the long run. Sure, we could redistribute income through tax policy, but that isn't going to happen. So why not try Mr. Reich's idea: Strengthen workers' ability to negotiate wages, severance, and security on their own behalf within the new economy.

Pie-in-the-sky? Maybe. But some way has to be found to persuade labor to loosen its grip on the door, and one way could be this bargain: You let go of the door and we'll empower you to better thrive with it open.

Where No Business Is Good Business

JACK EL-HAI

In a quiet office park in the Minneapolis suburb of Minnetonka, half hidden by a knoll, stands an unexceptional one-story office building. No sign identifies the building's purpose. Inside is a securities-trading floor with up-to-date computers, data lines to the world's major stock markets, and banks of telephones. Wall clocks tell the time in Singapore, Minneapolis, and London.

Not even on the busiest day of the year in the stock markets, typically, do the phones on this floor ring or the computer screens light up. Periodically, cleaners come in to wipe away the fine layer of dust that accumulates on the French Impressionist prints in the conference room, the kitchen counters in the break room, the tables, desks, and chairs, and the empty wastebaskets. Except for a skeleton crew of two in the front office, no one works here. Everyone is happy if the work stations that fill the building remain unused as much as possible. In the upside-down world of workplace-recovery centers, of which this building is an example, no business is good business.

The Minnetonka building, which is owned by Comdisco, of Rosemont, Illinois, will open its doors to subscribers when a power outage, a tornado, a fire, a blizzard, a flood, or some other interruption to business strikes. Subscribers—in particular, securities-trading firms—will simply forward their calls and move temporarily to Minnetonka. They will thus avoid the financial losses and ill will resulting from an inability to execute trades; few customers will ever know that any transfer of operations took place.

Although subscribers frequently visit in order to test their disaster-recovery plans and equipment, the Minnetonka facility has never in its four years under the current ownership been fired up in an emergency situation. Scores of other facilities around the country sit in a state of continuous anticipation, awaiting disasters that may never happen.

Subscribers annually pay $400 to $800 per work station for the right to occupy a recovery facility in an emergency, and they will be assessed additional fees (often covered by business-interruption insurance) if they actually begin using it. Today the biggest concentrations of such facilities are near the financial centers of the East Coast. But the business originated in the upper Midwest, when a Minneapolis consultant named Ken Israel, an expert in computer and communications recovery, realized that trillions of dollars in trades were endangered

Atlantic Monthly, August 2000. Reprinted with permission of the author. Jack El-Hai is the author of *Lost Minnesota: Stories of Vanished Places* and a freelance journalist.

every year because most financial-services firms lacked backup offices and equipment.

One day in 1988, as Israel was offering disaster-recovery recommendations to a large brokerage firm, the idea of workplace-recovery centers hit him. "I was highlighting the company's points of weakness, and I saw that data was not the important piece," Israel recalls. "They made their money via communications and trading, and they had a huge exposure [to losses]. They were spending hundreds of thousands of dollars backing up their mainframe computers, but that wasn't what they needed most."

Israel, a slight man who is visibly intense and energetic, conceived a simple, valuable idea: securities traders needed disaster-proof temporary quarters in the event of an emergency, with adequate equipment and connections to the world's securities markets—and he would build such quarters. At first, Israel had difficulty imagining what his facility would even look like. Then, searching the Twin Cities for a vacant building, he stopped at one place and peeked through a window. "I got a vision," he says.

His mind's eye showed him a miniature trading floor, a shrunken replica of the space in which his brokerage client conducted its daily business. The building would have satellite-linked phone service and diesel generators supplying backup power. Israel and a partner leased the building, got design assistance from the Securities and Exchange Commission, and established connections to 144 securities exchanges worldwide. They called their firm Exchange Resources, and they acquired several subscription-paying clients, including the company now known as American Express Financial Advisors.

One of the biggest pools of potential customers was in New York City, and in 1992 Israel persuaded J. P. Morgan and Company to buy a $30 million subscription that allowed Exchange Resources to build a facility on Staten Island. In the minds of New Yorkers at the time, terrorist attacks loomed larger than other disasters as threats to business, so the new facility was built "in the last place anyone would look," Israel says—right next to the Fresh Kills landfill, one of the world's biggest garbage dumps. The building has satellite uplinks, low windows designed to foil the assaults of terrorist sharpshooters, and a walk-in electrical generator "that could light up Broadway and still have juice left over for Hoboken," Israel says. "New York could have sunk, and we'd keep on trading."

Exchange Resources later opened workplace-recovery centers in Singapore and England. The English facility, built in an old cookie factory, concealed its true purpose by allowing a local baker to run the ovens, sending the aroma of freshly baked cookies over the neighborhood.

The company's technological capabilities did not remain untested for long. When the "storm of the century" hit New York City in December of 1992 and flooded the streets, a securities-trading subsidiary of National Westminster Bank lost its electrical power and telephone service. By 6:45 A.M. on the next business day seventy-five of the bank's securities traders were doing business out of Exchange Resource's Staten Island facility.

By then, however, Israel was starting to lose his love for the business. Exchange Resources prided itself on the extent to which it could replicate a client's home trading floor—complete with speed-dial numbers programmed into the telephones and framed photos of executives' families on the desks—but clients wanted more. They demanded exclusive space, emergency offices bigger than what their competitors were given, and menus of the catered food they would be served on days of emergency. "Monday had to be Chinese, Tuesday French, the next day pizza—and they were dead serious about this," Israel says. "They wanted eleven bagels toasted light, et cetera. This was ass-kissing and not staying focused on the business."

Meanwhile, the workplace-recovery business attracted well-financed new competitors with roots in the insurance and data-recovery fields, quickly reducing Exchange Resources from the industry leader to a poorly capitalized underdog. In 1995 Israel and his partner sold Exchange Resources to Comdisco.

Since then the industry has lost some of its romance. Power outages, dead phone lines, and crashed Internet servers are now possibilities more chilling to corporations than terrorist attacks. Although IBM, Comdisco, and SunGard, the big three in the industry, still have plenty of financial-services and securities-trading firms among their clients (federal regulations in fact require banks and many financial institutions to have disaster-recovery plans), other kinds of businesses now also use their services, including health-maintenance organizations, e-commerce enterprises, travel agencies, transportation companies, and automakers. Anyone who relies on the phone or the Internet to keep in touch with customers is a good prospect for a workplace-recovery center. Often the staff of a company's call center, which handles inquiries or orders from customers, occupies the desks when things go wrong.

This is not to say that only electronic glitches drive businesses to workplace-recovery centers. Industry studies show that, whereas power outages and computer hardware and software problems account for about 40 percent of companies' disaster declarations, hurricanes, floods, fires, explosions, and earthquakes cause most of the rest. When Hurricane Floyd soaked the East Coast last September, recovery facilities throughout the area experienced high demand for their dry and electrically self-sufficient offices.

In a hurricane or other disaster any plan to use a workplace-recovery center is doomed if the company doesn't repeatedly practice the relocation of its business operations and prepare for a sudden switchover. To be ready for such testing—let alone a real disaster—many clients keep backup software and disaster-recovery manuals in the recovery center's lockers. Some clients' lockers also hold T-shirts and caps that the lead recovery staffers will wear to maintain order during relocation and recovery.

When companies arrive for testing, which can happen several times a year for days at a time, workplace-recovery centers awaken. GMAC Residential Mortgage bused thirty employees from its customer-service center in Waterloo, Iowa, to a workplace-recovery facility in Illinois, forwarded some incoming calls, started up the computers and GMAC's proprietary software, and watched what happened. It all worked, and the employees were able to do their jobs. The company did its best to see that employees liked their new surroundings. "We were taking them away from their families," says Mark Kern, GMAC's vice president of corporate contingency planning and security, "so we got them a nice bus, kept them in a pretty nice hotel, and made them as comfortable as possible."

Repeated practice helped Mercedes-Benz USA, whose headquarters, in Montvale, New Jersey, endured its share of suffering during Hurricane Floyd. The heavy rains and flooding didn't damage the company's facilities, but they disrupted the electrical power and phone service. Mercedes-Benz runs a twenty-four-hour roadside-assistance center, which handles five thousand calls a day from stranded motorists; the company declared a disaster and quickly shifted the center's operations to a workplace-recovery facility. In just two hours employees were again taking calls on the toll-free line, twenty miles away from company headquarters. They remained there for three days while phone and electrical service were gradually restored in Montvale. "The key to success was testing, making employees comfortable, and defining their roles and responsibilities," says Gordon Michel, the company's disaster-recovery coordinator. "Going through the testing process was just another day at the office—but in another office."

Some companies publicize their subscription to workplace-recovery centers, hoping that customers will regard their preparedness as reassuring. Providing uninterrupted service to customers "is part of the values and ethics of my company," says Tonya York, the vice president of business-resumption services at the Charles Schwab and Company brokerage firm, which has contracts to occupy up to 2,200 work stations in recovery centers around the country in the event of an emergency. Although Schwab isn't likely to run an ad campaign featuring its disaster-backup plans, York says, "our customers and investors are becoming more educated every day, and to think they're not thinking about this is unreasonable."

Other firms—most, in fact—do not discuss their recovery plans in public. Few companies like to admit that they might experience a catastrophe, especially if they are dependent on a feeble and untested recovery program. All the firms that operate workplace-recovery centers keep their complete client lists confidential.

In the future, however, no doubt more and more companies will subscribe. Already many businesses cannot function without such third parties as telecommunications suppliers and Internet-service providers, and the growth of e-commerce will put even more businesses in a position of dependency. If its supplier fails, the business is in trouble unless it has somewhere else to go. "There's a greater expectation that you will be there all the time," York says. "You'll have to recover instantly [from a disaster] or have a redundant environment somewhere so that you will always be up."

Disasters of a magnitude sufficient to require companies to activate their workplace-recovery contracts remain infrequent. Many recovery facilities go for years without housing anybody in actual distress—and their owners make money regardless. During those times, staff members at the centers assist with testing, keep their places in working order, and give tours to prospective customers. Still, working in a sizable office building that is nearly empty must get lonely. "I'm used to it," says Matt Scribner, who runs Comdisco's facility in Minnetonka. All around him computers, fax machines, phones, printers, and coffee machines sit silent, awaiting their chance to come to life.

Dialogues with James Fallows

MICHAEL LEWIS AND JAMES FALLOWS

FROM: MICHAEL LEWIS
TO: JAMES FALLOWS
SUBJECT: RE: THE (NEXT) AGE OF THE INTERNET—PART TWO

Dear Jim:
The two themes you so politely question—"the rise of the young" and the "end of authority"—I think of as falling someplace between literary conceits and honest arguments. I suppose they are suggestions, made to the reader in a gentle, coaxing spirit with the help of stories that (I hope) will give him some pleasure—even if he finds my suggestions absurd. One of the things I wanted to do in the book was to dramatize the way that rapid technical change (of which the Internet is just one example) undermines authority and gives outsiders (of which kids are just an example) new powers. I didn't want to sell too hard the idea that fifteen-year-old boys will be chairing the Federal Reserve anytime soon, because I don't think they will.

On the other hand, I wouldn't dismiss out of hand the notion that fifteen-year-olds will have more and more economic power. In recent years—or since the time when I was a very young person—very young people have enjoyed fantastic economic opportunities, and it's worth asking why this is. (Especially since I think I know the answer.) I recall a conversation I had a few years back with Marc Andreessen, the cofounder of Netscape. He was marveling at the exploits of some teenage Canadian hacker who had turned up in the newspapers. I asked him at what age he would like to be able to hire people to work at Netscape. He said that, were it not for child-labor laws, twelve-year-olds could be very usefully employed as programmers. He said that for many programming tasks he'd prefer a bright teenager to a grown-up.

Now, I've never written computer code, but I've been told about six thousand times by people who do that the aptitude for it is something like an aptitude for mathematics. Mathematicians famously peak young, so perhaps computer programming, as big and growing a field as it is, should be treated as an exception to some general economic rule. But then I think back to my experience on

Excerpts from "Fallows@Large: Dialogues with James Fallows, Beyond the Tech Bubble," *Atlantic Monthly*, August 29, 2001. Reprinted with permission of the *Atlantic Monthly*. Michael Lewis is the author of several best-selling books, a contributing writer to the *New York Times Magazine*, and a visiting fellow at the University of California at Berkeley. James Fallows is an author, national correspondent of the *Atlantic Monthly*, and a contributor to various publications.

Wall Street in the 1980s. I arrived on the Salomon Brothers trading floor about the same time as the computer. Thanks to the computer, Wall Street—like many sectors of the economy—was becoming highly technically innovative. The computer enabled the creation and analysis of more and more complicated financial products. And, for reasons both obvious and mysterious, young people tended to be the ones who created them.

All of a sudden experience mattered a lot less on Wall Street. It's no accident that the 1980s gave us the twenty-six-year-old Wall Street millionaire. Or that, since then, finance has remained a province of youth, a business in which people come of age in their mid twenties and often retire in their late thirties. From the moment the computer hit the trading floor, perfectly ignorant young people (like me) were able to walk into big Wall Street firms and within six months make themselves expert on aspects of the business that the old guys did not fully understand.

I think this aspect of Wall Street life—rapid technical innovation inside an industry leading to a "youthening" of that industry—is a dramatic illustration of a force at work in any economy that makes a fetish, as ours does, of technical innovation. As you point out, it is now fashionable to pooh-pooh the youth-quake aspects of the Internet Boom. But it's interesting to stand back from the wreckage and ask: Who won? Who walked away with lots more money in his pocket than he had before? The answer is: the people who got in early and got out before the market tanked. And these, in the main, were very young people. (Think of the founders and first employees of Netscape, Yahoo, Excite, etc., etc.) The wise, gray-headed manager types now currently in fashion were also the ones who waited until just before the bubble burst to quit their jobs to work for dot-coms.

I agree with you that "the end of authority" is hardly an original theme. The reason the Internet is such a powerful force for social change is that it pushes society in a direction it was predisposed to travel. But if everything I wrote had to be wholly original I'd never write anything. And I did think it was useful to suggest—gently, coaxingly—the way new technology feeds the perpetual American desire for insurrection.

Best,
Michael

FROM: JAMES FALLOWS
TO: MICHAEL LEWIS
SUBJECT: THE (NEXT) AGE OF THE INTERNET—PART THREE

Greetings Michael:
We come to the end, and I have a couple of questions that will (gasp!) lead you away from the contents of your book itself. These are designed to let you put on your Savant's Cap and tell us how we should think about the following technology-financial events.

I know that Savantage—not a word, but it should be—is not your natural approach. But on the basis of *Liar's Poker*, *The New New Thing*, and *Next*, you're entitled. Together they form a kind of social history of the last two financial bubbles. And that leads me to the first question:

1. *Liar's Poker* described the bubble of the late 1980s, now remembered in shorthand as the Junk Bond days. *TNNT* and *Next* are about the ups and downs of the Internet-boom era. There are some obvious similarities between the two episodes. Greedy people with good timing got rich. Penny-ante people with worse timing were their victims. Excesses were excessed. The natural forces of gravity eventually set in. The first boom was "democratizing" in certain ways—the uncouth characters who traded bonds became richer than their social betters. The Internet is democratizing in other ways, or so you contend in *Next*.

There were obvious differences too. The first bubble seemed New York-centric. The second seemed Palo Alto-centric. Technology played only a small role in the first—mainly through adding "derivatives" to the portfolio list. Technology, and the different estimates of its ultimate impact, was the fundamental force behind the second. The lasting impact of the first boom is hard to detect. You argue that the lasting impact of the second is now being underestimated.

And so on. My request to you is: Compare and contrast! You lived inside the first boom and chronicled people at the center of the second one. What are the main useful, or simply interesting, conclusions to draw from the similarities and differences between them?

2. Let's talk about real shifts in power. Historically, a few kinds of technology really have changed the balance of power within and between societies. The combination of agriculture and simple advances in public health may have been the most important of them. Before, perhaps, the Dickensian era, one big advantage the upper classes had over the lower classes was that the people on top were more likely to survive! They had enough food, they didn't get as many diseases, they weren't as likely to freeze to death for lack of coal. Even these days it's obviously still healthier to be on the top of society than the bottom. But at least in America, the reasons for the difference are changing. (You can tell professional-class Americans by how few of them smoke and how few are fat.) And the absolute gap here is much smaller than it used to be. I don't have the exact statistics, but something like the following is true: at the turn of the twentieth century, the life-expectancy-at-birth for black males in America was about twenty years less than for white males. Now it's three or four years. Similarly, the balance of power between nations has obviously been changed by the invention of the first nuclear weapons. And the seemingly inevitable advent of cheap, deployable "weapons of mass destruction," from portable nukes to little anthrax vials, will change the balance of power again, putting big states more at the mercy of small ones. [I wrote the preceding sentence on September 10, having no idea of the horrifying way in which it would be illustrated the following day.]

Automobiles, by contrast, have socially democratized various cultures without *really* changing the balance of power. I mean, the car culture of southern California was part of its loose and easy nature (*American Graffiti* was basically all about this point). But as you look around the world, I don't think you can argue that cars basically changed the distribution of power—rich versus poor, government versus citizen, superpower versus piddling state. (Maybe you can argue this: be my guest!)

One main point of *Next* is that the Internet really will change the balance of power—young versus old, outsiders versus insiders, people in out-of-the-way places versus those at the command center. You mentioned in our second round that the idea of deep change spurred by the Internet was something between a literary conceit and a real contention. Could I put you on the spot to ask which it is? Is information technology going to be an interesting new adjunct to how we work and play? Or will it, in an important way, give power to some people and take it away from others?

3. Finally, a question that affects us both: how and when will the Internet work out a way of paying for "content"? The publications that rushed to give their articles away on the Internet are now feeling vaguely like chumps. They thought they were being modern and adding to "mindshare," but in many cases they were simply undercutting their own product. Newsstand sales of magazines in general have been declining for several years: the Internet must have something to do with that. The recording industry has won its battle against Napster, but it seems almost certain to lose the war. When it is *technically possible* for people to get "content"—software code, textual information, music—legal regulations don't usually stand in their way. Think of how early software companies had to drop their clumsy "copy protection" schemes.

I've assumed all along that the current "content is free" policy on the Internet was just a transition blip. *Eventually*, people have to be paid to compose songs or write books or develop code. And over the years people have been willing to pay some fee for this "intellectual property." When previous technical waves have threatened to wreck the existing payment model—when the Xerox machine meant students could copy an article rather than buy it, when the first tape recorders meant you could capture music coming over the radio—new payment systems have been worked out. The classic example is that the movie industry makes tons of money from the very VHS industry it once feared.

My question for you is: how, and when, will the current "content is free" anomaly resolve itself on the Internet? The optimistic scenario is that this will happen smoothly and quickly, perhaps through "micro-royalties." The bleak scenario is that there will be an overreaction against Web content of all kinds, as there is now an overreaction against Internet and tech investments in general, and it will take years to reach equilibrium. What's your view?

That's it from this end. Thanks for taking part, and good luck on whatever you write about next.

FROM: MICHAEL LEWIS
TO: JAMES FALLOWS
SUBJECT: RE: THE (NEXT) AGE OF THE INTERNET—PART THREE

Dear Jim:
All of a sudden everything that happens in the world happens in reference to last week's catastrophe, and I don't see why our exchange should be any different. We should let readers know that you have not—as it appears—ignored current events to indulge some deep abiding passion for my book. You wrote your half of the exchange just before the planes crashed, and I sat on it for a week, watching CNN, and feeling distinctly disadvantaged. Since then I've been told by our editor to ignore whichever of your questions I feel like ignoring. I've been doing that anyway, but guiltily. Now I'll do it self-righteously. I don't have any original content to add to the discussion about the future of Internet content. So let me try to say something useful about your first two questions.

I never really thought of the eighties as a financial bubble. Many of the trends that got up and running during the most frenzied days of the eighties—junk-bond financing, leveraged buyouts, twenty-six-year-old millionaires, globalization of finance—are still with us. I also don't think that the Silicon Valley nineties were financially distinct, but rather a natural extension of the ideas that undergirded the Wall Street eighties. The central insight that led to much of the turmoil on Wall Street in the eighties was Michael Milken's understanding that certain kinds of risky debt were systematically undervalued. The central insight of the nineties in financial terms was the Silicon Valley capitalists' understanding that certain kinds of risky equity was also systematically undervalued.

In both cases insights about risk led to a perhaps excessive financial appetite for risk. Too much capital went into junk bonds in the eighties, just as too much capital went into venture-capital funds in the nineties. But when the dust settles—which, with the collapse of the Twin Towers, may take a bit longer than previously thought—there will be huge and thriving industries devoted to investing in risky debt and equity. And these industries will be the cutting edge of American finance, the place where the smartest financiers want to work.

The eighties on Wall Street and the nineties in Silicon Valley were both periods in which businessmen projected themselves out of their usual narrow contexts and shaped the larger world in their image. But in each case the larger world responded differently to the businessman's influence. For instance, the people who got rich in Silicon Valley, unlike the people who got rich on Wall Street, didn't have a lot of annoying people telling them they didn't deserve their fortunes. The larger world identified its own interests in the interests of the Silicon Valley mogul. Wall Street just seemed like a lot of greedy young men getting rich at other people's expense. Silicon Valley has benefited from a trend in the moral climate of money—a trend that last week's bombings may have reversed. I think Maureen Dowd was the one who said that in the eighties people felt guilty for getting rich, while in the nineties people felt guilty for not getting rich. I'd like to steal that line, if I thought I could get away with it.

You also want to know if I really mean it when I say that the Internet gives some people power and takes power from others. I do. I think the Internet will permanently change big tracts of the economy. I think, for instance, that anyone whose power depends on privileged access to information is likely to find that power undermined. It may take a while, and so it may never come as a shock, but the end result, if it could be viewed right now, would appear shocking.

One of the things I tried to get across in the book was how new technology is always coming along to change the rules of the game, and, in doing this, often makes life easier for people who were losing under the old rules. It's true that the process is not static. Once the rules get broken, new rules are created to shore up the authority of those in power. It's also true that not all technology is a weapon in the hands of the weak. The atom bomb was in many ways great for established authority. (On the other hand it meant that the people in power could no longer insulate themselves from personal danger in war.) But many new technologies create momentary opportunities for people who do not have power to seize some. The Internet has already done this. It is now being tamed, and made less threatening.

By the way, I just finished reading the FBI's description of the people who staged last week's hijackings. Did you notice that most of them were as wired as Silicon Valley venture capitalists?

Mass of Newly Laid-Off Workers Will Put Social Safety Net to the Test

JASON DEPARLE

At the Beverly Hilton, 200 workers have lost their jobs and nearly 250 have been dismissed from the sparkling towers of the Westin Bonaventure. A Las Vegas casino company, Mandalay Resorts, will cut its workforce by more than 4,000.

The airline industry says 100,000 people will lose their jobs. Among hotel and restaurant workers, industry leaders say, the number of people with lost jobs or sharply reduced hours could reach a million. In their suddenness and severity, the layoffs that followed the September 11 attacks have shocked the economy. They will pose a significant new test of a revamped social safety net. The mass of newly unemployed workers will encounter a welfare system that was overhauled in 1996 and has never faced a recession. A system that moved from federal control to a patchwork of state programs has, until now, been shielded by prosperity and low unemployment.

About 2.5 million adults have left the welfare rolls in recent years, lured by good times and pushed by tough laws. Maids, waitresses, cooks, and clerks, most hold the kind of low-skilled jobs that quickly disappear when businesses tighten their belts. Many work in the very industries—travel and tourism—devastated by the terrorist attacks.

That was the message conveyed recently by Barry Sternlicht, head of Starwood Resorts and Hotels, as he discussed his company's fifteen thousand layoffs. "We're talking about hourly people," Mr. Sternlicht said. "People who have made the welfare-to-work leap and are really not equipped to take this kind of layoff."

In the past, the ability of these people to return to welfare was virtually assured, and federal financing automatically grew to meet demand. Now federal financing is fixed, recipients face time limits and work rules, and states have wide discretion in deciding whom to help.

Critics of the new welfare system have often warned that it would fail in a faltering economy. Faced with falling revenues and fixed federal money, they say, states will cut aid just when the poor need it most.

"It's going to be hard for administrators to go to their legislatures and ask for more money," said Mark Greenberg of the Center on Law and Social Policy,

New York Times, October 8, 2001. Reprinted with permission of the *New York Times.* Jason DeParle reports on welfare, health care, and social policy for the *New York Times.*

a Washington advocacy group. "They may be fearful about letting people back on the rolls."

But others argue the safety net is stronger than the one it replaced. Many more job seekers have recent résumés. They also have expanded access to child care and transportation. State bureaucracies have gotten better at helping the poor find work.

"Every state does a better job than it used to of getting people into jobs," said Jason A. Turner, the welfare commissioner in New York City. "The overall safety net functions better and provides higher levels of income than it did before."

As former welfare recipients lose their jobs, a big unknown is how many will qualify for unemployment insurance. In the past, most failed to work long enough or earn enough to qualify. In Nevada, for instance, a jobless person has to earn $5,600 in a three-month period to qualify for the average unemployment benefit. That is more than twice what a woman leaving welfare typically earns.

In the past, Mr. Greenberg said, only 10 to 15 percent of former welfare recipients were able to meet state thresholds like these. Since more people have recent work experience now, those percentages are expected to rise.

Even so, "no more than a third will get on unemployment insurance," said Harry Holzer, an economist at Georgetown University.

In Denver, Sonja Gonzalez, twenty-two, just started working at United Airlines early this year. Now laid off without welfare or unemployment aid, she said, "I need to find a job fast."

In theory, if some people return to welfare, states should have the money to help them. States still get the same amount of federal welfare money as they did six years ago—$16.5 billion a year—though they serve fewer than half as many clients.

But with creative accounting, states have used some of the windfall on tax cuts, roads, and prisons. They have also used it to finance new services for the poor, including housing, car loans, and mental health programs. The largest amounts have gone for child care. A decade ago, for instance, Michigan spent $20 million a year on child care subsidies. Now it spends $500 million.

As the economy slowed before the attacks, a notable trend was already taking shape. Though unemployment was rising, the welfare rolls continued to fall, in some places sharply. In Illinois the unemployment rate grew nearly a percentage point. But the welfare rolls fell 30 percent. Florida had already cut its rolls 74 percent. But as unemployment grew there, the rolls fell 5 percent more. Pennsylvania followed the trend: unemployment up, welfare down.

Critics say numbers like these show the system no longer responds to rising need. "It's been so hostile to clients for so many years, people aren't going there," says Charles Sheketoff of the Oregon Center for Public Policy, an advocacy group. As a truer gauge of economic need, Mr. Sheketoff points to food stamps, whose costs are fully paid by the federal government. While Oregon kept its cash welfare rolls flat, food stamps rose 34 percent.

But state officials offer a different explanation. Until recently, they note, most layoffs involved industries that employ few welfare recipients, like manufacturing and technology. Entry-level jobs by and large remained plentiful, especially among women. "Our clients are still getting jobs," said Karan Maxson, who runs the Illinois welfare program. Plus, officials say, the rise in food stamps is not a surprise: that program typically reacts faster to economic trends.

Not every state with growing unemployment followed the roll-cutting trend. In Nevada, the caseload has grown 34 percent since reaching a trough last year.

Some people worry that time limits have weakened the safety net. The economy is failing just as the first welfare families are reaching a five-year lifetime limit on aid. Some states set shorter limits that have already expired. But because few families have continuously stayed on the rolls, a small minority risk being cut off soon. All states can grant some exceptions. Nationwide, of those who have already left the rolls, more than 90 percent are thought to have time left on the clock.

What does seem clear is that few who left the welfare system seem eager to go back. Lou Ann Cataneo of New York, a self-described "poster child for the welfare-to-work movement," spent a decade living on welfare, using drugs, and running from a violent boyfriend.

After becoming sober, she joined a training program run by Marriott and became a concierge at the Marriott Financial Center near the World Trade Center. In August, she traveled to Washington to tell the Brookings Institution, a policy group, the new welfare laws worked well.

Now, the hotel where Ms. Cataneo worked is damaged and closed. Ms. Cataneo is filing for unemployment benefits and hoping that Marriott will find her another job. If not, she says, the welfare office will be the last place she will return. "I'm always on my soapbox telling people it's not like it used to be: you can't stay on welfare for a generation," she said. "I'll work in McDonald's. It wouldn't be the first time I said, 'Do you want fries with that?'"

Chapter 5

Ethics and Justice in the New Workplace

THE ISSUES OF FAIRNESS, justice, and rights in the workplace have at times been obscured by the media's interest in the new economy's growth, opportunity, and rewards. Even a modest economic decline can awaken us, however, to the importance of the social and legal compact between worker and employer and government. Much is at stake for human health and well-being, civil and human rights, and social stability in how we define and build expectations about the fair and appropriate ways for workers to exchange their labor for pay. The triumph of the new economy in the 1990s and the many consequences of globalism cast new light on existing struggles to set these standards in the workplace, and also entangle us in new categories of personal difficulty: conflicts between work and family, lack of pension security, access to lifelong learning and skills. In this collection of pieces addressing ethics and justice in the new workplace, we sought pieces from writers and scholars who have performed the earliest and most important work in identifying these new and old conflicts that are relevant for most workers.

In a report developed for Working Partnerships USA and the South Bay AFL-CIO Labor Council, Chris Benner describes how contingent employment is more widespread and growing faster in Silicon Valley than in the country as a whole, providing a picture of emerging dilemmas, challenges, and responsibilities for the future of contingent employment nationally. Barbara Ehrenreich, in an excerpt from *Nickel and Dimed*, describes her experiences and observations in a series of jobs typically held by the working poor, including a stint working for a corporate maid service in Maine. An excerpt from Katherine Newman's *No Shame In My Game*, a study of the hardworking inner-city poor in their struggles to find upward mobility through fast-food employment, describes the stress and stigma associated with this frontline retail work in low-income neighborhoods. Powerful remarks by Linda Chavez-Thompson of the AFL-CIO describe the phenomenon of child labor abuse in the United States among farmworkers and even more troubling trends abroad. Chavez-Thompson brings to our attention that even in the United States we find violations of some of the basic rights we assume to be universal in our nation and our workplace.

A series of pieces follow that explore the roles and purposes of loyalty and ethics in corporations. The highly praised business writer Jerry Useem is excerpted here in a biting, humorous *Fortune* article that explores the shaky state of business ethics and loyalty in high-rolling Silicon Valley during late 1999 and 2000—including interviews with many observers and executives who worried that greed and arrogance would hasten an economic fall. Deborah Roberts, writing for a leading trade newsletter, describes two companies that battled high turnover in the food business by building trust and loyalty among all employees. Concluding this section is Sue Shellenbarger's *Wall Street Journal* article, "Workplace Upheavals Seem to Be Eroding Employees' Trust," which explores the underreported power of maintaining trust in the workplace, and of employers demonstrating respect for basic human values and needs, despite business pressures.

Shock Absorbers in the New Economy

CHRIS BENNER

In the last fifteen years, there has been a rapid increase in various forms of contingent employment. Temporary, contract, freelance, and part-time workers are becoming an increasingly large part of the labor force. The reason for this rise in contingent employment, to a large extent, is corporations' increasing drive for "flexibility" in the face of escalating global competition and the rapidly changing economy. Since the 1970s, employers have accelerated the elimination of full-time, permanent jobs and turned instead to more "flexible" arrangements, in which a greater number of employees move from job to job and project to project without long-term ties to their employers. Major corporations are shrinking the size of their core workforce and using various forms of temporary, contracted, and subcontracting arrangements to respond to uncertain market conditions and rapidly changing niche markets.

Contingent employment is more widespread and growing faster in Silicon Valley than in the country as a whole. The region thus provides a picture of the future of employment for millions of Americans as information technology increasingly transforms the structure of work in our economy. For a minority of highly skilled employees who have learned how to negotiate decent wages for themselves and operate in contingent labor markets, these flexible employment patterns can be beneficial—making it easier to balance work and family responsibilities and to gain greater control of their own work schedules. But for the majority of both low- and high-skilled Silicon Valley residents, the rise in contingent employment means increasing economic insecurity, declining wages, little access to benefits and health care, and limited opportunities for advancement.

The Problem of Contingent Employment

It is difficult to measure exactly the extent of contingent employment in the economy, because current government statistics do not track contingent employment. However, if all categories of contingent workers are included—temporary, part-time, self-employed, and contract work—the best estimate is that from 27 percent to 40 percent of all employees in Santa Clara County are contingent

Executive Summary, Working Partnerships USA, May 1996. Reprinted with permission of Working Partnerships USA. Chris Benner is an assistant professor at Pennsylvania State University and former research associate at Working Partnerships USA.

workers. The contingent workforce is growing rapidly—two to four times as fast as overall employment—and nearly all net job growth in the county in the last ten years is accounted for by the growth of contingent employment.

The most visible sign of this increase in contingent work is the rapid rise of temporary agencies in the region:

- Between January 1991 and January 1995, employment in temporary agencies in Santa Clara County grew by 48 percent, while overall employment in the County declined by 2 percent. In the first nine months of 1995 alone, employment in temporary agencies grew by 41 percent.
- According to figures from the California Employment Development Department, since 1984, employment in temporary help agencies has grown by 150 percent, a rate more than fifteen times the overall employment growth in the region.
- Temporary agencies now employ more than 32,000 people in the county, out of a workforce of some 800,000. The percentage of the workforce employed in temporary agencies in the last ten years has grown from 1.5 percent to 4 percent. This is nearly triple the national average. There are more than 250 offices of temporary agencies operating in Silicon Valley. Manpower Temporary Services (now the largest employer in the United States with more than 800,000 employees) operates fifteen offices in Silicon Valley, placing more than 5,000 people a week.
- Between 1989 and 1994, wages for all temporary workers in the United States declined by an average of nearly 14.7 percent in real terms. The drop was greatest for precision production workers (31.9 percent decline) and for technical occupations, including computer programmers (27.9 percent decline).

The rise in employment in temporary agencies is only one strategy among many that corporations use to maintain "flexibility" in their hiring practices. Many corporations are increasingly hiring temporary employees directly. The use of part-time workers has also increased, growing from 15.6 percent of the workforce in 1972 to 17.5 percent in 1993. Nearly all of that growth is in involuntary part-time work.

Perhaps the most significant increase in contingent employment comes in the form of corporations outsourcing and contracting out functions that had previously been performed in-house. In software development (one of the fastest growing industries in the Valley), much of the core work is done by "software gypsies" who move from company to company. Much of the assembly work in the Valley is now done by a range of contract electronic assembly companies, employing large numbers of immigrant Asian women. Such contracting out helps corporations ramp up production of new products but leaves employees extremely vulnerable to shifts in the market.

The contingent workforce is a heterogeneous group in terms of employment conditions. What all workers in contingent employment share is that their terms of employment stand outside the standard employment relationship on which the framework of employment and labor law was built. The fact that all contingent employees are outside the standard employment relationship means that they are vulnerable to rapid economic change and have difficulty being represented.

Recommendations for Public Policy Reform

A wide range of reforms in public policy and social welfare could be implemented to provide increased protection for contingent employees. They include:

- Wage support, aimed at increasing wages for contingent workers and decreasing the disparity between permanent and contingent workers. This includes raising the basic minimum wage and passing civil rights legislation to ensure contingent workers are paid the same wages as permanent workers performing the same work;
- Increased access to health coverage, ideally through a universal health insurance system in which people have access to health coverage by virtue of being residents, not through an individual's employment relationship. Other more piecemeal efforts include increasing the health care tax exemption for self-employed persons, and various efforts designed to allow workers to maintain health coverage even during periods of periodic unemployment;
- Increased access to pensions, through various tax strategies to promote pension portability and adopt measures that allow workers to carry pension credits with them from job to job; and
- Increased access to unemployment insurance. Currently only 32.5 percent of all those who are unemployed receive benefits from the Unemployment Insurance (UI) system, and in many states independent contractors, temporary, part-time, and seasonal workers are denied benefits.

In addition, regulation of the temporary industry itself should be pursued, as is common practice in Japan and in most European countries. These regulations should be geared toward:

- Managing conditions for establishing a temporary help agency, including requiring licenses to operate and conducting regular reviews of operations. In some cases temporary help firms are prohibited from operating in particular sectors of the economy. This helps prevent abuses and provides channels for hearing grievances against corporations.
- Governing conditions for the use of temporary workers, ensuring that temporary workers are not used to replace permanent employees, limiting the

maximum number of jobs in an enterprise that can be filled by temporary workers, or limiting the duration of temporary assignments.
- Providing adequate social protection for workers in temporary agencies and ensuring adequate wages and social benefits. For instance in France, temporary workers are required to be paid the same wage as permanent workers, and upon conclusion of their assignment, temporary workers also benefit from a "precarious employment allowance," which is increased by 50 percent if the temporary help agency does not offer them a new assignment within a period of three days.

Recommendations for Unions

The rise in contingent employment calls for new thinking and innovations in organizing. There are numerous initiatives both in Silicon Valley and around the country that have begun trying to represent contingent workers' interests. These initiatives provide a measure of permanence and security for workers even as they are forced to move from job to job and employer to employer. The focus of these efforts for workers at all skill levels goes beyond organizing in a single worksite or with a single employer. Instead, they focus on building *career or employment security,* even if job security is impossible to achieve. The various initiatives outlined in this report point to the need to organize around both residential and occupational identity and the need to assist contingent workers in the following areas:

- Coordinated Training Programs: Because people change jobs repeatedly (and before downsizing hits) unions need to play a larger role in reaching out to contingent workers to provide apprenticeship training, retraining, skill certification, and job placement and to help build career job ladders. Through such an effort, unions would be able to guarantee quality work, build loyalty to the union throughout a person's career, and demand premium wages for their members even in the midst of industry restructuring and frequent job changes.
- Protection of Employee Rights: Employee rights have actually expanded over the last twenty-five years (for example, antidiscrimination and occupational safety and health legislation), while union membership has been declining. The problem is that without collective organization many workers remain unaware of their rights or lack the organizational strength to pursue grievances. Unions need to strengthen their efforts to provide education to unrepresented workers and to provide representation for members based on their legal rights, even without collective bargaining agreements.
- Multi-Employer Regional Collective Bargaining: Organizations representing contingent workers should aim toward developing multi-employer collective bargaining on a regional basis. To be effective, such organizing must

be built on providing representation for workers prior to being able to achieve collective bargaining. Such pre–collective bargaining representation can be achieved through an expanded associate membership program, or through representation in guild-type associations.

- Portable Benefits: These new organizations should provide workers with benefits, particularly health care and pension programs, that they can maintain as they move from employer to employer and even during periods of unemployment. Collective bargaining programs need to be geared toward employer contribution to these portable benefit plans.

Scrubbing in Maine

BARBARA EHRENREICH

After a day's training I am judged fit to go out with a team, where I soon discover that life is nothing like the movies, at least not if the movie is *Dusting*. For one thing, compared with our actual pace, the training videos were all in slow motion. We do not walk to the cars with our buckets full of cleaning fluids and utensils in the morning, we run, and when we pull up to a house, we run with our buckets to the door. Liza, a good-natured woman in her thirties who is my first team leader, explains that we are given only so many minutes per house, ranging from under sixty for a 1½-bathroom apartment to two hundred or more for a multibathroom "first timer." I'd like to know why anybody worries about Ted's time limits if we're being paid by the hour but hesitate to display anything that might be interpreted as attitude. As we get to each house, Liza assigns our tasks, and I cross my fingers to ward off bathrooms and vacuuming. Even dusting, though, gets aerobic under pressure, and after about an hour of it—reaching to get door tops, crawling along floors to wipe baseboards, standing on my bucket to attack the higher shelves—I wouldn't mind sitting down with a tall glass of water. But as soon as you complete your assigned task, you report to the team leader to be assigned to help someone else. Once or twice, when the normal process of evaporation is deemed too slow, I am assigned to dry a scrubbed floor by putting rags under my feet and skating around on it. Usually, by the time I get out to the car and am dumping the dirty water used on floors and wringing out rags, the rest of the team is already in the car with the motor running. Liza assures me that they've never left anyone behind at a house, not even, presumably, a very new person whom nobody knows.

In my interview, I had been promised a thirty-minute lunch break, but this turns out to be a five-minute pit stop at a convenience store, if that. I bring my own sandwich—the same turkey breast and cheese every day—as do a couple of the others; the rest eat convenience store fare, a bagel or doughnut salvaged from our free breakfast, or nothing at all. The two older married women I'm teamed up with eat best—sandwiches and fruit. Among the younger women, lunch consists of a slice of pizza, a "pizza pocket" (a roll of dough surrounding some pizza sauce), or a small bag of chips. Bear in mind we are not office workers, sitting

From *Nickel and Dimed: On Not Getting by in America*. Copyright © 2001 by Barbara Ehrenreich. Reprinted by permission of Henry Holt and Co., LLC. Barbara Ehrenreich is a widely published writer who frequently appears in *The Nation*, *Harper's*, and many other newsletters and mainstream periodicals and is the author of many distinguished books.

around idling at the basal metabolic rate. A poster on the wall in the office cheerily displays the number of calories burned per minute at our various tasks, ranging from about 3.5 for dusting to 7 for vacuuming. If you assume an average of 5 calories per minute in a seven-hour day (eight hours minus time for travel between houses), you need to be taking in 2,100 calories in addition to the resting minimum of, say, 900 or so. I get pushy with Rosalie, who is new like me and fresh from high school in a rural northern part of the state, about the meagerness of her lunches, which consist solely of Doritos—a half bag from the day before or a freshly purchased small-sized bag. She just didn't have anything in the house, she says (though she lives with her boyfriend and his mother), and she certainly doesn't have any money to buy lunch, as I find out when I offer to fetch her a soda from a Quik Mart and she has to admit she doesn't have eighty-nine cents. I treat her to the soda, wishing I could force her, mommylike, to take milk instead. So how does she hold up for an eight- or even nine-hour day? "Well," she concedes, "I get dizzy sometimes."

How poor are they, my coworkers? The fact that anyone is working this job at all can be taken as prima facie evidence of some kind of desperation or at least a history of mistakes and disappointments, but it's not for me to ask. In the prison movies that provide me with a mental guide to comportment, the new guy doesn't go around shaking hands and asking, "Hi there, what are you in for?" So I listen, in the cars and when we're assembled in the office, and learn, first, that no one seems to be homeless. Almost everyone is embedded in extended families or families artificially extended with housemates. People talk about visiting grandparents in the hospital or sending birthday cards to a niece's husband; single mothers live with their own mothers or share apartments with a coworker or boyfriend. Pauline, the oldest of us, owns her own home, but she sleeps on the living room sofa, while her four grown children and three grandchildren fill up the bedrooms.[1]

But although no one, apparently, is sleeping in a car, there are signs, even at the beginning, of real difficulty if not actual misery. Half-smoked cigarettes are returned to the pack. There are discussions about who will come up with fifty cents for a toll and whether Ted can be counted on for prompt reimbursement. One of my teammates gets frantic about a painfully impacted wisdom tooth and keeps making calls from our houses to try to locate a source of free dental care. When my—or, I should say, Liza's—team discovers there is not a single Dobie in our buckets, I suggest that we stop at a convenience store and buy one rather than drive all the way back to the office. But it turns out I haven't brought any money with me and we cannot put together two dollars between the four of us.

The Friday of my first week at The Maids is unnaturally hot for Maine in early September—ninety-five degrees, according to the digital time-and-temperature displays offered by banks that we pass. I'm teamed up with the sad-faced Rosalie and our leader, Maddy, whose sullenness, under the circumstances, is almost a relief after Liza's relentless good cheer. Liza, I've learned, is the highest-ranking cleaner, a sort of supervisor really, and said to be something of a snitch, but Maddy, a single mom of maybe twenty-seven or so, has worked for only three months and broods about her child care problems. Her boyfriend's sister, she tells me on the drive to our first house, watches her eighteen-month-old for fifty dollars a week, which is a stretch on The Maids' pay, plus she doesn't entirely trust the sister, but a real day care center could be as much as ninety dollars a week. After polishing off the first house, no problem, we grab "lunch"—Doritos for Rosalie and a bag of Pepperidge Farm Goldfish for Maddy—and head out into the exurbs for what our instruction sheet warns is a five-bathroom spread and a first-timer to boot. Still, the size of the place makes us pause for a moment, buckets in hand, before searching out an appropriately humble entrance.[2] It sits there like a beached ocean liner, the prow cutting through swells of green turf, windows without number. "Well, well," Maddy says, reading the owner's name from our instruction sheet, "Mrs. W. and her big-ass house. I hope she's going to give us lunch."

Mrs. W. is not in fact happy to see us, grimacing with exasperation when the black nanny ushers us into the family room or sunroom or den or whatever kind of specialized space she is sitting in. After all, she already has the nanny, a cooklike person, and a crew of men doing some sort of finishing touches on the construction to supervise. No, she doesn't want to take us around the house, because she already explained everything to the office on the phone, but Maddy stands there, with Rosalie and me behind her, until she relents. We are to move everything on all surfaces, she instructs during the tour, and get underneath and be sure to do every bit of the several miles, I calculate, of baseboards. And be mindful of the baby, who's napping and can't have cleaning fluids of any kind near her.

Then I am let loose to dust. In a situation like this, where I don't even know how to name the various kinds of rooms, The Maids' special system turns out to be a lifesaver. All I have to do is keep moving from left to right, within rooms and between rooms, trying to identify landmarks so I don't accidentally do a room or a hallway twice. Dusters get the most complete biographical overview, due to the necessity of lifting each object and tchotchke individually, and I learn that Mrs. W. is an alumna of an important women's college, now occupying herself by monitoring her investments and the baby's bowel movements. I find special charts for this latter purpose, with spaces for time of day, most recent fluid intake, consistency, and color. In the master bedroom, I dust a whole shelf of books on pregnancy, breastfeeding, the first six months, the first year, the first two years—and I wonder what the child care–deprived Maddy makes of all this. Maybe there's been some secret division of the world's women into breeders and drones, and those at the maid level are no longer supposed to be reproducing at all. Maybe this is why our office manager, Tammy, who was once a maid herself, wears inch-long fake nails and tarty little outfits—to show she's advanced to the breeder caste and can't be sent out to clean anymore.

It is hotter inside than out, unair-conditioned for the benefit of the baby, I suppose, but I do all right until I encounter the banks of glass doors that line the side and back of the ground floor. Each one has to be Windexed, wiped, and buffed—inside and out, top to bottom, left to right, until it's as streakless and invisible as a material substance can be. Outside, I can see the construction guys knocking back Gatorade, but the rule is that no fluid or food item can touch a maid's lips when she's inside a house. Now, sweat, even in unseemly quantities, is nothing new to me. I live in a subtropical area where even the inactive can expect to be moist nine months out of the year. I work out, too, in my normal life and take a certain macho pride in the *Vs* of sweat that form on my T-shirt after ten minutes or more on the StairMaster. But in normal life fluids lost are immediately replaced. Everyone in yuppieland—airports, for example—looks like a nursing baby these days, inseparable from their plastic bottles of water. Here, however, I sweat without replacement or pause, not in individual drops but in continuous sheets of fluid soaking through my polo shirt, pouring down the backs of my legs. The eyeliner I put on in the morning—vain twit that I am—has long since streaked down onto my cheeks, and I could wring my braid out if I wanted to. Working my way through the living room(s), I wonder if Mrs. W. will ever have occasion to realize that every single doodad and *objet* through which she expresses her unique, individual self is, from another vantage point, only an obstacle between some thirsty person and a glass of water.

When I can find no more surfaces to wipe and have finally exhausted the supply of rooms, Maddy assigns me to do the kitchen floor. OK, except that Mrs. W. is *in* the kitchen, so I have to go down on my hands and knees practically at her feet. No, we don't have sponge mops like the one I use in my own house; the hands-and-knees approach is a definite selling point for corporate cleaning services like The Maids. "We clean floors the old-fashioned way—*on our hands and knees*" (emphasis added), the brochure for a competing firm boasts. In fact, whatever advantages there may be to the hands-and-knees approach—you're closer to your work, of course, and less likely to miss a grimy patch—are undermined by the artificial drought imposed by The Maids' cleaning system. We are instructed to use less than half a small bucket of lukewarm water for a kitchen and all adjacent scrubbable floors (breakfast nooks and other dining areas), meaning that within a few minutes we are doing nothing more than redistributing the dirt evenly around the floor. There are occasional customer complaints about the cleanliness of our floors—for example, from a man who wiped up a spill on his freshly "cleaned" floor only to find the paper towel he employed for this purpose had turned gray. A mop and a full bucket of hot soapy water would not only get a floor cleaner but would be a lot more dignified for the person who does the cleaning. But it is this primal posture of submission—and of what is ultimately anal accessibility—that seems to gratify the consumers of maid services.[3]

I don't know, but Mrs. W.'s floor is hard—stone, I think, or at least a stonelike substance—and we have no knee pads with us today. I had thought in my middle-class innocence that knee pads were one of Monica Lewinsky's prurient fantasies, but no, they actually exist, and they're usually a standard part of our equipment. So here I am on my knees, working my way around the room like some fanatical penitent crawling through the stations of the cross, when I realize that Mrs. W. is staring at me fixedly—so fixedly that I am gripped for a moment by the wild possibility that I may have once given a lecture at her alma mater and she's trying to figure out where she's seen me before. If I were recognized, would I be fired? Would she at least be inspired to offer me a drink of water? Because I have decided that if water is actually offered, I'm taking it, rules or no rules, and if word of this infraction gets back to Ted, I'll just say I thought it would be rude to refuse. Not to worry, though. She's just watching that I don't leave out some stray square inch, and when I rise painfully to my feet again, blinking through the sweat, she says, "Could you just scrub the floor in the entryway while you're at it?"

I rush home to the Blue Haven at the end of the day, pull down the blinds for privacy, strip off my uniform in the kitchen—the bathroom being too small for both a person and her discarded clothes—and stand in the shower for a good ten minutes, thinking all this water is *mine*. I have paid for it; in fact, I have earned it. I have gotten through a week at The Maids without mishap, injury, or insurrection. My back feels fine, meaning I'm not feeling it at all; even my wrists, damaged by carpal tunnel syndrome years ago, are issuing no complaints. Coworkers warned me that the first time they donned the backpack vacuum they felt faint, but not me. I am strong, and I am, more than that, good. Did I toss my bucket of filthy water onto Mrs. W.'s casual white summer outfit? No. Did I take the wand of my vacuum cleaner and smash someone's Chinese porcelain statues or Hummel figurines? Not once. I was at all times cheerful, energetic, helpful, and as competent as a new hire can be expected to be. If I can do one week, I can do another, and might as well, since there's never been a moment for job-hunting. The 3:30 quitting time turns out to be a myth; often we don't return to the office until 4:30 or 5:00. And what did I think? That I was going to go out to interviews in my soaked and stinky postwork condition? I decide to reward myself with a sunset walk on Old Orchard Beach.

On account of the heat, there are still a few actual bathers on the beach, but I am content to sit in shorts and T-shirt and watch the ocean pummel the sand. When the sun goes down I walk back into the town to find my car and am amazed to hear a sound I associate with cities like New York and Berlin. There's a couple of Peruvian musicians playing in the little grassy island in the street near the pier, and maybe fifty people—locals and vacationers—have gathered around, offering their bland end-of-summer faces to the sound. I edge my way through the crowd and find a seat where I can see the musicians up close—the beautiful young guitarist and the taller man playing the flute. What are they doing in this rinky-dink blue-collar resort, and what does the audience make of this surprise visit from the dark-skinned South? The melody the flute lays out over the percussion is both utterly strange and completely familiar, as if it had been imprinted in the minds of my own peasant ancestors centuries ago and forgotten until this very moment. Everyone else seems to be as transfixed as I am. The musicians wink and smile at each other as they play, and I see then that they are the secret emissaries of a worldwide lower-class conspiracy to snatch joy out of degradation and filth. When the song ends, I give them a dollar, the equivalent of about ten minutes of sweat.

Notes

1. The women I worked with were all white and, with one exception, Anglo, as are the plurality of housecleaners in America, or at least those known to the Bureau of Labor Statistics. Of the "private household cleaners and servants" it managed to locate in 1998, the BLS reports that 36.8 percent were Hispanic, 15.8 percent black, and 2.7 percent "other." However, the association between housecleaning and minority status is well established in the psyches of the white employing class. When my daughter, Rosa, was introduced to the father of a wealthy Harvard classmate, he ventured that she must have been named for a favorite maid. And Audre Lorde reported an experience she had in 1967: "I wheel my two-year-old daughter in a shopping cart through a supermarket . . . and a little white girl riding past in her mother's cart calls out excitedly, 'Oh look, Mommy, a baby maid'" (quoted in Mary Romero, *Maid in the U.S.A.: Perspectives on Gender* [New York: Routledge, 1992], 72). But the composition of the household workforce is hardly fixed and has changed with the life chances of the different ethnic groups. In the late nineteenth century, Irish and German immigrants served the urban upper and middle classes, then left for the factories as soon as they could. Black women replaced them, accounting for 60 percent of all domestics in the 1940s, and dominated the field until other occupations began to open up to them. Similarly, West Coast maids were disproportionately Japanese American until that group too found more congenial options (see Phyllis Palmer, *Domesticity and Dirt: Housewives and Domestic Servants in the United States, 1920–1945* [Philadelphia: Temple University Press, 1989], 12–13). Today, the color of the hand that pushes the sponge varies from region to region: Chicanas in the Southwest, Caribbeans in New York, native Hawaiians in Hawaii, native whites, many of recent rural extraction, in the Midwest and, of course, Maine.

2. For the affluent, houses have been swelling with no apparent limit. The square footage of new homes increased by 39 percent between 1971 and 1996, to include "family rooms," home entertainment rooms, home offices, bedrooms, and often a bathroom for each family member ("Détente in the Housework Wars," *Toronto Star,* November 20, 1999). By the second quarter of 1999, 17 percent of new homes were larger than three thousand square feet, which is usually considered the size threshold for household help, or the point at which a house becomes unmanageable to the people who live in it ("Molding Loyal Pamperers for the Newly Rich," *New York Times,* October 24, 1999).

3. In *Home Comforts: The Art and Science of Keeping House* (New York: Scribner, 1999), Cheryl Mendelson writes, "Never ask hired housecleaners to clean your floors on their hands and knees; the request is likely to be regarded as degrading" (501).

No Shame in (This) Game

KATHERINE S. NEWMAN

In the early 1990s, the McDonald's Corporation launched a television ad campaign featuring a young black man named Calvin, who was portrayed sitting atop a Brooklyn stoop in his Golden Arches uniform while his friends down on the sidewalk passed by, giving him a hard time about holding down a "McJob." After brushing off their teasing with good humor, Calvin is approached furtively by one young black man who asks, sotto voce, whether Calvin might help him get a job too. He allows that he could use some earnings and that despite the ragging he has just given Calvin, he thinks the uniform is really pretty cool—or at least that having a job is pretty cool.

Every fast-food worker we interviewed for this book knew the Calvin series by heart: Calvin on the job, Calvin in the streets, Calvin helping an elderly woman cross the street on his way to work, Calvin getting promoted to management. And they knew what McDonald's was trying to communicate to young people by producing the series in the first place: that the stigma clings to fast-food jobs, that it can be overcome, and that even your best friends will come to admire you if you stick with it—after they've finished dissing you in public.

Americans have always been committed to the moral maxim that work defines the person. We carry around in our heads a rough tally that tells us what kinds of jobs are worthy of respect and what kinds are to be disdained, a pyramid organized by the income a job carries, the sort of credentials it takes to secure a particular position, the qualities of an occupation's incumbents—and we use this system of stratification (ruthlessly at times) to boost the status of some and humiliate others. This penchant for ranking by occupation is more pervasive in the United States than in other societies, where there are different ways of evaluating the personal worth of individuals. In these societies, coming from a "good family" counts heavily in the calculus of social standing. Here in America, there is no other metric that matters as much as the kind of job you hold.

Given our tradition of equating moral value with employment, it stands to reason that the most profound dividing line in our culture is that separating the working person from the unemployed. Only after this canyon has been crossed do we begin to make the finer gradations that distinguish white-collar worker

 Katherine S. Newman is a Ford Foundation Professor of Urban Studies at the Kennedy School of Government at Harvard University.

from blue-collar worker, CEO from secretary. We attribute a whole host of moral virtues—self-discipline, personal responsibility, maturity—to those who have found and kept a job, almost any job, and dismiss those who haven't as slothful or irresponsible.

We inhabit an unforgiving culture that is blind to the many reasons why some people cross that employment barrier and others are left behind. While we may remember, for a time, that unemployment rates are high, or that particular industries have downsized millions of workers right out of a job, or that racial barriers or negative attitudes toward teenagers make it harder to get a job at some times and for some people, in the end American culture wipes these background truths out in favor of a simpler dichotomy: the worthy and the unworthy, the working stiff and the lazy sloth.

These days, our puritanical attitudes owe some of their force to the resentment the employed bear toward the taxes they must pay to support those who cannot earn on their own. But it has deeper cultural dimensions. From the earliest beginnings of the nation, work has been the sine qua non of membership in this society. Adults who work are full-fledged citizens in the truest sense of the term—complete participants in the social world that is most highly valued. No other dimension of life—community, family, religion, voluntary organizations—qualifies Americans for this designation of citizen in the same way.

We express this view in a variety of ways in our social policies. Virtually all our benefits (especially health care but including unemployment insurance, life insurance, child care tax credits, etc.) are provided through the employment system. In Western Europe this is often not the case: health care is provided directly through the tax system, and benefits come to people who are political "citizens" whether they work or not. In the United States, however, those outside the employment system are categorized as unworthy and made to feel it by excluding them from these systems of support. To varying degrees, we "take care" of the socially excluded by creating stigmatized categories for their benefits—welfare and Medicaid being prime examples. Yet we never confuse the approved, acceptable Americans with the undeserving, and we underscore the difference by separating them into different bureaucratic worlds.

For those on the positive side of the divide, those who work for a living, the rewards are far greater than a paycheck. The employed enter a social world in which their identities as mainstream Americans are shaped, structured, and reinforced. The workplace is the main institutional setting in which individuals become part of the collective American enterprise that lies at the heart of our culture: the market. We are so divided in other domains—race, geography, family organization, gender roles, and the like—that common ground along almost any other lines is difficult to achieve. Indeed, only in wartime do Americans tend to cleave to their national origins as a major feature of their self-concept. The French, by contrast, are French whether they work or not. But for our more diverse and divided society, participation in the world of work is the most powerful source of social integrations.

It is in the workplace that we are most likely to mix with those who come from different backgrounds, are under the greatest pressure to subordinate individual idiosyncrasy to the requirements of an organization, and are called upon to contribute to goals that eclipse the personal. All workers have these experiences in common; even as segregation constrains the real mix of workers, conformity is expected to a greater degree for people who work in some kinds of jobs than in others, and the organizational goals to which they must subscribe are often elusive, unreachable, or at odds with personal desire.

The creation of an identity as a worker is never achieved by individuals moving along some preordained path. It is a transformation worked by organizations, firms, supervisors, fellow workers, and the whole long search that leads from the desire to find a job to the end point of landing one. This is a particularly dramatic transformation for ghetto youth and adults, for they face a difficult job market, high hurdles in convincing employers to take a chance on them, and relatively poor reward—from a financial point of view—for their successes. But the crafting of an identity is an important developmental process for them, just as it is for their more privileged counterparts.

Powerful forces work to exclude minorities from full participation in American society. From a school system that provides a substandard education for millions of inner-city kids, to an employment system rife with discrimination, to a housing market that segregates minority families, there is almost no truth to the notion that we all begin from the same starting line. Precisely because this is the case, blasting one's way through the job barrier and starting down that road of acquiring a common identity as a mainstream worker is one of the greatest importance for the young. It may be one of the few available pipelines into the core of American society, and the one with the greatest payoff, symbolic and material.

The Social Costs of Accepting Low-Wage Work

Even though we honor the gainfully employed over the unemployed, all jobs are not created equal. Fast-food jobs, in particular, are notoriously stigmatized and denigrated. "McJob" has become a common epithet for work without much redeeming value. The reasons for this are worth studying, for the minority workers who figure in this book have a mountain of stigma to overcome if they are to maintain their self-respect. Indeed, the organizational culture they join when they finally land a job at Burger Barn is instrumental in generating conditions and experiences that challenge a worker's self-esteem.

As Robin Leidner has argued, fast-food jobs epitomize the assembly-line structure of de-skilled service positions: they are highly routinized and appear to the casual observer to be entirely lacking in discretion—almost military in their scripted nature. The symbolic capital of these assembly-line jobs can be measured in negative numbers. They represent the opposite of the autonomous entrepreneur who is lionized in the popular culture, from *Business Week* to hip-hop.

Burger Barn workers are told that they must, at whatever cost to their own dignity, defer to the public. Customers can be unreasonably demanding, rude, even insulting, and workers must count backwards from a hundred in an effort to stifle their outrage. Servicing the customer with a smile pleases management because making money depends on keeping the clientele happy, but it can be an exercise in humiliation for teenagers. It is hard for them to refrain from reading this public nastiness as another instance of society's low estimation of their worth. But they soon realize that if they want to hold on to their minimum-wage jobs, they have to tolerate comments that would almost certainly provoke a fistfight outside the workplace.

It is well known among ghetto customers that crew members have to put up with whatever verbal abuse comes across the counter. That knowledge occasionally prompts nasty exchanges designed explicitly to anger the worker, to push him or her to retaliate verbally. Testing those limits is a favorite pastime of teenager customers in particular, for this may be the one opportunity they have to put a peer on the defensive in a public setting, knowing that there is little the victim can do in return.

It is bad enough to be on the receiving end of this kind of abuse from adults, especially white adults, for that has its own significance along race lines. It is even worse to have to accept it from minority peers, for there is much more personal honor at stake, more pride to be lost, and an audience whose opinion matters more. This, no doubt, is why harassment is a continual problem for fast-food workers in Harlem. It burns. Their age mates, with plenty of anger bottled up for all kinds of reasons extraneous to the restaurant experience, find counterparts working the cash register convenient targets for venting.

Roberta is a five-year veteran of Burger Barn who has worked her way up to management. A formidable African American woman, Roberta has always prided herself on her ability to make it on her own. Most of her customers have been perfectly pleasant; many have been longtime repeat visitors to her restaurant. But Roberta has also encountered many who radiate disrespect.

> *Could you describe some of the people who came into the store during your shift?*
>
> The customers? Well, I had alcoholics, derelicts. People that are aggravated with life. I've had people that don't even have jobs curse me out. I've dealt with all kinds. Sometimes it would get to me. If a person yelled out [in front of] a lobby full of people . . . "Bitch, that's why you work at [Burger Barn]," I would say [to myself], "I'm probably making more than you and your mother." It hurts when people don't even know what you're making and they say those things. Especially in Harlem, they do that to you. They call you all types of names and everything.

Natasha is younger than Roberta and less practiced at these confrontations. But she has had to contend with them nevertheless, especially from customers her age who at least claim to be higher up the status hierarchy. Though she tries, Natasha can't always control her temper and respond the way the firm wants her to.

> It's hard dealing with the public. There are good things, like old people. They sweet. But the younger people around my age are always snotty. Think they better than you because they not working at [Burger Barn]. They probably work at something better than you.
>
> *How do you deal with unfriendly customers?*
>
> They told us that we just suppose to walk to the back and ignore it, but when they get in your face like that, you get so upset that you have to say something . . . I got threatened with a gun one time. 'Cause this customer had threw a piece of straw paper in the back and told me to pick it up like I'm a dog. I said, "No." And he cursed at me. I cursed at him back, and he was like, "Yeah, next time you won't have nothing to say when I come back with my gun and shoot your ass." Oh, excuse me.

Ianna, who had just turned sixteen the summer she found her first job at Burger Barn, has had many of the same kinds of problems Natasha complains of. The customers who are rude to her are just looking for a place to vent their anger about things that have nothing to do with buying lunch. Ianna recognizes that this kind of thing could happen in any restaurant but believes it is a special problem in Harlem, for ghetto residents have more to be angry about and fewer accessible targets. So cashiers in fast-food shops become prime victims.

> What I hate about [Burger Barn] is the customers, well, some of them that I can't stand. . . . I don't want to stereotype Harlem . . . but since I only worked in Harlem that's all I can speak for. Some people have a chip on their shoulders . . . Most of the people that come into the restaurant are black. Most of them have a lot of kids. It's in the ghetto. Maybe, you know, they are depressed about their lifestyles or whatever else that is going on in their lives and they just . . . I don't know. They just are like, urff! And no matter what you do you cannot please them. I'm not supposed to say anything to the customer, but that's not like me. I have a mouth and I don't take no short from nobody. I don't care who it is, don't take anybody's crap.

Despite this bravado, Ianna knows well that to use her mouth is to risk her job. She has had to work hard to find ways to cope with this frustration that don't get her in trouble with management.

> I don't say stuff to people most of the time. Mostly I just look at them like they stupid. Because my mother always told me that as long as you don't say nothin' to nobody, you can't never get in trouble. If you look at them stupid, what are they going to do? If you roll your eyes at somebody like that, I mean, that's really nothing [compared to] . . . cursing at them. Most of the time I try to walk away.

As Ianna observes, there is enough free-floating fury in Harlem to keep a steady supply of customer antagonism coming the way of service employees every day of their work lives. The problem is constant enough to warrant official company policies on how crew members should respond to insults, on what managers should do to help, on the evasive tactics that will work best to quell an ugly situation without losing the business. Management tries to minimize the likelihood of incidents by placing girls on the registers rather than boys, in the apparent belief that young women attract less abuse and find it easier to quash their anger than young men.

Burger Barn does what it can to contend with these problems in the workplace. But the neighborhood is beyond their reach, and there, too, fast-food workers are often met with ridicule from the people they grew up with. They have to learn to defend themselves against criticism from people they have known all their lives. As Stephanie explains, here, too, she leans on the divide between the worker and the do-nothing:

> People I hang out with, they know me since I was little. We all grew up together. When they see me comin', they laugh and say, "Here come Calvin, here come Calvin sister." I just laugh and keep on going. I say, "You're crazy. But that's okay 'cause I got a job and you all standing out here on the corner." Or I say, "This is my job, it's legal." Something like that. That Calvin commercial show you that even though his friends tease him he just brushed them off, then he got a higher position. Then you see how they change toward him.

Tiffany, also a teen worker in a central Harlem Burger Barn, thinks she knows why kids in her community who don't work give her such a hard time. They don't want her to succeed because if no one is "making it," then no one needs to feel bad about failing. But if someone claws her way up and it looks as if she has a chance to escape the syndrome of failure, it implies that everyone could, in theory, do so as well. The teasing, a thinly veiled attempt to enforce conformity, is designed to drag would-be success stories back into the fold.

> What you will find in any situation, more so in the black community, is that if you are in the community and you try to excel, you will get ridicule from your own peers. It's like the "crab down" syndrome. . . . If you put a bunch of crabs in a big bucket and one crab tries to get out, what do you think the other crabs would do now? According to my thinking, they should pull 'em up or push 'em or help 'em get out. But the crabs pull him back in the barrel. That's just an analogy for what happens in the community a lot.

Keeping everyone down protects against that creeping sense of despair which comes from believing things could be otherwise for oneself.

Swallowing ridicule would be a hardship for almost anyone in this culture, but it is particularly hard on minority youth in the inner city. They have already logged four or five years' worth of interracial and cross-class friction by the time they get behind a Burger Barn cash register. More likely than not, they have also learned from peers that self-respecting people don't allow themselves to be "dissed" without striking back. Yet this is precisely what they must do if they are going to survive in the workplace.

This is one of the main reasons why these jobs carry such a powerful stigma in American popular culture: they fly in the face of a national attraction to autonomy, independence, and the individual's "right" to respond in kind when dignity is threatened. In ghetto communities, this stigma is even more powerful because—ironically—it is in these enclaves that this mainstream value of independence is most vigorously elaborated and embellished. Film characters, rap stars, and local idols base their claim to notoriety on standing above the crowd, going their own way, being free of the ties that bind ordinary mortals. There are white parallels, to be sure, but this is a powerful genre of icons in the black community, not because it is a disconnected subculture but because it is an intensified version of a perfectly recognizable American middle-class and working-class fixation.

It is therefore noteworthy that thousands upon thousands of minority teens, young adults, and even middle-aged adults line up for jobs that will subject them, at least potentially, to a kind of character assassination. They do so not because they start the job-seeking process with a different set of values, one that can withstand society's contempt for fast-food workers. They take these jobs because in so many inner-city communities, there is nothing better in the offing. In general, they have already tried to get better jobs and have failed, landing at the door of Burger Barn as a last resort.

Social stigma has other sources besides the constraints of enforced deference. Money and mobility matter as well. Fast-food jobs are invariably minimum-wage positions. Salaries rise very little over time, even for first-line management. In ghetto areas, where jobs are scarce and the supply of would-be workers chasing them is relatively large, downward pressure on wages keeps these jobs right down at the bottom of the wage scale.

The public perception (fueled by knowledge of wage conditions) is that there is very little potential for improvement in status or responsibility either. Even though there are Horatio Algers in this industry, there are no myths to prop up a more glorified image. As a result, the epithet "McJob" develops out of the perception that fast-food workers are not likely to end up in a prestigious job as a general manager or restaurant owner; they are going to spend their whole lives flipping burgers.

As it happens, this is only half true. The fast-food industry is actually very good about internal promotion. Workplace management is nearly always recruited from the ranks of entry-level workers. Carefully planned training programs make it possible for employees to move up, to acquire transferable skills, and to at least take a shot at entrepreneurial ownership. McDonald's, for example, is proud of the fact that half of its board of directors started out as crew members. One couldn't say as much for the rest of the nation's Fortune 500 firms.

However, the vast majority never even get close to management. The typical entry-level worker passes through his or her job in short order, with an industry-average job tenure of less than six months. Since this is an average, it suggests that a large number of employees are there and gone in a matter of weeks. It is this pattern, a planned operation built around low skills and high turnover, that has given fast-food jobs such a bad name. In order for the industry to keep functioning with such an unstable labor force, the jobs themselves must be broken down so that each step can be learned, at least at a rudimentary level, in a very short time. A vicious circle develops in which low wages are attached to low skills, encouraging high departure rates. Hence, although it is quite possible to rise above the fray and make a very respectable living as a general manager overseeing a restaurant, most crew members remain at the entry level and leave too soon to see much upward movement. Observing this pattern on such a large scale—in practically ever town and city in the country—Americans naturally conclude that one can't get anywhere in a job like this, that there is no real future in it, and that anyone with more "on the ball" wouldn't be caught dead working behind the counter. Mobility isn't necessarily that limited, but since that is not widely known, the negative impression sticks.

The stigma also stems from the low social status of the people who hold these jobs: minorities, teenagers, immigrants who often speak halting English, those with little education, and (increasingly in affluent communities afflicted with labor shortages) the elderly. To the extent that the prestige of a job refracts the social characteristics of its average incumbents, fast-food jobs are hobbled by the perception that people with better choices would never purposely opt for a "McJob." Entry-level jobs of this kind are undeserving of this scorn: more skill, discretion, and responsibility are locked up in a fast-food job than is apparent to the public. But this truth hardly matters where public perception is concerned. There is no quicker way to indicate that a person is barely deserving of notice than to point out he or she holds a "chump change" job at Kentucky Fried Chicken or Burger King. We "know" this is the case just by looking at the age, skin color, or educational credentials of the people already on the job: the tautology has a staying power that even the smartest public relations campaign cannot shake.

Ghetto youth are particularly sensitive to the status degradation entailed in stigmatized employment. As Elijah Anderson (in *Streetwise* [University of Chicago Press, 1990]) and others have pointed out, a high premium is placed on independence, autonomy, and respect among minority youth in inner-city communities—particularly by young men. No small amount of mayhem is committed every year in the name of injured pride. Hence jobs that routinely demand displays of deference force those who hold them to violate "macho" behavior codes that are central to the definition of teen culture. There are, therefore, considerable social risks involved in seeking a fast-food job in the first place, one that the employees and job seekers are keenly aware of from the very beginning of their search for employment.

Abusive Child Labor Practices

LINDA CHAVEZ-THOMPSON

I am one who knows something about child labor. I grew up in west Texas . . . and beginning when I was ten years old, I spent every summer weeding cotton, Monday through Friday, ten hours a day. When other kids were on the playground—or taking vacations—I was working in ninety- and one-hundred-degree heat in the cotton fields, making thirty cents an hour. It was like that every year. It lasted that way until I was fifteen. Then, my father took me out of school, and I started both hoeing and picking cotton.

It wasn't just summers that I was in the fields. I saw what this kind of life did to my family. My mother had to work in the fields . . . and she had to leave the four youngest kids at home alone when they were four to eight years old, with no family and no babysitter to care for them. I'll never forget that. And I'll never forget watching my father . . . who was the biggest man in my life . . . standing silent with his hat in his hands as he was being screamed at and humiliated by the field boss.

No child should have to work like I worked. No child should have to see what I saw. I'd like to tell you that this no longer happens in America. I'd like to tell you that—but I can't. The truth is that hundreds of thousands of children . . . no one knows exactly how many . . . are working in fields and orchards all across the country.

As Human Rights Watch tells us, they pick lettuce and cantaloupe . . . they weed cotton fields, like I did . . . they climb rickety ladders in cherry orchards . . . they stoop low over chili plants . . . and they pitch heavy watermelons, hour after hour. Do they work ten-hour days, like I did? Many don't—many actually work twelve-hour days. That means that they have no chance of staying in school . . . no chance of using their talents and moving ahead . . . no chance of a brighter future.

No one knows exactly how many thousands of children and teens are working in agriculture, and no one knows exactly how little they are all paid. But a third of those who were interviewed by Human Rights Watch were earning much less than the minimum wage . . . some of them only two or three dollars an hour.

When I was a child hoeing cotton, I damaged my back and still have a spinal curvature. I was one of the lucky ones. Plenty of children and teens are hurt worse than I was. They are crippled in accidents with heavy equipment, or falls

Remarks from the Forum on Abusive Child Labor, May 10, 2001. Reprinted with the permission of the AFL-CIO. Linda Chavez-Thompson is the executive vice president of the AFL-CIO.

from ladders, or sharp knives. Some lose their lives. In fact, agricultural work is one of the three most dangerous industries in America, along with mining and construction . . . and children account for 20 percent of all farm fatalities.

With all the problems—all the suffering—all the deprivation that these kids face . . . the fact is that they actually have *less* legal protection than kids in other workplaces. For instance, under the Fair Labor Standards Act, children working on farms can be employed at a lower age—twelve years old—than in other workplaces . . . *and* there's no limit on how many hours they may work . . . *and* there's no requirement that they be given overtime pay . . . *and* they can be put into hazardous work two years earlier than in other workplaces. It's a terrible double standard . . . one standard for kids who work for McDonald's or a shop in the mall, and another standard for kids who work for a farm or orchard. It's not right—it's not fair. The law should be changed.

That's why it's great news that Senator Harkin is introducing the Children's Act for Responsible Employment—the CARE Act of 2001. It stiffens the penalties for child labor violations that involve serious injury or death of a minor . . . and it ends the double standard of lower protection for children working in large-scale agriculture. This is a fine piece of legislation. It would correct some terrible wrongs against millions of young people.

I promise you here and now that it will have the full support of the thirteen million women and men in the AFL-CIO . . . and I urge all of you here to join us. As bad as child labor is in this country . . . it's often much worse abroad. The International Labor Organization estimates that in developing countries alone, there are some 250 million children between the ages of five and fourteen who go to work every day instead of school. Of those, 120 million are working full time. They are toiling in mines and quarries . . . they are exposed to dangerous agrochemicals in the fields . . . they are squatting for hours every day in positions that cripple them as they weave rugs and carpets . . . and they are traumatized and abused in the commercial sex trade.

We in the AFL-CIO have been fighting against child labor around the world for years. Our Solidarity Center runs child labor programs everywhere from Kenya to Indonesia to Brazil to Bangladesh . . . and we worked hard to get the United States to ratify ILO Convention 182, which bans the worst forms of child labor.

Let me offer a few observations on how we in the union movement look at this awful problem. First, all of our experiences tell us that child labor is not a problem that's isolated all by itself. Some people argue that it's arrogant to say that children shouldn't work when their families need that income. But the truth is that child labor is tied very closely to adult labor. We've seen over and over again that when adults have jobs that pay decent wages . . . when they're not underpaid and underemployed . . . they're much more likely to keep their kids *out* of the workplace and *in* school. And good jobs for adults are the number one goal of union movements worldwide. Time after time, in one nation after another, you can see a clear pattern: strong union movements . . . good, well-paying jobs for adults . . . and less child labor all go together.

My second observation is that kids belong in school, not at work. School is the best place for children to be . . . no matter what their social status, no matter what their country. We all know that basic education is necessary to lift families and communities and nations out of poverty . . . and it's just as necessary to end child labor. That's why the AFL-CIO and other union movements around the world call on the IMF and the World Bank to promote policies that lead to more access to schools for more children . . . rather than forcing governments to slash education and impose fees for primary schooling. We believe that such fees should be ended as a condition for all World Bank lending programs.

Third, the fight against child labor is really part of a larger campaign for basic core standards for every worker around the world. Dozens of nations around the world have joined together in the International Labor Organization to set out these standards . . . the right to reject child labor and forced labor, the right to work free from discrimination, the right to a free choice to join a union. These are all strands in the same fabric . . . a fabric of justice and fairness for all workers. But the fact is that many workers have never even heard that they have these protections. We in the AFL-CIO want to change that.

Just this month, we kicked off a new campaign to post the ILO's Declaration on Fundamental Principles and Rights at Work in workplaces, union halls, and government offices in 148 nations. We want to spread the word so more working people can know their rights. And we want our trade and investment agreements to protect those rights instead of undermining them.

I can tell you that all of us in the union movement will keep on doing everything we possibly can to end child labor, both in America and around the world. I can also tell you that there is no way that our efforts by themselves will be enough. This crusade . . . and that's what it really is . . . is going to take the effort and energy and vision of all of us . . . whether we're in unions, or the government, or human rights organizations, or schools.

Together, we can make a world where children can grow and play and learn as they should. Together, we can make a world where the blight of child labor is brought to an end. Together, we can make a world where justice is finally done. If we don't do it, nobody will—and we will.

New Ethics or No Ethics?

Questionable Behavior Is Silicon Valley's Next Big Thing

JERRY USEEM

Back when greed was good, in the 1980s, a lot of rapacious capitalists got together and decided it was okay to do some bad things, like selling junk bonds to each other and doing insider trading and playing racquetball and stuff (this on top of that whole S&L debacle), which is to say that Wall Street's Decade of Greed was a carnival of immorality that is a stain on our national conscience or something.

Whew, thank goodness that's over! Today, by contrast, we have Silicon Valley and the Internet boom—a deeply wholesome movement of idealistic risk takers who are out to change the world and who, incidentally, all look like Jeff Bezos. These good folks and their IPOs have been blessedly free of the sort of shady doings that characterized those ugly predators and their LBOs. And if our TV screens are full of people declaring "I feel the need for greed," well, that's only a game show.

Nice story. But we're not so sure we buy it anymore. For the articles that follow, *Fortune* explored a series of increasingly common business practices in the Internet world that, while not yet the stuff of a Michael Douglas movie, collectively don't smell right.

The first story, Jeremy Kahn's "Presto Chango! Sales Are Huge!" examines the woolly accounting methods by which many dot-coms inflate their revenues. Melanie Warner delves into the world of friends-and-family stock—and reports how one company used it to reward key employees at what was then its only customer. Mark Gimein scrutinizes the decisions of CEOs who unload big chunks of their own stock, and Peter Elkind asks whether dot-coms' insiderish boards of directors are a corporate governance disaster waiting to happen. Finally, Erick Schonfeld shows how the "objective" opinions of Wall Street's Internet analysts may not be as objective as you think.

Together, they present a portrait of an industry awash in . . . what? Greed, certainly. But something else too: an inverted dynamic, born of a stock market gone mad, in which entrepreneurs have begun to regard the capital market not as a disciplining force but as the customer. Companies are created, hyped, and sold with less concern for attracting real customers than for lining one's pockets with investors' money. The result is that participants can wear a set of ethical blinders, behaving in ways that might seem perfectly acceptable within this

 Jerry Useem is a senior writer at *Fortune*.

insular context but that, when viewed with a modicum of objectivity, look borderline at best. One can already imagine the postmortem articles that will follow any Internet crash. SiliconValley.con, they'll call it.

"The bull market has attracted a huge number of people for whom money is the only motivating factor," says Roger McNamee of Integral Capital Partners, a Menlo Park, California, investment firm. He's not alone in voicing such concerns. "We're getting to the stage where the frauds are going to come in," warns Bill Joy, Sun Microsystems' cofounder and chief scientist. "There will be handwringing afterward. We've seen this movie before." Only this time the sums at stake are much, much larger, making the end of the '80s look like kindergarten. Move over, *Bonfire of the Vanities.*

For the most part, they're not talking about latter-day Michael Milkens. (Though the Valley has had its share of out-and-out frauds, as when MiniScribe shipped bricks instead of disk drives. More recently, the Securities and Exchange Commission accused software maker Informix of booking sales that were . . . well, not exactly sales.) Among the common infractions: companies stealing one another's intellectual property, cheating employees out of promised stock options (as two former execs have accused iVillage of doing), or intercepting private e-mail, as when Interloc, the corporate predecessor of rare-book company Alibris, started collecting messages sent from Amazon.com to its customers.

But before we talk further about business ethics, plural, a bit about the business ethic, singular, that has evolved along the fertile crescent between San Francisco and San Jose. The story starts, unsurprisingly, with the stock market and its recent tendency to grant to barely-off-the-drawing-board concepts—BlowYourNose.com, TheseDarnPants.com, what have you—market caps large enough to acquire most of the UN's nonaligned bloc. With every IPO, every newly minted billionaire, the message gets louder: You're supposed to be getting rich, you chump. The hope of getting wealthy has morphed into something like expectation, often tinged with desperation. "They all think they have a God-given right to be a millionaire," says Lise Buyer, an Internet analyst at Credit Suisse First Boston. "The greed has grown, as it does at the top of any market," agrees Arthur Rock, widely credited with inventing high-tech venture capital. "People want their share, or unfair share."

Most Valleyites protest, predictably, that they're not in it for the money. And insofar as they have never had much use for mansions and helicopters, the claim is not a wholly disingenuous one. The thing is, money isn't just for buying things; it also functions as a scorecard. As in: If he's a billionaire, then I've got to be worth at least $500 million. So the perpetual refrain—"It's not about the money"—doesn't really carry much moral suasion. "We used to be able to say it with a very straight face," says Randy Komisar, the former head of LucasArts Entertainment and a self-styled "virtual CEO" who has helped run such companies as WebTV and TiVo. "Nowadays, it sounds stupid."

Yet it's the knowledge of just how quickly it all could end that lends everything a slightly kooky quality—like the manic laugh of the old man at the end of *The Treasure of Sierra Madre,* when he realizes the Mexicans have let the gold dust blow all over the prairie. "There's a gnawing anxiety right now in Silicon Valley. Everybody has this nasty knot in their stomach," says Joe Costello, ex-CEO of software giant Cadence Design Systems and now head of Think3, a start-up that makes 3-D design software. Many companies, Costello notes, face the terrifying task of having to "grow into" those nosebleed valuations, and that requires the appearance of momentum: a constantly rising line of revenues, eyeballs, buzz, and so forth. "We've all learned to play the momentum game," says Costello. "But underneath, everyone knows it's something of a sham. People know these [valuations] are absolutely wild excursions to the upside. . . . There's going to be a day where people say, 'Okay, we want to see profits.' And I don't want my net worth being judged on that day of reckoning."

"That," he says, "generates a fast-money mentality: Dodge in and out—you know, If I can get out now, I'll never have to meet that day. It is the carrot and stick of fear and greed. But they're at such epic proportions that it creates a very, very strange psychology." Here, for instance, is how Komisar describes entrepreneurs pitching ideas to venture capitalists these days: "People walk into a VC presentation and their first line is about exit strategy. They're not talking about the investors—they're talking about themselves. How will they cash out? And this raises a subtle point: These founders don't think of themselves as CEOs of operating companies. They think of themselves as investors."

It's a complaint voiced more and more often these days, especially among high-tech veterans: Instead of building sustainable companies with long-term economic value, today's Internet entrepreneurs are more interested in playing the capital markets for the quick buck—pumping a concept, "flipping" it to an acquirer, then hopping to the next hot opportunity like a day trader riding momentum stocks. (Komisar calls it "momentum employment.") Some venture capitalists even have a name for these sorts of companies: burgers—built to be flipped.

Of course it's easy to roll one's eyes at Valleyites, their millions safely socked away, who are suddenly shocked, shocked to learn the arrivistes are motivated by—gasp—money! "I think every generation says, 'Boy, when I was doing it, people had values, people worked for it,'" notes Guy Kawasaki, a former Apple executive and now CEO of Garage.com. "I bet [Digital Equipment founder] Ken Olsen said that about Steve Jobs." But at the risk of sentimentalizing a past that had its share of money lust, it's hard to brush away the feeling that something has changed. "There wasn't this evanescent sense of 'We'll catch the wave today, hit it, and go away,'" says Fred Hoar, who served as communications director at Fairchild, Apple, and Genentech before becoming chairman of PR firm Miller/Shandwick Technologies. "We never had this expectation of instantaneous riches beyond the dreams of Croesus that permeates, not to say infects, the culture . . . . There's been a tectonic shift." Lest one be tempted to dismiss such remarks as the they-don't-build-'em-like-they-used-to natterings of an older generation, listen to Justin Kitch, the twenty-seven-year-old founder and

CEO of free Website-building company Homestead.com: "It used to be that people started companies because they wanted to change the world. Now they start them to change their pocketbooks."

This situation does not in itself constitute an ethical transgression, of course. But it does create a context in which ethically dubious behavior can seem, well, normal. "Because momentum is everything, you start to do whatever it takes not to break it," says Connie Bagley, a Stanford Business School lecturer who studies Internet law. "People tell themselves, 'I'm making incredible value for my shareholders, I'm making great money for my employees.' And that gets very dangerous."

Many companies, for instance, have become clever about finding ways to recycle their balance sheets through their income statements: recording barter deals as revenue, investing in companies that turn around and buy advertising on their Web sites, and so on. "It's not shipping bricks," says a venture capitalist, "but it's the online version of it." The thing is, because so much in the Internet economy is circular and self-fulfilling (for example, a hot stock causes more customers to buy your product, having more customers causes more people to buy your stock, etc.), such tricks have a certain corrosive logic—deceiving people into thinking you're more successful than you are may, in fact, cause you to be more successful.

Lest we come down too hard on the entrepreneurs, though, let's take a closer look at the venture capitalists' role in all this. They, like the entrepreneurs, are theoretically in the business of developing and nurturing sustainable companies and bearing much of the risk along the way. That's in theory. In practice, they're now taking start-ups public long before anyone can say whether those companies have a workable approach. By making such an early (and often insanely lucrative) exit, the VCs shift most of the risk onto the public market. And that risk is considerable. "The potential losses are gigantic," notes Costello. "It's not right. The venture guys should be thinking about building long-term, self-sustaining companies, but they're off to the races on something new. This is just a pyramid game here, a pump-and-dump Ponzi scheme . . . . It's become a completely internal loop, with the public markets paying the bill."

Venture capitalists' main function thus becomes, in a sense, marketing: making their firm's own brand name so strong that the best deals flow their way and then using that imprimatur to sell as-yet-unproven concepts to the public. "It's a money-printing machine," says Costello. "The risk used to be the business model, and whether it could perform. Now the risk is, 'Did I get enough of my money in the deal?' And [the VCs] will kill to make that happen. They are clawing each other and stabbing each other in the back and screwing each other."

Sometimes it's the entrepreneurs who get stabbed. "Last week I saw the most outrageous thing I've ever seen in my life in this Valley," says Randy Komisar. "VCs are throwing term sheets on the table that aren't real term sheets, just to lock up the deal. The entrepreneurs, of course, don't know that." And when the venture capitalists decide they don't like the deal after all, the entrepreneurs "end up high and dry." (One might think, with venture returns being what they are right now—namely, ludicrous—that such cutthroat tactics would abate. But alas, it's a relative game, and the pressure to produce rates of return in line with other venture firms' is intense.)

Lest we unfairly single out the venture capitalists, though, consider that everyone else remotely involved with the money machine is also trying to squeeze lucre out of it. Consulting firms like Andersen and McKinsey are taking equity instead of cash for their services. Despite warnings of conflicts of interest, so are law firms. Even executive search firms are forming venture-capital funds to invest in companies in which they place executives. "Everybody in the world is trying to touch a piece of this dot-com bonanza," says Regis McKenna, Silicon Valley's Uber-marketer.

Consider the case of one software start-up that was recently about to go public. According to a member of its board, the company's two largest customers called and said they'd, uh, like some pre-IPO shares. "I've never seen anything like it," says the board member. "It was extortion, a shakedown. They know we're going public, know they've got the muscle to screw it up, and so they cleverly exploit their position. What is [the start-up] going to say? Um, no?" According to the board member, one of the corporate customers made $70 million off the deal. "Every single company that's going public, they knock up for stock," the board member adds. "And they're not alone; everybody's doing it. People were crawling all over this thing to find ways to get money out of it."

Meanwhile, those who hew to quaint notions of building for the long haul can find themselves walking into a stiff headwind, says Homestead.com CEO Kitch. "People say, 'Wait, you're not doing it? You're doing this barter deal and not reporting it as revenue?' I say no, that I'm thinking about what this organization is going to look like twenty years from now. Is doing this barter deal going to make the company better? In fact, it's going to make it worse, because I'm going to have to undo it and find another $100,000 of real revenue." Does he feel pressured toward such tactics frequently? "Totally," says Kitch. "Five times a day."

To hear business ethicists tell it, the sheer speed of activity may be partly to blame. "One of the problems is that ethics implies deliberation," says Dennis Moberg, director of the Markkula Center for Applied Ethics at Santa Clara University. "It implies periods of contemplation and deliberation, and working through a moral calculus." Who has time for such navel-gazing when everyone is "moving @ Internet speed"? "It's not that these are evil people; it's just that in the rush, a lot of things just don't get reflected upon," says Kirk Hanson, a senior lecturer in ethics at Stanford. "You see gold in the vein, and jumping the claim or grabbing the idea you hear from somebody else becomes much more tempting. So there's a coarsening of standards."

Yet, is it possible that the Internet economy could provide some safeguards against chicanery that the old economy couldn't? For one thing, there's the presence of experienced venture capitalists and angel investors on boards of directors, whose ongoing goodwill is needed if one is ever to raise money again. Then, too, the Internet itself can be a force for transparency; incriminating information that was once limited to file cabinets and a few people's heads nowadays has a way of appearing online. "There may be some corrective mechanisms emerging," speculates Joseph Badaracco, a professor of ethics at Harvard Business School. "It does involve a high degree of transparency, but it doesn't necessarily involve the SEC and all its mechanisms. It's a different kind of governance system—a self-regulating one."

Could be. The Old West developed a set of frontier ethics independent of the government and all its mechanisms. But frontier ethics can be problematic. "It becomes a wonderful context to validate your behavior," notes Jeffrey L. Seglin, assistant professor of ethics at Emerson College in Boston and author of *The Good, the Bad, and Your Business: Choosing Right When Ethical Dilemmas Pull You Apart*. "You can chalk it up to the New Economy." Many Net companies caught in wrongdoing have simply stopped the practice, shrugged, and said they weren't aware they were doing anything wrong.

Indeed, if there's anything that characterizes periods of economic upheaval—the Internet boom, the Wall Street boom, the industrial boom—it's the ineffable sense that old rules no longer apply, that the laws governing the universe have been suspended. From there, is it such a leap to conclude that the old rules of ethics have been suspended too? "The robber barons who lit up $100 bills to light cigars for guests, they were in a world where the old rules didn't apply," says Tom Donaldson, a professor of ethics at Wharton. "Eventually, our deeper values catch up to the new worlds we create. In the meantime, there will be a lot of shenanigans."

Bill Joy is right. We have seen this movie before.

Two Companies Battle High Turnover and Win!

DEBORAH S. ROBERTS

Once the average employee wanted only decent benefits, a pension plan, and a long-term future. Today, the average employee wants more—and above-average employees more still.

Keeping talented people is a challenge for every employer. But perhaps nowhere is the challenge more evident than in the restaurant industry, where service can mean the difference between being a hot spot . . . or a has-been.

New York City's Tavern on the Green seems to meet that challenge. The famed eatery boasts annual sales topping $34 million, clientele such as Barbra Streisand, and a secure place on the *Restaurants and Institutions* magazine list of top independents.

Most important, Tavern maintains a strong core of skilled workers in an industry known for high turnover.

"We average 425 employees," says Tavern's training director Laura Vaughan. "About 150 have been here more than ten years and some more than twenty."

Success in the hospitality industry depends on finding and keeping top-quality workers, Vaughan says. This is particularly true for Tavern, which builds its reputation on making customers feel like honored guests.

For years Tavern's training program consisted only of letting new hires "trail" other workers. Then about two years ago Tavern management put new emphasis on creating a stronger workforce. That's when Vaughan was hired. She created an employment process that includes:

- a prescreening telephone application
- at least four interviews with department heads
- personality and drug testing
- a five-hour orientation

About forty hours of classroom training covers such subjects as food, spirits, guests, and conflict management. Finally, new hires still trail other workers for two to five days.

The priority, Vaughan says, is to find people with enthusiasm.

The Employee Retention and Recruitment Newsletter, 2000. Reprinted with the permission of the Lawrence Ragan Communications, Inc. Deborah S. Roberts is the editor of the Ragan Publication *The Employee Recruitment and Retention Newsletter.*

"It comes down to the desire to take care of guests," she says. "If we're interviewing waiters, we may ask about dishwashing. The answers tell us if they want to be part of a team or just stay in their box."

Because Tavern is a union shop, benefits are provided through the union, though Tavern contributes. But an important benefit the union can't provide is making employees feel the company cares.

"When I was hired, I said what we needed more than anything was a paid listener," Vaughan says. "When we're busy, we are so busy. Even a manager who wants to listen has three other things going on and people feel brushed off."

Now employees know they can come to Vaughan to find a willing ear. More important, she says, they can come to managing director Allan Kurtz, whose door is open to every staffer.

"That's the way things have to be in this day and age," Vaughan says. "The restaurant industry in particular is really in the Stone Age—it's 'them and us.' I don't think managers who feel like that are long for this world.

"If you want people to give their top performance, to make sure every last spot is cleaned off the crystal, you must treat them with dignity and respect."

Listening is only the first step. Vaughan says Tavern management also has been generous in supporting a number of incentive programs.

The restaurant provides free "family meals" for employees three times daily. Workers order from a special menu that includes staff favorites.

Last year, Vaughan introduced a program called "Training Bucks." With a budget of $13,500, she printed fake dollars supervisors could give employees for a job well done; ten bucks would buy a gift certificate for such vendors as Macy's, The Gap, or Tower Records.

"The program was not perfect in a lot of ways," Vaughan says. "One obstacle was to convince managers the bucks didn't have to go to someone they liked or someone who jumped over the dishwasher to give the Heimlich maneuver to a customer. If you just say you appreciate their hustle that day, it might encourage them to try harder. The point was recognition."

This year Vaughan has started a new program called "Tavern All Stars," which invites all employees to nominate one manager and six line professionals for recognition each quarter. A secret committee chooses winners who receive a seventy-five-dollar Tavern gift certificate and an engraved brass star; a special celebration will be held at year's end.

Vaughan likes to find big ways to recognize employees, but she still appreciates small touches—like making the rounds with her smiley-face bucket, depositing candy at server stations or into dishwashers' pockets.

Recognizing the importance of those small touches is a philosophy Vaughan shares with Alan and Katherine Pool, owners of On the Corner Seafood Grill in Clermont, Florida.

The Corner Grill is miles from Tavern on the Green—and not just geographically. While Tavern is known for its extravagance, the Corner Grill, like its Florida environs, is laid-back. The restaurant is less than six years old and boasts about 10 percent of Tavern's staff, topping off at around forty employees.

But the Pools have two things in common with Tavern: First, they operate in a highly competitive environment. Clermont, a once sleepy citrus town, is now a booming bedroom community of Orlando. Nearby are the sprawling Disney theme parks, Universal Studios, and dozens of resorts. All beckon the workers in Clermont's employee pool—a pool diluted by a heavy presence of retirees.

And, second, despite the competition, the Corner Grill has also found a way to hang on to its best workers, many of whom have been with the Pools since the doors opened.

"The number one thing is hands-on management," says Alan Pool. Pool and his wife juggle virtually all management duties, although a head waitress handles scheduling.

"Big companies have a lot of workers available. They don't have to help their employees because there's someone else right behind that employee waiting to take the job," Pool says. "But here, we're basically a retirement community. It's tough to get people."

How does he keep the ones he finds? Simple: "I appreciate my staff very much and tell them they do a great job."

Like Tavern, Pool also feeds his employees. Sometimes if an employee comes in for dinner with the family, he'll pick up the tab. And each year, he puts on a big Christmas party for the staff. But when it comes to more traditional benefits, the budget is limited.

"I hear of different companies sending employees on weekend trips to the Bahamas, but I can't do that myself," Pool laughs. He also can't yet provide health care. But he does provide less traditional help.

Pool has bailed two employees out of jail and provided a crying shoulder for workers going through everything from divorces to child-custody problems. Server Nancy Appleton marvels that he held her job when she was sidelined for a two-month illness just three weeks after being hired. And, he keeps a spiral notebook in his desk filled with notations on personal loans and cash advances for the staff.

"I've only had one or two people who didn't pay me back," he says. "Shame on them. But you still have to have faith in people. I don't have any incentive programs, but I'm good to my employees every day.

"It all goes back to treating people like you want to be treated."

Tavern's Laura Vaughan seconds that. "And," she adds, "hopefully you want to be treated very well."

BUILDING BONDS

What's the quickest way to strengthen the bond between employees and management? Improve communication, says Tavern on the Green's Laura Vaughan. She offers these suggestions for opening communication—and closing the revolving door:

1. Hold open forums. Set up monthly—or at least quarterly—forums in which workers can talk with decision makers on issues important to them. At first, Vaughan says, expect a lot of general griping. But if you make the effort to address issues—and report progress—meetings will become more productive. "Initially, people will only tell you what's wrong," she says. "But then they'll tell you why it's happening, and soon they'll tell you what you can do about it. Finally they'll become partners in fixing it."
2. Improve credibility. Do what you say you are going to do or offer a good reason why you can't. Even if it's something trivial, Vaughan says, you lose face with workers when you don't keep a promise.
3. Find ways to communicate. Tavern on the Green has a quarterly employee newsletter, the *Tavern Times.* And Vaughan puts out special editions when the occasion warrants. The publication includes a letter from the managing director, who also routinely sends employees thank-you letters of recognition that are copied into their personnel files.
4. Eliminate fear of reprisal. "Employees should be able to voice their ideas, concerns, or complaints without fear," Vaughan stresses. Tavern uses suggestion boxes as an anonymous way to let employees speak out. Of course, Vaughan says, some suggestions are silly—for example, "I want the owner to buy each employee a new car." But she also finds gems among the rubbish.
5. Share important information. Finally, Vaughan says, treat employees as partners. Communicate numbers—good and bad. Don't hoard data on successes that might make workers feel a sense of accomplishment, or on problems that might encourage them to go the extra mile. These suggestions aren't new, Vaughan says. They're just common sense.

Workplace Upheavals Seem to Be Eroding Employees' Trust

SUE SHELLENBARGER

A former finance-department employee of a multinational manufacturer recalls the day his trust in his employer was shattered.

A devastating earthquake in Turkey had killed and injured thousands of people. He and his coworkers were panicked because they couldn't reach fellow employees there. At that time, he overheard his boss of three months telling the finance manager to revise sales projections for Turkey downward because they were likely to suffer—sales that accounted for only a fraction of 1 percent of the company's total.

"Ten thousand people, including possibly some of our own employees, were missing or dead, and she was worried about hitting sales targets," says the employee, who asked that his name not be used because he fears retaliation. "I gave my notice the following week."

Management gurus pretty much agree that trust in the workplace has been eroding since the 1980s, largely due to the layoff and acquisition binges and the accelerating pace of change. A study of 1,800 workers by Aon's Loyalty Institute, Ann Arbor, Michigan, set for release today, says more than one in eight, or 13 percent, of U.S. workers distrust their employers on the most basic level—that is, they don't feel free from fear, intimidation, or harassment at work. Watson Wyatt Worldwide, Bethesda, Maryland, found in a study of 7,500 employees that only half trusted their senior managers.

Now that it's gone, many workplace experts are waking up to how important trust is, especially in a tight labor market. The Aon research shows that trust is such a basic requirement that without it a company's other benefits and programs won't raise employee commitment very much. Watson Wyatt also found a correlation between trust and profit. Companies where employees trusted top executives posted shareholder returns forty-two percentage points higher than companies where distrust was the rule.

A common view among managers is that it's unwise, impractical, or impossible to try to cultivate trust amid nonstop change and reorganizations. But that's a misfire, says the Loyalty Institute's David Stum. "The American worker knows quite well that change is never-ending. How it's handled is what can lead the

 Sue Shellenbarger is the award-winning "Work and Family" columnist who writes for the *Wall Street Journal.*

worker to be secure or insecure." The basic question, Mr. Stum says, is, "Do I trust my company to be fair and honest as it goes through changes?"

Based on my mail, it's the small gestures that often matter most to employees. The rules for building trust at work are actually pretty simple—the kinds of things we try to teach kids in elementary school. Dennis and Michelle Reina, coauthors of the 1999 book *Trust and Betrayal in the Workplace,* cite such behaviors as respecting others, sharing information, admitting mistakes, giving constructive feedback, keeping secrets, avoiding gossip and backbiting, being consistent, and involving others in decision making.

A former operations director for a Virginia aircraft-maintenance concern recalls a particularly harsh violation of the "tell-the-truth" maxim. He first caught wind of it on a tip from a friend in human resources: "You should ask to see your confidential personnel file." He did, and discovered to his alarm several memos from his boss blaming him for problems he didn't believe he had caused. When the operations director began filing rebuttals, his boss flew into a rage—not at his supposed poor performance, but at the person who had tipped him. The operations director soon left the company.

Trust is reciprocal. To paraphrase Henry Stimson, FDR's war secretary and a famed diplomat, the surest way to make employees untrustworthy is to distrust them, and to show it. Bart Rhoten says his former employer, the credit-card unit of a banking concern, forbade after-hours or weekend work unless a supervisor was present. "They thought we'd sit around racking up overtime and eating doughnuts," he says—even though employees' in-baskets were visibly jammed with backed-up work. The company also fired people for returning late from lunch and never promoted from within. The atmosphere of mistrust so demoralized workers that annual turnover in the three-hundred-employee unit soared to 400 percent, says Mr. Rhoten, now a senior consultant for another company.

Betrayal has a powerful emotional effect, Ms. Reina says. It can cause employees to withdraw or to vent frustration and anger on their families. Often, family members will blow the whistle. "The cost becomes so high at home that a spouse or child may say, 'Hey, we can't take this any more.'"

Some companies are consciously taking steps to build trust. SRA International, a Fairfax, Virginia, systems consultant, requires all two thousand of its employees to take mandatory training on respect, fairness, ethics, and honesty.

For employers with patience, the payoff is worth the effort. The Reinas, organizational development consultants in Stowe, Vermont, tell of a manufacturing plant in a small New England town where managers had to lay off 100 of 420 employees. They held meetings to share information. They hung out on the shop floor on all three shifts to answer employees' questions and to hear their worries. They set up outplacement centers and invited other employers to the plant to meet their people.

Not surprisingly, Ms. Reina says, when jobs opened up again at the plant, more than 80 percent of the layoff victims came running back.

Chapter 6

Balancing Work and Family

BALANCING WORK AND FAMILY has grown into a national social and policy concern that involves every worker and every decision maker. The spectacular growth and wealth creation of the United States' "new economy" of the 1990s came with a price—an intense squeeze on time and resources generated by dual-parent families, high-productivity workplaces, and the commitments of home and family. The work-life balance is no longer seen as solely a human resources issue, but as *the* human resources issue—and a paramount concern for corporate leaders, academics, and policy makers. The implications range far beyond the stress felt by individuals "choosing" to have a career and raise a family. Employees suffering from too much stress and overwork affect not only themselves and their families (which is serious indeed) but also their employers, who need talent, the social institutions that benefit from engaged citizens, and a shared future in which children will become adults. The first part of this section relies on leading advocates and analysts to describe the scope of the debate; the second part features a set of pieces that relate how various public and private organizations can and have developed policy responses to this uniquely American problem.

Ellen Galinsky's "The Daily Grind," concisely summarizes the National Work and Family Institute's major research findings on stress and overwork in today's organization. Ann Crittenden's "An Accident Waiting to Happen" documents the economic penalties exacted on mothers by employers and public policy in the United States, detailing how Washington policy makers rewrote laws governing at-home child care that by inference and by background testimony were changed explicitly to punish mothers for working outside the home. Barbara Carton's front-page *Wall Street Journal* article, "Day Care Is Moving to the Night Shift," illustrates how low-income women and their children struggle under the intense work-family juggling act.

Alden Hayashi's "Mommy-Track Backlash," a *Harvard Business Review* case study, illuminates the challenges facing corporate managers seeking to provide flexible policies that are fair for working parents *and* their childless colleagues. Some experts, including Carl Van Horn and Duke Storen of the Heldrich Center, believe telework is among the most promising policy tools available on the work-life front. In a major presentation, "Is Telework Coming of Age?," created for the U.S. Department of Labor, these authors explore the benefits of telework policies and the barriers organizations face in making these policies work. Leading journalist Susan Garland (now freelancing) of *Business Week* discusses the pros and cons of at-home telework in "Work at Home? First, Get Real." Finally, in "Child Care, the Perk of Tomorrow?" Steven Greenhouse's *New York Times* coverage of the Ford/United Auto Workers family centers captures why "Ford's plan is widely viewed as the most comprehensive effort by an American corporation to help rank-and-file workers handle the balancing act."

The expansion of domestic partner benefits marks additional important progress in developing smart, fair policies, and we have included Hewlett-Packard's domestic partner benefits policy, which is regarded as the gold standard of its kind. Also, the executive summary of the Human Rights Congress' annual report, "The State of the Workplace for Lesbian, Gay, Bisexual, and Transgendered Americans, 2000," explains the progress of this issue.

The Occupational Safety and Health Administration (OSHA) has become a locus of growing controversy during the 1990s, and we have included two pieces that argue different sides of the most public and polarizing OSHA decisions. The first article, "Should Washington Implement National Ergonomic Standards?" by conservative Edward Potter of *Insight,* decries OSHA's proposed ergonomics standard. The next article, "Home-Office Debate Isn't New," by Eileen Boris and Nelson Lichtenstein, defends OSHA's late 1990s ruling to place the home office under the same health and safety standards as any other workplace. A Communications Workers of America union fact sheet, "Right to Refuse Unsafe Work," captures the difficulty workers face in factory and manufacturing workplaces where managers have the leverage to order them to perform jobs that may be unsafe. And two intriguing documents, "Fishing for a Living Is Dangerous Work," by Dino Drudi, and "Logging Is Perilous Work," by Eric F. Sygnatur, combine analysis and anecdote to describe the perils of the fishing and logging trades. A final piece from HR.com, "What Is Stress and Why Is It Hazardous?" provides an overview of stress management in the workplace from the perspective of human resources.

The Daily Grind

Catch a Break from a Stressed-Out World

ELLEN GALINSKY

As president of a nonprofit organization that conducts research on the changing workforce, family, and community, my job is to detect critical societal changes that are starting to crest and conduct studies on them. One such change is people feeling overworked and stressed. The signs are all around. Perhaps the most compelling finding that led me to take a deeper look at what's going on comes from the World Health Organization. It reports that by 2020, clinical depression is expected to outrank cancer and follow only heart disease in causes of death and disability worldwide.

Thus, in the beginning of this year, my colleagues at the Families and Work Institute, Stacy Kim and Terry Bond, and I set out to look at the factors in our lives that precede feelings of being overworked. With PricewaterhouseCoopers funding, we conducted a national study of 1,003 employees.

Feelings of being overworked are pervasive. We found 28 percent of those surveyed felt overworked or overwhelmed by work often or very often in the past three months. These feelings take a toll on home and work lives. As one employee says, "If I'm worrying about work all the time, things at home suffer."

If we feel more overworked, our study found, we experience more conflict between work and home life and feel less successful in relationships. Says a survey participant: "My biggest fear is that my kids are going to grow up, leave home, and I'm going to look around and know no one."

The more overworked we feel, the study also found, the more likely we won't take proper care of ourselves, will lose sleep, and have poorer health and higher stress levels.

What's to be done? We can ignore these findings. Or feel guilty but continue the way we've been working, saying, "it's only for a few more days, weeks, years." But the bottom line is employers have a responsibility to make changes, and so do we.

We need to confront our assumptions about how we work. If we think the only way to succeed is to keep pushing ourselves harder, then it's likely we won't take action.

Our results reveal we can change many of the antecedents of feeling overworked, which could have positive consequences for us and our employers. Try

 Ellen Galinsky is president and cofounder of the Families and Work Institute.

to work a schedule closer to the hours and days you prefer; don't interrupt others or let yourself be interrupted; limit multitasking to a reasonable level; create a more supportive and flexible work environment for yourself, your coworkers, and those you supervise; work to improve the quality of jobs at your workplace (for example, jobs with more autonomy and less low-value work).

Also, set reasonable limits on using technology during nonwork hours; go on vacation; take care of your health; and set aside time for those outside of work who are important to you and encourage the same of coworkers.

I hope this study is a clarion call to all of us, employers and employees, to examine how we're working in this 24/7 economy and to find creative ways to work that benefit us and our employers. It can be a win-win situation.

An Accident Waiting to Happen

ANN CRITTENDEN

Child monitor (domestic ser.): Observes and monitors play activities or amuses children by reading to or playing games with them. Prepares and serves meals or formulas. Sterilizes bottles and other equipment used for feeding infants. Dresses or assists children to dress and bathe. Accompanies children on walks or other outings. Washes and irons clothing. Keeps children's quarters clean and tidy. Cleans other parts of home . . . May be designated Baby Sitter (domestic ser.) when employed on daily or hourly basis.
—U.S. government's definition of child care in a private home

In the fall of 1997, a nineteen-year-old English girl was convicted in Boston of killing a baby who was under her care. The girl, Louise Woodward, was a teenager who had minimal qualifications to care for an infant. And yet she had been admitted into the country for the express purpose of caring for two young children, an eight-month-old and his three-year-old brother.

The outrage on both sides of the Atlantic that accompanied Woodward's trial and conviction included criticism of the murdered child's mother, an optometrist who had had the audacity to leave her baby for a few hours a day, three days week, to practice her profession. But the anger that was so aggressively directed at the two women never quite focused on the real issue: Why on earth was the United States allowing immature kids into the country to take responsible jobs caring for young children?

Working parents still don't realize that their enormous difficulties in finding qualified, responsible caregivers to work in their homes are the direct result of an obscure immigration law that ranks trained nannies as "unskilled" labor. This strange state of affairs began in 1990, when Congress passed an immigration bill that drastically reduced the number of unskilled immigrants allowed to enter the United States. Since nannies and child-care workers were defined under the new law as unskilled, they were effectively shut out of the country, unless they came under the au pair program, which allows foreign students to work in exchange for bed, board, and a stipend. After 1990, if Mary Poppins tried to get an American work permit, she would be denied.

The new law virtually guaranteed that there would be insufficient trained, legal caregivers to meet the rapidly growing demand for in-home child care. Since the law has been passed, countless working parents who need support have either had to hire unqualified people, including many of the teenagers who are

 Ann Crittenden is a former reporter for the *New York Times*, *Fortune*, and *Newsweek* and the author of *Killing the Sacred Cows: Bold Ideas for a New Economy*.

admitted as au pairs, or break the law. As a result, working women face a terrible choice: They can go to work and risk leaving their children in unsafe hands, or stay at home and risk losing their livelihood and financial independence. The official disregard for child care affects every child's safety and every mother's peace of mind, regardless of income or class.

The immigration bill was a bipartisan effort, drafted by Senators Ted Kennedy and Alan Simpson in 1988. Kennedy was then chairman of the Senate Subcommittee on Immigration and Refugee Affairs, and Simpson, the previous chairman, was a passionate advocate of greater restrictions on immigration. At the time, approximately 27,000 unskilled people were entering the United States legally every year, including women who were coming to fill jobs as housekeepers and nannies. Democratic staffer Eugene Pugliese told me he remembers saying to his Republican counterpart, "'Why are we taking in 27,000 unskilled workers a year, when we get at least that many every day or every month coming in across the border illegally?' We weren't confident that there was a need for visas for these workers," he added.[1]

According to a female aide with firsthand knowledge of the negotiations, when one of the senators' male staffers asked who would be affected by the elimination of visas for the unskilled, the answer was "maids and rich matrons in Beverly Hills." In other words, no one we need worry about.

Warren R. Leiden, executive director of the American Immigration Lawyers Association, claims the senators were fully aware that such a restriction would have adverse effects on working mothers. "I was told, behind closed doors, that if women want to leave the home and go to work, then let them pay $45,000 a year for the privilege," he said. "Let them be put to that trial. There was a real hostility to working women."

"But there's also a real irony in Congress voting this in," Leiden continued. "Lots of senators, congressmen, and their staffers, who have working wives are trying to bring in foreign home-care workers."[2]

The first step an employer has to take to bring in a worker is to apply to the Labor Department for a certification that no American can be found to fill the job. The agency then has to classify the applicant as to skill level, using the government's *Dictionary of Occupation Titles,* a compilation of more than 21,000 salaried occupations.

The *Dictionary* became infamous in the 1970s when a study revealed that it rated many "women's" jobs at the lowest possible level of complexity. Paid occupations resembling traditional women's work, like nursery school teacher, were classified as custodial or menial labor—far below such elevated tasks as marine mammal handler, barber, and bus driver. The government ranking also overemphasized formal education, so that occupations requiring "people skills," jobs like clergyman or dean of boys, received higher ratings than foster mother, a demanding job often involving work with troubled children. Jobs in the caring field, including home nursing and child care, were not even listed. There was, for example, no such thing as a "nanny."

The 1970s study had concluded that the *Dictionary* "systematically—though not purposely—discriminated against virtually all nondegreed, people-oriented women's jobs . . . jobs suffering most are the salaried derivatives of homemaking and mothering, particularly those at the paraprofessional level in the fields of health, education, and welfare."[3]

In response to this critique, some changes were made. All job titles were made gender-neutral, so that the occupation of "governess" became "children's tutor." And many traditional women's occupations were moved up from the notorious .878 code, which had branded them as devoid of any significant skill. But mysteriously, the Department of Labor still considers even British-trained nannies with two-year diplomas from training colleges as unskilled workers for the purpose of immigration. They have to be classified either as a "child monitor," whose job description (quoted above) is that of a menial, or as a "children's tutor," a job that is also given an unskilled ranking.

The new Kennedy-Simpson immigration bill didn't in the end eliminate all visas for unskilled workers, but it did reduce the annual allocation to 10,000. The change meant that after 1991, when the law went into effect, only about 4,000 to 5,000 individuals intending to work as a nannies were granted permission to do so in the United States each year.

To put these numbers in perspective, in 1990 there were an estimated 325,000 nannies in the United States, including roughly 75,000 who were in their employers' homes. According to the Census Bureau, by 1995, half a million American children under the age of five were being cared for by nannies. The demand for at-home care, not just for young children but the elderly, is expected to skyrocket in the coming years. With most working-age women now unavailable for full-time unpaid child care, the Bureau of Labor Statistics has predicted that residential care will be the fastest-growing industry in the country in the next decade.

In short, the decision to shut off the legal supply of people willing to care for family dependents in a home was bound to affect hundreds of thousands of American families, not just a few rich matrons in Beverly Hills

When I spoke with Eugene Pugliese in 1995, he denied that his legislative handiwork had contributed to a nanny shortage. "They say about child care that 'an American won't do it.' But there isn't anything you can't get an American to do, if you pay them enough. If you pay *me* enough, *I'd* do it."

One female staffer working for Democratic congressman Charles Schumer saw the issue differently. "I had a baby in 1989," she told me in a telephone interview, after being assured anonymity. "I had just been through the experience of looking for a nanny in the Washington area, as well as having friends who were going through it. I *knew* that it was not true that you could find Americans for these jobs. I had placed an ad, not mentioning salary, in the *Washington Post* for a housekeeper, and out of about seventy calls, *two* were from Americans. About 90 percent of the responses were from illegals. You can't talk to anyone who doesn't know about this—my neighbor, my friends, all of them have illegal help.

I even had one employment agency say to me, 'It's too bad you have to have somebody who's legal—we have some great Filipinas.'"

Like other mothers, I too had discovered that Americans don't want these jobs. And no wonder: the hours are long, the pay is low, the conditions are lonely, and the societal respect is nil. Many of the women who might be interested have children of their own, and no one to care for them. Black Americans in particular are understandably dead set against repeating their mothers' and grandmothers' unhappy history of working for white women in servile, dead-end jobs. In 1972, 40 percent of full-time domestic workers were black—more than 500,000 women. By 1995, fewer than 17 percent of household workers were black—137,000 women.

Many immigrants come from a different, more desperate place. They have left their own children back home and are more than willing to put in a few years in other people's homes in return for a chance at a better life. Some actually prefer to live in, because they can save money faster and feel relatively secure from the Immigration and Naturalization Service. The work is frequently unpleasant and exploitative, but that has been the history of the immigrant in the United States from the beginning, and people who see a job as a stepping-stone are more willing to endure it for a while than those who see it as a trap.

In sum, reducing the number of nannies legally admitted from abroad effectively dried up the supply of legal, in-home care providers in the United States. But not a peep of protest was heard from the American women who would be affected.

Every previous restriction on immigration had brought the affected American employers to Washington, D.C., to object, more often than not successfully. When agricultural growers complained about a 1986 ban on hiring undocumented workers, for example, the government responded by allowing more than one million undocumented farmworkers to qualify for legal status. The 1990 law itself opened the doors wider to foreign professionals, including managers, computer programmers, and marketing specialists, in response to complaints from corporations that they needed employees from abroad for those well-paying jobs.

But the restrictions on at-home caregivers, a serious impediment to the livelihood of a large percentage of professional women in this country, were not challenged by a single women's organization. "There was no letter, no phone calls, nothing submitted to any congressman on this subcommittee, saying that because of what you guys are doing, it's going to be harder than ever for working women to find reasonable child care, to keep their jobs," Pugliese told me. "Nobody's called about this but you."

The only voices raised came from the immigration bar, which makes a living helping clients bring workers into the country. One attorney, Carolyn Killea, appeared on a Washington, D.C., radio show in the summer of 1990 and accurately predicted what was going to happen. "Working women, who are trying to get care for their children, for older family members, and handicapped family members, are going to feel these provisions the most," she declared prophetically, "because they are relying on largely immigrant women to enable them to work . . . This law is an accident waiting to happen."

"I told anyone who would listen that we were going to do ourselves out of the next generation of women leaders," she later recalled. "I never expected to be proven right so soon, with the Zoe Baird case."[4]

Zoe Baird was general counsel at Aetna Life and Casualty when President Bill Clinton, before his inauguration, announced that she was his choice for attorney general. Shortly thereafter, Baird herself revealed that she had hired two illegal aliens as domestic staff and failed to pay the required Social Security taxes on their wages. This was a civil violation, and one of Baird's advisers had told her that it might be similar to a parking ticket. Years before, back in the early 1970s, it had come out that William Ruckelshaus, then deputy attorney general, had a foreign woman with an improper visa working in his home. His wife, Jill, was blamed for the oversight, and the matter was quickly passed over.

The offense was not something that had been red-flagged by the FBI's routine background checks, and it was not something that any male appointee had ever thought important enough to bring up. The hearing on Baird's confirmation on January 1993 revealed, however, that her maternal obligations were of great interest to the Senate Judiciary Committee, the same all-male body that had grilled Anita Hill. The senators were particularly curious about how many hours Baird spent away from her four-year-old son, Julian, inquiring when she left home in the morning and when she got home at night. "I must have been out of the room when those questions were being asked of Ron Brown," commented Delissa A. Ridgway, president of the Women's Bar Association of the District of Columbia.

Zoe Baird's interrogators were unaware of the lengths to which Baird and her husband, Paul Gewirtz, a constitutional law professor at Yale, had gone to find legal child care. In 1990, the year after Julian was born, Baird had been named the top lawyer for Aetna, at a salary of $507,105. (The couple's combined income was $660,345.) The pair obviously could afford a full-time nanny, and they originally hired an American citizen who worked for them for five months before quitting with two weeks' notice.[5]

The couple then placed this ad in three local newspapers:

> Child Care Nanny. Live-in Nanny for 7 Mo. Old Boy in warm family setting. Light housekeeping, cook dinners. Long term position with appreciative family in beautiful home. Nonsmoker. Driver. Citizen or green card only. Require child care references.

They received not one response.

They contacted an agency and flew in an American candidate from Texas at their own expense. She refused the job, she explained, because she didn't feel comfortable working for a Jewish family. There followed a series of frustrating interviews with other applicants sent by agencies. One said that she had decided not to leave her current job; one took another job before the scheduled interview;

one had a negative reference from her employer; one admitted that she smoked. The couple finally hired a woman who quit after a few days, explaining that she was homesick.

An acquaintance who had lunch with Baird around this time told me that she was not surprised to learn that Baird and Gewirtz had "nanny problems." It appeared to her that the couple was looking for someone to be on duty virtually every waking hour, a person who would be a de facto parent to the infant. This woman remembers thinking, "She's not going to find someone like that, even a live-in."

Finally, an agency sent a Peruvian woman named Lilian Cordero, who, Baird felt, would make a suitable caretaker of Julian. Cordero wanted to negotiate a job for her husband as well, so Baird and Gewirtz agreed to take him on as a driver, even though they didn't think they really needed one.

This was the summer of 1990. Professor Gewirtz was not teaching, so he assured his busy wife that he would handle the legal work involving the Corderos—whereupon he stepped into a Kafkaesque legal and bureaucratic maze that confounded even a Yale law professor.

Gewirtz was first told by an immigration lawyer that he couldn't pay Social Security taxes on the Corderos' wages until they had Social Security numbers, and they couldn't have numbers until they had permanent residency status, or green cards. Several months later, Gewirtz filed for a labor certification for Lilian Cordero (certifying that no American citizen had been found for the job). This was approved, and he then filed an application with the INS for a green card. In October 1992 Cordero was approved for a green card, to be issued when her number in the visa application waiting list came up. But by this time, her husband had deserted her, and in November she too left the household. After Baird was nominated attorney general, the couple paid about $12,000 in back taxes and fines.

That was Zoe Baird's crime. But hiring illegal help, a civil violation, was not her real transgression. A few weeks after her nomination was rejected by the Judiciary Committee, her mentor, Lloyd Cutler, told me, "It was women who killed her appointment. The committee was deluged with angry calls and letters from women, denouncing her in the worst possible terms."

The grassroots attack on Baird was in stark contrast to the utter silence with which women had greeted the passage of the immigration law. Some female writers opined that Baird came across as a cold person. ("Compared to whom? Warren Christopher?" wondered one Washington female attorney.)

Other working women betrayed their resentment over the fact that Baird had not made the kinds of career sacrifices that they had—turning down promotions or choice assignments—in order to have more time with their children. Women who followed the drama closely told me they believed that this was what hounded Zoe Baird out of Washington more than anything else. There was a "we've paid, now she has to" quality to the attacks on her. (Baird's workaholism was never in question; she had called presidential aide Howard Paster at 8:00 P.M. on Christmas Eve to strategize about her confirmation, to the disgust of Paster's wife.)

Not one major women's organization stepped up to the plate for Baird, despite the blatant double standard that was being applied to her case. With their own memberships bitterly divided over the affair, no national group wanted to risk taking a controversial stand on behalf of a beleaguered corporate attorney who had never been particularly active in women's causes.

Then there was the liberal guilt factor, as thick as smoke at a barbeque. "There was some skittishness about the class thing," Warren Leiden told me. "I met with some women at the American Bar Association who were very interested in doing something about the housekeeper/nanny shortage. But there was this sense that it was somehow selfish and inappropriate for women to be seeking solutions just for themselves, for what many saw as a privilege."

I ran across this guilt phenomenon one day while skimming the Internet. I came across an ongoing conversation among female academic economists on the touchy subject of household help. Constance Newman of the University of California at Davis has suggested that to be entirely politically correct, a professional woman should consider not hiring any domestic help. Newman's proposal had unleashed an anguished uproar from computers from coast to coast. One correspondent logically noted that "short of doing all the household and childcare oneself, which is clearly not possible, the only alternative to offending Constance's sensibilities is to hire men to do those tasks."

Once Baird's case achieved notoriety, no one, male or female, who had ever hired an undocumented worker or failed to pay Social Security taxes for an employee could be safely considered for top public offices. A new penalty was added to all the others attached to motherhood. A friend of mine, a forty-year-old public policy analyst, saw this immediately. "Just when we are on the verge of moving into real power," she lamented, "they invented a new reason to keep us out."

Kimba Wood, the next candidate for attorney general, had broken no laws at all, but because she had hired an undocumented child-care worker before 1986, when it was legal to do so, she was forced to withdraw.

The legacy of the Baird fiasco continues to punish working parents. Women—and some men—with young children are still being disqualified for judgeships and high government positions because they have a "Zoe Baird problem," shorthand for having run afoul of one of the myriad laws regulating household workers. In 1994 I had a conversation with Clarine Riddle, a former attorney general of Connecticut, who was then assisting Sen. Joseph Lieberman in selecting candidates for the next available federal judgeship in that state. "I interviewed about twenty-five people, the overwhelming majority of them women," she told me, "and more than half had some kind of nanny problem in the past, mostly the failure to pay Social Security taxes." Riddle explained that the new disqualifier hurt women far more than men, because virtually every working mother needs a nanny, while many men can count on their wives to take care of the kids. She believes that the number of women appointed to judgeships in the 1990s was significantly lower than it might have been had this controversy never erupted.

Interestingly, the issue of immigration restrictions never became a focus of media attention at the time of the Zoe Baird affair. Attorney Killea says that she was contacted by several women television reporters who wanted to do a show on the immigration roadblock, but "then they'd say, 'by the way, I have a nanny. Should I do this show?' I would tell them the INS will look at you, and if something is not completely [on the] up-and-up, they cold put your nanny into deportation proceedings and cite you for employer sanctions. And then what happens to your kid?" No one did the show.

It would be absurdly simple to alleviate the shortage of legal nannies. If home-care workers were simply reclassified—correctly—as skilled, they would fall into a category for which visas are readily available. One wonders why this solution did not occur to any of the American women's organizations. It did occur to one woman, however.

When the 1990 immigration law began to take effect, Priscilla Labovitz, an immigration lawyer in suburban Washington, D.C., decided to challenge the Department of Labor's definition of a nanny's job. One of her cases involved an English nanny who wanted to enter the United States to work for a couple in northern Virginia. The woman had two years of formal training in the care and development of children and seven years of child-care experience. Labovitz filed an application for labor certification, asking that the applicant be considered a "nanny," which she described as a skilled occupation. She explained that the job's purpose was "to care for, and supervise the development (physical, intellectual, moral) of, children during most of their waking hours." The various tasks included teaching two young children social skills, conferring with their doctors, transporting them to appointments, preparing nutritious meals; in short, all of the services that parents provide.[6]

In her statement on the application, the mother explained that she was the owner and operator of a publishing company and had to take three- to four-day business trips about twice a month. Her husband, an investment banker, also had to travel frequently and unexpectedly. The mother stated that "because of our national failure to place sufficient value on the early development of children," she had encountered a shortage of professionally trained American nannies. She said that she had called every one of the fourteen nanny programs in the country and been told that there were lengthy waiting lists for their graduates. While waiting to find the right person, both she and her husband had cut their jobs back to thirty hours a week. Labovitz's effort to certify the English woman as a skilled worker was denied on the grounds that the parents, by asking for a person with two years of training plus experience, were asking for more than the job required.

In the meantime, Labovitz had applied to the Department of Labor requesting that the "new" occupation of "nanny" be established and coded as "skilled," requiring two years of formal training plus child-care experience. Normally, requests for new occupational categories take a couple of weeks to be OK'd. In this case, several months went by before the request finally came back in April of 1994. It had been approved.

"I was ecstatic," Labovitz recalled during an interview in her office. "The decision was published in the newsletter of the American Immigration Lawyers Association, and I got calls from all over the country. It meant that people meeting the standards would have to wait only about a year for a visa.

"The first thing I did was call the Department of Labor and ask them to reconsider [the English nanny's] application in light of the change. The woman I spoke with congratulated me and said, 'I thought you were right all along.'"

"Then about fifteen minutes later, the woman called back. 'We're going to deny the cert,' she said, 'and he [her superior in the regional labor certifying office in Philadelphia] says we'll fight you all the way.'"

A week later, the Department of Labor officially reversed its decision to create a new occupational category. In a letter to Labovitz, a bureaucrat in the department's occupational analysis center explained that the original decision was "based on insufficient fact-finding and research." According to immigration attorneys, there is little chance that Congress will remedy the situation given the current climate of hostility toward immigration.

Labovitz says that she now tells people who are working as nannies and who want to get a green card to go to college and study something other than early childhood development for two years and then apply as a skilled worker. As she puts it, "We've created an absolute disincentive for foreign-born workers to get training in child care."

With qualified caregivers shut out of the country, the only in-home workers who are currently allowed to enter are au pairs. Originally intended to be a form of cultural exchange, the au pair program offered girls a chance to live with an American family and study at a local institution in return for some service. But over the years, it has become more of a conveyor belt bringing in female teenagers to serve as cheap domestic help. These girls are allowed to care for infants after only twenty-four hours of instruction in child development and one day of safety training. Their contracts allow them to work ten hours a day, forty-five hours a week, at wages of little more than three dollars an hour, plus room and board and a small educational stipend.

Three years before the Louise Woodward case in Boston, another nineteen-year-old au pair, a Dutch girl, was accused of shaking an eight-week-old baby to death in Virginia. The jury deadlocked in the girl's trial for manslaughter, and she was subsequently convicted of a misdemeanor and sent home. In the wake of that incident, the federal government imposed much tougher standards for au pairs. But 3,500 people, most of them mothers, wrote letters complaining that the new rules would increase the cost of au pairs and limit the hours they could work. Faced with this outcry, the government backed down and dropped a couple of the imposed new requirements. One of these would have prevented anyone under the age of twenty-one from caring for infants of less than two years old.[7]

Had this regulation been adopted, Louise Woodward and Matt Eappen would never have met.

Notes

1. Eugene Pugliese, personal communication, 1995.
2. Warren R. Leiden, personal communication, 1995.
3. "Women's Work—Up from .878," report of the DOT Research Project, University of Wisconsin, Extension Women's Education Resources, 1975, p.11.
4. Carolyn Killea, personal communication, 1995.
5. Sidney Blumenthal, "Adventures in Babysitting," *New Yorker,* February 15, 1993.
6. This and the following information was provided by Priscilla Labovitz, 1995.
7. Debbi Wilgoren, "New Regulations on Au Pairs Draw Criticism, Support," *Washington Post,* December 17, 1994. Additional details of this story were provided by Stanley Colwin of the State Department, the agency that administers the au pair program. Personal communication, 1997.

Day Care Is Moving to the Night Shift

BARBARA CARTON

There are plenty of places to sleep at the Children's Choice Learning Center in North Las Vegas, Nevada, but nine-year-old Najah Finch isn't napping.

Wearing a pink "I am Boy Crazy" T-shirt, she cartwheels around the floor, breaks for juice and popcorn, then settles down at the TV for a Muppet video. Najah's mom isn't due to pick her up for another three hours.

At 3:30 A.M.

A good number of Najah's fifty playmates won't leave until the wee hours, either. Others will stay all night at the round-the-clock facility. Many of the children's parents are cashiers, dealers, and others working the busy weekend shifts at the Texas Station Gambling Hall and Hotel next door, but some 40 percent work as hospital technicians, nurses, and call-center operators.

As more single parents and working couples cope with a twenty-four-hour economy, day care is making an uneasy transition to night care. Employers are building round-the-clock centers to attract and keep employees. State and local governments are also supporting extended-hour and night-care initiatives, partly because they feel obliged to help the single mothers they sent to work under welfare reform.

"If we could have the kind of life that our parents had, where I would go to work nine to five, Monday through Friday, and my wife was able to stay home with the children, we'd much rather do that," says Randy Donahue, a security guard whose wife is a night-shift nurse. "But in today's world, it takes two incomes to make it work." Mr. Donahue arrives at Children's Choice near midnight to pick up his children after work.

In Florida, the number of providers offering child care sometime between 6 P.M. and 7 A.M. has grown 14 percent to more than 1,500 since the end of 1999. Illinois last month extended a two-year, $1 million pilot project that encouraged ten day-care centers across the state to offer subsidized odd-hour care.

In Philadelphia, Cynthia Higgins, forty-one, a former teenage mother, says "absolutely tremendous" need led her to open a small day-care chain called Dusk-2-Dawn 24/7 Quality Childcare. She serves 140 children. Typically, 45 children spend all or part of each night.

Over the past decade or so, there have been scattered efforts to offer odd-hour child care. Some have stumbled, mostly because of parental squeamishness

Wall Street Journal, July 6, 2001. Barbara Carton is a staff reporter for *Wall Street Journal*.

about putting children to bed in an institution, however nice. There are indications, though, that popular attitudes may be changing. A generation ago, day care of any sort was widely shunned. Today, centers say they are under increasing pressure from parents who—even if they still balk at night care—are demanding greater flexibility to accommodate early-morning commutes and later evenings at work.

Ford Motor Company, auto-parts maker Visteon Corporation, and the United Auto Workers are building thirteen facilities that could stay open round-the-clock. The first center, scheduled to open in Dearborn, Michigan, later this year, has 1,090 applications for 220 available slots.

Sears, Roebuck and Company plans a six-city program to encourage day-care operators to stay open as late as 11 P.M. Britt Berrett, chief executive of Medical City Dallas Hospital, says he is eagerly awaiting this fall's completion of the center's new $4 million, twenty-four-hour child-care center, which he says will give him an edge in recruiting nurses.

A place to leave the kids any time is even touted as a lure by the 100-acre Coventry housing development in Valparaiso, Indiana, which promises homebuyers a "24-hour day care" center on site. The subdivision is near Bethlehem Steel Corporation's Burns Harbor plant and other round-the-clock employers.

Although the move toward expanded hours and overnight care is widely regarded as a necessity mandated by new economic realities, it leaves some providers and childhood experts uncomfortable about lengthening periods of parental separation and lack of adequate sleep, especially for preschoolers. At Children's Choice, on the night Najah Finch left at 3:30, at least eight children stayed thirteen hours or more, including a preschooler dropped off at 6:19 Friday evening and picked up at 10:18 the following morning.

If work schedules leave parents no choice but institutional overnight care, "we'd better rethink our whole system so that parents do have choices," says T. Berry Brazelton, a Harvard Medical School pediatrician and author of popular child-rearing books.

Kyle Pruett, a professor of psychiatry at the Yale University Child Study Center, says children are especially vulnerable and prone to anxiety at bedtime. With the high staff turnover in day care, children may face a changing cast tucking them in, says Dr. Pruett, who questions "whether we are asking just too much of our kids in those settings."

Lots of families don't think so—and, in any case, they say they don't have a choice.

Natalie Biggs, thirty-eight, a single mother who works a rotating day/night schedule as a cashier, is thrilled to have found Children's Choice. "I've seen other day cares," she says, "but not as nice as this." Her son, Donovan, five, spends two nights a week at the center while she works 11:30 P.M. to 7:30 A.M.

"It's nice to be a couple of hundred yards away from your child," says Ron Santisteban, forty-nine, a waiter who works the 4 P.M. to midnight shift at a nearby steak house while daughter Angela, ten, goes to Children's Choice. "If anything goes wrong, they know where I'm at. I can be here in two minutes."

Judy Harden, who has fought for overnight facilities as family-care coordinator for the United Auto Workers, says "people who criticize . . . don't understand the reality of today's workplace." At Ford, that reality was summarized in a "needs assessment" conducted before the 1999 contract talks that led to expanded overnight facilities.

Ford built a twenty-four-hour center in 1993 for 175 of its employees' children in Livonia, Michigan. But the new survey showed more need: 31 percent of Ford's 86,100 Detroit-area employees were hourly employees in night jobs and 58 percent were younger than forty-six. In Kansas City, half of Ford's workers were hourlies in night jobs, with two-thirds under forty-six.

One of the reasons Ford supported the idea, says Renee Lerche, then the company's director of workplace development, is that much of its worker absenteeism is caused by parents' need to stay home with sick children.

Nationally, the U.S. Department of Labor says that about one in six workers had evening, night, or rotating-shift schedules in 1997, the last year it collected such figures. The ratio had been steady for about a decade.

But that was before the changes in welfare rules became widespread, requiring mothers to return to work. Often, because they have limited qualifications, ex-welfare moms get the work no one else wants, including night shifts. In Washington State, the number of children whose parents are seeking night or weekend care from community referral agencies has surged 53 percent to 12,588 since 1996, when welfare reform was enacted.

Many manufacturers, meanwhile, have been consolidating and adding shifts at existing plants rather than building new ones, according to William G. Sirois, chief operating officer of Circadian Technologies Inc., a Cambridge, Massachusetts, consultancy that specializes in round-the-clock business. Mr. Sirois says there is an "explosion" in round-the-clock telephone-call centers, computer-facility sites, and retailers that close late at night, or not at all.

Longer commutes also stretch day care. Sara Murphy, a twenty-three-year-old loan officer, drops her one-year-old, Cecily, at the twenty-four-hour Little Sandbox Daycare near her Oakley, California, home by 6 A.M. and sometimes as early as 4 A.M. Unless she starts early, she says, she can't get a parking space at the train station to get to her credit-union job in Oakland. Her total commute time: an hour and forty-five minutes.

Ms. Murphy, whose husband has a longer commute, says she has looked for work nearby, "but this is a really small town and pay isn't good at all. And the company I work for is a really great company—they're helping me develop into what I want to do in the future, which is be a branch manager."

Many states and localities limit the lengths of stays in day care, and providers also set maximums, but these rules reflect little agreement on what is best for a child. Connecticut limits care to twelve hours in a twenty-four-hour period. Kentucky allows up to sixteen. Several others, including Pennsylvania and

Michigan, merely state that the care cannot encompass an entire twenty-four hours. In the Ford-Visteon-UAW centers, the limit will be twelve hours.

In Nebraska, several day-care providers have urged hours limits because some parents are virtually abandoning their children to day care, even during hours or vacation days when they aren't at work, bringing them home only to sleep overnight, says Pat Urzedowski, Nebraska's child-care licensing administrator. She says providers are concerned that children are "missing out on an important part of childhood—being with their family."

"I've had to tell more than one parent, 'You're leaving your child too much,'" says Elvira Monsalve, who provides child care in her Boston home. She says that on occasion, parents on business trips have left children for two or three weeks at a time. She declines to give their names. Massachusetts sets no limit on child-care hours.

Seeing the changing work landscape as an opportunity, Leslie Wulf started Children's Choice Learning Centers Inc. in 1998. Its business plan: building and operating twenty-four-hour centers for employers. Its corporate slogan: "Child Care That Is Always There."

Mr. Wulf targets fast-growing markets in the Sun Belt and the South, where the workforce includes large numbers of newcomers or transients living far away from parents and siblings. Employers in these locales "are finding there is no family infrastructure," says Mr. Wulf, formerly the president of the Grandma Lee's restaurant chain. "And the less family infrastructure there is, the harder it is for employees to balance work and family."

Children's Choice daily rates vary, according to the child's age and the hours used. For example, an infant kept up to three hours costs seven dollars an hour, versus four dollars an hour for children six to twelve years old. An infant left for the maximum twelve hours to fourteen hours would cost forty dollars a day, whereas a six- to twelve-year-old kept for the same period costs twenty-six dollars. Siblings get a 5 percent discount off the oldest child's tuition rate.

Children's Choice has built five twenty-four-hour centers and is under contract to build seven more. Four of the centers were built for Station Casinos Inc., which operates a chain of gambling parlors. Half of its eleven thousand employees are women, many of them single parents laboring at dead-of-night jobs. The four centers enroll three thousand children, with 25 percent of usage occurring overnight, and also have contracts with other twenty-four-hour employers in the Las Vegas area, including three hospitals, a call center, and a drug-testing laboratory.

The Texas Station center, one of the four, looks like a bright elementary school by day, with colorful murals and brand-new equipment. By 10 P.M. one spring night, however, lights in most classrooms had already been dimmed. The fifty children being looked after are divided into various groups—infants age six weeks and up, toddlers, and those that are older.

Most of the younger group are asleep in cribs or pint-size cots, where Children's Choice workers have tucked them in. Some are clutching blankets from home, with pictures of their parents hung on the walls nearby. But two of them are still up, including a ten-month-old whose parents want him awake in parallel with their work cycle and asleep in the daytime. He crawls silently across the floor in an orange Space Exploration sweatshirt, his path illuminated by nightlights.

Down the hall, laughter erupts from the brightly lighted activities room, where the seventeen older kids, including James Novak, are still wide awake. "I've never been to a cool day care like this," says the ten-year-old, who lives with his grandmother, a casino dealer. "We've got computers. All we had at the old place was board games."

On school nights, dormitory-style rows of Murphy beds are pulled down in a Sleep Room and lights go out at 9 P.M. On weekends, beds don't go down until 1 A.M.—also with parents' permission—and a slumber-party atmosphere reigns.

After exercise, Legos, computer games, and a video, the group breaks for a snack. Meanwhile, weary parents come and go, picking up and dropping off children.

Just before midnight, Mr. Donahue, the security guard, lifts his sleepy four-year-old son, Kyle, to one shoulder while daughter Emily, who is eight, pads along beside in a Strawberry Shortcake nightgown as the family heads out into the parking lot. Mr. Donahue's wife, Lorna, won't be home from her nursing shift until breakfast.

Tonia Jones, a single mother and X-ray technician at a local medical center, drops off Tristian, a six-year-old kindergartner. She'll pick him up when she gets off work at 7:30 A.M. "Before this," she says, "I had to struggle to see who would keep him. I alternated days with relatives. My cousin and my mom took their turns." But arrangements often broke down, so she turned to Children's Choice, where she says the care is more reliable.

By the time Najah Finch's mother shows up after her casino-dealer shift, the fourth-grader is already fast asleep, curled up with her favorite stuffed dolphin. Staffers tucked her in, but they didn't hug or kiss her goodnight. They say the rules forbid that.

Mommy-Track Backlash

ALDEN M. HAYASHI

Everyone at ClarityBase seemed to understand when one account manager—a working mother—got a special deal: Fridays off, limited travel, easy clients. But when other employees—namely, nonparents—started asking for similar treatment, the company found itself on the brink of an organizational firestorm.

"Please don't tell me that I need to have a baby to have this time off."

Those words were still ringing in the ears of Jessica Gonon an hour after a tense meeting with one of her key managers. As she sat in her office trying to make sense of a recent customer survey, Jessica, the vice president of sales and customer support at ClarityBase, was having trouble concentrating on the bar graphs and pie charts in front of her. Snippets from her earlier conversation kept interrupting her thoughts.

The issue seemed simple enough. Jana Rowe, an account manager in the sales support department, had requested a lighter workload: she wanted a four-day workweek, and for that she was willing to take a corresponding 20 percent cut in pay. Those were the simple facts, but the situation at ClarityBase was anything but straightforward.

Just last week, Davis Bennett, another account manager, had made a similar request. He wanted a lighter workload so he could train for the Ironman Triathlon World Championship, the premier competition held each October in Hawaii. He was a world-class athlete, and his ultimate goal was a spot on the U.S. Olympic team in 2004. Davis had said he didn't need to begin training full throttle until mid-spring, so Jessica had asked him for a couple weeks to figure out how ClarityBase might best accommodate his training schedule.

A complicating factor was that both Davis and Jana were well aware that Megan Flood, another account manager, had been working a reduced schedule for nearly two years. When she was hired, Megan had requested Fridays off to spend time with her two young boys, and Jessica had agreed.

In her meeting with Jessica, Jana had declined to explain why she wanted the reduced hours, citing "personal reasons." When Jessica had paused, wondering what those reasons might be, Jana added, "All I'm asking for is the same deal that Megan has. Please don't tell me that I need to have a baby to have this time off." Jana was married and had no children. Davis was single and also without children.

Harvard Business Review, March 2001. Reprinted with the permission of HBS Publishing Corp. Alden M. Hayashi is senior editor with the *Harvard Business Review*.

There were other subtle issues. A reduced workweek for Jana and Davis meant much more than just that. From Jessica's conversations with them, she inferred that any official reduction in hours—having a day off every week in Jana's case—would also mean they wouldn't have to work the occasional nights and weekends that the other account managers did, all except Megan.

ClarityBase, headquartered in Reston, Virginia, sold large database applications that helped companies run their operations, including human resources, manufacturing, and order fulfillment. The eight account managers—Jana, Davis, and Megan among them—were in charge of helping the company's largest customers install and maintain the software, which required no small amount of hand-holding and coddling. Because Megan had an abbreviated workweek, the other account managers were assigned the more demanding clients.

Davis, in particular, seemed to have the toughest customers, most notably St. Elizabeth's Hospital in Philadelphia, which required him to be available around the clock. Once, when its system failed on Christmas Day, Davis took the train to Philadelphia to help get the hospital's crucial patient database up and running. If Jessica agreed to a shorter workweek for Jana and Davis, who would take over clients like St. Elizabeth's? And what would happen if the other account managers began asking for similar deals?

It was Monday morning—what a way to start the week, thought Jessica. She had promised Jana that she'd get back to her by Friday, so at least she had the whole week to sort things out. That was plenty of time, or so she hoped.

Trading Places

Jessica had had second thoughts before hiring Megan—she had made so many demands in the interview. Her children, said Megan, were paramount to her, and she wanted a very flexible schedule. Not only did she want the freedom to come in late and leave early occasionally, she also wanted Fridays off. She wasn't amenable to any business travel, and she wouldn't be able to attend after-hours meetings except when her personal schedule allowed.

But Megan had come highly recommended. Her three years of experience at Dawson Software, ClarityBase's chief competitor, would be a huge asset; her technical skills were superb; and her professional and friendly demeanor would surely impress customers. And, last but certainly not least, Jessica had looked for months to hire someone of Megan's caliber. None of the other candidates had come remotely close. So after thinking about it over a weekend, Jessica decided to offer her the job.

Still, Megan's demands had left Jessica feeling uneasy. Part of the reason, Jessica realized later after much introspection, was because she had had it much tougher when she was starting her career in the early 1970s—a different era before flexible work hours, on-site day care centers, and the Family and Medical Leave Act. At that time, women like Jessica, who held a bachelor's degree in computer programming from Penn State, simply couldn't have it all, both career and children. So Jessica and her husband, who was on the partner track at his architectural firm, had decided that she would quit her job as a supervisor in the MIS department for Capital Insurance when they had their first child.

Nine years later, after their youngest child had started kindergarten, Jessica reentered the workforce as a sales assistant at ClarityBase. She took classes at night to get up to speed on the computer industry and slowly rose to become a sales rep, then account manager, and then head of the Northeast sales region. At the age of fifty-two, she was promoted to her current position of vice president of sales and customer support. The road had been long, and having children had been a substantial detour. But just because Jessica had had to make trade-offs between career and family, should Megan have to as well?

Hidden Tensions

It was nearly 7 P.M. when Jessica finally crammed the customer survey reports into her briefcase and started to head home. As she walked through the sales support group, she was reminded of a conversation she happened to overhear in this corridor last week: "I honestly don't know if I can force myself to smile through yet another precious baby shower," said a woman's voice from the other side of a cubicle wall. At the time, Jessica paid little attention to the comment, but now, those words made her stop and think.

ClarityBase prided itself on its progressive work-life policies. The company offered all employees family medical insurance, adoption assistance, and paid maternity and paternity leave. But perhaps the thing that ClarityBase was most proud of was the on-site child-care center that the company subsidized. Bill Welensky, vice president of human resources, liked to brag that such perks helped ClarityBase keep employee turnover to less than 5 percent annually, unheard of in the software industry. But had the company become too pro-parent at the expense of other employees?

A year and a half ago, as Labor Day approached, tension between the two groups surfaced. Ed Fernandez—whom Jessica had just hired to supervise ClarityBase's call center—had drawn up the schedule for the holiday weekend in what he thought was the fairest way: people who hadn't worked over a holiday for the longest time would be the first to be called to duty. Many mothers were on the short list because the previous supervisor had never scheduled them to work on holidays. When the assignment was posted, the mothers were peeved, and their reaction irritated other employees.

Fortunately, Ed was able to strike a compromise. The assignments for Labor Day would be done as they had been in the past, with special consideration given to mothers. From that point on, though, every employee would have to work his or her fair share of holidays, regardless of past status or history. The only consideration would be for seniority: newer employees, whether they were parents or not, would be the first to serve.

That solution seemed to prevent a fracture in the workplace between parents and nonparents. But could it be that a dangerous rift did exist, with only a fragile veneer of social decorum to conceal it? Jessica did an about-face and headed back to her office to reboot her computer. She composed two e-mails, one to Jana and the other to Davis, requesting that she meet with each of them as soon as possible to discuss their requests further.

Gathering Information

At lunch the next day, Jessica waited until she and Jana had comfortably settled into their booth and ordered their meals before asking the delicate questions. "I want to understand your situation, why you've requested a shorter workweek," she started. "Yesterday, you cited 'personal reasons.' The last thing I want to do is pry into your personal life, but is there anything else you would feel comfortable telling me?"

Jessica watched as Jana swallowed her food and collected her thoughts. "I don't mean to be disrespectful," Jana began. "Honestly, I don't. Nor do I mean to be mysterious. But I really don't think I should have to explain why I want the time off. Suffice it to say that it's very, very important to me."

"I see," replied Jessica. "I'm sorry to have asked. I just wanted to understand your situation better."

The two women ate in silence for a few minutes. Then Jana put her fork down and looked at Jessica intently. "The thing that gets me," Jana said, "is that somehow all the family stuff is deemed more important— the soccer games, the school plays, the graduations. Well I have important things going on in my life, too. They just don't involve children."

"Do you think that parents are treated with favoritism at ClarityBase?" Jessica asked.

"I'd like to think not," Jana replied. "But is it so hard to believe that my reasons for wanting a lighter workload might be just as important to me as Megan's children are to her?" Before Jessica could say anything, Jana added, "Don't get me wrong. I think Megan's great. She's one of our best account managers, so I have no qualms about the deal she has. I'm just saying that I think I deserve the same deal."

On her drive home that night, Jessica thought more about what Jana had said. She had heard of companies with a no-explanation policy for time off, but that blanket policy seemed unfair to her. Some people might need more consideration at specific times—for example, the birth of a child—whereas others could postpone their plans—for instance a college course could be taken in the fall instead of in the spring. On the other hand, a blanket no-explanation policy would certainly make her job easier—she wouldn't have to make value judgments about whose reasons were more important.

Breakfast the next morning with Davis went more smoothly. When Jessica asked him whether he felt that parents at ClarityBase were treated with favoritism, he replied, "I've never felt like a second-class citizen, if that's what you're asking. I really don't mind helping out someone who's having some kind of family emergency, because working parents have it tough. I have no idea how they juggle everything. I'd be a nut case."

"Thanks for your great attitude," said Jessica.

"Well, we're all on the same team."

"I guess what I need to know from you," Jessica continued, "is how much flexibility you might have. Excuse my ignorance, but I know very little about triathletes, and I'm not sure how much time off you'll need to train."

"It varies; everyone seems to have a different training regimen," said Davis. "But here's what I think would work best for me: for the summer, I'd like to leave work at three on Tuesdays and Thursdays. Then, during the fall, I'd want to leave early maybe four days a week. But on the days I left early, I could definitely come in at 6 A.M. to make up some of that time, or I could stay later on the other days."

"I appreciate that," said Jessica, "and I've always been grateful for your willingness to go the extra mile. But with this new schedule, do you think you could keep up with the needs of your clients?"

"I've thought about that a lot, and to be honest with you, I don't know," Davis admitted. "I realize that the customer comes first, but I'd also like to think that most of them would be willing to make adjustments—and I think they'd be minor ones—to accommodate my new hours. Of course, I have no idea if everything would work out as smoothly as I'm hoping."

"This particular triathlon is really important to you?" Jessica asked, almost rhetorically.

"Well, I've won a few local ones, but nothing big," said Davis. "And the Ironman is big; it's the Superbowl. My goal is to place in the top twenty. And yes, it's very important to me. In fact, I suppose I've never wanted anything as badly in my entire life."

Jessica thought back to when she had hired Davis more than five years ago. What impressed her most about him was his passion. Davis was clearly the type of person who threw himself into everything he did, and it was evident in his work. So it was hardly surprising that he would want extra training time to prepare for the Ironman.

Decision Time

As Jessica pulled into ClarityBase's parking lot, she noticed a Honda with a bumper sticker that proudly declared "Child-free (not child-less) . . . and loving every minute of it." Could that car belong to the woman she had overheard the other night?

Before heading to her office, Jessica decided to stop by the HR department to talk with Bill Welensky. "Bill, do you have a few free minutes?" she asked.

Bill, who was Jessica's mentor and one of her biggest supporters at ClarityBase, listened carefully as she told him about Jana, Davis, and her earlier arrangement with Megan. "I know that we don't have any official policy that specifically addresses these issues," she said, "but I was hoping for some advice."

"I'm not sure exactly what to say," said Bill. "As you know, ClarityBase prides itself on its progressive views on work-life issues, and we try to accommodate people as much as possible. But we really don't have any policies at all regarding flex time."

When Jessica told Bill about what Jana had said—that she felt parents got special consideration at ClarityBase—he paused before speaking. "That's not the first time that sentiment has been expressed," he offered. "But as far as flex time or shorter workweeks are concerned, we certainly don't have any guidelines with regard to parents versus nonparents. Supervisors just have to make those kinds of decisions on a case-by-case basis."

Jessica thought about that for a few seconds. "The problem," she started, "is that I feel like I somehow have to make value judgments about what's more important, someone's parenting needs versus someone else's personal achievement goals. And I don't feel comfortable doing that."

Bill looked at Jessica. "Have you tried taking a different perspective?" he asked. "Think of it as two employees who both want raises but your budget will allow just one. What would you do?"

Without hesitation, Jessica replied, "I'd make a judgment about just how valuable—and irreplaceable—each employee was. But my situation is so much more complicated than that. With salary requests, I could compare apples with apples. With work-life issues, I feel like I have to compare an apple with a hammer with a vase."

"Then let me speak to you as a friend and not as the HR director," Bill said. "And let me be frank with you: the reason you were promoted to vice president is precisely because of your ability to compare apples with hammers and vases. You run a large department and, yes, it's not always easy to meet the needs of your staff while also making your quarterly numbers. So, no, you can't go out and hire two more account managers to cover for the people who want flex time. There is no simple, tidy solution here."

As Jessica left Bill's office, she tried to reassure herself that it was just Wednesday; she still had until Friday to figure out what to do. The problem, though, was that with each day she was becoming increasingly confused.

Is Telework Coming of Age?

Evaluating the Potential Benefits of Telework

CARL E. VAN HORN AND DUKE STOREN

Computers, the Internet, and other forms of information technology have already changed the way we work and live. The mass infusion of information technology into the economy has profound impacts on labor supply and demand, and on the education and training institutions preparing people for work. Our "digital economy" could revolutionize the way we communicate, learn, and work. It could also alter the way our society addresses such social problems as unemployment and illiteracy.

Information technology now profoundly shapes American culture, at least for the middle class. Daily examples of information technology's grip on the nation include technology sections in every broad circulation newspaper and magazine, intense attention to the ups and downs of dot-com stocks, and television advertisements for Internet job sites during mass culture events, such as the Olympics and the Superbowl. The exchange of e-mail addresses in addition to, or instead of, phone numbers is now common practice for many Americans.

Eight years of sustained economic growth, low unemployment, high labor-force participation rates, increasing real wages, and increasing workweeks for many have created new "challenges." Namely, the American worker who is stressed out and looking for new strategies to accomplishing their 24 by 7 by 365 jobs while still enjoying their personal and family lives.

These two powerful trends—widely available information technology and workers hoping to balance work and family—have generated strong interest in the potential value of telecommuting to work or "telework." There is no commonly accepted definition of *telecommuting* or *telework* within the scholarly literature or within government agencies or private firms. The popular media typically use *telecommuting* and *telework* interchangeably to describe any non-traditional work arrangement. Academics and other experts apply narrower definitions for the purpose of measurement.

In this essay, the term *telework* is defined as working at home, away from an employer's place of business, using information technology appliances, such as the Internet, computers, or telephones. Teleworkers include people who work at home full time or part time and those who work at a remote location other than

From *Telework: The New Workplace of the Twenty-first Century* (Washington, D.C.: U.S. Department of Labor, 2000). Carl E. Van Horn is a professor and director of the John J. Heldrich Center for Workforce Development. Duke Storen was a senior project director at the Heldrich Center, and now is director of public benefits for the Commonwealth of Virginia.

their employer's central office full time or part time. Excluded from our definition are people who own home-based businesses and conduct much of their work from their private residences and the purely mobile workforce, the traveling sales force and consultants of the twenty-first century.

Teleworkers have been part of the workforce for a long time, albeit using low-tech information technology. Ever since there was paperwork to be brought home and a telephone to call colleagues and clients, telework has been conducted in the United States. What is new, of course, is that the widespread availability of contemporary information technology devices. Millions of people are now able to accomplish, from their residences, a wide range of complex tasks in collaboration with colleagues and others around the world. Equipped with laptop computers, handheld Internet appliances, fax machines, voicemail, e-mail, and other technologies, a new "anytime, anywhere" work culture is emerging.

Although estimates vary, the consensus view is that approximately 10 percent of the workforce in 2000 are teleworkers (using the above-stated definition). The ranks of teleworkers could increase dramatically in the coming years if technology continues to improve and if workers and their managers fully embrace new models of work.

Gaining a better understanding of telework is important for several reasons. First, increases in teleworkers could have profound impacts on worker behavior and satisfaction, employer profitability, and preferred management practices. To remain competitive in the global market, American workers and employers must continue productivity gains. Telework arrangements may represent an opportunity to increase productivity and worker satisfaction. If further research establishes the positive benefits of telework, traditional management models will have to change. The question then becomes, what management practices will be most effective in the new digital culture?

Second, the digital economy generates millions of jobs that could be conducted in workers' homes either all or part of the workweek. More than two-thirds of all workers use a computer in the workplace every day, according to research conducted by the John J. Heldrich Center for Workforce Development.[1] The explosive growth of e-commerce and the Internet have created strong demands for workers with information technology skills. These high-end information sector jobs, and their retail counterparts, such as customer service support and data processing, represent major growth sectors in the economy with "teleworkable" jobs. One important question for future research should be How will we prepare the workforce and businesses to take advantage of these new opportunities and develop career paths for the teleworker?

Third, aggressive marketing of inexpensive, high-bandwidth, secure Internet connections (DSL, cable, satellite) means that telework is much more affordable than it was just two or three years ago. Millions more workers are able to access high-bandwidth, secure Internet sites because their corporate LANs and phone systems can be accessed remotely at affordable prices. The percentage of Internet users with broadband access is expected to triple from

Table 1. Projected Percentage of Internet Users with Broadband Access, 1999–2003

Year	*Millions of Broadband Users*	*Millions of Internet Users*	*% Internet Users with Broadband*
1999	2.5	58	4
2000	5.51	75.75	7
2001	10.98	90	12
2002	17.77	103.88	17
2003	25.09	118.25	21

Note: These projections could increase substantially if American businesses decide to promote telework options for large numbers of their employees.

7 percent to 21 percent from 2000 to 2003, according to an analysis reported in *Business 2.0* (table 1).[2]

Fourth, telework can have important implications for helping low and moderate-income workers and potentially bridging the digital divide. Despite the strong economy and overall low unemployment rate, millions of residents in urban and isolated rural and Native American communities remain unemployed and three out of every four severely disabled Americans are unemployed. Telework could provide promising opportunities to these and other groups on the wrong side of the digital divide by helping them overcome traditional transportation barriers and bringing access to technology into their communities. These workers would be able to work from home or from neighborhood telework centers that would link them with valuable job opportunities as well as bring technology infrastructure into low-income communities. Telework may also provide a viable solution for working parents who cannot afford to pay childcare expenses. Given its potential benefits, there is a strong public interest in learning more about how telework can be effectively applied to ameliorate important social problems.

Finally, increasing telework may be a valuable component in reducing traffic congestion and air pollution, especially in urban communities. Telework has been shown to have positive impacts by reducing work trips and overall travel, but little is known about the long-term effects of these changes in travel behavior and residential choice decisions. It is possible that telework may promote further deconcentration of housing in the long run and thus increase vehicle miles traveled for nonwork trips while reducing congestion in peak hours during the work commute.

The Triple Bottom Line

Telework holds the potential to affect the "triple bottom line" of financial, environmental, and social goals.[3]

The Human Resource and Financial Bottom Line. Increasing telework opportunities may positively affect employee recruitment, retention, absenteeism, and productivity and thus improve the financial bottom line. Recent studies also claim that telework programs reduce building and parking costs. The flexibility afforded by teleworking enables employees to attend to emergent problems, such as a sick child, and to continue working during inclement weather.

The research is far from definitive, but several studies evaluating the impact of teleworking are promising. One study concluded that employees who telework save their employers up to $10,000 per year in reduced absenteeism and retention costs.[4] Another found that telework reduces absenteeism costs by 63 percent, or an average savings of more than $2,000 per employee.[5]

Evidence about the impact of telework on productivity is also encouraging. Workers and employers tell survey researchers that they are more productive when permitted to telework for at least part of the workweek. In a series of national *Work Trends* surveys conducted by the John J. Heldrich Center for Workforce Development at Rutgers University and the Center for Survey Research and Analysis at the University of Connecticut (hereafter referred to as Work Trends), 40 percent of American workers say that their productivity increased when working outside the office, and another 30 percent said they were at least as productive at home as they were in the office.[6] Similarly, in surveys conducted by the America National Telework Study, close to half (47 percent) of teleworkers claimed they are more productive working at home than at their conventional work locations; 42 percent said their productivity remains the same.[7]

Employers also report productivity gains from teleworkers. An evaluation of the state of Arizona's telecommuting program found that senior managers cited increased efficiency, greater productivity, and enhanced employee morale as the greatest benefits of the program.[8] In addition, an assessment of twelve pilot telework programs operated in the private and public sectors (including Apple Computer, AT&T, and the state of California) found that, "by all measures, productivity changes were positive" and that most supervisors reported increased or the same productivity among their teleworking employees.[9]

Telework may also be a valuable tool in attracting and retaining employees. The Work Trends national survey found that 59 percent of employees would telework for all or part of the week if offered the option by their employer.[10] In another national study by Telework America, more than half (53 percent) of teleworkers surveyed said it is "important" or "extremely important" to have the ability to work at home at least some of the time when considering a new employer.[11] In addition to attracting new talent, existing employees may be more likely to remain at their current job if given the opportunity to telework all or part of the week.

Telework programs can also lower overhead expenses for companies, according to telework consultant Gil Gordon.[12] For some firms, telework programs have reduced office space needs. AT&T, for example, estimates that its telework program saved them $500 million since 1991.[13] IBM reported savings of $1 billion on real estate costs from 1992 to 1997.[14] While some companies can realize immediate overhead savings, most companies will use telework to save on future real estate costs. For example, American Express Travel reports significant reductions in space needs due to increases in teleworking by their workforce.

Research Issues. The limited collection of available research suggests that telework effectively addresses many important human resource challenges faced by employers in the new economy. However, more research must be conducted to assess telework's impact on productivity, recruitment, retention, and absenteeism, especially in the long term. Also needed are more careful evaluations of the management practices that measure and bolster the productivity of teleworkers.

Social Bottom Line. Telework strategies can also be used to address workforce equity issues facing the country, such as high unemployment in low-income urban and rural communities, high unemployment among individuals with disabilities, bridging the digital divide, and the child care challenge of working parents.

Individuals with disabilities and low-income individuals in many urban and rural communities share a common barrier to success in the labor market—transportation. With the dispersion of jobs to the suburbs, many working poor and unemployed individuals from low-income urban communities cannot afford to own and operate the automobile necessary for an urban to suburban commute. Few transportation networks available to individuals with disabilities provide adequate service to suburban employment locations.

In a *Work Trends* study of the working poor (defined as those earning at or below 200 percent of the poverty level), respondents said that that their location presented a significant barrier to their success in the labor market. Nearly nine in ten (88 percent) of the working poor expressed the need for better jobs in their community. In looking to solutions, working-poor Americans look favorably on policies designed to address the mismatch between where they live and where desirable jobs are located. Nearly two-thirds said they would telework if given the option, and three-fourths said they would use on-site childcare if it were available. Forty-one percent stated they would take public transit if it met their work commute needs.[15]

The U.S. Department of Commerce study, *Falling Through the Net II,* reports on the computer "haves" and "have-nots." Households earning more than $75,000 annually are nine times as likely to have home computer access compared to households earning less than $15,000.[16] College educated individuals are sixteen times more likely to have Internet access than are individuals lacking a high school education. Whites are twice as likely as blacks and Hispanics to have home computer access. Accordingly, lower income, less educated, and racial minorities are the least likely groups to have access to technology and the Internet. The technology gap further isolates already racially and economically segregated communities, thus exacerbating an already distressed situation. The Office of Technology Assessment (OTA) described this effect as "the concentration of poverty and the de-concentration of opportunity."[17]

The advent of new technologies enables companies to decentralize their operations to suburban locations close to skilled labor forces. This "spatial mismatch" leaves individuals who might otherwise use technology on the job and develop technical skills without the opportunity to do so. Without access to information technology tools, residents are unable to acquire the necessary skills for the new economy, which subsequently impedes future economic development for the entire community.

Furthermore, telecommunications tools can be used to encourage civic engagement. As suggested by the Benton Foundation,

> any of the associations people form to address specific issues can facilitate coordination and communication, foster the emergence of leaders who can help generate collective action . . . the resulting "social capital" can enable communities to deal more successfully with social problems. Communities without access to communications networks may find it more difficult to sustain the civic engagement that can lead to these improved outcomes.[18]

If already isolated communities are expected to sustain and grow, they need access to the benefits of information technology.

Telework may have the capacity to overcome geographic isolation from desired labor markets and help bridge the digital divide. Such strategies could not only consist of working from residences but also include establishing neighborhood telework. The creation of urban telework centers can counteract the dispersal of jobs from urban areas by creating opportunities for employers to relocate their customer service and back office functions to central cities or rural communities. Some of the advantages telework centers offer to this particular workforce include close proximity to workers' homes, flexible work hours, comparatively low entry-level skill requirements in typing and computer competence, a professional environment for skill development and increased marketability, and potential job-laddering opportunities within the call center industry. "High end" customer services call center workers can earn thirteen to twenty dollars per hour. In addition, telework centers can bring much-needed technology infrastructure into "digitally divided" communities. This fixed capital investment can be used in nonwork hours to provide computer skills training, access to distance education, and access to the Internet.

Research on the impact of telework for individuals with disabilities is also promising. For example, Doug Kruse and Mary Anne Hyland's analysis of 1991 and 1997 Current Population Survey (CPS) data found that the "growth of paid home-based work has been greater among workers with disabilities, resulting in 15% doing such work in 1997 compared to 10% of workers without disabilities."

They suggest that "there remains large potential to expand employment opportunities for people with disabilities through home-based work," and that the use of computers in home-based work can offer special advantages to people with disabilities such as ameliorating or making irrelevant some of the limitations created by disability. However, the low level of computer use among home-based employees with disabilities suggests that employers and employees are not taking full advantage of these opportunities.[19]

Research Issues. The idea of increasing employment rates in urban and rural communities by encouraging telework is a promising, if untested, strategy. The proliferation of customer service, e-commerce call centers provides an opportunity to study their impact on low-income job seekers when such centers locate in urban communities or in isolated rural communities. Federal and state governments may wish to encourage and then evaluate this economic development strategy by partially funding public-private partnerships to conduct feasibility studies and capitalize telework centers that employ low-income individuals.

In addition, more research about the potential for telework to employ individuals with disabilities needs to be conducted. A more detailed understanding of the specific occupations and associated skills/proficiencies that would be appropriate for individuals with different types of disabilities is necessary to move from theory to practice.

Environmental Bottom Line. Reducing congestion and the associated environmental benefits are often cited as the principal reasons for initiating telework programs. While there is some evidence about short-term environmental benefits, long-term benefits are less clear. Several telework pilot programs have achieved significant reductions in work trip vehicle miles, which reduce the amount of carbon dioxide (CO_2) released into the environment.[20] For example, the Puget Sound Telecommuting Demonstration travel log data show reductions of thirty-six miles per telecommuting occasion (each day a person teleworks), a 61 percent reduction in daily travel. Using various models for measuring the reduction in pollutant emissions, daily reductions of 50–70 percent occur on teleworking days. A pilot conducted by the Southern California Association of Governments (SCAG) found that teleworking reduced travel by an average of forty-six miles per trip; in Hawaii, almost all (93 percent) of employees reported a reduced number of work trips and an average drop of fuel consumption by 29 percent over the course of a year.[21]

Research Issues. While short-term studies of the environmental impacts of teleworking are encouraging, they cannot predict the long-term effects of these programs on residential and employment location decisions or travel behavior. Telework enhances flexibility, dispersion, and mobility and cannot be viewed solely as a substitution for travel to the office. For example, teleworkers may choose to live farther away from employers because they commute only a couple of days or no days at all. A more dispersed population increases vehicle miles traveled and could actually increase congestion. Telework, therefore, actually acts more as a demand management strategy than a travel reduction strategy. Future research must carefully assess the long-term impacts of telework.

Notes

1. John J. Heldrich Center for Workforce Development at Rutgers University, Center for Survey Research and Analysis at the University of Connecticut, *Work Trends V—Nothing but Net: American Workers and the Information Economy* (New Brunswick, N.J., 2000), 4.
2. Gil Gordon, "Gil's News and Views: Interesting Statistics from the Broadband Battleground," *Telecommuting Review,* September 26, 2000. Reference at http://www.gilgordon.com/review/index.htm.
3. Brad Allenby and Deanna J. Richards, "Applying the Triple Bottom Line: Telework and the Environment," *Environmental Quality Management* (summer 1999): 3.
4. Telework America, Telework America On-line Curriculum; employers save $10,000 per teleworker in reduced absenteeism and retention costs. Teleworkers increase to 10 percent of U.S. adults. September 19, 2000.
5. American Management Association, "The Latest Cost Savings Stats on Telework," *HR Focus,* January 2000, http://proquest.umi.com.
6. John J. Heldrich Center, *Nothing But Net*, 10.
7. Joanne Pratt, *1999 Telework America National Telework Survey: Cost Benefits of Teleworking to Manage Work/Life Responsibilities* (International Telework Association and Council, 1999).
8. State of Arizona, "ADOA Travel Reduction Programs," *State of Arizona Telecommuting Evaluation* (State of Arizona, 1996).
9. Joanne Pratt, "Telecommuting: Productivity Issues and Results of Pilot Programs," *ITCA Yearbook 1994,* found at http://www.joannepratt.com/bibliography.htm#TCgProduc.
10. John J. Heldrich Center, *Nothing But Net,* 1. Pratt, *1999 Telework.*
11. Interview with Gil Gordon of Gil Gordon and Associates, March 2000. Gordon is a telework consultant and creator of www.gilgordon.com, which is a resource for managers and teleworkers that offer up-to-date news, resources, FAQ's, tips on how to implement advice, and updates on the state of the current market.
12. Allanby and Richards, "Applying the Triple Bottom Line," 5.
13. U.S. Department of Transportation, Federal Transit Administration, Office of Technical Assistance and Safety, Office of Mobility Enhancement, Service Assistance Division, Telecommuting: Description.
14. John J. Heldrich Center for Workforce Development at Rutgers University, Center for Survey Research and Analysis at the University of Connecticut, *Work Trends II—Working Hard but Staying Poor: A National Survey of the Working Poor and Unemployed* (New Brunswick, N.J., 1999).
15. National Telecommunications and Information Administration, *Falling Through the Net II: New Data on the Digital Divide* (Washington, D.C.: U.S. Department of Commerce, 1998).
16. Benton Foundation, *Losing Ground Bit by Bit* (Washington, D.C., 1998).
17. Ibid.
18. Douglas Kruse and MaryAnne Hyland, *Telecommuting and Other Home-Based Work: Differences by Disability Status* (New Brunswick, N.J., 1998).

19. Cooperative Extension, Washington State University Energy Program, "Travel Characteristics and Impacts,"http://www.energy.wsu.edu/telework/travel.htm.

20. U.S. Department of Transportation, Federal Transit Administration, Office of Technical Assistance and Safety, Office of Mobility Enhancement, Service Assistance Division, Telecommuting: Description.

21. U.S. Census Bureau, "Working At Home: 1990," table 1, "All Workers and Workers Who Worked at Home: 1960–1990," http://.census.gov/population/www/socdemo/workathome/wkhtab1.html.

Work at Home?

First, Get Real

SUSAN B. GARLAND

Every day, moms and dads quit their jobs in the hope of becoming part of that popular image of the work-at-home parent, the one where they are smiling at the computer while their adorable little baby crawls underfoot. I wish I could tell you that this picture squares with reality. But it doesn't. In fact, it's pure fantasy. Last November, after twelve years as a full-time Washington correspondent for *Business Week,* I resigned to become a freelance writer, setting up shop in my basement. I wanted to spend more time with my daughter, Kristina, who was then five. But like many who had made this move before me, I had unrealistic expectations about how much I could accomplish with only a carpet commute.

Of the 37.8 million households with dependent children, there are 11.6 million that have at least one parent who works from home, says International Data Corporation, based in Framingham, Massachusetts, which provides market data on information technology. For parents out there who are thinking of trading in their power suits for sweat suits, managing expectations is critical. Figure out at the start how you can spend more time with your child. Will you need a reduced workload? Are you also looking for a better quality of life, with a spectrum of other activities, such as more time at the gym? Or do you simply plan to transfer a full-time workload to a home office? To help you plan, here are ten tips for the prospective at-home working parent: NO WORK, NO PAY. If you telecommute with a regular salary, you may have time to play with your child, get a haircut, and putter in your garden. But if you plan to be a free agent, remember: Money coming in depends directly on doing the work. Yes, you can put in a load of wash while your PC is booting up. But every hour you spend running errands means lost income.

Beware the 24/7 Week

The great advantage of working at home is that you can work at 3 A.M. if necessary. That's the disadvantage, too—work is always there. It's hard to turn down jobs that will bring in money, and it's hard to pit your child's needs against those of your clients. But if you don't set limits, there's no point being home. "When

BusinessWeek, September 18, 2000. Reprinted with the permission of *BusinessWeek*. Susan B. Garland is a freelance journalist and former correspondent for *BusinessWeek*.

my daughter was twelve, she wrote a message on my [computer] screen because she knew that's where I looked: 'Can you please pick me up?' That's when I knew it was bad," recalls Lisa Roberts, who runs www.en-parent.com.

Establish a Routine

Thought you were leaving behind scheduled meetings and set hours? The choices that come with being home can be overwhelming, so set regular hours. That could mean working from 9 A.M. to noon, taking the rest of the day off to go to the gym and care for kids, then working again from 9 P.M. to midnight. Or work from 9 A.M. to 3 P.M. and take Fridays off for chores and downtime. Your life can turn chaotic unless you stick to a schedule that's as predictable as the office was.

Allow for Emergencies

Routines are great, but they can easily fall apart. Plan for the unplanned—such as a child's illness. I had daydreamed that if my child fell ill, I would read aloud by her bedside and feed her chicken soup. But when Kristina was sick on the same day a work assignment was due, she had to spend several hours upstairs by herself, miserable. If you pace your work, you can keep minidisasters to a minimum.

Be Realistic About Money

Whatever your lowball earnings projections are, deduct 20 percent just to be safe. Unless you're telecommuting for an employer, you're probably forgoing health insurance, retirement-plan contributions, paid vacations, and expense accounts. Calculate conservatively the time you can put in. I thought I could easily work twenty-five hours a week—9 A.M. to 3 P.M., with an hour off a day for errands. I underestimated the time it took for chores, doctors' visits, and other responsibilities.

Just Say No

So you want to be president of the PTA? Becoming an integral part of your child's school may seem alluring from the distance of your downtown office. But volunteering can eat into your paid hours. Valerie Finberg, a Boulder, Colorado, mother of two—who, until recently, worked at home full time as a management consultant—ran a book program for her child's class. "I was a miserable failure at it," she says. "It required constant attention." So volunteer for an occasional field trip, but be careful not to overcommit.

Don't Fire the Nanny

If you have a baby or toddler, you may be able to get some work done during nap time, but not much. The best bet is to hire a part-time sitter if you have young children and want to get in extra hours without working at 3 A.M. I set my office hours while my daughter is in school, giving her my full attention at other times. But that doesn't always work. I recently had to schedule a phone interview while my daughter was home with a play date. The six-year-olds promised not to interrupt unless there was an emergency. The emergency? They wanted candy NOW.

Get Even More Reinforcements

When I left my full-time job, I let the nanny go without realizing how much housework I would have to take on. Besides caring for Kristina, she had folded my daughter's laundry, cleaned her room, and straightened the family room. I spent the first hour of every workday on those chores. But I could earn more—and reduce my stress—by adding a second day for a cleaning person. As Roberts writes in *How to Raise a Family and a Career Under One Roof*: "Take the time you would have spent, say, cleaning the house or mowing the lawn, and earn money at something you are really good at."

Give Yourself a Break

You would think that Jeralynn Burke, forty-two, would know something about stress reduction. Burke, of Des Plaines, Illinois, runs E-scent-ials, a Web site that sells aromatherapy products. A year ago, she suffered from palpitations, shortness of breath, and chest pains. Between caring for two preschoolers, running her house, and setting up her home business, she hadn't taken a day off from work for eight months. "Now, I'm taking some time off each day," she says, "even if it's fifteen minutes sitting on the porch with a cup of tea."

Get Out and About

For me, the first few weeks of working at home were euphoric. Without the distractions of the office, my productivity soared. But then I started talking to myself for prolonged periods. I was suffering from isolation—a common affliction of the at-home worker. So, despite the pressures, see a friend for lunch. Meet a client face to face even if it would be quicker to do business by phone.

Most important, don't forget why you wanted to become a work-at-home parent. The chance to test new skills, build a business, and assert more control over your life are all important goals. But strengthening bonds with your children tops the list. As long as you're prepared, you can find that right balance.

Advice from the Front

Online

Web sites that offer guidance to work-at-home parents, plus links to other sites:
www.en-parent.com for "the entrepreneurial parent"
www.wahm.com for "work-at-home moms"
www.ivillage.com/work for "stay-at-home parents"
www.slowlane.com for "stay-at-home dads"

Books

How to Raise a Family and a Career Under One Roof by Lisa Roberts
The Work at Home Balancing Act: The Professional Resource Guide for Managing Yourself, Your Work, and Your Family at Home by Sandy Anderson
Working at Home while the Kids Are There, Too by Loriann Hoff Oberlin
Mompreneurs: A Mother's Practical Step-by-Step Guide to Work-at-Home Success by Ellen Parlapiano and Patricia Cobe

Child Care, the Perk of Tomorrow?

STEVEN GREENHOUSE

During the flush times of the 1990s, many blue-chip and high-tech companies began giving elite employees perks like stock options and country club memberships.

But a new program developed by the Ford Motor Company may create a whole new kind of perk, dedicated to nonelite, often blue-collar, workers. And it has everything to do with family. Ford has broken ground in several cities as part of an ambitious plan to create dozens of centers to provide child care, summer camps, and tutoring, as well as activities for teenagers and retirees. With American workers complaining increasingly about the difficulties of balancing job and family, Ford's plan is widely viewed as the most comprehensive effort by an American corporation to help rank-and-file workers handle the balancing act.

The United Auto Workers pressed Ford to establish the centers partly because the United States, given its long tradition of privileging private responsibility, furnishes far fewer public child care programs than Western European governments.

"Ford is filling a gap because we as a country haven't responded to the social revolution in which working mothers moved massively into the workplace," said Faith Wohl, president of the Child Care Action Campaign, a New York–based advocacy group. "We're the only country to address a major social problem—child care—through the private sector rather than through some public solution."

In its thirty Family Service and Learning Centers, Ford, working closely with the UAW, will provide after-school care for preteens and recreation programs for teenagers. If a child is mildly sick, a worker can drop that child off at the center and not have to miss work. Some centers will offer round-the-clock child care, with emergency help available to a midnight-shift employee whose spouse has to rush off to Florida to care for an ailing parent. There will be tutoring for teenagers who have fallen behind in school, and for retirees there will be reading groups and museum trips. The centers' services will be available to more than 300,000 people, not just union members but also salaried employees and retirees.

Other companies have done part of what Ford plans. IBM is spending $50 million to help develop child-care programs, while J.C. Penney has budgeted

New York Times, May 13, 2001. Reprinted with permission of the *New York Times*. Steven Greenhouse reports on labor and workforce issues for the *New York Times*.

$12 million to help communities set up after-school programs, like homework help and recreational basketball.

But Ford's program is by far the broadest. "It's leading the way," said Ellen Galinsky, president of the Families and Work Institute. "It pulls a lot of things together in a more comprehensive way than a lot of companies are doing."

Carl Van Horn, director of the Heldrich Center for Workforce Development at Rutgers University, predicted that more companies would adopt such programs because they recognize that employees focus better on their work and are less likely to leave when companies address family needs, like after-school care.

"Companies realize more than they did ten or fifteen years ago that it is important to help their workers balance work and family," he said.

Since the early 1900s, Ford, indeed all of Detroit's automakers, have set the trend for the nation's companies—and workers—on pay and benefits. Henry Ford played a pivotal role in creating America's middle class by making sure that his assembly-line workers earned enough to purchase the cars that his factories churned out.

The Big Three, pushed by the United Auto Workers, later led the way in providing health coverage and pensions to rank-and-file workers. More recently, Ford was the first major nonelectronics company to provide its rank-and-file workers with another essential part of middle-class life: home computers.

All these measures were designed not merely to enrich Ford's workers but also to create a stable, satisfied workforce dedicated to Ford and reluctant to jump to the employer across the street. In the same vein, Ford executives say they are establishing the new centers for hard-nosed business reasons. The company is within spitting distance of surpassing GM to become the world's biggest automaker, a position it lost back in 1930, when Henry Ford was still in charge.

"Clearly we see it as a competitive advantage," said Dennis Cirbes, Ford's executive director of corporate labor affairs and co-chairman of the family centers' board of directors. "We see these centers now and in the future as helping us be an employer of choice."

Of course, no development is without its downside. Some people think a better solution would be less pressure to work constantly rather than more child care. And while many children's advocates applaud Ford, they acknowledge that the automaker's plan will further a trend that they frown upon—the widening gaps between the child-care offerings made to well-paid workers and poorly paid workers and between workers at large, profitable companies and those at companies that are smaller or have thin profit margins.

"There's always been a gap between large firms and small enterprises with regard to health insurance coverage and pensions, and now we're seeing it with child care," said Sheila Kamerman, director of the Columbia University Institute on Child and Family Policy. "Ford's plan will be great for employees who have access, but it underscores the inadequacy of the provision of child care generally."

The State of the Workplace for Lesbian, Gay, Bisexual, and Transgendered Americans, 2000

HUMAN RIGHTS CAMPAIGN

Employers across the country are continuing at a rapid pace to implement policies and programs aimed at treating gay, lesbian, bisexual, and transgender workers more equally. Two important bellwethers tracked closely by the Human Rights Campaign Foundation's WorkNet project—nondiscrimination policies and domestic partner benefits—increased markedly during the period covered in this report (August 2000–August 2001).

Employers and Sexual Orientation Nondiscrimination Policies

As of August 15, 2001, HRC WorkNet had identified 2,001 companies, colleges and universities, state and local governments, and federal agencies that had written nondiscrimination policies covering sexual orientation. This represents an increase of 293 employers, or 17 percent, in one year.

At this writing, 294, or 59 percent, of Fortune 500 companies include sexual orientation in their nondiscrimination policies. This represents an increase of 39 companies, or 15 percent, over the prior year.

The closer a company is to the top of the Fortune 500 list, the more likely it is to have such a policy. A total of 79 percent of the Fortune 100 and 88 percent of the Fortune 50 prohibit sexual orientation discrimination.

Employers and Domestic Partner Benefits. The number of employers that provide domestic partner health insurance benefits has increased by a full 50 percent from 2,856 employers in August 1999—the first year in this series of reports—to 4,285 in August 2001. These employers include private companies, colleges and universities, and state and local governments.

That number is up from 3,572 employers in August 2000. This was an increase of 713 employers, or 20 percent, in the twelve months covered by this report.

It appears that the economic slowdown resulting from the bursting of the high-tech bubble has not had an impact on the rate of domestic partner benefits implementation—but it may be too early to tell. Even in the absence of local

Executive Summary, Human Rights Campaign (HRC). Reprinted with permission of HRC, a national lesbian and gay political organization that promotes equal rights and protection under the law. It lobbies, provides campaign support to candidates for federal office, and works to educate the public.

contracting laws requiring companies to provide benefits, the pace of employers adding the benefits has accelerated. The Human Rights Campaign Foundation has identified more employers that have added the benefits so far in 2001—independent of city contracting laws requiring them to do so—than in any year since the HRC Foundation has tracked the trend.

The trend toward offering domestic partner benefits is clearest in the Fortune 500 companies, where America's largest companies are increasingly making domestic partner benefits a standard practice. The number of Fortune 500 companies offering domestic partner benefits has more than doubled in the past three years, from 61 in 1998 to 145 in 2001. In fact, more Fortune 500 companies—36—added domestic partner benefits in 2001 than in any year since the HRC Foundation has tracked the trend.

The closer a company is to the top of the Fortune 500 list, the more likely it is to provide domestic partner health benefits. While 29 percent of Fortune 500 companies provide domestic partner benefits, 54 percent of Fortune 50 companies offer them.

Sexual Orientation Nondiscrimination Laws. Because there is no federal law explicitly prohibiting discrimination based on sexual orientation or gender identity, lesbian, gay, bisexual, and transgender workers are covered by a patchwork of state and local laws—if they are covered at all.

Eleven states, the District of Columbia, and 122 cities and counties ban antigay discrimination in private workplaces, as well as in public-sector jobs. The states are California, Connecticut, Hawaii, Massachusetts, Minnesota, Nevada, New Hampshire, New Jersey, Rhode Island, Vermont, and Wisconsin. Only two—Minnesota and Rhode Island—extend protections to individuals based on gender identity. An additional ten states and 106 city and county governments and agencies—for a total of 250 state and local governments—protect their own public employees from discrimination based on sexual orientation.

In the period covered by this report, one state—Maryland—passed a law prohibiting sexual orientation discrimination in employment, housing, and public accommodations. (That law will not go into effect as slated this year because a conservative coalition has filed petitions seeking a referendum on the law in November 2002. The petition signatures are currently being challenged in court.)

The number of localities that are providing workplace protections has been steadily rising since the 1970s.

Government bodies in at least eight other jurisdictions enacted laws banning antigay discrimination in public and private employment during the period covered in this report. They are Atlanta, DeKalb County, Georgia; Des Moines, Iowa; Fort Worth, Texas; Nassau County, New York; Peekskill, New York; Rochester, New York; and Summit County, Ohio. These gains include the first municipalities in Georgia and the second city in Texas (after Austin) to enact such protections.

Three states enacted laws protecting public employees from job discrimination based on sexual orientation: Indiana, Montana, and Delaware.

At least seven municipalities enacted laws protecting their public employees from this type of discrimination: Fairfax County, Virginia; Greenburgh, New York; Houston; Lake Worth, Florida; Monroe County, Florida; Orlando, Florida; and San Luis Obispo County, California.

Domestic Partner Benefits Laws. Eight states and 105 city and county governments or quasi-government agencies provide health insurance benefits to their employees' domestic partners, for a total of 113 state and local governments.

Since August 2000, two states passed measures to provide domestic partner health insurance benefits: Maine and Rhode Island.

During the same period, at least ten local governments or quasi-governmental agencies added or announced domestic partner benefits: Concord, California; DeKalb County, Georgia; Eastchester, New York; Mansfield, Connecticut; Mission Viejo, California; Milwaukee; Scottsdale, Arizona; Summit County, Colorado; Ventura, California; and the Washington, D.C., Metropolitan Area Transit Authority.

Gender Identity Issues and Employment

In the past year, HRC WorkNet observed increased interest among employers regarding gender identity issues. Much of this appears to have been the result of individual employees raising the issue and/or seeking to transition, in varying degrees, from one sex to the other while continuing to work. In addition, several gender identity organizations have been actively working for several years to change nondiscrimination policies and health insurance benefits to protect and assist gender-variant employees. Plus, HRC WorkNet has sought to raise awareness of the issue with human resources groups and in the media, resulting in articles in the past year in both trade and mainstream publications, including the *Washington Post* and the *Wall Street Journal.*

HRC WorkNet has provided advice and assistance to numerous employers grappling with these questions. The project has created Web-based resources (see www.hrc.org/worknet) that address in detail issues related to gender transitioning on the job. A complete list of employers prohibiting gender identity discrimination is also available through the Web site.

Gender Identity and the Law. Two states—Minnesota and Rhode Island—the District of Columbia, and thirty-two local governments have enacted laws that provide protections for transgender employees in either the public or private sector.

During the twelve months covered by this report, Rhode Island and at least five municipalities enacted laws to protect gender-variant people. De Kalb,

Illinois, Madison, Wisconsin, and Portland, Oregon, enacted new laws to cover employees in public and private workplaces. Houston and Multnomah County, Oregon, banned discrimination against transgender employees in the public workforce.

Three other states have extended protections to transgender people on the job, but not through legislative action. Connecticut's Commission on Human Rights and Opportunities decided in 2000 that transsexual people may bring a claim under that state's nondiscrimination law. Also, a New Jersey appeals court ruled on July 3, 2000, that transsexuals and other gender-variant people are covered by the state law against gender and disability discrimination. In New York, a few courts have held that transsexual people are protected under the state's sex discrimination law.

Gender Identity and Workplace Policies. HRC WorkNet has identified twenty private employers that expressly prohibit discrimination based on gender identity. Among these are five Fortune 500 companies: AMR (parent company of American Airlines), Apple Computer, Lexmark International, Lucent Technologies, and Xerox Corporation. Other employers that provide such protections include Agere Systems Inc., Avaya Inc., Trillium Asset Management, and the law firm Patterson, Belknap, Webb and Tyler LLP.

GENERAL DESCRIPTION OF HEWLETT-PACKARD'S DOMESTIC PARTNER BENEFITS

Hewlett-Packard Company has offered benefits to the domestic partners of its employees since January 1997. Domestic partners of the same and opposite gender and their eligible children are covered, and benefits include health, life insurance, and relocation, among others. The company added "sexual orientation" to its equal employment opportunity and harassment policies in 1992. At twelve different locations, there are employee network groups for gay, lesbian, bisexual, transgender, and allied employees. The oldest has been in existence for more than twenty years.

"The extension of benefits to domestic partners continues HP's ongoing efforts to create an inclusive environment," said Lewis Platt, chairman and CEO. "We're also enhancing our competitiveness as a great place to work so we can attract and retain top talent."

To be eligible for most benefits, employees must submit a declaration of domestic partnership and meet the following criteria:

There must be an ongoing and committed spouselike relationship intended to exist indefinitely, which has existed for at least six months

The partners are not related by blood to a degree of closeness that would prohibit legal marriage in the state in which they reside

Both have shared the same residence for at least six months, are responsible to each other for the direction and financial management of their household, and are jointly responsible for each other's financial obligations.

The following benefits are available:

Declaration Required

- Health plans (HP Medical, HMOs, and Dental Plan)
- Retiree medical
- Group universal life
- Long-term care
- Relocation benefits
- Adoption assistance
- Unpaid leave of absence to care for partner or dependent
- Up to twelve weeks per year of unpaid, job-protected time off to care for a domestic partner with a serious health condition. HP has implemented this policy because FMLA does not provide for time off to care for a domestic partner.
- Children of domestic partners are eligible for employee scholarship program.

No Declaration Required

- Employee assistance program
- LifeWorks
- Bereavement leave
- Credit Union membership

The company's goal is "spousal equivalency," so additional benefits are being considered on an ongoing basis. Currently, they are available only to the employees in the United States, but coverage in other countries is under consideration. Because of IRS rules, the amount that HP pays toward the premium for a domestic partner and his/her children is considered taxable income to the employee. If a domestic partnership ends, the employee must notify the company within thirty days and remove the former domestic partner and his or her dependents from the benefit plans, for which they are no longer eligible. There is a six-month waiting period before a new domestic partner is eligible for benefits.

Should Washington Implement National Ergonomic Standards?

EDWARD POTTER

"We're from the government, and we're here to help," is probably the oral equivalent of nails scratching a blackboard for most citizens of the United States.

Yet, most likely with this credo in mind, federal bureaucrats from the Department of Labor's Occupational Safety and Health Administration, or OSHA, busily have been holding public hearings and sifting through thousands upon thousands of comments regarding its proposal to regulate workplaces throughout the nation in an effort to prevent "ergonomic" injuries.

Ergonomics is the study of how our bodies interact with the space that surrounds us: how far we have to reach for our car radio from the driver's seat, or at what level our keyboard sits compared to our chair.

OSHA, with the best of intentions, wants to police millions of workplaces to protect workers from ergonomic injuries, which also are known as musculoskeletal disorders, or MSDs. The concept is a good one: Attention to ergonomic design can benefit employees and employers with greater comfort, endurance, and efficiency. It is the practical implementation of ergonomic ideas that is more problematic—even the experts disagree about what works. Comfort is highly subjective and often reflects psychological factors as much as physical ones.

The uncertainty surrounding ergonomic design is not a problem as long as application of the concept is a free choice: People can try different approaches and adopt what seems to work for them. Ergonomic uncertainty is a big problem when government regulators give ergonomic notions the force of law.

OSHA claims its ergonomics protections will affect more than twenty-seven million jobs—but that number is just a very conservative estimate of the people whose jobs will be regulated. Potentially ninety-three million workers could have their jobs regulated by OSHA's ergonomic inspectors. How will the regulation work? For example, in a typical office, all workers involved in manufacturing or manual handling—which could be mailroom workers involved in document production and delivery—will be subject to the regulation, as well as anyone else in any job where someone develops an MSD that is caused or aggravated by work. The employer must put in ergonomic fixes immediately or risk a citation or a fine from OSHA. If a worker who uses a keyboard reports an injury, all employees

Insight, August 7, 2000. Copyright © 2000 News World Communications, Inc., in association with the Gale Group and LookSmart. Reprinted with permission of *Insight on the News* and News World Communications, Inc. Edward Potter is president of the Employment Policy Foundation.

using the same motion must be ergonomically refitted. The OSHA police also can inspect you at any time.

OSHA, like, all federal regulatory agencies, was required to publish for public comment a cost-benefit analysis for its ergonomics program. Unfortunately, OSHA did not check its math before publishing its ergonomics treatise. We found it contained innumerable errors, omissions, and unsupported assumptions. Correcting for just seven of those mistakes, this regulation will cost more than it benefits anyone—to the tune of as much as $100 billion per year (or up to twenty-five times more than OSHA estimated). OSHA also made mistakes in the calculation of benefits to workers and employers. It calculated $10 billion, but the correct figure is less than $5 billion.

What kind of mistakes are we talking about? One miscalculation that stands out in particular is the amount of time it would take managers to familiarize themselves with the regulation (in other words, those in charge of implementing it). OSHA estimated it would take one hour to understand its prescription—but the regulatory text and explanation that OSHA published is 100,000 words—about the length of Tolstoy's *War and Peace,* but not nearly as interesting. Even assuming a rapid reading rate of 110 words per minute (which would be a fast rate of comprehension for regulatory material), it would take fifteen hours to read the material. Thus, familiarization costs could be as high as $3.3 billion alone—not the $200 million OSHA estimated in its line-item tally of costs. Time does, in fact, equal money—something lifelong bureaucrats may not realize.

OSHA also mistakenly assumes that laypersons charged with implementing the new rules will perform as efficiently as ergonomic experts. It claims that its regulation will reduce ergonomic-injury cases by half, but its data are derived from studies of programs supervised by professional "ergonomists." No trials have been done on shop managers—again, those who will have direct responsibility for identifying and fixing ergonomic hazards in the workplace (the same people OSHA thinks can read regulatory text at the pace of Superman).

The regulation also is problematic because it assumes that businesses—large and small—simply will implement the changes and suck up the increased costs themselves. What is most likely to happen is that businesses will be forced to pass on their costs somewhere, either by lowering future wage increases, reducing benefits, forcing layoffs, passing the costs on to their customers, or slowing growth of new jobs. At a time when American business needs to maintain its competitive edge, OSHA's regulation sets medical benefits for ergonomic injuries (workers' compensation) at the 90 percent level of pay for up to six months—hardly an inducement to get back to work in a reasonable amount of time. Because of the nature of MSDs, which are hard to diagnose and confirm as to when they have healed, hypochondriacs could have a picnic with OSHA's regulation, with their employers picking up the tab. Ironically, OSHA seems to be promoting automation to eliminate ergonomically challenged jobs. At a recent hearing on Capitol Hill, OSHA's administrator responded to a question about solving the ergonomic problems of people who wash dishes in restaurants by suggesting that the owner buy an automatic dishwashing machine. With the North American Free Trade Agreement and other free-trade imperatives, it entirely is plausible that OSHA will create an additional incentive for certain jobs to be outsourced overseas. So, OSHA may end up protecting workers to the point of protecting them out of jobs.

Despite what you might think, the workers most lacking in ergonomic protections are in the very government agencies responsible for writing these regulations, such as OSHA itself. Anyone taking a ten-minute stroll inside OSHA offices will discover numerous ergonomic injuries waiting to happen—computer monitors placed precipitously on phone books, keyboards on desks, chairs adjusted to the wrong level, etc. Perhaps before OSHA tries to regulate the rest of us, it should turn itself into an MSD-free zone—a shining example for the rest of us to follow—and a test of the real costs and ease of implementation.

There also is the question of whether this regulation is needed in the first place. Interestingly, the rate of MSDs has declined 22 percent during the past five years, according to OSHA's own analysis. This trend should continue, eliminating the ergonomic problem during the next decade without any government regulation. In other words, the private sector doesn't always need federal bureaucrats to intervene and solve its problems. Of course businesses have a strong interest in making sure their workers are healthy—which is why employers and employees have been working together quietly, privately, and successfully for twenty years to solve ergonomic problems—long before the government thought about ergonomic regulations.

Every boss in America has a stake in making sure his or her employees are healthy, particularly in today's tight labor market. Gone are the days of the Dickensian factory where workers stood powerless against abuses by the boss: Today, workers and their employers have a strong mutual interest in making sure the other is on firm ground.

OSHA's proposal will force companies to abandon their effective, individually tailored, and need-focused ergonomics efforts to follow a prescription that requires the same response to every complaint no matter how big or small. The OSHA plan will cause protection resources to be spread thinly across the workplace instead of being focused on the most important problem areas. The result will be less protection at a higher cost.

But like a dog on a bone, the staff at OSHA is doing nothing but ergonomics—even though there are much more serious workplace hazards to remedy. For perspective, there are 17,000 non-MSD injuries every day compared to 1,600 ergonomic-related problems—more than ten times as many. And, while OSHA concentrates its resources mandating footrests and wrist supports for aches and pains, there are sixteen deaths per day from occupational injury.

But unions have made ergonomics one of their top legislative priorities, and the political calculus is such that the Clinton administration—in its drive to lock up the union vote for Vice President Al Gore—is putting all its OSHA weight behind this regulation, no matter what the economic reality is.

Unions will be one of the biggest winners in the ergonomic battle (aside from professional ergonomists whose business will boom from the regulation). With an ergonomics standard in hand, union leaders virtually can file ergonomic complaints with OSHA all day long and use threats to pressure companies to unionize.

For all these reasons, Congress, in its proper role of creating checks and balances, repeatedly has expressed skepticism about OSHA and its ergonomics regulations for several years. Last month, both the House and Senate voted to strip OSHA's funding for implementation of its ergonomics program—but Labor Secretary Alexis Herman blasted the move, and Clinton has vowed a veto unless the funding is restored.

The bond of trust between government and the people dissipates when government regulators do not present intellectually honest explanations and accurate assessments of the consequences of their proposals. By ignoring abundant, credible, objective, empirical data from firms that already have implemented ergonomic programs, OSHA has unleashed on the public capricious, arbitrary regulations. OSHA, quite simply, has not done its homework on the issue. The regulations, while well intended, could become the most expensive government employment mandate since the founding of the United States, all for a problem that seems to be improving dramatically without government intervention.

Home-Office Debate Isn't New

EILEEN BORIS AND NELSON LICHTENSTEIN

"A Big Brother-like overreach," fumed the American Electronics Association. "An outrageous extension of the Washington bureaucracy into the lives of working men and women across America," charged House Majority Leader Dick Armey (R-Texas). "Simply foolish," agreed Rep. Pete Hoekstra (R-Mich.).

Thus did a firestorm of criticism envelop a recent ruling by the Occupational Safety and Health Administration that placed the home office under the same health and safety standards as any other workplace. The OSHA advisory letter made employers liable for the working conditions of telecommuters, much to the chagrin of those, like a Fairfax, Virginia, proprietor of a small marketing firm, who asserted, "My workplace is no one's business but my own." Faced with such outrage, Labor Secretary Alexis M. Herman quickly caved. By Thursday, she was merely calling for a "national dialogue on the subject." But we've had that dialogue: It has been going on for more than a hundred years. At the turn of the last century, America was the world leader in an industry, not unlike that of the Internet, that valued salesmanship, product innovation, and long hours of dedicated work. In an ever-changing market, hard-driving entrepreneurs found it easy to set up shop and tap into a huge pool of consumers, many of whom shopped at new, fixed-price department stores. Naturally, many start-up businesses relied on home production because of its flexibility, low overhead, and willing supply of workers, largely women with young children.

These were the garment trades, out of whose thousands of shops and factories came a stream of colorful, fashionable, and inexpensive dresses, hats, gloves, pants, and shirtwaists, enough to make turn-of-the-century U.S. residents the best clothed in the world. But this cornucopia came with a high price: low wages, long hours, and unsanitary working conditions. Pressured by ferocious competition, entrepreneurs moved the most time-consuming manufacturing tasks—hemming seams, sewing buttons, and making lace—into crowded tenements, unsafe lofts, and isolated farmhouses.

Reformers called this kind of "industrial homework" sweatshop labor, because it was inherently unhealthy and poorly paid. It bred child labor, self-exploitation, and filthy living conditions. Florence Kelley, Frances Perkins, and

Los Angeles Times, January 9, 2000. Reprinted with permission of the authors. Eileen Boris is Hull Professor of women's studies at the University of California at Santa Barbara and author of *Home to Work: Motherhood and the Politics of Industrial Homework in the United States.* Nelson Lichtenstein is a professor of history at the University of Virginia and author of *The Most Dangerous Man in Detroit: Walter Reuther and the Fate of American Labor.*

Eleanor Roosevelt all campaigned for the regulation, or, when possible, for the abolition of such home production. "We not only want a fair wage for the workman," declared the National Consumers' League, "but sanitary quarters for them also." As one reformer declared, "The state cannot afford to sink knee deep in evil for the sake of a fur cape on the shoulders of a society belle." In 1938, the Fair Labor Standards Act, of President Franklin D. Roosevelt's New Deal, banned outright much home production; in 1972, OSHA further extended the government's right to regulate a safe and healthful working environment.

But businessmen and manufacturers ridiculed such reform efforts from the start. In 1900, garment manufacturers and cigar firms dependent on home production used language almost identical to that of today's Internet capitalists to denounce even the most timid government efforts to regulate such work. "A man's dwelling place is his castle," declared New York opponents of a law prohibiting home production of cigars. Antisweatshop laws were "unconstitutional," railed the makers of buttons and artificial flowers when the New Deal first sought to prohibit children from joining their mothers at the kitchen table. Just as today, these petty capitalists found plenty of hard-pressed mothers to complain that without the right to take their work home, they would have to leave the kids unattended.

Telecommuting entrepreneurs will undoubtedly claim it is absurd to compare the working conditions of a computer-literate home worker in the exurbs to the grinding labor of a tenement-house sewing-machine operator on the Lower East Side in New York City. But it is not the character of the technology alone that determines the well-being of the workers or the level of their wages. When today's computerized homebodies find themselves with a pain in their wrist, fatigue in their neck, or a crick in the lower back, the cause is remarkably similar to that of their sweatshop ancestors: inadequate equipment, self-exploitation, and overwork.

These are some of the reasons that our health and safety standards, as well as contemporary labor law, apply to all employees—including telecommuters. So as we open a dialogue about the workplace of the future, let's not leave behind the advances of the past. These include the guarantee of decent work in an environment that nurtures the worker instead of destroying the soul.

Right to Refuse Unsafe Work

COMMUNICATIONS WORKERS OF AMERICA

Thousands of workers die or are injured because of on-the-job accidents each year. Many more are exposed to unhealthy conditions that cause serious illnesses years later.

When does a worker have the right to refuse dangerous work? On February 26, 1980, the U.S. Supreme Court issued a landmark ruling that more clearly defined a worker's right to refuse work where an employee(s) has (have) reasonable apprehension that death or serious injury or illness might occur as a result of performing the work. The unanimous decision came in a 1974 case against Whirlpool Corporation in which two workers refused to crawl out on a screen from which a coworker had fallen to his death only nine days earlier. A Cincinnati, Ohio, appeals court ruled in favor of the worker's rights in *Whirlpool* and the Supreme Court affirmed that decision. (At the time the Supreme Court took the *Whirlpool* case, there were two other appeals court decisions that had gone the other way. These cases were by courts in New Orleans in 1977 and Denver in 1978.)

The two workers in the *Whirlpool* case were told to go out on a screen twenty feet above the floor to retrieve small appliance parts that had fallen from a conveyor belt system above. The screen was in place to protect workers in the plant from falling parts. The retrieval assignment had resulted in other workers falling partially or completely through the screen. Claiming that the screen was unsafe, two employees refused to carry out the assignment. Whirlpool supervisors sent the workers home for the day and withheld about six hours pay.

The Court, in its decision, emphasized that the OSHA act provides a worker with the right to choose not to perform an assigned task due to reasonable apprehension of death or serious injury coupled with a reasonable belief that no less drastic alternative is available. Further, the Court held that a worker who utilizes this OSHA protection may not be discriminated against for such action.

However, the Court also indicated that an employee who refused work based on the regulation runs the risk of discharge or reprimand in the event a court subsequently finds that he/she acted unreasonably or in bad faith.

As noted, the employer docked the two workers about six hours pay in the *Whirlpool* case. The Supreme Court ruled that the OSHA act does not require an employer to pay a worker who refuses to perform an assigned task in the face

Fact Sheet 14, Communications Workers of America, Workers and Industries, AFL-CIO, CLC, 2001. Reprinted with permission of the AFL-CIO.

of imminent danger. Rather, the act simply provides that in such cases the employer may not discriminate against the involved worker(s). Thus, the Court has left this issue to be decided by labor and management through collective bargaining. Members of unions that do not negotiate the necessary protective language in their contracts should not expect to be paid for the refusal to work period. This will be true even where an employer is found guilty of violating the OSHA act.

In light of the Supreme Court's decision, what should CWA members who are faced with an imminent danger situation do? The Supreme Court has said that a worker may refuse unsafe work where he/she has refused the job in good faith. Good faith may be interpreted as an honest belief that the job was unsafe and where the job was unusually and objectively dangerous.

Good faith can be demonstrated by the manner in which you refuse unsafe work:

- Explain the hazard to the supervisor and your steward;
- Offer to do other, safe work until the hazard is corrected;
- Give management a chance to respond before doing anything else;
- If the condition isn't corrected, call OSHA and request an "imminent danger" inspection;
- Do not walk off the job. If management won't fix the hazard, force them to take the next step. Make sure you have expressed your reasons for refusing the job and your willingness to do other work, clearly and in the presence of your steward or other workers.

If you're fired or disciplined:

- file a grievance immediately; file an unfair labor practice charge with the NLRB immediately but within 180 days;
- file a section 11(c) discrimination complaint with OSHA immediately but within 30 days.

The bottom line is to stay cool. Don't let management provoke you into rash actions that could hurt your case later. Proving that your job was "abnormally and objectively dangerous" is a matter of documentation:

- Was the job one you'd never done before? Or, had the conditions of the job changed recently?
- Did you protest the job before?
- Did other workers protest the job before? Did others refuse to do the job?
- Was the company in violation of OSHA, state, or local health and safety regulations?
- Many chemicals and conditions are clearly dangerous but aren't covered by any standards. Have workers been injured or made sick doing your job? Just what chemicals were you working with?

If any CWA member refuses unsafe work, he/she should notify the local union president. In turn, this information should be made available to the CWA representative, and the CWA Occupational Safety and Health Department.

What can you do? All CWA members should make sure that their employer is maintaining a safe and healthful workplace. The key to making the workplace safe for all CWA members is strong, active local safety and health committees. The committee can identify dangerous conditions at the workplace and discuss them with management. If the company refuses to cooperate, the committee can request an OSHA inspection. The committee should always coordinate its activities through the local officers, the CWA representative, and negotiated safety and health committees.

In addition, CWA members may obtain information and assistance by contacting:

CWA Occupational Safety and Health Department
501 Third Street, N.W.
Washington, D.C. 20001-2797
Phone: (202) 434-1160

Fishing for a Living Is Dangerous Work

DINO DRUDI

Fishing has consistently ranked as the most deadly occupation since 1992, when the Bureau of Labor Statistics started publishing fatality rates by occupation. Workers in this occupation face unique life-threatening hazards—vessel casualties, falling overboard, and diving incidents.

Each year during the nineteenth century, Gloucester, Massachusetts, typically lost to the sea about two hundred men employed in fishing—4 percent of the town's population. Since 1650, the sea has claimed an estimated ten thousand Gloucester residents. Sometimes a storm would hit the Grand Banks and half a dozen fishing ships would go down—one hundred men lost overnight. On more than one occasion, Newfoundlanders awoke to find their beaches strewn with the storm-tossed corpses of those who toiled on New England fishing boats.[1]

While fishing, like almost all other occupations, has become less dangerous in recent years, the Bureau of Labor Statistics' Census of Fatal Occupational Injuries (CFOI), since its inception in 1992, has reported fishing as the single most deadly occupation.[2] Persons engaged in this work typically face a risk of suffering a fatal job injury twenty to thirty times greater than the risk for all occupations. For the years 1992 through 1996, the most recent year for which data are available, there were between 50 and 100 fishing fatalities annually. This translates into 140 fatalities per 100,000 workers engaged in the occupation for the five-year period. By contrast, the fatality rate for all occupations during this same period was 5 per 100,000.

Although in the nineteenth century more than 1 out of 25 Gloucester fishermen were killed on the job each year, for the period 1992 through 1996, the number of commercial fishing workers killed on the job annually averaged 1 out of 716. This translates into 61 fatal injuries per 1,000 workers over a forty-five-year fishing work lifetime.[3]

This article discusses fatal occupational injuries to fishers for 1992–96 and does not include any analysis of their nonfatal occupational injuries and illnesses.

U.S. Department of Labor, Bureau of Labor Statistics, *Compensation of Working Conditions* (summer 1998).
Dino Drudi is an economist in the Office of Safety, Health and Working Conditions, Bureau of Labor Statistics, U.S. Department of Labor.

Vessel Casualties

Commercial fishing vessels often travel a long way from their home ports, and great distances from shore, in search of ever dwindling fish stocks. Perils to fishing vessels include storms, which can produce "rogue waves"—also known as "freak seas" or "nonnegotiable waves"—over 100 feet (30 meters) high and fog that hinders safe navigation.

Rogue waves often are several ordinary waves that get "in step" to form veritable piles of water, or they are leftover waves from earlier storms that circumnavigate the globe and strike in otherwise relatively calm seas. They have incredibly destructive power. To illustrate, in 1973, a 12,000-ton ship broke in half on her maiden voyage after being struck by a rogue wave. The following year, a 132,000-ton tanker fell into a huge trough caused by a rogue wave. A crew member remarked, "There was no sea in front of the ship, only a hole." The ship then took an equally huge wave over her bow, which crumpled a 1-inch (2 1/2-centimeter) thick steel plate, twisted railroad-gauge I-beams into knots, and tore off the entire bow bulb! Rogue waves have the power to devastate a typical fishing boat.[4]

Rogue waves are not the only ocean peril that can sink or capsize ships. Ships might, for example, strike a submerged rock or collide with another vessel in the fog. Vessel casualties were the leading cause of fishing fatalities and often involved multiple deaths. From 1992 through 1996, half of fishing fatalities—197 cases—involved vessel casualties, such as sinkings, capsizings, or collisions. Often the bodies of the deceased are never found, particularly if they go down with the ship, wash ashore in some remote place, or enter the food chain of higher-level marine life.

"Person Overboard!"

It isn't only rogue waves that are capable of washing fishers overboard or tilting the deck enough to cause them to slip into the water. Lesser waves also wash fishers overboard. But wave action is not the only way a fisher can go overboard, as the following accounts demonstrate:

> A fisherman on board a 113-foot (34-meter) crabbing vessel was thrown overboard when a crab pot line he was straddling suddenly tightened.[5]
>
> Baiting has all the glamour of a factory shift and considerably more of the danger. The line is spooled on a big drum. It crosses diagonally over the deck, passes through an overhead block, and then bends straight back toward the stern. A steel ring guides it over the rail and into the water. That's where the baiters stand. There's a bait table on top of the stern rail—basically a wooden well with squid and mackerel [baitfish] in it—and a leader cart on either side. The leader carts are small drums spooled with hundreds of lengths of seven-fathom line called gangions. Each gangion has a #10 hook at one end and a stainless steel snap on the other. . . . The baiter reaches behind him and takes a

> gangion from his back-up man, who's peeling them off the leader cart one at a time. The baiter impales a squid or mackerel onto the hook, snaps the gangion onto the mainline, and throws the whole thing over the side. The hook is easily big enough to pass through a man's hand, and if it catches some part of the baiter's body or clothing, he goes over the side with it. . . . The crew's looking the other way, the hook's got you, and suddenly you're down at the depth where swordfish feed.[6]

Going overboard as a consequence of slipping on a wet or icy deck, being pulled overboard when lines wrap around one's legs, being washed overboard by a wave, pulled overboard by a hook, or flung overboard by a line suddenly tightening are examples of incidents classified as "falls from ship or boat." These types of falls accounted for seventy fatalities—almost one-fifth of the total during the 1992–96 period.

Fishers who go overboard into very cold water are at risk of hypothermia—the cooling of the core body temperature. This condition causes shivering, loss of muscle coordination, unconsciousness, and even death.[7] Unless wearing a survival suit or a personal flotation device (life jacket), a fisher could not withstand more than six or seven minutes immersed in very cold water before succumbing.

Diving—An Emerging Hazard

Diving fatalities are beginning to be recognized as an emerging hazard in the fishing industry.[8] Sometimes crewmembers with little formal diving training or experience are called on to dive below water to untangle nets or lines that have snagged on the ocean floor or in the boat's propellers. Even experienced, certified scuba[9] divers hired to dive for sea cucumbers and other aquatic life often face numerous hazards such as adverse sea and weather conditions,[10] murky water, unexpected shifts in underwater currents, entanglement of air lines, scuba equipment malfunction, decompression problems, and encounters with dangerous marine life.[11] The sixty drownings that occurred during 1992–96 accounted for one-sixth of fishing fatalities. Most of these drownings involved diving activities.

A variety of other hazards that tend to be more typical of workplaces generally—such as electrocutions, being caught in winches and other machinery, homicides, and aircraft crashes—accounted for the remaining fishing fatalities.

Economic and Demographic Characteristics

Commercial fishing vessels, often capable of hauling a catch weighing many tons, and sometimes having onboard processing facilities, require a crew with a wide range of specialized skills. As a prerequisite, fishers must be in good health and possess physical strength and coordination. They must also possess the mechanical aptitude to operate, maintain, and repair onboard machinery and fishing gear and the perseverance to perform strenuous outdoor work and endure long hours at sea often under difficult conditions.[12]

Often the proceeds from the fish catch are apportioned among the crew based on the market price the catch brings when landed in port—an elaborate kind of piecework pay scheme. The pay can be quite rewarding—$4,000 or more per month. Many of the individuals employed in fishing, such as college students taking fishing jobs during the summer to meet high tuition bills,[13] are highly motivated to face these risks and withstand these rigors because the pay is so attractive. Others are highly motivated because they find themselves unemployable in other lines of work and they end up in fishing as a last resort, while still others fall in love with fishing as a line of work and a way of life.[14] These factors may work in tandem to produce a workforce more motivated and able to push limits that would dissuade or disable workers in other industries.

Fishing in cold waters is inherently riskier because of hypothermia. Alaska, with one of the nation's smallest workforces, accounted for the largest number of fishing fatalities during the 1992–96 period. Moreover, some specific Alaska fishing activities are particularly hazardous. For example, harvesting most commercial crab species in Alaska takes place during the winter, when air and water temperatures are colder; high winds, snow, sleet, and ice are more prevalent; daylight hours shorter; and high seas are more common.[15]

Other cold-water states—such as Massachusetts, Oregon, Washington, and Maine—also had disproportionately high numbers of fishing fatalities.

Industry analysis suggests that persons engaged in commercial shellfishing are more at risk of dying on the job than those engaged in commercial finfishing.[16] During 1992–96, shellfishing, with 160 fatalities, accounted for one-third more deaths than finfishing, with 119 fatalities, despite the fact that the shellfishing industry employed only three-fifths as many workers as the finfishing industry[17] and the weight for the commercial shellfish catch was less than one-sixth that for finfish. The commercial dollar value of the shellfish catch, however, is nearly equal to that of the finfish catch, in part as a consequence of the greater risk involved in shellfishing.[18] In addition, there were sixteen commercial fishing fatalities in the miscellaneous marine products industry (sea cucumbers, sponges, seaweed, sea urchins, etc.), and fifty-five in general commercial fishing. Miscellaneous amusement and recreation services, which includes fishing guides, accounted for ten fatalities. The remainder were scattered over various industries.

While Current Population Survey data show self-employed individuals compose at least three-fifths of employment in fishing occupations, they accounted for just over a third of the fatalities during this period. This may be due to a variety of factors, such as self-employed fishers being limited by economies of scale to more familiar local waters. Moreover, because some types of fish can only be taken at certain times of the year, many self-employed fishers engage in fishing on a part-time basis.

During 1992–96, fishing fatalities tracked age group employment fairly closely, except that the twenty-five to thirty-four age group experienced a disproportionately high share of the fatalities, while the fifty-five to sixty-four age group experienced a slightly lower share. Non-Hispanic persons from racial categories other than white and black—such as Asians, Pacific Islanders, American Indians, Eskimos, and Aleuts—comprise 7 percent of fishing employment but at least 16 percent of fishing fatalities.[19]

Conclusion

This article builds on the research undertaken by the National Institute for Occupational Safety and Health (NIOSH), which has published several special studies, most of which have focused on the fishing industry in Alaska.[20] Census of Fatal Occupational Injuries (CFOI) data supplement the NIOSH studies and provide information on hazards facing those engaged in commercial fishing occupations throughout the United States.

Because fish are believed to have various dietary benefits, per capita fish consumption in the United States has increased by 20 percent over the past two decades. Overall per capita fish use—which includes both food consumption and industrial fish products such as fishmeal and crushed oyster shells—has increased 30 percent.[21]

Although the United States is still a net importer of fish, exports of edible fish products have tripled in weight and doubled in dollar value during the past decade, while imports have remained stable. During this time, exports of industrial fish products increased nearly sixtyfold to more than $5 billion, while the dollar value of industrial fish product imports barely doubled.[22]

Fishing employment has declined from an estimated 59,000 in 1992 to 47,000 in 1996.[23] This decline, which has taken place in the face of an increased demand for fish, is a consequence mainly of the declining supply of fish due to overfishing. But, as the demand for fish grows, and meeting that demand requires ever longer voyages and greater efforts, these factors working in tandem have the potential to increase the hazards of fishing occupations and negate any fatality decreases that stricter safety regulation may have afforded. Indeed, in 1996, when the CFOI all-employment fatality rate reached its lowest level since the program began, the rate for fishers jumped to 178 fatalities per 100,000 employment—the highest it has been since the CFOI program began collecting data in 1992. In 1996, the fatality rate for fishing occupations—which include fishers, captains, and other fishing vessel officers—reached its highest level in three years.

Technical Note

The lifetime risk for a specific industry or occupation was calculated using an equation proposed by the Occupational Safety and Health Administration in 1995:

$$WLTR = [1 - (1 - R)^y] \times 1{,}000,$$

where

WLTR = working lifetime risk
R = probability of a worker having a work-related fatal injury in a given year
1 – R = probability of a worker not having a work-related fatal injury in a given year
y = years of exposure to work-related injury
$(1 - R)^y$ = probability of surviving *y* years without a work-related fatal injury
$1 - (1 - R)^y$ = probability of having a work-related fatal injury over *y* years of employment

In this study, *y* was set at 45 years. This assumes workers are exposed to work-related injury hazards for approximately 45 years, starting at age 20.

The formula is then multiplied by 1,000 to derive the number of fatal occupational injuries per 1,000 workers, as follows:

R = 0.0014 = 140 fatalities per 100,000 employment = a 0.14 percent probability of a worker having a work-related fatal injury in a given year

1 – R = 1 – 0.0014 = 0.9986 = a 99.86 percent probability of a worker not having a fatal occupational injury in a given year

$(1 - R)^{45} = 0.9986^{45} = 0.9389$ = a 93.89 percent probability of surviving 45 years without having a work-related fatal injury

$1 - (1 - R)^{45} = 1 - 0.9389 = 0.0611$ = a 6.11 percent probability of having a work-related fatal injury over 45 years of employment

While it is tempting to view the inverse of 0.0611 (1:16) as the probability a worker faces of suffering a fatal occupational injury over a theoretical 45-year fishing career, because of such factors as turnover, the risk should be expressed on a per 1,000 worker basis, as follows:

$[1 - (1 - R)^{45}] \times 1{,}000 = 0.0611 \times 1{,}000 = 61$ fatalities per 1,000 employment over a 45-year period comprising a working lifetime

Notes

1. Sebastian Junger, *The Perfect Storm* (New York: W. W. Norton, 1997), 44–45.
2. For 1996, the occupation with the next highest rate is timber cutters at 157, followed by airplane pilots (88), structural metal workers (85), and extractive occupations (67).
3. For a good explanation of the methodology used to derive this statistic, see David E. Fosbroke, Suzanne M. Kisner, and John R. Myers, "Working Lifetime Risk of Occupational Fatal Injury," *American Journal of Industrial Medicine* 31 (1997): 460–61. See "Technical Note" at the end of this article.
4. Junger, *The Perfect Storm,* 114–15, 123, 150.
5. National Institute for Occupational Safety and Health, *NIOSH Alert: Request for*

Assistance in Preventing Drownings of Commercial Fishermen, Publication No. 94-107, April 1994, p. 4.

6. Junger, *The Perfect Storm,* 52, 70.

7. NIOSH, *NIOSH Alert,* 2.

8. National Institute for Occupational Safety and Health, "Commercial Fishing Fatalities in Alaska: Risk Factors and Prevention Strategies," *Current Intelligence Bulletin* 58 (September 1997): 12.

9. *Scuba* is an acronym for "self-contained underwater breathing apparatus."

10. NIOSH, "Commercial Fishing Fatalities in Alaska," 12.

11. Bureau of Labor Statistics, *Occupational Outlook Handbook, 1998–99 Edition,* Bulletin 2500, January 1998, 417.

12. Ibid., 416–18.

13. National Institute for Occupational Safety and Health, *NIOSH Update: College Students May Be Risking Their Lives on Fishing Vessels: Working in the Alaska Fishing Industry Is One of the Nation's Most Hazardous Jobs,* Publication No. 94-111, April 1994.

14. For a fuller discussion, see Junger, *The Perfect Storm,* 15, 48–49.

15. NIOSH, "Commercial Fishing Fatalities in Alaska," ix, 2.

16. Shellfish include cephalopods such as squid, crustaceans such as lobster and shrimp, and univalve and bivalve mollusks such as abalone and clams, whereas finfish—such as shark, tuna, and salmon—are all vertebrates. Some of the hazards confronting shellfishers are different from those confronting finfishers. For example, shellfishing for king crab is done using cages called "pots"—some weighing more than 700 pounds (318 kilograms)—which are stored on the deck, where they might fall on someone, whereas finfishers do not use pots. Many types of finfishing, such as longlining, however, make use of numerous hooks, which can puncture and pull a fisher overboard.

17. Industry employment figures are from the Covered Employment and Wages (also known as the ES-202) program. See the annual publication *Employment and Wages, Annual Averages,* for the years 1992 through 1996.

18. National Marine Fisheries Service, *Fisheries of the United States, 1996,* Current Fishery Statistics No. 9600, July 1997, iv, 10–13. Weights for all fish are reported in round weight (defined as weight of fish as taken from the water, the complete or full "live" weight when caught), except for univalve and bivalve mollusks, which are reported in meat weight (excluding the shell).

19. Employment data for race and age are derived from the Current Population Survey.

20. See Fosbroke, Kisner, and Meyers, "Working Lifetime Risk"; Richard D. Kennedy and Jennifer M. Lincoln, "Epidemiology of Fatal Injury in the U.S. Commercial Fishing Industry," *Safety and Health in Agriculture, Forestry, and Fisheries* (Rockville, Md.: Government Institutes, 1997), 557–70; Patricia G. Schnitzer, Deborah D. Landen, and Julie C. Russell, "Occupational Injury Deaths in Alaska's Fishing Industry, 1980 through 1988," *American Journal of Public Health,* 83, no. 5 (May 1993): 685–88; NIOSH, *NIOSH Alert;* NIOSH, *NIOSH Update.*

21. National Marine Fisheries Service, *Fisheries of the United States,* 125, 127.

22. Ibid., 98, 106.

23. Employment data are derived from various sources including the Current Population Survey; the *Occupational Outlook Handbook,* 417; and CFOI.

Logging Is Perilous Work

ERIC F. SYGNATUR

Despite the risks involved in logging, timber is a multibillion dollar industry in the United States. Products and structures made from trees are so prevalent that their origin is scarcely noticed. Yet, in 1997, logging was the most dangerous occupation in the country.

Logging was the second most dangerous occupation (behind fishing) during 1992–96, according to data from the Bureau of Labor Statistics' Census of Fatal Occupational Injuries (CFOI). With more than 128 deaths per 100,000 workers, logging surpassed fishing as the most dangerous occupation in 1997.[1]

Homes and furniture, paper and pencils, some cloth fibers, even many medicinal extracts are derived from wood. According to one report, "an average American uses wood and paper products equivalent to what can be produced from one 100-foot, 18-inch tree every year."[2] Trees provide the convenience of the Sunday paper just as readily as they provided previous generations with fuel in the winter. In fact, it takes a cord of wood (an 8′ × 4′ × 4′ stack) to produce 250 copies of a typical Sunday edition of *The New York Times*.[3]

Timber resources come at a price, however: Each year, between 100 and 150 loggers lose their lives according to the CFOI, and many more suffer nonfatal injuries. Loggers face a risk of fatal work injury approximately twenty-seven times greater than the average for all occupations. During 1992–97, loggers suffered, on average, 128 fatalities per 100,000 workers compared to 5 per 100,000 for all occupations. Over the six-year period, 1 out of every 780 loggers lost his life to a work injury, which translates into 57 fatal injuries per 1,000 workers over a forty-five-year lifetime of timber cutting.[4]

Working Conditions

Logging occupations are physically demanding, involving lifting, climbing, and other strenuous activities in remote locations, frequently isolated from readily available medical services.[5] In addition, because the work is performed outdoors, loggers must often face adverse weather conditions, irregular terrain, and con-

U.S. Department of Labor, Bureau of Labor Statistics, *Compensation and Working Conditions* (winter 1998). Eric F. Sygnatur is an economist in the Office of Safety, Health and Working Conditions, Bureau of Labor Statistics, U.S. Department of Labor. Guy Toscano, Office of Safety, Health and Working Conditions, provided technical guidance.

tend with swarms of mosquitoes, blackflies, and deerflies. Long hours and six-day workweeks are also common.[6] None of these conditions, however, is as menacing to the well-being of a logger as the trees themselves; of the 772 fatal injuries to loggers in 1992–97, 70 percent resulted directly from contact with trees and logs. The magnitude of this number is significant, as skidders and tractors,[7] the next most common sources of injury, together only accounted for 6 percent of total fatalities. The remaining 24 percent were from a variety of sources (such as dump trucks, the ground, and pickup trucks), none of which individually accounted for more than 2 percent of the logging fatalities.

Trees pose a number of hazards to loggers. Wind, structural irregularities in the tree, wet or sloped terrain, and structural failures within the tree such as heart rot, splits, breaks, and cracks may cause the tree to fall at unexpected times in unexpected directions. Felled trees can become entangled in other trees or, less obviously and more commonly, broken tree limbs can be caught in nearby trees where they dangle capriciously, often falling onto unsuspecting loggers. The latter scenario is so common that hanging limbs are often referred to as "widow makers." Falling trees can also hit overhead power lines and telephone poles, or vines and other dense vegetation, resulting in erratic falls, fires, or entanglement. "Fishtailing" trees sweep a large surface area as they swing sideways, and "mousetraps" sometimes occur when a felled tree strikes another, perhaps concealed log, which in turn strikes the logger. Even when the tree is settled it poses dangers when limbs become locked or bent. Loggers who cut these limbs must guard against slingshot effects, which can throw large limbs up to fifty feet.[8]

Some 65 percent of logging fatalities occurred as a result of being struck by falling objects, almost all of which were trees and logs. Various types of non-roadway vehicular accidents, including those caused by tractors and skidders, accounted for 7 percent of fatalities; loggers crushed or struck by rolling logs accounted for 5 percent; and falls from trees, 2 percent. In 95 percent of the cases where the time of the incident was reported, they occurred between the hours of 7 A.M. and 5 P.M.[9]

Economic and Demographic Characteristics

Many regions of the United States boast a rich sylvan heritage—the huge Douglas firs and redwoods of the Pacific Northwest, the hearty maples of the upper Midwest, the white pines of the Northeast, and the southern pines (longleaf, shortleaf, slash, and loblolly) of the South are some of the most well known. Logging of these trees is a multibillion dollar industry practiced in all states. Some regions (those characterized by the types of trees they harvest, the levels of mechanization used, and other economic factors) have natural advantages over others.

Weather and climate, and the percent of logging employment, are important factors to consider when comparing regional fatality numbers. The southern region, as defined by the Bureau of the Census,[10] had 413 logging fatalities, about 54 percent of the total between 1992 and 1997. In this region, North Carolina, with fifty-five deaths, had the most fatalities of any state; this represents 7.1 percent of all logging fatalities, although North Carolina only accounts for 2.9 percent of all loggers. Logging is a flourishing industry in the South, "[where] timber harvesting costs . . . are among the lowest in the world, and perhaps the lowest."[11] New mechanization procedures in the South for whole-tree (longwood) harvesting have decreased average costs and increased efficiency, shifting the production output dramatically over the 1979–87 period. The number of less efficient pulpwood (short-wood) firms decreased by half over the eight-year period, and average pulpwood harvesting costs declined significantly in real terms.[12]

The rich soils, ample rain, and mild climate of the West Coast make it an ideal location to practice silviculture (the care and tending of forest vegetation).[13] In 1991, California's timber harvest value exceeded $900 million, and California, Oregon, and Washington combined produce nearly fourteen million board feet of lumber per year.[14] These three states accounted for 97 deaths, or 13 percent of the total, for the 1992–97 period. The western region had 186 deaths, or 24 percent of all logging fatalities, from 1992 to 1997.

The remaining two regions, the Northeast and Midwest, accounted for eighty-three and eighty-nine deaths, or 11 and 12 percent, respectively. In these two regions, only Pennsylvania ranked among the top fifteen states in fatalities, with thirty-three, or 4.3 percent of the total. Fifteen states experienced 70 percent of all logging fatalities, and the top five states, 30 percent.

During the 1992–97 period, less than 1 percent of the logging fatalities involved women, who made up about 3 percent of the logging industry workforce. Blacks made up between 7 and 12 percent of the workforce but were slightly overrepresented in fatalities, with between 11 and 17 percent. Whites, who made up 83 percent of the workforce, also constituted 83 percent of the fatalities. The remaining races, who comprise only a small fraction of those employed, incurred very few fatalities.

About one-third of logging workers are self-employed, a much higher proportion than in most occupations.[15] These workers incurred about one-third of the logging fatalities between 1992 and 1997.[16] Employees working for compensation or pay constitute the overwhelming majority of remaining fatalities, with very few fatalities among those working in family businesses or volunteering their efforts. In the competitive logging industry, the median weekly earnings for full-time wage and salary earners in the forestry and logging occupations was $443, compared to $490 for all occupations.[17]

Data for Nonfatal Injuries

Logging injuries that do not result in a fatality but require time away from work to recuperate most often occur to the trunk of the body and the lower extremi-

Table 2. Number of Occupational Injuries and Illnesses Involving Time Away from Work, 1996

Nature of Injury	*Number of Cases*	*Percent of Total Cases*
Total cases	2,136	100
Sprains, strains	713	33
Fractures	359	17
Bruises	305	14
Cuts, punctures	209	10
Bodily pain	87	4
All other	463	22

Source: U.S. Bureau of Labor Statistics.

ties. In 1996, the most recent year for which data are available, there were an estimated 2,136 cases involving time away from work (table 2). However, this statistic does not account for the self-employed, government workers, or workers in agricultural establishments with fewer than eleven employees.[18] As table 2 shows, the injuries most often reported in 1996 for timber cutters, including supervisors, were sprains and strains, followed by fractures and bruises.

About half of the nonfatal injuries in 1996 were caused by events such as being struck or crushed, followed by falls, which accounted for about one-quarter. Between 1992 and 1996, more than 30 percent of the logging injury cases resulted in thirty-one or more lost workdays and almost 17 percent resulted in three to five days away from work. The median number of days away from work for the five-year period was eleven. As the following tabulation shows, an important trend seems to have developed, as the number of nonfatal injury cases involving lost workdays has steadily dropped from more than 4,500 in 1992 to 2,136 in 1996 (see table 3).

Table 3. Number of Injured Workers, 1992–96

Year	*Number of Injuries*
1992	4,537
1993	4,522
1994	3,479
1995	2,779
1996	2,136

Conclusion

Loggers comprise 1/2 of 1 percent of the total workforce in America, yet they account for nearly 2 percent of all fatalities. This astounding ratio is an indication of the unpredictable dangers involved in logging.

Employment levels and the demand for wood have been relatively stable over the past six years, and any future increases in the demand for wood products is expected to be offset by improvements in technology rather than increases in employment.[19] Recent history reveals a disturbing pattern of regularity to logging fatalities that does not appear to be changing. Perhaps developments in logging techniques, training, and equipment will provide a boost in safety. Significant decreases in the number of nonfatal injuries requiring time away from work is encouraging, certainly, but logging still has the highest fatality rate among all occupations.

Technical Note

The lifetime risk for a specific industry or occupation was calculated using an equation proposed by the Occupational Safety and Health Administration in 1995:

$$WLTR = [1 - (1 - R)y] \times 1{,}000,$$

where

$WLTR$ = working lifetime risk
R = probability of a worker having a work-related fatal injury in a given year
$1 - R$ = probability of a worker not having a work-related fatal injury in a given year
y = years of exposure to work-related injury
$(1 - R)y$ = probability of surviving y years without a work-related fatal injury
$1 - (1 - R)y$ = probability of having a work-related fatal injury over y years of employment

For this article, y was set at 45 years. This assumes workers are exposed to work-related injury hazards for approximately 45 years, starting at age 20.

The number of fatal occupational injuries per 1,000 workers is derived as follows:

$R = 0.00128$ = 128 fatalities per 100,000 workers, which is equal to a .128 percent probability of a worker having a work-related fatal injury in a given year

$1 - R = 1 - 0.00128 = 0.99872$, which is equal to a 99.87 percent probability of a worker not having a fatal occupational injury in a given year

$(1 - R)\ 4\ 5 = 0.9987\ 4\ 5 = 0.9431$, which is equal to a 94.31 percent probability of surviving 45 years without having a work-related fatal injury

1 – (1 – R) 4 5 = 1 – 0.9431 = 0.0569, which is equal to a 5.69 percent probability of having a work-related fatal injury over 45 years of employment

Although it is tempting to view the inverse of 0.0569 (1:18) as the probability a worker faces of suffering a fatal occupational injury over a theoretical 45-year logging career, risk should be expressed on a per 1,000 worker basis to account for such factors as turnover, as follows:

[1 – (1 – R) 4 5] × 1,000 = 0.0569 × 1,000, which is equal to 57 fatalities per 1,000 workers over a 45-year period comprising a working lifetime

State and region-specific employment estimates were obtained using the Current Population Survey's Federal Electronic Research and Review Extraction Tool (FERRET) for the years 1994–97, corresponding with the earliest year for which FERRET microdata is available, and the latest year for which CFOI numbers are available. Given the stable employment numbers and markets for loggers between 1992 and 1997, this average estimate for 67 percent of the period should prove reliable for employment composition by state over the whole 1992–97 period. Additional information on FERRET can be obtained from the Bureau of Labor Statistics Internet site at *http://ferret.bls.census.gov/cgi-bin/ferret*. See "Explanatory Notes and Estimates of Error" in the January 1998 *Employment and Earnings* for an explanation of CPS sampling and estimation methodology and standard error computations. The relative standard error of the CPS employment estimates can be used to approximate confidence ranges for the fatality rates.

Notes

1. The Census of Fatal Occupational Injuries has collected occupational fatality data since 1992, using diverse data sources to identify, verify, and profile fatal work injuries. Information about each workplace fatality (occupation and other worker characteristics, equipment being used, and circumstances of the event) is obtained by cross-referencing source documents, such as death certificates, workers' compensation records, and reports to federal and state agencies. This method assures counts are as complete and accurate as possible.
2. Washington Contract Loggers Association, "Washington State Timber Facts, Figures and Issues for Concerned Citizens," http://www.loggers.com/timber_facts.htm.
3. Ibid.
4. For an explanation of the methodology used to derive this statistic, see David E. Fosbroke, Suzanne M. Kisner, and John R. Myers, "Working Lifetime Risk of Occupational Fatal Injury," *American Journal of Industrial Medicine* 31 (1997): 460–61. Also see technical note at the end of this article.
5. Bureau of Labor Statistics, *Occupational Outlook Handbook, 1998–99 Edition,* Bulletin 2500, 1998, p. 420.
6. John Gagnon, *Hard Maple, Hard Work* (Marquette, Mich.: Northern Michigan University Press, 1996), 63–65.
7. Skidders are tractorlike vehicles used to drag logs through forest terrain.

8. Gerald F. Beranek, *The Fundamentals of General Tree Work* (Fort Bragg, N.C.: Beranek Publications, 1996), 362–83.

9. Ninety-four percent of the cases reported the time of incident.

10. Bureau of the Census regional designations:

Northeast: CT, ME, MA, NH, NJ, NY, PA, RI, and VT.
Midwest: IL, IN, IA, KS, MI, MN, MO, NE, ND, OH, SD, and WI.
South: AL, AR, DE, DC, FL, GA, KY, LA, MD, MS, NC, OK, SC, TN, TX, VA, and WV.
West: AZ, AK, CA, CO, HI, ID, MT, NV, NM, OR, UT, WA, and WY.

11. Douglas R. Carter et. al., "Southern Pulpwood Harvesting Productivity and Cost Changes Between 1979 and 1987," Research Paper NC-318, U.S. Department of Agriculture, North Central Forest Experiment Station, St. Paul, Minn., 1994, pp. 31–32.

12. Ibid.

13. Earl Roberge, *Timber Country* (Caldwell, Idaho: Caxton Printers, 1973), 1.

14. Little Hoover Commission, *Timber Harvest Plans: A Flawed Effort to Balance Economic and Environmental Needs* (Sacramento, Calif., 1994), 10–12.

15. Bureau of Labor Statistics, *Occupational Outlook Handbook, 1998–99,* 420.

16. Two-thirds of the fatality records in the 1992–97 period indicated the size of the establishment that employed the decedent. Eighty-two percent of those indicating employment size employed between one and ten workers.

17. Bureau of Labor Statistics, *Employment and Earnings,* January 1997, table 39, 206–10.

18. The Survey of Occupational Injuries and Illnesses (SOII) collects information from a random sample of about 200,000 establishments representing most of private industry, with the exception of the self-employed. Worker characteristics are collected only for those workers sustaining injuries and illnesses that require days away from work (with or without restricted work activity) to recuperate. Because the scope and methodology of CFOI and SOII are slightly different, comparison of the fatal and nonfatal data is problematic. Additional information on either CFOI or SOII can be obtained from the Bureau of Labor Statistics Internet site at http://www.bls.gov/iif/.

19. Bureau of Labor Statistics, *Occupational Outlook Handbook, 1998–99,* 421.

What Is Stress and Why Is It Hazardous?

HR.com

Stress, as defined by Edwards (1996) is a "consequence of or a general response to an action or situation that places physical or psychological demands, or both, on a person." While we have all, undoubtedly, complained about our stress levels "going through the roof" on several occasions, do we actually know what stress can do to our bodies and what we can do to manage stress at the workplace? Our bodies are designed to enable us to encounter stress in our daily lives. Not only does our fight-or-flight response allow us to survive stressful situations, but stress can also have motivating powers. Too little stress can lead to boredom and the lack of fulfillment or motivation to accomplish one's tasks. Studies have demonstrated that there is an optimal point at which stress can enhance performance. Individuals differ as to the level at which optimal functioning results from the interaction between stimuli and performance. In the workplace, one must find the appropriate occupation for which they are suited in order to achieve congruence. Studies have demonstrated that occupations having high demands but low decision-making latitude, such as assembly-line workers, are sources of stress, as are those occupations that have high decision-making latitude but deal with a multitude of variables simultaneously, such as nurses and police officers. When stress becomes unmanageable, physiological, emotional, and behavioral outcomes result. Stress overload can lead to anxiety, fatigue, headaches, hypertension, depression, alcoholism, drug abuse, and cardiovascular or gastrointestinal disease. At the workplace, stress-related disability claims are a rapidly growing form of occupational illness within the workers' compensation system. Moreover, stress can generate increased costs due to lost productivity from stress-related disease and illness, as well as increased health insurance premiums. As those employees having low levels of work-related stress miss fewer days of work due to injury and illness, reducing stress in the workplace can generate cost savings for those organizations that actively promote stress management.

Work/Life Balance: What's All the Fuss?

There is no doubt that we have all experienced stress at some time in our lives. Job interviews, rapidly approaching deadlines, and corporate presentations are often wrought with feelings of anxiety and tension. While stress-ridden

HR.com, April 20, 2001. Reprinted with permission of HR.com.

situations such as these cannot simply be eliminated from our working lives, stress at the workplace need not be a no-win situation. From daycare to eldercare, sabbaticals to fitness centers, employers have myriad options from which to choose to help ease the burdens of their workers.

Work/life balance may be defined as the repackaging and restructuring of work to alleviate the conflicting demands of one's personal and professional life. Policies and programs developed to assist employees in alleviating their work-life conflict allow organizations to benefit from a less stressed and more productive, efficient, and satisfied workforce. The notion of a necessary balance between one's work and family life has become especially salient as women have secured a permanent position in the labor market and as the baby boom generation nears retirement. Coupled with a supportive corporate culture and climate, these initiatives enable organizations to benefit in the areas of attraction and retention, absenteeism and productivity. As globalization has led to increased labor market competition, those organizations that actively promote work-life balance are at a competitive advantage in attracting and retaining top talent in the new millennium.

According to the Institute of Personnel and Development's annual survey of one thousand workers, 40 percent of employees surveyed stated that work demands often get in the way of nonwork commitments. Similarly, in a survey of employees at a global high-tech firm, "volume of work" was cited as the main obstacle to obtaining proper work-life balance. Managers must learn to control the demands they place on their staff and understand that flexible work arrangements may be necessary to reduce their employees' work-life conflict. One must remember that "face time" does not necessarily translate into "work time"!

Combatting Stress at the Workplace: Flexible Work Arrangements

Organizations implement flexible work arrangements to provide individually negotiated conditions of employment with regard to the place, scope, or timing of work. To ensure the success of a flexible work arrangement program, managers and employees must operate in an environment in which trust and respect prevail. The organizational culture provides the framework for effective programs and policies that reduce stress. The goals of the company and the needs of its employees must be in alignment to encourage participation and to ensure the ultimate success of alternative work arrangements. Following are some options for managers to assist workers in achieving harmony in their personal and professional lives:

Flexible Hours: employees work full time with core office hours but flexible start and finish times. The most common alternative work arrangement, flexible hours enable employees to modify their schedules to suit their childcare and transportation needs.

Telecommuting: employees perform work outside of the office for an agreed-upon portion of the workweek. Telecommuting allows for office space and utilities savings with no impact on salary or benefits.

Compressed Workweek: employees work a typical workweek, but work more hours on certain days and less hours or no hours on other days. For example, an employee works from eight to six Monday through Thursday and has an extra day of leisure at the end of each week.

Part-time Work: employees are considered part-time if employed less than thirty hours in their main work role. Such an arrangement allows for increased compatibility between employee availability and workload.

Job Sharing: Two part-time employees share the responsibility and functions of one full-time position, allowing the workers to maintain their seniority and career development.

One should be aware that there are potential drawbacks that may be incurred with the implementation of these programs, such as communication and isolation concerns for off-site employees, additional administrative costs, and the potential for decreased productivity at the end of a long workday in the case of the compressed workweek. However, the benefits of alternative work arrangements, which include increased employee motivation, morale and organizational commitment, enhanced efficiency and job satisfaction, as well as reduced stress and absenteeism, most certainly outweigh the drawbacks of a flexible work arrangement policy.

Stress Busters

Role conflict, which may be defined as the incompatibility of one's expectations and demands, and role overload, which occurs when an employee perceives that his or her cumulative demands exceed his or her ability and motivation to perform a task, are frequently the cause of an individual's work-related stress. Aside from running away to a remote, sun-splashed tropical island, there are simple ways for managers and employees to combat stress that arises from role conflict and role overload.

Firstly, an employee should assess her environment to ensure that she is employed in a role that best suits her needs. While some workers thrive and excel in fast-paced, hectic environments, others are more suited for more steady and relaxed working conditions. Learning to say no, and that you cannot do absolutely everything, may actually be simpler than you think. By dividing overwhelming duties into easy-to-conquer tasks and crossing off priorities on a master list, you may find that you have accomplished much more than you had imagined. Taking mini workout breaks at the office, such as a run up the stairs, or a quick set of sit-ups to get the blood flowing, can give you the extra bit of energy you seek during a stressful day.

To assist their employees in decreasing their stress levels, organizations can implement programs that educate employees on stress management techniques, such as relaxation therapy, yoga, and meditation. Wellness programs, such as fitness and nutrition education also serve to combat stress in the workplace. Many proactive corporations are introducing such programs as noon hour "fit-walks" around the office building, health and safety fairs, and back health education. Tuition reimbursement, family leave, resource libraries, employee assistance programs, and career development programs are other available options that many employees are able to take advantage of within those organizations that value the importance of a stress-free environment.

Chapter 7

Technology on the Job

HOW WILL TECHNOLOGY AFFECT the workforce and workers in terms of e-business and e-learning, and aging workers? The pieces in this chapter illuminate the psychological and social boundaries between the speed and adaptability of technology and the basic human capacities of workers. Silicon Valley generates wealth—as well as stress and fatigue. Knowledge management systems link workers around the world but do not change the basic rules of human face-to-face conduct. Truck drivers must do more than drive; now they master laptops to stay on the road. Older workers struggle to remain relevant in the technology-obsessed workplace. For decades to come, resolving conflict between the possibilities of technology and the capacity of workers to manage stress will endure as a core challenge of the workplace.

Our first selection features the executive summary to the seminal Merrill Lynch report on the education and training economy, "The Knowledge Web." Here, Michael Moe argues that in today's knowledge-based global marketplace, human capital has replaced physical capital as the source of competitive advantage and that organizations—educational ones—that nurture and expand this resource will become increasingly vital. Jon Gordon's "The Long Boom" describes how the technology boom in northern California has exacted worrisome tolls on quality of life and affordability. "Twelve Learning Interventions That Combat Technophobia" provides a humorous discussion of the battles waged by the millions of frontline workers to adapt to the wired workplace, including substantive advice on overcoming the problems of late adopters. In "E-Business 2.0," John Thompson of IBM provides a vision of the coming transformation of enterprises and industry being driven by e-business (the use of Internet technologies throughout the sales and marketing process). A *New York Times* article, "Rig de Rigueur: Eighteen Wheels and a Laptop," by Robert Strauss, illustrates Thompson's thesis in his examination of the role of technology and e-business applications in the trucking industry. Next we look to those who think about the intersection of knowledge, e-learning, and work. In "A Vision of E-Learning for America's Workforce," experts at the American Society of Training and Development and the National Governors Association Center for Best

Practices provide the policy-eye view of the importance of e-learning to government policy makers and the private sector, as well as the need for cohesive strategies to remove barriers to networks of learning among schools, colleges, workplaces, health care institutions, and homes.

The Knowledge Web

MICHAEL MOE

Take our twenty best people away, and I can tell you that Microsoft would become an unimportant company.
—Bill Gates

When the puck goes in the net, all the sticks go in the air. Likewise, attributing what or who deserves the credit for the incredible economic boom we are experiencing is a crowded stage. Silicon Valley, Alan Greenspan, the fall of the Berlin Wall, and, of course, the Internet are all lead actors amongst the cast of thousands in the New Economy script.

Technology is the driver of the New Economy, and human capital is its fuel. In today's world, knowledge is making the difference not only in how an individual does but also in how well a company does and, for that matter, in how well a country does. While the future possibilities of the knowledge economy look both exciting and, at the same time, daunting, the transformation to a knowledge economy is now evident.

Most striking—the dramatic pay gap between those with education and those without has more than doubled in less than twenty years. Looked at another way, the purchasing power of a thirty-year-old man with a high school diploma has dropped by more than one-third over the past two decades.

Also significant—our analysis illustrating a seismic shift in how the market values companies, discounting traditional analysis of earnings derived from physical capital and replacing it with analysis of earnings power derived from human capital.

Finally, the structural changes that have occurred in our economy mean that the new jobs being created today are service and skill-based jobs rather than manufacturing jobs. In 1950, unskilled jobs constituted 60 percent of all jobs, with professional and skilled jobs representing the remainder. Fast forward the clock to today, and it is expected that 65 percent of all new jobs created will be skilled jobs and that by 2005 skilled jobs will represent 85 percent of all new jobs created. Fundamental to the investment opportunity is the significant demand imbalance for knowledge workers versus the supply of skill-based jobs.

In today's knowledge-based global marketplace, human capital has replaced physical capital as the source of competitive advantage. A key result of the confluence of technology and the Internet Economy is the need for better, faster,

Excerpts from Executive Summary, Merrill Lynch, 2000. Reprinted with permission of Merrill Lynch.
Michael Moe is founding partner of ThinkEquity Partners and former director of Global Growth Stock Research and a managing director at Merrill Lynch.

and smarter workers. The reality of a 4 percent unemployment rate in the United States, the "free agent" mindset of the most talented workers, and the fact that only 21 percent of the U.S. adult population has a college degree is making this task more difficult than ever before. E-commerce forces even traditional businesses to operate at Internet speed, with "time-to-competency" now a major factor determining the competitiveness of all companies.

The truly revolutionary impact of the Internet is just beginning to be felt. In the old economy, geographic distance needed to be mastered to shop, be serviced, or to learn. In the new economy, distance has been eliminated. We are rapidly evolving into one economy and one market.

We see the e-knowledge market being the next major growth phase of the Internet, following huge business and investment opportunities in business-to-consumer (B2C) e-commerce and business-to-business (B2B) commerce and services.

At no previous time has human capital been so important, meaning finding, developing, and retaining knowledge workers will be mission-critical functions—and high-growth sectors—in the new economy. Accordingly, we look at the continuum of human capital solutions holistically—a Knowledge Web—and believe the most important companies will have an appreciation for and/or involvement in a comprehensive solution. We believe those companies that can link different elements of the human capital value chain—stretching from recruiting to assessment to training and through retention—while leveraging the Internet's capabilities to deliver a total solution, will be the big winners.

Unleashing the Killer App

The death of distance and the compression of time have powerful implications in the knowledge-based economy. The biggest investment ideas are often where there is a problem—and the bigger the problem, the bigger the opportunity. There is no bigger problem in the global marketplace today than how to obtain, train, and retain knowledge workers. Seventy percent of Fortune 1000 CEOs cite the ability to attract and keep adequately skilled employees as a major issue for growth and competitiveness. Given that essentially all of the twenty million net new jobs that were created in the past twenty years were from small- and mid-sized companies, obtaining, training and retaining talent is even more critical to what has become the growth engine of the new economy.

The killer app for the next decade is talent acquisition and retention.
—John Doerr
Kleiner, Perkins, Caufield & Byers

The next big killer application for the Internet is going to be education.
— John Chambers, CEO
Cisco Systems

Nowhere is the importance of people more evident than with technology professionals, or "techies." Techies are the heroes of the New Economy: they influence the spending of $1 trillion of annual purchases; they are mission-critical for any organization; and they are in extremely short supply. In fact, there are currently 700,000 open IT jobs, or one-third of the total of all IT jobs, with the shortage expected to more than double in the next five years. Compounding the complexity of dearth of IT professionals is that Moore's Law is alive and well, making IT skills obsolete at the blink of an eye.

Fast-forward the clock five years and, unfortunately, the supply of students coming out of America's schools doesn't promise much relief. Twelfth-graders in U.S. schools in the most recent international comparisons finished dead last and next to last in the key new economy subjects of math and science, respectively.

Hence, the fundamental and massive problem of global competitiveness and obtaining knowledge workers reaches all the way down to the K–12 level. As the human capital demand funnel is triggered, global corporations need to more effectively recruit knowledge workers and provide lifelong learning for their employees and create supply for the future by improving the K–12 education system. The Internet acts as a major enabler linking corporations to people, providing management systems, anytime/anywhere learning, and a catalyst to help revolutionize a failing primary education system.

Mind Over Matter: Human Capital in the Knowledge Economy

Throughout history, whether in preindustrial or industrial times, great nations developed based on their access to physical resources or their ability to surmount physical barriers: England and Spain crossed the oceans, Germany turned coal and iron into steel, and the United States exploited a wealth of agricultural and industrial resources to become the world's breadbasket and industrial superpower.

The advent of the personal computer, the Internet, and the electronic delivery of information have transformed the world from a manufacturing, physically based economy to an electronic, knowledge-based economy. Whereas the resources of the physically based economy are coal, oil, and steel, the resources of the new, knowledge-based economy are brainpower and the ability to acquire, deliver, and process information effectively.

> We spend all our time on people. The day we screw up the people thing, this company is over.
> —Jack Welch

With some of the greatest developments in new technologies arriving late in the twentieth century, widespread optimism surrounding the twenty-first century has yielded futurists predicting a period of rapid growth at the magnitude of the industrial revolution, if not greater, with the advent of the knowledge-based economy. In this new economy, knowledge workers form the cornerstones of successful businesses, emerging industries, and economic growth. In this new environment, however, the labor force is presented with an unprecedented challenge as it must now gain and continuously upgrade its skills. Companies are increasing R&D expenditures, and employees must continue to "upgrade" their skills in order to keep pace with the innovation. Case in point, the number of patents being issued in the United States is almost twice the amount granted only ten years ago, and the pace of patent applications is accelerating.

Growing Pay Gap Rewards Knowledge Workers

In today's economy, companies' earnings power rises due to returns on human capital. Companies, in turn, must reward employees with their "productivity wages" or risk losing them to competitors. The result is that the earnings power of knowledge employees rises in the job market. Those without the necessary education, however, do not reap similar rewards. Accordingly, we have seen the income gap between those with a bachelor's or higher degree and those with just a high school education widen significantly, and we expect this trend to continue as long as the marketplace continues to reward knowledge-intensive companies.

Moreover, the computer is replacing many "left brain" task-oriented jobs as it performs these functions faster, cheaper, and better. A significant challenge and opportunity is the necessity to create knowledge workers from today's existing labor pool.

"Capital is accessible, and smart strategies can simply be copied. The half-life of technology is growing shorter all the time. For many companies today, talented people are the prime source of competitive advantage."
—Ed Michaels, Director
McKinsey & Co.

Recognition of Human Capital Driving Market: Valuations of Knowledge Enterprises

Growth companies today are dependent on human capital. Those companies that have created growth by leveraging their "off balance sheet" human capital assets have, in turn, seen their share prices rewarded with higher valuations. It is illustrative to look at valuations of the largest ten companies in the old economy and compare them with the largest ten companies in the new economy. In the old economy, price-to-book was a useful valuation measure, as it was physical capital that companies leveraged into earnings power. What matters in the new economy, however, is human capital. In 1980, the price-to-book of the largest companies in the United States was 1.2×. Today the price-to-book is 12.1×, or ten times greater.

There is a clear relationship between the effectiveness of a company's human capital and the creation of superior shareholder returns.
—Watson Wyatt, Human Capital Index Study

Growth Jobs Are Knowledge and Service Jobs. During the industrial revolution, the labor force was already equipped with the skills to enter into manufacturing sector employment, where the assembly line merely required the theory of work organization to be put into practice. Workers were required to do no more than perform specific tasks and later operate specialized machinery that performed the actual work. Nonetheless, the changes that this innovation brought were enormous. By 1950, 40 percent of the American workforce was employed in the manufacturing sector and, as a result, productivity increased fifty-fold. Workers accrued the majority of the benefits—half in the form of sharply reduced working hours and the other half in a twenty-five-fold increase in real wages.

The rise of the knowledge worker, those succeeding the industrial worker, began fifty years ago with roots in the GI bill, the "Management Revolution," and the rise of the services sector. Since 1950, employment in the manufacturing sector has fallen from nearly 40 percent of total employment to less than 18 percent currently, while service sector employment has risen from less than 14 percent to more than 35 percent, essentially flip-flopping from where it had been in 1950.

During this period, demands for an educated workforce grew. Increased competition from abroad, and particularly from emerging economic regions, has resulted in continued substitution in the manufacturing sector away from workers and toward technology, increasing the productivity of remaining workers. Domestically, the service sector has attracted the more highly skilled workers away from the manufacturing sector. Lower-skilled factory jobs have been absorbed by less developed countries.

Today with the emergence of the information age, the strength of a country is based on knowledge. National greatness will arise not from our natural resources or our factories, but from our people—people with new ideas and skills.
— Michael Milken, *Fueling America's Growth, Education, Entrepreneurship and Access to Capital*

Just as gains in manufacturing productivity, greater access to higher education, and an affluent middle-class fueled the transition from a manufacturing to a services-based economy, the extensive adoption of information technology is now creating the need for a highly skilled knowledge-based economy. While service sector job growth has been growing overall, the more technology-intensive industries have experienced the most rapid growth. In fact, traditional services sector employment, retail and wholesale trade, financial services, and leisure services, has experienced slower job growth than the total job market. Knowledge jobs such as IT, health, and business services, on the other hand, are growing three to six times as fast as economy-wide job growth.

The growth of the knowledge workforce heralds the potential for far greater opportunities for today's workers, companies, and the economy. The resulting demand for an educated workforce, however, also presents a sizable challenge for today's workers. With rapid technological advances and the continued proliferation of computers and the numerous applications that are required to be mastered, employers are demanding more from their current and prospective employees.

The challenge to workers, companies, and economies in realizing this practically open-ended economic growth opportunity (where we are limited only by "gray matter," that is, brainpower) is in preparing today's workforce for tomorrow's jobs. Coming generations of workers must accomplish far more in terms of educational attainment, and companies will have to invest heavily in training if "the greatest boom in history" is to become a reality. As a consequence, we believe this dynamic will be accompanied by a significant growth in the knowledge services industry, creating tremendous growth opportunities for investors.

Fast Facts: The New Economy

- The pay gap separating a high school graduate from a college graduate was 50 percent in 1980. Today, it has reached 111 percent. Looked at another way, a thirty-year-old male with a high school diploma earns just two-thirds of what he earned twenty-five years ago. Even so, only 21 percent of American adults over the age of twenty-five have a bachelor's degree or better.
- In 1980, the price-to-book ratio of the ten largest publicly traded companies in the United States was 1.2x. Today, the price-to-book is 12.1x, or ten times greater. This multiple expansion correlates directly with the increased productivity of a company's intangible assets—its human capital.
- On average, each employee at the leading "New Economy" companies is "worth" $38 million based on market cap-per-employee. In contrast, each employee at the leading "Old Economy" companies is worth about $689,000, or less than 2 percent of employee value at the New Economy companies.
- Venture capital funding in knowledge enterprises amounted to over $3 billion since January 1999, or about triple the total invested in the previous nine years.

- At the end of 1999, more than 196 million people were using the Internet worldwide. The number of global Internet users is expected to more than triple to 638 million by 2004, a 27 percent CAGR.
- The "free agent" mindset of today's knowledge worker is evidenced by the fact that the average person entering the workforce today will work for between eight and ten different employers versus four to six a decade ago. Only 15,000 businesses currently recruit online, but this figure is expected to increase to 124,000 by 2003.
- Worldwide, the Internet economy is expected to mushroom from $361 billion in 1998 to more than $2.8 trillion in 2003.
- In 1999, nearly 720,000 IT positions went unfilled. Today, one of every five IT jobs remains unfilled, and nearly 75 percent of new openings fail to receive interested and qualified candidates.
- Worldwide business-to-business (B2B) commerce dwarfs B2C commerce in both size and growth. Total B2B Internet revenue is expected to top $2 trillion in 2004, up from $80 billion in 1999, a 91 percent CAGR.
- Firms are stepping up their e-commerce outsourcing initiatives as they move from building stand-alone sites to Internet-enabled supply chains and customer service systems. The result is a rising median outsourcing budget, from $750,000 in 1999 to a projected $1.5 million in 2001.
- The amount spent on online advertising is expected to increase tenfold from $3.3 billion in 1999 to $33 billion in 2004, a 58 percent CAGR.
- At the end of 1998 there were approximately eighty-eight Internet stocks. Currently, there are approximately four hundred with nearly a half trillion dollars of market cap.
- Approximately 50 percent of the total Internet market cap is accounted for by the five largest Internet companies, providing evidence for the belief that, on the Internet, the winners "take all."
- Studies show that effective management of human capital can improve shareholder value by up to 30 percent.
- By our estimates, the e-knowledge market will reach $53.3 billion by 2003 from $9.4 billion in 1999, growing at a CAGR of 54 percent.
- Reflecting the transformation of technology in our economy, in 2000, skilled jobs will represent 65 percent of all jobs. This is expected to expand to 85 percent by 2005, up from just 20 percent in 1950.
- Knowledge Services—education and corporate learning for the new economy—is a $885 billion industry in the United States and a $2 trillion industry globally.
- Web-based corporate learning should enjoy explosive growth, measuring $11.4 billion by 2003, up from $550 million in 1998, an 83 percent CAGR.
- By 2002, technology-based training will capture the majority of dollars for IT training, at 55 percent versus the 45 percent share captured by instructor-led methods.

- In 1996, 44 percent of higher-ed students were adults over twenty-four, up from 28 percent in 1970.
- The ratio of students to computers in our nation's K–12 schools is rapidly improving, falling from 16 to 1 in 1992 to approximately 6 to 1 in 1999.
- Nearly every K–12 school in the country (96 percent) has at least one Internet-linked computer. To date, 51 percent of classrooms have Internet-connected computers.
- The number of K–12 students with Internet access has grown from virtually zero in 1994 to ten million in 1996 and is projected to grow to forty million by 2002.
- Forty-seven percent of sixteen- to twenty-two-year-olds are on the Web and control $37 billion in spending. Forty percent have bought and paid for something online. By 2003, 62 percent of sixteen- to twenty-two-year-olds will be on the Web.
- The domestic broadband market will expand to 2.3 million homes this year, up 200 percent from approximately 750,000 in 1998. By 2004, we expect broadband to reach 48 percent of Internet users, or 30 million households.

The Long Boom: Boom Fatigue

JON GORDON

You'd be hard-pressed to argue that the current economic boom is a bad thing. But it has a downside. We're working harder, seeing our families less, and coping with busier airports, freeways, and retail stores. One researcher has given a name to the stress that good economic times can produce: "boom fatigue." That fatigue is evident in the epicenter of the boom, San Francisco and Silicon Valley.

In a recent study, Rutgers University Professor Carl Van Horn looks at how American workers feel about the economic expansion. Van Horn conducts the survey every year, and for two years running he's found that even though Americans are generally glad for the economic boom, they're increasingly dissatisfied with their jobs and their lives.

"When you look at the surface, it's the most positive economic situation you can imagine," Van Horn says. "When you dig a little deeper, you realize there are problems—problems in terms of people feeling pressure and stress."

There's certainly lots of pressure and stress in the Silicon Valley housing market, where the technology-led boom is driving home prices to astronomical levels. On a recent Saturday, a guitar-playing duo called "Los Compadres" entertained a crowd of about one hundred near downtown Campbell, a well-to-do Silicon Valley city nestled at the foot of the Santa Cruz Mountains. People gathered to hoot and holler about the rarest of commodities: two affordable houses; brand new four-bedroom, two-bath houses selling for $110,000 each. The lucky buyers are getting the homes from Habitat for Humanity, a charity that usually sells houses to the poor for about $45,000.

But this is Santa Clara County, where the median price of housing is pushing $500,000 dollars. The buyers have good jobs and make enough money to live comfortably in the Twin Cities and many other places. But middle-class income just doesn't cut it in the Bay Area.

Theresa Jackson is buying one of these subsidized houses. She's an accountant with three young daughters. Jackson says until she started working with Habitat for Humanity, the overheated housing market—a product of Silicon Valley's economic boom—had worn her down. "I've gone to mortgage companies and have been laughed at, told 'no way,'" she says. "For a person in my position, it is impossible in this area. I have a lot of friends who are commuting

Transcript, "Marketplace Radio," Public Radio International, 2000. Reprinted with permission of Minnesota Public Radio. Jon Gordon is a correspondent for Marketplace Radio and host of the network's program "Future Tense."

in from Tracy and places real far away, taking two or three hours one way just so they can afford a house. But for us it would have been impossible, especially for a single parent needing to be close to school."

In Palo Alto, about twenty miles from Theresa Jackson's new house, Web designer Ann Bradley is desperately looking for a modest apartment to share with her teenage son. She's grown tired of going to open houses where more than one hundred apartment-seekers compete for the right to rent a room in a house for $1,500 a month. So just the other day she placed a unique ad in the *Palo Alto Daily News.*

> Will trade domain name "thiswiredhouse.com" or "etakeout.com" for Palo Alto living situation. That's right; my dotcom address for your street address.

"I saw an ad for a place for $995 dollars a month," Bradley recalls. "It was a room in a house, it had a small kitchen and half a bath. And half a bath is just not acceptable at $995 a month. You have to have a place to take a shower."

No one has taken Bradley up on her offer so far. Higher prices for apartments and houses are just one of the expansion-related phenomena that causes stress.

Denise Sullivan, a third-generation San Franciscan, says the boom has transformed her city for the worse. Over coffee in a Mission District café, Sullivan laments that San Francisco now aggravates her. "I don't like to go out as much anymore," she says. "I certainly don't consider going to a movie on a Friday or a Saturday. There's no way I would do that. Everything is too crowded."

Five years ago, before the dot-comification of San Francisco, it was a mellower scene. "It was a friendly place to live and work," Sullivan recalls. "It wasn't about survival, it wasn't about being the first person when you see that vacancy for that apartment and then bidding over the asking price for the apartment. People are willing to pay more rent than advertised."

"This all contributes to the difficulty people report in balancing work and family, because when they leave work, it's harder to get home at night, it's harder to get to work in the morning," says researcher Carl Van Horn. "So what they are looking for is, how do I achieve a better balance?"

Van Horn says many people are tired of the expansion, but not so weary they wish for the opposite: recession. "Overall Americans are satisfied with their jobs and they're very happy with the current state of the economy. They want to see it continue. But they're saying OK, with this new economy, how do we come up with a better way to achieve positive economic growth without driving us into the ground?"

Van Horn says the boom-fatigued would benefit from more flexible work schedules and widespread telecommuting. He says people would feel better about their jobs and home life if they could be off the roads at busy times and with their families more often. What people are seeking, he says, is a better balance between work and their personal lives—something that's often missing in this long boom.

Twelve Learning Interventions That Combat Technophobia

LINDA RISTOW PUETZ

Are you ready to sustain technology's eager adopters, nurture its resisters, and encourage the prove-its? Here are twelve workplace interventions that can help.

If I touch this button, will the computer explode? You've heard that one, right? How about this: A woman calls the help desk with a printer problem. The techie asks her whether she's running it under Windows. The woman responds, "No, my desk is next to the door. But that's a good point. The man sitting next to me is sitting under a window, and his computer is working just fine."

Why do people have difficulty using the technology provided at such great expense by our organizations? Michelle Weil and Larry Rosen, clinical psychologists based in California, have done extensive research over the past fifteen years to explore technology and its effect on people. They describe three distinct technology attitude groups:

Eager adopters love technology. They have the latest cellular phones, big-screen TVs, disc players, and computers. They love tinkering with the newest and most modern technologies available and will spend hours experimenting with new tricks and methods.

Resisters don't like technology; it's intimidating. They feel awkward, overwhelmed, scared, and angry when forced to deal with it.

Prove-its sit on the sidelines, not actively resisting technology but waiting to be shown how it can make their lives easier.

Studies show that a consistent 10 to 15 percent of people are eager adopters, 50 to 60 percent are hesitant prove-its, and 30 to 40 percent are resisters. That means 85 to 90 percent of an organization's employees may be uncomfortable with new technology and are technophobic, to some degree.

According to Weil, "This wouldn't be so bad if we could opt out [of new technology], but people don't have much of a choice anymore. All of a sudden you have to weigh your own fruit on the digital scale and buy gasoline at the pump with electronic fund transfers. And, there's voice mail. It's an indication of how little choice we have now. Technology isn't going away."

American Society for Training and Development (ASTD), *Learning Circuits* (learningcircuits.org), March 2000. Reprinted with permission of ASTD and Learning Circuits. Linda Ristow Puetz is a continuing education consultant and facilitator at Children's Mercy Hospital in Kansas City, Missouri. She also has fifteen years' experience as a neonatal and pediatric critical care nurse.

So how can we sustain the eager adopters, nurture the resisters, and encourage the prove-its when technological changes occur in the workplace? Here are some effective training interventions.

1. Assess the attitudes of end users, then place them in appropriate learning groups. Split the group into hesitant prove-its, diehard resisters, and eager adopters. Each group has its own special learning needs and effective approaches. Keeping everyone together in one group often causes eager adapters to become bored if gradual instruction is geared toward resisters; resisters may tremble watching the eager adopters race through the technology if instruction is rapid. Remember to personalize the introduction of technology.
2. Learn new technology from someone who's skilled in using it and can explain it without jargon. Even when instructors understand the technology thoroughly, they may transfer an anxiety to learners. Training should be down-to-earth with no more than one or two concepts presented at a time. It's important to use teaching exercises and concepts that learners will find motivating and interesting.
3. Make sure that technology instruction is hands-on for all users. Technophobia is intensified when an instructor stands in front of a passive learning group and rapidly clicks his or her mouse, selects menus, and whizzes from screen to screen remarking to the group, "See? Isn't this easy?" Users need hands-on time to practice and play with the technology from the start because it reduces anxiety and builds confidence and motivation to learn.
4. New technology is best learned together, using a sequence of skills geared to the new user's knowledge level and attitude. A one-on-one buddy system—pairing a new learner with a knowledgeable (and patient) expert—is very effective, especially with resisters. Some eager adopters can learn new technologies from manuals, but the majority of persons learn much more quickly and effectively when someone is there to help walk and talk them though the new information. Small groups of matched-level learners working with an expert can also progress effectively when the instructor gives individual attention as needed and evaluates each group member's progress.
5. Limit instruction time to what the new user can assimilate and retain. This time frame varies widely depending on the user group's level of expertise and attitude, but almost no one can withstand an eight-hour-long instruction session, even with breaks. You'll find more effective retention and improved learning outcomes with short periods of instruction of no more than two hours. This is especially true when working with resisters.
6. Don't move into new instruction areas until current information is clearly understood and mastered. A slow-paced, unhurried atmosphere will increase learner self-confidence by providing successful experiences—

especially in the early stages. Don't assume that all is well when no one asks questions. Continue to assess new learners frequently and encourage questions. Resisters often feel they're the only ones who don't understand and that mistakes are always their fault, so sharing your own difficult technology experiences and how you successfully problem-solved will often help them.

7. Prior to introducing new technology, staff responsible for its administration should become thoroughly familiar with its use and the organization's implementation process. Prior to implementation, anticipate common questions and have answers ready. Provide detailed troubleshooting instruction to all administrators, help-desk personnel, and on-the-job experts. Expert support help should be available whenever new learners are working with new technology.
8. Have specific instructional needs in mind. Assess ahead of time what users need to know to perform their jobs most effectively, then provide examples that include those needs. Prove-its particularly like this approach because it shows them immediately how learning new technology will help them do their jobs better. If learner anxiety is high, consider easing resisters into learning by using educational games or simple word processing. For example, the Solitaire game found in Windows is an effective mouse-skills instructor. It provides immediate feedback, and moving cards around on a computer screen adds to the fun.
9. Use the identical version of the new user's hardware and software programs for training. Resisters and prove-its may find learning from different software or hardware frustrating and may tune out instruction because they can't make the connection to their own work setup.
10. Whenever possible, hold training onsite at the workers' job location. If that isn't possible, the next best option is to hold instruction in a well-designed technology center within the organization. If you've exhausted available internal learning options, consider external vendor classes and seminars.
11. Create and maintain easy access to an expert user after training. The ideal situation is to have an expert close at hand in every work area to handle questions. On-the-job expert help demonstrates organizational commitment to the new technology.
12. Employers need to value the technology and the people expected to use it. Because 85 to 90 percent of employees may have reservations about any new technology, it's important to ensure that it will be successfully integrated into every part of the organization. According to Michelle Weil, "If employers don't take into consideration that there will be company resisters and technophobes for whom they have done nothing to help, then they're going to suffer reduced worker productivity, lower job satisfaction, their profits and their efficiency are going to decrease companywise, and there will be more mistakes and errors with higher employee absenteeism."

Taking care to recognize and implement different training interventions for different worker attitudes and expertise levels better ensures desired outcomes: improved productivity, cost savings, and job satisfaction. By reducing workplace technophobia, you'll be well on your way to more effective technology implementation and use. And, you'll be doing your part to reduce those "exploding computer key" fears.

For Further Information

R. Heverly, "Training Helps Employees Overcome 'Technophobia,'" *Capital District Business Review: Focus, Office Quarterly.*

M. Marquardt and G. Kearsley, *Technology-Based Learning: Maximizing Human Performance and Corporate Success.* ASTD Press.

J. Shreve, "Overcoming Fear, Loathing of Computers," *San Francisco Examiner.*

E-Business 2.0

The Real Transformation Begins

JOHN THOMPSON

I'd like to pass on a few observations and some real-world examples that you can apply to your information technology plans going forward. I'll focus on three things. First, the technology advances you can expect over the next five to ten years. Second, how these advances are going to affect e-business and the institutions that you represent. Third, what you need to consider as you build your applications and infrastructure.

Let me start with technology advances. There's been a lot written about Moore's Law, which you know is the ability to continue to improve the price/performance of computing by a factor of two about every eighteen months, done by shrinking the size of silicon and transistors. Recently, a school of thought has developed that perhaps Moore's Law no longer holds true, that the shrinking may slow down as we go through future technological change.

I don't believe that for a minute. We clearly have some challenges ahead, but I think that you will see today's rates of price/performance continue to improve, at least for the next ten years at the systems level. And that's because it's really about more than just the silicon itself.

I would say that about 70 percent of the potential we have for overall systems-level improvements come from things like new circuit designs, architectural improvements, better packaging, faster subsystems, more efficient multi-processing, new compilers, and better-tuned operating systems and middleware.

Let me give you a few examples of things you're likely to see when you package all these technologies together to create computers.

At one end of the scale, today's best laptops, which run at about .8 giga-flops today, will grow to about 10 giga-flops by the end of the decade. That's serious power—plenty for handwriting recognition, audio capture and speech, full language translation, and 3D graphics. They'll probably also be able to run off batteries for a year. And depending on the power needed, they will fit into many form factors, from pens to wearable computers to many kinds of handheld or embedded devices.

At the other end of the scale, we have massively parallel supercomputers. These will reach somewhere on the order of a peta-flop, or a million giga-flops,

Speech presented at the Intel E-XCHANGE Industry Show, 2000. Reprinted with permission of Vital Speeches of the Day and IBM. John Thompson is the vice-chairman of the board of directors for IBM.

by 2005 or 2006. To put that into perspective, it moves us close to the processing power of the human brain. Now these machines aren't going to be able to think. I don't want to suggest that. But they do approximate human levels in terms of raw operations processed per second. We've come a long way. A few years ago we created something called "Deep Blue" to play Kasparov in chess. It had the operational speed of a lizard's brain.

Right now, Intel and IBM are building something called the ASCI systems, which are being installed at the U.S. Department of Energy. They're up to about the level of a mouse's brain in operations. And at our place, we've got something on the drawing boards called "Blue Gene." It will help the study of the human genome and, more important, how proteins fold. This is the kind of system that will have more humanlike speeds in terms of processing by around 2005.

Somewhere between these two poles—laptops and massively parallel supercomputers—come Web servers. The best way to put this in perspective is to talk a little bit about size and price/performance.

First of all, servers are going to shrink. The University of Massachusetts has already produced some experimental Web servers that are about the size of a match head. In fact, when I walk around the halls of our labs these days there are people muttering about "smart dust." I don't know exactly what that is, but suffice it to say that processors are going to get very, very small.

On the price front, if you apply Moore's Law, a server that costs around $30,000 today will probably be built for a few hundred dollars by 2010. That's assuming, of course, that servers process the same programs that they process today. And given the price economics, it's not surprising that all the computer companies are working overtime to figure out all kinds of exotic things to fill up this newfound capacity.

Storage. The price/performance of storage devices is generally driven by improvements in areal density magnetics. This is the number of bits that you can store in a square inch. Historically, this rate has been improving at about 60 percent a year. And like silicon, there still are a few hills to climb. But at this point, IBM's labs are predicting that areal densities can improve by about a hundred times. In other words, we're going to see this 60 percent growth in price/performance continue over the next ten years.

Size will also be greatly affected. Take the Microdrive. It's the size of a book of matches, and it already holds a gigabyte of information and will continue to grow in the years ahead. We know how to extend that technology. Imagine some of the possibilities in consumer products. In a digital camera, for instance, the Microdrive can hold over a thousand high-resolution photographs. As the density goes up, that could easily rise by an order of magnitude.

Bandwidth and connectivity. It takes about one megabit per second to stream good quality video to a single person. Over the last ten years we've seen enough fiber and multiplexing capability installed in the telecom backbone to stream real-time video to every man, woman, and child in North America—simultaneously.

This doesn't include the "last mile." But we're seeing a rapid roll out now of cable, satellite, and DSL connections for the linkage between this backbone and digital broadband into the house and office. That means that at least 70 percent, maybe even closer to 100 percent, of all organizations in the United States will have access to that capability by the end of next year.

Wireless. Today, most of the wireless data connectivity is what we call "second generation." It runs at about ten kilobits—pretty slow. That's roughly equivalent to the old 9600-baud modems. "Third-generation" wireless starts at about 50 kilobits to 100 kilobits. That's more like today's 56KB modems. That service is available today in Japan over something called iMode and is in the process of being rolled out in the United States. You'll probably see it available by the end of 2003.

This same third-generation technology will ramp up to one or two megabits, which will allow for full video streaming over wireless in the next few years. By the way, Japan is doing trials on this as we speak. By 2007, we should see the "fourth generation." It will support about ten megabits per second over wireless and will allow full multichannel video streaming.

All of this technology is, of course, only interesting in terms of the applications and solutions that it enables. Many of the characteristics of the new computing environment are going to grow out of these technologies. Let me go through a couple of them.

First, connectivity through the Internet will become pervasive. One of the biggest drivers will be wireless devices. They will far outnumber today's connection of personal computers and servers. This, in turn, will lead to an unprecedented volume of transactions, all based on Internet technologies.

Second, rich media and content. They will bring real-time collaboration capabilities and knowledge transfer. The amount of data digitized here is going to absolutely explode. Why? Because of the volume of all these transactions and devices that are producing information. And also because of the availability of cheap storage.

All this, together with the availability of very high processing performance, is leading to what we at IBM call "Deep Computing." This entails all sorts of new modeling, grand challenge problems, data mining, and new management tools that can be used to create competitive advantage.

Enough about technology. How will these advances affect e-business? We are entering a new phase of e-business. If this were a software release, we'd probably call it something like e-Business 2.0.

e-Business 2.0 is going to fundamentally change business processes. Think of it this way. A few years ago, we started out with simple Web publishing. That grew reasonably quickly into islands of Web applications. For example, we saw a lot of stand-alone sites for e-commerce and procurement. And these all tended to be single applications that were dedicated to a specific part of the business. They weren't integrated into the rest of the organization's business processes.

Today the emphasis has shifted to application integration—the integration of all of these e-business applications into related processes. Take procurement, supply-chain optimization, and production scheduling and put them together to create a supply-chain management system using e-business techniques. Or, perhaps more broadly, link supply-chain management with e-commerce and customer relationship management and create an end-to-end business process.

This kind of integration is having a tremendous impact on bottom lines because we are collapsing cycle times and eliminating a lot of process steps as we do it. But it is still integration, because it doesn't really change or create whole new ways of doing things.

The next phase will entail fundamental business model innovation. We are creating some entirely new business models and, beyond that, entirely new industry models. This is what I really mean by e-Business 2.0. It's about creating business processes without technological or organizational boundaries. The Internet affords us that.

This capability, in turn, is leading to a virtual enterprise model where organizations can begin to outsource components of their business processes to others who can do that particular component better. We're already seeing this model throughout the financial industry. We'll often see a single company, like a discount broker, offering its clients full banking services through a portal. And that portal links, in turn, to a mortgage company, insurance company, full banking service, mutual funds. And yet the customer that's doing business there sees all of this as a single brand, because the linkages are transparent.

E-markets are another good example of virtual organizations. They're happening more at an industry level than at a single company level.

Another characteristic of the next phase of e-business will be the advent of expert organizations. These organizations will transform vast amounts of collected information and turn it into business intelligence that will help organizations run their businesses more effectively. They will also keep track of individual skills and the knowledge of their people. Through real-time collaboration, they will bring the right expertise to bear to meet specific customer needs.

Let me give you two examples of leading-edge work that we're doing with customers—with virtual enterprises and expert organizations.

In an effort to support its small and medium businesses, the state of Pennsylvania asked us to help them prototype a virtual industrial park. It works something like this. A buyer can submit an electronic RFQ for a finished product to a Web site. The site matches the request with vendors that can provide different parts of the solution. A virtual consortium is created from the best responses from these individual companies, and the RFQ is answered.

The initial prototype that we're working on is being constructed for the powdered metal industry, which happens to be very important to Pennsylvania and to the automotive companies. In the area of knowledge management, St. Paul Reinsurance has an interesting project under way that will turn them into an expert organization.

In the first phase, which is working now, they are using Lotus' Discovery Server to automatically analyze e-mails, scanned documents, internal and external Web sites, and databases. The system categorizes and indexes all this information so that it can be linked together to satisfy an employee's search for information.

The information is accessed through a new Lotus technology called K-Station, which lets them set up instant "knowledge windows" to support a community of workers. For instance, if a hurricane were to occur, an instant portal can be created that tracks the weather, written reports, spreadsheets estimating damages, and databases of insured properties—all in real time. In the next phase of the project they will add skill profiles of employees to the system, so that they can locate specific expertise when needed.

We've talked about the new technology landscape and how e-business is changing as a result. As we move forward, I think there are some important factors to bear in mind as you build new applications and the infrastructure to support them.

The first is that the networked world will become pervasive. Everyone and everything will be connected. By 2003 wireless devices—handheld and embedded—will represent two-thirds of all Internet access devices. That means about 700 million PCs will share the Net with two billion other networked devices.

Now think about this. Today more than 80 percent of all computing applications are designed for PCs. So the race is on. The ability to access your applications from pervasive devices is going to be a huge competitive advantage.

I know at least one CEO who has figured this one out. The CEO of TD Waterhouse, one of the largest discount brokers, told me last month that his company is planning for 70 percent of all stock trades to be placed from digital wireless phones or PDAs. Today, they're very busy redesigning their systems.

Here is another good example. SwissAir is prototyping a system to recognize registered frequent flyers when they walk into the airport with their digital phones turned on. The server, which interfaces with all of the airline's other systems, checks the traveler in, can do seat selection, and provides them with the latest gate and departure information, all over the phone. Applications like these will put tremendous demand on infrastructure.

Now, I never thought I'd say that infrastructure is sexy, but these days it is. And that means you need to think about whether or not your infrastructure is sexy. Is it designed to handle the explosive growth in volumes of transactions? The proliferation of devices?

To put this in perspective, our Web site for the Atlanta Olympic games four years ago handled 187 million hits. Two years ago at Nagano the number grew to 634 million. Two weeks ago we finished up at Sydney with 11.3 billion hits during the games. That's a 1,700 percent increase.

And while the absolute scale may not apply to many of you, the trend probably does. There are a few other things worth thinking about when it comes to your infrastructure. The network itself is becoming far more intelligent. In addition to containing switches and routers, there are now specialized servers and software for tasks like caching, directory, and security. You can take advantage of these by using dedicated appliance servers or by buying these functions from a service provider.

The second factor is that as you scale Web servers to handle the huge growth in transactions you can gain a lot of flexibility and capacity by constructing your topology in a layered way that puts the right capability in the right place and provides optimal response times. It also helps to segregate serious hi-speed data and transaction processing into secure, back-end servers.

The third factor is that you won't have to put all the infrastructure together yourself. That's because of a third factor we call e-sourcing. It's a whole lot more than simple outsourcing. For some time now a number of organizations have outsourced technology, usually their data centers and sometimes their entire IT shops. This is most often a binary decision. But the Internet's connectivity has made it possible to take a far more granular approach. As a result, we have seen the rise of more specialized e-sourcing like Web hosting and application processing through ASPs. But that's really just the beginning. There is a whole new class of infrastructure services that are being offered as utilities over the Internet. If you need improved network security, consider e-sourcing it. If you need to enhance Web performance, e-source to a caching service. If you need more disk capacity, e-source it from a storage utility. With time and skills being at such a premium, I think we're going to see a lot of this.

The fourth factor is open standards. The future is about being able to interconnect everything—devices, infrastructure, applications, and business processes. Pervasive devices are heterogeneous and depend on open standards. Network and server infrastructures need real cross-platform connectivity, not just simple gateways to interconnect Windows, Linux, and mainframe systems. Application and business process integration and e-sourcing all depend on XML and new emerging e-commerce standards. And like the Internet itself, none of this interconnectivity is possible without adopting open standards.

The final factor I'd like to mention is the importance of middleware—middleware that embraces open standards. I'm talking about database technology, Web transaction software, system management, enterprise integration and application development tools. One reason this is important is that middleware is the carrier of most of the open standards and is where they are implemented. Another reason is that the right middleware is cross platform and provides a common base for applications to run on multiple operating systems. That's why picking the right middleware is more important than picking an operating system.

Let me close with one final story, which illustrates some of the factors that I talked about. The Sydney Olympics was a monumental undertaking because we had to build the equivalent of an entire IT system for a Fortune 500 company in a little over a year's time. For starters, we deployed over 7,300 IBM PCs and

600 servers in thirty-nine locations, all attached to scoreboards, timers, pervasive devices, and the media and real-time Web feeds.

The application code totaled thirteen million lines, all to capture the myriad sporting rules and to manage results for three hundred individual events. We accredited, provided accommodations for, and tracked information on 260,000 members of the Olympic Family. That's analogous to hiring, maintaining, and releasing 260,000 employees in just over a four-week period. It was a big job.

An Intranet for the Olympic Family was created and handled more than a million daily inquiries. Then there was the official Web site, the one that handled the 11.3 billion hits. And an e-commerce site that automated all the ticketing and merchandising sales.

All of this was designed to interface with pervasive devices through open standards. Having the right infrastructure in place left us prepared for the unexpected. Take the women's marathon. The runners had radio chips in their shoe laces that allowed us to track their progress in real time. One of the leaders decided to take her shoes off and run in her bare feet, which really puzzled us for a while when she just stopped moving in the system. We were able to recover by updating her progress from a digital cellular phone on the course.

We managed system performance for the entire Olympics by layering the infrastructures. All of the information from the venues was layered into three groups of servers to ensure that the data and the transactions were kept at the right point in the system to optimize the performance. Information at the sites was handed off between three layers of servers to ensure that the right capabilities were in the right place. We used open standards and a lot of Java, not only to support the pervasive devices but for everything that might need to be changed at the last moment. For instance, all the programming that described the rules and scoring for each event had to be flexible because the sporting federations changed rules right up to the night before a competition.

Finally, we took full advantage of middleware. Most of the systems had to be developed independently, but we were able to integrate and synchronize them through the use of our MQSeries software. We used a common DB2 database and common WebSphere software on all of the platforms—Intel, RISC, and mainframe—that greatly eased data replication and integration.

By the way, I forgot to mention that in our free time at the Olympics we also hosted the NBC Web site—yet another interesting case of e-sourcing.

Well, we've covered a lot of territory—the relentless progress of technology, the transformation of enterprises and industries, the factors affecting every major IT decision you face. It all points to one inescapable conclusion: the last five years were nothing but a preamble. The true e-business revolution is just beginning.

Rig de Rigueur: Eighteen Wheels and a Laptop

ROBERT STRAUSS

A few years ago, Scott Barnes was a computer novice, not knowing a laptop from a lapdog. He is a long-haul independent truck driver, and the technological revolution was being fought far from the cab of his big rig.

But here was Mr. Barnes tap-tap-tapping away at the Cyber Stop at the Petro Truck Plaza in this central New Jersey crossroads. "You had better not be scared of computers any more if you drive a truck for a living," he said. "It's how you communicate, how you find your next load, how you do your accounts, how other people find you."

While Mr. Barnes used computers at the truck stop to send e-mail messages to his family and to some clients, his primary destinations in cyberspace are what are known in the trucking business as loadboards. These are Web sites where shippers and brokers post freight, in either full or partial truckloads, in hope of getting truck drivers to deliver the loads.

The Internet is transforming the truck stop into a wired communications hub. For example, the Cyber Stop has five computer workstations open twenty-four hours and a computer-trained attendant. The truck stop also sells computer equipment and cell phones.

On this day, Mr. Barnes was surfing Web sites, looking for freight that his truck could carry back to his home in Barton, Florida.

"Right now, I could find something, but they don't seem to be paying enough," he said, scanning a few offers on Getloaded.com, one of about a dozen online loadboards. "But this is still better than making phone calls and crossing your fingers that one would work out."

The amount of goods being moved through the sites is relatively small in the overall scheme of things, with many of the shipments from occasional shippers.

The granddaddy of loadboard purveyors is DAT Services, founded twenty-two years ago as Dial-A-Truck by Al Jubitz, a truck stop owner in Portland, Oregon. The trucking industry had been deregulated in the 1970s, encouraging independent truck drivers and small companies to find extra loads rather than returning empty.

Mr. Jubitz noticed drivers hanging around his stop after the usual meal and shower, hoping to find a load. So he decided to start signing up brokers and shippers who needed freight hauled from Portland. He listed the loads on a monitor at his truck stop and charged the drivers a nominal fee to get the phone

New York Times, December 13, 2000. Reprinted with permission of the *New York Times*. Robert Strauss is a staff writer for the *New York Times*.

number of the company wanting to move the freight. By the 1980s, DAT monitors could be found in hundreds of truck stops around the country, with 17,000 truck drivers and shippers subscribing.

"DAT is still the Microsoft of our industry," said Ken Hammond, the vice president for marketing for Getloaded.com, founded two years ago in Richmond, Virginia. "But the Internet is changing things—the monitor was, in effect, a monopoly. The Internet has allowed us to cut into that."

DAT, while keeping its television monitors in place, has edged onto the Internet. It hopes to leverage that seventeen-thousand-subscription base into an online service called DAT Conexus (www.datconexus.com). The new service not only finds loads for truckers to haul, it also lists drivers and companies with extra rigs for use or rental.

DAT makes money from subscriber fees from truckers, freight brokers and shippers. Subscription prices vary depending on use and the size of the company. DAT also earns some revenue from online advertising for trucking supplies and used equipment.

Getloaded.com, on the other hand, charges truckers thirty-five dollars a month for unlimited use of the Web loadboards, but shippers and brokers can list loads free.

"If a shipper can get on our boards for free and has to pay someone else, who do you think they will go to?" Mr. Hammond said. "In any case, we needed to develop a big database, and this is the way to do it. We couldn't have challenged DAT when it was the monitor loadboards, but with the Internet, the overhead just isn't there anymore."

Mr. Hammond said Getloaded.com started making money this year, with sixteen thousand drivers or trucking companies subscribing for at least one month through the end of the year. But he said that he thought only a few companies would survive in the Internet load-matching market.

In any case, said Randy Garber, vice president for operation services practice at the consulting company A. T. Kearney, the business seems more of a niche market than one that will take over the trucking industry.

"The hangup is that trucking is still a relationship business," Mr. Garber said. "As much as the layperson may think of these things as commodities, if I am a shipper, I'll be damned if I want the last piece in the supply chain to my customer to be handled by any Joe Blow. A small part of my business? Perhaps. Some internal freight? Yes. But I don't think Wal-Mart is going to subcontract its trucking to loadboards any time soon."

Linda Willis, the dispatcher for Admiral Truck Services, a small flatbed-trucking company in Waller, Texas, near Houston, said that Internet loadboards like Getloaded.com had been a lifesaver for her company.

"We get loads out, but not many coming back, and they can be to different places all the time," she said. "Fresno one day, Denver the next. Now I can get on the computer and find my guys a load back home instead of them just waiting and waiting around a truck stop."

Efforts have been made to use similar services with ocean and air shipping, Mr. Garber said, but they have not fared well, in part because those industries are more centralized. Getloaded.com's Mr. Hammond sees an advantage for smaller companies like his in the fragmentation of the trucking industry, especially as independent operators get more computer savvy.

Bob Johnson, an independent driver from Bangor, Maine, was in the Bordentown Petro Cyber Stop with his laptop, which he uses to keep accounts and send e-mail messages home. Mr. Johnson said he had used DAT from time to time but was a bit skeptical.

"Seems people use them out of desperation," he said. "The only way to stay afloat is to have steady business." But he noted: "There are the times I am in Alabama, and I want to get home and I need a load. Now that I have my laptop, I'd at least be more inclined to use it to get that load. It may not be the thing that saves the trucking industry, but at least it gets a few more loads moved, and that can't be all bad."

A Vision of E-Learning for America's Workforce

THE COMMISSION ON TECHNOLOGY AND ADULT LEARNING, AMERICAN SOCIETY FOR TRAINING AND DEVELOPMENT / NATIONAL GOVERNORS ASSOCIATION CENTER FOR BEST PRACTICES

Recent technological advances have laid the foundation for a learning revolution that will clearly take place in the years ahead. The Commission on Technology and Adult Learning believes that e-learning will play a vitally important role in equipping workers with the skills they need to succeed in the twenty-first-century digital economy.

What Is E-Learning?

E-learning can be defined as instructional content or learning experiences delivered or enabled by electronic technology. The Commission on Technology and Adult Learning has focused its attention on adult-centered and work-related e-learning—that is, technology-enabled learning designed to increase workers' knowledge and skills so they can be more productive, find and keep high-quality jobs, advance in their careers, and have a positive impact on the success of their employers, their families, and their communities.

E-learning has the potential to revolutionize the basic tenets of learning by making it individual- rather than institution-based, eliminating clock-hour measures in favor of performance and outcome measures, and emphasizing customized learning solutions over generic, one-size-fits-all instruction. It is this transformational potential of e-learning that the commission believes America must recognize and embrace in the years ahead.

Making the Case for E-Learning

The economic case for building a successful e-learning future hinges in part on the efficiency of e-learning and its role in shortening the amount of time it takes

Excerpted from a report of the Commission on Technology and Adult Learning, American Society for Training and Development (ASTD)/National Governors Association (NGA) Center for Best Practices, June 2001. Reprinted with the permission of ASTD/NGA Center for Best Practices.

to get workers up to speed on new products and processes. Improvements in the quality of education and training are an equally important economic benefit of e-learning, which offers potentially universal access to best-in-class learning content, as well as a wide variety of content available anywhere in the world. E-learning also holds enormous potential as a tool for reducing the costs of workplace-related education and training.

Economic reasons, however, are not the only justification for aggressively supporting e-learning. At a time when many Americans express concern about growing economic disparities among different segments of the population, e-learning holds the potential to broaden access to high-quality education and training opportunities and, in turn, boost income growth at all levels.

A Vision of America's E-Learning Future

The Commission on Technology and Adult Learning foresees a future in which e-learning allows learning to become a continuous process of inquiry and improvement that keeps pace with the speed of change in business and society. With e-learning, the learner has convenient, just-in-time access to needed knowledge and information, with small content objects assembled and delivered according to the learner's specific needs.

The commission foresees increased reliance on new means of assessing and certifying learning results that emphasize individual skills and knowledge rather than courses taken or credit hours earned. We also see the continued rise of an e-learning market based on common technical standards, "open design," and the widespread sharing of information across states and sectors about successful and innovative approaches.

This vision of e-learning is evolving at a fast pace. By acting together now, government, business, and education have the opportunity to shape America's e-learning future.

Technology and the Learning Revolution

The twenty-first-century economy places a premium on innovation, customization, new business models, and new ways of organizing work. In order to succeed—and even survive—in this new environment, individuals and organizations must continually acquire new skills and new ways of managing knowledge and information. Just as technology is driving many of the revolutionary changes that are occurring in the world of work, it also holds the potential of helping people and organizations keep pace with change. Technology—and, more specifically, e-learning—opens the door to a learning revolution that could help to create unprecedented opportunity, productivity, and prosperity in the years ahead.

What Is E-Learning?

E-learning can be defined as instructional content or learning experiences delivered or enabled by electronic technology. Functionally, e-learning can include a wide variety of learning strategies and technologies, from CD-ROMs and computer-based instruction to videoconferencing, satellite-delivered learning, and virtual educational networks. In other words, it is not just Web-based instruction or distance learning but also the many ways in which individuals exchange information and gain knowledge.

For the purposes of this report, e-learning is adult centered and work related. More broadly, it is technology-enabled learning that is designed to increase workers' knowledge and skills so they can be more productive, find and keep high-quality jobs, advance in their careers, and have a positive impact on the success of their employers, their families, and their communities.

The E-Learning Universe

Distance learning
CD-ROMs
Videoconferencing
Computer-based instruction
Satellite downlinks
Interactive TV lectures
Computerized diagnostic assessment and evaluation
Competency certification
Electronic portfolios
Virtual educational networks
Corporate universities
Communities of learners
Group- and project-based learning technologies

Why Should Governors and CEOs Care?

Governors and CEOs should care about e-learning because of the very real and quantifiable benefits it can deliver for individuals, organizations, and society as a whole. E-learning has the potential to play a critical role in equipping workers with the skills they need to succeed in the digital economy—and, in turn, boost economic competitiveness and growth.

Today's job market places a premium on higher levels of skills and knowledge. Eighty-five percent of new jobs require education beyond high school, up from 65 percent in 1991. And yet, employers across the country are having trouble finding the highly educated, highly skilled workers they need. A recent American Management Association survey found that nearly four out of every ten job applicants tested for basic skills by U.S. corporations in 1999 lacked the necessary reading, writing, and math skills to do the jobs they sought.

E-learning has the potential to help reduce the skills gap that continues to stand in the way of individual and organizational success. And, by promoting speed, accessibility, and an environment for continuous learning, e-learning can help workers keep pace with today's rapidly changing business and work environments.

As strong as the potential of e-learning is, it is neither a quick nor an easy fix for longtime educational and societal problems. Ensuring the quality of e-learning and developing new content and systems takes time and money. Furthermore, while technology provides new opportunities to make learning a more integral part of Americans' work and lives, technology cannot do this on its own. Reaping the true benefit of e-learning for our citizens, our economy, and our democracy will require changing societal attitudes and broader educational policies and practices that have resisted reform.

What Makes E-Learning Different?

E-learning can emphasize solutions and learning results. A gradual transformation is under way in today's workplaces, one in which "training" is giving way to "learning solutions." This transformation is based on the fact that in an e-learning environment, access to just-in-time information, advice, and performance support is as central to learning as the traditional classroom event was for earlier generations. The e-learning experience is based on the recognition that technology offers the opportunity to integrate learning with work in order to enhance performance in a dynamic, interactive, and measurable way.

E-learning is also learner-focused. Technology can personalize content and anticipate learners' future information and learning needs by recognizing patterns in how people learn. It also can match content with each individual's learning style, experience, and skills. Personal electronic "tutors" can offer different pathways (sound, virtual depictions, alternative explanations) to help learners grasp what was not clear the first time around. And visualization technologies enable instructors and learning content providers to model and present many different kinds of information in dynamic ways that help people learn more rapidly and effectively by doing rather than observing. Flight simulators, for example, allow student pilots to learn to fly in dangerous weather conditions without risk and with the benefit of advice from experienced aviators.

In addition, by creating communities of learners, e-learning can help people share information in both formal and informal ways. It can happen anytime and anywhere. In contrast to traditional forms of work-related learning that require participation in specific courses at specific times and locations, e-learning can take place anytime and anywhere—and from any source. One important benefit is that e-learning allows learning to take place at the work site and in the context of an individual's job responsibilities. This enables learners and organizations to tailor learning to workers' unique needs, interests, and schedules.

At the same time, e-learning's "anytime, anywhere" approach places different responsibilities on the individual learner, who must now be able to find, analyze, integrate, store, and retrieve information in new and more self-directed ways. In an e-learning environment, individuals also must take added responsibility for keeping their skills up to date.

It creates new models for the provision of learning. The demand for greater customization of information and learning, together with technology's role in meeting this demand, increasingly removes the intermediary in transactions between producers of information and the individual user. This can make it easier to reach a larger audience. Technology also can help break down the barriers of space and time and offer unprecedented access to opportunities for information sharing and peer-to-peer learning.

E-learning changes the traditional business model for education, which relies on physical plant, professors and curricula, libraries, and laboratories. One result is that at least some of the core capabilities of postsecondary institutions are likely to be disaggregated and provided by new businesses.

Another consequence of these emerging learning models is that new strategies for promoting and protecting investments in research, writing, and other forms of intellectual property will be required in the more competitive and fluid learning environment of the future. E-learning also creates a need for new and different ways of measuring the quality of learning. New credentials that validate what an individual knows and is able to do are already beginning to challenge traditional certifications based on courses taken and credits earned.

The Case for E-Learning

Building a successful e-learning future should be a priority for both the public and private sectors because doing so can contribute to both economic *and* social progress. One of the most important benefits that can accompany a commitment to e-learning is a large-scale boost in the quality of the learning opportunities available to American workers.

The Economic Case. The economic case for forcefully addressing this issue hinges on the dynamic relationship that links e-learning, the individual learner, and organizational performance. Simply put, people can learn more efficiently through e-learning—in large part because it makes learning more personalized and more accessible. Numerous studies have shown that workers learn faster with multimedia training; they more accurately recall what they learned over a longer period of time; and they are better able to transfer what they learned to actual performance. Enhancing the quality of e-learning so that these benefits are more widely available is thus a vitally important priority for the years ahead.

High-quality e-learning creates an economic advantage for both individuals and organizations by improving speed to capability—or shortening the amount of time it takes to get workers up to speed on new products and processes. As *Fortune Magazine* put it, "Training that used to take 6 to 9 months will be compressed to just 2 to 3 weeks, thus assuring faster time-to-market with products, and greater productivity." This creates a strong economic incentive for the business community to embrace e-learning.

E-learning also offers potentially universal access to best-in-class learning content, as well as a wide variety of content available anywhere in the world. This, in turn, opens doors to dramatic gains in economic performance for individuals and organizations everywhere.

In addition to quality and performance improvements, e-learning holds enormous potential as a tool for reducing the costs of workplace-related education and training. Once the up-front infrastructure and development costs are met, the marginal cost of serving additional students is close to zero. At technology giant Cisco, e-learning programs in manufacturing have resulted in savings of $1 million per quarter thanks to improved processes, as well as an 80 percent increase in speed to competence. Evidence of the economic promise of e-learning comes in the results of a 1999 report by W. R. Hambrecht and Company. Corporate e-learning, according to the report, is one of the fastest growing and most promising markets in the education industry today. "Technology-based training solutions are changing the way corporations deliver training in nearly all segments of the business process," the report states. It continues: "corporations save between 50–70 percent when replacing instructor-led training with electronic content delivery. Opting for e-training also means that courses can be pared into shorter sessions and spread out over several days so that the business would not lose an employee for entire days at a time. Workers can also improve productivity and use their own time more efficiently, as they no longer need to travel or fight rush-hour traffic to get to a class." Once again, however, these benefits will only be available on a wide scale if the public and private sectors engage in good-faith efforts to improve the quality of e-learning.

The Social Case. The social case for e-learning is equally compelling. At a time when many Americans express concern about growing economic disparities among different segments of the population, e-learning holds the potential to broaden access to high-quality education and training opportunities. This, in turn, can boost income growth while nurturing a contributing citizenry.

More than ninety million Americans have low levels of literacy and are therefore unable to meet the needs of the changing workplace, according to the 1999 U.S. Department of Commerce report, *Twenty-first Century Skills for Twenty-first Century Jobs.* E-learning can play a crucial role in bridging skill, education, and income gaps by making high-quality learning experiences more widely available and by tailoring them to individual workers' needs.

Not only will an expanded commitment to e-learning help people obtain and keep jobs, but it also will equip them to meet the needs of their families and communities. E-learning can help to strengthen democracy and community by broadening access to the information people need to improve their lives and the lives of those around them.

E-learning, of course, is not a panacea for America's social and economic challenges. Rather, it can and must be an integral part of a larger system of practices and policies crafted to broaden access to the opportunities our society offers.

Chapter 8

The Changing Face of the Workforce

THE LAST CHAPTER COLLECTS a group of influential pieces regarding the effects of age, immigration, and technology on the workforce and public policy. If the new economy period erased many expectations of the worker-employer compact, the tidal demographic shifts of age and immigration will continue to clear out the last vestiges of lifelong employment and workplace entitlement known to previous generations.

Thomas Stewart's article, "Gray Flannel Suit? Moi?" portrays the ascension of knowledge as the corporate coin of the realm and the pathway to success and power. In "New Opportunities for Older Workers," an excerpt from the Committee for Economic Development's study of the aging workforce, policy recommendations are made regarding older workers. And, in "Finished at Forty," Nina Munk describes the realities and implications of age in the workforce.

Finally, we take a look at technology's implications for immigrant labor. In "The Working Caste," Leah Platt tackles a little-discussed aspect of globalization and immigrant labor—the role of guest or imported workers in many countries, welcomed to fill the need for certain kinds of low-skilled or undesirable labor but given few rights of citizenship. Suzette Brooks Masters and Ted Ruthizer's "The H-1B Straitjacket" marshals a series of arguments in favor of the H-1B visa program, which provides for a large number of overseas technical and professional workers to work in the United States. Finally, "Labor Movement," by Joel Millman and Will Pinkston, provides a surprising and unexpected perspective on immigrant labor in America that raises critical questions in the wake of September 11 and a renewed and intense review of immigration policy in the United States.

Gray Flannel Suit? Moi?

THOMAS STEWART

Yes, *vous*. Ties between employees and companies are looser. But powerful new forces link them together. Smart people—and smart companies—should exploit both continuity and change.

He's gone, right? The man in the gray flannel suit, briefcase in hand, fedora on head, waiting on the platform for the 7:37 to go downtown. Stable, conservative, educated but not too clever, slightly behind his time rather than slightly ahead of it, the Organization Man seems more passe than a Rob Roy before lunch.

Fortune's William H. Whyte, who named Organization Man, described his kind in 1956: "They are all, as they so often put it, in the same boat. Listen to them talk to each other over the front lawns of their suburbia and you cannot help but be struck by how well they grasp the common denominators which bind them . . . They are keenly aware of how much more deeply beholden they are to organization than were their elders. They are wry about it, to be sure; they talk of the 'treadmill,' the 'rat race,' of the inability to control one's direction. But they have no great sense of plight; between themselves and organization they believe they see an ultimate harmony."

The new orthodoxy is that there is no such orthodoxy. There are no implicit contracts and not many explicit ones. No loyalty. No common lot. No harmony of interests, no trust that what's good for General Motors is good for us, personally. No one who can promise anyone a job, except a customer—and customers force us to apply for our jobs again and again; not faithful wives but fickle mistresses, customers daily remind us that they will leave for a younger guy with thicker hair if we don't bring bigger roses at a lower price. And since no one promises us a job, the only promise we make to an employer is to take him for all he's got.

Yet, two full generations after Whyte christened Organization Man, his hold on our collective imagination remains powerful. In the flesh he was anything but memorable; bland was the whole point. But he is vivid in our minds.

We respond to him because he is still us. Organization Man did not die; he morphed. The hat's gone. The briefcase contains a laptop. The 737 is probably a plane at O'Hare, not a train at Winnetka. He underwent a sex change too: In 1956, 85 percent of civilian men were in the labor force, versus only 37 percent of women; by 1997, men's participation rate had fallen to 75 percent, women's

 Thomas A. Stewart is editorial director of *Business 2.0* magazine and a contributor and member of the board of editors of *Fortune*.

risen to 60 percent. (No, Desmond isn't living off Molly: Men's lower participation chiefly reflects a larger retiree population.) The attachment between the Organization and the Organization (Wo)Man has changed as well, in both profound and superficial ways.

In cataloging the alterations, however, we risk ignoring deep continuities. This is a mistake. People and companies that figure out how to use both—how to catch the waves of change and also ride the tides of continuity—can prosper from the knowledge.

There is still, to start with a small example, that shared sense of running a rat race; we're proud of it, though we worry that the exercise shrivels the soul to the dimensions of a rodent's. In a remarkable diary, Thomas Asacker, founder of Humanfactor, a New Hampshire medical devices company, writes: "I'm amazed at how few interesting people I meet in my business life—for me a redundant expression. It seems that most of the people I run into simply want enough money and free time for things like annual vacations, watching television, surfing the Net, or kibitzing about this or that. Questioning the way things are and trying to improve them appears to be nothing but a waste of their 'downtime.' Business people seem particularly prone to this status quo way of living. We're running so fast that we often forget to stop, take a breath, look at the map, and question the route."

Also like our 1950s forebears, we show an easy grasp of the "common denominators" that connect us regardless of industry or geography; perhaps we're less likely to chat across suburban front lawns—who's home anymore?—but in airport lounges, at offsite after offsite, conference after conference, whether we work for Russell Reynolds, Reynolds and Reynolds, or Reynolds Metals, we talk about the boat we're all in. We chat about golf and upgrades rather than lawn seed and Chevrolets, but that's a difference of degree rather than of kind, what you'd expect given a 240 percent rise in real GDP since 1956. The backbiting between Generation X and middle aged baby-boomers is almost word-for-word the same as it was when parents complained: "I don't know what's wrong with these kids today. . . . Noisy, crazy, sloppy, lazy loafers" (Bye Bye Birdie, 1960); and their offspring returned the disfavor: "Your sons and your daughters are beyond your command; your old road is rapidly agin'" (Bob Dylan, 1964).

Significantly, we share a jargon—phrases like "actionable plans" and "jump to a new S-curve"—that is a sure mark of a common culture. The words themselves change, but business jargon is as universal today as when E. B. White derided it in *The Elements of Style* (1959).

Yet clearly today's Organization Man is not just yesterday's without the skinny necktie. Business types, for all their bluster and (more jargon) "bias toward action," tend to be more acted upon than acting. They still "do it the company way," like J. Pierpont Finch, hero of *How to Succeed in Business Without Really Trying*. Dilbert resents the obedience demanded of him—but he relents.

If we're to understand the new shape of Organization Man, therefore, we must learn what bent him. There are two big causes of the change—drivers, in our lingo. First: the acceleration of the rate of change itself. "I've been in business for thirty-five years, and I've never seen change of such complexity, pace, scale, and speed," says Vincent DiBianca, who spent two decades at Touche Ross, then founded DiBianca Berkman, a consulting firm he sold to CSC Index in 1993. "How quickly our competitors can copy us," confides Asacker in his diary—not that this is a secret from anyone in business today. In information technology, the already punishing rate of change expressed by Moore's Law—which says that computing power per dollar doubles every eighteen months—is now being pushed even faster by advances in chip design. In the swiftest of all industries, financial services, products have the life span of weird subatomic particles; they might be designed and introduced in a matter of minutes, and might disappear in a matter of hours. Says Sir Brian Pittman, chief executive of Lloyds TSB in Britain: "If we introduce a new consumer banking product in the morning, we know if it is a success before we go to lunch."

Supersonic change warps managerial roles and structures. When advantage is fleeting, one must exploit it stat. This demands that one rapidly move people and resources both inside corporations and among them, creating teams where there's not time to set up departments, alliances where there's not time to build capabilities. DiBianca tests agility by asking executives how long their companies would need to get a smallish group of people (a dozen or two) up and running on a new project in a new location—the whole setup, including getting the funds, picking the people, getting their bosses to sign off, backfilling their old jobs, preparing facilities, running in phones and local-area networks, etc. Answers run the gamut from six months to six weeks. But some companies—Warner Lambert is one—say they've got it down to just six days.

Change loosens the tie between Organization Man and the Organization; there is less routine to hitch to. What knots there are might be retied overnight, as happened in 1997 for 2,600 information-system employees of Du Pont who, after an outsourcing deal, are doing the same work, in the same offices, for paychecks that now say Computer Sciences Corporation.

There is a second big reason Organization Man has taken on a new form: a change in the character of the capital of which managers are custodians. Says Elizabeth Lanier, a self-described "recovering lawyer" who is chief of staff of Cinergy, the $3.2-billion-in-sales gas, electric, and energy services company based in Cincinnati: "Organization Man was on a short leash because there was a relative shortage of capital. When you are capital constrained, you want people who think like you and use capital just like you. Capital markets themselves were much narrower—just banks and bonds and insurance companies—and more narrow-minded."

Lots of that capital was tied up in facilities—factories, stores, refineries, warehouses, offices—and Organization Man, in turn, was tied to them. Says Richard M. Zavergiu, a transportation consultant in Canada: "Manual workers as well as highly skilled managers were rooted in physical place." Sometimes this was because a place was specially designed for one kind of work—a factory, a refinery. But even a drone in a generic office beehive had to be there. It was impossible—or impossibly expensive—to work together without being together physically. Long-distance phone calls were exotic enough that you'd leave a meeting to accept one; in a world where memos circulated because they could not be photocopied, where phone calls came through a switchboard and international communications through a bulky telex in the mailroom, you had to be downtown. Today, with Albuquerque a mouse-click away from Zimbabwe, it's easy to forget that voice mail and fax machines were novelties a dozen years ago.

Now capital is not scarce and not rooted in a place. It is, says Lanier, "democratically abundant" from all kinds of sources. Moreover, the financial and physical capital that companies need is less valuable than their intellectual capital. When it seemed as if physical capital was most valuable—and when human beings couldn't communicate at a distance greater than a few hundred feet—Organization Man went to a central place, like Mohammed to the mountain. Now, says Zavergiu, "the capital value of knowledge exceeds the capital value of fixed assets for many corporations." The worker is worth more than his tools. The mountain must come to Mohammed. In New England, in Portland, Maine, two semiconductor labs—one owned by National Semiconductor, the other by Fairchild Semiconductor—stand next to each other. Why Maine? Quality of life: Many skilled workers like Maine's lifestyle. In Old England, the trains between London and Amsterdam are full of software programmers. Why? Says Keith Bradley, professor at Britain's Open University Business School: "In London we have a great need for smart programmers, but Holland has become the hot place for them to live because Dutch dope laws are so liberal. A lot of software companies are starting up in Holland."

In a knowledge economy, then, technology untethers the man. At the same time, he is less beholden to the organization for capital. As the value of human capital rises compared with the value of fixed assets, the organization becomes more beholden to the man. Says Lanier: "I could quit my job today and go back to law. I don't need Cinergy. Cinergy needs me."

That's also what twentysomethings say who have never known anything other than the new economy in boomtime. Mind you, legions of U.S. managers who were kicked in the teeth by their employers in the 1980s and 1990s—and legions in Europe who face the same boot in the next decade—will dispute the notion that the company needs them. But it does, and that is a major change. The Organization never did need Organization Man, though it employed him in vast numbers. It needed a certain amount of output, pushed paper mostly. Dilbert's creator, Scott Adams, has talent worth tens or hundreds of millions of dollars. His former employer, Pacific Bell, needed someone in the job he held, but it had no need for Adams, no way to use his talent. So Adams left as others did—some who jumped, some who were pushed.

The transition has been ugly; transitions usually are. Consider how the reputation of General Electric's John F. Welch changed. A dozen years ago he was "Neutron Jack"—the man who kept the buildings and fired the people; now he is the CEO of America's most admired corporation, a man who is believed when he says, "None of this is about squeezing anything at all—it is about tapping an ocean of creativity, passion, and energy." The Organization needs you. Maybe not for long, but for now.

Out of these changes—an economy that rewards agility and a company that needs our minds and souls—has emerged the notion of a "new contract" between employer and employee. The old contract supposedly promised employment: If you do it the company way, if executive policy is okay by you, you will still be here. The new contract supposedly goes like this: Rather than promising employment, we will strive to make you employable by offering a challenge and the chance to learn valuable skills.

That's not hogwash, but it's not a pure, cool, mountain stream of truth either. For one thing, there never was an old contract legally or in any other sense. U.S. labor markets are—and always have been—the freest in the developed world. "Employment at will" (the employer's will) is a matter of law in many states; if anything it's harder to fire someone in the United States today than it was in the 1950s, the supposed heyday of employment for life.

Furthermore, the employability stuff, which does a fine job of rationalizing quitting and firing, doesn't explain why people yearn to stay. And yearn they do; even the most gung-ho players in the wild, wired new economy, if they had their druthers, would prefer to have one employer than hop-skip-and-jump from one knowledge-worker gig to another. By a two-to-one ratio, according to a survey taken for *Wired* magazine and Merrill Lynch, "superconnected" people—who regularly exchange e-mail and use a laptop, cell phone, beeper, and home computer—would rather stick with one employer for twenty years than have five jobs for four years each, even if the money and responsibilities were the same.

What, then, does tie us to the company? Ask people with a choice why they choose to stay. A good answer in the 1950s, says Brent Snow, an organizational development consultant, would have emphasized the safety and resources big groups offer small individuals: "It's a good company; I have an opportunity to move up; I have a future here." Recently, Snow has been asking employees at Oracle why they work there. The response? "Every one of them, I suspect, could be making more money. But they all start talking about the challenges, the chance to do interesting work on the cutting edge."

Learning is a piece of the "new contract" that people truly buy. Listen, for example, to a trio of thirtysomethings at PriceWaterhouse consulting:

JOHN WATERMAN, thirty: "I'm here because I keep learning. Whenever I start to get a little bored, a new project comes along with opportunities for learning."

TRACY AMABILE, thirty-three: "The people and the learning are what's primary. I've been provided a lot of opportunities, lots of challenging work in different industries."

ED GERMAIN, thirty-five: "I've had a lot of training, a lot of project opportunities. For me stagnation would lead to restlessness."

Leaders at another Big Six (or Five, or Four) consulting firm talk about "knowledge handcuffs." At a time when these fast-growing firms are offering big bonuses to poach the others' talent, they have found people often stay because they feel bound to the knowledge of their firm—the networks, electronic and (chiefly) human, of experts and expertise upon which they rely.

Learning has taken on such psychic importance that schooling—or at least credentials—has begun to take the place of promotions. Quasi-professional certification exams are showing up in all kinds of general management areas, such as project management, management consulting, and human resources management. The newly flat and lean HR department may no longer have "benefits managers" and "senior benefits managers," but you can take a test (offered by the Human Resources Certification Institute) and become a "professional of human resources," then take a harder test and become a "senior professional of human resources." In 1997 about nine thousand people sat down for the HR exams, ten times the number in 1990. When asked why they came, the No. 1 reason they offered was "I did it for personal growth."

And for a fringe benefit of potential gain too: The sheepskin helps you get work. John Bishop, chairman of the human resources studies department at Cornell University, has discerned a fascinating nascent trend in U.S. labor markets. People are beginning to have more different employers (no surprise) but fewer different occupations. In the old dispensation, IBM might have hired you as a salesperson, then over the years moved you into marketing, manufacturing, finance: One company, four occupations. That still dominant pattern is starting to evolve toward one in which you stay in marketing but move from IBM to Procter and Gamble to Ameritech to Wells Fargo. Credentials can help you make such leaps: By gum, the next applicant in the waiting room is a senior human resources professional. Says Peter Capelli of the Wharton School: "Increased mobility across companies means that investments in skills pay off relatively more for individuals and relatively less for companies."

Cinergy has changed how it trains and develops people to recognize that individuals must be the prime investors and beneficiaries in learning. Gone are executive and leadership development; in their place is "talent development," and it's available to everyone. Says Lanier: "The premise is that we want to have the smartest people in every layer in every job. If it's a janitor in a power plant, I want him smarter than any other janitor." If you recruit and train only high-potential leaders for the organization, says Lanier, you not only run the very high risk that your best talent will take your investment to the competition but "you get a high piss-off factor. You tick off all existing employees. Our business is changing fast. Our ability to respond to opportunities is not a function of how well we recruit MBAs but of how many smart people we have that we can lateral to and say run with it." You stay, then, because the Organization, so long as it needs you, gives you a way to invest in skills you truly want.

A second powerful force that ties Man to Organization: The company gives you a field on which to strut your stuff. Paradoxically, that is, you are dependent on the organization to provide the arena in which to be independent. Explains David Witte, CEO of the Ward Howell International executive search firm: "Freedom and responsibility are the very best golden handcuffs there are." For example, in the oil business, says Witte, "I can easily take people from bureaucratic companies like Amoco or Exxon, but there's no way in hell I can steal from Joe Foster." Foster, when he was at Tenneco Oil, was one of the first in the energy business to offer employees the freedom and authority of self-managing teams; in 1989 he and twenty-two others left Tenneco to start up Newfield Exploration Company in Houston (1996 sales: $149 million), built on the philosophy that independence and equity ownership are the keys to retaining expert employees, who are, in turn, the key to success.

This independence is not the same as—is dramatically at odds with—the "You Inc." view of the new contract, which holds that we are each of us on our own, and which would substitute fluid, internal labor markets for the old organization's hierarchies. To rely chiefly on market mechanisms to allocate talent is to admit being unable to do it yourself, says Howard Stevenson, a professor at Harvard Business School. "The myth of atomistic man is wrong, and companies that are acting on it are wrong. Markets result when organizations fail, not the other way around."

In chaotic times, Stevenson argues, some people become lone wolves (the You Inc. approach); others join cults, following a leader who offers simplistic solutions (the guru du jour approach); and some form tribes. Tribal loyalty—along with learning and independence—is the third great rope tying the New Man to the Organization. The tribe is not the organization as a whole (unless it is relatively small) but rather teams, communities of practice, and other groups within the company or one's occupation.

Tribalism explains an otherwise baffling phenomenon: If the employment "contract" has shifted from paternal and permanent to individualistic and transactional, why have we become so obsessively concerned with interpersonal relationships at the office? Why do we care about "fit" and culture? Why not just snarl at one another eight hours a day and be done with it?

Brian Hall, CEO of Values Technology in Santa Cruz, California, has documented a shift in people's emotional expectations from work. Hall has taken speeches, letters, interview transcripts, and brochures from the entire history of two long-lived companies (a midsized financial services company and a global electronics giant), scanned them into a computer, and searched for words and phrases that refer to values such as independence, entrepreneurship, loyalty, etc. In both companies Hall finds a "massive transition" in progress. From the 1950s on, a "task-first" relationship to the company—"tell me what the job is, and let's get on with it"—dominated employee attitudes. Emotions and personal life were checked at the door; you might have worked thirty years with strangers, or be like the Boston banker Hall met who never told his colleagues he had developed Parkinson's disease.

In the past few years, a "relationship-first" set of values has risen to challenge the task orientation, and Hall believes it will become dominant: Employees want to share attitudes and beliefs as well as workspace, want to establish the relationship (with one another and with the company) before buckling down to the task.

That's not touchy-feely. When the task changes abruptly and often, people need to cling to something that has continuity. As Stevenson points out, "We have to know each other, know how we work together, so that when a crisis comes we don't have to spend a long time coordinating." At Hewlett-Packard, for example, tasks change constantly; more than 50 percent of the company's orders derive from products that did not exist two years ago. The performers, however, don't change. HP's employee attrition rate is usually half the average in the labor markets where it operates; in the 1990s attrition has actually fallen by a third. "I get benchmarked on this frequently," says Sally Dudley, a manager of human resources and a twenty-four-year HP veteran. "We don't do anything special. We're 'among the leaders' on pay. Our total compensation package is fairly traditional for a large company." HP's magic lies in the primacy of relationships over tasks. Says Dudley: "I've done fourteen different jobs here. Those who have spent most of their careers at HP—and most of us have—don't identify with doing the same thing."

So learning supplants security; freedom to maneuver supplants power; and relationship supplants task. But there is one price the Organization exacts as implacably as ever: conformity, though with a characteristic fin-de-siècle twist. The Organization these days demands a stereotype of original thinking, an orthodoxy of the unorthodox. Change management is a discipline, its practitioners experts in something called the "change piece": "Tell me how you did the change piece," they ask one another. The definition of the ideal manager may be different from what it was in 1958, but it is just as rigid. See how far you'd get in a job interview if you proclaimed yourself an "inside-the-box thinker."

Says headhunter Witte: "For a huge percentage of searches, the client asks for the same thing: 'I want someone who has been in consumer goods for ten years and telecom for five years. I want that guy—find me him. I want him to come into my steel mill, into my chemical plant, into my whatever.'" "It's not that they want someone from Procter and Gamble or Pacific Telesis in particular, Witte says. Instead, they want a "change agent"—another piece of jargon—which Witte defines as follows: "Someone who has had a lot of change, been promoted quickly, has shown he can change industries, identify new opportunities, throw them into a business plan, and deliver on it."

It seems sensible until you wonder, Why do we all want to be different in the same way? Orthodoxies come, it seems, and orthodoxies go, but the fact of orthodoxy—that remains.

ESCAPE FROM THE CULT OF PERSONALITY TESTS

Several years ago I visited an AlliedSignal factory in Virginia where managers wore name badges color-coded to reveal how they had scored on a test of personality type. The idea was that people could communicate better if they understood their interlocutors' characters. To be labeled by personality type is perhaps the inevitable result of the primacy of relationship over task in employee-employer dealings. No wonder sales are at an all-time high for the granddaddy of these instruments, the Myers-Briggs Type Indicator; that's the one people have taken who tell you "I'm an ENTJ"—an extroverted intuitive thinking judger, a born leader—or "I'm an ISFP"—an introverted sensing feeling perceiver, a loyal follower. About a third of the time, the Myers-Briggs is administered by colleges or career counselors; most often it's given by companies to employees or job candidates.

Test publishers caution against using their instruments to judge applicants or candidates for promotion—these are tools for counseling, team building, and development, they say—but it's an open secret that they're used to screen candidates. One Fortune 100 company routinely gives a battery of standardized tests to would-be executives; others mix tests among other assessments, ranging from good old-fashioned interviews to unstructured group situations where a trained observer watches to see if you assume the role of leader, consensus-builder, nuisance, or what. Applicants might spend a fictional day on the job, going through an inbox full of "problems," interrupted by "subordinates." The best approach, says Dee Soder, president of CEO Perspective Group, who coaches executives and evaluates job candidates for companies, is to consider what character traits matter most—stability, adaptability, quickness of learning, whatever—then design an assessment process that includes at least two different ways to get at each trait.

It's possible to cheat on standardized tests. "Just ask my client, who is now an executive vice president at [the Fortune 100 company]," one psychologist says, anonymous because psychology, like most professions, considers it wrong—or bad business practice—to share trade secrets with the laity. On the Gordon Personal Profile, never forget that you "take the lead in group activities," are "able to make important decisions without help," or find it "easy to influence other people." You will get credit for a trait called "ascendancy," which, test developer Leonard Gordon says, "has been a consistent predictor of managerial success."

Tests have questions that trip up phonies, but there's a difference between fakery and shifts of emphasis. The best advice for beating the tests comes from William H. Whyte in *The Organization Man:* Stay in character. Gild the lily, but don't pretend to be a magnolia. On the 16PF test, for example, you'll look more like a leader if you answer questions as if you were just a tad more outgoing, a bit bolder, and little livelier than you ordinarily are, and just a smidgen less anxious and self-reliant. (Leaders, say the authors of this test, are independent but not self-reliant. If you get the difference, you can game these tests.)

But why fool the tests? You'll only get yourself a job at which you'll fail, right? That assumption is, at least to a contrarian INTP (with a strong streak of J) like me, more troubling than the mystique surrounding testing. It's a tenet of America's faith that anyone can become anything. Whether we start in a log cabin or a mansion, graduate from Harvard or the William Morris mailroom, Americans are not what we are: We are what we can become. Self-help books—starting with Dale Carnegie's 1938 *How to Win Friends and Influence People*—find a bigger audience in America than anywhere else. In F. Scott Fitzgerald's novel

This Side of Paradise, the young hero, Amory Blaine, says, "We're not personalities, but personages." A personality, he explains, "is what you thought you were. . . . A personage, on the other hand . . . is never thought of apart from what he's done. He's a bar on which a thousand things have been hung—glittering things, sometimes." Whether it's scientifically right or wrong, the determinism that lurks behind tests of personality type is, in other words, downright un-American. I can be whatever I want: Just give me the chance.—T. A. S.

New Opportunities for Older Workers

COMMITTEE FOR ECONOMIC DEVELOPMENT

America is getting older—a simple observation with far-reaching implications. By now, the first wave of baby boomers has received invitations to join AARP.[1] While the boomers themselves may choose to ignore those invitations for a few more years, the challenges posed by an aging society cannot wait that long. As today's workers evaluate their own retirement security, and as policymakers and business leaders assess the viability of the nation's aging-related programs and policies, they must recognize the need for significant changes in attitudes and practices.

Work will be central to this process of change. During this century, retirement has become increasingly important in the lives of most Americans, as reflected in their declining average age of withdrawal from the workforce. Today, retiring with many years of life remaining is regarded as a just reward for a working life. In contrast, life after work was not something to look forward to in earlier eras. It was associated with severe economic insecurity, and often seen as a precursor to death. But the past half century has seen sustained growth in the U.S. economy, the growth of public and private retirement systems, improvements in the health of older individuals, and increases in life expectancy. As a result, Americans now measure retirement in decades rather than years.

However, as the baby boom generation grows older, it is doubtful that ever-longer retirement will continue to be beneficial and affordable for individuals or the nation. CED strongly believes that additional years of work in some form—not necessarily full-time, career employment—will be increasingly desirable for a growing number of older Americans and for our society.

The Economic Imperative

The aging of the American workforce will have major effects on our economy. Labor force growth will slow dramatically as the baby boom generation retires. Fewer workers relative to nonworkers imply lower national saving and investment. As a result, the growth of productivity and our standard of living will suffer. One prominent observer highlights the economic implications of what he calls the "gray dawn," arguing that aging populations will become "the transcendent political and economic issue of the twenty-first century."

Executive Summary, Committee for Economic Development (CED), October 1999. Reprinted with permission of the CED.

Aging lies at the heart of two of the most difficult policy challenges we face today: reforming Social Security and Medicare. Reform debates already have been rancorous, pitting older and younger generations against one another. These are not false divisions; Social Security and health care benefits for retirees require tax revenues from younger, working Americans. With fewer workers relative to retirees, the burden placed on younger generations will grow. Extending work lives would help reduce this burden.

However, the work "solution" must be kept in perspective. An aging America will present considerable economic and social challenges. Longer work lives will not solve all of these problems—but they will help to alleviate many of them. And unlike the reform of Social Security and Medicare, which will necessarily produce winners and losers, an effective pro-work agenda for older Americans can be a win-win for all parties involved—older workers, businesses, and government.

Removing Barriers to Work for Older Americans

Our goal should be increased work opportunities and incentives for older Americans that meet the needs of these workers and their employers. Older Americans who want to work currently face numerous obstacles: pension plans that strongly discourage them from working, workplace attitudes and practices that hinder their employment, federal regulations that inhibit flexible work arrangements, and sometimes unrealistic expectations on the part of workers themselves.

Employer attitudes and policies must change if older workers are to remain in the workforce longer. Businesses have heretofore demonstrated a preference for early retirement to make room for younger workers. But this preference is a relic from an era of labor surpluses; it will not be sustainable when labor becomes scarce. A stagnant labor supply will force many employers to rethink their attitudes toward older workers and reverse policies that inhibit their employment. It is in the nation's economic interest that businesses make these changes sooner rather than later. This report is, in part, a wake-up call to business (and others), urging them to avoid a future game of "catch up" and the considerable economic losses that will come with it.

This policy statement defines the challenges ahead of us—why encouraging work is important, what stands in the way, and how to overcome these barriers. Reforms must encompass public and private sector policies. Our recommendations do not rely merely on goodwill or employer sacrifice. Rather, we strongly believe that changes in employer practices are as much a matter of self-interest as national interest. Older workers are a neglected but valuable resource in today's economy and will be even more valuable in the future. It is time for employers, policy makers, and older workers themselves to recognize this fact and act on it.

Major Findings

1. Americans are retiring earlier and living longer, healthier lives. As a result, they spend more time in retirement than ever before. In 1965, a typical male worker could expect to spend thirteen years in retirement; today, he will spend eighteen years. For working women the retirement span has increased from sixteen years to more than twenty.
2. The workforce is aging. The disproportion between the retired baby boomers and workers supporting them will be unprecedented. In 1950, there were seven working-age persons for every person age sixty-five and older in the United States; by 2030, there will be fewer than three.
3. These two trends have tremendous economic implications. In coming decades, employers will face tight labor markets as fewer new workers enter the labor force. Economic growth will be reduced by lower national saving, due in particular to the exploding costs of our old-age entitlement programs.
4. Encouraging older Americans to work longer and facilitating longer work lives will alleviate this economic burden. Just as important, it will expand options for the growing number of workers who are not ready to retire at today's average retirement age of sixty-two.
5. Older Americans currently face barriers to work on several fronts, including financial disincentives to work, workplace discrimination, and inadequate training. Ever-younger retirement ages have been, in part, a reflection of these barriers. Older workers' experiences in the job market indicate problems as well; unemployment becomes more persistent as workers age, and job opportunities are often limited. Very few older workers have the option to scale back employment in a long-held, career job (that is, "phased retirement").
6. Financial considerations often strongly discourage work. Many private pensions penalize work after some age, frequently as low as fifty-five. Work after this age creates an implicit "tax" (often exceeding 50 percent) due to the decline in value of lifetime pension benefits. Similarly, some Social Security provisions—such as earnings limits for beneficiaries—create disincentives to work.
7. Employers' willingness to hire and retain older workers depends, in part, on the availability of labor. As growth in the labor supply slows, employers will look to nontraditional sources, including older persons, to alleviate shortages.
8. Employers' willingness to employ older workers also depends on the workers' productivity and cost. There are, in fact, no discernible differences between the intrinsic abilities (measured as physical and mental ability and capacity to learn) of most older workers and those of their younger counterparts for most jobs today. Many older workers offer distinct advantages in terms of experience, company loyalty, and job flexibility.

9. However, productivity also depends on skill levels, and older workers often fail to maintain and upgrade their skills. Older employees can also cost more as a result of practices related to earnings, health insurance, and pensions. Government regulation of employee benefits also imposes costs and may discourage the employment of older workers.
10. Some older workers face discrimination in the workplace and job market. Older workers who believe they are likely to face discrimination are less inclined to remain in the workforce.

Summary of Recommendations

Our "pro-work" agenda for employers, policy makers, and older workers includes detailed recommendations in six areas:

1. Getting the Financial Incentives Right. As a means of retaining valued older employees, CED encourages employers to reassess their pension offerings and consider changes that would make them neutral between work and retirement. Major changes in public policies necessary to encourage longer work lives include:

eliminating the Social Security earnings test,
increasing Social Security's normal and early retirement eligibility ages, and
eliminating the employer first-payer provision in Medicare.

We call on employers, employer associations, government, unions, and seniors' groups to educate workers about financial planning for retirement. Many workers lack a clear understanding of the financial resources required for a twenty- or thirty-year retirement. With a better understanding of their retirement needs, these workers would likely avoid the early retirement trap.

2. Replacing Stereotypes about Older Workers. CED urges employers to address age discrimination in the workplace and hiring practices through training sessions and workshops, following the model of race- and gender-oriented initiatives. As a matter of self-interest, employers should abandon stereotypes about older workers in favor of honest assessments of value.

3. The Training Imperative. Older workers themselves have the primary responsibility to acquire and maintain their own skills. However, employers who offer training should recognize the value of training their older workers and ensure equal access to training for them.

We urge higher education and other training institutions to recognize the need for work-oriented learning among older Americans and expand their offerings to this largely untapped customer market.

4. Rethinking the Organization of Work. CED calls on companies to explore innovative ways to reorganize work for long-tenure employees in order to avoid career plateaus.

We believe that phased retirement is a promising, but vastly underutilized means of extending work lives. Successful implementation of phased retirement may require a change in company pension and benefit rules and changes to federal regulations governing employee benefits.

5. Getting Older Workers into New Jobs. Better opportunities for older job seekers are required. To identify and encourage older applicants, CED believes that employers should revise their recruiting practices with older candidates in mind by identifying promising recruiting markets, orienting recruiting material toward older candidates, and partnering with seniors' groups to advertise positions.

Older workers looking for new employment should update their job search skills and recognize the increasing importance of computer-based job searches.

Federal law governing employee benefits should be amended to allow greater flexibility in hiring older workers for contingent and part-time work. Older workers who want to work in flexible arrangements should be permitted to opt out of traditional benefit packages.

CED calls on employers to consider greater use of cafeteria-type flexible benefit packages to facilitate the hiring of older workers in flexible work arrangements.

6. A Strong and Flexible Safety Net. Social Security Disability Insurance (DI) should be reformed to promote work by DI recipients, many of whom are older Americans, while maintaining an adequate safety net of benefits. Our recommended reforms to DI illustrate how public safety net programs can serve their intended populations while also promoting work.

Note

1. Peter Peterson, *Gray Dawn: How the Coming Age Wave Will Transform America—and the World* (New York: Random House, 1999).

Finished at Forty

NINA MUNK

In the new economy, the skills that come with age count for less and less. Suddenly, forty is starting to look and feel old. America is no place to age gracefully. Of course, basketball players, dancers, and fashion models are finished young; mathematicians and chess players peak early too. So do construction workers and coal miners. Once you're fifty-five, it's almost impossible to find a job in business. But a new trend is emerging: In corporate America, forty is starting to look and feel old.

Since the early 1980s big companies have been getting rid of people. For a long time, though, seniority mattered. Hierarchy was respected too. If people had to be fired, the younger, junior people were usually the first to go. That's no longer true. The working world has changed. It has become faster and more efficient and, for many people, crueler. The unemployment rate hovers at thirty-year lows; even so, companies announced the elimination of some 600,000 U.S. jobs last year, according to Challenger, Gray and Christmas, an outplacement firm that tracks such depressing data. There's no way to tell how many of those people are over forty, but this much is sure: Companies today have less and less tolerance for people they believe are earning more than their output warrants. Such intolerance, or pragmatism, hits older workers hardest. The older an employee, the more likely it is he can be replaced by someone younger who earns half as much. "For my salary the company could hire two twentysomethings," says a forty-one-year-old we spoke to. "I'm good at what I do. But am I better than two people? Even I know that's not true." Today, for many people, the longer you've been at one company, the more disposable you are.

Here's a sign of the times: At Westech Career Expos, the nation's biggest technology-related job fairs, the registration form asks attendees to indicate their "professional minority status." One option is "Over 40." ("Until I filled out that form, I never knew I was a minority," remarked a forty-three-year-old white male attendee at a Westech expo.)

Perhaps technology is to blame. Maybe in this "new" economy, the old ways of doing business are indeed anachronistic—if the economy is new, who needs experience? Whatever the reason, in America today the skills that come with age and experience appear to count for less and less. It's hard to demonstrate with numbers, but a lot of people over forty sense it: Youth, with its native optimism,

 Nina Munk is a contributing editor at *Vanity Fair* and a freelance journalist.

is what companies want now. "The bar is lowering on what is considered old," says David Opton, executive director of Exec-U-Net, a network of five thousand executives looking for leads on new jobs. "I often tell people who are between forty and forty-five and thinking of getting a new job to hurry, because the door closes at forty-five."

In some industries the door closes earlier. The half-life of computer engineers, for example, is especially short, and getting shorter. "It used to be that when you talked about age challenges in employment, it was people age fifty, fifty-five, or above. Now, well, I've had people in their late thirties tell me they've had people look at them and say, 'Wow, you're kind of old for a programming job, aren't you?'" says Paul Kostek, president of the Institute of Electrical and Electronic Engineers-USA.

That so many workers are over forty compounds the problem. In just four years, for the first time ever, there will be more workers over forty than there are workers under forty. All those people—the seventy-eight million baby boomers—are competing for a limited number of top jobs. For those who have made it (status, money, fan mail, a title, a corner office), there's no problem; but for the millions who are just decent, everyday performers, it's another story. These people are squeezed: They can't rise to the top (there's no room), and right behind, ready to overtake them, is another generation. In years gone by, executives in this position spoke of reaching a plateau—if their path no longer led upward, at least they were in a stable, safe place. Now the plateau is a narrow ledge. Suddenly, at an age when they expected to be at the peak of their careers, growing numbers of fortysomethings are slipping backward.

Debbie Brown is a software engineer who recently lost her job after fourteen years at Northrop Grumman. Since last June, when Brown first knew she'd lose her job, she has sent out about three hundred resumes. Her yield so far: four phone interviews, one in-person interview, and not a single job offer. Brown is forty-four. She earned a master's degree in software engineering from the University of California at Irvine in 1983 and has twenty-three years of industry experience. According to headhunters, however, she's obsolete—not because she's worked in the defense business (although that probably doesn't help), but largely because she moved into management in an era when fortysomething middle managers are a dime a dozen. As for her technical skills, well, people half her age are better qualified. To get a job offer, she must be prepared to cut her $88,500 salary in half, headhunters advise. Either that or go back to school. "I came to Northrop thinking that I'd retire here," she says. "And now here I am, at forty-four, out of work and useless."

It's not only high-tech firms that are slamming the door on people over forty. In older industries, too, as the lives of products get shorter and as the speed of change gets faster, it can be awfully hard to keep up unless you have the stamina of a twenty-five-year-old. "Just as the product life cycle is shortening, so too is the career cycle of the average employee," wrote two organizational psychologists

Douglas Hall and Philip Mirvis in a 1994 essay titled "The New Workplace and Older Workers."

Last year, when management consulting firm Watson Wyatt Worldwide asked 773 CEOs at what age they felt people's productivity peaked, the average response was: forty-three.

There are advantages to age. Older employees have more experience than younger workers; they also have better judgment, have a greater commitment to quality, are more likely to show up on time, and are less likely to quit—that's what a recent study commissioned by the American Association of Retired Persons found. Younger workers, by contrast (in this case defined as under fifty), were found to be more flexible, more adaptable, more accepting of new technology, and better at learning new skills. It may seem that there are as many advantages in hiring older workers as in hiring younger ones. But as the AARP study discovered, increasingly what matters to companies is potential, not experience; street smarts, not wisdom. "The traits most commonly desired for the new world of work are flexibility, acceptance of change, and the ability to solve problems independently—performance attributes on which managers generally did not rate older workers highly," notes the AARP study. "The message is consistent: Managers generally view older workers as less suitable for the future work environment than other segments of the workforce."

To discover, after years of being promoted, that all of a sudden you are "less suitable" for your job than people younger than you is not easy. On January 6, 1998, FedEx delivered letters to the homes of 389 Gerber Products salespeople telling them they were out of work. Of those 389 employees, nearly 70 percent were over forty. One of them was Tom Johnson. He had been selling Gerber baby food for twenty-seven years; he started with the company when he was twenty-one. Shouldn't he have known he was vulnerable? "Right up until D-day, I was convinced I wouldn't be hit, what with me calling on national accounts and all," Johnson says.

It's human nature that causes us to be blindsided: No matter how often we hear stories of corporate ruthlessness, of forty-five-year-olds being replaced by twenty-eight-year-olds, we believe it won't happen to us. Sitting in his living room in Mesquite, Texas, in his La-Z-Boy, Johnson opened up that FedEx letter and felt sick. "I sat in my chair and read it eight times and couldn't believe it, I just couldn't believe it. It was like someone grabbed me and hit me as hard as they could right in the stomach. I thought, 'God, all I've done and all I've worked, and it doesn't mean a thing.'" His unemployment insurance checks, at $476 every two weeks, ran out months ago. When we last spoke to him, he had sent out about four hundred resumes, and still he hadn't found a job. If truth be told, his chance of finding anything that comes close to paying what he earned at Gerber is probably zero.

To compete in an industry that's cutthroat, Gerber, which is owned by the Swiss pharmaceuticals giant Novartis, decided to replace its in-house sales force with outside grocery brokers, big, anonymous, national sales firms. But Johnson thinks there's more to it. "They didn't just put us out to pasture, they put a bullet through us," agrees one of his former colleagues, Bob Butcher. Johnson and Butcher have filed an age-discrimination lawsuit against Gerber.

For many people over forty, it's getting harder to hold on to jobs that let them maintain their standard of living. Mike Bellick is forty-six. Until recently he was among the 2.3 percent of working-age Americans who earn over $100,000 a year: As the head of sales and marketing for a small Kansas City firm, he pulled in $130,000. All of a sudden, this past September, Bellick was let go and replaced by a twenty-eight-year-old who, presumably, earns far less than Bellick did ("I became the big target," he explains. "I was the guy making all the money"). True, Bellick didn't have too much trouble finding a new job; he has twenty years' experience in sales and marketing. But today, once you're over forty, it's one thing to find work and another to find a job that pays enough to support the lifestyle to which you have become accustomed.

When we spoke to Bellick in early December, he had had two job offers. One was for about the same salary he had earned before, but in his view it was a lower-level position, and worse, it was in San Jose, California, where the cost of living is far, far higher than in Kansas. The other position was in Kansas City, his hometown, but the salary was some 40 percent less than that of his old job. Meanwhile, and typically for someone his age, Bellick's living expenses have never been higher: His children's college expenses will run him $17,000 this year; then there's the mortgage on his four-thousand-square-foot home and the cost of maintaining three cars.

It's hard to feel sorry for someone earning $75,000 a year in Kansas City. But the point is, Bellick's gone about as far as he can go. "My salary has not grown in three years, and now it's going down," he says. "Should I go out and retrain myself? Perhaps. But how can I? I am supporting two kids in school. I support my wife. You get caught between a rock and a hard place. You say, 'Man, I've got to work, and $75,000 a year is better than going to work at a grocery store.'"

No longer is it unusual for a fortysomething like Bellick to be replaced by a twenty-eight-year-old. "The market is so fast moving that for some reason it's reduced the premium these [older] guys have," notes a New Yorker who runs a hedge fund. Callously, but realistically, he explains his preference for younger employees this way (and for obvious reasons he won't let his name be used): "The way I look at it, for $40,000 or $50,000, I can get a smart, raw kid right out of undergrad who's going to work seven days a week for me for the next two years. I'll train him the way I want him, he'll grow with me, and I'll pay him long-term options so I own him, for lack of a better word. He'll do exactly what I want—and if he doesn't, I'll fire him. . . . The alternative is to pay twice as much for some forty-year-old who does half the amount of work, has been trained improperly, and doesn't listen to what I say."

It's a sentiment a lot of baby boomers talk about, at least behind closed doors. "People my age are very insecure about the younger workforce; at this health club

I go to we talk about it, we worry about it," confessed a forty-four-year-old executive we spoke to. What unnerves these fortysomethings is that in a world increasingly dominated by information technology, people in their twenties and early thirties (Generation X) are more technically savvy than most baby boomers. Even more, many Gen Xers work sixty or seventy hours a week, mostly because their job is their whole life. But so what? From the perspective of an employer, such single-mindedness, such devotion to the company, makes Gen Xers all the more valuable. It also makes for unflattering comparisons to the fortysomething employee who leaves the office right at 6 P.M. to pick up the children from day care. As one highly placed human resources manager put it, "The attitude is, Why not hire someone who's young and idealistic and will work eighty hours a week?"

Lately it is becoming acceptable for this attitude to be explicit. Giving young people positions of power is a defined strategy at Consolidated Graphics, a $430 million firm that owns fifty commercial printing companies. Last year the company was ranked No. 87 on *Fortune*'s list of fastest-growing companies, and CEO Joe Davis believes the firm's success is largely due to his young, driven executives. "These twenty-year-olds believe they can do anything, and that kind of attitude is uplifting and very successful in a business that's been chugging along the same way for fifteen years," Davis, fifty-five, explains. "They introduce fresh ideas. Suddenly the energy level at these plants changes. At 6 P.M. you look around, and they're the only people left at the office.'

In an economy where the rules seem to shift every day, it's the risk takers, the people who believe they can do anything, who are being rewarded. And after all, who's more likely to take risks—a forty-six-year-old with a mortgage and two kids in college or a thirty-year-old with nothing to lose? (Freedom may be just another word for not having a mortgage.) Robert Michlewicz is the president of one of Consolidated Graphics' biggest plants, Houston-based Chas. P. Young Company, with sales of $20 million. He's thirty, oversees a staff of 150 people, and works seventy hours a week. When he started with the company, just out of Texas A&M, Michlewicz wouldn't be constrained by the printing industry's traditional ways of doing business. "When I got into sales here, there was this rule of thumb that once you sold $1 million worth of printing, you were an established, veteran salesperson," he explains. "I did $500,000 in my first year, $1.5 million in my second year, and $6.1 million in 1995. . . . I had no preconceived notions. That million-dollar threshold didn't mean anything to me."

The harder Gen Xers work, the more they tend to resent all those forty-four-year-olds who put in half as many hours and earn more money. "A large percentage [of us] have decided not to buy into a corporate system clogged with entrenched boomers who won't make way for people who are more efficient and have better ideas," writes twenty-eight-year-old "Delsyn" in an Internet posting on the Boomer Board chat room. Younger generations may have always felt thus; what's different now is that Delsyn, or someone like her, may be your next boss.

"You have to do more for young people because they are likely to turn over more quickly than older workers. Consequently, a lot of companies are putting young people on the fast track, so you have twenty-eight-year-olds running entire departments that twenty years ago were run by fifty-five-year-olds," explains Joe Gibbons, a human resources consultant at William M. Mercer. "That's a big change—it's a sea change."

What this change has done above all is upset the expected career paths of boomers. Increasingly, fortysomethings who have followed a good, steady career path find themselves competing with thirtysomethings on the fast track. "Imagine you're looking to hire someone, and you've got this thirty-two-year-old fast-tracker and a normal forty-two-year-old manager in the same position," says Neal Lenarsky, who runs his own career-management firm, Strategic Transitions, based in Woodland Hills, California. "It makes you wonder. You start to say, 'Why has this forty-two-year-old not made it to the next level?'" The next level! Suddenly, that good, steady career path looks dangerous, full of thorns and briars.

At the very top levels of corporate America, among the chief executive officers of the Fortune 500, youth is still rare: The average Fortune 500 CEO is fifty-six. Still, these CEOs are getting younger. Back in 1980, 69 percent of Fortune 500 CEOs were over fifty-five; in 1998 the figure had dropped to 61 percent. Meanwhile, the number of CEOs in their thirties and forties increased by 17 percent.

If the very top people are getting younger, then presumably those just below the top tier—people at the senior vice president level, say—are younger still. Why does this matter? Because, it is said, people hire people who look like them, or who are like them. Women and minorities have long complained that such partisanship is one reason they are shut out of traditional, white, male-dominated companies. If this is so, consider what it means to anyone over forty that, more and more, the people doing the hiring are young. The very last thing a thirty-one-year-old manager wants to feel is that he's hiring his uncle, or . . . his mother. One senior executive says that when he was interviewing for the CFO job at a fast-growing high-tech company last year, he felt self-conscious about his age for the first time; he was thirty-seven. "I expected, in my full day of interviews, to be talking to some silver-hairs eventually, but they just didn't exist," he says. "These kids, people age twenty-six and twenty-seven, were interviewing me. I wasn't intimidated by their youth, but I did feel old."

Anyone who hasn't been job hunting in the past five years is in for a shock, so quickly have these changes occurred. Bob, a forty-five-year-old senior vice president at a national insurance company, has been looking for a new position for about a year. (Because he's job hunting, he doesn't want his full name used.) After a long and successful career at his firm, he presumed that finding a more fulfilling job in this buoyant labor market would be simple. He was wrong. "I've been with this company sixteen years, and I always looked at that as a good thing, a sign of my stability, but at one [job] interview they held that against me. They said, 'You just haven't had enough diversity of experiences and ideas,' and I thought to myself, 'That's really not what this is about; this is about me being forty-five years old.' At another interview I met with a younger management group, in their thirties and forties. They asked me, 'What are your normal work hours? What do you do on the weekends?' I said, 'Oh, I like to watch football,' and one of them replied, 'Oh, yeah, I'm a couch potato too.' I felt like they were trying to establish a pattern or a lifestyle for somebody who's older."

As the onset of "old age" occurs earlier and earlier in corporate America, it is no surprise that more fortysomethings are filing age-discrimination lawsuits. In a study of all the age-bias suits filed in federal courts in 1996, Howard Eglit, a law professor at Chicago-Kent College of Law, found that 26 percent were brought by plaintiffs in their forties. That's up from 18 percent in an earlier study that looked at age-discrimination suits filed between 1968 and 1986.

Sandra McHugh was forty-two when she was fired by her employer, an Arizona firm called Impra that sells medical devices. She sued. In court Impra claimed McHugh was fired for not meeting her sales quota. Presenting evidence that younger sales people at the firm were not fired for failing to meet their quotas, McHugh's lawyer argued that Impra had engaged in age discrimination. Her lawyer also noted that once, at a sales award meeting, back when McHugh was surpassing her quotas, her boss had presented her with the firm's President's Award, saying, "It's nice to see that someone over forty can do something." Last June a Florida jury awarded McHugh $1.1 million, plus legal fees. (Under the Florida Civil Rights Act of 1992, those damages were recently capped at $265,000. Impra is appealing.)

Most companies looking to dump older employees don't leave traces. Richard Posner, chief judge of the U.S. Court of Appeals for the Seventh Circuit and author of *Aging and Old Age* (University of Chicago Press, 1995), explains why: "Within companies [the Age Discrimination in Employment Act] has forced a vocabulary purge—we know now we can't say, 'We need new blood,' but we can't be prevented from thinking it. If you believe you have too many old people, you can simply offer them early retirement. And it's said that if you want to fire an older person, you just fire a disposable younger person along with him in order to avoid a lawsuit."

One reason age-bias suits are hard to win is that older employees are indeed different from younger ones. For one thing, they make more money. The implicit wage contract is that employees are often underpaid at the beginning of their careers, then well paid in their thirties and forties, and usually overpaid as they hit their fifties. It has long been understood that late in their careers, as long as they perform satisfactorily, employees continue to receive annual raises and better perks—this even after their productivity has peaked or perhaps declined. Today, however, this social contract has made the overpaid older employee a walking target. "The economy is now so dynamic that older people are going to be at a disadvantage unless they have extraordinary skills that compensate for age," says Posner.

Older employees don't just earn more. Granting more vacation time costs money. The costs of medical benefits and insurance, too, rise with age. And the older an employee, and the longer he's been with the firm, the more expensive it becomes to support his pension plan. If length of work experience really counted for something, these extra costs wouldn't be an issue; but several studies have shown that differences in job performance between someone with twenty years' experience and someone with just five years are often negligible. That is to say that a twenty-eight-year-old with six years on the job may perform as well as a forty-eight-year-old with twenty-six years on the job. The twenty-eight-year-old, however, earns $45,000, while the forty-eight-year-old makes $120,000 (assuming a 5 percent raise every year).

These points were raised in an age-discrimination lawsuit filed against Ernst and Young. During an eighteen-month period after the 1989 merger of Arthur Young and Ernst and Whinney, 99 partners over forty were fired, while 112 under forty were hired. One of those fired partners was LaRue Simpson; he was then forty-six and making $196,000 a year. In court Simpson's lawyer pointed out that E&Y saved $5.5 million a year in salaries alone by replacing older partners with younger ones. She argued that E&Y fired Simpson because he was approaching the age when his retirement benefits would be vested. Simpson won $3.7 million ($5.2 million after interest and legal fees); the court ruled that the firm fired older partners to reduce its unfunded pension liability.

Suing for age bias is expensive, emotionally exhausting, and rarely successful. It took six years for Simpson's case to wind its way through the courts. Through it all, he endured round after round of public humiliation: The defense tried to prove he was a bungling, incompetent accountant who was unable to attract big clients and thwarted in his ambitions to become a managing partner. How hard were those six years? "Let me put it this way," Simpson says. "In 1982 I was diagnosed with a brain tumor and I had to wait six months for surgery before I could be sure that it was benign. Relative to my ordeal with Ernst and Young, that brain tumor was a piece of cake."

If companies discard older workers because they're earning more than they deserve, then perhaps the solution is to change the way people are being paid: Pay them what they're worth. It's self-evident, but it's rarely the way companies compensate people. "The solution is to develop compensation plans that pay for ideas, not tenure; that pay for contribution, not hierarchy," declares George Bailey, who until recently was head of Watson Wyatt's human-capital group.

Implementing performance-based compensation plans isn't easy. The key is figuring out how to value the performance of every employee ("If you can't find a way to measure [a job's value], you can probably eliminate it," declares Bailey). How many new ideas did she think up this year? How much money did she save? What did she do to help meet our goals? Did she accomplish the goals we set for her? It's a lot of work, but it beats rewarding people just because they've been with the firm for a long time.

A pure performance-based compensation plan means that an average employee may have to assume that at some point, probably in his mid-forties, maybe sooner, maybe later, he will face a pay cut. And rather than receive four weeks' vacation, he may now receive just three. Sounds harsh. But not if the alternative is being fired, laid off, offered "early retirement," or downsized because a twenty-seven-year-old has replaced you.

Here and there, pay is already largely performance driven. But in most of corporate America, the incentives built into salary and benefits plans are at odds with a firm's goals. Consider the traditional pension plans offered by most Fortune 500 companies: Relics from the days of corporate paternalism, they're designed to reward people, especially unproductive people, for sticking around forever. Take an average manager earning $100,000 who retires at sixty-five. If he stays with one company his entire career, he'll receive as pension $60,000 a year, according to calculations made for us by William M. Mercer. If, instead, he changes jobs just once in his career, he receives only $41,307 a year after retirement. If he's a modern job hopper, working for a new company every five years, he winds up with only $29,725. This anomaly explains why a growing number of companies—among them AT&T, Empire Blue Cross Blue Shield, and Owens Corning—have dumped the traditional pension plan in favor of a so-called cash-balance plan that neither rewards long-timers nor penalizes job hoppers. Rather than have a pension based on length of service, most cash-balance plans grant everyone the same annual credit (between 4 percent and 8 percent of salary) plus interest toward an eventual pension, and if an employee leaves, he typically takes his "cash balance" with him. "These new plans pay people for what they're bringing to the firm today, not for what they brought to the firm yesterday," explains Ethan Kra, chief actuary at William M. Mercer. "Basically, they're designed to take away the incentive to stay a long time."

Taking a cut in salary and benefits isn't the only way to remain competitive. Dean Keith Simonton, a psychologist at the University of California at Davis, argues that many signs of age that employers complain about—less productivity, less creativity, less enthusiasm—are in fact signs of boredom. "What I have found is that there is a trajectory in a career: It rises, rises, then peaks and falls. Basically, what happens is that you get everything there is to know about a job down cold, and then you run out of challenges and eventually reach a point where everything becomes a little too easy," he explains. "That's not a function of your chronological age; it's a function of your career age." The solution, he advises, is to change jobs, switch disciplines, get on another path before boredom sets in and before you become the sort of employee that companies want to eliminate. "If you start a new career, you reset the clock," Simonton says.

Don Naab reset his clock that way. About two years ago, as an executive at Kidde International, a $1.1 billion fire protection company, Naab looked around and realized that too many senior executives didn't have enough to do and, moreover, that he was one of them. He had just turned forty-four. Instead of waiting to see how things would turn out, he decided to start over. Naab left his job and started searching. For eighteen months he met with headhunters, called on former colleagues and business acquaintances, and interviewed with seventy companies, more or less. To cover his family's living expenses, he and his wife sold their home in Eden Prairie, Minnesota, invested the money, and lived off the income.

Last June, Naab was named president and chief operating officer of Pacific Research and Engineering, a $12 million public company in Carlsbad, California, that makes equipment for radio stations, such as mixers, cabinets, and consoles. He took a pay cut, but what mattered to him was finding a job that would keep him young and curious. "I'm as driven today as I was in the 1970s when I was in my twenties and thirties," he says. "If I have to put in a fifteen-hour day, I'm not burned out at the end of it. And I actually like getting up in the morning knowing that I have to deal with problems at work."

Question: When will older workers get some respect? Answer: when they're needed. Consider this: By 2003, more than half the nation's workers will be forty and over. Who will replace them? Generation X (born between 1965 and 1977) numbers only forty-five million; Generation Y (the echo boomers) is huge, but it won't be noticeable in the workforce for another decade or so. The bottom line: At some point—probably around 2011, when boomers start turning sixty-five—companies will become desperate for workers, even older workers, according to the Hudson Institute's Richard Judy, a coauthor of *Workforce 2020.*

But for companies that think quarter to quarter, 2011 is a very long way away.

SUSPECT AGE BIAS? TRY PROVING IT

The Age Discrimination in Employment Act was passed by Congress in 1967, making workers who are forty and over a protected class. But even though everyone knows, or suspects, that age discrimination is widespread, it's very difficult to prove. In 1997 the Equal Employment Opportunity Commission handled 18,279 complaints filed under the ADEA. Of those, however, 61 percent were found to have "no reasonable cause." Besides, to receive severance pay and severance benefits, most workers who are fired or take "early retirement" are required to sign away their right to sue.

Even if an employee manages to take his case to court, it's unlikely he will win, partly because of a 1993 U.S. Supreme Court decision. In that case *(Hazen Paper Co.* v. *Biggins),* the court suggested this: Just because a company takes an action that happens to be more harmful to older workers than to younger workers, it does not necessarily constitute age discrimination. Many lower courts have interpreted the decision broadly: If a company fires everyone, say, who makes over $100,000—thus only people over forty are purged—the company is not guilty of age bias. "As soon as a firm says, 'It wasn't about age, it was really about cost,' the courts seem to say, 'Okay, case closed,'" complains Laurie McCann, a staff attorney for the American Association of Retired Persons. "Sure, it may be about cost, but it's not about cost alone. But the courts are closing the doors because they don't let employees prove that second step."

In a 1998 survey conducted by the Society for Human Resource Management and the AARP, an astounding one in five companies said they had been hit by an age-discrimination claim in the past five years. Those charges are rarely made public because an estimated 90 percent of all age-discrimination charges are settled long before any complaints are filed with the EEOC. Companies know that if a case actually makes it before a jury, the plaintiff has an excellent chance of winning. In law professor Howard Eglit's research of 325 cases filed in federal court in 1996, only nineteen went before a jury, but of those, seventeen were decided in favor of the plaintiff.

Mark Cheskin, a partner with Steel Hector and Davis who represents companies in age-bias suits, has a rule of thumb: If a company settles with a disgruntled employee immediately, a settlement worth one- to three-months' salary should do the trick; that is, get him or her to sign away any rights to sue. If the company lets the complaint ride and then receives a demand letter from the employee's lawyer, it can usually settle for between three- and six-months' salary. However, as soon as an employee has actually filed a lawsuit, the company is in trouble, according to Cheskin: "Once an employee has taken that mental step of filing, they want $1 million."

Under the federal statute, recovery is limited to back pay (an employee's salary and the value of his benefits since he was fired), possibly front pay (if it's clear the employee will have a hard time finding another job), and attorney's fees. If the jury decides the discrimination was "willful," which juries often do, back-pay damages are doubled. The big money begins with state statutes, some of which permit punitive damages as well as damages for emotional distress. In California, for example, $1.5 million in damages is not considered unusual for someone who, when fired, was making $100,000. That is to say, the chance of getting an age-discrimination case to court is slim, but if a case makes it through, damages can be huge.

The Working Caste

LEAH PLATT

Tel Aviv's city bus number four runs down Allenby Street through the heart of secular Israel's glittering urban showcase. Just visible in one direction is the crowded Mediterranean coast, dotted with international hotels and frolicking sunbathers. A few blocks in the other direction are the cafés and boutiques of Dizengoff Street. As the bus pulls southward and heads farther inland, the scene out the window becomes seedier and, in a country not known for its clean streets, even dirtier. Trendy shops are replaced by open-fronted stores displaying luggage and trinkets, carts piled with vegetables and candied nuts, and placards advertising peep shows. This is South Tel Aviv, an area populated by members of Israel's large and growing community of foreign workers.

At the end of a workday, Romanian men still dusty from the job gather on benches to drink bottled beer. African men sit in threes and fours on folding chairs outside international calling centers that advertise rates to Kenya, Ecuador, Moldova, and Ukraine. A few older Filipino women rest on crates, displaying bunches of vegetables before them on blankets. The only Israeli in view is a man in a knitted *kippah* selling adult videos and assorted electronic goods.

According to the Israeli Central Bureau of Statistics, there are approximately 125,000 non-Palestinian foreign workers in the country today—roughly 50,000 of them undocumented. Israeli businesses recruit workers from all over the world: Thais for fieldwork, Romanians for construction jobs, Filipino women as nannies and home health care providers. Illegal workers arrive from Nigeria, Ghana, Colombia, Chile, Peru, and the former Soviet Union.

The presence of foreign workers is a relatively new phenomenon in Israel, a society that prides itself on being a haven for Jewish immigrants—and Israel is not alone. From Japan to Germany to Singapore, migration for employment is a growing trend. The category of "migrant worker"—as distinguished from "immigrant" on the one hand and "refugee" on the other—is somewhat hazy, so no one knows exactly how many of these workers there are worldwide. The International Labor Organization (ILO) pegs the total at around forty-two million: Indian computer programmers in Silicon Valley, Pakistani laborers in Saudi Arabian oil fields, and Filipino maids cleaning fashionable apartments in Tel Aviv, among many others.

American Prospect 12, no. 8 (May 7, 2001). Reprinted with permission of *American Prospect*, 5 Broad Street, Boston, MA 02109. Leah Platt is a writing fellow at *American Prospect*.

The International Confederation of Free Trade Unions (ICFTU) warns that the number of migrant workers will only increase over the next twenty years, as whole groups of people in the developing world are displaced by civil conflict and environmental degradation. Migrant labor probably will increase, but migrants may not be pushed from poor nations so much as pulled by rich ones. The populations of most countries in the industrialized world (the United States being one notable exception) are projected both to shrink and to age dramatically in the next generation. Importing foreign workers, a process dubbed "replacement migration" in a recent United Nations report, may be the only way for developed countries to sustain economic prosperity without drastically scaling back entitlements.

But industrialized countries will need to balance their appetite for foreign labor against their reluctance to open their doors to outsiders. Even at current levels of migration, foreign workers are the favorite scapegoat for economic strain—more than a million were deported from Malaysia and South Korea after the 1998 Asian financial crisis—and their increasing visibility will only enhance their vulnerability.

Blood Citizenship

Nowhere, perhaps, has the political impact of migrant labor been more acute than in Germany, which is currently home to 7.3 million foreigners. Many of these foreign residents are the children or grandchildren of Turkish, Italian, and Yugoslavian *Gastarbeiters* ("guest workers") recruited by the government in the 1950s and 1960s. Because the recruitment program's inception in 1955 coincided with postwar economic expansion, the government was slow to enforce rotation requirements and other measures designed to restrict permanent settlement. According to Douglas Klusmeyer, an associate at the Carnegie Endowment's program on international migration, policy makers were focused on the short-term economic benefits of a stable workforce, which, unlike a rotating system, does not require the constant training of new recruits.

By 1973, when the oil crisis and ensuing recession led to a freeze on new recruits, the number of guest workers had grown to 2.7 million. Over the next few years, the government offered financial rewards to workers who agreed to return home, but few accepted. The bargain was too little, too late; despite the moratorium on new guest workers, there were more foreigners living in Germany in 1983 than in 1973.

Germany has historically defined citizenship solely according to bloodlines or heritage instead of birthplace; the citizenship law of 1913 (which was reinstated after World War II, but has since been revised) provides automatic German citizenship only to children with a German father. U.S. citizenship law, by contrast, is a mixed system based on parentage and birthplace. Both the child born to an illegal Mexican migrant in El Paso and the child born to a U.S. citizen in Mexico City are automatically citizens of the United States.

Like Germany, Israel operates under a strict system of jus sanguinis, or citizenship by blood. Israeli immigration policy, codified in the 1950 Law of Return, is explicitly targeted at the "return" of the world Jewish community to its ancestral land. As Ze'ev Rosenhek, a professor of sociology at the Hebrew University of Jerusalem, puts it: "Israel is not an immigration country; it is an *aliyah* country. Non-Jewish immigrants are not considered prospective members of society." *Aliyah,* which literally means "ascending," denotes purely Jewish immigration to Israel.

A similar right of return affirmed in Germany's federal constitution allows ethnic Germans whose families settled in Russia and other parts of Eastern Europe in the eighteenth century to return with full citizenship. The number of ethnic German *Aussiedlers* ("resettlers") arriving from Eastern Europe each year is not insignificant; while it has fallen from its peak of 397,000 in 1990, it remains at roughly 100,000 a year.

Before 1990, second- and third-generation foreigners, most of whom had attended German schools and could speak the language fluently, were denied the opportunity to naturalize as German citizens. Children whose parents, or even grandparents, were of foreign origin inherited their family's "foreignness." By the early 1990s, 100,000 such native foreigners were being born every year and, if the government had not acted, could have lived in Germany for many more generations as technical outsiders. The first citizenship reforms, authorized by then–Chancellor Helmut Kohl, were modest; they extended the option of naturalization to foreign workers who had been living in Germany for at least fifteen years.

In 1999 Chancellor Gerhard Schröder proposed a far more sweeping revision of the citizenship regime: reducing the residency minimum from fifteen years to eight and permitting newly naturalized Germans to hold dual citizenship. Pressed by the center-right Christian Democratic Union (CDU)—which, in an unprecedented operation, collected nearly five million signatures on a "yes to integration, no to dual nationality" petition—Schröder's Red-Green government was forced to jettison some of the more progressive elements of the proposal. The final legislation abandoned the prospect of dual citizenship: Foreigners who wish to become German citizens must relinquish their original citizenship, but children of foreign-born parents may hold dual citizenship until the age of twenty-three, at which time they must choose between the two.

For all its restrictions, Germany is downright welcoming compared to Japan, a country known for being particularly insular and intolerant of foreigners. The native-foreigner problem there—most of Japan's 630,000 noncitizen permanent residents are descended from Korean workers who have lived in the country since World War II or before—has not been addressed. A measure that would give permanent residents the right to vote in Japanese elections is pending in the Diet, the nation's parliament. But despite small reforms, Japanese politicians and their constituents are wary of what they see as an increasing foreign presence. Tokyo's Governor Shintaro Ishihara caused a minor international scandal when he publicly accused "*sangokujin* and other foreigners" of committing "atrocious crimes." (*Sangokujin* is a derogatory term that literally means "people from third countries" and usually refers to Koreans or Taiwanese.)

International Solutions

Migration is by definition a global issue, but the movement of people is, for the most part, regulated at the national level. There are a few exceptions. The European Union allows citizens of its member states to move and settle freely throughout the union (though it does not yet have a coherent policy on welcoming immigrants from outside the union). But when Mexico's new president, Vicente Fox, recently suggested an expansion of the North American Free Trade Agreement to include the free movement of *people,* not just goods, his northern neighbors in the United States and Canada laughed uncomfortably and then politely ignored him.

With regional organizations turning a blind eye to the problem, the task of protecting migrant workers has been left to the (relatively weak) instruments of the United Nations and the International Labor Organization. The ILO's Migration for Employment Convention, drafted in 1949, is sorely outmoded. In a recent e-mail, Gloria Moreno Fontes Chammartin, an ILO official in Geneva, wrote that while "the principles enshrined in these instruments are still valid today," many of the specific provisions need to be updated. "The ILO instruments were drafted with state-organized migration in mind," she said, and they have little to say about "clandestine migration and undocumented employment," which have become much larger problems.

While the ILO is in the process of rethinking its convention, the United Nations is moving—very, very slowly—toward the enactment of the International Convention on the Protection of the Rights of All Migrant Workers and Members of Their Families, which was adopted by the General Assembly in 1990. The text of the convention is little more than a reiteration of two covenants included in what is known in diplomatic parlance as the International Bill of Human Rights: the International Covenants on Civil and Political Rights and on Economic, Social and Cultural Rights. Migrant workers, along with women, racial and ethnic minorities, and children, need their own convention, the thinking goes, because in practice they are often not afforded the rights promised them by more universal human rights language.

As part of international law, the convention would establish minimum standards for the protection of migrant workers, regardless of their legal status, including freedom from slavery or forced labor and from arbitrary arrest and detention. States could be held accountable for their mistreatment of undocumented workers at border crossings and police stations; under the current system, such mistreatment is considered an internal matter. (Unless a large number of their countrymen work abroad, as with Koreans in Japan and Indians in the Gulf states, sending countries are slow to protest abuses.) The convention would go even further in extending rights to documented migrants—most notably, the right to "equality of treatment" with nationals in access to education, housing, and a variety of workplace protections.

It is hard to consider the migrant workers' convention (MWC) a "major human rights instrument," as it was hailed at the 1993 World Conference on Human Rights: More than ten years after its drafting, it has yet to go into effect. A UN convention can enter into force only after twenty countries have ratified it. The MWC, which has sixteen ratifications and ten signatures (a signature is the first step toward ratification), is in diplomatic limbo. Patrick Taran, who coordinates the global campaign for ratification of the MWC, is hopeful that the convention will come into force within the next few months. The easiest short-term solution, he says, would be to lean on the ten signatory countries to ratify the convention as quickly as possible.

But the campaign, a consortium of fifteen nongovernmental organizations (including Migrants Rights International, of which Taran is director), does not have the resources to carry out such a coordinated effort. The process has been held back by understaffing, caused in turn by underfinancing. As Taran wrote in the *European Journal of Migration and Law* last summer, "There is not one person anywhere in the world, in any international organization, in any government, or any civil society group engaged with full-time responsibilities related to promoting this convention. There is simply no one yet taking up on a full-time basis the huge tasks of information distribution, coordination, advocacy, etc., that promoting adoption of a major international treaty requires."

If the convention were to come into effect in a few months, or even a few years, a huge problem would still remain: All of the countries that have signed on are developing nations that, on balance, send their citizens to work abroad. Egypt, Mexico, and the Philippines have all ratified the treaty; Turkey, Guatemala, and Bangladesh are at the signature phase. To date, none of the industrialized countries—countries that are largely responsible for the mistreatment of migrants—has so much as expressed interest in the treaty.

This divide between developed and developing countries was obvious last year at a meeting on the topic of "Rights of Migrant Workers, Minorities, Displaced Persons, and Other Vulnerable Groups" that was held by the United Nations commissioner for human rights. Representatives from developing countries like Senegal, El Salvador, Morocco, and Venezuela spoke about the need for international standards to address the plight of migrant workers. The United States and European countries talked instead about minorities and "other vulnerable groups" like gays and lesbians and people with mental disabilities, ignoring the topic of migrant workers completely. Belgium brought up the not wholly related topic of child pornography. The only direct response came from Singapore, whose representative, Margaret Liang, asserted that migrants ought not to have guarantees of equal treatment because "the labor market should be allowed to find its own equilibrium."

Activists are not surprised that industrialized countries, many of whom are dependent on migrant labor in their agricultural or service sectors, are not interested in backing an international treaty for migrants' rights. Patrick Taran likes to say that "Chile under Pinochet and Iran under the shah did not rush to sign the treaty on torture." Shirley Hune, who sat in on the convention's drafting process for the Quaker United Nations Office, remembers the U.S. representative insisting that the treaty had little to do with the American immigration experience. But the convention states that any migrant—documented or undocumented—who is engaged in "remunerated activity," or any member of such a migrant's family, is entitled to certain fundamental human rights. This would include the seasonal farmworkers, more than one million of them, who cross the U.S.-Mexican border to pick tobacco and lettuce and apples, as well as the undocumented migrants who work in restaurants and factories in U.S. cities.

Wanted but Not Welcome

Whether or not the industrialized countries choose to ratify the MWC, they will be forced to reconsider their policies on migrant labor over the next few years as they find their social insurance running up against the strain of an aging population. According to a UN report on replacement migration released last year, the demographic situation is so dire that in order to offset the aging population, the necessary level of new immigration will need to be "extremely large, and in all cases entail vastly more immigration than occurred in the past." Consider the case of Japan, whose population is projected to decline by 17 percent by 2050, from 127 million to 105 million, at the same time that the percentage of the population over sixty-five is expected to nearly double from 17 percent to 32 percent. In order to maintain the current balance between workers and retirees, Japan would have to open its doors to an unprecedented ten million migrants a year over the next fifty years. Just to keep the size of the labor force at the 1995 level would require 600,000 new migrants a year. And similarly radical levels of immigration would be necessary to safeguard retirement benefits throughout Europe.

Changing deep-rooted attitudes toward immigration, though, is easier said than done. Throughout the industrialized world, public reaction to the presence of foreign workers has been anything but welcoming. Switzerland, which has the largest percentage of foreigners of any European country—in part because of its restrictive citizenship policies—held a referendum in September on a proposal to cap the number of foreigners at 18 percent of the population. The proposal lost 64 percent to 36 percent. If it had been adopted, it would have been summarily deported.

The climate in Switzerland is not much more extreme than in the European Union. While member states have successfully harmonized their policies toward movement within the union, they are finding it much more difficult to agree on a common set of immigration laws. Douglas Klusmeyer of the Carnegie Endowment notes that efforts to establish a set of European Union–wide guidelines on the acceptance of what are known as third-country nationals—most recently at a conference in Tampere, Finland—have been "focused on the prevention of asylum seekers and illegal immigration, and the crime associated with those groups. It is striking that there was so little said in Tampere about the positive contributions of immigrants to European societies since World War II and next to nothing about the demographic problems."

In Israel some conservative politicians have seized on the problem of foreign workers as one that threatens everything from jobs to the solvency of the welfare system to the Jewish character of the state. In December of last year, Zevulun Orlev, a member of Israel's parliament, the Knesset, for the mainstream National Religious Party, called for the deportation of all undocumented foreign workers. His words could have been taken from the debate five years earlier in California over Proposition 187, the controversial ballot initiative to deny state social services to illegal immigrants. Orlev told the *Jerusalem Post* that "the children of foreign workers demand resources which should be given to Israeli children. I am not in favor of punishing a child because of the sins of his parents, but I cannot understand why we do not . . . expel them from the country."

The irony, of course, is that many of the very workers accused of overrunning the country were recruited by local businesses. Until the early 1990s, Israeli businesses were dependent on Palestinian day laborers to work in their fields and build block after block of concrete apartment buildings. That changed in 1993 when a series of bus bombings encouraged the Israeli government to close the border with the territories and impose curfews, sometimes for weeks at a time. Because Palestinians were no longer a reliable source of labor, Israeli businesses quietly lobbied the labor and agriculture ministries for permission to recruit workers from abroad. The policy and its possible implications were never debated in the Knesset.

Aristide Zolberg, director of the International Center for Migration, Ethnicity and Citizenship and a professor of politics at the New School University, calls this discrepancy between business interest and nationalist sentiment the "wanted but not welcome paradox." As he explains in *Citizenship and Exclusion,* "The very qualities that make a group suitable for recruitment as 'labor' demonstrate its lack of qualifications for 'membership.'" But foreign workers are not merely labor; they are also human beings who put down roots and start families in their host country. Efforts to prevent temporary workers from settling more permanently—limiting slots to single men and women, rotating recruitment, and restricting options in employment (often to a single employer)—have failed, almost without exception.

Even if a country were able to monitor its legal foreign workforce closely, there still would be the matter of illegal entrants. In Israel undocumented workers, who are not bound by set visa time limits, are even more likely than their legal counterparts to stay in the country for long stretches of time. "Wages are low in their home country. They cannot make a living," notes sociology professor Ze'ev Rosenhek, who—along with Erik Cohen, also of the Hebrew University—is conducting the first academic study of Israeli migrant-worker communities. "Some have already stayed for ten years; they have families and kids here. They've established a 'normal life.' Kids play in the streets. Families walk to church on Sunday."

While illegal migrants do live with the fear of being deported—the Israeli government deported 5,200 illegal workers in 1999, up from 950 in 1995—they often have more freedom than legally recruited migrants in their choice of work. Illegal migrants can work for any company willing to hire labor under the table, while legal workers are often restricted on official work permits to a single employer. This structure worries Dana Alexander, an attorney with the Association for Civil Rights in Israel, who calls legal foreign workers "one of the most vulnerable groups in Israeli society." Because workers are bound to a single employer, they "have no bargaining power," Alexander says. "They cannot stand up to their employers for abuses like illegal deductions, withholding pay, or receiving less than minimum wage," for fear of deportation. (This process is not unlike the H1-B visa program in the United States, which is used to recruit skilled foreign labor. An H1-B visa authorizes computer programmers and techies to work for a particular employer; workers can be deported if they quit or get fired. See Alexander Nguyen, "High-Tech Migrant Labor," *American Prospect* [December 20, 1999].)

A better solution, argues Dana Alexander, would be to issue a work permit for a certain area of employment—say, agriculture or construction—for a given period of time. With work authorization separated from employment at a specific company, foreign workers could join the open labor market, and employers would be forced to treat their workers fairly or risk losing them entirely. Decoupling work permits from specific jobs would also eliminate the most egregious abuses of human rights, such as the confiscation of a worker's passport or the withholding of pay until the end of a worker's stay—both common strategies that companies use to retain control over "their" corps of foreign workers.

This is exactly the kind of reform that would be encouraged by the UN convention on migrant workers. It remains to be seen, though, if countries like Israel, Germany, and the United States will comply with the convention's guidelines, or if they will, in the words of Singapore's Margaret Liang, allow the labor market to "find its own equilibrium," exploitation and all.

The H-1B Straitjacket: Why Congress Should Repeal the Cap on Foreign-Born Highly Skilled Workers

SUZETTE BROOKS MASTERS AND TED RUTHIZER

Executive Summary

American industry's explosive demand for highly skilled workers is being stifled by the federal quota on H-1B visas for foreign-born highly skilled workers. The quota is hampering output, especially in high-technology sectors, and forcing companies to consider moving production offshore.

The number of H-1B visas was unlimited before 1990, when it was capped at 65,000 a year. In 1998 the annual cap was raised to 115,000 for 1999 and 2000, but industry is expected to fill the quota several months before the end of the fiscal year. The shortage shows no sign of abating. Demand for core information technology workers in the United States is expected to grow by 150,000 a year for the next eight years, a rate of growth that cannot be met by the domestic labor supply alone.

Fears that H-1B workers cause unemployment and depress wages are unfounded. H-1B workers create jobs for Americans by enabling the creation of new products and spurring innovation. High-tech industry executives estimate that a new H-1B engineer will typically create demand for an additional three to five American workers.

Reports of systematic underpayment and fraud in the program are false. From 1991 through September 1999, only 134 violations were found by the U.S. Department of Labor, and only 7, or fewer than 1 per year, were found to be intentional. The lack of widespread violations confirms that the vast majority of H-1B workers is being paid the legally required prevailing wage or more, undercutting charges that they are driving down wages for native workers. Wages are rising fastest and unemployment rates are lowest in industries in which H-1B workers are most prevalent.

Trade Briefing Paper, CATO Institute, Center for Trade Policy Studies, March 3, 2000. Reprinted with permission of the CATO Institute. Suzette Brooks Masters is an attorney and a member of the board of directors of the National Immigration Forum. Ted Ruthizer is a partner and the head of the Immigration Law Group at the New York law firm of Robinson Silverman Pearce Aronsohn & Berman, LLP. He teaches immigration law at Columbia Law School and is former president and general counsel of the American Immigration Lawyers Association.

Congress should return to U.S. employers the ability to fill gaps in their workforce with qualified foreign national professionals rapidly, subject to minimal regulation, and unhampered by artificially low numerical quotas.

Introduction

For almost fifty years the U.S. economy has benefited from the contributions of people admitted with the H-1B status, which permits qualified foreign national professionals to work for U.S. employers on a temporary basis.[1] By using the H-1B visa, employers have been able to quickly plug holes in their domestic workforce with capable and often exceptional professionals from abroad in a wide range of fields, including information technology, finance, medicine, science, education, law, and accounting. Yet, as U.S. employers, large and small alike, struggle to find enough skilled professionals, particularly in the high-tech sector,[2] the H-1B status is being strangled. Unnecessary and inadequate H-1B quotas have put this vital immigration status in jeopardy and threaten to undermine the competitiveness of U.S. companies in the global marketplace.

The puzzling question is why the use of H-1B professionals has been subject to such virulent attack. How is it that this long-established visa category can be championed by virtually all employers and by most economists who have studied its effects on the economy and, at the same time,[3] be reviled by much of organized labor and labor's supporters in Congress and the executive branch?

To understand that enigma, one must examine the major questions—both factual and rhetorical—underlying the H-1B debate:

Do H-1B professionals benefit the domestic economy?

Do H-1B professionals displace U.S. workers or depress wages?

Without a strict quota, will employers hire foreign nationals before U.S. citizens?

Does the availability of H-1B professionals diminish the willingness of U.S. companies to train and educate our domestic workforce for technical and scientific positions?

Our study of each of those questions leads us to the firm conclusion that H-1B hiring has contributed significantly to the growth and continued good health of our economy and has helped, not harmed, the U.S. worker. Although labor organizations and their political allies have continued to perpetuate the myth of underpaid foreign professionals damaging our economy and destabilizing our domestic workforce, the facts tell us otherwise. The challenge for Congress is to move beyond this restrictionist mind-set and recognize the important benefits of using foreign professionals to fill specific employment positions. That requires a rethinking of the numerical caps now crippling the H-1B status.

Foreign Professionals: A Boon to the U.S. Economy

The United States is the economic envy of the world. Our dynamic tradition of accepting and successfully integrating successive waves of immigrants has made us the beneficiary of the world's most talented and renowned research scientists, economists, engineers, mathematicians, computer scientists, and other professionals. Those immigrants have made major contributions to the U.S. economy, particularly in the high-tech sector.[4] Recent studies that have measured the magnitude of those contributions have confirmed that immigration creates wealth and increases the size of the economy overall.

One of the most widely respected of those studies, a 1997 report by the National Research Council of the National Academy of Sciences, found that immigrants raise the incomes of U.S.-born workers by at least $10 billion per year.[5] And some people believe that those estimates are understated because they do not account for the domestic economic impact of immigrant-owned businesses or of highly skilled foreign national workers on overall U.S. productivity.[6]

Over time, the benefits of immigration are even greater. James P. Smith, chairman of the National Research Council's Panel on Immigration and an economist at the RAND Corporation, testified in 1997 before the Immigration Subcommittee of the Senate Judiciary Committee that if the $10 billion annual gain from immigrants were discounted by a real interest rate of 3 percent, the net present value of the gains from immigrants who have arrived in the United States since 1980 would be $333 billion.[7]

Of all the foreign workers coming to the United States, no category provides such an instant boost to the economy as do H-1B professionals. Although they are here no longer than six years, H-1B professionals, like their permanent counterparts, satisfy unmet labor needs and provide a diverse, skilled, and motivated labor supply to complement our domestic workforce and spur job creation. But unlike their permanent counterparts, H-1B professionals offer the very important advantage of enabling employers to meet immediate labor needs. Employers can hire H-1Bs in months or even weeks. In contrast, it can take four years or more to qualify a worker for permanent "green card" status.[8]

With unemployment at a peacetime, postwar low of 4.1 percent, the resulting tight labor market has made the H-1B status even more important to U.S. companies of all stripes and sizes. In recent years, H-1B usage by financial and professional service firms has risen sharply, reflecting the increased globalization of those industries. Multinational companies often must draw on the skills and talents of professionals from their operations abroad. In information technology, management consulting, law, accounting, engineering, and telecommunications, companies are increasingly using international teams to work on transnational projects to meet the needs of their global clients.[9]

Across the board, in virtually all the professions, skilled and talented foreign nationals bring fresh perspectives and special expertise to American companies. For example, in the important field of advertising, British nationals have led the way in introducing the important new discipline of account planning. In the fifteen years since British account planners "exported" that new way of looking at advertising from the consumers' point of view, virtually all major U.S. advertising agencies have established account planning departments, which follow the precepts taught by the British account planners who first came here with the H-1B status. When French or German H-1B corporate lawyers use their knowledge of European civil law or EU law to analyze complex legal issues, they not only benefit their U.S. law firm employers but also enrich our economy in ways beyond simply filling a job for which competent professionals are in short supply. Similar examples abound in countless other fields, in which H-1Bs bring to their U.S. employers new ways of thinking about technology, processes, and problem solving.

Perhaps no industry presents a stronger case for increased usage of H-1Bs than does information technology (IT). The evidence is overwhelming that there is currently a serious shortage in the United States of IT professionals, one that is projected to become increasingly severe over the next several years.[10] Two years ago, the Information Technology Association of America and Virginia Polytechnic Institute released preliminary findings on the shortage of IT workers, estimating that as of January 1998 there were 346,000 IT vacancies;[11] there is no sign that the shortage has abated since then. Currently, the IT sector remains the most dynamic in the U.S. economy and is driving much of its growth, contributing more than one-third of our real economic growth between 1995 and 1997. The increase in the number of IT workers in the U.S. economy has vastly outpaced the overall U.S. job growth rate. For example, between 1983 and 1998 jobs for systems analysts and computer scientists soared by 433 percent, or nearly fifteen times the comparable national rate of job growth of 30 percent.[12]

The explosive growth of high-tech jobs will likely continue through the next decade. In its June 1999 report, "The Digital Work Force," the U.S. Department of Commerce's Office of Technology Policy underscored the importance of the IT sector to the U.S. economy and noted that the need for IT workers cuts across all industries, from manufacturing, services, and health care to education and government.[13] The OTP predicts that 1.4 million new workers, nearly 150,000 a year, will be required to meet the projected demand for core information technology workers in the United States between 1996 and 2006,[14] and that the domestic pipeline of potential workers will not meet that demand. In November 1999 the U.S. Department of Labor projected that the five fastest growing occupations between 1998 and 2008 would all be in computer-related fields. Three of those occupations—systems analysts, computer engineers, and computer support specialists—were also among the top fifteen in projected numerical growth. The Labor Department expected the total number of workers in those three core high-tech occupations to increase from 1,345,000 in 1998 to 2,685,000 in 2008, a 100 percent increase compared to a growth rate in overall employment of 14 percent. "The demand for computer-related occupations will continue to increase as a result of the rapid advances in computer technology and the continuing demand for new computer applications, including the Internet, Intranet, and World Wide Web applications," the Labor Department noted.[15]

Information technology companies depend on H-1B professionals to compete in a rapidly changing marketplace. In 1995 about one-quarter of H-1B professionals were in IT-related fields. Not surprisingly, by 1997 approximately half of the H-1Bs were in IT-related fields.[16] Several aspects of the way the IT industry functions account for its particular need for H-1B professionals. First, quick turnaround time inevitably drives employers to hire professionals who already possess the needed technical skills and experience and can work productively at once. Second, product proliferation creates demand, which changes suddenly and often, for specialized knowledge and skills. Combined, those pressures produce the need for "the right worker, with the right skills, at the right time."[17] Because of those constraints, if there is no readily available U.S. worker, the H-1B professional becomes critical to continued economic growth. Yet, despite the demonstrated contributions of those workers to America's welfare, the Clinton administration and some members of Congress have gone out of their way to make it difficult, and sometimes impossible, to hire H-1B professionals.

H-1B Availability Has Been Sharply Curtailed

The H-1B visa category was designed to be an asset to American industry, and for almost forty years there was no limit on the number of H-1B "nonimmigrant" petitions granted in any given year. In its 1992 report reviewing the history of the H-1B status, the U.S. General Accounting Office explained the economic benefit provided by H-1B professionals: "One of the major purposes of nonimmigrant work-related visas is to enable U.S. businesses to compete in a global economy. Increasingly, U.S. businesses find themselves competing for international talent and for the 'best and the brightest' around the world. The nonimmigrant visa program can be a bridge or a barrier to successful international competition."[18]

What had been a bridge suddenly became a barrier with the passage of the Immigration Act of 1990.[19] At the same time that Congress expanded the levels of permanent employment-based immigration (raising the annual maximum numerical quota from 54,000 to 140,000), it reduced the future availability of temporary H-1B professionals by imposing, for the first time, a cap on annual visas. The rationale driving the 1990 act's seemingly inconsistent expression of public policy was the erroneous assumption that, with an increase in the number of slots made available for permanent immigrants, there would be reduced demand for temporary professionals.[20] And many members of Congress were swayed by organized labor's fears about the weak economic bargaining power of the temporary professionals and the possible displacement of U.S. workers.[21] The 1990 law imposed a cap of 65,000 on the annual number of new H-1B professionals permitted entry into the United States and required U.S. employers hiring such foreign workers to make a variety of attestations to ensure that those hires would have no adverse effect on the wages and working conditions of U.S. workers.[22] Employers were also prohibited from using foreign workers as strikebreakers and were required to notify their employees of the proposed hiring of a foreign temporary worker.

In 1997, when the cap was reached for the first time, U.S. employers began to clamor for more H-1B visas. In 1998 the cap was again reached, this time in May, only seven months into the fiscal year.[23] Finally, in October 1998 Congress responded to the employer outcry by enacting the American Competitiveness and Workforce Improvement Act,[24] which increased the number of H-1B professionals to 115,000 for fiscal years 1999 and 2000, and 107,500 for FY01. The new law also provided for a return to the 65,000 cap in FY02. Unfortunately, the increase soon proved insufficient. Because of pent-up demand and an economy chugging along in high gear, the increased numbers for FY99 were once again exhausted by the spring of 1999, months before the September 30 end of the fiscal year.[25] The situation for FY00 seems even worse—the 115,000 cap is likely to be reached several months before the fiscal year ends.

H-1B Professionals Create Opportunities for U.S. Workers

In an intensely competitive global environment, with constant pressure placed on employers to cut expenses and increase productivity, the H-1B visa category has become a convenient target for critics who try to draw a connection between immigration and domestic layoffs. Although it is true that large U.S. corporations have been laying off workers in record numbers,[26] many employers are firing one type of worker and hiring other workers with different skills. H-1B professionals are not the cause of those layoffs and hiring practices but an important source of flexibility in the labor market. The need for H-1B professionals is another manifestation of the inexorable pressure on companies to adapt quickly to changing market conditions. Constraining H-1B hiring won't end corporate downsizing. It will simply force employers to shift more and more of their operations abroad, where they can get the resources they need, including all-important human capital, to maintain production.[27]

When the demand for workers cannot be met domestically, which is the case today, U.S. companies must look elsewhere. Ideally, they would hire foreign workers and integrate them into their existing U.S. operations. But if U.S. companies are unable to gain access to the workers they need because of limits on H-1B hiring, then some are left with only one choice: hire the workers they need abroad with a corresponding offshore shift in domestic operations. Asked how Motorola Inc. would respond to the hiring crisis caused by inadequate numbers of H-1B visas, Motorola's head of global immigration services recently stated: "If we have to do that [shift work overseas], we will, but that's not a very practical business approach to the problem. . . . And it's not very good for American workers."[28]

This phenomenon, known as offshore outsourcing, can be harmful to the U.S. economy and U.S. workers, especially in the more knowledge-intensive industries. The hiring of foreign-born highly skilled workers can have a positive ripple effect not only on the companies that hire the workers but on the economy as a whole. Highly skilled workers are able to create new products and, in some cases, whole new sectors of an industry, creating opportunities for other workers. T. J. Rodgers, president and CEO of Cypress Semiconductors, testified before Congress that for every foreign-born engineer he is allowed to hire, he can hire five other workers in marketing, manufacturing, and other related areas.[29] At Sun Microsystems, both the Java computer language and the innovative SPARC microprocessor were created by engineers first hired through the H-1B program; their work then opened opportunities for thousands of other workers.[30]

In the critical IT sector, companies that can't hire the professionals they need are going abroad in increasing numbers. In recent testimony before the Senate Subcommittee on Immigration investigating this problem, witness after witness spoke to this growing phenomenon. Susan Williams DeFife, CEO of women-CONNECT.com, a leading Internet site for women in business, asked: "What happens when companies like mine can't hire the workers we need? We have to delay projects and in the Internet industry where change occurs daily and competitors are springing up all around you, waiting to execute on a project can be lethal."[31] DeFife told the subcommittee that denying companies the ability to hire H-1B professionals would leave companies with three less-than-satisfactory options: limit the company's growth, "steal" employees from competitors, or move operations offshore.

In a similar vein, Sen. Spencer Abraham (R-Mich.), chairman of the Senate Immigration Subcommittee and main sponsor of the 1998 bill raising the H-1B cap, echoed the concern about forcing American industry to export jobs abroad: "[F]oreign countries are stepping up their own recruitment efforts, including a pitch by the Canadian government for U.S. high-tech companies to move to Canada so as to avoid the problem of hitting the H-1B cap year after year here in America. The CEO of Lucent Technologies stated this summer at a Capitol Hill technology forum that it has placed hundreds of engineers and other technical people in the United Kingdom in response to an insufficient supply of U.S.-based workers—keeping many related jobs from being created in America."[32]

Shall we close our eyes to globalization and take the myopic view that a job that cannot be filled with an American is not a job worth saving? Such a policy would be harmful not only to the individual businesses affected but also to America's general economic well-being.

H-1B Enforcement Problems Minimal

The most common argument against H-1Bs is that they allegedly displace U.S. workers and depress wages. In response, Congress has spun an elaborate web of laws resulting in complex regulations supposedly to protect native workers from any such impact. But nothing in theory, wage and job trends, or law enforcement data indicates that the H-1B status has a negative impact on the U.S. labor market.

The U.S. Department of Labor, one of the major critics of the H-1B status, has carefully tracked the program's so-called abuses. We obtained and reviewed H-1B enforcement data from the Wage and Hour Division of DOL and were surprised by what we found.[33] From 1991, at the inception of the H-1B caps and labor condition attestations, through September 30, 1999, DOL received a total of 448 complaints alleging underpayment of H-1B professionals, and other employer violations (an average of fewer than 60 complaints nationwide each year). Of those 448 complaints, only 304 resulted in a DOL investigation. During that period, nearly 525,000 H-1B nonimmigrant petitions were granted.[34] Clearly, the complaint rate for a program supposedly rife with abuse is minuscule.

A violation was found in only 134 of the 159 DOL investigations that have been completed to date. Back wages found due over the entire eight-year period amounted to $2.7 million spread over 726 employees. That amount averages $337,500 a year in total underpayments, or less than $5 a year in underpayments for each H-1B visa issued during the period. In relation to the $4.2 trillion in total wage and salary disbursements paid to U.S. workers in 1998,[35] the average annual underpayment to H-1Bs amounted to 0.000008 percent—or about forty cents for every $50,000 paid in wages and salaries. With H-1B workers accounting for such a small share of total U.S. workers, the impact of these rare cases on the overall wage level is insignificant.

Infractions of DOL wage rules appear to be not only rare but random, with no discernible pattern of intentional abuse. Of the 134 violations, only 7 were determined to be "willful,"[36] an average of about one intentional violation per year. The fact that more than 94 percent of the small number of violations were unintentional demonstrates that the problem is not with employers but with a law that is needlessly complex, arbitrary, and cumbersome.

Given all the attention lavished by H-1B critics on the "job shops" (that is, companies providing temporary professional personnel to high-tech employers on a contract basis), one would expect to find large numbers of cases involving IT-sector employers failing to pay the prevailing wage. In fact, the authors' analysis of DOL enforcement data shows that, over the eight-year period in question, only 231 employees in the high-tech sector, now estimated to employ between 2 million and 3.5 million people,[37] were owed back wages. This constitutes less than one-third of the total number of H-1B employees in all specialty occupations found by DOL to be due back wages.

What is most striking about the low level of enforcement activity is that an aggrieved party (that is, the largely mythical American worker who loses a job to an underpaid temporary foreign worker) has but to make a call to DOL to start the ball rolling. Complaints don't require lawyers, simply a phone call. And DOL is champing at the bit to find abusive employers. In this environment, one would expect every "displaced" U.S. worker and every "underpaid" foreign worker to clamor for justice. Workers talk to one another, and job hopping and raiding are commonplace. If abuse were prevalent, it would be impossible to hide. The enforcement data simply do not support allegations of the displacement of U.S. workers or the underpayment of H-1B professionals by employers.[38]

The tame enforcement picture contrasts sharply with the widespread but unproven accusations of pervasive fraud in the H–1B visa process. According to some opponents of the H-1B status, the alleged fraud is occasioned by employers who knowingly file visa petitions for persons who fail to meet the statutory criteria, prospective H-1B applicants who falsify their academic credentials, and government employees on the take who further those criminal acts. But the evidence of H-1B visa fraud is exclusively anecdotal. Given the small number of those visas available every year and the overwhelming need for such visas by legitimate employers complying with the law, vague, largely unsubstantiated allegations of abuse should not be accepted without hard evidence, and they must not obscure the very real benefits provided by this important category of visa holders.

In House Immigration Subcommittee hearings held on the topic of nonimmigrant visa fraud in May of 1999, senior Immigration and Naturalization Service official William Yates testified that "anecdotal reports by INS Service Centers indicate that INS has seen an increase in fraudulent attempts to obtain benefits in this category [H-1B]. These fraud schemes appear to be the result of those wishing to take advantage of the economic opportunities in the U.S."[39] Given the small base number of proven frauds, the alleged increase hardly seems a vigorous call to action. In a similar vein, the inspector general of the U.S. Department of Justice, Michael R. Bromwich, testified that "there is very little hard data available to gauge the magnitude of visa fraud, a point noted by [the General Accounting Office] in its reports on this subject. . . . This lack of comprehensive statistics hinders the ability of the State Department and the INS to appropriately respond to visa fraud."[40] Moreover, the three cases cited in the inspector general's testimony as ongoing fraud investigations all involved criminal activity by INS employees. No reasonable person condones immigration fraud of any type, but the allegation of significant H-1B fraud is simply unsupported by the facts.

H-1B Professionals Do Not Depress U.S. Wages

Despite the absence of evidence that H-1B workers are paid less than the market wage, critics persist in arguing that H-1B workers are paid less than their U.S. counterparts, which exerts downward pressure on wages. Yet the facts are that wage growth is strong in the United States and that H-1B professionals' pay is on a par with that of their domestic counterparts. We know that H-1B workers are paid well because the law mandates that they be paid at least the prevailing wage or the actual wage paid to those who are similarly situated. And we also know from reviewing the enforcement evidence that an overwhelming majority of employers of H-1B workers are complying with the law. Those few cases in which the law is violated are relatively easy to detect and report to the relevant authorities. Given the desperate need employers have for skilled workers to meet their skills gaps, the high costs associated with H-1B hiring, and the extremely low incidence of violations detected by DOL, there is no basis for speculating that H-1B workers are being paid less than the going rate.

Compound that with the fact that H-1B professionals are only a tiny fraction of the U.S. labor force, and claims of wage erosion become increasingly fanciful. The stock of H-1B professionals in the United States (six years' worth of annual flows) accounts for only about one-third of 1 percent of the domestic workforce. To illustrate the point, assume conservatively that 15 percent of the U.S. labor force, or 21 million people based on a civilian labor force of 140 million,[41] turns over every year. If we assume also that there are 240 working days per year, that means 88,000 workers are leaving their jobs every day. The influx of an entire year's worth of H-1B professionals would be equivalent to less than two days' worth of labor turnover, or 1 new H-1B worker for every 184 native workers leaving their jobs. With this much labor market activity, the effect of the annual influx of H-1B professionals on the overall labor market is insignificant.

The Commerce Department's OTP reviewed the major competing sources of wage and salary data and concluded with respect to IT workers (the sector that H-1B critics claim has been most harmed by the H-1B professionals) that salaries have been high and rising, and that those with hot skills have been seeing faster salary growth.[42] U.S. employers are paying top dollar to hire and retain the right workers and believe the investment is worthwhile. In addition to raiding other people's workers, they offer finder's fees, sign-on bonuses, and substantial salaries to potential hires, as well as quality-of-life improvements and other fringe benefits. Those who don't offer competitive salary and benefit packages will watch their workers be lured away.[43]

Everyone agrees that wages are rising in the IT sector, but people differ in their estimates. Government surveys show a moderate rate of wage growth of 3 to 4 percent a year but do not include fringe benefits, bonuses, and stock options, even though they are often key components of an overall compensation package.[44] In contrast, many private-sector surveys that do include those elements of compensation show a considerably faster pace of growth, in the range of 7 to 9 percent.[45] Hot specialties, as expected, are seeing double-digit growth.[46] With the unemployment rate down to 1.4 percent in the IT market (one-third of the overall 4.1 percent unemployment rate), there are innumerable forces militating against low pay for H-1Bs.[47]

Even outside the H-1B arena, there is no evidence to suggest that immigration generally has a depressing effect on the wages of native workers. It seems inevitable that there should be because every student is taught in Economics 101 that when the supply of something increases, and all other factors are held constant, then its price must fall. Immigration, however, changes more than the labor supply. It stimulates domestic demand for food, clothing, housing, and other consumer goods, thus raising the demand for labor. Immigration can also lead to new products, lower prices, and more innovative ways of doing business, raising the overall level of productivity and actually raising the general wage level.

That counterintuitive result is borne out in study after study. In an exhaustive 1995 survey, "Immigration: The Demographic and Economic Facts," the late economist Julian Simon reviewed the theoretical and econometric literature on the impact of immigration on wages and found only negligible effects on native wages.[48] The prominent Columbia University economist Jagdish Bhagwati commented recently in the *Wall Street Journal* that labor economists "have long puzzled over the minuscule effect on wages of even large-scale immigration (if there is an effect at all, which is debatable)."[49] He believes the explanation lies in the way immigrants are absorbed into the labor force in open economies.

In a recent paper pursuing this approach, economists Gordon Hanson and Matthew Slaughter applied the principles of international trade theory to labor market functioning, tested their hypothesis, and concluded that immigration has no adverse impact on regional wages in the United States. Specifically, Hanson and Slaughter hypothesized that if an increase in the relative supply of workers through immigration increased the output of goods and services that used labor relatively intensively and decreased the output of at least some other goods and services that used labor less intensively, then the relative demand for labor would increase—because of rising demand for its products—and thus downward pressure on wages would be eliminated. And the data they looked at for fifteen states between 1980 and 1990 bore out their hypothesis.[50]

The compelling econometric evidence on the absence of a depressing wage effect should alleviate fears that foreign professionals are hurting the earning power of domestic workers. If overall permanent immigration (both family- and employment-based) to the United States, which accounts for upwards of 800,000 new permanent residents annually, has at most a marginal effect on native wages, then it goes without saying that the effect of H-1B professionals will be inconsequential. The debate about the H-1B category should properly dispense with rhetorical arguments about caps, all of which are statistically irrelevant, and focus instead on how to help expand the U.S. economy.

Employers Pay a Premium for H-1B Professionals

Employers don't petition for H-1B professionals on a whim. The statutory and regulatory maze through which employers must navigate is difficult, time-consuming, and expensive. It is instructive to spell out exactly how expensive and burdensome it is to hire an H-1B professional, particularly since the real transaction costs have been grossly underestimated by the Department of Labor, the agency charged with monitoring and enforcing the wage and working-condition aspects of the H-1B process.[51]

To handle the complex H-1B process, employers generally must use specialized immigration counsel, knowledgeable human resources staff schooled in the finer points of immigration law, compensation and benefits experts, and educational evaluators expert in reviewing and analyzing foreign degrees and professional credentials. Employers must develop an objective wage system justifying the salary levels for every position and an actual wage system showing how the salary to be paid to the prospective H-1B employee fits within this framework, locate a published wage survey or other "legitimate source of wage information" that meets strict DOL criteria for the correct prevailing wages paid by all employers in the same geographic area or areas for the position offered at the same level of education and experience, and update these prevailing wage determinations every two years. Employers must also comply with internal posting requirements at the employers' work sites and at the work sites of other employers, observe complex "no benching" rules for H-1B employees,[52] and document their own H-1B dependency status if applicable. Employers must maintain and make available for public inspection files of labor-condition attestation records and maintain internal files documenting compliance with the many record-keeping requirements in the Labor Condition Application, a preliminary requirement before an H-1B worker can be hired. For heavy users of the H-1B visa, the compliance costs are even greater.

Following the Labor Department's certification of the LCA, immigration lawyers, working with in-house counsel or human-resource directors, must prepare the H-1B petition and supporting papers. The papers submitted to the INS Regional Service Center must establish the bona fides of the employer, the professional-degree-requiring nature of the position offered, and the professional credentials of the foreign national. Generally, an independent educational evaluator must be involved to evaluate the foreign degrees and, in some cases, to weigh the foreign national's education and employment experience to determine if they equal the required U.S. university degree.

For each petition, the INS charges a steep $610 filing fee, $500 of which is allotted to U.S. worker "retraining" and scholarships. In addition, the employer must pay the expense of recruitment and, in many cases, help pay relocation costs for the employee and any immediate family members. Those hefty transaction costs are even more burdensome for smaller employers.

If the foreign national and his or her family are overseas, they must obtain H-1B and the corresponding H-4 accompanying-family-member visas from a U.S. consulate abroad in order to enter the United States to work for an H-1B-sponsoring employer. This process requires the preparation of visa applications, the payment of separate visa processing fees, and the submission to U.S. consular officials stationed at U.S. consular posts abroad of proof of the legitimacy of the petition previously approved by the INS. Depending on the volume of cases and the numbers of employees assigned to visa work at U.S. consulates, this process can add considerable time and expense to the successful hiring of an H-1B professional.

After the expiration of the initial three-year H-1B petition, the employer must begin the H-1B process anew and go through all of the onerous procedures again. And if the H-1B professional has not been able to qualify for permanent resident status (a process that routinely takes four years) before the six-year maximum period in H-1B status elapses, the employer must say goodbye to that valued professional, despite all the previous costs and burdens.

Not too surprisingly, U.S. employers uniformly bemoan the costliness and difficulty of hiring H-1B professionals. According to Michael Murray, a human-resources executive at Microsoft: "Finding and employing foreign workers is far more time consuming, burdensome, and costly than hiring locally. For example, relocation and visa processing generally cost between $10,000 and $15,000 per foreign employee."[53]

If U.S. workers were available, it seems obvious that U.S. employers would prefer them and look to foreign workers only for unique skills unlikely to be found domestically.

H-1B Hiring Complements Training and Education

Another charge against the H-1B program is that it discourages U.S. companies from adapting to the domestic skills shortages by investing in training of the domestic workforce. In practice, however, American industry is pouring money into training programs and technical education. Hiring H-1Bs and educating and training domestic workers are not mutually exclusive but complementary: both are essential to preserving the competitive edge of U.S. companies in a global economy.

The reasons for training are obvious: retaining existing employees, keeping pace with new product lines and technological advances, and boosting skill levels of new hires. And U.S. companies are responding to the call for new training initiatives. According to Phyllis Eisen, executive director of the National Association of Manufacturers' Center for Workforce Success, U.S. industry currently invests between $60 billion and $80 billion in training annually.[54] U.S. companies are not only training their own employees but also educating America's youth in order to create a suitably trained workforce for the future.

On the basis of its 1998 survey on training issues, NAM's Center for Workforce Success reports that one-third of manufacturers offer programs to teach computer technology, and fully one-quarter of them are upgrading their workers' math and problem-solving skills. The vast majority of companies (more than 80 percent) also offers supplemental educational opportunities beyond remedial training.[55] Half of survey respondents spend between 2 and 5 percent of their payroll on training, a huge jump since 1991. In the high-tech sector, companies spend even more on training, between 4 and 6 percent of payroll, according to NAM's Eisen. Microsoft, a company that petitions for many H-1B IT professionals, invests heavily in training its own employees ($54 million in FY98) and supports the use of technology in schools throughout the country. In FY97 it contributed nearly $250 million to promote those broad training efforts.[56]

The need to train the next generation of U.S. workers and to retool current American workers to help meet the demand for professionals in the IT and other sectors makes training a high priority for U.S. companies. In a fiercely competitive global environment, H-1B professionals help U.S. companies remain in the game while they invest in their workforce and their future.[57]

Congress Should Unfetter H-1B Hiring

Meanwhile, on Capitol Hill, Congress struggles to achieve consensus on whether and how much to raise the H-1B cap, largely ignoring the overwhelming evidence that attempts to "control" the H-1B inflow are not only unnecessary but counterproductive.

"Increase the H-1B cap" bills have been introduced in the Senate and the House and are awaiting action while the available FY00 visas evaporate. The American Competitiveness in the Twenty-first Century Act, introduced in February 2000 by Senators Phil Gramm (R-Tex.), Spencer Abraham (R-Mich.), Slade Gorton (R-Wash.), and Orrin Hatch (R-Utah), would raise the cap on H-1B visas to 195,000 in fiscal years 2000–2002. It would exclude from the caps foreign-born workers employed by universities and those with advanced degrees.

Another proposal involves creation of a new immigration visa category (the so-called T visa) for foreign-born technology professionals, in recognition of the national shortage of qualified high-tech workers. Under the proposed BRAIN Act (H.R. 2687) introduced by Rep. Zoe Lofgren (D-Calif.) in August 1999, a foreign professional would need a bachelor's degree or higher in mathematics, science, engineering, or computer science and the offer of a job paying at least $60,000 a year to qualify for this new visa status. Eligibility would be limited to recent graduates of U.S. undergraduate or postgraduate programs who are currently in the United States on student visas. A similar Senate bill (S. 1645) was introduced in September 1999 by Sen. Charles Robb (D-Va.). Although the Lofgren and Robb bills acknowledge the need to fix the serious, chronic problem of too few visas, the $60,000 threshold seems arbitrarily drawn and too high an amount to cure the problem of insufficient numbers. Creating a new, separate category of visa would also require a whole new set of regulations, needlessly complicating the hiring process and introducing more delays and uncertainty into the system, rather than working within the already established H-1B procedures.

In late October 1999, Sen. John McCain (R-Ariz.) became the first member of Congress to propose doing away with the H-1B cap altogether. The Twenty-first Century Technology Resources and Commercial Leadership Act (S. 1804) would suspend the cap on H-1B nonimmigrants for the next six years, through FY06. It would also require the INS to give priority to processing H-1B petitions on behalf of students graduating from U.S. universities with advanced degrees in technical disciplines. Congress will likely consider some variation of these proposals in 2000.

Let the Market Decide H-1B Supply

Should Senator McCain's bill become law, for the first time since 1991 the U.S. government would let the market determine how many H-1Bs were needed. Since the evidence does not support claims of job displacement, wage erosion, or failure to invest domestically in training, what is the real fear? That the floodgates will fly open and millions of H-1B professionals will invade our shores? That is extremely unlikely. Before 1990 there were no caps on H-1B entrants and the numbers were always modest. Even in the early days of caps, demand for H-1B professionals never reached the permissible limit. It was not until 1997 that the legislated cap of sixty-five thousand was first met, a reflection of a strong economy's need for those valuable professionals.

The argument for raising the cap cuts across party and ideological lines. Laura D'Andrea Tyson, former chief economic adviser to President Clinton, made the case in a *Business Week* column last year that the current restrictions on H-1B visas are impeding employment and output in a rising number of regions and economic sectors. She pointed to evidence that immigrants have been a major source of job and wealth creation in Silicon Valley's thriving high-tech sector, bringing with them skills, creativity, human capital, and links to global markets. She concluded: "Conditions in the information technology sector indicate that it's time to raise the cap on H-1B visas yet again and to provide room for further increases as warranted. Silicon Valley's experience reveals that the results will be more jobs and higher income for both American and immigrant workers."[58]

One of the great strengths of the American economy today is its openness—to the flow of goods, services, capital, and people. The warnings from left and right that more trade and immigration would throw native Americans out of work, destroy jobs, and drive down real wages have proven to be spectacularly wrong as economic expansion continues. In the last decade, trade and investment flows have reached record levels while the influx of legal immigrants has averaged close to one million per year. During that period, unemployment has fallen to a thirty-year low, fifteen million net new jobs have been created, real wages have been rising all across the income scale, and the current economic expansion has just set a record as the longest in U.S. history. Our openness to trade and immigration has been an integral part of our economic success.

America's economic health should not be jeopardized by an arbitrary quota on foreign-born professionals. It is time to return to U.S. employers the ability to fill gaps in their workforce with qualified foreign national professionals rapidly, subject to minimal regulation, and unhampered by artificially low numerical quotas. We advance neither U.S. workers nor the U.S. economy by denying our employers the ability to continue to bring to our shores the best professional talent available in the world. Sound policy dictates that Congress should abolish the caps and let the market determine the need for H-1B professionals.

Notes

1. The H-1B visa provides a quick, lawful way for U.S. employers to hire foreign national professionals on a temporary basis. See § 101(a)(15)(H)(i)(b) of the Immigration and Nationality Act (INA), 8 U.S.C. § 1101(a)(15)(H)(i)(b) (1952, as amended). H-1B professionals are defined as persons coming to work in a "specialty occupation" (i.e., an occupation requiring at least the equivalent of a bachelor's degree in the field of specialty) for up to six years. INA, § 214(i), 8 U.S.C. § 1182(i). Typical examples of persons hired with H-1B status are engineers, scientists, professors, accountants, researchers, lawyers, physical therapists, economists, financial analysts, and computer professionals. See "The H-1B Program: America's Home Court Advantage in Global Competition," American Immigration Lawyers Association Issue Paper, November 3, 1999.

2. See, for example, Matt Richtell, "Need for Computer Experts Makes Recruiters Frantic," *New York Times,* November 18, 1999.

3. The H-1B status was originally introduced as part of the INA in 1952 (at which time it was classified simply as "H-1"; the "B" classification was added much later to reflect the addition of a separate visa category for nurses, the "H-1A"). It has remained in the law, albeit with major changes, since that time. Until 1990 the statutory language reserved the H-1 status for persons deemed to be of "distinguished merit and ability" coming to the United States "to perform services of an exceptional nature requiring such merit and ability." Although never defined by statute, the term *distinguished merit and ability* had long been understood and applied by the Immigration and Naturalization Service to include persons with bachelor's or higher degrees (i.e., professionals), as well as persons of prominence. In short, the H-1B status has been available to U.S. employers for almost fifty years and is hardly the ephemeral, Johnny-come-lately program that its critics pretend it to be. For an insightful history of the H-1B status, see Charles G. Gordon, Stanley M. Mailman, and Stephen Y. Yale-Loehr, *Immigration Law and Procedure* (New York: Matthew Bender, 1999), §§ 20.08 (2)(a)–(f).

4. See T. J. Rodgers, president and CEO of Cypress Semiconductor Corp., Testimony and prepared statement in support of testimony, in Senate Committee on the Judiciary, *Hearing on the High-Tech Worker Shortage and U.S. Immigration Policy,* 105th Cong., 2d sess., February 25, 1998, Serial no. J-105-76, 30–39; Stephen Moore, "Immigration Reform Means More High-Tech Jobs," *Today's Commentary,* Cato Institute, September 24, 1998, postulating that, in aggregate, the largest immigrant-founded high-tech companies generated about seventy thousand jobs and $28 billion in annual revenues in 1996; and Scott Thurm, "Asian Immigrants Are Reshaping Silicon Valley," *Wall Street Journal,* June 24, 1999, discussing the results of research showing that Asian immigrants have started, and own and direct, nearly 25 percent of high-tech companies started in Silicon Valley since 1980 and that their companies had sales of $17 billion and employed nearly sixty thousand people in 1998.

5. National Research Council, *The New Americans: Economic, Demographic, and Fiscal Effects of Immigration* (Washington: National Academy Press, 1997).

6. Moore, "A Fiscal Portrait of the Newest Americans."

7. James P. Smith, Response to Questions Posed by Sen. Spencer Abraham, in Subcommittee on Immigration of the Senate Committee on the Judiciary, *Hearing on the Economic and Fiscal Impact of Immigration,* 105th Cong., 1st sess., September 9, 1997, Serial no. J-105-45, appendix, 21.

8. For a lively and insightful discussion of the very lengthy and difficult process entailed in qualifying for U.S. permanent residence status, see Barry Newman, "In Canada, the Point of Immigration Is Mostly Unsentimental," *Wall Street Journal,* December 9, 1999.

9. Austin T. Fragomen, chairman of the American Council on International Personnel, Testimony, in Subcommittee on Immigration and Claims of the House Committee on the Judiciary, *Hearings on the H-1B Professional Worker Program,* 106th Cong., 1st sess., August 5, 1999.

10. U.S. Department of Commerce, Office of Technology Policy, "America's New Deficit: The Shortage of Information Technology Workers," Fall 1997; OTP, "Update: America's New Deficit," January 1998; OTP, "The Digital Work Force: Building Infotech Skills at the Speed of Information," June 1999, cited hereafter as "The Digital Workforce"; and Senate Committee on the Judiciary, *Hearing on the High-Tech Worker Shortage and U.S. Immigration Policy.*

11. Virginia Polytechnic Institute, "Help Wanted: A Call for Collaborative Action for the New Millennium," March 1998.

12. Ibid., 21.

13. "The Digital Work Force," 5.

14. Ibid., 25.

15. Douglas Braddock, "Occupational Employment Projections to 2008," *Bureau of Labor Statistics Monthly Labor Review* (November 1999): 55.

16. "The Digital Work Force," 5.

17. Ibid., 9.

18. U.S. General Accounting Office, "Immigration and the Labor Market: Nonimmigrant Alien Workers in the United States," GAO/PEMD-92-17, April 1992, 10.

19. The changes made by the Immigration Act of 1990 (Pub. L. No. 101-649) went into effect in October 1991.

20. This view soon proved completely unfounded and misguided. Backlogs of employment-based permanent residence cases to be processed and approved increased to as long as four years, making it wholly unrealistic to expect that any employer could wait that long to bring a badly needed professional to the United States without first relying on the H-1B status.

21. Based on November 9, 1999, telephone interview with former U.S. representative Bruce Morrison, chairman of the House Subcommittee on Immigration at the time of the passage of the Immigration Act of 1990.

22. Those attestations are included in the Labor Condition Application, which is submitted to the U.S. Department of Labor.

23. "The Digital Work Force," 16.

24. American Competitiveness and Workforce Improvement Act (ACWIA), Title IV, Pub. L. no. 105-277. In addition to setting new caps, ACWIA imposed a battery of new restrictions on employers, particularly those deemed to be "H-1B dependent." To silence protectionist voices alleging that foreign workers displace U.S. workers and that exploitative employer practices hurt both domestic and foreign national professionals, Congress included sweeping new recruitment and employment restrictions in the legislation. Employers who violate any of the ACWIA provisions face stiff penalties, including fines of up to $35,000 for severe violations and debarment from further use of the H-1B status for up to three years. In addition, the De-

partment of Labor has been given greater authority to investigate complaints and initiate random "spot checks" of employers with past violations. The proposed regulations implementing ACWIA were published by DOL in the *Federal Register* on January 5, 1999, but are not expected to become final before early 2000.

25. The U.S. Immigration and Naturalization Service stopped approving new H-1B petitions in the spring of 1999 and apparently erroneously approved petitions in excess of the 115,000 cap for FY99. Current demand far outstrips the supply of H-1Bs. See letter dated October 5, 1999, from Sen. Spencer Abraham, chairman of the Senate Immigration Subcommittee, to Doris Meissner, commissioner of the INS, copy in authors' files; and Diane Lindquist, "INS Handed Out High-Tech Visas Lavishly, May Have Exceeded Legal Cap by as Many as 20,000," *San Diego Tribune,* October 9, 1999.

26. Michael M. Weinstein, "Economic Scene: Cream in Labor Market's Churn: Why Job Losses Are Rising amid Job Hunters' Nirvana," *New York Times,* July 22, 1999.

27. Fragomen, *Hearings on the H-1B Professional Worker Program.*

28. Quoted in Rob Kaiser, "Visa Shortage Boosts Business Overseas," *Bergen Record,* December 13, 1999.

29. Rodgers, *Hearing on the High-Tech Worker Shortage,* 35.

30. Kenneth M. Alvares, Testimony, in Senate Committee on the Judiciary, *Hearing on the High-Tech Worker Shortage and U.S. Immigration Policy,* 54.

31. Susan Williams DeFife, Testimony, in Subcommittee on Immigration of the Senate Committee on the Judiciary, *Hearing on American's Workforce Needs in the Twenty-first Century,* 106th Cong., 1st sess., October 21, 1999.

32. Spencer Abraham, Opening remarks before the Senate Subcommittee on Immigration, *Hearing on American's Workforce Needs in the Twenty-first Century,* 106th Cong., 1st sess., October 21, 1999.

33. The data were obtained in electronic format from Tom Schierling, DOL Wage and Hour Administration, in October 1999. This information is compiled by DOL for presentation at quarterly meetings with the Information Technology Association of America

34. The total number of visas is based on INS quarterly data submitted to Congress on H-1B petitions granted, as reported in a November 9, 1999, telephone interview with Theresa Cardinal Brown of the American Immigration Lawyers Association:

FY92: 48,645
FY93: 61,591
FY94: 60,279
FY95: 54,178
FY96: 55,141
FY97: 65,000
FY98: 65,000
FY99: 115,000 (estimated, number may actually be higher)
Total: 524,834

35. Joint Economic Committee of Congress, *Economic Indicators,* November 1999, 5.

36. See DOL enforcement data referenced previously. "Willful" violations are now defined as those in which there is a "willful failure" to pay the correct wages or a "willful misrepresentation of material fact" in connection with the very complex wage and record-keeping requirements of the statute and Labor Department regulations. INA, § 212(n)(2)(C). Before the recent ACWIA changes, the standard for finding willful violations was "substantial failure" to comply.

37. Estimates of the size of the IT workforce vary. The 2 million estimate comes from "The Digital Work Force," 24. By contrast, the February 1997 Information Technology Association of America–Virginia Polytechnic Institute study, *Help Wanted: The IT Workforce Gap at the Dawn of a New Century* (Arlington, Va.: ITAA, 1998), estimated the core IT workforce at 3.5 million.

38. Stuart Anderson, "Widespread Abuse of H-1Bs and Employment-Based Immigration? The Evidence Says Otherwise," *Interpreter Releases,* May 13, 1996.

39. William R. Yates, Testimony, in Subcommittee on Immigration and Claims of the House Committee on the Judiciary, *Oversight Hearing on Non-immigrant Visa Fraud,* 106th Cong., 1st sess., May 5, 1999.

40. Michael R. Bromwich, Testimony, in Subcommittee on Immigration and Claims of the House Committee on the Judiciary, *Oversight Hearing on Non-immigrant Visa Fraud.*

41. According to the Bureau of Labor Statistics, the seasonally adjusted civilian labor force figure for November 1999 was 139.8 million. Regarding turnover, see Bolaji Ojo, "Tighter Labor Market Costly to Tech Sector," *Electronic Buyers News,* September 6, 1999.

42. "The Digital Work Force," 41–46.

43. Ojo discusses BLS reports of labor market tightening in the high-tech sector. Because of tight market conditions and raiding by competing employers, the annual turnover rate in Silicon Valley is between 20 percent and 30 percent, well above the national average of 13 percent to 18 percent. See Michael Murray, vice president for Human Resources at Microsoft, Prepared statement in support of testimony, in Senate Committee on the Judiciary, *Hearing on the High-Tech Worker Shortage and U.S. Immigration Policy,* 19–30.

44. "The Digital Work Force," 41. Assumptions about biases in government wage surveys are based on a telephone interview with Theresa Cardinal Brown of the American Immigration Lawyers Association, November 9, 1999.

45. The 1999 private surveys discussed in "The Digital Work Force," 43–46, include those of the Institute of Electrical and Electronics Engineers; *Information Week;* Datamasters; *Computerworld;* and the Systems Administration, Networking and Security Institute.

46. Bronwyn Fryer, "Two Years after IT Salaries and Bonuses Skyrocketed to Record Highs, Managers Report Again They Have Put a Stop to the Madness, Giving Traditional Increases to All but a Prized Few," *Computerworld,* September 6, 1999.

47. "The Digital Work Force," 47; Robert Petersen and James Forcier, "The Economics of the Information Technology Worker Shortage," *San Francisco Examiner,* April 25, 1998.

48. Julian Simon, "Immigration: The Demographic and Economic Facts," Cato Institute and the National Immigration Forum, December 1995. The extensive literature reviewed by Simon includes research studies by George J. Borjas, David Card, Michael Fix, and Jeffrey S. Passel. For a full listing, consult the bibliographic references in Simon.

49. Jagdish Bhagwati, "A Close Look at the Newest Newcomers," *Wall Street Journal,* September 28, 1999. See also Jagdish Bhagwati, "Immigration Debate Takes Skill," *Wall Street Journal,* October 13, 1999.

50. Gordon H. Hanson and Matthew J. Slaughter, "The Rybczynski Theorem, Factor Price Equalization, and Immigration: Evidence from U.S. States," National Bureau of Economic Research Working Paper 7074, April 1999. The Slaughter-Hanson paper covers small regions, such as states, groups of states, or small countries. It remains unclear what conclusions can be drawn about the impact on the United States as a whole. This is a subject for future research.

51. In its comments on the Notice of Proposed Rulemaking issued by DOL regarding the H-1B program, dated February 19, 1999, the American Immigration Lawyers Association criticized DOL's estimate of employer compliance costs as "groundless."

52. Under ACWIA, an employer must pay an H-1B worker for any nonproductive time after employment begins. This means that, during temporary economic downturns, an employer would need to terminate the employee rather than simply place the employee on unpaid leave or temporarily reduce the work schedule. For a discussion of these and other regulatory burdens imposed by ACWIA, see A. James Vazquez-Azpiri and Alan Tafapolsly, "The Practical Impact of the New Employer Obligations of the American Competitiveness and Workforce Improvement Act," *Bender's Immigration Bulletin* 4, no. 1 (January 1, 1999).

53. Murray, *Hearing on the High-Tech Worker Shortage,* 26.

54. Based on telephone interview with Phyllis Eisen on November 9, 1999. See also National Association of Manufacturers' Center for Workforce Success and Grant Thornton, LLP, *The Skills Gap* (Washington: NAM, 1998).

55. Ibid.

56. Murray, *Hearing on the High-Tech Worker Shortage.*

57. See "The Digital Work Force," chap. 8.

58. Laura D'Andrea Tyson, "Open the Gates Wide to High-Skilled Immigrants," *Business Week,* July 5, 1999, 16.

Labor Movement

Mexicans Transform a Town in Georgia—and an Entire Industry

JOEL MILLMAN AND WILL PINKSTON

Making carpets has been very good to Emiterio Fraire. The Mexican immigrant recently moved his family into the Frazier Acres subdivision here, leaving a rental to buy a $104,000 house. He loves his new, forest-green Ford Expedition and the backyard patio that's perfect for Mexico-style Sunday grilling.

Mr. Fraire and his immediate family, who hold five jobs in the nearby carpet mills, were their cul-de-sac's first Mexicans. Now two more Mexican clans have arrived, also carpet workers who have leveraged multiple incomes from the mills to leap from Third World poverty to suburban security.

"I'm surprised how much this feels like home," says the fifty-three-year-old Mr. Fraire, who has spent a quarter century toiling amid the whirring looms of about fifteen different Dalton carpet makers. "I guess as long as I'm doing this work, I'm never leaving."

He could be speaking for an entire industry. Here, in this Appalachian foothill town of 28,000 that calls itself "the carpet capital of the world," there's little concern that the North American Free Trade Agreement will siphon off U.S. jobs to Mexico, as opponents warned a decade ago. In carpet's case, the labor went to the industry instead of the industry going to the labor. Carpet mills now rely on thousands of Mexican immigrants such as the Fraires to replace an aging, mostly white, rural workforce.

Carpet's concentration in Dalton and surrounding northwest Georgia has made the industry a case study in a phenomenon sweeping the American interior: the Mexican company town. Mexicanization has spread from the meat processors of Kansas to the poultry centers of Arkansas during the past decade as more than three million Mexican workers, most of them illegal, swarmed over the border to fill gaping labor shortages.

This increasingly symbiotic relationship makes Dalton just the kind of place politicians have in mind these days when they talk about doing something to "legalize" the status of Mexican workers in the United States—a topic at the top of the agenda when Mexican President Vicente Fox and George W. Bush meet next week in Washington.

 Joel Millman and Will Pinkston are staff reporters for the *Wall Street Journal*.

While a blanket amnesty for illegal workers has largely been ruled out, the leaders hope to announce a preliminary agreement on a "guest worker" program that will allow Mexican workers with long-standing ties to their U.S. employers to legalize their status. Congress would then have to sign off on the deal.

"Everyone's getting their papers together," hoping to qualify for whatever immigration reform comes along, says Mr. Fraire, himself a beneficiary of an amnesty law passed in 1986, the last time the nation dealt broadly with the issue. He says he knows dozens of illegal workers who could benefit this time around, including members of his family.

But what works for Mexicans faces mixed reviews in the community and carpet mills. Two weeks ago, Dalton's Carpet and Rug Institute trade group considered endorsing amnesty but decided it was too dicey an issue to touch. The largest mills aren't speaking out, knowing support for a relaxed immigration policy could upset white residents already unnerved by rapid change in Dalton. "They don't want to generate more resentment," says Randall Patton, a carpet-industry historian and professor at Georgia's Kennesaw State University. "But on the other hand they need the labor. They're in a difficult situation."

Just as mechanization kept U.S. jobs at home in decades past, the arrival of thousands of Mexican workers gave Dalton's carpet industry a chance to refill labor pools being thinned as aging American workers educated their children for better opportunities than they had. Lured by good wages in the mills—entry-level pay starts around $21,000 a year and can rise quickly—Mexicans poured into Dalton.

While countless textile and apparel factories have fled the South for cheap labor in Mexico, Dalton's biggest producers have closed operations in other regions, choosing to hunker down even deeper in their familiar north Georgia hills.

All of the Big Three carpet makers—Shaw Industries Inc., Mohawk Industries Inc., and Beaulieu of America LLC—are based in the vicinity. Roughly three-quarters of all U.S. carpet production comes from Georgia, mostly in the northwest corner. U.S. wholesale shipments run about $12 billion a year.

It didn't make sense to leave. Carpet mills here have made huge investments in giant tufting machines that stitch yarn into plastic backing and dye tanks that soak color into bolts of weave the length of football fields. Even if the mills cut labor costs by moving offshore, they'd still face the added expense of shipping heavy carpet back to their major market. Dalton is within a twenty-four-hour drive of about 85 percent of all U.S. buyers. Industry consolidation during the past two decades strengthened carpet makers' ties to the area, not only making Dalton a one-industry town but also making carpets a one-town industry. So, with the industry's roots entrenched, Mexico has come to Georgia. With one in five residents now identified as Hispanic, surrounding Whitfield County boasts the highest Hispanic concentration in the Southeast. That ratio reflects both immigration and the movement of thousands of white residents to outlying counties.

From fewer than 1,500 Spanish-speakers recorded by the 1990 Census, Dalton's Hispanic population swelled to 11,200 by the latest tally. Last year, one-third of the 2,400 babies born in Dalton's Hamilton Medical Center came from Hispanic homes. Hispanic children now make up a majority of all incoming kindergarten pupils in the city school system.

The sights and sounds of rural Mexico are everywhere along Dalton's main drag, Walnut Street, where accordion-rich music from Mexico's north blares from quick-stop taco shops. Posters and fliers in Spanish tout at least twenty different agencies offering ways for recent migrants to send money home. Each morning, a refrigerated truck of an Atlanta-based food distributor, El Maizal, darts in and out of the local strip malls, stocking more than two dozen Mexican restaurants and convenience stores.

Florists, funeral homes, and pharmacies all promise walk-in customers that "se habla español"—Spanish is spoken here. Dionisio Duarte's tortilla shop does a brisk business with the mill hands emerging from the Shaw Industries plant nearby. "I move 100 or 150 packages of tortillas just in the hour after a shift change," he says. His second store will open soon.

The transformation of Dalton's streets pales in comparison with what's happened in its factories. City fathers helped trigger the change in the mid-1980s. Lamenting the community's perennial designation as one of Georgia's least literate locales, they urged carpet mills not to hire teenagers who hadn't completed high school. The upshot: More local teens earned diplomas—and found better jobs.

Before long, Mexican immigrants began learning about the wealth of jobs going begging in Dalton. They started in the most menial positions: creelers, who feed yarn into tufting machines, and "roll-ups," who stoop to squeeze 1,000-foot lengths of carpet into long packing tubes.

Emiterio Fraire arrived in 1976, well ahead of the curve, after an acquaintance from his home state of Zacatecas told him about the good pay Dalton's carpet mills were offering. He left a construction job in south Texas and caught a Greyhound bus for Georgia. Finding work without a proper immigration document, or "green card," wasn't easy at first, but rapid turnover helped him climb the ladder from part-time to full-time employment.

With a churn of 20 percent a year in workers at some mills, demand for replacement hands was constant. "Ten years ago, if you didn't like the work at one mill, you'd just go to another," recalls Beaulieu Chairman Carl Bouckaert. "You want to go deer hunting? You just quit and got another job when you came back."

Managers routinely lost staff to deer season or weekend jaunts to the Talladega, Alabama, stock-car raceway. That made them prize Mexicans—typically single males with a single-minded purpose of working hard and sending their wages home to Mexico. They never seemed to make excuses for not showing up and never declined an extra shift. Gradually, the new hires moved from the night shifts to the day shifts.

"Our workforce went from basically 0 percent Hispanic in 1990 to 12 percent by 2000," says Julius Shaw, executive vice president at Shaw Industries and son of one of the founders of the company, which was taken over last year by Warren Buffett's Berkshire Hathaway Inc.

Inside the mills, older white workers grew resentful. Some accused carpet mills of actively recruiting workers from Mexico, a charge the industry denied. A series of well-publicized factory raids by the U.S. Immigration and Naturalization Service, dubbed Operation SouthPAW (for "Protecting American Workers"), only deepened Anglo residents' perception that Dalton had been overrun by aliens. "Quit employing them, quit renting to them, quit educating them," a bitter Dalton native fumed in a letter to the *Daily Citizen-News* on July 4, 1995, part of an avalanche of angry letters the paper received that summer before editors quit publishing anti-Mexican comments.

By then, Mr. Fraire was working for Shaw. His two sons, Carlos and Jose, had come to Dalton with their mother in 1984—eight years after their father had arrived. Their family was still without papers, but Mr. Fraire's bosses liked him and immigration officials arrested him only once. He agreed to a "voluntary departure." But he didn't actually have to leave the country because in 1986 Congress passed the Immigration Reform and Control Act, which included a broad amnesty provision.

That allowed Mr. Fraire, his brothers and about ten other family members to get their green cards. Amnesty would eventually help more than fifty Fraire family members settle near Dalton's carpet mills.

Further relaxation of immigration policy would help ease labor pressures that persist in Dalton today despite the economic slowdown. Consider Beaulieu of America, where Carlos and Jose Fraire operate forklifts in the distribution center. Beaulieu, with 11,000 workers, will hire 2,500 new employees this year even though carpet sales are down. The reasons: an aging of the native workforce and Beaulieu's growing difficulty finding and keeping skilled legal immigrants.

Hunched over a job application at Beaulieu's hiring center on Chatsworth Highway on a recent morning, a young Latino man struggled to answer each question. He insisted he's from Puerto Rico, a U.S. territory, which means Beaulieu can hire him without a green card. Before filling in the top of the application—for name and present address—the young man reached into his shirt to remove an official-looking document he had wrapped in a plastic bag. "Hiram Gonzalez," he read slowly. "Born in Arecibo, Puerto Rico, on 3 June 1969."

Later, in the parking lot, the applicant admitted to a reporter he is really Santiago Solis from Guatemala. Mr. Solis said he paid $650 for his fake birth certificate, obtained from a broker he met through a friend at his last job, a North Carolina poultry plant.

Beaulieu turned him down because he answered "no" when asked on the application if he could prove his legal residency. Undeterred, he's convinced his $650 investment will land him a job. "Everyone says they need lots of men at the carpet mills in Dalton," he says.

Beaulieu's managers say they do all they can to keep illegals such as Mr. Solis out of their mills. Yet the same day in June the hiring center rejected his application, Beaulieu's human resources department learned that of ten thousand Social Security numbers it submitted to Washington for verification, more than five hundred were rejected. Most of the rejects, the company says, were because of clerical errors made by Beaulieu. But the company concedes some came as a result of job-seekers using false identification or stolen work cards.

Ann Dorsey, a Beaulieu official, says the company faces a "damned if we do, damned if we don't" situation. Demanding Latino applicants postpone work while their Social Security numbers are checked leaves the company open to charges of discrimination and "racial profiling," she says. She concedes that some holders of illegal documents are hired inadvertently.

In theory, amnesty would help companies such as Beaulieu reduce their exposure to document fraud. But it wouldn't solve another looming problem: finding skilled workers. Even among legal applicants, "the question is, 'Are they qualified?'" says Mike O'Neill, human resources director for Mohawk Industries. He says some tasks, such as converting polypropylene pellets into yarn, require special analytical abilities. And when it comes to career advancement, he says, "lack of English skills will be a barrier."

The children of immigrants such as Mr. Fraire are learning English, but another round of relaxed immigration policies may not be as effective as the 1986 amnesty in prolonging the Mexicanization of the carpet industry.

Increasingly, the new generation of immigrants seem as unlikely as the children of Anglos to follow their fathers into the mills. Mr. Fraire's son Carlos makes $30,000 a year driving a forklift. But the twenty-one-year old, who started at Beaulieu as a tenth grader, considers this year his last in the mill. By December, he says he'll have completed classes in computer maintenance at Dalton State College, and he'll be ready to quit the sweltering heat of the factory for an air-conditioned office. Eventually, he hopes to study dentistry.

Emiterio Fraire has even higher hopes for his youngest child, nine-year-old Mayra. His Dalton-born daughter, a U.S. citizen who will never need a green card, shouldn't have to work the way he did, he says. "I want my daughter to study, study, and study. If it's up to me, she'll never work in a mill."

Bibliography

Adams, S., and D. Neumark. 2000. *Do Living Wage Ordinances Reduce Urban Poverty?* NBER Working Paper No. 7606. Michigan State University, East Lansing.

Addison, T., D. Fox, and C. Ruhn. 1995. "Trade and Displacement in Manufacturing." *Monthly Labor Review* 118, no. 4 (April): 58–68.

AFL-CIO. "Runaway CEO Pay: What's Happening and What You Can Do About It." <http://www.aflcio.org> (2001).

Allen, K. 2001. *Health Insurance: Characteristics and Trends in the Uninsured Population—Testimony and Statement.* Washington, D.C.: U.S. General Accounting Office.

Alsalam, N. 1998. *The Economic Effects of Federal Spending on Infrastructure and Other Investments.* Washington, D.C.: Congressional Budget Office.

American Association of Community Colleges. "National Community College Snapshot." <http://www.aacc.nche.edu/allaboutcc/snapshot.htm>.

American Society for Training and Development (ASTD). 2001. "A Vision of E-Learning for America's Workforce—Report of the Commission on Technology and Adult Learning." Washington, D.C.: Virginia and National Governors Association.

American Society for Training and Development. 2001. "The 2000 ASTD State of the Industry Report Says Training Investments Reach New Heights." Press release.

Barrington, L. 2000. *Does a Rising Tide Lift All Boats?* New York: Conference Board.

Bartik, T. 2000. *Employment as a Solution to Welfare: Employment Research* 7, no.1. Kalamazoo, Mich.: W. E. Upjohn Institute for Employment Research.

Bassi, L., and M. Van Buren. 1999. *Sharpening the Leading Edge.* Alexandria, Va.: American Society for Training and Development.

———. 1999. *State of the Industry Report.* Alexandria, Va.: American Society for Training and Development.

———. 2000. *State of the Industry Report.* Alexandria, Va.: American Society for Training and Development.

Beder, H. 1999. *The Outcomes and Impacts of Adult Literacy Education in the United States.* Cambridge, Mass.: National Center for the Study of Adult Learning and Literacy.

Beneria, L. 1998. *The Impact of Industrial Relocation on Displaced Workers: A Case Study of Cortland, NY.* Community Development Reports, vol. 6, no. 1. New York: Cornell Community and Rural Development Institute.

Benson, G. 1997. "A New Look at EPSS." *Training and Development* (January): 48–49.

Bergman, B. 1996. *In Defense of Affirmative Action.* New York: Basic Books.

Bernstein, A. 2000. "Too Much Corporate Power: The Twenty-first Century Corporation." *Business Week,* September 11.

Bernstein, J. 2000. *The Living Wage Movement: Pointing the Way toward the High Road.* Washington, D.C.: Economic Policy Institute.

Bernstein, J., and J. Schmitt. 2000. *The Impact of the Minimum Wage: Policy Lifts Wages, Maintains Floor for Low-Wage Labor Market—Briefing Paper.* Washington, D.C.: Economic Policy Institute.

Bingman, M. 1999. *Changes in Learners' Lives on Year after Enrollment in Literacy Programs: An Analysis from the Longitudinal Study of Adult Literacy Participants in Tennessee.* Report no. 11. Cambridge, Mass.: National Center for the Study of Adult Learning and Literacy.

Bishop, J. 1994. "The Impact of Previous Training on Productivity and Wages." *Training and the Private Sector: International Comparisons*, ed. Lisa M. Lynch. Chicago: University of Chicago Press.

Bluestone, B. 1996. "Rewarding Work: Feasible Antipoverty Policy." *American Prospect* 7, no. 26 (May–June): 40.

Boards of Governors of the Federal Reserve System. 2001. *Consumer Credit Report, Federal Reserve Statistical Release.* Washington, D.C.: Federal Reserve System.

Brauner, S., and P. Loprest. 1999. *Where Are They Now? What States' Studies of People Who Left Welfare Tell Us, New Federalism: Issues and Options for States.* Series A, no. A-32. Washington, D.C.: Urban Institute.

Brock, T., et al. 1997. *Creating New Hope: Implementation of a Program to Reduce Poverty and Reform Welfare.* La Follette, Wisc.: School of Public Affairs.

Bronson, D., and S. Rousseau. 1995. "Working Paper on Globalization and Workers' Human Rights in the APEC Region." Rights and Democracy, International Center for Human Rights and Democratic Development, Montreal, Canada.

Brown, J. 2000. "Digital Education." *Government Technology: Solutions for State and Local Government in The Information Age* 13 (October): 28–34.

Brull, S. 2000. "What's So Bad About a Living Wage? Paying above the Minimum Seems to Do More Good Than Harm." *Business Week*, September 4.

Bruno, A. 1999. *Affirmative Action: Congressional and Presidential Activity: 1995–1998. CRS Report for Congress.* Washington, D.C.: Library of Congress.

"The Business Week Executive Compensation Scoreboard." 2001. *Business Week,* Special Issue, April 16.

Byrne, J. 2000. "Management by Web: The Twenty-first Century Corporation." *Business Week,* August 21/28.

Campbell, J., C. M. Hombo, and J. Mazzeo. 2000. *Three Decades of Student Performance: NAEP 1999 Trends in Academic Progress.* Washington, D.C.: U.S. Department of Education.

Carnevale, A., and D. Desrochers. 1999. *Getting Down to Business: Matching Welfare Recipients' Skills to Jobs That Train.* Princeton, N.J.: Educational Testing Service.

Carol, A., and J. Sergeant. 1999. *The Digital Work Force: Building Infotech Skills at the Speed of Innovation.* Washington, D.C.: U.S. Department of Commerce, Office of Technology Policy.

Cattagni, A., and E. Farris. 2001. *Internet Access in the U.S. Public Schools and Classrooms: 1994–2000, Statistics in Brief.* Washington, D.C.: U.S. Department of Education, National Center for Education Statistics.

Center for Budget and Policy Priorities. 2000. *Health Care after Welfare: An Update of Findings from State-Level Leaver Studies.* Executive Summary. Washington, D.C.

———. 2001. *Poverty Rates Fell in 2000 As Unemployment Reached Thirty-one-Year Low: Upturn in Unemployment Combined with Weaknesses in Safety Net Raise Red Flags for 2001.* Washington, D.C.

Challenger, J. 2000. "Worker-Starved Firms Turn to Telecommuting." *Chicago Sun-Times,* August 20.

Child Trends. 2001. *CTS Facts at a Glance.* Washington, D.C.: Child Trends.

Children's Defense Fund. 2000a. "CDF Releases New Report on Hardships Faced by Low-Income Working Families Who Have Left Welfare since 1996." Press release.

———. 2000b. "Child Care and Early Education Basics." Press release.

———. 2000c. "Families Struggling to Make It in the Workforce: A Post Welfare Report." Press release.

Ciulla, J. 2000. *The Working Life: The Promise and Betrayal of Modern Work.* New York: Times Books.

Clines, F. 2001. "Safety Net Helps Make Leaving the Welfare Rolls Permanent." *New York Times*, March 19.

Committee for Economic Development. 1996. *American Workers and Economic Change*. New York: Committee for Economic Development.

Compa, L. 2001. *Unfair Advantage*. New York: Human Rights Watch.

Conference Board. 1998. *Technology's Effect on Work/Life Balance, Work-Family Roundtable* 8, no. 2. New York: Conference Board.

Cooper, P., and B. S. Schone. 1997. "More Offers, Fewer Takers for Employment-Based Health Insurance: 1987–1996. *Health Affairs* 16 (6): 142–149.

Costello, C., and A. Stone. 2001. *The American Woman, 2001–2002, Getting to the Top*. Washington, D.C.: The Women's Research and Education Institute.

Coy, P. 2000. "The Creative Economy: The Twenty-first Century Corporation." *Business Week*, August 21/28.

"Creating an Informal Learning Organization: Power of Ideas @ Work." 2000. *Harvard Management Update: Harvard Business School* 5, no. 7 (July): 2–4.

Crittenden, A. 2001. *The Price of Motherhood: Why the Most Important Job in the World Is Still the Least Valued*. New York: Henry Holt and Co.

D'Amico, C., and R. Judy. 1997. *Workforce 2020*. Indianapolis: Hudson Institute.

Dean, S., and S. Parrott. 1999. *Food Stamps Can Help Low-Income Working People Put Food on the Table*. Washington, D.C.: Center on Budget and Policy Priorities.

Deibel, M. 2001. *New Century Workers: Educated, Self-Reliant, Older*. Washington, D.C.: Scripps Howard News Service.

Devol, R. 2001. *Metropolitan Economies in the Wake of September 11*. Los Angeles: Milken Institute.

Doyle. R. 2001. "U.S. Workers and the Law: Labor Rights of Americans Lag behind Those of Other Nations." *Scientific American*, August.

Eck, A. 1993. "Job-Related Education and Training: Their Impact on Earnings." *Monthly Labor Review* 116, no. 10.

Economic Policy Institute. 2001. *Living Wage: Facts at a Glance*. Washington, D.C.

Elliot, M., M. Grote, and O. M. Levin-Waldman. 2001. "Income Inequality in New York City: Deepening Disparity." *Public/Private Ventures*, September.

Elstrom, P. 2000. "Needed: A New Union for the New Economy." *Business Week*, September 4.

Employee Benefit Research Institute. 2001. *The Basics of Social Security*. Washington, D.C.: Employee Benefit Research Institute.

Employee Benefit Research Institute and Research Fund. 1997. "Social Security and Medicare." Retirement Confidence Survey. Washington, D.C.: Employee Benefit Research Institute and Research Fund.

Employment Policy Foundation. 2001. "Women Breaking through Male-Dominated Fields." Press release. Washington, D.C.

Fagnoni, C. 1999. *States' Implementation and Defects on the Workforce Development System. Welfare Reform: Testimony*. Washington, D.C.: U.S. General Accounting Office.

Families and Work Institute. 1998. *Business Work-Life Study*. Executive Summary. New York: Families and Work Institute.

Federal Reserve Bank of St. Louis. 2001. *Accounting for Computers: National Economic Trends*. Missouri: Federal Reserve Bank of St. Louis.

Fish, S. 1993. "Reverse Racism or How the Pot Got to Call the Kettle Black." *Atlantic Monthly Review* 272 (November).

Fleming, S. H. 2001. "OSHA at Thirty: Three Decades of Progress in Occupational Safety and Health." *Job Safety and Health Quarterly Magazine* (spring): 23–33.

Fletcher, J. D., and D. E. Hawley, and P. K. Piele. 1990. "Costs, Effects and Utility of Microcomputer Assisted Instruction in the Classroom." *American Educational Research Journal* 27: 783–806.

Fraser, J. 2001. *White-Collar Sweatshop: The Deterioration of Work and Its Rewards in Corporate America*. New York: W. W. Norton & Co.

Freedman, S., and D. Friedlander. 1995. *The JOBS Evaluation: Early Findings on Program Impacts in Three Sites*. New York: Manpower Demonstration Research Corporation.

Freeman, R. B. 1981. "Black Economic Progress after 1964: Who Has Gained and Why?" *Studies in Labor Markets*, ed. Sherwin Rosen. Chicago: University of Chicago Press.

Friedlander, D., D. Greenberg, and T. Robins. 1997. "Evaluating Government Training Programs for the Disadvantaged." *Journal of Economic Literature* 35 (4): 1809.

Friedman, P. 2000. *Career Opportunities and Support Services for Low-Income, Post-High School Young Adults*. Washington, D.C.: Workforce Information Network.

Fullerton, H. 1999. "Labor Force Projections to 2008." *Monthly Labor Review* 122, no. 11 (November): 19–34.

Galinsky, E., S. Kim, and J. Bond. 2001. *Feeling Overworked: When Work Becomes Too Much*. New York: Families and Work Institute.

Ganzglass, E., C. King, B. Narver, and C. Van Horn. 2001. *Building a Next Generation Workforce Development System*. Washington, D.C.: National Governors Association.

Ganzglass, E., et al. 2001. *Transforming State Workforce Development Systems: Case Studies of Five Leading States*. Washington, D.C.: National Governors Association Center for Best Practices.

Gardyn, R. 2000. "Who's the Boss?" *American Demographics: Consumer Trends for Business Leaders* (September): 54.

Geoghegan, T. 1991. *Which Side Are You On*? New York: Plume.

Girion, L. 2000. "Pierced, Dyed, Tattooed, and Hired: Tongue Studs and Inked Skin Are Showing Up in Traditional Offices As Bosses Struggle to Fill Jobs." *Los Angeles Times*, September 24.

Golonka, S., and L. Matus-Grossman. 2001. *Opening Doors: Expanding Educational Opportunities for Low-Income Workers*. Washington, D.C.: Manpower Demonstration Research Corporation; New York: National Governors Association.

Golub, S. 1998. "International Labor Standards: Are They an Appropriate Response to Global Competitiveness?" *U.S. Information Agency Electronic Journal* 3, no. 1 (February).

Greenspan, A. 2000. *The Economic Importance of Improving Math-Science Education—Testimony*. Washington D.C.: Federal Reserve Board.

Greenstein, R., and I. Shapiro. 1998. *New Research Findings on the Effects of the Earned Income Tax Credit*. Washington, D.C.: Center on Budget and Policy Priorities.

Guerrero, J. F., et al. 1990. "Honing in on the Target: Who among the Educationally Disadvantaged Benefits Most from What CBI?" *Journal of Research on Computing in Education* (summer): 381–403.

Hall, B. 2000. "What You Need to Know about Executive Stock Options." *Harvard Business Review* (March–April): 121–129.

Helwig, R. T. 2001. "Worker Displacement in a Strong Labor Market." *Monthly Labor Review* 124, no. 6 (June): 13–29.

Henry J. Kaiser Family Foundation. 2000. *The Uninsured and Their Access to Health Care: The Kaiser Commission on Uninsured Facts*. Washington, D.C.: Henry J. Kaiser Family Foundation.

Hershey A., et al. 1999. *Expanding Options for Students: Report to Congress on the National Evaluation of School-to-Work Evaluation*. Prepared for U.S. Department of Labor, Department of Education, by Mathematica Policy Research, Princeton, N.J.

Hipple, S. 2001. "Contingent Work in the Late 1990s." *Monthly Labor Review* 124, no. 3 (March): 3–27.

Hobbie, R., D. Wittenburg, and M. Fishman. 1999. "Temporary Assistance for Low-Wage Workers: Evolving Relationships in Work, Welfare, and Unemployment Insurance." *Rethinking Income Support for the Working Poor: Perspectives on Unemployment Insurance, Welfare, and Work.* Washington, D.C.: National Governors Association.

Hoff, D. 2001. *Access for All: A Resource Manual for Meeting the Needs of One-Stop Customers with Disabilities.* Boston: Institute for Community Inclusion.

Holahan, J. 1999. *The Uninsured: Variations among States and Recent Trends.* Washington, D.C.: Urban Institute.

Hollenbeck, K. 2001. *Education and the Economy: Employment Research.* Kalamazoo, Mich.: W. E. Upjohn Institute for Employment Research.

Holzer, H., and D. Neumark. 1996. *Are Affirmative Action Hires Less Qualified? Evidence from Employer-Employee Data on New Hires.* Cambridge, Mass.: National Bureau of Economic Research.

Howland, M. 1988. *Plant Closings and Worker Displacement: The Regional Issues.* Kalamazoo, Mich.: W. E. Upjohn Institute for Employment Research.

Human Rights Campaign. 2000. "HRC Hails Automakers' Unprecedented Move to Offer Domestic Partner Benefits to Same Sex Partners." <http://www.hrc.org>.

Hussar, W. 1997. *Projections of Education Statistics to 2007.* Washington, D.C.: National Center for Education Statistics, Office of Educational Research and Improvement, U.S. Department of Education.

Information Technology Association of America. 2000. *Task Force Report: Building the Twenty-first Century Information Technology Workplace—Underrepresented Groups in the Information Technology Workforce.* Arlington, Va.: Information Technology Association of America.

"Innovation and Technology: A Statistical Look at the Roots—and Fruits—of Technological Advances around the World." 2000. *Wall Street Journal,* September 25.

Institute for Policy Studies. 2001. *New CEO/ Worker Pay Gap Study: Labor Day Report Reveals Layoff Leaders Cushioned from Downturn.* Washington, D.C.

Internet Business Network. 1999. *Electronic Recruiting Index.* Mill Valley, Calif.: Internet Business Network.

Jacobson, L., R. LaLonde, and D. Sullivan. 1993. *The Costs of Worker Dislocation.* Kalamazoo, Mich.: W. E. Upjohn Institute for Employment Research.

Jeffress, C. 2000. "Uniform Workplace Protections Are a Win-Win Proposition." *Insight on the News,* August 7.

Jones, K., 2000. *Application of the Occupational Safety and Health Act (OSHA) to Teleworkers—CRS Report for Congress.* Washington, D.C.: Congressional Research Service, Library of Congress.

Kaufman, P., et al. 1999. *Dropout Rates in the United States, 1998: Statistical Analysis Report.* Washington, D.C.: National Center for Education Statistics, U.S. Department of Education.

Kaye, D., and S. Nightingale. 2000. *The Low Wage Labor Market: Challenges and Opportunities for Economic Self-Sufficiency.* Executive Summary. Washington, D.C.: U.S. Department of Health and Human Services.

Kennedy, R. 1991. "Persuasion and Distrust." *Racial Preference and Racial Justice.* Washington, D.C.: Ethics and Public Policy Center.

Kerrey, R., et. al. 2000. *The Power of the Internet for Learning: Moving from Promise to Practice.* Report of the Web-based Education Commission to the president and Congress of the United States. Joint Congressional–White House Commission, Washington, D.C.

Kim, K. and S. Creighton. 2000a. *Participation in Adult Education in the United States, 1998–*

1999: Statistics in Brief. Washington, D.C.: National Center for Education Statistics, U.S. Department of Education.

———. 2000b. *Education Statistics Quarterly* (spring). Washington, D.C.: National Center for Education Statistics, U.S. Department of Education.

Kim, K., et al. 1995. *Forty Percent of Adults Participate in Adult Education Activities: 1994–1995 Statistics in Brief.* Washington, D.C.: National Center for Education Statistics, U.S. Department of Education.

Kleiman, N. 2000. *The Skills Crisis: Building a Jobs System That Works.* New York: Center for an Urban Future.

Klein, N. 1999. *No Logo: Taking Aim at the Brand Bullies.* New York: Picador U.S.A.

Kletzer, L., and R. Litan. 2001. *A Prescription to Relieve Worker Anxiety.* Washington, D.C.: Brookings Institution.

Knell, S. 1992. *Fine Tuning the Mechanics of Success for Families: An Illinois Family Literacy Report.* Champaign, Ill.: Illinois Literacy Resource Development Center.

Kodrzycki, Y. 1997. "Training Programs for Displaced Workers: What Do They Accomplish?" *New England Economic Review.* (May): 39–47.

Koralek, R., et al. 2001. *Recent Changes in New Jersey Welfare and Work, Child Care, and Child Welfare Systems.* Washington, D.C.: Urban Institute.

Korb, R., and A. Lin. 1999. *Postsecondary Institutions in the United States: 1997–1998.* Washington, D.C.: National Center for Education Statistics, U.S. Department of Education.

Koretz, G. 2000. "Health Plans Feel the Boom: Tight Labor Fuels Wider Coverage." *Business Week,* October 2.

Kuhn, P., and M. Skuterud. 2000. "Job Search Methods: Internet versus Traditional." *Monthly Labor Review* (October): 2–12.

Kulish, N. 2001. "Snapshot of America 2000." *Wall Street Journal,* August 6.

LaLonde, R. *The Returns of Going Back to School for Displaced Workers.* Chicago: Center for Human Potential and Public Policy, Irving B. Harris Graduate School of Public Policy Studies. <http://www.jcpr.org/newsletters/vol5_no4/articles.html#story_5> (2002).

Leete, L., N. Bania, and C. Coulton. 1997. *City or Suburbs? Job and Residential Location of Welfare Exiters in 1996: Briefing Report.* No. 9907. Cleveland: Center on Urban Poverty and Social Change, Case Western Reserve University.

Leigh, D., and K. D. Gifford. 1999. "Workplace Transformation and Worker Upskilling." *Industrial Relations* 38, no. 2 (April): 174-191.

Leigh, D., and A. Gill. 1997. "The Effect of High-Performance Workplace Practices on Individual Workers' Productivity." Paper presented at the Third Annual Conference—What Skills Matter in the Economy, University of British Columbia.

Leonhardt, D. 2001. "Executive Pay: A Special Report." *New York Times,* April 1.

Lerman, R., and S. Schmidt. 2000. "An Overview of Economic, Social and Demographic Trends Affecting the U.S. Labor Market: Globalization." *Futurework: Trends and Challenges for Work in the Twenty-first Century.* Washington, D.C.: U.S. Department of Labor.

Levine, L. 2000. *Employer-Provided Training: CRS Report for Congress.* Washington, D.C.: Congressional Research Service, Library of Congress.

Levy, F. 1998. *The New Dollars and Dreams: American Incomes and Economic Change.* New York: Russell Sage Foundation.

Long, S., and M. S. Marquis. 1999. "Stability and Variation in Employment-Based Health Insurance Coverage, 1993–1997." *Health Affairs* 18 (6): 133–139.

Loprest, P. 1999a. *Families Who Left Welfare: Who Are They and How Are They Doing? Assessing the New Federalism.* Washington D.C.: Urban Institute.

———. 1999b. *How Families That Left Welfare Are Doing: A National Picture, New Federalism:*

National Survey of America's Families. Series B, no. B-1. Washington, D.C.: Urban Institute.

Lynch, L., and S. Black. 1995. "Beyond the Incidence of Training: Evidence from a National Employers Survey." NBER Working Papers 5231. Cambridge, Mass.: National Bureau of Economic Research.

Martinez, B. 2001. "Behind the Curtain: How Do Insurers Decide What Gets Covered?" *Wall Street Journal*, February 21.

Mateyaschuk, J. 1999. "1999 National IT Salary Survey: Pay Up," *InformationWeek*, April 26.

McMurrer, D., and A. Chasanov. 1995. "Trends in Unemployment Insurance Benefits." *Monthly Labor Review* 118, no. 9 (September).

McMurrer, D., I. Sawhill, and R. Lerman. 1997. *Welfare Reform and Opportunity in the Low-Wage Labor Market: "Opportunity in America."* Washington D.C.: Urban Institute.

Mendel, R. 1994. *The American School-to-Career Movement: A Background Paper for Policy-makers and Foundation Officers.* Washington, D.C.: U.S. Department of Education.

Mishel, L., J. Bernstein, and J. Schmitt. 1999. *The State of Working America, 1998–1999.* New York: Cornell University Press.

Moe, M. 1998. *The Book of Knowledge.* San Francisco: Merrill Lynch Growth Group.

———. 2000. *The Knowledge Web.* San Francisco: Merrill Lynch Growth Group.

Mogensen, V. L. 1999. "Ergonomic Inaction: Congress Puts OSHA's Ergonomic Standard on Hold." <http://www.tifaq.com/articles/ergonomic_inaction-jan99-vernon_mogenscn.html> (2002).

———. 1996. *Office Politics: Computers, Labor, and the Fight for Safety and Health.* New Brunswick: Rutgers University Press.

Moss, P., and C. Tilly. 2001. *Stories Employers Tell: Race, Skill and Hiring in America.* New York: Russell Sage Foundation.

National Alliance of Business. 1997. "Who Does It, Who Gets It, and Does It Pay Off?" *Workforce Economics* 3 (2): 26-30.

National Council on Disabilities. 1995. *Study on Financing of Assistive Technology Devices and Services for Individuals with Disabilities: A Report to the President of the United States.* Washington, D.C.

National Employment Law Project. 2001. *Part-Time Workers and Unemployment Insurance: Expanding UI for Low-Wage Part-Time Workers.* New York: National Employment Law Project.

National Institute for Literacy. 2000. "A Blueprint for Creating A More Literate Nation: Literacy Skills for Twenty-first Century America." Draft report for the National Literacy Summit 2000, Washington, D.C.

Newman, K. 1999. *No Shame in My Game: The Working Poor in the Inner City.* New York: Russell Sage Foundation and Alfred A. Knopf.

Nussbaum, K. 1997. *Working Women Say . . . .* Washington, D.C.: American Federation of Labor, Congress of Industrial Organizations.

O'Neill, D. M., and J. O'Neill. 1992. "Affirmative Action in the Labor Market." *Annals of the American Academy of Political and Social Science* 523 (September): 88–103.

Olsen, P. 2002. "Dot.Com Meets Dot.Edu: Trends in Learning Partnerships," *Learning Circuits, ASTD* <http://www.learningcircuits.org/jul2000/olesen.html>.

Orr, L. L., et al. 1994. *The National JTPA Study: Impacts, Benefits, and Costs of Title II-A.* Bethesda, Md.: Abt Associates.

Osterman, P. 1992. "New Lessons for State Training," *Spectrum* (summer): 7-14.

Pakko, M. R. 2002. *The High-Tech Investment Boom and Economic Growth in the 1990s. Review* (March): 3–18.

Peters, J. 1997. *When Mothers Work: Loving Our Children without Sacrificing Ourselves.* Cambridge, Mass.: Perseus Books.

Petzinger, T., Jr. 1999. *The New Pioneers: The Men and Women Who Are Transforming the Workplace and Marketplace.* New York: Simon and Schuster.

Political Economy Research Institute. 2000. *Living Wage Ordinances That Cover Contractors and Subsidy Recipients: 1991–2000.* Amherst: University of Massachusetts.

Porter, K., and A. Dupree. 2001. *Poverty Trends for Families Headed by Working Single Mothers: 1993–1999.* Washington, D.C.: Center on Budget and Policy Priorities.

Porter, K., and W. Primus. 1999. *Recent Changes in the Impact of the Safety Net on Child Poverty.* Washington, D.C.: Center on Budget and Policy Priorities.

Porter, S. 2002. *CenterPoint.* Washington, D.C.: American Council on Education.

Primus, W., et al. 1999. *The Initial Impacts of Welfare Reform on the Incomes of Single-Mother Families.* Washington, D.C.: Center on Budget and Policy Priorities.

Progressive Policy Institute. 1998–2002. *The New Economy Index Reports.* Washington, D.C.: Progressive Policy Institute.

Public Papers of the Presidents of the United States: Lyndon B. Johnson 1965. Washington, D.C.: Government Printing Office, 1966.

Rappaport, E. 2000. *OSHA Reform: Partnership with Employers—CRS Issue Brief.* Washington, D.C.: Congressional Research Service, Library of Congress.

Regional Technology Strategies and National Governors Association. 1999. *A Comprehensive Look at State-Funded, Employer-Focused Job Training Programs.* Washington, D.C.

Relave, N. 2000. *Collaboration between the Welfare and Workforce Development Systems—Issue Notes* 4, no. 2. Washington D.C.: Welfare Information Network.

Research and Policy Committee of the Committee for Economic Development. 1999. *New Opportunities for Older Workers.* Washington, D.C.: Committee for Economic Development.

Rocha, C., and F. McCant. 1999. "Closing Time: Workers' Last Call." Forum: For Applied Research and Public Policy, Tennessee Valley Authority.

Rodgers, W. M. 2000. *The Nature and Scope of the U.S. Skills Shortage.* Washington, D.C.: Office of the Chief Economist, U.S. Department of Labor.

Rodgers, W. M., and W. Spriggs. 1996. "The Effect of Federal Contractor Status on Racial Differences in Establishment-Level Employment Shares." *American Economic Review* 86 (May): 290–293.

Sachs, J. 1996. "Globalization and Employment." Speech before the International Labour Organization and the World Trade Organization, Geneva, Switzerland, March.

Schor, J. 1993. *The Overworked American.* New York: Basic Books.

Schultz, E. 2001a. "Raw Deals—Companies Quietly Use Mergers and Spinoffs to Cut Worker Benefits," *Wall Street Journal.* January 17.

———. 2001b. "Big Send Off: As Firms Pare Pensions for Most, They Boost Those for Executives." *Wall Street Journal,* June 20.

Sennett, R. 1998. *The Corrosion of Character.* New York: W. W. Norton & Co.

Shapiro, I., R. Greenstein, and W. Primus. 2001. *Pathbreaking CBO Study Shows Dramatic Increases in Income Disparities in 1980s and 1990s: An Analysis of the CBO Data.* Washington, D.C.: Center on Budget and Policy Priorities.

Smallwood, S. 2001. "Survey Points to Mismatch between Ph. D. Students, Their Programs, and Their Potential Employers." *Chronicle of Higher Education.* January 16.

Smith, D., and S. Woodbury. 1999. *The Low Wage Labor Market: Challenges and Opportunities for Economic Self-Sufficiency—The Business Cycle and Regional Differences.* Washington, D.C.: Office of the Assistant Secretary for Planning and Evaluation.

Smith, J., and F. Welch. 1984. "Affirmative Action and Labor Markets." *Journal of Labor Economics* 2 (April): 276.

Smith, J., and F. Welch. 1986. *Closing the Gap.* Santa Monica: Rand Corporation.

"Snapshot of America 2000: Small Census Survey Finds Richer, More Educated, Multilingual Nation." 2001. *Wall Street Journal*, August 6.

Soupata, L. "The Knowledge Imbalance: Free-Market Strategies for Bridging the Skills Gap." Paper delivered to the Council for Urban Economic Development, Annual Convention, Atlanta.

"Special Report—For the Boss Happy Days Are Still Here." 2001. *New York Times,* April 1.

St. Pierre, R. G., and M. Noonan. 1998. *Analysis of Federal Even Start Expenditures and Selected Comparisons.* Cambridge, Mass.: Abt Associates.

Steele, S. 1990. *The Content of Our Character.* New York: St. Martin's Press.

Stevens Institute of Technology. 1995. *The Knowledge Economy: Who Will Win?* Hoboken, N.J.: Stevens Institute of Technology.

Stillman, J. 1999. *Working to Learn: Skills Development Under Work First.* Philadelphia: Public/Private Ventures.

Stroh, L. 1994. "Fathers Whose Wives Stay Home Earn More and Get Ahead, Studies Find." *The Price of Motherhood* by Ann Crittenden. New York: Metropolitan Books, 2001.

"Study: CEOs Rewarded As More Workers Get the Ax." 2001. *USA Today*, August 28.

Super, D. 2001. *Background on the Food Stamp Program.* Washington, D.C.: Center on Budget and Policy Priorities.

Sweeney, E., and E. Schott. 2000. *Windows of Opportunity*. Washington, D.C.: Center on Budget and Policy Priorities.

Tannen, D. 1994. *Talking from Nine to Five: Women and Men in the Workplace—Language, Sex, and Power.* New York: Avon Books.

U.S. Bureau of Labor Statistics. 2001. *Union Members in 2000: Union Summary*. Washington, D.C.

U.S. Census Bureau. 2000. *Fastest Growing Cities in the U.S. between 1990 and 1998 in Percent Change amongst Cities Bigger than 100,000 People*. Washington, D.C.

U.S. Census Bureau, Department of Commerce. 2000a. *Demographic Data.* Washington, D.C.

———. 2000b. *Historical Income Tables.* Washington, D.C.

———. 2001. *Poverty in the United States 2000. Current Population Reports: Consumer Income*. Washington, D.C.

U.S. Department of Commerce. October 2000. *Falling through the Net: Toward Digital Inclusion.* Washington, D.C.

U.S. Department of Education, Center for Education Statistics. 1998. *Internet Access in Public Schools: Issue Brief.* Washington, D.C.

U.S. Department of Education, National Center for Education Statistics. 1999. *Internet Access in Public Schools and Classrooms, 1994–1998: Issue Brief.* Washington, D.C.

———. 2000. *Digest of Education Statistics.* Washington, D.C.

———. 2001. *Digest of Education Statistics.* Washington, D.C.

U.S. Department of Education, Office of Educational Research and Improvement. 2000. *National Center for Educations Statistics: Statistics in Brief.* Washington, D.C.

U.S. Department of Education, Office of Educational Technology. 2000. *e-Learning: Putting a World-Class Education at the Fingertips of All Children.* Washington, D.C.

U.S. Department of Health and Human Services, Administration for Children and Families. 1999. "Estimates of Child Care and Development Fund Eligibility and Receipt." Washington, D.C.

U.S. Department of Labor. 1995. *What's Working (and What's Not): Summary of Research on the Economic Impacts of Employment and Training Programs.* Washington, D.C.

———. 1999a. "Employee Benefits in Medium and Large Private Establishments—1997." Press release. Washington, D.C.

———. 1999b. *Futurework: Trends and Challenges for Work in the Twenty-first Century*. Executive Summary. Washington, D.C.

———. 1999c. *Overview of Report on the American Workforce*. Washington, D.C.

———. 1999d. *The Occupational Safety and Health Act of 1970 (OSH Act): Small Business Handbook-Safety and Health Standards*. Washington, D.C.

U.S. Department of Labor. 2000. *Telework and the New Workplace of the Twenty-first Century*. Washington, D.C.: U.S. Department of Labor.

U.S. Department of Labor, Bureau of Labor Statistics. 1995. *Survey of Employer-Provided Training*. Washington, D.C.

———. 1997. *Contingent and Alternative Employment Arrangements—February 1997*. Technical Note. Washington, D.C.

———. 1999a. *BLS Releases New 1998–2008 Employment Projections*. Washington, D.C.

———. 1999b. *Employment Projections*. Washington, D.C.

———. 1999c. *Just-in-Time: Report on the American Workforce*. Washington, D.C.

———. 2000a. "Employment Experience and Other Characteristics of Youths: Results from a New Longitudinal Survey." Press release. Washington, D.C.

———. 2000b. *Labor Force Participation Rates*. Washington, D.C.

———. 2000c. *National Compensation Survey: Occupational Wages in the United States*. Bulletin 2529. Washington, D.C.

———. 2000d. *Union membership, analysis of CPS data*. Washington, D.C.

———. 2001a. *Job Growth by States*. Washington, D.C.

———. 2001b. *Report on the American Workforce*. Washington, D.C.

———. 2001c. *Contingent and Alternative Employment Arrangements— February 2001*. Technical Note. Washington, D.C.

U.S. Department of Labor, Employment and Training Administration. 2000. *Strategic Plan: Fiscal Years 1999–2004*. Washington, D.C.

U.S. Department of Labor, Employment and Training Administration, and John J. Heldrich Center for Workforce Development. 2001. *Promising Practices under WIA*. New Brunswick, N.J.: John J. Heldrich Center.

U.S. Department of Labor, U.S. Department of Commerce, National Institute of Literacy, and the Small Business Administration. 1999. *Twenty-first Century Skills for Twenty-first Century Jobs*. Washington, D.C.

U.S. General Accounting Office. 1999. *Welfare Reform: Information on Former Recipients' Status*. Report # HE-HS-99-48. Washington, D.C.

———. 2000. *Unemployment Insurance—Role as Safety Net for Low-Wage Workers Is Limited*. Washington D.C.

Van Horn, C. 1995. *Enhancing the Connection between Higher Education and the Workplace: A Survey of Employers*. Denver: State Higher Education Executive Officers and the Education Commission of the States.

———. 1996. *No One Left Behind: The Report of the Twentieth Century Fund Task Force on Retraining America's Workforce*. New York: Twentieth Century Fund Press.

———. 1999. *Working Hard but Staying Poor: A National Survey of the Working Poor and Unemployed—Work Trends: Americans' Attitudes About Work, Employers, and Government*. New Brunswick, N.J.: John J. Heldrich Center for Workforce Development at Rutgers University.

Van Horn, C., and B. Erlichson. 1999. "School to Work Governance: A National Review—Final Draft." Consortium for Policy Research in Education, University of Pennsylvania, Philadelphia.

Van Horn, C., and K. Dautrich. 1998. *Work Trends I—The Economy and Job Security*. New

Brunswick, N.J.: John Heldrich Center for Workforce Development at Rutgers University and Center for Survey Research and Analysis at the University of Connecticut.

———. 1999a. *Work Trends II—Work and Family: How Employers and Workers Can Strike the Balance.* New Brunswick, N.J.: John Heldrich Center for Workforce Development at Rutgers University and Center for Survey Research and Analysis at the University of Connecticut.

———. 1999b. *Work Trends III—Working Hard but Staying Poor: A National Survey of the Working Poor and Unemployed.* New Brunswick, N.J.: John Heldrich Center for Workforce Development at Rutgers University and the Center for Survey Research and Analysis at the University of Connecticut.

———. 1999c. *Work Trends IV—Who Will Let the Good Times Roll? A National Survey on Jobs, the Economy, and the Race for President.* New Brunswick, N.J.: John Heldrich Center for Workforce Development at Rutgers University and the Center for Survey Research and Analysis at the University of Connecticut.

———. 2000a. *Work Trends V—Nothing but Net: American Workers and the Information Economy.* New Brunswick, N.J.: John Heldrich Center for Workforce Development at Rutgers University and the Center for Survey Research and Analysis at the University of Connecticut.

———. 2000b. *Work Trends VI—Making the Grade? What American Workers Think Should Be Done to Improve Education.* New Brunswick, N.J.: John Heldrich Center for Workforce Development at Rutgers University and the Center for Survey Research and Analysis at the University of Connecticut.

———. 2000c. *Work Trends VII—Second Wind: Workers, Retirement, and Social Security.* New Brunswick, N.J.: John Heldrich Center for Workforce Development at Rutgers University and the Center for Survey Research and Analysis at the University of Connecticut.

———. 2001a. *Work Trends VIII—Holding On: Americans Assess a Changing Economic Landscape.* New Brunswick, N.J.: John Heldrich Center for Workforce Development at Rutgers University and the Center for Survey Research and Analysis at the University of Connecticut.

———. 2001b. *Work Trends Special Release: Workers Respond to Terrorism and Its Impact.* New Brunswick, N.J.: John Heldrich Center for Workforce Development at Rutgers University and the Center for Survey Research and Analysis at the University of Connecticut.

———. 2002. *Work Trends X: A Workplace Divided.* New Brunswick, N.J.: John Heldrich Center for Workforce Development at Rutgers University and the Center for Survey Research and Analysis at the University of Connecticut.

Vroman, W. 1998. *Effects of Welfare Reform on Unemployment Insurance: New Federalism—Issues and Options for States.* No. A-22. Washington, D.C.: Urban Institute.

Wagner, S. 2000. *Winning the War for Talent through Training.* Arlington, Va.: American Society for Training & Development.

Wandner, S., and T. Stengle. 1997. "Unemployment Insurance: Measuring Who Receives It." *Monthly Labor Review* (July): 15–24.

Wartzman, R. 2001. "Falling Behind, Bare Minimum: Support Erodes for an FDR-Era Program." *Wall Street Journal,* July 19.

Watson Wyatt Worldwide. 2001. *Cost of Typical Benefits Package Up 18 Percent in Just Two Years—2000/2001.* New York: Watson Wyatt Worldwide, Data Services News.

Weisbrot, M., and M. Sforza-Roderick. 1998. *Baltimore's Living Wage Law: An Analysis . . . Costs of Baltimore City Ordinance 442.* Washington, D.C.: Preamble Center for Economic Policy and Research.

Wertheimer, R. May 2001. *Working Poor Families with Children: Leaving Welfare Doesn't Necessarily Mean Leaving Poverty.* Washington, D.C.: Child Trends.

Whalen, C. 2000. "The Skinny on Downsizing: Economic Trends." *Business Week,* August 28.

Wiatrowski, W. 1995. "Who Really Has Access to Employer-Provided Health Benefits?" *Monthly Labor Review* (May): 15–21.

Wilson, A. 2000. *The World Trade Organization: The Debate in the United States—CRS Report to Congress.* Washington, D.C.: Foreign Press Centers, U.S. Department of State.

Wolff, E. 2000. *A Plan for Increasing Personal Savings: Idea Brief No. 3.* New York: Century Foundation.

"Women Breaking through Male-Dominated Fields, Paid Equally." 2000. Human Resources <http://www.hr.com>.

Wood, D. 1998. "Fastest Growth in the West. " *Christian Science Monitor,* January 26.

Wright, E., and R. Dwyer. 2000. *The American Jobs Machine.* Boston: Copper Canyon Press.

Zachary, G. 2000. "People Who Need People: With Skilled Workers in High Demand, Employers Are Hunting Them Down, No Matter Where They Live." *Wall Street Journal,* September 25.

Zachary, G., and R. Frank. 2000. "High-Tech Hopes: Countries Are Pinning Their Economic Dreams These Days on a New Truism—Innovation Can, and Does, Happen Anywhere." *Wall Street Journal,* September 25.

Zedlewski, S. 1999. *Work Activity and Obstacles to Work among TANF Recipients, New Federalism: National Survey of America's Families.* Series B, no. B-2. Washington, D.C.: Urban Institute.

———. 2001. *Former Welfare Families and the Food Stamp Program: The Exodus Continues, New Federalism: National Survey of America's Families.* Series B, no. B-33. Washington, D.C.: Urban Institute.

Internet References

AFL-CIO: *www.aflcio.org*
American Society of Training and Development: *www.astd.org*:
Americans United for Affirmative Action: *www.auaaa.org*
American with Disabilities Act: *www.usdoj.gov/crt/ada/adahom1.htm*
Bureau of Labor Statistics: *http://stats.bls.gov/blshome.htm*
Census Bureau home page: *www.census.gov*
Center on Budget and Policy Priorities: *www.cbpp.org*
Employee Benefit Research Institute: *www.ebri.org*
EconData.net: Your Guide to Regional Economic Data: *http://www.econdata.net*
Economic Policy Institute *www.epinet.org*
Income page: *www.census.gov/hhes/www/income.html*
NewWork News: *www.newwork.com*
Office of Civil Rights, U.S. Department of Education: *www.ed.gov/offices/OCR*
School-to-work: *http://www.stw.ed.gov*:
Workers with Disabilities: *www.worksupport.com*

Index

References to figures are printed in italic type.

About the Authors

Herbert A. Schaffner has held a series of senior-level positions in communications and publications at national organizations, including the John J. Heldrich Center for Workforce Development, where he currently oversees the center's communications and marketing activities, including media relations, event planning, publications design and promotion, audience development, and outreach. Schaffner develops public education and awareness strategies for the center and its partners in the workforce development system. He has also supervised communications operations and strategies for the Center on Budget and Policy Priorities at Stevens Institute of Technology and for a variety of labor, political, and nonprofit groups and clients. Schaffner served as special assistant for communications to the governor of New Jersey from 1990 to 1993 and has worked as an editor and writer on books and magazines. He is also the coeditor of *Work in America*, an encyclopedia of labor history, and the author of three books on fishing.

Carl E. Van Horn is a widely recognized expert on workforce, human resources, and employment policy issues, with extensive experience in public and private sector policy making. Van Horn is the founding director of the Heldrich Center and chairs the University's Workforce Development Coordinating Council—a group that includes all major training and research units concerned with preparing and improving the workforce.

A member of Rutgers' graduate faculties of political science, management and labor relations, urban planning, and education, his credits also include more than seventy-five articles and twelve books, including *No One Left Behind: Economic Change and the American Worker* and *Turning Brownfields into Jobfields*. Van Horn's status makes him a noted speaker at national and regional conferences, as well as a frequent source on labor, workforce, and economic issues for the national media. Prior to coming to the Heldrich Center, Van Horn held several senior-level positions in government and universities, including those with policy-making responsibility. He has been director of policy for the state of New Jersey, senior economist at the Joint Economic Committee of the U.S. Congress, chair of the Public Policy Department at the Bloustein School of Planning and Public Policy, and director of the Eagleton Institute at Rutgers. Van Horn has advised the National Science Foundation and was appointed by President Clinton to a presidential emergency board to mediate disputes between labor and management in the railroad industry.